Oxford

English-Chinese
Chinese-English Minidictionary

牛津英汉
汉英小词典

新版
New Edition

外语教学与研究出版社
FOREIGN LANGUAGE TEACHING AND RESEARCH PRESS
北京 BEIJING
牛津大学出版社
OXFORD UNIVERSITY PRESS

图字：01 - 2004 - 2958

published by Oxford University Press, Great Clarendon Street, Oxford

© Boping Yuan and Sally Church 2000, 2001

This reprint of Oxford Chinese Minidictionary originally published in English in
2001 is published by arrangement with Oxford University Press for distribution
in Chinese Mainland only and not for export therefrom

Oxford is a registered trademark of Oxford University Press

图书在版编目(CIP)数据

牛津英汉汉英小词典 / 牛津大学出版社编 . — 北
京：外语教学与研究出版社，2004.3
ISBN 7 - 5600 - 4074 - 8

Ⅰ. 牛… Ⅱ. 牛… Ⅲ. ①英语—词典 ②词典—英、
汉 Ⅳ. H316

中国版本图书馆 CIP 数据核字(2004)第 025259 号

出 版 人：李朋义
责任编辑：周懿行
出版发行：外语教学与研究出版社
社　　址：北京市西三环北路 19 号 (100089)
网　　址：http: // www.fltrp.com
印　　刷：中华商务联合印刷(广东)有限公司
开　　本：787×1092　1/64
印　　张：11
版　　次：2004 年 9 月第 1 版　2006 年 12 月第 5 次印刷
书　　号：ISBN 7 - 5600 - 4074 - 8
定　　价：17.90 元

如有印刷、装订质量问题出版社负责调换
制售盗版必究　举报查实奖励
版权保护办公室举报电话：(010)88817519

牛津英汉汉英小词典
出 版 前 言

《牛津英汉汉英小词典》是牛津大学出版社新近推出的一部质量上乘的英汉汉英双向词典。它保持了牛津词典权威可靠、释义简明的品牌特色，还具有以下几个鲜明的特色：

一、英文翻译地道，语言富有现代气息，英语语料全部来自语料库。

二、例句典型丰富，贴近日常生活，注重口语和惯用法，便于模仿学习。

三、所收词条全为英汉两种语言的核心词汇，释义精当贴切，浓缩英汉双语学习的精华。

四、编排更加科学，汉语词条全部标注词性。

五、突出汉语搭配，并针对汉语量词复杂难用的特点，设计了同类词典中独有的汉语量词搭配。

参加编校的人员有：周懿行、李少林、董燕萍、赵岩华、丁文娟等。

学术与辞书部

外语教学与研究出版社

Contents 目录

Proprietary terms
专利名称

This dictionary includes some words which are, or are asserted to be, proprietary names or trade marks. Their inclusion does not imply that they have acquired for legal purposes a non-proprietary or general significance, nor is any other judgement implied concerning their legal status. In cases where the editor has some evidence that a word is used as a proprietary name or trade mark, this is indicated by the symbol ®, but no judgement concerning the legal status of such words is made or implied thereby.

本词典收了一些被称为专利名称或者商标的词语。收录这些词语不意味着它们从法律上讲已经不是专有商标词,已经获得了普遍意义了,也不意味着对它们的法律地位作出了任何判断。编者有证据证明某个词语被用作专有商标词或商标时,则用"®"这个符号加以说明,但是这绝不是也不意味着对这些词语的法律地位作出了任何判断。

Introduction
序言

The *Oxford English-Chinese Chinese-English Minidictionary* represents a major departure from traditional bilingual dictionaries on several fronts. It approaches the specific needs of the English-speaking learner of Chinese from a very different angle.《牛津英汉汉英小词典》在多个方面与传统的双语词典有着显著的区别。它从迥然不同的角度来满足英语使用者学习汉语时的特定需要。

It looks different 它与众不同

The dictionary page is refreshingly uncluttered, with streamlined typeface and symbols providing a consistent structure for the information both in English and Chinese. Subdivisions of text are clearly indicated using Arabic numerals. Points of basic grammar are reinforced using the ! sings, and informal or colloquial usage is marked* for Chinese. 词典页面清晰简洁,英语和汉语的信息,统一使用改良了的字体和符号表示。正文的细分部分都以阿拉伯数字清晰标明。基本语法点用叹号(!)进行了强调,汉语中的非正式或者口语用法都用 * 号予以标记。

It provides essential information in a new way 以新方式提供必要信息

Every effort has been made to approach the foreign language from the point of view of the beginner who may be unfamiliar with the conventions of the more traditional bilingual dictionary. 初学者可能并不熟悉传统一些的双语词典的惯常做法,因此编者千方百计地从他们的角度出发来对待汉语这门外语。

Parts of speech and grammatical terms are all given in abbreviated form with a glossary providing explanations and examples of different parts of speech in use. More complex grammatical issues are dealt with in short notes at appropriate points in the text. All Chinese headwords and examples are presented in both *pinyin* (the Chinese phonetic system) and Chinese characters to make the dictionary more user-friendly for beginners. Only simplified characters are used. 词性和语法术语均以缩减形式给出，术语集注解释和举例说明不同词性的用法。较为复杂的语法问题在词典正文中的适当位置以简短注释予以解决。所有汉语词条和例证均以拼音和汉字两种形式出现，从而使本词典更加便于初学者使用。所用汉字均为简化字。

The language used in examples and in sense indicators (or signposts to the correct translation) is carefully screened and reflects current English and Chinese as it is based on up-to-date corpus information. 示例和释义标记（或者正译译文的标记）中所使用的语言以最新的语料库信息为基础，经过精心甄别，反映了当代英汉两种语言的时代特色。

Both varieties of English—British and American—are covered and clearly labelled on the English-Chinese side, while users on both sides of the Atlantic will recognize the appropriate English-language equivalent for items in the Chinese-English part of the dictionary. 英语的两种变体—英国英语和美国英语—均有收录，并在英汉部分予以清晰标明。同时，大西洋两岸的使用者都将会在本词典的汉语部分找到与汉语条目相对应的贴切的英语表达。

The two sides of the dictionary have distinct functions 词典的两部分各司其职

Each side of the dictionary is shaped by its specific

function. The Chinese-English side is designed to capitalize on what English speakers know about their language, hence the more streamlined presentation of English speakers know about their language, hence the more streamlined presentation of English-language information. The *Oxford English-Chinese Chinese-English Minidictionary* provides generous coverage of those aspects of Chinese which are less easy to decode for English speakers. 本词典的英汉与汉英两部分各有其独特的功能。汉英部分旨在利用英语使用者有关自己语言的知识，进一步改进英语信息的最大限度的表达。《牛津英汉汉英小词典》大量收录了英语使用者不大容易解读的汉语问题。

The English-Chinese side is longer, providing the user of the foreign language with maximum guidance in the form of detailed coverage of essential grammar, clear signposts to the correct translation for a particular context, and lots of examples. 英汉部分篇幅较长，为汉语这门外语的使用者提供了最大限度的指导，其形式包括详尽的基本语法说明、特定语境下正确译文的明确标示以及众多的示例说明。

The *Oxford English-Chinese Chinese-English Minidictionary* is unique as an accessible and user-friendly introduction to the Chinese language.《牛津英汉汉英小词典》对初学汉语者来说方便易用，因而独领风骚。

How to use the dictionary
本词典使用说明

The English into Chinese side 英汉部分

The English into Chinese side of the dictionary attempts to give full guidance on how to write and speak correctly in Chinese. Plenty of examples are given to demonstrate not only the translation of words into Chinese but also hints about their usage in Chinese sentences. You will find additional information on grammatical points, such as the use of words in certain contexts, in the grammatical notes that occur within the entries on certain words. These notes are designed to help you produce correct Chinese in areas where mistakes are frequently made. Information about alternative pronunciations is also given in these notes. 本词典的英汉部分全面指导如何正确运用英语写作和对话。大量的例句不仅展示英语的汉译, 更提示汉语句子中的用法。在本词典中, 读者可发现在某些词条中的用法说明部分外的语法点信息, 如特定语境下的词汇用法。这些用法说明旨在帮助读者在汉译中经常出错的地方使用正确用法。同时, 用法说明中还包含词条的异读音。

If you are unable to translate an English word into Chinese because you cannot find it in the wordlist, try to use another word with the same or a similar sense, or choose another form of wording which will enable you to find what you're looking for. For instance, if you want to translate the adjective *complex* but cannot find it in the dictionary, you could try *complicated* as an alternative, which gives *fùzá* 复杂 as the Chinese equivalent. 如果读者在词典中查不到需要从英文翻译成汉语的词汇, 请尝试查找该词的同义词或近义词, 或者该词的另一种说法也

有助于帮助您找到需要的词汇。比如，你在词典中找不到你想翻译的形容词"complex"，就可以试着查"complicated"，从而知道它在汉语中的意思是"复杂"。

The Chinese into English side 汉英部分

The Chinese into English side of the dictionary is organized alphabetically by *pinyin* spellings. If you already know the *pinyin* romanization for a word, you can go straight to the Chinese-English side and look it up alphabetically. Words that have the same *pinyin* spelling but different tones are arranged according to tone, with the first tone first, followed by the second, third, fourth, and neutral tones. (See the section on **Tones in Mandarin Chinese** for information on tones.) Thus *fān* will come before *fǎn*, and *bǎ* will come before *bà*. Words beginning with the same character are grouped together to give a sense of the semantic range of that character. Words that begin with different characters having the same romanization and tone are arranged according to the number of strokes in the character, with the smaller number first. Thus *jiān* 尖 comes before *jiān* 肩 because the former has six strokes and the latter eight strokes. If words or compounds begin with the same character, romanization, and tone, they are arranged alphabetically according to the first letter of the second syllable or word in *pinyin*. For example, *miànqián* comes before *miàntiáor*. 本词典的汉英部分按照汉语拼音的字母顺序排列。如果读者已经知道某个词的汉语拼音拼写方式，就可直接翻到本词典的汉英部分按照字母顺序进行查询。词条音若同音异调，则按声调排列，首先是阴平，然后是阳平、上声、去声、轻声（汉语拼音的知识见"普通话的声调"部分）。所以 fān 在 fǎn 之前，bǎ 在 bà 之前。以同一单字开头的词放在一起，以显示该单字所包含的意义。同音、调同而形不同的词条

按笔画顺序排列，笔画少的排在前面。所以"尖"在"肩"之前，因为"尖"是 6 画而"肩"是 8 画。词组和合成词如果第一个字的字形、拼音字母和声调都相同，则按拼音中第二个音节或字的首字母的顺序排列。比如，"miànqián"就放在"miàntiáor"的前面。

In the cases of *yi* 一 — (*one*) and *bu* 不 (*not*), where the tone of the character changes depending on the character that follows it (see the subsection on **Tone Changes** in the section on **Tones in Mandarin Chinese**), all words and compounds beginning with the character in question are listed together, regardless of tone, and are arranged alphabetically by the *pinyin* romanization of the second character in the word or compound. For instance, *bùguǎn* 不管 is listed before *búyào* 不要 because *g* comes before *y* in the alphabet, even though *bu* in the first has a fourth tone and *bu* in the second has a second tone. 在"一"和"不"两个字的特例中，它的声调随后面所跟字的不同发生变化(参见"普通话的声调"部分下的"声调的变化"小节)。而在本词典中所有以"一"和"不"开始的词组和合成词都放在一起，不因声调的变化而变化，并按照词组或合成词的第二个字的拼音字母顺序排列。例如："bùguǎn 不管"就排在"búyào 不要"的前面，因为"g"在"y"之前，即使"不管"中的"不"是去声，而"不要"中的"不"是阳平。

If you have only the Chinese character but do not know how it is pronounced, or spelled in *pinyin*, you can use the **Radical Index** and the **Character Index** in the **Index** section to find the pronunciation. 如果读者只知道词条的字形而不知道其发音和拼音的拼写形式，可在索引部分的部首目录和检字表中查询该词条的发音。

How to use the Index 如何使用检索

The **Index** is divided into the **Radical Index** and the **Character Index**. The **Character Index** lists every character that is either a headword or the first character of a headword in the dictionary. It lists them by radical and provides their *pinyin* romanization, which is the key to finding them in the Chinese-English side. 检索分为部首目录和检字表。检字表中按部首列出了字典中收录的所有偏旁或字条的首字，按部首列出，并给出了罗马体的拼音，以方便汉英部分的查阅。

To find a character in the **Character Index**, you need first to identify the radical under which the character is categorized. The **Radical Index** provides a list of radicals and their numbers in order of their appearance in the **Character Index**. These radicals are listed according to the number of strokes used to write them, with the smallest number of strokes coming first. When you have identified the most likely radical of a character, note its radical number in the **Radical Index**, and use this number to find the radical in the **Character Index**. Because it is sometimes difficult to figure out which radical is used to categorize any given character, the **Character Index** lists some characters under more than one radical for your convenience. For example, the character 胃 is listed both under the 田 radical and the 月 radical in the **Character Index**. 要在检字表中查到某字，首先要确定某字的部首。部首目录中列出了各个部首及其在检字表中的编码。部首依据其笔画的多少排列，笔画最少的位置最前。确定某字最可能的部首后，记下部首目录中该部首的编码，然后根据此编码在检字表中找到该部首。由于有时所给汉字的部首难以确定，所以，检字表中有些字被列在几个部首下，以便于查找到。例如，在检字表中"胃"字既列在"田"部内，也列在"月"部内。

The **Character Index** lists each radical by number, followed by all the characters categorized under that radical. The characters under each radical are listed according to the number of strokes beyond those needed to write the radical portion of the character. For instance, supposing you are looking for the character 树 in the **Index**. You guess that it is probably listed under the radical (木), which is often called the *tree radical*. This radical is Number 81 in the **Radical Index**. To find the pronunciation of 树, first find where radical 81 is in the **Character Index**. You will see all the characters having this radical listed below it. The *tree radical* has four strokes. Now count the number of strokes that remain after you have written those four strokes. The answer is five. If you look down the list of characters to the subsection entitled "Five Strokes", you will see that the character 树 is listed within that group. The listing tells you that the character is pronounced *shù*; now you can look up *shù* in the Chinese-English side. 检字表按编码列出了各个部首，各个部首下列有含该部首的所有汉字。汉字按除部首以外其他部分的笔画数排列。例如，要在检字表中查找"树"字，猜测它可能列在"木"字旁下。"木"字旁在部首目录中的编码为81，在检字表中找出81号部首后，可以看到所有含"木"字旁的汉字都列在其下方。"木"字旁有四画，除去这四画，其他部分为五画。在列表下方找到标有"五画"的部分，从中可以找到"树"字。从列表中可知"树"字念"shù"，然后就可以在汉英部分查找"shù"。

By following this procedure, you should be able to find any character you are looking for, providing that it is in the dictionary as a headword or the first character of a headword. If you have trouble finding a character in the **Character Index**, first check above or below in the list under that radical, in case your stroke count was incorrect. It is best to write the character down as you count, being sure to write it using the proper strokes and stroke order. If you still cannot find it, the character is probably listed under a different radical, and you will need to start again from the beginning of the process described above, looking under a different radical.

Beginners sometimes find this process frustrating, but if you keep trying, it will become easier. 只要是词典中收录的词条或词条的首字，通过这些步骤就可以查找到。如果在检字表中未找到某字，先检查此部首项下列表的上下方，看是不是因为数错了笔画。最好是边写边数，并确定使用了正确的笔画和笔顺。如果仍未查到，那么该字可能列于另一部首下，需在另一部首下重复上述过程。初学者有时会觉得这个过程非常令人沮丧，但只要不断练习，查字就会变得容易了。

Each Chinese character corresponds to a syllable in *pinyin*, but a Chinese word can consist of more than one character. There is no obvious way to distinguish word boundaries in a written text unless one knows what the characters and words mean. Because only headwords and first characters of headwords are indexed in this dictionary, the absence of a character from the **Index** does not mean that it is not in the dictionary. It could be the second or third character in a word or expression, whose first character is in the **Character Index**. If the character you are looking for happens to be such a second, third, or fourth character, you may not find it in the **Index**. In that case you must look back at your text to see if it might be the latter part of a word beginning with a different character. For instance, if you find the character 壁 *bì* in your text, and try to look it up in the dictionary, you will not find it in the **Index** or under *bì* in the Chinese into English side. However, after looking again at your text you may find that it occurs after the character 隔 *gé*, as the second character of the word 隔壁 *gébì* (= next door). You can then try looking up 隔壁 *gébì* under *g* in the dictionary. Sometimes the **Character Index** gives you more than one pronunciation. It is best to check all the different pronunciations until you learn which one is used for the meaning of the character you are looking for.

每个汉字对应拼音中的一个音节，但中文的词可能含有几个字。除非知道字、词的意思，否则没有明显的方法来分辨书面文字中词的界线。检索中缺少某个字并不表示该字未收录在词典中，因为本词典只将词条和词条的首字收入在检索里。这个字可能是某个词或词组的第二或第三个字，而在检字表中只能找到该词的首字。如果要查的字正好属于此类，就无法在检索中查到。出现这种情况，必须再看看那段文字，查看该字是否处于某词的首字之后。比如，要查找一段文字中的"壁"字，而在检索或汉英部分的"bi"项下没有该字。但是查看原文后发现它用在"隔"字的后面，是"隔壁（＝ next door）"一词的第二个字，于是可以试着在字典的"g"部分查找"gébì 隔壁"。有时检字表会给出几个读音，这时最好是查看所有不同的读音，以确定哪一个用来表达所查字的意义。

Tones in Mandarin Chinese
普通话的声调

Chinese is a tonal language. In Mandarin Chinese, there are four tones, indicated respectively by the tone marks – ˊ ˇ and ˋ. 汉语是声调语言。普通话有四个声调,分别由 – ˊ ˇ ˋ 这几个符号表示。

Tone 声调	Tone mark 调号	Description 调号说明	Example 例子
First tone 阴平	–	high, level pitch 高平调	tī 踢 = kick
Second tone 阳平	ˊ	starting high and rising 高升调	tí 提 = lift
Third tone 上声	ˇ	falling first, then rising 先降后升	tǐ 体 = body
Fourth tone 去声	ˋ	starting high and falling 高降调	tì 替 = replace

As can be seen from the fourth column above, the tone is marked above the vowel in the romanized syllable. It is marked only in the *pinyin* romanization, not in the characters. Some words have unstressed syllables. These are toneless, and are not given tone marks. For example, in *wǒmen* 我们 (= we, us), the syllable *men* is toneless and therefore has no tone mark on it. This type of syllable is often called a neutral tone syllable. 从上面第四栏的例子可看出,声调标注在罗马体音节的元音上。声调只会在拼音上出现,不会标在汉字上。有些词没有重读音节,无声调,所以拼音上没有调号。例如,"wǒmen 我们(= we, us)"这个词中,"men"音节无声调,因此没标调号。这类音节常被称作轻声音节。

Tone Changes 声调的变化

Sometimes the tone of a syllable or a word changes

according to the tone of the syllable that follows it，有时候音节或词的声调会随着其后面音节的声调而发生变化。

1．The negative adverb *bù* 不（= not）否定副词"不（= not）"

Normally，the negative adverb *bù* 不 is pronounced in the fourth tone：通常，否定副词"不"读去声：

wǒ **bù** tīng yīnyuè 我不听音乐
= *I don't listen to music*

wǒ **bù** xué Zhōngwén 我不学中文
= *I don't study Chinese*

wǒ **bù** mǎi Zhōngwénshū 我不买中文书
= *I don't buy Chinese books*

However，when it is followed by a fourth-tone syllable，its tone changes to the second tone。但是，当"不"字后面的音节读去声时，"不"的声调就要变成阳平。

wǒ **bú** shì Zhōngguórén 我不是中国人
= *I'm not Chinese*

2．The numeral *yī* 一（= one）数词"一（= one）"

When read in isolation，in counting，or in reading numbers，the numeral *yī* 一 is pronounced in the first tone。数词"一"在单独使用、在数数或读数字时读作阴平。

yī，èr，sān，sì... 一，二，三，四... = *1，2，3，4...*

yījiǔjiǔbā 一九九八 = *1998*

However，when the numeral *yī* 一 precedes a first-，second-，or third-tone syllable，its tone changes to the fourth tone。但是，如果数词"一"后面的音节为阴平、阳平或上声，"一"的声调就要变成去声。

yī zhāng zhǐ 一张纸 = *a piece of paper*

yì pán cídài 一盘磁带 = *a tape*

yì běn shū 一本书 = *a book*

When it is followed by a fourth-tone syllable，its tone

changes to the second tone. 如果"一"字后面的音节读去声,"一"的声调就要变成阳平。

    yí liàng qìchē 一辆汽车 = *a car*

3. A third-tone syllable preceding another third-tone syllable 一个上声音节后有另一个上声音节

    When a third-tone syllable precedes another third tone, it is pronounced in the second tone even though the tone mark remains the same. 如果一个上声音节的后面跟着另一个上声音节,那么前一个上声音节读阳平,但其调号保持不变。

wǔ běn shū 五本书 = *five books*

nǐ hǎo! 你好! = *hello*!

hǎohǎo xuéxí 好好学习 = *study well*

The structure of English-Chinese entries
英汉词条体例

词条 —— **cool** /kuːl/ adj (fresh, not hot) liáng de 凉的; —— 拼音
liángkuài de 凉快的; a cool drink yí fèn lěngyǐn 汉字

词条的 —— 一份凉饮; it's much cooler today jīntiān —— 译文
各义项 liángkuài duō le 今天凉快多了; (calm)
lěngjìng de 冷静的; (fashionable) kù de 酷的*; —— 语法提
语法类 示符
别编号 —— **dance** /dɑːns/ **1** vb tiàowǔ 跳舞 **2** n a dance
yí gè wǔdǎo 一个舞蹈 —— 数量词

director /dɪˈrektə(r)/ n (of a film or play)
词条各 dǎoyǎn 导演; a director yí gè dǎoyǎn 一个导演;
义项的 a director (of a research institute or
解释 department) yí gè suǒzhǎng 一个所长,
yí gè zhǔrèn 一个主任; (of a factory) yí gè
词性 chǎngzhǎng 一个厂长; (of a company)
标注 —— yí gè zǒngcái 一个总裁

except /ɪkˈsept/ prep chúle... (yǐwài)... dōu —— 可有可
除了...(以外)...都 无的成分

单列词 —— **fireman** /ˈfaɪəmən/ n a fireman yí gè
条的复 xiāofángyuán 一个消防队员
合词 —— **fire station** /ˈfaɪə ˌsteɪʃən/ n a fire station
yí gè xiāofángzhàn 一个消防站

kick /kɪk/ vb tī 踢; to kick someone tī mǒu
rén 踢某人; he didn't kick the ball tā méi tī qiú
短语 他没踢球; kick off (in a football match) kāiqiú
动词 —— 开球; kick out to kick someone out bǎ mǒu rén
gǎn chūqù 把某人赶出去

说明生 —— **plenty** /ˈplentɪ/ pron to have plenty of [time |
成结构 money | friends...] yǒu hěn duō [shíjiān | qián | péngyou...]
的例证 —— 有很多 [时间 | 钱 | 朋友...]

正确的 —— **population** /ˌpɒpjuˈleɪʃən/ n rénkǒu 人口
语法用 ! Note that rénkǒu 人口 is uncountable and
法提示 does not have a measure word; a population of
one million yìbǎi wàn rénkǒu 100万人口

The structure of Chinese-English entries
汉英词条体例

词条 保护 **bǎohù** 1 *vb* protect, safeguard ···· 译文
语法类 **2** *n* protection
别编号
拼音 词性
汉字 北边 **běibian** *n* the North, the north 标注
side, on the north ! *This term can also
be used to refer either to the northern
border or what is north of the border;*
注释 **Měiguó de běibian shi Jiānádà 美国**
用法示例 **的北边是加拿大** north of the United
States of America is Canada

词条互见 上面 **shàngmian** ▶ 上边 **shàngbian** 可有可
无的成
圣诞(节) **Shèngdàn (Jié)** *n* 分
Christmas (Day)

研究 **yánjiū** 1 *vb* study, do research;
*(for problems, suggestions,
applications)* consider, discuss **2** *n*
research, study; **yánjiūhuì 研究会**
research association; **yánjiūshēng**
词条末的 研究生 research student,
复合词 postgraduate student; **yánjiūsuǒ**
研究所 research institute

词条的 员 **yuán** *n* (of a profession, party, or
义项的 *other organisation)* member, personnel,
解释 staff; [dǎng | hǎi | chuìshì | shòuhuò] yuán
说明生 [党 | 海 | 炊事 | 售货] 员 party member |
成结构 sailor | cook | shop assistant] 词用用
的例证 法的互
zhāng 张 *mw* ▶ 623 (for flat things 见页码
such as paper, paintings, tables, etc.)

Glossary of grammatical terms
语法术语集注

This section explains the basic terms that are used in this dictionary to help you to find the information that you need. 这部分阐释说明了本词典中所使用的基本术语，以帮助读者找到所需信息。

Adjective 形容词

An adjective is used to add extra information to a noun — *an **experienced** worker*, *a **beautiful** girl*, *a **black** cat*. In Chinese: *yí gè yǒu jīngyàn de gōngrén* 一个有经验的工人，*yí gè piàoliang de gūniang* 一个漂亮的姑娘，*yí zhī hēimāo* 一只黑猫。As can be seen in the examples above, the Chinese adjective is often followed by *de* when used to modify a noun. In some Chinese grammar books, some Chinese adjectives are called stative verbs, because the adjective in dictates the state of the subject, and the Chinese equivalent of the verb *be* is not used. 形容词为名词增加额外信息，如：*an **experienced** worker*（yí gè yǒu jīngyàn de gōngrén 一个**有经验的**工人），*a **beautiful** girl*（yí gè piàoliang de gūniang 一个**漂亮的**姑娘），*a **black** cat*（yì zhī hēimāo 一只**黑**猫）。从以上示例可看出，修饰名词时，汉语的形容词后常跟"de 的"。由于形容词用于描述事物的状态，所以有些汉语语法书把某些形容词称为状态动词。在汉语中，与英文动词 be 对应的词经常都被省略。

*he is **tired*** = tā __ lèi le 他__累了
*these students are very **intelligent*** = zhèxiē xuéshēng __ hěn cōngmíng 这些学生__很**聪明**

Adverb 副词

An adverb is used to add extra information to a verb, an adjective, or another adverb — *to walk **slowly***, *extremely satisfied*, *quite frequently*. In Chinese: *hěn mànde zǒu* 很慢地走，*fēicháng mǎnyì* 非常满意，*xiāngdāng pínfán* 相

当频繁. When used to modify a verb, the Chinese adverb is often followed by de 地. 副词为动词、形容词或其他词增加额外信息,如:to walk slowly(hěn màn de zǒu 很慢地走),extremely satisfied(fēicháng mǎnyì 非常满意),quite frequently(xiāngdāng pínfán 相当频繁). 修饰动词时,汉语的副词后常跟"de 地"。

Auxiliary verb 助动词

An auxiliary verb is a verb, such as be, do, have, which is used to form a particular tense or grammatical function of another verb, or to form an interrogative, negative, or imperative sentence. Here are some English examples: it is raining; did you see him?; she didn't come; he has left; don't go!. 助动词(如 be,do,have)是动词的一种,用以构成另一动词的某种时态的语法功能形式,或者用以构成疑问、否定、祈使等句式。以下是一些英文示例:it is raining; did you see him?; she didn't come; he has left; don't go!。

Comparative 比较级

The comparative, as its name indicates, is the form of the adjective or adverb which enables us to compare two or more nouns or pronouns. In English, this is usually done by putting more, less, or as before the appropriate adjective or adverb, or by changing the base form to the comparative form ending in -er. Chinese adjectives and adverbs do not have comparative forms. The comparison is usually indicated by bǐ 比, the Chinese equivalent of than, as can be seen in the following examples: 比较级,顾名思义,就是可以对两个或两个以上的名词或代词进行比较的形容词或副词的一种形式。英语中表示比较:通常是在适当的形容词或副词前加 more, less 或 as,或者是在形容词或副词的原形后加-er。汉语的形容词或副词没有比较级形式。汉语中的比较通常是用与英文单词"than"对应的词"bǐ 比"来表示。例如:

my mother is more patient (than my father) = wǒ

māma(**bǐ** wǒ *bàba*)nàixīn 我妈妈(比我爸爸)耐心

*he has **less** money（**than** I have）* = tā de qián(**bǐ** wǒ de)shǎo 他的钱(比我的)少

*Tom is taller（**than** his father）* = Tāngmǔ(**bǐ** tā bàba) gāo 汤姆(比他爸爸)高

*he walked **more** slowly（**than** my mother）* = tā(**bǐ** wǒ māma)zǒu de màn 他(比我妈妈)走得慢

*he is **as** tired **as** I am* = tā **hé** wǒ yíyàng lèi 他和我一样累

Note that when the comparison is implied, that is, when **bǐ** 比(= *than*) is not used, the Chinese adjective has a sense of comparison by itself, as in the example below.

注意：当句子中暗含比较的意思而未使用"bǐ 比(= than)"时，汉语的形容词本身就有比较的意义，例如：

A：*Of you two, who is **older**?* = nǐmen liǎ rén shéi dà? 你们俩人谁大？

B：*I'm **older*** = wǒ dà 我**大**

C：*Yes. I'm **younger*** = duì, wǒ xiǎo 对, 我小

If the sentence describes the state or condition of the subject, and no comparison is implied, it is necessary to add the adverb **hěn** 很(= *very*) before the adjective, as in the example below. Otherwise, the sentence has a sense of comparison. 如果句子是描述事物的状态而不含比较的意思，则需要在形容词前加上副词"**hěn** 很(= *very*)"，否则句子中就会有比较的意义。示例如下：

she is tall = tā hěn gāo 她很高

Conditional 条件从句

A conditional sentence is one in which the statement contained in the main clause can only be fulfilled if the condition stated in the subordinate clause is also fulfilled. This condition is usually introduced by *if* in English and *rúguǒ* 如果 in Chinese. 只有满足了从句中所描述的条件，主句中所包含的状态才能实现，这样的从句称为条件从句。条件通常由英语中的"if"和汉语中的"rúguǒ 如果"引出。

If it is fine tomorrow，we'll go to the seaside = rúguǒ míngtiān tiānqì hǎo, wǒmen jiù qù hǎibiān 如果明天天气好,我们就去海边

I would go travelling if I had lots of money = rúguǒ wǒ yǒu hěn duō qián,wǒ jiù qù lǚxíng 如果我有很多钱,我就去旅行

Conjunction 连词

A conjunction can be either (i) a word like *and* or *but* which is used to join words or simple sentences together, or (ii) a word like *when*, *although*, *if*, *where*, which is used to form a complex sentence. Note that *and* is not translated into Chinese when it joins two simple sentences or two verbal phrases. See the following examples: 连词既可以是用于连接词语或简单句子的词(如"and"和"but"),也可以是用于构成复杂句的词(如 when, although, if, where)。注意"and"用于连接两个简单句或两个动词短语时无需翻译成中文,见以下示例:

(i) *Britain **and** China* = Yīngguó hé Zhōngguó 英国和中国
*he is tired **but** happy* = tā hěn lèi **dànshì** hěn gāoxìng 他很累但是很高兴
*I went to Beijing **and** she went to Shanghai* = wǒ qùle Běijīng,__ tā qùle Shànghǎi 我去了北京,__ 她去了上海
*she went to the shop **and** bought some apples* = tā qù shāngdiàn __ mǎile yìxiē píngguǒ 她去商店 __买了一些苹果

(ii) *he has agreed to help me **even though** he is busy* = suīrán tā hěn máng,dàn tā tóngyì bāngzhù wǒ **虽然** 他很忙,但他同意帮助我
***when** I was about to go out，the telephone rang* = wǒ zhèngyào chūqù **de shíhou**,diànhuàlíng xiǎng le 我正要出去的时候,电话铃响了

Determiner 限定词

A determiner is used before a noun in order to identify more precisely what is being referred to. Here are some examples：限定词用于名词前以更准确地描述所指的内容。请见以下示例：

the book = zhè běn shū 这本书

my book = wǒ de shū 我的书

that book = nàběn shū 那本书

these books = zhèxiē shū 这些书

some books = yìxiē shū 一些书

Note that the English determiner *a* is usually translated into Chinese as a numeral plus an appropriate nominal measure word：

注意：英语的限定词翻译成中文，通常都翻成数词加上名词性量词的形式，如：

a book = yì běn shū 一本书

Exclamation 叹词

An exclamation is a word or phrase conveying a reaction such as surprise, shock, disapproval, indignation, amusement, etc. In both English and Chinese, it is usually followed by an exclamation mark. 叹词是用于表示惊讶、震惊、反对、愤慨和愉悦等反应的单词或短语。英语和汉语的叹词后面经常都用感叹号。

Excellent ! = Hǎo jí le ! 好极了！

What nice weather! = Duōme hǎo de tiānqì a 多么好的天气啊！

Imperative 祈使句

An imperative sentence is used to indicate an order, command, prohibition, suggestion, etc. 祈使句用于表示命令、指示、禁止和建议等。

come here quickly = kuài lái 快来

don't go out = bié chūqù 别出去

let's go = zánmen zǒu ba 咱们走吧

Infinitive 不定式

The infinitive is a form of the verb which has no indication of person or tense. In English, it is often preceded by *to*, as in *to walk*, *to run*, *to read*, *to receive*.

In Chinese, there is no word like *to* or any change of form to indicate the infinitive. 不定式是一种不含人称和时态标志的动词形式,在英语中不定式常接在 to 后面,如 to walk,to run,to read,to receive。汉语里没有类似 to 的词,也没有表示不定式的任何词类形式的变化。

Measure word 量词 ▶ Nominal measure word 名词性量词,Verbal measure word 动词性量词

Nominal measure word 名词性量词

In Chinese, a numeral cannot quantify a noun by itself. It has to be accompanied by the measure word that is appropriate for the noun that is being used. Each noun has a specific measure word or set of measure words that can be used with it. There is often a link between the measure word and the shape of the object. In expressions of quantification, the numeral comes first, followed by the measure word and the noun. When the determiner *this* or *that* is used, an appropriate measure word is also required. As can be seen in the examples below, we have put the numeral/determiner and the measure word together as one word in *pinyin* to correspond to the numeral or the determiner in English. Note that some nominal measure words can also be used as verbal measure words. (For a list of commonnominal measure words) and examples of their use, see the section on **Measure Words** on page 623)在汉语里,数词本身不能表示一个事物的数量,必须与名词相匹配的量词连用。每一个词都有一个或一组可与之搭配的量词。量词通常与被描述物体的外形有关。在表述名词的数量时,首先是数词,其后接量词和名词。使用 this 或 that 等限定词时,也需要用恰当的量词。如以下例句中,数词/限定词和量词在拼音中被放在一起作为一个词以对应英语中的数词或限定词。注意:某些名词性量词也可用作动词性量词。(参见 623 页词部分的常见名词性量词及其用法示例列表。)

a computer = yī **tái** jìsuànjī 一台计算机

four dictionaries = sì běn cídiǎn 四本词典
this student = zhège xuésheng 这个学生
that river = nà tiáo hé 那条河

Noun 名词

A noun is used to identify a person, an animal, an object, an idea, or an emotion. It can also be the name of an individual, a company, or an institution. 名词用于表示人、动物、物体、想法或情感等,也可用作个人、公司或机构的名称:

student = xuésheng 学生
dog = gǒu 狗
table = zhuōzi 桌子
plan = jìhuà 计划
happiness = xìngfú 幸福
Peter = Bǐdé 彼得
America = Měiguó 美国

Number 数词

A number, as a part of speech, refers to numerical figures, such as *five*, *twenty*, *thousand*, etc., or words indicating quantity. As a grammatical concept, it refers to the state of being either singular or plural. Nouns in English usually change to their plural forms by adding -s to the end: *a table*, *two tables*. Chinese nouns usually do not change to form singular and plural. 作为一种词类,数字是指计数符号,如 *five*, *twenty*, *thousnd* 等,或者是表示数量多少的词。而从语法概念上来说,它是指单数或复数的状态。英语名词要变成复数形式时通常在词尾加-s,如:*a table*, *two tables*,而汉语的名词通常没有单复数形式的变化。

a table = yī zhāng zhuōzi 一张桌子
two tables = liǎng zhāng zhuōzi 两张桌子

Occasionally, -men 们 can be attached to the end of a noun to mark the plural form, but it is optional and applies only to nouns referring to animate entities: 有时句中在名词后加"men 们"来表示复数形式,但并非必须且仅适用于表

示有生命的实体名词。

> *students* = xuésheng(men)学生（们）
> *workers* = gōngrén(men)工人（们）

Object 宾语

The object of a sentence is the word or group of words which is immediately affected by the action indicated by the verb. In the following English sentence, the word *child* is the subject, *broke* is the verb and *a cup* is the object. Similarly, in the Chinese translation, *zhège háizi* 这个孩子 is the subject, *dǎpòle* 打破了 is the verb and *yíge chábēi* 一杯茶 is the object. 句子中的宾语是指受到动作所指动作直接影响的一个词或一组词。在下面的英文句子中，child 一词是主语，broke 是动词，a cup 是宾语。同样，在汉语译文里，"zhège háizi 这个孩子"是主语，"dǎpòle 打破了"是动词，"yí gè chábēi 一个茶杯"是宾语。

> *the child broke a cup* = zhège háizi dǎpòle yí gè chábēi
> 这个孩子打破了一个茶杯

There may be two kinds of object in a sentence, a direct object and an indirect object. In the example above, *a cup* and *yígè chábēi* 一个茶杯 are strictly direct objects. However, in the following English sentence, *he* is the subject, *gave* is the verb, *the child* is the indirect object and *a cup* is the direct object. Similarly, in the Chinese translation, *tā* 他 is the subject, *gěile* 给了 is the verb, *zhège háizi* 这个孩子 is the indirect object and *yígè chábēi* 一个茶杯 is the direct object. In general terms, the indirect object indicates the person or thing which 'benefits' from the action of the verb upon the indirect object. 一个句子中可能有两种宾语，即直接宾语和间接宾语。上述例句中的 a cup "yí gè chábēi 一个茶杯" 无疑是直接宾语。但在下面的英文句子中，"he"是主语，"gave"是动词，"the child"是间接宾语，而 a cup 是直接宾语。同样，在汉语译文里，"tā 他"是主语，"gěi le 给了"是动词，"zhège háizi 这个孩子"是间接宾语，"yí gè chábēi 一个茶

杯"是直接宾语。一般来说,间接宾语是指从施加在直接
宾语上的动作中"受益"的人或物。

he gave the child a cup = tā gěi le zhège háizi yí gè chábēi
他给了这个孩子一个茶杯

Phrasal verb 短语动词

A phrasal verb is a verb combined with a preposition or
an adverb and having a particular meaning. For example,
to run away, meaning to flee, and *to see to something*,
meaning to ensure that something is done, are phrasal
verbs. If you look up *to run away* for example, you will
see that the phrasal verbs beginning with the word *run* are
listed after all the other meanings of the word *run*, in
alphabetical order of the following adverb or preposition. 短
语动词是指与介词或副词搭配并具有特定含义的动词,比
如 to run away(逃跑)和 to **see to** something(确定已做某
事)都是短语动词。查找 to **run away**,会发现词典在列出
run 一词的所有其他含义后,按其后副词或介词的字母顺
序列出了以 run 打头的短语动词。

Pinyin 拼音

Designed in the People's Republic of China during the
mid-1950s, *pinyin* is a phonetic system of the Chinese
language. It adopts the roman alphabet to represent
phonemic sounds in Mandarin Chinese. In this dictionary,
all Chinese headwords, translations, and examples are
given first in *pinyin* and then in Chinese characters.
拼音是汉语的音标系统,由中华人民共和国在 20 世纪 50 年代
中期制定。它用罗马字母代表普通话中音素的发音。在
本词典中,所有汉语词条、翻译和示例都是先列出拼音,然
后给出汉字。

Preposition 介词

A preposition is a word, such as *under*, *beside*, *across*,
in, which is usually followed by a noun in English. In
Chinese, the preposition often consists of two parts, such
as *zài*… *xiàmian* 在…下面(= *under*),and the noun is

placed between them, as in the examples below. 介词是一个单词，如 *under*、*besides*、*across*、*in* 等，在英语中介词后常跟名词短语。汉语的介词经常由两部分构成，如 "*zài···xiàmian* 在···下面(=under)"，名词则位于两部分之间，例如：

> *under the table* = zài zhuōzǐ xiàmian 在桌子**下面**
>
> *beside the road* = zài lù pángbiān 在路**旁边**
>
> *in the garden* = zài huāyuán li 在花园里

Most preposition + noun groups indicate movement

绝大多数介词＋名词词组表示运动

> *he ran **towards the house*** = tā cháo nà zuò fángzi pǎo qù 他**朝那座房子**跑去

position 位置

> *your books are **on the table*** = nǐ de shū zài zhuōzi **shang** 你的书在**桌子上**

or time 或时间

> *I'll be there **at 4 o'clock*** = wǒ sì diǎn zhōng huì dào nár 我 **4 点钟**会到那儿

Pronoun 代词

A pronoun is used instead of a noun in order to avoid repeating it unnecessarily. There are the personal pronouns *I*, *you*, *he*, *she*, *it*, *we*, *you*(plural), *they*; the possessive pronouns *mine*, *yours*, *his*, *hers*, *its*, *ours*, *yours* (plural), *theirs*; the interrogative pronouns used in questions *who*, *which*, *what*; the demonstrative pronouns *this*, *that*, *these*, *those*; the relative pronouns used in relative clauses *who*, *which*, *whose*; and the reflexive pronouns *myself*, *yourself*, *himself*, *herself*, *itself*, *ourselves*, *yourselves*, *themselves*. To find the Chinese equivalents of these pronouns, please look them up in the English-Chinese side of the dictionary. 代词用于代替名词以避免不必要的重复。代词分为人称代词，如 I, you, he, it, we, you(复数); they; 物主代词，如 mine, yours, his, hers, its, ours, yours(复数); theirs; 用于问句中的

疑问代词 who，which，what；指示代词 this，that，these，those；用于关系从句的关系代词 who，which，whose，以及反身代词 myself，yourself，himself，herself，itself，ourselves，yourselves，themselves。要找到这些代词的中文对应词，请查阅本词典的英汉部分。

Reflexive pronoun 反身代词 ▶Pronoun 代词
Relative pronoun 关系代词 ▶Pronoun 代词

Subject 主语

The subject of a sentence is often the word or group of words which performs the action indicated by the verb. In the sentence *John laughed*，*John* is the subject of the verb *laughed*. Of course, the verb doesn't necessarily express an action as such. For example, in the sentence *John is tall*，*John* is the subject of the verb *is*. In the Chinese sentence *Yuēhàn xiào le* 约翰笑了，*Yuēhàn* 约翰 is similarly the subject of the verb *xiào le*，and in the sentence *Yuēhàn hěn gāo* 约翰很高，*Yuēhàn* 约翰 is the subject of *hěn gāo* 很高。句子的主语通常是完成动词所指动作的一个词或一组词。在"*John laughed.*"这个句子中，"*John*"是动词 laughed 的主语。当然，动词不一定表示这样的动作。例如在"*John is tall.*"这个句子里，John 是动词 is 的主语。类似地，在"*Yuēhàn xiào le* 约翰笑了"这个中文句子中，"*Yuēhàn* 约翰"是动词"*xiào le* 笑了"的主语；在"*Yuēhàn hěngāo* 约翰很高"这个句子中，"*Yuēhàn* 约翰"是"*hěn gāo* 很高"的主语。

Superlative 最高级

The superlative is the form of the adjective or adverb which is used to express the highest or lowest degree. In English, the adjective or adverb is usually preceded by *most* or *least*. Some adjectives and adverbs (usually of one syllable) have their own form: *best*，*worst*，*biggest*，*smallest*，*fastest*，*slowest*，etc. In Chinese, the superlative is formed by putting *zuì* 最 before the adjective or adverb. 最高级是形容词或副词用于表示最高或最低程度的一种

形式。在英语中形容词或副词通常位于 most 或 least 之后。有些形容词或副词（通常是单音节词）本身有最高级形式，如 best、worst、biggest、smallest、fastest、slowest 等。在汉语里，最高级是通过在形容词或副词前加"zuì 最"来表示的。

most important = zuì zhòngyào 最重要

least important = zuì bú zhòngyào 最不重要

most carefully = zuì zǐxì 最仔细

least carefully = zuì bù zǐxì 最不仔细

smallest = zuì xiǎo 最小

Tense 动词时态

The tense of a verb expresses whether the action takes place in the past, present, or future. Unlike English verbs, Chinese verbs do not have any particular form to express tense; the time of the action is usually indicated by the adverb or in the context. 动词的时态表明动作是发生在过去、现在还是将来。与英语动词不同，汉语的动词没有特定的形式表示时态；动作发生的时间通常由副词表示或隐含在上下文中。

Present tense 现在时

he is telephoning his friends = tā zài gěi tā de péngyou dǎ diànhuà 他在给他的朋友打电话

Past tense 过去时

I didn't go = wǒ méi qù 我没去

Future tense 将来时

they will come tomorrow = tāmen míngtiān lái 他们明天来

Tone 声调

Please see the section on Tones in Mandarin Chinese on page 17. 请参见第 17 页"普通话的声调"部分。

Verb 动词

The verb propels the sentence along, telling us what is happening. Note these examples：动词推动着句子，说明正在发生的事情。请看下列例句：

Paul bought a new car = Bǎoluó mǎile yí liàng xīnchē 保

罗买了一辆新车

The flood caused a lot of damage = shuǐzāi zàochéngle hěn dà de sǔnhài 水灾造成了很大的损害

Sometimes, of course, the verb doesn't describe an action, but rather a state of affairs：当然，有时动词描述的不是动作，而是事件的一种状态：

He has a problem = tā yǒu yí gè wèntí 他有一个问题

The damage appears quite serious = shǔnhài kànlái xiāngdāng yánzhòng 损害看来相当严重

I am ill = wǒ bìng le 我病了

Note that the verb *am* in the sentence *I am ill* is not translated into Chinese. See the entry on **Adjective** in the glossary above. 注意"I am ill"译成中文时动词"am"不译。参见上述集注中形容词部分的说明。

Verbal measure word 动词性量词

Verbal measure words are generally used to indicate the number of times an action or state occurs. As in the case of nominal measure words, the numeral and verbal measure word are spelled together as one *pinyin* word in this dictionary. The numeral + measure word unit is preceded by the verb and is usually followed by the object, if there is one (i. e. if the verb is transitive). For a list of common verbal measure words and examples of their use, see the section on **Measure words** on page 623. 动词性量词通用来表示某个动作或某种状态所出现的次数。与名词性量词的情况一样，本词典将数词与动词性量词拼在一起作为一个拼音词，动词位于数词＋量词单位之前，如果有宾语(即动词是及物动词时)，通常接在数词＋量词单位之后。参见 623 页"量词"部分的常见动词性量词及其用法实例列表。

I've been to Hong Kong twice = wǒ qùguo liǎng **cì** Xiānggǎng 我去过两**次**香港

he nodded his head several times = tā diǎnle jǐ **xià** tóu 他点了几**下**头

Index 索引

1. Radical Index 部首目录

2. Character Index 检字表

(1)
、

之 zhī
为 wéi；wèi
头 tóu
主 zhǔ
半 bàn
农 nóng
良 liáng
举 jǔ

(2)
一

一 yī

一至
二画

七 qī
三 sān
干 gān；gàn
于 yú
下 xià
上 shàng
丈 zhàng
万 wàn
与 yǔ
才 cái

三画

丰 fēng
天 tiān
夫 fū

开 kāi
井 jǐng
无 wú
专 zhuān

五画

五 wǔ
不 bù
丑 chǒu
互 hù
牙 yá

四画

平 píng
未 wèi
正 zhèng；
zhèng
世 shì
可 kě；kè
册 cè
东 dōng
丝 sī

五至
六画

夹 jiā
亚 yà
再 zài
百 bǎi
而 ér
来 lái
严 yán
更 gèng
束 shù
两 liǎng
求 qiú

七画
以上

表 biǎo
事 shì
甚 shèn
歪 wāi
面 miàn
哥 gē
整 zhěng

(3)
丨

三至
六画

丰 fēng
中 zhōng
内 nèi
北 běi
旧 jiù
电 diàn
由 yóu
出 chū
师 shī
曲 qū
肉 ròu

七或
八画

非 fēi
临 lín

古	gǔ
考	kǎo
毕	bì
华	huá
协	xié
克	kè
直	zhí
卖	mài

七画
以上

南	nán
真	zhēn
韩	hán

(12)
厂

厅	tīng
历	lì
压	yā
厕	cè
厘	lí
厚	hòu
原	yuán
厨	chú

(13)
匚

区	qū
匹	pǐ
巨	jù
医	yī

(14)
卜（⺊）

卡	kǎ
占	zhàn
外	wài
卧	wò
桌	zhuō

(15)
刂

二至
五画

列	liè
划	huá；huà
刚	gāng
则	zé
创	chuàng
判	pàn
别	bié
利	lì

六至
八画

刻	kè
刺	cì
到	dào
制	zhì
刮	guā
刷	shuā
前	qián
剧	jù

九画
以上

副	fù
割	gē
剩	shèng

(16)
冂

同	tóng
网	wǎng
肉	ròu
周	zhōu

(17)
八（丷）

八	bā

二至
五画

公	gōng
分	fēn；fèn
半	bàn
只	zhǐ；zhǐ
兴	xīng
	xìng
关	guān
并	bìng
共	gòng
兵	bīng
弟	dì

八画

倍	bèi
借	jiè
值	zhí
倒	dǎo;
	dào
倾	qīng
俱	jù
健	jiàn

九画
以上

停	tíng
偏	piān
做	zuò
偶	ǒu
偷	tōu
假	jiǎ; jià
傍	bàng
傲	ào
催	cuī
傻	shǎ
像	xiàng

(20)
勹

勺	sháo
匀	yún
勿	wù
句	jù
匆	cōng
包	bāo
够	gòu

(21)
儿

儿	ér
元	yuán
允	yǔn
兄	xiōng
充	chōng
光	guāng
先	xiān
克	kè
党	dǎng

(22)
几

几	jī; jǐ
凡	fán
凭	píng
凳	dèng

(23)
厶

允	yǔn
去	qù
台	tái
县	xiàn
参	cān
能	néng

(24)
又(ㄡ)

又	yòu

一至
五画

叉	chā
支	zhī
友	yǒu
反	fǎn
双	shuāng
劝	quàn
圣	shèng
对	duì
戏	xì
观	guān
欢	huān
发	fā; fà

六画
以上

变	biàn
取	qǔ
叔	shū
受	shòu
艰	jiān
叙	xù
难	nán

(25)
廴

延	yán
建	jiàn

汗	hàn
污	wū
江	jiāng
汤	tāng
沉	chén
沙	shā
汽	qì
没	méi

五画

注	zhù
浅	qiǎn
法	fǎ
河	hé
泪	lèi
油	yóu
沿	yán
治	zhì
泥	ní

六画

浑	hún
浓	nóng
洪	hóng
洒	sǎ
洞	dòng
测	cè
洗	xǐ
活	huó
派	pài

七画

流	liú
浪	làng
酒	jiǔ
消	xiāo
浮	fú

涂	tú
浴	yù
海	hǎi
涨	zhǎng

八画

淡	dàn
深	shēn
清	qīng
添	tiān
淋	lín
渐	jiàn
混	hùn

九画

渡	dù
游	yóu
港	gǎng
湖	hú
湿	shī
温	wēn
渴	kě
滑	huá

十画以上

滚	gǔn
满	mǎn
演	yǎn
滴	dī
漂	piāo; piǎo
漏	lòu
澳	ào
激	jī

(33)
忄

一至六画

忙	máng
怀	huái
快	kuài
性	xìng
怕	pà
怪	guài
恢	huī
恰	qià
恨	hèn

七至九画

悄	qiāo
惊	jīng
情	qíng
惭	cán
惨	cǎn
愤	fèn
慌	huāng
愉	yú

十画以上

慷	kāng
慢	màn
懂	dǒng
懊	ào
懒	lǎn

扣 kòu　　　抬 tái　　　推 tuī
托 tuō　　　掀 pī　　　掀 xiān
执 zhí　　　招 zhǎo　　掏 tāo
扫 sǎo；sào　　　　　　据 jù

四画　　　　六画　　　　九至
　　　　　　挖 wā　　　十画
抗 kàng　　按 àn
护 hù　　　挤 jǐ　　　　搁 gē
扶 fú　　　拼 pīn　　　搭 dā
技 jì　　　挥 huī　　　提 tí
扰 rǎo　　挂 guà　　　插 chā
拒 jù　　　挡 dǎng　　握 wò
找 zhǎo　　拾 shí　　　搞 gǎo
批 pī　　　挑 tiāo；tiǎo　摸 mō
抄 chāo　　挺 tǐng　　　摆 bǎi
抢 qiǎng　 指 zhǐ　　　摇 yáo
折 zhé　　　挣 zhèng　 搬 bān
抓 zhuā　　　　　　　摊 tān
投 tóu　　　七画
抛 pāo　　　捞 lāo　　十一画
扭 niǔ　　　捕 bǔ　　　以上
把 bǎ　　　捉 zhuō
报 bào　　　捆 kǔn　　摘 zhāi
　　　　　　损 sǔn　　摔 shuāi
五画　　　　捡 jiǎn　　撕 sī
　　　　　　换 huàn　　撒 sǎ
拉 lā　　　挨 āi；ái　　撞 zhuàng
拦 lán　　　　　　　　操 cāo
抹 mǒ　　　八画　　　擦 cā
拔 bá　　　控 kòng　　攒 zǎn
拣 jiǎn　　接 jiē
担 dān；dàn　探 tàn
抽 chōu　　捧 pěng　　　　**(49)**
拐 guǎi　　措 cuò　　　　小（⺌）
拍 pāi　　　描 miáo
拆 chāi　　排 pái
拥 yōng　　掉 diào　　小 xiǎo
抱 bào　　　　　　　　少 shǎo；shào

嘴	zuǐ
器	qì
嚷	rǎng

(51)

口

四	sì
团	tuán
因	yīn
回	huí
园	yuán
围	wéi
困	kùn
国	guó
图	tú
圆	yuán
圈	quān

(52)

巾

市	shì
布	bù
师	shī
吊	diào
希	xī
帮	bāng
带	dài
常	cháng
幅	fú
帽	mào
幕	mù

(53)

山

山	shān
岁	suì
岛	dǎo
岸	àn
崇	chóng
崭	zhǎn

(54)

彳

行	háng; xíng
彻	chè
往	wǎng; wàng
征	zhēng
待	dài; dāi
律	lǜ
很	hěn
得	de; dé; děi
街	jiē
微	wēi
德	dé

(55)

彡

形	xíng
参	cān
彩	cǎi
影	yǐng

(56)

夕

名	míng
岁	suì
多	duō
梦	mèng

(57)

夂

冬	dōng
处	chǔ; chù
各	gè
条	tiáo
复	fù
夏	xià

(58)

犭

犯	fàn
狂	kuáng
犹	yóu
狗	gǒu
狮	shī
独	dú
狼	láng
猜	cāi
猪	zhū
猫	māo
猴	hóu

幻 huàn
幼 yòu

(67)
子（孑）

子 zǐ
孔 kǒng
存 cún
孙 sūn
学 xué
享 xiǎng
孤 gū
孩 hái

(68)
纟

一至
四画

纠 jiū
红 hóng
纤 xiān
约 yuē
级 jí
纪 jì
纺 fǎng
纯 chún
纷 fēn
纸 zhǐ
纽 niǔ

五至
六画

线 xiàn
练 liàn
组 zǔ
细 xì
织 zhī
终 zhōng
统 tǒng
结 jiē；
   jié
绕 rào
给 gěi
绝 jué

七画
以上

继 jì
综 zōng
绳 shéng
维 wéi
绿 lǜ
编 biān
缓 huǎn
缩 suō

(69)
马

马 mǎ
闯 chuǎng
骂 mà
骄 jiāo
骑 qí

骗 piàn

(70)
巛

巢 cháo

(71)
灬

点 diǎn
热 rè
煮 zhǔ
然 rán
照 zhào
熊 xióng
熟 shóu；shú

(72)
斗

斗 dòu
斜 xié

(73)
文

文 wén
齐 qí

(79)
王

一至
四画

主	zhǔ
玉	yù
全	quán
弄	nòng
玩	wán
环	huán
现	xiàn

五至
六画

皇	huáng
玻	bō
班	bān
望	wàng
球	qiú
理	lǐ
琴	qín

(80)
韦

韩	hán

(81)
木

木	mù

一至
二画

本	běn
末	wèi
朴	pǔ
杀	shā
机	jī
朵	duǒ
杂	zá
权	quán

三画

床	chuáng
杆	gān
村	cūn
材	cái
束	shù
条	tiáo
极	jí

四画

枕	zhěn
枝	zhī
杯	bēi
果	guǒ
采	cǎi
松	sōng
枪	qiāng
板	bǎn
构	gòu

五画

染	rǎn
亲	qīn
标	biāo
某	mǒu

查	chá
相	xiāng；xiàng
树	shù
架	jià

六画

校	xiào
样	yàng
栽	zǎi
桌	zhuō
桃	táo
桥	qiáo
格	gé
根	gēn

七至
八画

渠	qú
检	jiǎn
梨	lí
桶	tǒng
棋	qí
植	zhí
森	sēn
椅	yǐ
棵	kē
棍	gùn
集	jí
棉	mián

九画
以上

楼	lóu
概	gài
榜	bǎng
模	mó；mú
横	héng

晾	liàng
普	pǔ
景	jǐng
晴	qíng
暑	shǔ
量	liáng; liàng
暂	zàn
暗	àn
暖	nuǎn

(91)

日(⊟)

曲	qǔ
冒	mào
曾	céng
替	tì
最	zuì

(92)

贝

二至
四画

则	zé
负	fù
贡	gòng
财	cái
员	yuán
责	zé
败	bài
贫	pín
货	huò

质	zhì
贯	guàn

五至
七画

贴	tiē
贵	guì
贸	mào
费	fèi
资	zī

八画
以上

赔	péi
赛	sài
赚	zhuàn
赞	zàn

(93)

见

见	jiàn
观	guān
现	xiàn
规	guī
觉	jué

(94)

父

父	fù

爷	yé
爸	bà

(95)

牛(牜 牛)

牛	niú
告	gào
牧	mù
物	wù
牵	qiān
特	tè
牺	xī
靠	kào

(96)

手

手	shǒu
承	chéng
拳	quán
拿	ná
掌	zhǎng
摩	mó

(97)

毛

毛	máo
尾	wěi
毫	háo
毯	tǎn

(114)
示

票	piào
禁	jìn

(115)
石

石	shí

二至
五画

矿	kuàng
码	mǎ
研	yán
砖	zhuān
砍	kǎn
砸	zá
破	pò

六画
以上

硬	yìng
确	què
碗	wǎn
碎	suì
碰	pèng
碑	bēi
磁	cí
磨	mó

(116)
龙

龙	lóng

(117)
业

业	yè

(118)
目

目	mù
相	xiāng; xiàng
省	shěng
盼	pàn
看	kān; kàn
睁	zhēng
眼	yǎn
睡	shuì
瞎	xiā
瞧	qiáo

(119)
田

田	tián
由	yóu
电	diàn

二至
四画

亩	mǔ
男	nán
思	sī
胃	wèi
界	jiè

五画
以上

留	liú
略	lüè
累	lèi
富	fù

(120)
罒

四	sì
罚	fá
罪	zuì

(121)
皿

盆	pén
盏	zhǎn
盐	yán
盖	gài
盒	hé
盘	pán

(130)
疋（疋）

蛋 dàn
疑 yí

(131)
皮

皮 pí

(132)
衣

衣 yī
表 biǎo
袋 dài
装 zhuāng
裁 cái

(133)
羊（⺷⺶）

羊 yáng
养 yǎng
差 chà
美 měi
着 zháo；
zhe

(134)
米

米 mǐ
类 lèi
粉 fěn
粒 lì
粘 zhān
粗 cū
粮 liáng
精 jīng
糊 hú
糖 táng
糟 zāo

(135)
耒

耕 gēng

(136)
老

老 lǎo
考 kǎo

盖 gài
羡 xiàn
善 shàn
群 qún

(137)
耳

耳 ěr
取 qǔ
耶 yē
闻 wén
聋 lóng
职 zhí
聊 liáo
联 lián
聪 cōng

(138)
臣

卧 wò

(139)
西（覀）

西 xī
要 yāo；yào
票 piào

(140)
页

页 yè
顶 dǐng
项 xiàng

顺 shùn
烦 fán
顾 gù
顿 dùn
预 yù
领 lǐng
颗 kē
颜 yán
题 tí
颠 diān

---

(141)
虍

虚 xū

---

(142)
虫

虫 chóng
虾 xiā
虽 suī
蚊 wén
蛇 shé
蛋 dàn
蜂 fēng
蜜 mì
蜡 là

---

(143)
缶

缺 quē

罐 guàn

---

(144)
舌

舌 shé
乱 luàn
甜 tián
舒 shū
辞 cí

---

(145)
竹(⺮)

竹 zhú
笔 bǐ
笑 xiào
笨 bèn
符 fú
第 dì
筐 kuāng
等 děng
策 cè
答 dā；dá
筷 kuài
简 jiǎn
筹 chóu
签 qiān
管 guǎn
算 suàn
箭 jiàn
篇 piān
箱 xiāng
篮 lán

---

(146)
臼

舅 jiù

---

(147)
自

自 zì
臭 chòu

---

(148)
血

血 xiě；xuè

---

(149)
舟

航 háng
舱 cāng
盘 pán
船 chuán
艘 sōu

---

(150)
羽

羽 yǔ

(163)
里

里　lǐ
厘　lí
重　chóng;
　　zhòng
野　yě
量　liáng;
　　liàng

(164)
足（⻊）

足　zú
距　jù
跌　diē
跑　pǎo
跨　kuà
跳　tiào
路　lù
跪　guì
跟　gēn
踢　tī
踩　cǎi
踏　tà
蹲　dūn

(165)
豸

貌　mào

(166)
谷

欲　yù

(167)
采

番　fān

(168)
身

身　shēn
射　shè
躲　duǒ
躺　tǎng

(169)
角

角　jiǎo
解　jiě

(170)
青

青　qīng
静　jìng

(171)
其

其　qí
甚　shèn
基　jī
期　qī
欺　qī

(172)
雨（⻗）

雨　yǔ
雪　xuě
雷　léi
零　líng
雾　wù
雹　báo
需　xū
露　lòu; lù

(173)
齿

龄　líng

(174)
金

金　jīn

Abbreviations
略语表

adjective（形容词）	adj
adjectival noun（形容词性名词）	adj n
adverb（副词）	adv
auxiliary verb（助动词）	aux vb
conjunction（连词）	conj
determiner（限定词）	det
measure word（量词）	mw
nominal measure word（名词性量词）	nmw
verbal measure word（动词性量词）	vmw
noun（名词）	n
number（数词）	num
preposition（介词）	prep
pronoun（代词）	pron
reflexive pronoun（反身代词）	ref pron
relative pronoun（关系代词）	rel pron
verb（动词）	vb
prefix（前缀）	prf
exclamation（感叹词）	exc
particle（小品词）	pt
suffix（后缀）	suf

Pronunciation table
发音表

Consonants 辅音

b	*b*ut	m	*m*easure	z	*z*oo
d	*d*og	n	*n*o	ʃ	*sh*e
f	*f*ew	p	*p*en	ʒ	mea*s*ure
g	*g*et	r	*r*ed	θ	*th*in
h	*h*e	s	*s*it	ð	*th*is
j	*y*es	t	*t*op	ŋ	ri*ng*
k	*c*at	v	*v*oice	tʃ	*ch*oice
l	*l*eg	w	*w*e	dʒ	*j*oke

Vowels 元音

æ	*ca*t	ɔ:	*saw*	eɪ	*da*y
ɑ:	*ar*m	ʌ	r*u*n	əʊ	n*o*
e	*be*d	ʊ	p*u*t	eə	*hai*r
ɜ:	*he*r	u:	*too*	ɪə	*nea*r
ɪ	*si*t	ə	*a*go	ɔɪ	*bo*y
i:	*see*	aɪ	*m*y	ʊə	*poor*
ɒ	*ho*t	aʊ	*how*		

Aa

a /强 eɪ;弱 ə/, **an** /强 æn;弱 ən/ *det* ▶623 yī 一; a dog yì tiáo gǒu 一条狗; an exhibition yí gè zhǎnlǎnhuì 一个展览会; a crowd of people yì qún rén 一群人

able /'eɪbl/ *adj* (*used as a modifier*) nénggàn de 能干的; an able nurse yí gè nénggàn de hùshi 一个能干的护士; (*having enough strength, skills or knowledge*) néng 能; **to be able to** [walk|type|translate] néng [zǒu|dǎzì|fānyì] 能 [走|打字|翻译]

aboard /ə'bɔːd/ *adv* ! Note that the type of vehicle needs to be specified in Chinese; **to go aboard** shàng [qìchē|huǒchē|fēijī] 上[汽车|火车|飞机]

about /ə'baʊt/ ! Often *about* occurs in combinations with verbs, for example: bring about, run about *etc*. To find the correct translations for this type of verb, look up the separate dictionary entries at bring, run, *etc*. **1** *prep* guānyú 关于; a book about China yì běn guānyú Zhōngguó de shū 一本关于中国的书 **2** *adv* (*pre-modifier*) dàyuē 大约; Oxford is about 40 km from here Niújīn lí zhèr dàyuē sìshí gōnglǐ 牛津离这儿大约四十公里; (*post-modifier*) zuǒyòu 左右; he goes to bed at about 11 o'clock tā shíyī diǎn zuǒyòu shuìjiào 他 11 点左右睡觉 **3 to be about to** jiùyào…le 就要…了, kuàiyào…le 快要…了! Note that a sentence-final particle le 了 is needed here in Chinese; **to be about to** [leave|cry|fall asleep] jiùyào [líkāi|kū|shuìzháo] le jiùyào 就要[离开|哭|睡着]了

above /ə'bʌv/ **1** *prep* zài…shàngbian 在…上边; their office is above a shop tāmen de bàngōngshì zài yí gè shāngdiàn shàngbian 他们的办公室在一个商店上边 **2** *adv* zài shàngbian 在上边; his room is just above tā de fángjiān jiù zài shàngbian 他的房间就在上边 **3 above all** shǒuxiān 首先

abroad /ə'brɔːd/ *adv* guówài 国外；be abroad zài guówài 在国外；return from abroad cóng guówài huílái 从国外回来；go abroad chūguó 出国

absent /'æbsənt/ *adj* méi lái de 没来的，méi qù de 没去的，bú zài de 不在的；she is absent from work tā méi lái shàngbān 她没来上班；absent from classes quēkè 缺课

accent /'æksənt/ *n* kǒuyīn 口音

accept /ək'sept/ *vb* jiēshòu 接受

accident /'æksɪdənt/ *n* (causing injury or damage) an accident yí cì shìgù 一次事故；a car accident yí cì chēhuò 一次车祸；(by accident) ǒurán 偶然；I met him by accident wǒ ǒurán yùjiànle tā 我偶然遇见了他

accommodation /əˌkɒmə'deɪʃən/ *n* zhùchù 住处；look for accommodation zhǎo zhùchù 找住处

accompany /ə'kʌmpənɪ/ *vb* péitóng 陪同

account /ə'kaunt/ *n* (in a bank) an account yí gè zhànghù 一个账户；there's money in my account wǒ de zhànghù li yǒu qián 我的账户里有钱；(consideration) take travelling expenses into account kǎolǜ lǚxíng de huāfèi 考虑旅行的花费

accountant /ə'kauntənt/ *n* an accountant yí gè kuàijì 一个会计

accuse /ə'kjuːz/ *vb* accuse someone of cheating zhǐzé mǒu rén qīpiàn 指责某人欺骗

across /ə'krɒs/ *prep* (to go across the road) guò mǎlù 过马路；to run across the road pǎoguò mǎlù 跑过马路；a journey across the desert chuānguò shāmò de lǚxíng 穿过沙漠的旅行；(on the other side of) zài…de nà yìbiān 在…的那一边；he lives across the street tā zhù zài mǎlù de duìmiàn 他住在马路的对面

act /ækt/ *vb* (to do something) xíngdòng 行动；(to play a role) bànyǎn 扮演

activity /æk'tɪvətɪ/ *n* huódòng 活动

actor /'æktə(r)/ *n* an actor yí gè nányǎnyuán 一个男演员

actress /'æktrɪs/ n an actress yí gè nǚyǎnyuán 一个女演员

actually /'æktʃʊəlɪ/ adv shíjìshang 实际上，shìshíshang 事实上；actually, she's a very good athlete shíjìshang, tā shì yí gè hěn hǎo de yùndòngyuán 实际上，她是一个很好的运动员

adapt /ə'dæpt/ vb shǐ…shìyìng 使…适应；I must adapt myself to the new environment wǒ yídìng yào shǐ zìjǐ shìyìng xīn de huánjìng 我一定要使自己适应新的环境

add /æd/ vb jiā 加

address /ə'dres/ n dìzhǐ 地址

admire /əd'maɪə(r)/ vb qīnpèi 钦佩，zànshǎng 赞赏

admit /əd'mɪt/ vb (to own up or recognize as being true) chéngrèn 承认；he admitted that he was wrong tā chéngrèn tā cuò le 他承认他错了；to be admitted to (the) hospital zhùjìn yīyuàn 住进医院

adolescent /ædəʊ'lesənt/ n qīngshàonián 青少年

adopt /ə'dɒpt/ vb cǎiyòng 采用，cǎinà 采纳

adult /'ædʌlt/ n chéngniánrén 成年人，dàren 大人

advantage /əd'vɑːntɪdʒ/ n (a benefit) hǎochù 好处；(a favouring condition) yǒulì tiáojiàn 有利条件；(superiority over another) yōushì 优势；at the beginning of the game, the advantage was with the blue team bǐsài kāishǐ de shíhou, lánduì zhàn yōushì 比赛开始的时候，蓝队占优势；to take advantage of… lìyòng… 利用…

adventure /əd'ventʃə(r)/ n an adventure yí cì màoxiǎn 一次冒险

advertise /'ædvətaɪz/ vb wèi…dēng guǎnggào 为…登广告；to advertise goods wèi shāngpǐn dēng guǎnggào 为商品登广告

advertisement /əd'vɜːtɪsmənt/ n guǎnggào 广告

advice /əd'vaɪs/ n zhōnggào 忠告，quàngào 劝告

advise /əd'vaɪz/ vb quàngào 劝告，jiànyì 建议

aerial /'eərɪəl/ n tiānxiàn 天线

aerobics /eə'rəʊbɪks/ n yǒuyǎng jiànshēncāo 有氧健身操

affect /ə'fekt/ *vb* yǐngxiǎng 影响

afford /ə'fɔːd/ *vb* (*to bear the expense*) mǎi de qǐ 买得起;he [can | cannot] afford to buy this car tā [mǎi de qǐ | mǎi bù qǐ] zhè liàng chē 他 [买得起 | 买不起] 这辆车;(*to have the time*) chōu de chū 抽得出;I [can | cannot] afford the time to go to the cinema wǒ [chōu de chū | chōu bù chū] shíjiān qù kàn diànyǐng 我 [抽得出 | 抽不出] 时间去看电影 ! *Note that to negate,* de 得 *in* mǎi de qǐ 买得起 *and* chōu de chū 抽得出 *has to be replaced with the negative particle* bù 不.

afraid /ə'freɪd/ *adj* (*fearful*) hàipà de 害怕的,pà de 怕的;she is afraid of dogs tā hàipà gǒu 她害怕狗;she is afraid to lose this opportunity tā pà diū zhège jīhuì 她怕丢了个机会;(*regretfully thinking*) kǒngpà 恐怕 ! *Note that in this usage, if the subject of the main clause is a first-person singular pronoun* (I wǒ 我), *it has to be phonetically silent and the subject of the embedded clause can often be moved to the main clause;* I'm afraid that I won't be able to go kǒngpà wǒ bù néng qù le 恐怕我不能去了,wǒ kǒngpà bù néng qù le 我恐怕不能去了;I'm afraid that he has left tā yǐjīng líkāi le 恐怕他已经离开了,tā kǒngpà yǐjīng líkāi le 他恐怕已经离开了

Africa /'æfrɪkə/ *n* Fēizhōu 非洲

African /'æfrɪkən/ **1** *adj* Fēizhōu de 非洲的 **2** *n* Fēizhōu-rén 非洲人

after /'ɑːftə(r)/ **1** *prep* (zài)…yǐhòu (在)…以后;after breakfast zǎofàn yǐhòu 早饭以后;the day after tomorrow hòutiān 后天 **2** *conj* …yǐhòu …以后;after we had eaten, we went for a walk chīle fàn yǐhòu, wǒmen chūqù sànbù 吃了饭以后,我们出去散步;they went in after the film had started diànyǐng kāishǐ yǐhòu tāmen cái jìnqù 电影开始以后他们才进去 **3 after all** bìjìng 毕竟

afternoon /ˌɑːftə'nuːn/ *n* xiàwǔ 下午

afterwards /'ɑːftəwədz/ , **afterward** /'ɑːftəwəd/ (*US*

English) *adv* yǐhòu 以后；(*when talking about a past event*) hòulái 后来

again /ə'gen/ *adv* (*when the repetition has already happened*) yòu 又；**he has come again** tā yòu lái le 他又来了；(*when the repetition is to happen*) zài 再；**please try it again** qǐng zài shì yí cì 请再试一次

against /ə'genst/ *prep* (*in the sense of being opposed to something*) fǎnduì 反对；**I am against this plan** wǒ fǎnduì zhège jìhuà 我反对这个计划；(*to resist the wind*) dǐng 顶；**the ship is sailing against the wind** chuán zhèng dǐngzhe fēng xíngshǐ 船正顶着风行驶；(*to resist a water current*) nì 逆；**she swam against the current** tā nìshuǐ yóuyǒng 她逆流水游泳；(*to put pressure upon*) kào 靠，yǐ 倚；**I was standing against the wall** wǒ kàozhe qiáng zhànzhe 我靠着墙站着

age /eidʒ/ *n* suì 岁，niánjì 年纪，niánlíng 年龄

aged /'eidʒɪd/ *adj* (*advanced in age*) lǎo de 老的，(*of the age of*) …suì de …岁的；**children aged 10** shí suì de háizi 10 岁的孩子

ago /ə'gəu/ *adv* yǐqián 以前；**two weeks ago** liǎng gè xīngqī yǐqián 两个星期以前；**long ago** hěn jiǔ yǐqián 很久以前

agree /ə'gri/ *vb* (*to have the same opinion*) tóngyì 同意，zàntóng 赞同；**I don't agree with you** wǒ bù tóngyì nǐ de yìjiàn 我不同意你的意见；(*to consent to do*) dāying 答应，yīngyǔn 应允；**he agrees to help us** tā dāying bāngzhù wǒmen 他答应帮助我们；(*to decide jointly*) shāngdìng 商定，yuēdìng 约定；**we have agreed on the date for the meeting** wǒmen shāngdìngle huìyì de rìqí 我们商定了会议的日期

agriculture /'æɡrɪkʌltʃə(r)/ *n* nóngyè 农业

ahead /ə'hed/ *adv* (*location*) zài…qiánmian 在…前面；**he is ahead of others** tā zài biérén qiánmian 他在别人前面；(*direction*) xiàng qián 向前；**look ahead** xiàng qián kàn 向前看

Aids /ˈeɪdz/ n àizībìng 艾滋病

aim /eɪm/ **1** n an aim (an object aimed at) yí gè mùbiāo 一个目标; (a purpose aimed at) yí gè mùdì 一个目的 **2** vb (to be directed at) to be aimed at young people zhēnduì niánqīngrén 针对年轻人; (when using a weapon) to aim a rifle at someone yòng qiāng miáozhǔn mǒu rén 用枪瞄准某人

air /eə(r)/ n kōngqì 空气; in the air zài kōngzhōng 在空中

air force /ˈeə fɔːs/ n kōngjūn 空军

air hostess /ˈeə ˌhəʊstɪs/ n (British English) an air hostess yí wèi kōngzhōng xiǎojiě 一位空中小姐

airmail /ˈeəmeɪl/ n to send a letter by airmail jì yì fēng hángkōngxìn 寄一封航空信

airport /ˈeəpɔːt/ n an airport yí gè fēijīchǎng 一个飞机场

alarm clock /əˈlɑːm klɒk/ n an alarm clock yí gè nàozhōng 一个闹钟

alcohol /ˈælkəhɒl/ n (chemical term) jiǔjīng 酒精; (drink containing alcohol) jiǔ 酒

alive /əˈlaɪv/ adj huózhe de 活着的

all /ɔːl/ **1** det (whole) zhěnggè 整个; I spent all week working wǒ zhěnggè xīngqī dōu gōngzuò 我整个星期都工作; (every) suǒyǒu de 所有的, quánbù de 全部的; all the men have left suǒyǒu de nánrén dōu líkāi le 所有的男人都离开了 **2** pron (people) suǒyǒu de rén 所有的人; all of us wǒmen suǒyǒu de rén 我们所有的人; (things) yíqiè 一切, suǒyǒu de yíqiè 所有的一切; these are all I have zhè shì wǒ yōngyǒu de yíqiè 这是我拥有的一切; that's all wán le 完了 **3** adv to be all alone dúzì yì rén 独自一人; he didn't go all along the street tā méiyǒu yìzhí yánzhe mǎlù zǒu 他没有一直沿着马路走

allow /əˈlaʊ/ vb yǔnxǔ 允许, zhǔnxǔ 准许; to allow someone to [work|play|leave...] yǔnxǔ mǒu rén [gōngzuò|wán|líkāi...] 允许某人 [工作|玩|离开…]; smoking is not allowed jìnzhǐ xīyān 禁止吸烟

all right /ɔːl 'raɪt/ *adj* (*when giving your opinion*) búcuò de 不错的, hái kěyǐ de 还可以的; the film was all right zhè bù diànyǐng búcuò 这部电影不错; (*when talking about health*) are you all right? nǐ hǎo ma?, nǐ hái xíng ma? 你还好吗?, 你还行吗?; (*when asking someone's opinion*) is it all right if I come later? wǒ wǎn diǎnr lái xíng ma? 我晚点儿来行吗?; come at about nine, all right? dàyuē jiǔ diǎn lái, xíng ma? 大约9点来,行吗?; (*when agreeing*) xíng 行, hǎo hǎo 好好

almond /'ɑːmənd/ *n* xìngrén 杏仁

almost /'ɔːlməʊst/ *adv* jīhū 几乎, chàbuduō 差不多; I almost forgot wǒ jīhū wàng le 我几乎忘了

alone /ə'ləʊn/ **1** *adj* dāndú de 单独的, dúzì yì rén de 独自一人的; to be all alone dúzì yì rén 独自一人; leave me alone! bié guǎn wǒ! 别管我!, bié dòng wǒ! 别动我! **2** *adv* [to work | to live | to travel...] alone dúzì yì rén [gōngzuò | shēnghuó | lǚxíng...] 独自一人 [工作 | 生活 | 旅行...]

along /ə'lɒŋ/ *prep* yánzhe 沿着; there are trees along the river yánzhe hébiān yǒu yìxiē shù 沿着河边有一些树

aloud /ə'laʊd/ *adv* dàshēng de 大声地; to read aloud lǎngdú 朗读

already /ɔːl'redɪ/ *adv* yǐjīng 已经; it's ten o'clock already yǐjīng shí diǎn le 已经10点了

also /'ɔːlsəʊ/ *adv* (*likewise*) yě 也; he also agrees with me tā yě tóngyì wǒ de yìjiàn 他也同意我的意见; (*in addition*) hái 还; I also bought a bottle of wine wǒ hái mǎile yì píng jiǔ 我还买了一瓶酒

although /ɔːl'ðəʊ/ *conj* suīrán 虽然, jǐnguǎn 尽管; although she's strict, she's fair suīrán tā hěn yángé, dàn tā hěn gōngpíng 虽然她很严格,但她很公平

always /'ɔːlweɪz/ *adv* (*every time*) zǒngshì 总是, lǎoshi 老是; I always go to China in (the) summer wǒ zǒngshì xiàtiān qù Zhōngguó 我总是夏天去中国; (*ever*) yǒngyuǎn 永远; I'll always remember him wǒ jiāng yǒngyuǎn jìzhù tā 我将永远记住他

amazed /ə'meɪzd/ *adj* jīngyà de 惊讶的，jīngqí de 惊奇的

amazing /ə'meɪzɪŋ/ *adj* lìngrén jīngyà de 令人惊讶的，liǎobuqǐ de 了不起的

ambition /æm'bɪʃən/ *n* (*aspiration for success or advancement*) bàofù 抱负，xióngxīn 雄心；(*inordinate desire for power，fame*) yěxīn 野心，shēwàng 奢望

ambitious /æm'bɪʃəs/ *adj* (*aspiring*) yǒu bàofù de 有抱负的，yǒu xióngxīn de 有雄心的；(*inordinately longing for power，fame*) yǒu yěxīn de 有野心的

ambulance /'æmbjuləns/ *n* jiùhùchē 救护车

America /ə'merɪkə/ *n* Měiguó 美国

American /ə'merɪkən/ **1** *adj* Měiguó de 美国的 **2** *n* Měiguórén 美国人

among /ə'mʌŋ/，**amongst** /ə'mʌŋst/ *prep* (*in the middle of*) zài…zhōngjiān 在…中间；she was sitting among the students tā zuò zài xuésheng zhōngjiān 她坐在学生中间；(*in a particular group*) zài…zhōng 在…中；unemployment among young people zài niánqīngrén zhōng de shīyè qíngkuàng 在年轻人中的失业情况

amount /ə'maʊnt/ *n* shùliàng 数量

amusement arcade /ə'mjuːzmənt ɑːˌkeɪd/ *n* diànzǐ yóuxìtīng 电子游戏厅

amusement park /ə'mjuːzmənt ˌpɑːk/ *n* yóulèchǎng 游乐场

an /强 æn；弱 ən/ ▶ **a**

ancestor /'ænsestə(r)/ *n* zǔzōng 祖宗，zǔxiān 祖先

and /强 ænd；弱 ən/ *conj* hé 和；father and mother bàba hé māma 爸爸和妈妈；(*and is not translated when it is used to connect two verb phrases or two sentences*) she went to the shop and bought some fruit tā qù shāngdiàn mǎile yìxiē shuǐguǒ 她去商店买了一些水果；(*in numbers，and is not translated*) three hundred and sixty-five sānbǎi liùshíwǔ 365

anger /'æŋgə(r)/ *n* fènnù 愤怒，qìfèn 气愤

angry /'æŋgrɪ/ *adj* to be angry shēngqì 生气；to be

angry with someone duì mǒu rén shēngqì 对某人生气

animal /'ænɪməl/ n dòngwù 动物; farm animals sìyǎng de dòngwù 饲养的动物

ankle /'æŋkl/ n huáiguānjié 踝关节, jiǎobózi 脚脖子

announcement /ə'naʊnsmənt/ n an announcement yí gè tōnggào/tōngzhī 一个通告/通知

annoy /ə'nɔɪ/ vb shǐ…shēngqì 使…生气, shǐ…nǎohuǒ 使…恼火; to annoy someone shǐ mǒu rén shēngqì 使某人生气

annoyed /ə'nɔɪd/ adj to be annoyed with someone duì mǒu rén shēngqì 对某人生气

another /ə'nʌðə(r)/ 1 det another zài…yī 再…一, lìng …yī 另…一; another cup of coffee? zài hē yì bēi kāfēi? 再喝一杯咖啡? I'll buy another ticket for her wǒ gěi tā lìng mǎi yì zhāng piào 我给她另买一张票; (different) biéde 别的, lìngwài de 另外的; there's another way of doing it hái yǒu biéde fāngfǎ zuò zhè jiàn shì 还有别的方法做这件事; he has become another person tā wánquán biànle yí gè rén 他完全变了一个人 2 pron I don't like [this pen | this book | this coat...]; please show me another wǒ bù xǐhuan [zhè zhī bǐ | zhè běn shū | zhè jiàn shàngyī …]; qǐng ná [lìng yì zhī | lìng yì běn | lìng yí jiàn…] gěi wǒ kànkan 我不喜欢 [这支笔 | 这本书 | 这件上衣…], 请拿 [另一支 | 另一本 | 另一件…] 给我看看! Note that it is necessary to use an appropriate measure word after lìng yī…另一…, when another is translated as a pronoun.

answer /'ɑːnsə(r)/ 1 n dáfù 答复, huídá 回答; did you get an answer? nǐ dédào dáfù le ma? 你得到答复了吗?; there's no answer (at the door) méi rén huídá 没人回答; (solution) dá'àn 答案; answers to the exercises liànxí dá'àn 练习答案 2 vb huídá 回答; to answer a question huídá yí gè wèntí 回答一个问题; to answer the phone jiē diànhuà 接电话

answering machine /'ɑːnsərɪŋ məʃiːn/ n an answering machine yí bù lùyīn diànhuà 一部录音电话

ant /ænt/ *n* an ant yì zhī mǎyǐ 一只蚂蚁

antique /æn'ti:k/ *n* an antique yí jiàn gǔwù 一件古物, yí jiàn gǔdǒng 一件古董

antique shop /æn'ti:k ˌʃɒp/ *n* an antique shop yì jiā gǔwù shāngdiàn 一家古物商店, yì jiā gǔdǒngdiàn 一家古董店

anxious /'æŋkʃəs/ *adj* (*uneasy with fear*) dānxīn de 担心的, jiāolǜ de 焦虑的; I'm anxious about her safety wǒ wèi tā de ānquán dānxīn 我为她的安全担心; (*eager*) jíqiè de 急切的, kěwàng de 渴望的; she is anxious to go with me tā jíqiè de xiǎng gēn wǒ yìqǐ qù 她急切地想跟我一起去

any /'enɪ/ **1** *det* (*in questions*) shénme 什么! *Note that it is often unnecessary to translate any in questions*; do you have any questions? nǐ yǒu (shénme) wèntí ma? 你有(什么)问题吗?; (*with the negative*) rènhé 任何; I didn't have any friends wǒ méiyǒu rènhé péngyou 我没有任何朋友; (*whatever*) rènhé 任何; any pen will do rènhé bǐ dōu xíng 任何笔都行 **2** *pron* do any of you know his telephone number? nǐmen shéi zhīdào tā de diànhuà hàomǎ ma? 你们谁知道他的电话号码吗?; do you have any? nǐ yǒu ma? 你有吗?; he doesn't have any tā méiyǒu 他没有! *Note that it is often unnecessary to translate any when it is used as a pronoun in an object position*.

anyone /'enɪwʌn/ *pron* (*also* **anybody** /'enɪˌbɒdɪ/) rènhé rén 任何人; did you meet anyone? nǐ yùjiàn rènhé rén le ma? 你遇见任何人了吗?; anyone could do it rènhé rén dōu néng zuò zhè jiàn shì 任何人都能做这件事

anything /'enɪθɪŋ/ *pron* (*in questions or with the negative*) shénme shì 什么事, rènhé shì 任何事; can I do anything for you? wǒ néng wèi nǐ zuò diǎnr shénme shì ma? 我能为你做点儿什么事吗?; there isn't anything to do here zhèr méiyǒu rènhé shì kě zuò 这儿没有任何事可做; (*everything*) rènhé shìqing 任何事情, yíqiè 一切; he is willing to do anything for her tā yuàn wèi tā zuò rènhé shìqíng 他愿为她做任何事情

anyway /'enɪweɪ/ adv fǎnzhèng 反正；I didn't want to go there anyway fǎnzhèng wǒ běnlái yě bù xiǎng qù nàr 反正我本来也不想去那儿

anywhere /'enɪhweə(r)/ adv (in questions or with the negative) nǎr 哪儿，nǎli 哪里；can you see a telephone anywhere? nǐ néng kànjiàn nǎr yǒu diànhuà ma? 你能看见哪儿有电话吗？；you can't go anywhere nǐ nǎr yě bù néng qù 你哪儿也不能去；(any place) zài rènhé dìfang 在任何地方；we can meet anywhere you like wǒmen kěyǐ zài rènhé dìfang jiànmiàn, suí nǐ biàn 我们可以在任何地方见面，随你便

apart /ə'pɑːt/ **1** adj they don't like being apart tāmen bú yuànyì fēnkāi 他们不愿意分开 **2** apart from chúle… (yǐwài) 除了…(以外)；apart from Tom, I don't know anyone there chúle Tāngmǔ (yǐwài), nàr wǒ shéi dōu bú rènshi 除了汤姆(以外)，那儿我谁都不认识

apartment /ə'pɑːtmənt/ n an apartment yí tào yōngyù fángjiān 一套公寓房间

apartment block /ə'pɑːtmənt blɒk/ n an apartment block yì pái gōngyùlóu 一排公寓楼

apologize /ə'pɒlədʒaɪz/ vb dàoqiàn 道歉；did you apologize to him? nǐ xiàng tā dàoqiàn le ma? 你向他道歉了吗？

apology /ə'pɒlədʒɪ/ n dàoqiàn 道歉，rèncuò 认错；to make an apology to him for coming late wèi láiwǎnle xiàng tā dàoqiàn 为来晚了向他道歉

appear /ə'pɪə(r)/ vb (to seem) kàn qǐlai 看起来，hǎoxiàng 好像；(to come into view) chūxiàn 出现，xiǎnlù 显露

appetite /'æpɪtaɪt/ n shíyù 食欲，wèikǒu 胃口；to have a good appetite shíyù hǎo 食欲好

apple /'æpl/ n an apple yí gè píngguǒ 一个苹果

apple juice /'æpl dʒuːs/ n píngguǒzhī 苹果汁

appliance /ə'plaɪəns/ n qìjù 器具，yòngjù 用具；an appliance yí jiàn qìjù 一件器具

application /ˌæplɪ'keɪʃn/ n an application yí fèn shēn-qǐng 一份申请

apply /ə'plaɪ/ vb shēnqǐng 申请；to apply for a pass-port shēnqǐng yì běn hùzhào 申请一本护照

appointment /ə'pɔɪntmənt/ n yuēhuì 约会；to make an appointment with someone gēn mǒu rén yuēhuì 跟某人约会

appreciate /ə'priːʃɪeɪt/ vb I'd appreciate it if you could let me know rúguǒ nǐ néng gàosu wǒ, wǒ huì fēicháng gǎnxiè 如果你能告诉我，我会非常感谢

approach /ə'prəʊtʃ/ vb jiējìn 接近，kàojìn 靠近

approve /ə'pruːv/ vb pīzhǔn 批准，tōngguò 通过；to approve of someone zànchéng mǒu rén 赞成某人

apricot /'eɪprɪkɒt/ n an apricot yí gè xìng 一个杏

April /'eɪprəl/ n sìyuè 四月

architect /'ɑːkɪtekt/ n an architect yí gè jiànzhùshī 一个建筑师

area /'eərɪə/ n (a region) dìqū 地区；an area yí gè dìqū 一个地区；(an academic field) lǐngyù 领域；an area yí gè lǐngyù 一个领域

area code /'eərɪə ˌkəʊd/ n (US English) yóuzhèng biānmǎ 邮政编码

argue /'ɑːɡjuː/ vb zhēnglùn 争论，biànlùn 辩论；to argue about politics zhēnglùn zhèngzhì 争论政治

argument /'ɑːɡjʊmənt/ n an argument yí gè lùndiǎn 一个论点，yí gè lǐyóu 一个理由；to have an argument with someone gēn mǒu rén zhēnglùn 跟某人争论

arm /ɑːm/ n the arm gēbo 胳膊，gēbei 胳臂

armchair /'ɑːmtʃeə(r)/ n an armchair yí gè fúshǒuyǐ 一个扶手椅

armed /ɑːmd/ adj wǔzhuāng de 武装的

arms /ɑːmz/ n wǔqì 武器

army /'ɑːmɪ/ n jūnduì 军队；to join the army cānjūn 参军

around /əˈraʊnd/ ! *Often* around *occurs in combinations with verbs, for example:* run around, turn around, *etc. To find the correct translations for this type of verb, look up the separate dictionary entries at* run, turn, *etc.* **1** *prep* zài ··· zhōuwéi 在 ··· 周围；there are trees all around the garden zài huāyuán zhōuwéi dōu shì shù 在花园周围都是树；the people around me were speaking Chinese zài wǒ zhōuwéi de rén shuō Hànyǔ 在我周围的人说汉语；to go around the world zhōuyóu shìjiè 周游世界 **2** *adv* (*nearby*) zhōuwéi 周围；he looked around tā xiàng zhōuwéi kàn le kàn 他向周围看了看；(*approximately*) dàyuē 大约；we'll be there at around four o'clock wǒmen dàyuē sì diǎn zhōng dào nàr 我们大约 4 点钟到那儿

arrange /əˈreɪndʒ/ *vb* (*to make plans in advance*) ānpái 安排；to arrange a break in Italy ānpái zài Yìdàlì xiūxi yíxià 安排在意大利休息一下；to arrange to have lunch together ānpái yìqǐ chī wǔfàn 安排一起吃午饭；(*to put in order*) zhěnglǐ 整理；to arrange his books zhěnglǐ tā de shū 整理他的书

arrest /əˈrest/ *vb* dàibǔ 逮捕

arrive /əˈraɪv/ *vb* dàodá 到达，dào 到；we arrived at the station at noon wǒmen zhōngwǔ dàodá chēzhàn 我们中午到达车站

arrow /ˈærəʊ/ *n* (*missile*) jiàn 箭；an arrow yì zhī jiàn 一支箭；(*mark or object*) jiàntóu 箭头；an arrow yì gè jiàntóu 一个箭头

art /ɑːt/ *n* yìshù 艺术

art gallery /ˈɑːt ˌgæləri/ *n* an art gallery yí gè měishùguǎn 一个美术馆

artificial /ˌɑːtɪˈfɪʃəl/ *adj* réngōng de 人工的，rénzào de 人造的

artist /ˈɑːtɪst/ *n* an artist yí gè yìshùjiā 一个艺术家

arts /ɑːts/ *n* arts and humanities rénwén xuékē 人文学科

arts and crafts /ˌɑːts ænd ˈkrɑːfts/ *n* gōngyì měishù 工艺

美术

as /强 æz; 弱 əz/ **1** *conj* as ànzhào 按照；do as he does ànzhào tā de yàngzi zuò 按照他的样子做；(*at the time when*) …de shíhou …的时候；the phone rang as I was getting out of the bath wǒ zhèng cóng zǎopén chūlái de shíhou, diànhuàlíng xiǎng le 我正从澡盆出来的时候，电话铃响了；I used to live there as a child wǒ xiǎo de shíhou zhù zài nàr 我小的时候住在那儿；(*because, since*) yīnwèi 因为，yóuyú 由于；as you were out, I left a note yīnwèi nǐ chūqù le, suǒyǐ wǒ jiù liúle zhāng tiáo 因为你出去了，所以我就留了张条；(*when used with the same*) gēn…yíyàng 跟…一样，hé…yíyàng 和…一样；my coat is the same as yours wǒ de shàngyī gēn nǐ de yíyàng 我的上衣跟你的一样 **2** *prep* she's got a job as a teacher tā zhǎodàole yí gè jiàoshī de gōngzuò 她找到了一个教师的工作；he was dressed as a sailor tā chuān de xiàng yí gè shuǐshǒu 他穿得像一个水手 **3** *adv* as [intelligent | rich | strong…] as he is hé tā yíyàng [cōngmíng | yǒuqián | qiángzhuàng…] 和他一样 [聪明 | 有钱 | 强壮…]；go there as fast as you can nǐ jìnkuài qù nàr 你尽快去那儿；I have as much work as you wǒ de gōngzuò hé nǐ de yíyàng duō 我的工作和你的一样多；he plays the piano as well as his younger sister tā tán gāngqín tán de hé tā mèimei yíyàng hǎo 他弹钢琴弹得和他妹妹一样好 **4 as usual** xiàng wǎngcháng yíyàng 像往常一样，zhàolì 照例

ashamed /ə'ʃeɪmd/ *adj* to be ashamed gǎndào cánkuì 感到惭愧，gǎndào hàisào 感到害臊

ashes /'æʃɪz/ *n* huī (jìn) 灰 (烬)；(*of a cigarette*) yānhuī 烟灰；(*of a dead body*) gǔhuī 骨灰

ashtray /'æʃtreɪ/ *n* an ashtray yí gè yānhuīgāng 一个烟灰缸

Asia /'eɪʃə/ *n* Yàzhōu 亚洲

Asian /'eɪʃən/ **1** *adj* Yàzhōu de 亚洲的 **2** *n* Yàzhōurén 亚洲人

ask /ɑːsk/ *vb* to ask wèn 问；he asked me my name tā wèn wǒ jiào shénme 他问我叫什么；I'll ask them if they want to come wǒ yào wèn tāmen xiǎng bù xiǎng lái 我要问他们想不想来；to ask a question wèn wèntí 问问题；(*to request*) ràng 让，jiào 叫，yāoqiú 要求；to ask someone to [phone | come | do the shopping...] ràng mǒu rén [dǎ diànhuà | lái | mǎi dōngxi...] 让某人 [打电话 | 来 | 买东西...]；to ask to speak to someone yāoqiú gēn mǒu rén jiǎnghuà 要求跟某人讲话；to ask for money yào qián yòng 要钱用；(*to invite*) yāoqǐng 邀请，qǐng 请；to ask some friends to dinner yāoqǐng yìxiē péngyou chīfàn 邀请一些朋友吃饭；(*to look for information*) xúnwèn 询问；did you ask about the tickets? nǐ xúnwèn piào de shìqing le ma? 你询问票的事情了吗?

asleep /əˈsliːp/ *adj* to be asleep zài shuìjiào 在睡觉；to fall asleep shuìzháo 睡着

assemble /əˈsembl/ *vb* (*to call together*) jíhé 集合；all the students assembled in the school hall xuésheng dōu zài xuéxiào lǐtáng li jíhé 学生都在学校礼堂里集合；(*to collect*) shōují 收集；she has assembled some materials tā yǐjīng shōují le yìxiē cáiliào 她已经收集了一些材料；(*to put together the parts of*) zhuāngpèi 装配；to assemble a machine zhuāngpèi jīqì 装配机器

assignment /əˈsaɪnmənt/ *n* a school assignment xuéxiào zuòyè 学校作业

assistant /əˈsɪstənt/ *n* an assistant yí gè zhùshǒu 一个助手；a shop assistant yí gè shòuhuòyuán 一个售货员；a teaching assistant yí gè zhùjiào 一个助教

at /强 æt；弱 ət/! *prep* There are many verbs which involve the use of at, like look at, laugh at, point at, etc. For translations, look up the entries for look, laugh, point, etc.；(*when talking about a position or place*) zài 在；we'll meet at the concert wǒmen zài yīnyuèhuì jiànmiàn 我们在音乐会见面；to be [at home | at school | at work...] [zài jiā | zài xuéxiào | zài shàngbān...] [在家 | 在学校 | 在上

班…]; **to be at one's desk** zài xuéxí 在学习，zài gōngzuò 在工作；(when talking about time and age)(zài)…(de shíhou)(在…的时候)；**the film starts at nine o'clock** diànyǐng jiǔ diǎn kāiyǎn 电影 9 点开演；**she was able to read at four years of age** tā (zài) sì suì (de shíhou) jiù néng kànshū le 她(在)4 岁(的时候)就能读书了；(when talking about speed and price) yǐ 以；**the car goes at seventy miles an hour** qìchē yǐ měi xiǎoshí qīshí yīnglǐ de sùdù xíngshǐ 汽车以每小时 70 英里的速度行驶；**at a low price** yǐ hěn dī de jiàqian 以很低的价钱

athlete /'æθliːt/ n **an athlete** yí gè yùndòngyuán 一个运动员，yì míng yùndòngyuán 一名运动员

athletics /æθ'letɪks/ n (in Britain) tiánjìng yùndòng 田径运动；(in the US) tǐyù yùndòng 体育运动

Atlantic /ət'læntɪk/ n **the Atlantic** Dàxīyáng 大西洋

atmosphere /'ætməsfɪə(r)/ n (the air) dàqì 大气，kōngqì 空气；(a mood, a feeling) qìfēn 气氛

attach /ə'tætʃ/ vb **to be attached to the wall** tiē zài qiáng shang 贴在墙上；**attach a basket to the bike** bǎ yí gè lánzi xì zài zìxíngchē shang 把一个篮子系在自行车上

attack /ə'tæk/ vb gōngjī 攻击，jìngōng 进攻

attempt /ə'tempt/ **1** vb shìtú 试图；**to attempt to break the record** shìtú dǎpò jìlù 试图打破纪录 **2** n chángshì 尝试，shìtú 试图

attend /ə'tend/ vb (to be present) cānjiā 参加，chūxí 出席；**to attend a meeting** cānjiā huìyì 参加会议；(to go regularly to) shàng 上；**to attend evening classes** shàng yèxiào 上夜校

attention /ə'tenʃən/ n zhùyì 注意；**to get someone's attention** yǐnqǐ mǒu rén de zhùyì 引起某人的注意；**to pay attention to the teacher** zhùyì tīng lǎoshī jiǎngkè 注意听老师讲课

attic /'ætɪk/ n gélóu 阁楼，dǐnglóu 顶楼

attitude /'ætɪtjuːd/ n tàidu 态度；**his attitude**

toward(s) me tā duì wǒ de tàidu 他对我的态度

attract /əˈtrækt/ vb to attract people xīyǐn rén 吸引人; to attract [attention|interest|appreciation]yǐnqǐ [zhùyì|xìngqù|zànshǎng] 引起 [注意|兴趣|赞赏]

attractive /əˈtræktɪv/ adj yǒu xīyǐnlì de 有吸引力的, yòurén de 诱人的

auburn /ˈɔːbən/ adj jīnzōngsè de 金棕色的

audience /ˈɔːdɪəns/ n (assembly of hearers) tīngzhòng 听众; (assembly of spectators) guānzhòng 观众

August /ˈɔːgəst/ n bāyuè 八月

aunt /ɑːnt/ n (father's sister) gūmǔ 姑母, gūgu 姑姑; (mother's sister) yímǔ 姨母, yí yí 姨; (a respectful form of address to an elderly woman) dàmā 大妈, dàniáng 大娘; (a respectful form used by children to address an adult woman) āyí 阿姨

au pair /ˌəʊˈpeə/ n an au pair yí gè bāngshǒu 一个帮手, yí gè bānggōng 一个帮工

Australia /ɒˈstreɪlɪə/ n Àodàlìyà 澳大利亚

Australian /ɒˈstreɪlɪən/ 1 adj Àodàlìyà de 澳大利亚的 2 n Àodàlìyàrén 澳大利亚人

Austria /ˈɒstrɪə/ n Àodìlì 奥地利

Austrian /ˈɒstrɪən/ 1 adj Àodìlì de 奥地利的 2 n Àodìlìrén 奥地利人

author /ˈɔːθə(r)/ n zuòzhě 作者

automatic /ˌɔːtəˈmætɪk/ adj zìdòng de 自动的

autumn /ˈɔːtəm/ n qiūtiān 秋天, qiūjì 秋季

available /əˈveɪləbl/ adj (obtainable through purchase) néng mǎidào de 能买到的, mǎi de dào de 买得到的; tickets for the concert are still available yīnyuèhuì de piào hái néng mǎidào 音乐会的票还能买到; (accessible for use) kěyǐ yòng de 可以用的; all the books are available to the students suǒyǒu de shū xuésheng dōu kěyǐ yòng 所有的书学生都可以用

average /ˈævərɪdʒ/ adj (mean) píngjūn de 平均的; (ordinary) pǔtōng de 普通的, tōngcháng de 通常的; the

average man pǔtōng de rén 普通的人

avoid /ə'vɔɪd/ vb (to prevent) bìmiǎn 避免; to avoid spending money bìmiǎn huāqián 避免花钱; (to stay away from) duǒkāi 躲开, huíbì 回避

awake /ə'weɪk/ adj to be awake (having slept) xǐng le 醒了; to stay awake shuì bù zháo 睡不着; to keep someone awake shǐ mǒu rén shuì bù zháo 使某人睡不着

award /ə'wɔːd/ n an award yí gè jiǎng(pǐn) 一个奖(品); she got the award for best actress tā huòdé zuìjiānǎyǎnyuánjiǎng 她获得最佳女演员奖

aware /ə'weə(r)/ adj to be aware of the [problem | danger | difficulty...] yìshí dào zhège [wèntí | wēixiǎn | kùnnan···] 意识到这个 [问题 | 危险 | 困难···]

away /ə'weɪ/ adv (absent) to be away bú zài 不在; she's away on business tā chūchāi le 她出差了; (when talking about distances) to be far away hěn yuǎn 很远; London is 40 km away Lúndūn lí zhèr sìshí gōnglǐ 伦敦离这儿 40 公里

awful /'ɔːfʊl/ adj (no good) zāotòu de 糟透了的, hěn zāogāo de 很糟糕的; I thought the film was awful wǒ juéde zhège diànyǐng zāotòu le 我觉得这个电影糟透了; (causing shock) kěpà de 可怕的; an awful accident yí gè kěpà de shìgù 一个可怕的事故; I feel awful wǒ gǎndào fēicháng nánshòu 我感到非常难受

awkward /'ɔːkwəd/ adj (describing a situation, a problem) jíshǒu de 棘手的, nán chǔlǐ de 难处理的; (embarrassed) gāngà de 尴尬的; I feel awkward about telling him gàosu tā wǒ juéde hěn gāngà 告诉他我觉得很尴尬

axe /æks/ n an axe yì bǎ fǔtou 一把斧头, yì bǎ fǔzi 一把斧子

Bb

baby /'beɪbɪ/ *n* a baby yí gè yīng'ér 一个婴儿

babysit /'beɪbɪsɪt/ *vb* zhàokàn háizi 照看孩子

back /bæk/! *Often* **back** *occurs in combinations with verbs, for example:* come back, get back, give back, *etc. To find the correct translations for this type of verb, look up the separate dictionary entries at* come, get, give, *etc.* **1** *n* (*part of the body*) the back bèibù 背部, bèi 背; I've hurt my back wǒ bèibù shòule shāng 我背部受了伤; (*the rear*) hòumian 后面; at the back of the supermarket zài chāojí shìchǎng hòumian 在超级市场后面; to sit in the back of the car zuò zài chē hòumian 坐在车后面 **2** *adv* to be back huílái 回来; I'll be back in five minutes wǒ guò wǔ fēnzhōng huílái 我过 5 分钟回来

back door /ˌbæk 'dɔː/ *n* the back door hòumén 后门

background /'bækgraʊnd/ *n* (*previous history of a person*) lǚlì 履历; (*upbringing of a person*) chūshēn 出身; (*of a picture or a story*) the background bèijǐng 背景

backpack /'bækpæk/ *n* a backpack yí gè bèibāo 一个背包

back seat /ˌbæk 'siːt/ *n* the back seat hòumian de zuòwèi 后面的座位

back to front /ˌbæk tʊ 'frʌnt/ *adv* fǎn 反; to put a sweater on back to front bǎ máoyī chuānfǎn le 把毛衣穿反了

backwards /'bækwədz/, **backward** /'bækwəd/ *adv* xiàng hòu 向后

bacon /'beɪkən/ *n* bacon xiánzhūròu 咸猪肉

bad /bæd/ *adj* huài de 坏的, bù hǎo de 不好的; a bad idea yí gè huài zhǔyi 一个坏主意; a bad film yí gè nánkàn de diànyǐng 一个难看的电影；I have some bad news wǒ yǒu yí gè huài xiāoxi 我有一个坏消息；to be bad at [maths | tennis | chess...] bú shàncháng [shùxué | dǎ wǎngqiú | xiàqí...] 不擅长 [数学 | 打网球 | 下棋...]；it's a bad time to go on holiday zhège shíjiān dùjià bù hǎo 这个时间度假不好；'was the film good?'—'not bad' "zhège diànyǐng hǎo ma?"—"búcuò" "这个电影好吗?"—"不错"；smoking is bad for you xīyān duì nǐ shēntǐ bù hǎo 吸烟对你身体不好；(serious) yánzhòng de 严重的；a bad accident yí gè yánzhòng de shìgù 一个严重的事故；to have a bad cold dé zhòng gǎnmào 得重感冒；(when talking about food) the milk has gone bad niúnǎi huài le 牛奶坏了；(not kind, not honest) bú dàodé de, 不道德的，huài de 坏的

badger /'bædʒə(r)/ n a badger yì zhī huān 一只獾

badly /'bædlɪ/ adv (not well) bù hǎo 不好；she slept badly tā shuì de bù hǎo 她睡得不好；(seriously) yánzhòng de 严重地；he was badly injured tā shāng de hěn yánzhòng 他伤得很严重；(naughty) tiáopí 调皮；this child behaves badly zhège háizi hěn tiáopí 这个孩子很调皮

badminton /'bædmɪntən/ n yǔmáoqiú 羽毛球

bad-tempered /ˌbæd'tempəd/ adj to be bad-tempered píqì hěn huài 脾气很坏

bag /bæg/ n a bag yí gè bāo 一个包

baggage /'bægɪdʒ/ n a piece of baggage yí jiàn xíngli 一件行李

bake /beɪk/ vb kǎo 烤

baker /'beɪkə(r)/ n a baker yí gè miànbāoshī 一个面包师

bakery /'beɪkərɪ/ n a bakery yì jiā miànbāodiàn 一家面包店

balance /'bæləns/ n (an instrument for weighing) chèng 秤，tiānpíng 天平；(equilibrium) pínghéng 平衡；to lose one's balance shīqù pínghéng 失去平衡

balcony /'bælkənɪ/ n a balcony yí gè yángtái 一个阳台

bald /bɔːld/ *adj* tūdǐng de 秃顶的, tūtóu de 秃头的

ball /bɔːl/ *n* a ball yí gè qiú 一个球; to play ball dǎqiú 打球

ballet /'bæleɪ/ *n* bālěiwǔ 芭蕾舞

balloon /bə'luːn/ *n* a balloon yí gè qìqiú 一个气球

ballpoint /'bɔːlpɔɪnt/ (*US English*) *n* a ballpoint pen yì zhī yuánzhūbǐ 一支圆珠笔

ban /bæn/ *vb* jìnzhǐ 禁止

banana /bə'nɑːnə/ *n* a banana yí gè xiāngjiāo 一个香蕉

band /bænd/ *n* (*a flat strip*) a band yì gēn dàizi 一根带子; (*a body of musicians*) yí gè yuèduì 一个乐队; (*a group*) qún 群; a band of football fans yì qún qiúmí 一群球迷

bandage /'bændɪdʒ/ *n* a bandage yì gēn bēngdài 一根绷带

bang /bæŋ/ **1** *n* (*a loud noise*) a bang pēng de yì shēng 砰的一声; (*US English*) (*fringe*) bangs liúhǎir 刘海儿 **2** *vb* (*to close with a bang*) pēng de guānshang 砰地关上; (*to strike with the head or body*) měng zhuàng 猛撞; (*to beat with the hand*) měng qiāo 猛敲; to bang one's fist on the table yòng quántou měng qiāo zhuōzi 用拳头猛敲桌子

bank /bæŋk/ *n* (*a financial institution*) a bank yì jiā yínháng 一家银行; (*blood bank*) a blood bank yí gè xuèkù 一个血库; (*of a river*) a river bank yí gè hé'àn 一个河岸

bank account /'bæŋk əkaʊnt/ *n* a bank account yí gè yínháng zhànghù 一个银行账户

bank holiday /bæŋk 'hɒlədeɪ/ *n* (*British English*) a bank holiday yí gè gōngjiàrì 一个公假日

bar /bɑː(r)/ *n* (*a place*) a bar yí gè jiǔbā 一个酒吧; (*made of metal*) an iron bar yì gēn tiěbàng 一根铁棒; (*on a cage or window*) a bar yì gēn zhàlan 一根栅栏; (*other uses*) a bar of soap yì tiáo féizào 一条肥皂; a bar of chocolate yí dà kuài qiǎokèlì 一大块巧克力

barbecue /'bɑːbɪkjuː/ n a barbecue yí cì shāokǎo yěcān 一次烧烤野餐

barely /'beəlɪ/ adv miǎnqiǎng 勉强; he was barely able to walk tā miǎnqiǎng nénggòu zǒulù 他勉强能够走路

bargain /'bɑːgɪn/ n a bargain yì bǐ jiāoyì 一笔交易

bark /bɑːk/ **1** n (of a tree) shùpí 树皮; (of a dog) the dog's bark gǒu jiào de shēngyīn 狗叫的声音 **2** vb the dog is barking gǒu zài jiào 狗在叫

barn /bɑːn/ n a barn yí gè gǔcāng 一个谷仓

barrel /'bærəl/ n a barrel of water yì tǒng shuǐ 一桶水

base /beɪs/ vb (use as a basis for) yǐ … wéi jīchǔ 以 … 为基础, yǐ … wéi gēnjù 以 … 为根据; to be based on a true story yǐ yí gè zhēnshí de gùshi wéi jīchǔ 以一个真实的故事为基础; (of a company or diplomatic mission) to be based in London chángzhù (zài) Lúndūn 常驻(在)伦敦

baseball /'beɪsbɔːl/ n bàngqiú 棒球

basement /'beɪsmənt/ n a basement yí gè dìxiàshì 一个地下室

basically /'beɪsɪkəlɪ/ adv jīběnshang 基本上

basin /'beɪsən/ n a basin yí gè pén 一个盆

basket /'bɑːskɪt/ n a basket yí gè lánzi 一个篮子

basketball /'bɑːskɪtbɔːl/ n a basketball yì gè lánqiú 一个篮球

bat /bæt/ n (in cricket or baseball) a bat yì gēn qiúbàng 一根球棒; (an animal) a bat yì zhī biānfú 一只蝙蝠

bath /bɑːθ/ n to have a bath xǐzǎo 洗澡; he's in the bath tā zài xǐzǎo 他在洗澡; (a bathtub) a bath yí gè yùpén 一个浴盆

bathroom /'bɑːθrʊm/ n a bathroom yí gè yùshì 一个浴室; (US English) (the toilet) to go to the bathroom shàng cèsuǒ 上厕所

battery /'bætərɪ/ n a battery (for a torch) yì jié diànchí 一节电池; (for a car) yí gè diànchí 一个电池

battle /'bætl/ n a battle yì chǎng zhàndòu 一场战斗

bay /beɪ/ n a bay yí gè hǎiwān 一个海湾

be /强 biː;弱 bɪ/ vb to be shì 是; he is a lawyer tā shì yí gè lǜshī 他是一个律师；(in the future tense or in the infinitive) chéngwéi 成为; Tom will be a film star Tāngmǔ jiāng chéngwéi yí gè diànyǐng míngxīng 汤姆将成为一个电影明星; my son hopes to be a footballer wǒ érzi xīwàng chéngwéi yí gè zúqiú yùndòngyuán 我儿子希望成为一个足球运动员；(when talking about travelling) I've never been to Japan wǒ cónglái méi qùguo Rìběn 我从来没去过日本; have you ever been to Africa? nǐ qùguo Fēizhōu ma? 你去过非洲吗?；(when talking about health) how are you? nǐ hǎo ma? 你好吗?; I'm very well nǐ hěn hǎo wǒ hěn hǎo 你很好我很好; how is your mother? nǐ māma hǎo ma? 你妈妈好吗?

beach /biːtʃ/ n a beach (on a sea) yí piàn hǎitān 一片海滩；(on a river) yí piàn hétān 一片河滩；(on a lake) yí piàn hútān 一片湖滩

beam /biːm/ n (in a building) a beam yì gēn liáng 一根梁；(a ray of light) a beam of light yí shù guāng 一束光，yí dào guāng 一道光

bean /biːn/ n a bean yí lì dòuzi 一粒豆子

bear /beə(r)/ 1 n a bear yì zhī xióng 一只熊 2 vb (to sustain) fūdān 负担，chéngdān 承担；(to endure) rěnshòu 忍受，róngrěn 容忍

beard /bɪəd/ n húzi 胡子

beat /biːt/ vb (to hit hard) dǎ 打；(in cooking) jiǎobàn 搅拌；(to win against) zhànshèng 战胜，dǎbài 打败; Scotland beat England two to one Sūgélán èr bǐ yī zhànshèngle Yīnggélán 苏格兰 2 比 1 战胜了英格兰

beautiful /ˈbjuːtəfʊl/ adj měilì de 美丽的，piàoliang de 漂亮的; a beautiful garden yí gè měilì de huāyuán 一个美丽的花园; a beautiful girl yí gè piàoliang de gūniang 一个漂亮的姑娘

beauty /ˈbjuːtɪ/ n měilì 美丽，měi 美

because /bɪˈkɒz/ 1 conj yīnwèi 因为; he didn't come

because he was ill yīnwèi tā bìng le, suǒyǐ tā méi lái 因 为他病了，所以他没来 **2 because of** yīnwèi 因为；**we didn't go out because of the rain** yīnwèi xiàyǔ, suǒyǐ wǒmen méi chūqù 因为下雨，所以我们没出去！*Note that the clause or phrase introduced by* yīnwèi 因为 *usually appears before the main clause. Note also that when* yīnwèi 因为 *is used, the main clause is often preceded by* suǒyǐ 所以 *which means therefore.*

become /bɪˈkʌm/ vb (*followed by a noun*) biànchéng 变成，chéngwéi 成为；**he has become an adult** tā biànchéng/chéngwéi dàren le 他变成/成为大人了；(*followed by an adjective*) biàn 变，biànde 变得；**it has become cold** tiān biànlěng le 天变冷了

bed /bed/ n a zhāng chuáng 一张床；**to go to bed** shàngchuáng shuìjiào 上床睡觉

bedroom /ˈbedrʊm/ n a bedroom yí gè wòshì 一个卧室，yí gè qǐnshì 一个寝室

bee /biː/ n a bee yì zhī mìfēng 一只蜜蜂

beef /biːf/ n niúròu 牛肉；**roast beef** kǎoniúròu 烤牛肉

beer /bɪə(r)/ n (*the product*) beer píjiǔ 啤酒；(*a glass of beer*) a beer yì bēi píjiǔ 一杯啤酒

beet /biːt/, **beetroot** /ˈbiːtruːt/ n (*British English*) tiáncài 甜菜

before /bɪˈfɔː(r)/ **1** prep (*referring to time*) zài…yǐqián 在…以前，…yǐqián …以前；**before 6 o'clock** (zài) liù diǎn yǐqián (在) 6 点以前；**the day before yesterday** qiántiān 前天；**the day before the exam** kǎoshì de qián yì tiān 考试的前一天；(*in front of*) zài…qiánmian 在…前面，zài…qiántou 在…前头；**he was before me in the queue** tā pái zài wǒ qiánmian 他排在我前面 **2** adv yǐqián 以前；**have you been to Beijing before?** nǐ yǐqián qùguo Běijīng ma? 你以前去过北京吗？**3** conj zài…yǐqián 在… 以前，zài…zhīqián 在 … 之前；**I'd like to phone him before he goes** (zài) tā zǒu yǐqián wǒ xiǎng gěi tā dǎ gè diànhuà (在)他走以前我想给他打个电话

beg /beg/ vb (for food，money，etc.) beg for 要 要，qǐtǎo 乞讨；(making requests)qǐqiú 乞求，kěnqiú 恳求

beggar /'begə(r)/ n a beggar yí gè qǐgài 一个乞丐，yí gè yàofàn de 一个要饭的

begin /bɪ'gɪn/ vb kāishǐ 开始；to begin ［working｜laughing｜raining］kāishǐ ［gōngzuò｜xiào｜xiàyǔ］开始 ［工作｜笑｜下雨］

beginner /bɪ'gɪnə(r)/ n a beginner yí gè chūxuézhě 一个初学者

beginning /bɪ'gɪnɪŋ/ n (of an event，of an activity) kāishǐ 开始，kāiduān 开端；a good beginning yí gè liánghǎo de kāiduān 一个良好的开端；(of a year，of a month) the beginning of ［the month｜the year｜May］［yuè｜nián｜wǔyuè］chū ［月｜年｜5 月］初边

behave /bɪ'heɪv/ vb (to act，to function) biǎoxiàn 表现；he behaved badly tā biǎoxiàn bù hǎo 他表现不好；(to conduct oneself well) shǒu guīju 守规矩；she always behaves (herself) tā zǒngshì hěn shǒu guīju 她总是很守规矩；behave yourself! guīju diǎn! 规矩点!

behaviour /bɪ'heɪvjə(r)/ (British English)，**behavior** (US English) n xíngwéi 行为，biǎoxiàn 表现

behind /bɪ'haɪnd/ **1** prep zài…hòumian 在…后面，zài…hòubian 在…后边；my house is behind the school wǒ de jiā zài xuéxiào hòumian 我的家在学校后面 **2** adv zài hòumian 在后面，zài hòubian 在后边；she is sitting behind tā zuò zài hòumian 她坐在后面

Belgian /'beldʒən/ **1** adj Bǐlìshí de 比利时的 **2** n a Belgian yí gè Bǐlìshírén 一个比利时人

Belgium /'beldʒəm/ n Bǐlìshí 比利时

believe /bɪ'liːv/ vb xiāngxìn 相信；believe in xìnrèn 信任

bell /bel/ n (in a church)zhōng 钟；(on a door or bicycle) líng 铃

belong /bɪ'lɒŋ/ vb (to be the property of) shǔyú 属于；that piece of land belongs to our college nà kuài dì shǔyú wǒmen xuéyuàn 那块地属于我们学院；(be a *member of*) **belong to a party** shì yí gè dǎng de dǎngyuán 是一个党的党员

belongings /bɪ'lɒŋɪŋz/ *n* (*luggage*) xíngli 行李;（*things that one owns*）dōngxi 东西; **his belongings** tāde dōngxi 他的东西

below /bɪ'ləʊ/ **1** *prep* (*in space*) zài … xiàmiàn 在 … 下面; **the kitchen is below my bedroom** chúfáng zài wǒ de wòshì xiàmian 厨房在我的卧室下面;（*in rank, age, degree, etc.*）(zài) … yǐxià（在）… 以下; **below 60 years old** liùshí suì yǐxià 60 岁以下; **10 degrees below zero** língxià shí dù 零下 10 度 **2** *adj* xiàmian de 下面的; **please do the exercises below** qǐng zuò xiàmian de liànxí 请做下面的练习

belt /belt/ *n* (*worn around the waist*) yāodài 腰带, pídài 皮带;（*in machinery*）chuándòng pídài 传动皮带

bench /bentʃ/ *n* chángdèng 长凳

bend /bend/ **1** *vb* (*to bend an object*) wān 弯, nòngwān 弄弯; **he bent the iron bar with his bare hands** tā yòng shǒu bǎ tiěbàng nòngwān le 他用手把铁棒弄弯了;（*to bend down or lower one's head*）dīxia 低下;（*to bend down one's head*）dīxia tóu 低下头;（*to bend down one's body*）wānxia 弯下; **he bent down to pick up the coin** tā wānxia shēnzi bǎ qián jiǎn qǐlai 他弯下身子把钱捡起来 **2** *n* zhuǎnwān 转弯, guǎiwān 拐弯; **there is a sharp bend in this road** zhè tiáo lù shang yǒu yí gè jízhuǎnwān 这条路上有一个急转弯

beneath /bɪ'niːθ/ *prep* zài … xiàmian 在 … 下面, zài … dīxia 在 … 底下

beside /bɪ'saɪd/ *prep* zài … pángbiān 在 … 旁边; **to sit beside me** zuò zài wǒ pángbiān 坐在我旁边; **to live beside the sea** zhù zài hǎibiān 住在海边

best /best/ **1** *adj* zuì hǎo de 最好的; **my best friend** wǒ zuì hǎo de péngyou 我最好的朋友; **this is the best hotel in the city** zhè shì zhège chéngshì zuì hǎo de lǚguǎn 这是这个城市最好的旅馆 **2** *adv* zuì hǎo 最好; **she**

sings the best tā chàng de zuì hǎo 她唱得最好；(*most*) zuì 最；I like tennis best wǒ zuì xǐhuan wǎngqiú 我最喜欢网球 3 *pron* the best zuì hǎo de ··· 最好的···；he's the best in his class tā shì bān li zuì hǎo de xuésheng 他是班里最好的学生；do one's best jìnlì 尽力，jìn zuì dà nǔlì 尽最大努力

bet /bet/ *vb* (*with money*) tóng ··· dǎdǔ 同 ··· 打赌；(*predict*) gǎn duàndìng 敢断定；I bet he'll win wǒ gǎn duàndìng tā huì yíng 我敢断定他会赢

better /'betə(r)/ 1 *adj* gèng hǎo de 更好的；they will have a better future tāmen huì yǒu yí gè gèng hǎo de wèilái 他们会有一个更好的未来；is she better today? tā jīntiān hǎo xiē le ma? 她今天好些了吗?；his Chinese is better than mine tā de Hànyǔ bǐ wǒ de hǎo 他的汉语比我的好 2 *adv* gèng hǎo de 更好地；he swims better than I do tā yóuyǒng yóu de bǐ wǒ hǎo 他游泳游得比我好；zuìhǎo 最好；we'd better go wǒmen zuìhǎo háishì zǒu ba 我们最好还是走吧；it's better to go by bus zuìhǎo zuò qìchē qù 最好坐汽车去

between /bɪ'twiːn/ *prep* zài ··· zhījiān 在 ··· 之间，zài ··· zhōngjiān 在 ··· 中间；there is a stream between the two gardens zài liǎng gè huāyuán zhījiān yǒu yì tiáo xiǎohé 在两个花园之间有一条小河；between 2 and 3 o'clock liǎng diǎn dào sān diǎn zhījiān 两点到三点之间

beyond /bɪ'jɒnd/ *prep* (*on the further side of*) zài ··· nàbiān 在 ··· 那边；beyond the mountain zài shān nàbiān 在山那边；(*out of reach of*) chāochū 超出；beyond my ability chāochū wǒ de nénglì 超出我的能力

bicycle /'baɪsɪkl/ *n* a bicycle yí liàng zìxíngchē 一辆自行车

big /bɪg/ *adj* (*large*) dà de 大的；a big garden yí gè dà huāyuán 一个大花园；(*important*) zhòngyào de 重要的；a big question yí gè zhòngyào wèntí 一个重要问题；(*serious*) yánzhòng de 严重的；a big mistake yí gè yánzhòng cuòwù 一个严重错误；(*heavy, thick*) hòu de

厚的，zhòng de 重的；**a big book** yì běn hěn hòu de shū 一本很厚的书

bill /bɪl/ n (for gas , electricity , telephone) dān 单；[gas | electricity | telephone] bill [méiqìfèi | diànfèi | diànhuàfèi] dān [煤气费 | 电费 | 电话费] 单；(in a restaurant or hotel) zhàngdān 账单；**here is your bill** zhè shì nín de zhàngdān 这是您的账单；**could we have the bill, please?** qǐng gěi wǒmen jié yíxià zhàng hǎo ma? 请给我们结一下账好吗?；(US English) (money) chāopiào 钞票；**a 10-dollar bill** yì zhāng shí měiyuán de chāopiào 一张 10 美元的钞票

billiards /'bɪljədz/ n billiards táiqiú 台球

bin /bɪn/ n (British English) **a bin** yí gè lājītǒng 一个垃圾桶

biology /baɪ'ɒlədʒɪ/ n biology shēngwùxué 生物学

bird /bɜːd/ n **a bird** yì zhī niǎo 一只鸟

biro® /'baɪərəʊ/ n (British English) **a biro**® yì zhī yuánzhūbǐ 一支圆珠笔

birth /bɜːθ/ n **a birth** chūshēng 出生, dànshēng 诞生；**a place of birth** chūshēngdì 出生地

birthday /'bɜːθdeɪ/ n birthday shēngrì 生日；**happy birthday!** shēngrì kuàilè! 生日快乐!

biscuit /'bɪskɪt/ n (British English) **a biscuit** yí kuài bǐnggān 一块饼干

bit /bɪt/ **1** n **a bit of** [cheese | bread | paper] yìdiǎnr [nǎilào | miànbāo | zhǐ] 一点儿 [奶酪 | 面包 | 纸] **2** a bit (British English) **a bit** [early | hot | odd] yǒudiǎnr [zǎo | rè | qíguài] 有点儿 [早 | 热 | 奇怪]

bite /baɪt/ vb yǎo 咬

bitter /'bɪtə(r)/ adj kǔ de 苦的

black /blæk/ adj hēi de 黑的

blackberry /'blækbərɪ/ n hēiméi 黑莓；**a blackberry** yí gè hēiméi 一个黑莓

blackboard /'blækbɔːd/ n **a blackboard** yí kuài hēibǎn 一块黑板

blackcurrants /ˌblæk'kʌrənts/ n hēi pútáogān 黑葡萄干

blade /bleɪd/ n (of a knife, a sword) dāorèn 刀刃，dāokǒu 刀口；a blade of grass yí piàn cǎoyè 一片草叶

blame /bleɪm/ **1** vb zébèi 责备，zéguài 责怪 **2** n to take the blame fùzé 负责，shòuguò 受过

blank /blæŋk/ adj (describing a page) kòngbái de 空白的；(describing a cassette) kōng de 空的

blanket /ˈblæŋkɪt/ n a blanket yì tiáo tǎnzi 一条毯子

blaze /bleɪz/ n huǒyàn 火焰

bleed /bliːd/ vb chūxuè 出血；my nose is bleeding wǒ de bízi zài chūxuè 我的鼻子在出血

blind /blaɪnd/ **1** adj shīmíng de 失明的，xiā de 瞎的 **2** vb (destroy someone's sight) shǐ … shīmíng 使 … 失明；he was blinded in an accident tā zài yí cì shìgù zhōng shīmíng le 他在一次事故中失明了；(to dazzle) shǐ … kàn bú jiàn 使 … 看不见 **3** n a blind yí shàn bǎiyèchuāng 一扇百叶窗

blink /blɪŋk/ vb zhǎ yǎnjīng 眨眼睛

blister /ˈblɪstə(r)/ n a blister yí gè pào 一个疱

block /blɒk/ **1** n (a building) a block of apartments yí zhuàng gōngyùlóu 一幢公寓楼；(a group of houses) a block of houses yí gè jiēqū 一个街区；(a large piece) a block of ice yí dà kuài bīng 一大块冰 **2** vb zǔsè 阻塞，dǔsè 堵塞；to block a road zǔsè mǎlù 阻塞马路

blond, blonde /blɒnd/ adj jīnsè de 金色的；he has blond hair tā de tóufa shì jīnsè de 他的头发是金色的

blood /blʌd/ n xuè/xiě 血

blouse /blaʊz/ n a blouse yí jiàn (nǚshì) chènshān 一件（女式）衬衫

blow /bləʊ/ **1** vb (if it's the wind or a person) chuī 吹；the wind blew the door shut fēng bǎ mén chuī de guānshang le 风把门吹得关上了；to blow a whistle chuīshào 吹哨；to blow one's nose xǐng bízi 擤鼻子 **2** n a blow yí gè dǎjī 一个打击；**blow away** to be blown away chuīzǒu le 吹走了；**blow down** to be blown

down chuīdǎo le 吹倒了；**blow out** chuīmiè 吹灭；to blow out a candle chuīmiè làzhú 吹灭蜡烛；**blow up** (to destroy) zhàhuǐ 炸毁，zhàdiào 炸掉；to blow up a car zhàhuǐ yí liàng qìchē 炸毁一辆汽车；(to put air into) chōngqì 充气

blue /bluː/ adj lánsè de 蓝色的

blush /blʌʃ/ vb liǎnhóng 脸红

board /bɔːd/ **1** n (a piece of wood) mùbǎn 木板；a board yí kuài mùbǎn 一块木板；(in chess, draughts, checkers) qípán 棋盘；a board yí kuài qípán 一块棋盘；(a blackboard) a board yí kuài hēibǎn 一块黑板 **2** vb to board a ship shàng chuán 上船 **3** on board [a ship a train a plane...] zài [chuán | huǒchē | fēijī...]shang 在 [船 | 火车 | 飞机...]上

boarding school /'bɔːdɪŋ skuːl/ n a boarding school yì suǒ jìsù xuéxiào 一所寄宿学校

boast /bəust/ vb zìwǒ chuīxū 自我吹嘘，zìkuā 自夸，chuīniú 吹牛

boat /bəut/ n a boat yì tiáo chuán 一条船

body /'bɒdɪ/ n(the body) shēntǐ 身体；(a dead body) shītǐ 尸体

boil /bɔɪl/ vb (an action done by a person)；to boil water shāo kāishuǐ 烧开水；to boil an egg zhǔ jīdàn 煮鸡蛋；(referring to water or milk) kāi 开；the water is boiling shuǐ kāi le 水开了

boiled egg /bɔɪld eg/ n a boiled egg yí gè zhǔjīdàn 一个煮鸡蛋

boiler /'bɔɪlə(r)/ n a boiler yí gè guōlú 一个锅炉

boiling /'bɔɪlɪŋ/ adj (when describing water or milk) fèiténg de 沸腾的；(when describing the weather) hěn rè de 很热的

bomb /bɒm/ **1** n a bomb yì kē zhàdàn 一颗炸弹 **2** vb hōngzhà 轰炸

bone /bəun/ n a bone (in the body, in meat) yí kuài gǔtou 一块骨头；(in fish) yì gēn yúcì 一根鱼刺

bonnet /'bɒnɪt/ n (*British English*) the bonnet (*in a car*) qìchē yǐnqínggài 汽车引擎盖

book /bʊk/ **1** n a book yì běn shū 一本书 **2** vb yùdìng 预订; to book a room yùdìng yí gè fángjiān 预订一个房间; the flight is fully booked zhè cì hángbān quánbù dìngmǎn le 这次航班全部订满了

booking /'bʊkɪŋ/ n a booking yùdìng 预订

bookshop /'bʊkʃɒp/, **bookstore** /'bʊkstɔː(r)/ n a bookshop, a bookstore yí gè shūdiàn 一个书店

boot /buːt/ n (*worn on the feet*) a boot yì zhī xuēzi 一只靴子; a pair of boots yì shuāng xuēzi 一双靴子; (*British English*) (*of a car*) the boot xínglǐxiāng 行李箱

border /'bɔːdə(r)/ n a border yì tiáo biānjiè 一条边界; to cross the border yuèguò biānjiè 越过边界

bore /bɔː(r)/ vb shǐ … yànfán 使 … 厌烦; her speech bored everyone tā de jiǎnghuà shǐ dàjiā dōu gǎndào yànfán 她的讲话使大家都感到厌烦

bored /bɔːd/ adj to be bored, to get bored gǎndào yànfán 感到厌烦

boring /'bɔːrɪŋ/ adj lìngrén yànfán de 令人厌烦的

born /bɔːn/ adj to be born chūshēng 出生; he was born in February tā èryuè chūshēng 他 2 月出生; she was born in Italy tā chūshēng zài Yìdàlì 她出生在意大利

borrow /'bɒrəʊ/ vb jiè 借; to borrow some money from someone xiàng mǒu rén jièqián 向某人借钱

boss /bɒs/ n the boss lǎobǎn 老板

both /bəʊθ/ **1** det liǎng … dōu … 两 … 都 …; both girls have blonde hair liǎng gè gūniang dōu shì jīnsè de tóufa 两个姑娘都是金色的头发; both my daughter and my son came wǒ de nǚ'ér hé érzi dōu lái le 我的女儿和儿子都来了 **2** pron liǎng … dōu …; you are both wrong, both of you are wrong nǐmen liǎng gè rén dōu cuò le 你们两个人都错了

bother /'bɒðə(r)/ vb (*to take the trouble*); don't bother calling back búbì huí diànhuà 不必回电话; (*to worry*, *to upset*) shǐ … fánnǎo 使 … 烦恼，shǐ … cāoxīn 使 … 操心；her health bothers her a lot tā de shēntǐ shǐ tā hěn fánnǎo 她的身体使她很烦恼；(*in polite apologies*) I'm sorry to bother you duìbuqǐ，dǎrǎo nín 对不起，打扰您

bottle /'bɒtl/ n a bottle yí gè píngzi 一个瓶子；a bottle of [wine|beer|water]yì píng [jiǔ|píjiǔ|shuǐ] 一瓶 [酒|啤酒|水]

bottle-opener /'bɒtl,əupənə(r)/ n a bottle-opener yí gè píngqǐzi 一个瓶起子

bottom /'bɒtəm/ **1** n (*the lowest part*) dǐ(bù) 底(部)；the bottom of a bottle píngzi dǐ(bù) 瓶子底(部)；at the bottom [of the lake or the sea|of the river...] zài [hú hǎi|hé...] dǐ 在 [湖海|河...] 底；(*of a mountain*) jiǎo 脚；the bottom of the hill shānjiǎo 山脚；(*of a page*) xiàduān 下端；at the bottom of the page zài nà yí yè de xiàduān 在那一页的下端；(*of a garden or street*)jìntóu 尽头；at the bottom of the garden zài huāyuán de jìntóu 在花园的尽头；(*at the lowest position*) zuìhòu yì míng 最后一名；to be at the bottom of the class quánbān zuìhòu yì míng 全班最后一名；(*part of the body*) the bottom pìgu 屁股 **2** adj zuì dìxià de 最下的；the bottom [shelf|drawer...] zuì dìxià de [yì céng shūjià|chōutì...] 最底下的 [一层书架|抽屉...]

bound /'baʊnd/ : to be bound to vb kěndìng 肯定，bìdìng 必定；it's bound to create problems zhè kěndìng huì zàochéng yìxiē wèntí 这肯定会造成一些问题；she's bound to complain tā kěndìng huì bàoyuàn 她肯定会抱怨

bow¹ /bəʊ/ n (*a knot*) a bow yí gè húdiéjié (lǐngdài) 一个蝴蝶结(领带)；(*a weapon*) a bow yí zhāng gōng 一张弓；(*used for playing a stringed instrument*) a bow yì zhāng qíngōng 一张琴弓

bow² /baʊ/ vb jūgōng 鞠躬；to bow one's head dīxia tóu 低下头

bowl /bəʊl/ n a bowl yí gè wǎn 一个碗

bowling /'bəʊlɪŋ/ n bǎolíngqiú 保龄球

box /bɒks/ n hézi 盒子，xiāngzi 箱子；a box yí gè hézi 一个盒子

boxing /'bɒksɪŋ/ n quánjī 拳击

boy /bɔɪ/ n a boy yí gè nánháir 一个男孩儿

boyfriend /'bɔɪfrend/ n a boyfriend yí gè nánpéngyou 一个男朋友

bra /brɑː/ n a bra yí gè rǔzhào 一个乳罩

bracelet /'breɪslɪt/ n a bracelet yí gè shǒuzhuó 一个手镯

braid /breɪd/ n (US English) a braid yì gēn biànzi 一根辫子

brain /breɪn/ n nǎozi 脑子

brake /breɪk/ n a brake yí gè zhá 一个闸，yí gè zhìdòngqì 一个制动器，yí gè shāchē 一个刹车

branch /brɑːntʃ/ n a branch (of a tree) yì gēn shùzhī 一根树枝，(of a river) yì tiáo zhīliú 一条支流，(of a bank) yí gè fēnháng 一个分行，(of a department store) yí gè fēndiàn 一个分店

brand-new /'brænd'njuː/ adj zhǎnxīn de 崭新的

brandy /'brændɪ/ n báilándì 白兰地

brave /breɪv/ adj yǒnggǎn de 勇敢 的

Brazil /brə'zɪl/ n Bāxī 巴西

bread /bred/ n bread miànbāo 面包

break /breɪk/ 1 vb (to be damaged) [the window | the teapot | the bowl...] broke [chuānghu | cháhú | wǎn...] pò le [窗户 | 茶壶 | 碗...] 破了；[the leg of the chair | the needle | the rope...] broke [yǐzituǐ | zhēn | shéngzi...] duàn le [椅子腿 | 针 | 绳子...] 断了，(to crack, to smash or damage) to break [the window | the teapot | the bowl...] bǎ [chuānghu | cháhú | wǎn...] dǎpò 把 [窗户 | 茶壶 | 碗...] 打破；to break [the leg of the chair | the needle | the rope...] bǎ [yǐzituǐ | zhēn | shéngzi...] nòngduàn 把 [椅子腿 | 针 | 绳子...] 弄断，(to injure) to break one's arm bǎ gēbo nòngduàn le 把胳膊弄断了；(not to keep) to break a promise wéibèi nuòyán 违背诺

言；to break the rules wéifǎn guīzé 违反规则 **2** n（a short rest）xiūxi 休息；（at school）kèjiān xiūxi 课间休息；to take a break xiūxi yíxià 休息一下；（a holiday）xiūjià 休假；**break down**（if it's a TV, a car）huài le 坏了，（to stop, as a negotiation or meeting）tíngzhǐ 停止，zhōngzhǐ 中止；（in health or spirit）kuǎ xiàlái 垮下来；（to get upset）**break down crying** shīshēng-tòngkū 失声痛哭；**break into（a house）** chuǎngrù 闯入；to be broken into by someone bèi rén pòmén'érrù 被人破门而入；**break out**（if it's a fire）fāshēng 发生；a fire broke out fāshēngle huǒzāi 发生了火灾；（if it's violence）bàofā 爆发；**break up**（to break up a crowd）qūsàn 驱散，（if it's a couple breaking up by themselves）fēnshǒu 分手；to break up with someone gēn mǒu rén duànjué láiwǎng 跟某人断绝来往，（if it's a third party breaking up a couple）chāisàn 拆散；（to end）jiéshù 结束；the meeting didn't break up until eight o'clock huìyì bā diǎn cái jiéshù 会议8点才结束

breakfast /'brekfəst/ n zǎofàn 早饭；to have breakfast chī zǎofàn 吃早饭

breast /brest/ n a breast（of a female）yí gè rǔfáng 一个乳房；（of a male or an animal）yí gè xiōngpú 一个胸脯

breath /breθ/ n hūxī 呼吸；to be out of breath shàngqì bù jiē xiàqì 上气不接下气；to hold one's breath bù chūshēng 不出声，bǐngzhù qì 屏住气

breathe /briːð/ vb hūxī 呼吸；**breathe in** xīrù 吸入；**breathe out** hūchū 呼出

breeze /briːz/ n a breeze wēifēng 微风

brick /brɪk/ n a brick yí kuài zhuān 一块砖

bride /braɪd/ n a bride yí gè xīnniáng 一个新娘

bridegroom /'braɪdɡrʊm/ n a bridegroom yí gè xīnláng 一个新郎

bridge /brɪdʒ/ n a bridge yí zuò qiáo 一座桥

brief /briːf/ adj（in time）duǎnzàn de 短暂的；（in content）jiǎnduǎn de 简短的

bright /braɪt/ adj (describing colours, light) xiānyàn de 鲜艳的; a bright red dress yí jiàn xiānhóng de yīfu 一件鲜红的衣服; (having plenty of light, sun) míngliàng de 明亮的; this room is not very bright zhège fángjiān bú tài míngliàng 这个房间不太明亮; (intelligent) cōngmíng de 聪明的

brilliant /'brɪljənt/ adj (very intelligent) zhuóyuè de 卓越的, cáihuá-héngyì de 才华横溢的; (British English) (informal, for emphasis) tài hǎo le 太好了, miào jí le 妙极了

bring /brɪŋ/ vb dàilái 带来; to bring someone a present gěi mǒu rén dàilái yí jiàn lǐwù 给某人带来一件礼物; it will bring us good luck tā jiāng gěi wǒmen dàilái hǎo yùnqi 它将给我们带来好运气; **bring about** dàilái 带来, zàochéng 造成; to bring about a change dàilái biànhuà 带来变化; **bring back** dài huílái 带回来; he brought me back some perfume tā gěi wǒ dài huílái yìxiē xiāngshuǐ 他给我带回来一些香水; **bring up** péiyǎng chéngrén 培养成人; to bring up a child bǎ yí gè háizi péiyǎng chéngrén 把一个孩子培养成人

Britain /'brɪtən/ n Yīngguó 英国

British /'brɪtɪʃ/ **1** adj Yīngguó de 英国的 **2** n the British Yīngguórén 英国人

broad /brɔːd/ adj (wide) kuān de 宽的; (covering a wide range) guǎngdà de 广大的

broadcast /'brɔːdkɑːst/ vb guǎngbō 广播; to be broadcast live shíkuàng zhíbō 实况直播

brochure /'brəʊʃə(r)/ n a brochure yì běn xiǎocèzi 一本小册子

broke /brəʊk/ adj fēnwén méiyǒu de 分文没有的, pòchǎn de 破产的

broken /'brəʊkən/ adj (if it's a window, a teapot, or a bowl) pò de 破的, suì de 碎的; (if it's a leg, a needle, or a rope) duàn de 断的; (if it's a car, a machine, or a watch) huài de 坏的

bronze /brɒnz/ *n* qīngtóng 青铜

brother /'brʌðə(r)/ *n* a brother yí gè xiōngdi 一个兄弟; a younger brother yí gè dìdi 一个弟弟; an elder brother yí gè gēge 一个哥哥

brother-in-law /'brʌðərɪnlɔ:/ *n* (*the husband of a younger sister*) mèifu 妹夫; (*the husband of an elder sister*) jiěfu 姐夫

brown /braʊn/ *adj* zōngsè de 棕色的, kāfēisè de 咖啡色的

bruise /bru:z/ *n* yí kuài qīngzhǒng 一块青肿, yí kuài shānghén 一块伤痕

brush /brʌʃ/ **1** *n* (*for clothes, shoes, hair, and for sweeping up*) shuāzi 刷子; a brush yì bǎ shuāzi 一把刷子; a toothbrush yì bǎ yáshuā 一把牙刷; (*for painting*) huàbǐ 画笔; a brush yì zhī huàbǐ 一支画笔; (*for writing*) máobǐ 毛笔; a writing brush yì zhī máobǐ 一支毛笔 **2** *vb* shuā 刷; to brush one's teeth shuāyá 刷牙

Brussels /'brʌsəlz/ *n* Bùlǔsài'ěr 布鲁塞尔

bubble /'bʌbl/ *n* a bubble yí gè shuǐpào 一个水泡

bucket /'bʌkɪt/ *n* a bucket yí gè shuǐtǒng 一个水桶

Buddhism /'bʊdɪzəm/ *n* fójiào 佛教

Buddhist /'bʊdɪst/ **1** *adj* fójiào de 佛教的, fó de 佛的 **2** *n* a Buddhist yí gè fójiàotú 一个佛教徒

build /bɪld/ *vb* (*to construct as a house or a railway*) jiàn 建, jiànzào 建造; (*to establish as a society or a system*) jiànlì 建立, jiànshè 建设

building /'bɪldɪŋ/ *n* a building yí gè jiànzhùwù 一个建筑物

bull /bʊl/ *n* a bull yì tóu gōngniú 一头公牛

bullet /'bʊlɪt/ *n* a bullet yì kē zǐdàn 一颗子弹

bulletin /'bʊlɪtɪn/ *n* a bulletin yì fèn gōngbào 一个/份公报; a news bulletin yì tiáo xīnwén bàodǎo 一条新闻报导; a bulletin board yí gè gōnggàolán 一个公告栏

bully /'bʊlɪ/ *vb* qīfu 欺负, qīwǔ 欺侮

bump /bʌmp/ *vb* zhuàng 撞, pèngzhuàng 碰撞; he bumped his head against the wall tā de tóu zhuàngzàile

qiáng shang 他的头撞在了墙上；**bump into**（to hit）
zhuàng 撞、pèngzhuàng 碰撞；（to meet）yùjiàn 遇见、
pèngjiàn 碰见

bunch /bʌntʃ/ n a bunch of flowers yí shù huā 一束花；
a bunch of grapes yí chuàn pútáo 一串葡萄；a bunch of
keys yí chuàn yàoshi 一串钥匙

burger /'bɜːgə(r)/ n a burger yí gè hànbǎobāo 一个汉堡
包

burglar /'bɜːglə(r)/ n a burglar yí gè qièzéi 一个窃贼

burglar alarm /'bɜːglər əlɑːm/ n a burglar alarm yí gè
fángdào jǐngbàoqì 一个防盗警报器

burglary /'bɜːglərɪ/ n a burglary yì qǐ dàoqiè'àn 一起盗窃
案

burn /bɜːn/ **1** vb（to destroy, to get rid of）shāohuǐ 烧毁、
shāodiào 烧掉；to burn rubbish shāodiào lājī 烧掉垃圾；
（to injure by fire）shāoshāng 烧伤；（to injure by boiling
water or something hot）tàngshāng 烫伤；（to be on fire）
ránshāo 燃烧；（when cooking）shāojiāo 烧焦；（in the
sun）shàishāng 晒伤；to burn easily róngyì shàishāng 容
易晒伤；**burn down** shāohuǐ 烧毁、shāodiào 烧掉 **2** n（by
a fire）shāoshāng 烧伤；（by boiling water or something
very hot）tàngshāng 烫伤

burst /bɜːst/ vb（if it's a balloon）bào 爆；（if it's a water
pipe）liè 裂；（if it's a river dam）kuìjué 溃决；to burst
its banks juékǒu 决口；**burst into** to burst into [tears |
laughter] tūrán [kū | xiào] qǐlai 突然 [哭 | 笑] 起来；**burst
out** to burst out [laughing | crying] tūrán [xiào | kū] qǐlai 突
然 [笑 | 哭] 起来

bury /'berɪ/ vb（to put in the grave as a dead body）
máizàng 埋葬、mái 埋；（to hide in the ground）máicáng
埋藏、mái 埋

bus /bʌs/ n a bus yí liàng gōnggòng qìchē 一辆公共汽车

bus conductor /'bʌs kən'dʌktə(r)/ n a bus conductor
yí gè qìchē shòupiàoyuán 一个汽车售票员

bus driver /'bʌs draɪvə(r)/ n a bus driver yí gè

gōnggòng qìchē sījī 一个公共汽车司机

bush /buʃ/ n a bush yí gè guànmùcóng 一个灌木丛

business /'bɪznɪs/ n (commercial activities) shāngyè 商业、shēngyi 生意; to go to London on business qù Lúndūn chūchāi 去伦敦出差; (a company) a business yì jiā shāngdiàn 一家商店, yí gè gōngsī 一个公司; (when protecting one's privacy) that's my business nà shì wǒ de shì 那是我的事; it's none of your business nǐ shǎo guǎn xiánshì 你少管闲事

businessman /'bɪznɪsmæn/, **businesswoman** /'bɪznɪswʊmən/ n a businessman, a businesswoman yí gè shāngrén 一个商人

bus station /'bʌs steɪʃən/ n a bus station, a bus stop yí gè (gōnggòng)qìchēzhàn 一个（公共）汽车站

busy /'bɪzɪ/ adj máng de 忙的, fánmáng de 繁忙的; to be busy working mángzhe gōngzuò 忙着工作; a busy day fánmáng de yì tiān 繁忙的一天; to lead a busy life guòzhe mánglù de shēnghuó 过着忙碌的生活

but /强 bʌt;弱 bət/ conj dànshì 但是, kěshì 可是; he can read Chinese but he doesn't speak it tā néng kàndǒng Zhōngwén, dànshì tā bú huì shuō 他能看懂中文，但是他不会说

butcher /'butʃə(r)/ n a butcher (one selling meat) yí gè mài ròu de 一个卖肉的; (one whose business is to slaughter animals for food) yí gè túzǎi gōngrén 一个屠宰工人; (one who delights in bloody deeds) yí gè guìzishǒu 一个刽子手

butter /'bʌtə(r)/ n huángyóu 黄油

butterfly /'bʌtəflaɪ/ n a butterfly yì zhī húdié 一只蝴蝶

button /'bʌtən/ n a button; (on clothes) yí gè niǔkòu 一个纽扣; (on a machine) yí gè diànniǔ 一个电钮

buy /baɪ/ vb mǎi 买; to buy a present for someone gěi mǒu rén mǎi yí jiàn lǐwù 给某人买一件礼物; she bought herself a new coat tā gěi zìjǐ mǎile yí jiàn xīn wàitào 她给自己买了一件新外套

buzz /bʌz/ vb fāchū wēngwēng shēng 发出嗡嗡声

by /baɪ/ prep (by means of) to travel by [bus│train│plane│boat] zuò [qìchē│huǒchē│fēijī│chuán] lǚxíng 坐 [汽车│火车│飞机│船] 旅行; we went there by bicycle wǒmen qí zìxíngchē qù nàr 我们骑自行车去那儿; to pay by cheque yòng zhīpiào fùqián 用支票付钱; to book by phone dǎ diànhuà yùdìng 打电话预订; to come in by the back door cóng hòumén jìnlái 从后门进来; he succeeded by working hard tā tōngguò nǔlì gōngzuò chénggōng le 他通过努力工作成功了; (beside) zài ⋯ (páng)biān 在 ⋯ (旁)边; by the sea zài hǎibiān 在海边; by the side of the road zài lù(páng)biān 在路(旁)边; (along a route passing) jīngguò 经过; to go by the post office jīngguò yóujú 经过邮局; (indicating an author or painter) a book by Dickens Dígèngsī xiě de shū 狄更斯写的书; a painting by his father tā bàba huà de huà 他爸爸画的画; (in the passive voice) bèi 被, jiào 叫, ràng 让; he was bitten by a dog tā jiào yì tiáo gǒu yǎo le 他叫一条狗咬了; the house was burnt down by a fire nà zhuàng fángzi bèi yì chǎng huǒ shāohuǐ le 那幢房子被一场火烧毁了; (when talking about time) by next Thursday xiàge xīngqīsì yǐqián 下个星期四以前; he should be here by now xiànzài tā yīnggāi lái le 现在他应该来了; (when talking about figures, rates) to increase by 20% zēngjiā bǎi fēn zhī èrshí 增加20%; to be paid by the hour àn xiǎoshí fùqián 按小时付钱; 8 metres by 4 metres bā mǐ chéng sì mǐ 8米乘4米; (set phrases) by accident ǒurán 偶然, pèngqiǎo 碰巧; by chance ǒurán 偶然, pèngqiǎo 碰巧; [take... │ see... │ write...] by mistake [ná│kàn│xiě] cuò⋯ [拿│看│写] 错⋯; one by one yí gè jiē yí gè 一个接一个; by and large dàtǐshang 大体上; by oneself dāndú 单独

Cc

cab /kæb/ *n* a cab yí liàng chūzūchē 一辆出租车

cabbage /'kæbɪdʒ/ *n* juǎnxīncài 卷心菜; Chinese cabbage dàbáicài 大白菜

cable car /'keɪbl kɑ:(r)/ *n* a cable car yí liàng lǎnchē 一辆缆车

café /'kæfeɪ/ *n* a café yì jiā kāfēiguǎn 一家咖啡馆

cake /keɪk/ *n* a cake yí gè dàngāo 一个蛋糕; a piece of cake yí kuài dàngāo 一块蛋糕

calculator /'kælkjuleɪtə(r)/ *n* a calculator yí gè jìsuànqì 一个计算器

calendar /'kælɪndə(r)/ *n* a calendar yí gè rìlì 一个日历

calf /kɑ:f/ *n* (*the animal*) a calf yì tóu xiǎoniú 一头小牛; (*part of the leg*) the calf xiǎotuǐ 小腿

call /kɔ:l/ *vb* (*to name*) jiào 叫; he's called Mark tā jiào Mǎkè 他叫马克; it's called 'chá' in Chinese Zhōngwén zhège jiào "chá" 中文这个叫 "茶"; we call him 'Xiǎo Lǐ' wǒmen jiào tā "Xiǎo Lǐ" 我们叫他 "小李"; (*to describe as*) to call someone a coward rènwéi mǒu rén shì gè dǎnxiǎoguǐ 认为某人是个胆小鬼; (*to cry aloud*) hǎn 喊; the teacher is calling us at the window lǎoshī zài chuānghu nàr hǎn wǒmen 老师在窗户那儿喊我们; (*to phone*) dǎ diànhuà 打电话; he'll call me this evening tā jīntiān wǎnshang gěi wǒ dǎ diànhuà 他今天晚上给我打电话; (*to get to come*) qǐng 请; to call the doctor qǐng dàifu dàdài 大夫; (*to wake*) jiàoxǐng 叫醒; (*to pay a visit*) bàifǎng 拜访; I called at his house yesterday wǒ zuótiān qù tā jiā bàifǎng 我昨天去他家拜访; **call back** (*to command to return*) jiào huílái 叫回来; (*to phone back*) huí diànhuà 回电话; **call off** qǔxiāo 取消; **call on** they called on him to make a speech at the meeting tāmen qǐngqiú tā zài huì shang jiǎnghuà 他们请求他在会上讲话；**call out** to call out the numbers for the lottery dàshēng hǎn zhòngjiǎng hàomǎ 大声喊中奖号码

calm /kɑːm/ **1** adj (when talking about the weather, the sea) píngjìng de 平静的；(when talking about people) zhènjìng de 镇静的 **2** vb píngjìng 平静，shǐ …zhènjìng 使…镇静；**calm down** píngjìng xiàlái 平静下来，zhènjìng xiàlái 镇静下来

camcorder /ˈkæmˈkɔːdə(r)/ n a camcorder yí jià shèxiàngjī 一架摄像机

camel /ˈkæməl/ n a camel yì tóu luòtuo 一头骆驼

camera /ˈkæmərə/ n a camera (for taking photos) yí jià zhàoxiàngjī 一架照相机；(in a studio, for videos) yí jià shèyǐngjī 一架摄影机

camp /kæmp/ **1** n yěyíng 野营；a summer camp yí gè xiàlìngyíng 一夏令营 **2** vb yěyíng 野营；to go camping qù yěyíng 去野营

campsite /ˈkæmpsaɪt/ n a campsite yí gè yíngdì 一个营地

campus /ˈkæmpəs/ n a campus yí gè xiàoyuán 一个校园

can¹ /强 kæn；弱 kən/ vb (to have the possibility) néng 能；can he come? tā néng lái ma？他能来吗？；where can I buy stamps? wǒ zài nǎr néng mǎidào yóupiào？我在哪儿能买到邮票？；(to know how to) huì 会，néng 能；she can swim tā huì yóuyǒng 她会游泳；he can't drive yet tā hái bù huì kāichē 他还不会开车；can/do you speak Chinese? nǐ huì shuō Hànyǔ ma？你会说汉语吗？！Note that when talking about the ability to speak a language, whether or not can is used in English, huì 会 is required in Chinese；(to be allowed to) kěyǐ 可以。! Note that to negate, you have to use bù néng 不能 rather than bù kěyǐ 不可以；can I smoke? wǒ kěyǐ xīyān ma？我可以吸烟吗？；sorry, you can't smoke here duìbuqǐ, nǐ bù néng zài zhèr xīyān 对不起，你不能在这儿吸烟；we can't turn right here wǒmen zài zhèr bù néng xiàng yòu guǎi 我们在这儿不能向右拐；can/may I help you? xūyào wǒ bāngmáng ma? 需要我帮忙吗?；(when asked by a shop assistant) nín yào mǎi shénme dōngxi ma? 您要买什么东西吗?

can² /kæn/ n a can yì tīng guàntou 一听罐头

Canada /ˈkænədə/ n Canada Jiānádà 加拿大

Canadian /kəˈneɪdɪən/ **1** adj Jiānádà de 加拿大的 **2** n Jiānádàrén 加拿大人

canal /kəˈnæl/ n a canal yì tiáo yùnhé 一条运河

cancel /ˈkænsəl/ vb qǔxiāo 取消；he cancelled his room reservation tā qǔxiāole yùdìng de fángjiān 他取消了预订的房间

cancer /ˈkænsə(r)/ n cancer ái 癌，áizhèng 癌症

candle /ˈkændl/ n a candle yì zhī làzhú 一支蜡烛

candy /ˈkændɪ/ n (US English) candy tángguǒ 糖果；(a sweet) a candy yí kuài táng 一块糖

canoe /kəˈnuː/ n a canoe yì tiáo dúmùzhōu 一条独木舟

canoeing /kəˈnuːɪŋ/ n huá dúmùzhōu yùndòng 划独木舟运动

can-opener /ˈkænˈəʊpənə(r)/ n a can-opener yí gè kāiguànqì 一个开罐器

canteen /kænˈtiːn/ n a canteen；(a dining hall) yí gè shítáng 一个食堂；(a container of water) yí gè shuǐhú 一个水壶

Cantonese /ˌkæntəˈniːz/ **1** adj Guǎngdōng de 广东的 **2** n (the people) Guǎngdōngrén 广东人；(the dialect) Guǎngdōnghuà 广东话

cap /kæp/ n a cap yì dǐng màozi 一顶帽子；a baseball cap yì dǐng bàngqiúmào 一顶棒球帽

capable /ˈkeɪpəbl/ adj yǒu nénglì de 有能力的；a very capable nurse yí gè hěn yǒu nénglì de hùshi 一个很有能力的护士；to be capable of looking after oneself yǒu nénglì zhàogù zìjǐ 有能力照顾自己

capital /ˈkæpɪtəl/ **1** n shǒudū 首都；Beijing is the

capital of China Běijīng shì Zhōngguó de shǒudū 北京是中国的首都 **2** adj dàxiě de 大写的；**capital P** dàxiě de P 大写的 P

captain /'kæptɪn/ n (of a ship) chuánzhǎng 船长；(of a team) duìzhǎng 队长

car /kɑː(r)/ n (a vehicle driven on a road) qìchē 汽车，jiàochē 轿车；**a car** yí liàng qìchē 一辆汽车；(a vehicle for railway travelling) chēxiāng 车厢；**a sleeping car** yì jié wòpù chēxiāng 一节卧铺车厢；**a dining car** yì jié cānchē 一节餐车

caravan /'kærəvæn/ n (British English) **a caravan** yí liàng sùyíngchē 一辆宿营车

card /kɑːd/ n (for sending to someone) kǎpiàn 卡片；**a card** yì zhāng kǎpiàn 一张卡片；(for playing games) zhǐpái 纸牌；**a card** yì zhāng zhǐpái 一张纸牌；**to play cards** dǎ pūkèpái 打扑克牌

cardphone /'kɑːdˌfəʊn/ n **a cardphone** yí gè cíkǎ diànhuà 一个磁卡电话

care /keə(r)/ **1** n (watchfulness) xiǎoxīn 小心；**he takes great care crossing the street** tā guò mǎlù hěn xiǎoxīn 他过马路很小心；(charge) zhàoguǎn 照管；**to take care of someone** zhàoguǎn mǒu rén 照管某人 **2** vb (to be concerned) guānxīn 关心；**to care about the environment** guānxīn huánjìng wèntí 关心环境问题；(to look after) zhàogù 照顾，guānhuái 关怀；**to care for the students** zhàogù xuésheng 照顾学生；(to mind) zàihu 在乎；**I don't care** wǒ búzàihu 我不在乎

career /kə'rɪə(r)/ n (progress through life) shēngyá 生涯；(profession or occupation) zhíyè 职业

careful /'keəfʊl/ adj xiǎoxīn de 小心的，zǐxì de 仔细的；**he is very careful crossing the street** tā guò mǎlù hěn xiǎoxīn 他过马路很小心；**to make a careful study of the problem** duì zhège wèntí jìnxíng zǐxì de yánjiū 对这个问题进行仔细的研究

careless /'keəlɪs/ adj cūxīn de 粗心的，shūhu de 疏忽的

car ferry /'kɑː ferɪ/ n a car ferry yì sōu qìchē dùlún 一艘汽车渡轮

carnival /'kɑːnɪvəl/ n (British English) (a festival) a carnival yí gè kuánghuānjié 一个狂欢节; (US English) (a fair) a carnival yí gè yóuyì yúlèhuì 一个游艺娱乐会

car park /'kɑː pɑːk/ n (British English) a car park yí gè tíngchēchǎng 一个停车场

carpet /'kɑːpɪt/ n a carpet yì tiáo dìtǎn 地毯

car phone /'kɑː fəun/ n a car phone yí gè chēyòng diànhuà 一个车用电话

carrot /'kærət/ n a carrot yì gēn húluóbo 一根胡萝卜

carry /'kærɪ/ vb (with one's hand) tí 提; she was carrying a handbag tā tízhe yí gè shǒutíbāo 她提着一个手提包; (on one's shoulder) káng 扛; he was carrying a box on his shoulder tā kángzhe yí gè xiāngzi 他扛着一个箱子; (in one's arms) bào 抱; she was carrying her daughter in her arms tā bàozhe tā de nǚ'ér 她抱着她的女儿; (on one's back) bēi 背; she was carrying her daughter on her back tā bēizhe tā de nǚ'ér 她背着她的女儿; to carry a bookbag on one's back bēi shūbāo 背书包; carry on jìxù 继续

cartoon /kɑː'tuːn/ n a cartoon (a comic strip) yì zhāng mànhuà 一张漫画; (a film) yí bù dònghuàpiàn 一部动画片

case¹ /keɪs/: in case conj (in the event that) jiǎshǐ 假使, jiǎrú 假如; in case you can't come, please phone me jiǎshǐ nǐ bù néng lái, qǐng gěi wǒ dǎ diànhuà 假使你不能来,请给我打电话; (lest) miǎnde 免得, yǐfáng 以防; I remind him again in case he forgets wǒ yào zài tíxǐng tā yíxià, miǎnde tā wàng le 我要再提醒他一下,免得他忘了

case² /keɪs/ n a case; (a box) yí gè hézi 一个盒子; (luggage) yí gè xiāngzi 一个箱子

cash /kæʃ/ 1 n xiànjīn 现金, xiànkuǎn 现款; to pay in cash yòng xiànjīn fùkuǎn 用现金付款 2 vb duìhuàn chéng xiànjīn 兑换成现金

cash dispenser /'kæʃ dɪsˌpensə(r)/ n a cash dispenser yí gè zìdòng qǔkuǎnjī 一个自动取款机

cassette /kæ'set/ n a cassette yí gè hézi 一个盒子，yí gè lùyīndàihé 一个录音带盒

cassette player /kæ'set ˌpleɪə(r)/ n a cassette player yì tái lùyīndài bōfàngjī 一台录音带播放机

castle /'kɑːsl/ n a castle yí zuò chéngbǎo 一座城堡

cat /kæt/ n a cat yì zhī māo 一只猫

catch /kætʃ/ vb (to capture) zhuō 捉; to catch a fish zhuō yì tiáo yú 捉一条鱼; (to take hold of) zhuāzhù 抓住; catch my hand zhuāzhù wǒ de shǒu 抓住我的手; (to take hold of something in motion) jiēzhù 接住; he didn't catch the ball tā méi jiēzhù nàge qiú 他没接住那个球; (to pinch, to stick) he caught his finger in the door tā de shǒuzhǐ bèi mén jiázhù le 他的手指被门夹住了; my shirt got caught by a nail wǒ de chènshān bèi yí gè dīngzi guàzhù le 我的衬衫被一个钉子挂住了; (to be in time for) gǎn 赶; he was running to catch the train tā pǎozhe qù gǎn huǒchē 他跑着去赶火车; (to take by surprise, to come upon) to catch someone stealing fāxiàn mǒu rén tōu dōngxi 发现某人偷东西; (to become ill with) dé 得; he caught flu tā déle liúgǎn 他得了流感; to catch fire zháohuǒ 着火; catch up gǎnshàng 赶上; to catch up with someone gǎnshàng mǒu rén 赶上某人

cathedral /kə'θiːdrəl/ n a cathedral yí zuò dàjiàotáng 一座大教堂

cauliflower /'kɒlɪflaʊə(r)/ n càihuā 菜花

cause /kɔːz/ vb to cause damage zàochéng sǔnhuài 造成损坏; to cause someone a lot of problems gěi mǒu rén dàilái hěn duō wèntí 给某人带来很多问题; to cause one to be suspicious yǐnqǐ mǒu rén de huáiyí 引起某人的怀疑

cautious /'kɔːʃəs/ adj xiǎoxīn de 小心的

cave /keɪv/ n a cave yí gè shāndòng 一个山洞

CD /ˌsiː 'diː/, **compact disk** n a CD yì zhāng guāngpán

一张光盘

CD player /ˌsiː ˈdiː ˌpleɪə(r)/ n a CD player yì tái guāngpán bōfàngjī 一台光盘播放机

ceiling /ˈsiːlɪŋ/ n the ceiling tiānhuābǎn 天花板

celebrate /ˈselɪbreɪt/ vb qìngzhù 庆祝; to celebrate someone's birthday qìngzhù mǒu rén de shēngrì 庆祝某人的生日

celery /ˈseləri/ n qíncài 芹菜

cell /sel/ n (a unit of living matter) xìbāo 细胞; a cell yí gè xìbāo 一个细胞; (a small room) xiǎowū 小屋; a cell yì jiān xiǎowū 一间小屋

cellar /ˈselə(r)/ n a cellar yí gè dìjiào 一个地窖

'cello /ˈtʃeləʊ/ n a 'cello yì bǎ dàtíqín 一把大提琴

cement /sɪˈment/ n shuǐní 水泥

cemetery /ˈsemɪtəri/ n a cemetery yí gè gōngmù 一个公墓

centimetre /ˈsentɪˌmiːtə(r)/ (British English), **centimeter** (US English) n a centimetre yì gōngfēn 一公分, yì límǐ 一厘米

central heating /ˌsentrəl ˈhiːtɪŋ/ n jízhōng gōngnuǎn 集中供暖

centre /ˈsentə(r)/ (British English), **center** (US English) n zhōngxīn 中心; a leisure centre yí gè yúlè zhōngxīn 一个娱乐中心; near the centre of London kàojìn Lúndūn shìzhōngxīn 靠近伦敦市中心

century /ˈsentʃəri/ n a century yí gè shìjì 一个世纪

certain /ˈsɜːtən/ adj (sure) yídìng de 一定的; (some) mǒu 某; a certain person mǒu yí gè rén 某一个人

certainly /ˈsɜːtənli/ adv yídìng 一定, kěndìng 肯定

chain /tʃeɪn/ n a chain yì tiáo liànzi 一条链子

chair /tʃeə(r)/ n a chair yì bǎ yǐzi 一把椅子

chalk /tʃɔːk/ n fěnbǐ 粉笔

champagne /ʃæmˈpeɪn/ n xiāngbīnjiǔ 香槟酒

champion /ˈtʃæmpiən/ n a champion yí gè guànjūn 一个冠军; a tennis champion yí gè wǎngqiú guànjūn 一个网

球冠军

chance /tʃɑːns/ *n* (*a possibility*) kěnéng 可能；there is a chance that she'll have a job in Beijing yǒu kěnéng tā huì zài Běijīng zhǎodào gōngzuò 有可能她会在北京找到工作；(*an opportunity*) jīhuì 机会；to have a chance to meet him yǒu jīhuì jiàndào tā 有机会见到他；by chance ǒurán 偶然

change /tʃeɪndʒ/ **1** *n* a change yí gè biànhuà 一个变化；a change of temperature wēndù de biànhuà 温度的变化；(*cash*) língqián 零钱；have you got change for 50 pence? nǐ yǒu wǔshí biànshì língqián ma? 你有 50 便士零钱吗? **2** *vb* (*to become different*) biànhuà 变化；this city has changed a lot zhège chéngshì biànhuà hěn dà 这个城市变化很大；(*to make different*) gǎibiàn 改变；I've changed my mind wǒ yǐjīng gǎibiànle zhǔyì 我已经改变了主意；(*to replace, exchange, switch*) huàn 换；to change a wheel huàn lúnzi 换轮子；to change a shirt for a smaller size huàn yí jiàn xiǎo yìdiǎn de chènshān 换一件小一点的衬衫；to change places with someone gēn mǒu rén huàn dìfang 跟某人换地方；to change channels huàn píndào 换频道；to get changed huàn yīfu 换衣服；to change trains huànchē 换车；to change dollars into pounds bǎ měiyuán (duì) huànchéng yīngbàng 把美元(兑)换成英镑

changing room /'tʃeɪdʒɪŋ rʊm/ *n* a changing room yì jiān gēngyīshì 一间更衣室

channel /'tʃænəl/ *n* a TV channel yí gè diànshì píndào 一个电视频道

Channel /'tʃænəl/ *n* the (English) Channel Yīngjílì Hǎixiá 英吉利海峡

chapter /'tʃæptə(r)/ *n* a chapter yì zhāng 一章

charge /tʃɑːdʒ/ **1** *vb* that hotel charged him 10 pounds for the night nà jiā lǚguǎn yí yè shōule tā shí bàng 那家旅馆一夜收了他 10 镑；they'll charge you for the electricity tāmen huì xiàng nǐ shōu diànfèi 他们会向你

收电费 **2** *n*（*a fee, a price*）fèiyòng 费用，jiàqian 价钱；there is no charge miǎnfèi 免费 **3** in charge fùzé 负责，zhǎngguǎn 掌管，zhǔguǎn 主管；to be in charge of the money zhǎngguǎn qián 掌管钱

charming /ˈtʃɑːmɪŋ/ *adj* mírén de 迷人的，kě'ài de 可爱的

chase /tʃeɪs/ *vb* zhuīgǎn 追赶；**chase away** qūzhú 驱逐，qūgǎn 驱赶

chat /tʃæt/ **1** *vb* liáotiān 聊天，xiántán 闲谈 **2** *n* a chat liáotiān 聊天，xiántán 闲谈；**chat up**（*British English*）hǒngpiàn 哄骗

cheap /tʃiːp/ *adj*（*not expensive*）piányi de 便宜的；it's cheap zhè hěn piányi 这很便宜；（*of poor quality*）dīliè de 低劣的

cheat /tʃiːt/ *vb* piàn 骗，qīpiàn 欺骗

check /tʃek/ **1** *vb* jiǎnchá 检查；you should check whether it's true nǐ yīnggāi jiǎnchá yíxià zhè shìfǒu shì zhēn de 你应该检查一下这是否是真的；they didn't even check our passports tāmen shènzhì méiyǒu jiǎnchá wǒmen de hùzhào 他们甚至没有检查我们的护照 **2** *n*（*US English*）（*a bill*）zhàngdān 账单；a check yì zhāng zhàngdān 一张账单；（*US English*）（*a cheque*）zhīpiào 支票；a check yì zhāng zhīpiào 一张支票；**check in** dēngjì 登记；**check out** jiézhàng líkāi 结账离开

checkbook /ˈtʃekbʊk/ *n*（*US English*）a checkbook yì běn zhīpiàobù 一本支票簿

checkers /ˈtʃekəz/ *n*（*US English*）tiàoqí 跳棋

check-in /ˈtʃekɪn/ *n*（*at an airport*）bànlǐ dēngjī shǒuxù 办理登机手续；（*at a hotel*）bànlǐ zhùdiàn shǒuxù 办理住店手续

checkout /ˈtʃekaʊt/ *n*（*at a hotel*）bànlǐ lídiàn shǒuxù 办理离店手续

cheek /tʃiːk/ *n* miànjiá 面颊

cheeky /ˈtʃiːkɪ/ *adj* wúlǐ de 无礼的，hòuliǎnpí de 厚脸皮的

cheerful /'tʃɪəful/ adj kuàihuo de 快活的，gāoxìng de 高兴的

cheese /tʃiːz/ n nǎilào 奶酪，rǔlào 乳酪

chef /ʃef/ n chúshī 厨师

chemist /'kemɪst/ n (in a shop) a chemist yí gè yàojìshī 一个药剂师；(in a laboratory) a chemist yí gè huàxuéjiā 一个化学家，yí gè huàxué gōngzuòzhě 一个化学工作者

chemistry /'kemɪstrɪ/ n huàxué 化学

cheque /tʃek/ n (British English) a cheque yì zhāng zhīpiào 一张支票；to write a cheque for £50 xiě yì zhāng wǔshí yīngbàng de zhīpiào 写一张 50 英镑的支票

cheque book /'tʃek bʊk/ n (British English) a cheque book yì běn zhīpiàobù 一本支票簿

cherry /'tʃerɪ/ n a cherry yí gè yīngtáo 一个樱桃

chess /tʃes/ n xiàngqí 象棋

chest /tʃest/ n (of the human body) xiōng 胸，xiōngqiāng 胸腔；(furniture) guìzi 柜子；a chest yí gè guìzi 一个柜子

chestnut /'tʃestnʌt/ 1 n a chestnut yí gè lìzi 一个栗子 2 adj zǎohóngsè de 枣红色的；she has chestnut hair tā yǒu zǎohóngsè de tóufa 她有枣红色的头发

chew /tʃuː/ vb jiáo 嚼

chewing gum /'tʃuːɪŋ gʌm/ n kǒuxiāngtáng 口香糖

chicken /'tʃɪkɪn/ n (the bird) a chicken yì zhī jī 一只鸡；(the meat) jīròu 鸡肉

child /tʃaɪld/ n a child yí gè xiǎoháir 一个小孩儿

chilly /'tʃɪlɪ/ adj hánlěng de 寒冷的

chimney /'tʃɪmnɪ/ n a chimney yí gè yāncōng 一个烟囱

chin /tʃɪn/ n xiàba(kēr) 下巴(颏儿)

China /'tʃaɪnə/ n 中国

Chinese /ˌtʃaɪ'niːz/ 1 adj Zhōngguó de 中国的 2 n (the people) Zhōngguórén 中国人；(the language) Zhōngwén 中文，zhōngguóhuà 中国话，Hànyǔ 汉语

Chinese New Year /ˌtʃaɪniːz nju: 'jɜː(r)/ n Chūn Jié 春节，Zhōngguó Xīnnián 中国新年

Chinese New Year's Eve /ˌtʃaɪniːz ˌnjuː jɜːz ˈiːv/ *n* chúxī 除夕

chips /tʃɪps/ *n* (*British English*) (*fries*, *French fries*) tǔdòutiáo 土豆条, shǔtiáo 薯条; (*US English*) (*crisps*) tǔdòupiàn 土豆片

chocolate /ˈtʃɒkəlɪt/ *n* qiǎokèlì 巧克力; a box of chocolates yì hé qiǎokèlì 一盒巧克力

choice /tʃɔɪs/ *n* xuǎnzé 选择; he made a wrong choice tā zuòle yí gè cuòwù de xuǎnzé 他做了一个错误的选择

choir /ˈkwaɪə(r)/ *n* (*in a church*) chàngshībān 唱诗班; (*a chorus of singers*) gēyǒngduì 歌咏队, héchàngduì 合唱团

choke /tʃəʊk/ *vb* he choked on a fish bone tā bèi yì gēn yúcì qiǎzhùle hóulóng 他被一根鱼刺卡住了喉咙; he choked her to death tā bǎ tā qiàsǐ le 他把她掐死了

choose /tʃuːz/ *vb* xuǎnzé 选择, tiāoxuǎn 挑选

chopsticks /ˈtʃɒpstɪks/ *n* kuàizi 筷子; a pair of chopsticks yì shuāng kuàizi 一双筷子

chore /tʃɔː(r)/ *n* jiāwù 家务; to do the chores zuò jiāwù 做家务

Christian /ˈkrɪstʃən/ **1** *n* jīdūtú 基督徒 **2** *adj* jīdūjiào de 基督教的

Christian name /ˈkrɪstʃən neɪm/ *n* a Christian name yí gè jiàomíng 一个教名

Christmas /ˈkrɪsməs/ *n* Christmas (Day) Shèngdàn (Jié) 圣诞(节); Merry Christmas!, Happy Christmas! Shèngdàn kuàilè! 圣诞快乐!

Christmas carol /ˌkrɪsməs ˈkærəl/ *n* a Christmas carol yì shǒu Shèngdàn sònggē 一首圣诞颂歌

Christmas cracker /ˌkrɪsməs ˈkrækə(r)/ *n* (*British English*) a Christmas cracker yí gè Shèngdàn cǎisè bàozhú 一个圣诞彩色爆竹

Christmas Eve /ˌkrɪsməs ˈiːv/ *n* Christmas Eve píng'ānyè 平安夜

Christmas tree /ˈkrɪsməs ˈtriː/ *n* a Christmas tree yì kē shèngdànshù 一棵圣诞树

church /tʃɜːtʃ/ n (building) a church yí zuò jiàotáng 一座教堂; (a group of people) a church yí gè jiàohuì 一个教会

cider /'saɪdə(r)/ n guǒjiǔ 果酒

cigar /sɪ'gɑː(r)/ n a cigar yì zhī xuějiā 一支雪茄

cigarette /ˌsɪgə'ret/ n a cigarette yì zhī xiāngyān 一支香烟

cigarette lighter /sɪgə'ret ˌlaɪtə(r)/ n a cigarette lighter yí gè dǎhuǒjī 一个打火机

cinema /'sɪnəmə/ n (British English) a cinema yí gè diànyǐngyuàn 一个电影院

circle /'sɜːkl/ n a circle yí gè yuánquān 一个圆圈; we were sitting in a circle wǒmen zuòchéng yí gè yuánquān 我们坐成一个圆圈

circus /'sɜːkəs/ n a circus yí gè mǎxìtuán 一个马戏团

citizen /'sɪtɪzən/ n (of a country) a citizen yí gè gōngmín 一个公民; (of a city or town) a citizen yí gè shìmín 一个市民, yí gè jūmín 一个居民

city /'sɪtɪ/ n a city yí zuò chéngshì 一座城市

city centre /ˌsɪtɪ 'sentə(r)/ (British English), **city center** (US English) n the city centre shìzhōngxīn 市中心

civilized /'sɪvɪlaɪzd/ adj wénmíng de 文明的

civil servant /ˌsɪvɪl 'sɜːvənt/ n a civil servant yí gè gōngwùyuán 一个公务员

clap /klæp/ vb (to pat) pāi 拍; (to applaud) gǔzhǎng 鼓掌

clarinet /ˌklærɪ'net/ n a clarinet yí gè dānhuángguǎn 一个单簧管

class /klɑːs/ n (a group of students) a class yí gè bān 一个班; (a lesson) a class yì jié kè 一节课; a history class yì jié lìshǐkè 一节历史课; (a social group) a (social) class yí gè (shèhuì) jiējí 一个(社会)阶级

classical music /ˌklæsɪkəl 'mjuːzɪk/ n gǔdiǎn yīnyuè 古

典音乐

classmate /'klɑːsmeɪt/ *n* a classmate yí ge tóngxué 一个同学

classroom /'klɑːsrʊm/ *n* a classroom yì jiān jiàoshì 一间教室

clean /kliːn/ **1** *adj* gānjìng de 干净的，qīngjié de 清洁的；my hands are clean wǒ de shǒu hěn gānjìng 我的手很干净；to keep the room clean bǎochí fángjiān qīngjié 保持房间清洁 **2** *vb* bǎ…nòng gānjìng 把…弄干净! Note that the verb *nòng* 弄 can be replaced by another verb, such as xǐ 洗 (= to wash) or cā 擦 (= to wipe) depending on the way the object is cleaned; to have the clothes cleaned bǎ yīfu xǐ gānjìng 把衣服洗干净；I have cleaned the windows wǒ bǎ chuānghu cā gānjìng le 我把窗户擦干净了

clear /klɪə(r)/ **1** *adj* (*easy to understand, see, or hear*) qīngchǔ de 清楚的；is that clear? qīngchǔ ma? 清楚吗？his voice isn't clear tā de shēngyīn bù qīngchǔ 他的声音不清楚；your writing must be very clear nǐ bìxū xiě de hěn qīngchǔ 你必须写得很清楚；(*obvious*) xiǎnrán de 显然的，míngxiǎn de 明显的；it is clear that he is unhappy xiǎnrán tā bù gāoxìng 显然他不高兴；(*with no rain or cloud*) qínglǎng de 晴朗的；a clear day yí ge qíngtiān 一个晴天 **2** *vb* (*to empty, to remove from*) to clear the table shōushi zhuōzi 收拾桌子；to clear the house of everything in it qīngchú fángzi li suǒyǒu de dōngxi 清除房子里所有的东西；to clear the snow off the road qīngsǎo lù shang de xuě 清扫路上的雪；(*about the sky or the weather*) biànqíng 变晴

clever /'klevə(r)/ *adj* cōngming de 聪明的；she is a clever girl tā shì yí ge cōngming de gūniang 她是一个聪明的姑娘；clever at shàncháng 擅长；to be clever at mathematics shàncháng shùxué 擅长数学

cliff /klɪf/ *n* a cliff yí ge xuányá 一个悬崖，yí ge qiàobì 一个峭壁

climate /ˈklaɪmɪt/ *n* qìhòu 气候

climb /klaɪm/ *vb* (*to ascend by clutching with hands and feet*) pá 爬；to climb (up) a tree pá shù 爬树；to climb a mountain pá shān 爬山；to climb over a wall fānguò qiáng 翻过墙；(*to rise higher*) xiàng shàng pá 向上爬

climbing /ˈklaɪmɪŋ/ *n* pāndēng 攀登

clinic /ˈklɪnɪk/ *n* a clinic yí gè ménzhěnsuǒ 一个门诊所，yí gè yīwùshì 一个医务室

cloakroom /ˈkləʊkrʊm/ *n* a cloakroom yí gè xǐshǒujiān 一个洗手间，yí gè yīmàojiān 一个衣帽间

clock /klɒk/ *n* (*on a building*, *in a room*, *or as an ornament*) zhōng 钟；(*in sporting events*) miǎobiǎo 秒表

close¹ /kləʊs/ **1** *adj* (*near*) jìn de 近的；the station is quite close chēzhàn bǐjiào jìn 车站比较近；is the house close to the school? fángzi lí xuéxiào jìn ma? 房子离学校近吗？；(*as a relative*) jìnqīn de 近亲的；a close relative yí gè jìnqīn 一个近亲；(*as a friend*) qīnmì de 亲密的；a close friend yí gè qīnmì de péngyou 一个亲密的朋友 **2** *adv* to live close (*by*) zhù zài fùjìn 住在附近；to follow close behind someone jǐn gēn zài mǒu rén hòumian 紧跟在某人后面

close² /kləʊz/ *vb* (*if it's a door or a window*) guān 关；to close the window guān chuāng 关窗；the door closed suddenly mén tūrán guānshang le 门突然关上了；(*if it's the eye or the mouth*) bì 闭；close your eyes bìshang nǐ de yǎnjing 闭上你的眼睛；(*if it's a shop or a bank*) guānmén 关门；the shop closes at noon zhè jiā shāngdiàn zhōngwǔ guānmén 这家商店中午关门；close down guānbì 关闭，dǎobì 倒闭；the factory has closed down zhè jiā gōngchǎng guānbì le 这家工厂关闭了

closed /kləʊzd/ *adj* guānbì de 关闭的，guānmén de 关门的

cloth /klɒθ/ *n* (*material*) bù 布；a cloth (*for dusting*) yí kuài mābù 一块抹布；a table cloth yí kuài zhuōbù 一块桌布；a cloth (*for dishes*) yí kuài shuāwǎnbù 一块刷碗

布；(*for the floor*) yí kuài tuōbù 一块拖布

clothes /kləʊðz/ *n* yīfu 衣服；to put on one's clothes chuānshang yīfu 穿上衣服；to take off one's clothes tuōxia yīfu 脱下衣服；to have no clothes on méi chuān yīfu 没穿衣服

cloud /klaʊd/ *n* a cloud yì duǒ yún 一朵云

clown /klaʊn/ *n* a clown yí gè xiǎochǒu 一个小丑

club /klʌb/ *n* a club yí gè jùlèbù 一个俱乐部；a tennis club yí gè wǎngqiú jùlèbù 一个网球俱乐部；(*a nightclub*) a club yí gè yèzǒnghuì 一个夜总会

clue /kluː/ *n* a clue yì tiáo xiànsuǒ 一条线索

clumsy /'klʌmzi/ *adj* bènzhuō de 笨拙的

coach /kəʊtʃ/ **1** *n* (*British English*) (*a bus*) a coach yí liàng chángtú qìchē 一辆长途汽车；(*of a train*) (*British English*) a coach yì jié chēxiāng 一节车厢；(*a trainer in sports*) a coach yí gè jiàoliàn 一个教练；(*a private tutor*) a coach yí gè sīrén jiàoshī 一个私人教师 **2** *vb* (*in sports*) xùnliàn 训练；(*in academic studies*) fǔdǎo 辅导

coach station /'kəʊtʃ ˌsteɪʃən/ *n* a coach station yí gè chángtú qìchēzhàn 一个长途汽车站

coal /kəʊl/ *n* méi 煤

coast /kəʊst/ *n* hǎi'àn 海岸

coat /kəʊt/ *n* a coat yí jiàn wàitào 一件外套；(*of an animal*) pímáo 皮毛

coat hanger /'kəʊt ˌhæŋə(r)/ *n* a coat hanger yí gè yījià 一个衣架

cobweb /'kɒbweb/ *n* a cobweb yí gè zhīzhūwǎng 一个蜘蛛网

cock /kɒk/ *n* a cock yì zhī gōngjī 一只公鸡

cocoa /'kəʊkəʊ/ *n* (*the drink*) kěkěchá 可可茶；(*the product*) kěkěfěn 可可粉

coconut /'kəʊkənʌt/ *n* a coconut yí gè yēzi 一个椰子

cod /kɒd/ *n* xuěyú 鳕鱼

coffee /'kɒfi/ *n* (*the product*) kāfēi 咖啡；(*a cup of coffee*) a coffee yì bēi kāfēi 一杯咖啡

coffee machine /ˈkɒfɪ məʃiːn/ n a coffee machine (*an appliance*) yí gè kāfēiqì 一个咖啡器; (*a machine*) yì tái kāfēijī 一台咖啡机

coin /kɔɪn/ n a coin yí gè yìngbì 一个硬币; a ten-pence coin yí gè shí biànshì de yìngbì 一个 10 便士的硬币

coincidence /kəʊˈɪnsɪdəns/ n a coincidence yí gè qiǎohé 一个巧合

cold /kəʊld/ **1** adj lěng 冷的; I'm very cold wǒ hěn lěng 我很冷; it's cold in the classroom jiàoshì li hěn lěng 教室里很冷; a cold meal yí dùn liángfàn 一顿凉饭 **2** n (*the lack of heat*) hánlěng 寒冷; (*a common illness*) gǎnmào 感冒

collapse /kəˈlæps/ vb (*if it's a building, a wall*) dǎotā 倒塌; (*in health*) kuǎ 垮; (*when talking about a person falling down physically*) dǎoxià 倒下

collar /ˈkɒlə(r)/ n (*on a shirt or jacket*) a collar yí gè lǐngzi 一个领子; (*for a pet*) a collar yí gè jǐngquān 一个颈圈

colleague /ˈkɒliːg/ n a colleague yí gè tóngshì 一个同事

collect /kəˈlekt/ vb (*to gather*) jí jí, shōují 收集; to collect materials shōují cáiliào 收集材料; he collects stamps tā jíyóu 他集邮; (*to pick up or meet a person*) jiē 接; he is going to collect her son tā yào qù jiē tā érzi 她要去接她儿子; (*to collect money or rubbish*) shōu 收; to collect taxes shōushuì 收税; to collect my post qǔ wǒ de xìnjiàn 取我的信件

collection /kəˈlekʃən/ n (*a set*) shōují 收集; she has a great collection of posters tā shōujíle hěn duō zhāotiēhuà 她收集了很多招贴画; (*money collected*)shōu de qián 收的钱

college /ˈkɒlɪdʒ/ n a college yí gè xuéyuàn 一个学院; to go to college shàng dàxué 上大学; to be at college zài dàxué shàngxué 在大学上学

colour /ˈkʌlə(r)/ (*British English*), **color** (*US English*) **1** n a colour yì zhǒng yánsè 一种颜色; what colour is the car? chē shì shénme yánsè de? 车是什么颜色的？**2** vb gěi… zhuósè 给…着色；to colour the drawings (in…) (yòng…) gěi huà zhuósè (用…)给画着色

colourful /'kʌləfʊl/ (British English)，**colorful** (US English) adj yànlì de 艳丽的，sècǎi fēngfù de 色彩丰富的；a colourful shirt yí jiàn yànlì de chènshān 一件艳丽的衬衫

colour television /'kʌlə telɪ,vɪʒn/ (British English)，**color television** (US English) n a colour television yì tái cǎisè diànshìjī 一台彩色电视机

comb /kəʊm/ **1** n a comb yì bǎ shūzi 一把梳子 **2** vb to comb one's hair shū tóufa 梳头发

come /kʌm/ vb to come lái 来；she's coming today tā jīntiān lái 她今天来；we'll come by bike wǒmen qí zìxíngchē lái 我们骑自行车来；I'm coming wǒ zhè jiù lái 我这就来；is the bus coming? chē lái le ma? 车来了吗？；be careful when you come down the stairs xià lóutī de shíhou yào xiǎoxīn 下楼梯的时候要小心；to come through the city centre chuānguò shìzhōngxīn 穿过市中心；(to happen) fāshēng 发生；whatever comes, I won't change my mind búguǎn fāshēng shénme shì, wǒ dōu bú huì gǎibiàn zhǔyì 不管发生什么事，我都不会改变主意；(to reach) dào 到；turn left when you come to the traffic lights nǐ dàole jiāotōngdēng de shíhou xiàng zuǒ guǎi 你到了交通灯的时候向左拐；(to attend) cānjiā 参加；will you be able to come to the meeting? nǐ néng cānjiā huìyì ma? 你能参加会议吗？；(to be a native or a product of) láizì 来自；she comes from Japan tā láizì Rìběn 她来自日本；the strawberries all come from Spain zhèxiē cǎoméi quánbù láizì Xībānyá 这些草莓全部来自西班牙；(in a contest) dé 得；to come first dé dì-yī 得第1；**come around ▶ come round**；**come back** huílái 回来；when will you come back? nǐ shénme shíhou huílái? 你什么时候回来？；to come back home huíjiā 回家；**come in** (to enter) jìnlái 进来；(if it's a plane, a train) dàodá 到达；the tide's coming in zhèngzài zhǎngcháo 正在涨潮；come off diào diào 掉掉；a button came off my shirt wǒ de chènshān diàole yí lì kòuzi 我的衬衫掉了一粒扣子；come on (to start) kāishǐ 开始；(if it's heating) kāishǐ rè 开始热；(if it's a light) kāishǐ liàng 开始亮；(when encouraging someone) kuài 快, déla 得啦；come on, hurry up! kuài, gǎnjǐn! 快, 赶紧！；come on, you can do better than that! déla, nǐ néng zuò de bǐ nà gèng hǎo! 得啦, 你能做得比那更好！；come out (to leave a place) chūlái 出来；I saw him as I was coming out of the shop wǒ cóng shāngdiàn chūlái de shíhou kànjiànle tā 我从商店出来的时候看了他；(to become available) (if it's a film) shàngyǎn 上演；(if it's a book) chūbǎn 出版；(to wash out) xǐdiào 洗掉；(if it's a photo) the photo didn't come out zhè zhāng zhàopiàn méi zhàohǎo 这张照片没照好；(if it's smoke, fire) mào chūlái 冒出来；there are flames coming out of the windows yǒu yìxiē huǒmiáo cóng chuānghu li mào chūlái 有一些火苗从窗户里冒出来；come round (to visit) lái wán; (after a faint) sūxǐng guòlái 苏醒过来；come to (to total) gòngjì 共计；the meal came to 75 pounds fànfèi gòngjì qīshíwǔ bàng 饭费共计 75 磅；how much does it come to? gòngjì duōshao qián? 共计多少钱？；come up (to be discussed) tí chūlái 提出来；has this question come up? zhège wèntí tí chūlái le ma? 这个问题提出来了吗？；(if it's the sun) chūlái 出来

comfortable /ˈkʌmfətəbl/ adj shūfu de 舒服的, shūshì de 舒适的；do you feel comfortable? nǐ gǎnjué shūfu ma? 你感觉舒服吗？

comforter /ˈkʌmfətə(r)/ n (US English) a comforter；(if it's a person) yí gè ānwèizhě 一个安慰者；(if it's a blanket) yì tiáo tǎnzi 一条毯子

comic strip /ˈkɒmɪk strɪp/ n a comic strip yí tào liánhuán mànhuà 一套连环漫画

commercial /kə'mɜːʃəl/ **1** adj shāngyè de 商业的，shāngwù de 商务的 **2** n a commercial (on TV or radio) yí gè guǎnggào jiémù 一个广告节目

commit /kə'mɪt/ vb to commit [a crime | a mistake | a murder] fàn [zuì | cuò | móushāzuì] 犯 [罪 | 错 | 谋杀罪]

common /'kɒmən/ adj (public) gòngyǒu de 共有的，gòngtóng de 共同的；(ordinary) pǔtōng de 普通的，tōngcháng de 通常的

communicate /kə'mjuːnɪkeɪt/ vb (to pass, to impart) chuándá 传达，chuánsòng 传送；(to have communication) liánxì 联系，liánluò 联络；to communicate with someone by [letter | telephone | fax] yǔ mǒu rén tōngguò [xìnjiàn | diànhuà | chuánzhēn] liánxì 与某人通过 [信件 | 电话 | 传真] 联系

community /kə'mjuːnətɪ/ n a community yí gè shètuán 一个社团，yí gè tuántǐ 一个团体

company /'kʌmpənɪ/ n (a business) gōngsī 公司；a company yí gè gōngsī 一个公司；(a group of actors) jùtuán 剧团；a theatre company yí gè jùtuán 一个剧团；(other people) péibàn 陪伴；to keep someone company péibàn mǒu rén 陪伴某人；to part company with someone gēn mǒu rén fēnshǒu 跟某人分手

compare /kəm'peə(r)/ vb bǐjiào 比较；to compare China with Japan ná Rìběn gēn Zhōngguó bǐjiào 拿日本跟中国比较；she compares herself to her older sister tā ná zìjǐ gēn tā jiějie bǐjiào 她拿自己跟她姐姐比较

compass /'kʌmpəs/ n a compass yí gè zhǐnánzhēn 一个指南针

competition /ˌkɒmpɪ'tɪʃən/ n jìngzhēng 竞争；there's a lot of competition between the schools zài gè xuéxiào zhījiān yǒu hěn duō jìngzhēng 在各学校之间有很多竞争；(a contest) bǐsài 比赛；a drawing competition yí cì huìhuà bǐsài 一次绘画比赛

competitive /kəm'petətɪv/ adj jùyǒu jìngzhēngxìng de 具有竞争性的

complain /kəm'pleɪn/ vb bàoyuàn 抱怨；to complain

about the food bàoyuàn fàn bù hǎo 抱怨饭不好

complete /kəm'pli:t/ **1** adj (entire) wánquán de 完全的;
it was a complete disaster zhè wánquán shì yì chǎng
zāinàn 这完全是一场灾难；this is a complete waste
of time zhè wánquán shì làngfèi shíjiān 这完全是浪费时
间；(finished) wánchéngle de 完成的；the work must
be complete by 10 o'clock zhè ge gōngzuò shí diǎn
yǐqián bìxū wánchéng 这个工作 10 点以前必须完成 **2** vb
wánchéng 完成；the project has not been completed
yet zhè xiàng gōngchéng hái méiyǒu wánchéng 这项工程
还没有完成

completely /kəm'pli:tlɪ/ adv wánquán 完全

complicate /'kɒmplɪkeɪt/ vb shǐ⋯fùzá 使⋯复杂；this
has further complicated the situation zhè shǐ xíngshì
gèng fùzá le 这使形势更复杂了

complicated /'kɒmplɪkeɪtɪd/ adj fùzá de 复杂的

compliment /'kɒmplɪmənt/ **1** n a compliment zànyáng
zànměi de huà 赞扬赞美的话 **2** vb chēngzàn 称赞,
zànměi 赞美；to compliment someone chēngzàn mǒu rén
称赞某人

compulsory /kəm'pʌlsərɪ/ adj (if it's education or
military service) yìwù de 义务的；(if it's a school
subject) bìxiū de 必修的；(if it's a way of handling
something) qiángzhì de 强制的，qiǎngpò de 强迫的

computer /kəm'pju:tə(r)/ n a computer yì tái jìsuànjī 一
台计算机，yì tái diànnǎo 一台电脑

computer game /kəm'pju:tə geɪm/ n a computer game
yí gè jìsuànjī yóuxì 一个计算机游戏

computer programme /kəm'pju:tə 'prəʊgræm/ n a
computer programme yí gè jìsuànjī chéngxù 一个计算机
程序

computer programmer /kəm'pju:tə 'prəʊgræmə(r)/ n
a computer programmer yí gè biānchéngyuán 一个编程
员

computer scientist /kəm'pju:tə 'saɪəntɪst/ n a

computer scientist yí gè jìsuànjī kēxuéjiā 一个计算机科学家

computer studies /kəm,pjuːtə 'stʌdɪz/ n jìsuànjīxué 计算机学

concentrate /'kɒnsəntreɪt/ vb (to bring towards a centre) jízhōng 集中; (to direct one's thoughts towards one object) jízhōng jīnglì 集中精力

concert /'kɒnsət/ n a concert yì chǎng yīnyuèhuì 一场音乐会

concert hall /'kɒnsət hɔːl/ n a concert hall yí gè yīnyuètīng 一个音乐厅

concrete /'kɒnkriːt/ n hùnníngtǔ 混凝土

condemn /kən'dem/ vb (to censure or blame) qiǎnzé 谴责; (to sentence) pànchǔ 判处; to condemn someone to death pànchǔ mǒu rén sǐxíng 判处某人死刑

condition /kən'dɪʃən/ n (prerequisite) tiáojiàn 条件; conditions of success chénggōng de tiáojiàn 成功的条件; (a state) zhuàngkuàng 状况; the car is in good condition chē de zhuàngkuàng hěn hǎo 车的状况很好; on condition that rúguǒ 如果; you can go on condition that her parents drive you home rúguǒ tā fùmǔ kāichē sòng nǐ huíjiā, nǐ jiù kěyǐ qù 如果她父母开车送你回家, 你就可以去! Note that the conditional clause precedes the main clause in Chinese.

condom /'kɒndəm/ n a condom yí gè bìyùntào 一个避孕套

conductor /kən'dʌktə(r)/ n (in an orchestra or a choir) a conductor yí gè yuèduì zhǐhuī 一个乐队指挥; (in a bus) a conductor yí gè shòupiàoyuán 一个售票员; (in a train) a conductor yí gè lièchēyuán 一个列车员

conference /'kɒnfərəns/ n a conference yí cì huìyì 一次会议

confidence /'kɒnfɪdəns/ n xìnxīn 信心; (trust) xìnrèn 信任; to have confidence in someone xìnrèn mǒu rén 信任某人

confident /'kɒnfɪdənt/ *adj* yǒu xìnxīn de 有信心的

confidential /ˌkɒnfɪ'denʃəl/ *adj* (*given in confidence*) mìmì de 秘密的, jīmì de 机密的; (*admitted into confidence*) cānyù jīmì de 参与机密的; a confidential secretary yí gè jīyào mìshū 一个机要秘书

confiscate /'kɒnfɪskeɪt/ *vb* mòshōu 没收

conflict /'kɒnflɪkt/ *n* chōngtū 冲突

Confucian /kən'fjuːʃjən/ **1** *adj* Kǒngzǐ de 孔子的, Rújiā de 儒家的 **2** *n* Rújiā chéngyuán 儒家, Kǒngzǐ de méntú 孔子的门徒

confused /kən'fjuːzd/ *adj* hútu de 糊涂的

congratulate /kən'grætjuleɪt/ *vb* zhùhè 祝贺

congratulations /kənˌgrætjuˈleɪʃənz/ *n* (*also exc*) zhùhè 祝贺; congratulations zhùhè nǐ! 祝贺你!

connection /kə'nekʃən/ *n* guānxì 关系; it has no connection with the strike zhè yǔ bàgōng méiyǒu guānxì 这与罢工没有关系

conscientious /ˌkɒnʃɪ'enʃəs/ *adj* rènzhēn de 认真的

conscious /'kɒnʃəs/ *adj* (*aware*) yìshí dào de 意识到的; (*after an operation*) shénzhì qīngxǐng de 神志清醒的

construct /kən'strʌkt/ *vb* jiànzào 建造, jiànshè 建设

consult /kən'sʌlt/ *vb* (*to discuss*) shāngliang 商量; to consult with him gēn tā shāngliang 跟他商量; (*to ask advice of*) qǐngjiào 请教; to consult the teacher qǐngjiào lǎoshī 请教老师; (*to look up for information*) chá 查; to consult a dictionary chá zìdiǎn 查字典

contact /'kɒntækt/ **1** *n* to be in contact with someone gēn mǒu rén yǒu liánxì 跟某人有联系; to lose contact shīqù liánxì 失去联系 **2** *vb* to contact someone gēn mǒu rén liánxì 跟某人联系

contact lens /'kɒntækt lenz/ *n* yǐnxíng yǎnjìng 隐形眼镜

contain /kən'teɪn/ *vb* (*if it's a substance*) hányǒu 含有; sea water contains salt hǎishuǐ hányǒu yán 海水含有盐; (*if it's a container*) zhuāng 装; this box contains apples zhège xiāngzi zhuāngzhe píngguǒ 这个箱子装着苹

果；(if it's a room or a hall) róngnà 容纳；this room can contain 20 people zhège fángjiān néng róngnà èrshí gè rén 这个房间能容纳 20 个人

content /kən'tent/ adj (satisfied) mǎnyì de 满意的；(not wanting more) mǎnzú de 满足的

contest /kən'test/ n bǐsài 比赛，jìngsài 竞赛

continent /'kɒntɪnənt/ n (a large mass of land) a continent yí gè dàlù 一个大陆；(British English) (Europe) the Continent Ōuzhōu Dàlù 欧洲大陆

continue /kən'tɪnjuː/ vb jìxù 继续；to continue to talk, to continue talking jìxù tánhuà 继续谈话

continuous /kən'tɪnjuəs/ adj chíxù de 持续的，búduàn de 不断的；a continuous noise chíxù de zàoshēng 持续的噪声

contraception /ˌkɒntrəˈsepʃən/ n bìyùn 避孕

contract /'kɒntrækt/ n a contract yí gè hétong 一个合同；to have a two-year contract huòdé yí gè liǎng nián de hétong 获得一个两年的合同

contradict /ˌkɒntrəˈdɪkt/ vb (to oppose by words) fǎnbó 反驳，(to deny) fǒurèn 否认；(to be contrary to) yǔ … xiāng máodùn 与 … 相矛盾；this document contradicts that one zhège wénjiàn yǔ nàge wénjiàn xiāng máodùn 这个文件与那个文件相矛盾

contradiction /ˌkɒntrəˈdɪkʃən/ n a contradiction yí gè máodùn 一个矛盾

contrast /kən'trɑːst/ n duìbǐ 对比，duìzhào 对照

contribute /kən'trɪbjuːt/ vb (to give money) juān(xiàn) 捐(献)；to contribute one's share gòngxiàn zìjǐ de yí fèn lìliang 贡献自己的一份力量

control /kən'trəʊl/ n **1** kòngzhì 控制；to take control of a situation kòngzhì júshì 控制局势；to lose control of a car duì chē shīqù kòngzhì 对车失去控制 **2** vb kòngzhì 控制；to control a region kòngzhì yí gè dìqū 控制一个地区；to control traffic guǎnzhì jiāotōng 管制交通

convenient /kən'viːnjənt/ adj fāngbiàn de 方便的；it's

more convenient to take the bus zuò qìchē gèng fāngbiàn 坐汽车更方便；it's not convenient for me zhè duì wǒ bù fāngbiàn 这对我不方便

conversation /ˌkɒnvə'seɪʃən/ n tánhuà 谈话；to have a conversation with someone yǔ mǒu rén tánhuà 与某人谈话

convince /kən'vɪns/ vb (to persuade) shuōfú 说服；(to satisfy as to the truth of something) shǐ…xìnfú 使…信服，shǐ…quèxìn 使…确信；he convinced me of his innocence tā shǐ wǒ quèxìn tā shì qīngbái de 他使我确信他是清白的

cook /kʊk/ **1** vb zuòfàn 做饭；to cook a meal zuòfàn 做饭 **2** n a cook yí gè chúshī 一个厨师，yí gè chuīshìyuán 一个炊事员

cooker /'kʊkə(r)/ n (British English) a cooker yí gè lúzào 一个炉灶

cookie /'kʊkɪ/ n (US English) a cookie yí kuài bǐnggān 一块饼干，yí gè xiǎotiánbǐng 一个小甜饼

cooking /'kʊkɪŋ/ n pēngtiáo 烹调，pēngrèn 烹饪；to do the cooking zuòfàn 做饭

cool /kuːl/ adj (fresh, not hot) liáng de 凉的，liángkuai de 凉快的；a cool drink yí fèn lěngyǐn 一份冷饮；it's much cooler today jīntiān liángkuai duō le 今天凉快多了；(calm) lěngjìng de 冷静的；(fashionable) kù de 酷的；**cool down** (to get colder) biànliáng 变凉；(to calm down) píngjìng xiàlái 平静下来

cooperate /kəʊ'ɒpəreɪt/ vb hézuò 合作；to cooperate with someone yǔ mǒu rén hézuò 与某人合作

cope /kəʊp/ vb yìngfu 应付，duìfu 对付；can he cope with this work? tā néng yìngfu zhège gōngzuò ma? 他能应付这个工作吗？

copper /'kɒpə(r)/ n tóng 铜

copy /'kɒpɪ/ **1** n a copy yí gè fùzhìpǐn 一个复制品；(if it's photocopy) yí gè fùyìnjiàn 一个复印件，yí gè yìngyìnjiàn 一个影印件 **2** vb (to photocopy) fùyìn 复印，

yǐngyìn 影印；(to reproduce a painting, a videotape, an antique) fùzhì 复制；(to plagiarize) chāoxí 抄袭；(to imitate) mófǎng 模仿

cork /kɔːk/ n a cork yí gè ruǎnmùsāi 一个软木塞；cork ruǎnmù 软木

corkscrew /'kɔːkskruː/ n a corkscrew yì bǎ kāisāizuàn 一把开塞钻

corner /'kɔːnə(r)/ n (of a street) guǎijiǎo 拐角；(of a table, a room) jiǎo 角；the corner of a table zhuōjiǎo 桌角；(in football, hockey) jiǎoqiú 角球；a corner yí cì jiǎoqiú 一次角球

correct /kə'rekt/ 1 adj zhèngquè de 正确的 2 vb to correct a mistake gǎizhèng cuòwù 改正错误；to correct an essay xiūgǎi wénzhāng 修改文章

correction /kə'rekʃən/ n gǎizhèng 改正, xiūgǎi 修改

corridor /'kɒrɪdɔː(r)/ n a corridor yí gè zǒuláng 一个走廊

cost /kɒst/ 1 n fèiyòng 费用 2 vb how much does it cost? zhège duōshǎo qián? 这个多少钱？it will cost a lot of money zhè yào huā hěn duō qián 这要花很多钱

costume /'kɒstjuːm/ n a costume yì zhǒng zhuāngshù 一种装束

cosy /'kəʊzɪ/ (British English), **cozy** (US English) adj a cosy room yí gè wēnnuǎn shūshì de fángjiān 一个温暖舒适的房间

cot /kɒt/ n (British English) a cot yì zhāng értóngchuáng 一张儿童床

cottage /'kɒtɪdʒ/ n a cottage yì suǒ xiǎo biéshù 一所小别墅，yì suǒ cūnshè 一所村舍

cotton /'kɒtən/ n (the material) miánhuā 棉花；(the thread) miánxiàn 棉线

cotton wool /ˌkɒtən 'wʊl/ n (British English) tuōzhīmián 脱脂棉，yàomián 药棉

couch /kaʊtʃ/ n a couch yí gè chángshāfā 一个长沙发

cough /kɒf/ vb késou 咳嗽

could /强 kʊd; 弱 kəd/ vb (knew how to) néng 能; she could read at the age of three tā sān suì jiù néng kàn shū 她 3 岁就能看书; he couldn't type tā bú huì dǎzì 他不会打字! Note that here in the negative sentence, bú huì 不会 should be used instead of bù néng 不能; (when talking about speaking or writing in a foreign language) huì 会; he could speak Japanese but I couldn't tā huì shuō Rìyǔ kěshì wǒ bú huì 他会说日语可是我不会; (in the negative sentence when talking about seeing, hearing, understanding, could is not translated) I couldn't see those words wǒ kàn bú jiàn nàxiē zì 我看不见那些字; he couldn't hear me tā tīng bú jiàn wǒ de shēngyīn 他听不见我的声音; they couldn't understand English tāmen bù dǒng Yīngyǔ 他们不懂英语; (when implying that something did not happen) she could have become a doctor tā běnlái kěyǐ chéngwéi yí gè yīshēng 她本来可以成为一个医生; you could have apologized! nǐ dāngshí yīnggāi dàoqiàn! 你当时应该道歉!; (when indicating a possibility) kěnéng 可能; they could be wrong tāmen kěnéng cuò le 他们可能错了; it could be very cold in Shanghai Shànghǎi kěnéng hěn lěng 上海可能很冷; (when making a request or suggestion) could you tell me his address, please? qǐng nín gàosu wǒ tā de dìzhǐ hǎo ma? 请您告诉我他的地址好吗?; we could go back by bus wǒmen kěyǐ zuò chē huíqù 我们可以坐车回去

count /kaʊnt/ vb shǔ 数; count on to count on someone yīkào mǒu rén 依靠某人

counter /'kaʊntə(r)/ n (a surface for putting things on) a counter yí gè guìtái 一个柜台; (a device that counts) a counter yí gè jìshùqì 一个计数器

country /'kʌntri/ n (a state) a country yí gè guójiā 一个国家; (the countryside) nóngcūn 农村, xiāngxià 乡下; to live in the country zhù zài nóngcūn 住在农村

countryside /'kʌntrisaɪd/ n the countryside nóngcūn

农村，xiāngxia 乡下

couple /ˈkʌpl/ n (*husband and wife*) fūfù 夫妇，fūqī 夫妻；a couple yí duì fūfù 一对夫妇；(*when talking about the approximate number*) liǎng-sān 两三；a couple of days liǎng-sān tiān 两三天；a couple of books liǎng-sān běn shū 两三本书；(*two*, *a pair*) yí duì 一对；a couple of players yí duì xuǎnshǒu 一对选手

courage /ˈkʌrɪdʒ/ n yǒngqì 勇气

courageous /kəˈreɪdʒəs/ adj yǒnggǎn de 勇敢的

course /kɔːs/ n 1 (*a series of lessons or lectures*) kèchéng 课程；a course yì mén kèchéng 一门课程；a language course yì mén yǔyán kèchéng 一门语言课程；(*part of a meal*) yí dào cài 一道菜；what's the main course? zhǔcài shì shénme? 主菜是什么？2 of course dāngrán 当然

court /kɔːt/ n (*of law*) fǎyuàn 法院，fǎtíng 法庭；a court yí gè fǎyuàn 一个法院；to go to court qǐsù 起诉；(*for playing sports*) chǎng 场；a tennis court yí gè wǎngqiúchǎng 一个网球场；a basketball court yí gè lánqiúchǎng 一个篮球场

court case /ˈkɔːt keɪs/ n a court case yí gè fǎtíng ànjiàn 一个法庭案件

cousin /ˈkʌzən/ n (*a male cousin, older than oneself*) a cousin yí gè biǎogē 一个表哥；(*a male cousin younger than oneself*) a cousin yí gè biǎodì 一个表弟；(*a female cousin older than oneself*) a cousin yí gè biǎojiě 一个表姐；(*a female cousin younger than oneself*) a cousin yí gè biǎomèi 一个表妹

cover /ˈkʌvə(r)/ 1 vb gài 盖，fùgài 覆盖；he covered his daughter with his overcoat tā bǎ dàyī gài zài tā de nǚ'ér shēn shang 他把大衣盖在他的女儿身上；(*to cover a table, a bed*) pū 铺；he covered the bed with a white sheet tā bǎ yì tiáo bái chuángdān pū zài chuáng shang 他把一条白床单铺在床上；the table was covered with a blue cloth zhuōzi shang pūzhe yí kuài lán zhuōbù 桌子上铺着一块蓝桌布 **2** n（a lid）a cover yí gè gàizi 一个盖子；（for a cushion, a quilt）a cover yí gè tàozi 一个套子；（on a book, a magazine, an exercise book）the front cover fēngmiàn 封面；the back cover fēngdǐ 封底

cow /kaʊ/ n a cow yì tóu mǔniú 一头母牛

coward /'kaʊəd/ n a coward yí gè dǎnxiǎoguǐ 一个胆小鬼

cowboy /'kaʊbɔɪ/ n a cowboy yí gè mùtóng 一个牧童，yí gè niúzǎi 一个牛仔

cozy /'kəʊzɪ/ ▶ **cosy**

crab /kræb/ n a crab yì zhī xiè 一只蟹

crack /kræk/ vb（to fracture with the parts remaining in contact）nòngliè 弄裂；the accident has cracked the walls of the house zhè cì shìgù bǎ fángzi de qiáng nòngliè le 这次事故把房子的墙弄裂了；（to be fractured with the parts remaining in contact）liè 裂；the bottle cracked píngzi liè le 瓶子裂了；（to break partially and suddenly）dǎpò 打破；the ball cracked the window qiú bǎ chuānghu dǎpò le 球把窗户打破了

cradle /'kreɪdl/ n a cradle yí gè yáolán 一个摇篮

cramp /kræmp/ n a cramp chōujīnr 抽筋儿, jìngluán 痉挛

crash /kræʃ/ **1** n pèngzhuàng 碰撞；a car crash yí cì zhuàngchē shìgù 一次撞车事故 **2** vb to crash into a tree zhuàng zài shù shang 撞在树上；the plane crashed fēijī zhuìhuǐ le 飞机坠毁了

crayon /'kreɪən/ n a crayon yì zhī cǎibǐ 一支彩笔

crazy /'kreɪzɪ/ adj fāfēng de 发疯的，fākuáng de 发狂的

cream /kriːm/ n nǎiyóu 奶油

create /kriːˈeɪt/ vb chuàngzào 创造；to create employment chuàngzào jiùyè jīhuì 创造就业机会

credit /'kredɪt/ **1** n（honour, glory）shēngwàng 声望；a scholar of the highest credit yí gè jí yǒu shēngwàng de xuézhě 一个极有声望的学者；（financial reliability and *reputation*) xìnyù 信誉;（*belief, trust*）xiāngxìn 相信, xìnrèn 信任; **do you give credit to this report?** nǐ xiāngxìn zhè tiáo bàodào ma? 你相信这条报道吗?;（*merit*）gōngláo 功劳, gōngjì 功绩; **she deserves all the credit for this** zhè jiàn shì suǒyǒu de gōngláo dōu yīnggāi guī tā 这件事所有的功劳都应该归她 **2** *vb*（*to believe*）xiāngxìn 相信; **I don't credit his words** wǒ bù xiāngxìn tā de huà 我不相信他的话;（*to add to a bank account or financial statement*）**to credit the money to someone's account** bǎ qián jìrù mǒu rén de zhàng 把钱记入某人的账

credit card /'kredɪt kɑːd/ *n* **a credit card** yì zhāng xìnyòngkǎ 一张信用卡

cricket /'krɪkɪt/ *n* bǎnqiú 板球

crime /kraɪm/ *n* zuì 罪, zuìxíng 罪行

criminal /'krɪmɪnəl/ **1** *n* **a criminal** yí gè zuìfàn 一个罪犯 **2** *adj* fànzuì de 犯罪的

crisis /'kraɪsɪs/ *n* **a crisis** yí cì wēijī 一次危机

crisps /'krɪsps/ *n*（*British English*）yóuzhá tǔdòupiàn 油炸土豆片

critical /'krɪtɪkəl/ *adj*（*relating to criticism*）pīpíng de 批评的;（*relating to a turning point or a crisis*）guānjiànxìng de 关键性的, wēijí de 危急的

criticize /'krɪtɪsaɪz/ *vb* pīpíng 批评

crocodile /'krɒkədaɪl/ *n* **a crocodile** yì tiáo èyú 一条鳄鱼

crooked /'krʊkɪd/ *adj*（*bent like a crook*）wān de 弯的, wānqū de 弯曲的; **a crooked line** yì tiáo wānqū de xiàn 一条弯曲的线;（*deviating from a right position*）wāi de 歪的; **the picture is crooked** zhàopiàn wāi le 照片歪了

cross /krɒs/ **1** *vb*（*to go across*）**to cross the road**（chuān）guò mǎlù（穿）过马路; **to cross the Channel** dùguò Yīngjílì Hǎixiá 渡过英吉利海峡; **to cross the border** yuèguò biānjiè 越过边界;（*other uses*）**to cross one's legs** pántuǐ 盘腿; **our letters crossed** wǒmen de

xìn hùxiāng cuòguò le 我们的信互相错过了 **2** *n* (*a mark*)
a cross yí gè shízì (biāojì) 一个十字 (标记) ; (*of a
church or as a religious symbol*) a cross yí gè shízìjià 一个
十字架 **3** *adj* to get cross with someone duì mǒu rén fā
píqi 对某人发脾气 ; **cross out** huàdiào 划掉

crossroad /ˈkrɒsrəʊd/ *n* a crossroad yí gè shízì lùkǒu 一
个十字路口

crossword puzzle /ˈkrɒswɜːd ˌpʌzl/ *n* a crossword
puzzle yí gè zònghéng zìmí 一个纵横字谜

crow /krəʊ/ *n* a crow yì zhī wūyā 一只乌鸦

crowd /kraʊd/ *n* (*a large number of people*) a crowd yì
qún rén 一群人 ; crowds of people xǔduō rén 许多人 ;
(*watching a game*) the crowd guānzhòng 观众

crown /kraʊn/ *n* (*on a king's head*) wángguān 王冠 ; a
crown yì dǐng wángguān 一顶王冠 ; (*on a queen's head*)
huángguān 皇冠 ; a crown yì dǐng huángguān 一顶皇冠

cruel /ˈkruːəl/ *adj* cánkù de 残酷的

cruelty /ˈkrʊəltɪ/ *n* cánkù 残酷

cruise /kruːz/ *n* xúnyóu 巡游

crush /krʌʃ/ *vb* (*to squeeze together*) zhà zhà 榨 ; (*if it's an
object*) yāsuì 压碎 ; (*if it's a person*) yādǎo 压倒

crutch /krʌtʃ/ *n* a crutch yì gēn guǎizhàng 一根拐杖

cry /kraɪ/ **1** *vb* (*to weep*) kū 哭 ; (*to utter loudly*) hǎn 喊
2 *n* (*a sound of weeping*) kūshēng 哭声 ; (*a shout*)
hǎnshēng 喊声

cub /kʌb/ *n* a cub yì zhī yòuzǎi 一只幼仔

cuckoo /ˈkʊkuː/ *n* a cuckoo yì zhī bùgǔniǎo 一只布谷鸟

cucumber /ˈkjuːkʌmbə(r)/ *n* a cucumber yì gēn huánggua 一根黄瓜

cuddle /ˈkʌdl/ *n* yōngbào 拥抱 ; to give someone a
cuddle yōngbào mǒu rén 拥抱某人

culprit /ˈkʌlprɪt/ *n* a culprit yí gè fànrén 一个犯人

cultural /ˈkʌltʃərəl/ *adj* wénhuà de 文化的

culture /ˈkʌltʃə(r)/ *n* wénhuà 文化

cunning /ˈkʌnɪŋ/ *adj* (*describing a person*) jiǎohuá de 狡

猎的；(describing a plan) qiǎomiào de 巧妙的

cup /kʌp/ n a cup yí gè bēizi 一个杯子；a cup of coffee yì bēi kāfēi 一杯咖啡；(in sport) a cup yí gè jiǎngbēi 一个奖杯

cupboard /'kʌbəd/ n a cupboard yí gè wǎnchú 一个碗橱

curb /kɜːb/ n the curb lùyuán 路缘

cure /kjʊə(r)/ **1** vb zhìhǎo 治好, zhìyù 治愈 **2** n zhìhǎo 治好

curious /'kjʊərɪəs/ adj hàoqí de 好奇的

curly /'kɜːlɪ/ adj juǎnqū de 卷曲的；curly hair juǎnqū de tóufa 卷曲的头发

currency /'kʌrənsɪ/ n a currency yì zhǒng huòbì 一种货币；foreign currency wàibì 外币, wàihuì 外汇

curry /'kʌrɪ/ n a curry gālí 咖喱

curtain /'kɜːtən/ n a curtain yí gè chuānglián 一个窗帘；to draw the curtains lā chuánglián 拉窗帘

cushion /'kʊʃən/ n a cushion yí gè diànzi 一个垫子

custard /'kʌstəd/ n niúnǎi dànhú 牛奶蛋糊

custom /'kʌstəm/ n a custom yì zhǒng xíguàn 一种习惯

customer /'kʌstəmə(r)/ n a customer yí gè gùkè 一个顾客

customs /'kʌstəmz/ n hǎiguān 海关；to go through customs tōngguò hǎiguān 通过海关

customs officer /'kʌstəmz ˌɒfɪsə(r)/ n a customs officer yí gè hǎiguān guānyuán 一个海关官员

cut /kʌt/ **1** vb (if it's an object) qiē 切, gē 割；to cut an apple in two bǎ píngguǒ qiēchéng liǎng bàn 把苹果切成两半；(if it's part of the body) gēpò 割破；to cut [one's fingers|one's knee|one's foot...] gēpò [shǒuzhǐ|xīgài|jiǎo…] 割破 [手指|膝盖|脚…]；(to cut with scissors) jiǎn 剪；to cut cloth jiǎn bù 剪布；she got her hair cut tā jiǎn tóufa le 她剪头发了；he got his hair cut tā lǐfà le 他理发了 **2** n (of the body) shāngkǒu 伤口；(in finance, expense) xuējiǎn 削减；(in a film, a book) shānjié 删节；**cut down** (to bring down by cutting) kǎndǎo 砍倒；

(to reduce, curtail) xuējiǎn 削减；**cut out** to cut a photo out of a magazine cóng zázhì shang jiǎnxià yì zhāng zhàopiàn 从杂志上剪下一张照片；**cut up** qiēsuì 切碎

cute /kjuːt/ adj kě'ài de 可爱的，dòu rén xǐ'ài de 逗人喜爱的

CV /ˌsiː ˈviː/ n a CV yí fèn jiǎnlì 一份简历

cycle /ˈsaɪkl/ vb qí zìxíngchē 骑自行车；**to cycle to school** qí zìxíngchē shàngxué 骑自行车上学；**to go cycling** qù qí zìxíngchē 去骑自行车

cycle lane /ˈsaɪkl leɪn/, **cycle path** /ˈsaɪkl pɑːθ/ n a cycle lane yì tiáo zìxíngchēdào 一条自行车道

cycling /ˈsaɪklɪŋ/ n zìxíngchē yùndòng 自行车运动

cyclist /ˈsaɪklɪst/ n a cyclist yí gè qí zìxíngchē de rén 一个骑自行车的人

cynical /ˈsɪnɪkəl/ adj wánshì-bùgōng de 玩世不恭的，lěngcháo-rèfěng de 冷嘲热讽的

Dd

---

dad, Dad /dæd/ n bàba 爸爸

daffodil /ˈdæfədɪl/ n a daffodil yì kē shuǐxiānhuā 一棵水仙花

daisy /ˈdeɪzɪ/ n a daisy yì kē chújú 一棵雏菊

damage /ˈdæmɪdʒ/ **1** vb (to damage) huǐhuài 毁坏；**the building was damaged by the fire** fángzi bèi dàhuǒ huǐhuài le 房子被大火毁坏了；(to harm) sǔnhài 损害；**it can damage your health** zhè huì sǔnhài nǐ de jiànkāng 这会损害你的健康 **2** n sǔnhuài 损坏；(loss) sǔnshī 损失；(harm) sǔnhài 损害

damp /dæmp/ adj cháoshī de 潮湿的

dance /dɑːns/ **1** vb tiàowǔ 跳舞 **2** n a dance yí gè wǔdǎo

一个舞蹈

dancer /'dɑːnsə(r)/ n a dancer yí gè wǔdǎo yǎnyuán 一个舞蹈演员

dancing /'dɑːnsɪŋ/ n tiàowǔ 跳舞

danger /'deɪndʒə(r)/ n wēixiǎn 危险; to be in danger zài wēixiǎn zhōng 在危险中

dangerous /'deɪndʒərəs/ adj wēixiǎn de 危险的

Danish /'deɪnɪʃ/ **1** adj Dānmài de 丹麦的 **2** n Dānmàiyǔ 丹麦语

dare /deə(r)/ vb (to have the courage) gǎn 敢; (when testing someone) I dare you to criticise her wǒ gǎn shuō nǐ bù gǎn pīpíng tā 我敢说你不敢批评她; (when expressing anger) don't dare speak to me like that! nǐ zěnme gǎn zhèyàng gēn wǒ jiǎnghuà! 你怎么敢这样跟我讲话!

dark /dɑːk/ **1** adj (lacking light) àn de 暗的, hēi'àn de 黑暗的; it's getting dark tiān hēi xiàlái le 天黑下来了; (black) hēi de 黑的; he's got dark hair tā shì hēi tóufa 他是黑头发; (darkish) shēn de 深的; a dark blue dress yí jiàn shēnlánsè de yīfu 一件深蓝色的衣服 **2** n (if it's a colour) hēisè 黑色, ànsè 暗色; (absence of light) hēi'àn 黑暗

darts /dɑːts/ n fēibiāo 飞镖; a game of darts fēibiāo yóuxì 飞镖游戏

date /deɪt/ n (in a calendar) a date yí gè rìqī 一个日期; what date is today? jīntiān jǐ hào? 今天几号?; (with a friend) to go out on a date with someone gēn mǒu rén chūqù yuēhuì 跟某人出去约会

daughter /'dɔːtə(r)/ n a daughter yí gè nǚ'ér 一个女儿

daughter-in-law /'dɔːtərɪnlɔː/ n a daughter-in-law yí gè érxífu 一个儿媳妇

dawn /dɔːn/ n límíng 黎明; at dawn límíng shí 黎明时

day /deɪ/ n a day yì tiān 一天; what day is it today? jīntiān xīngqījǐ? 今天星期几?; during the day zài báitiān 在白天; we had a very nice day wǒmen dùguòle měihǎo de yì tiān 我们度过了美好的一天；the next day, the day after dì-èr tiān 第 2 天；the day before qián yì tiān 前一天；the day after tomorrow hòutiān 后天；the day before yesterday qiántiān 前天；New Year's Day Yuándàn 元旦，xīnnián 新年；Christmas Day Shèngdàn Jié 圣诞节

daylight /'deɪlaɪt/ *n* rìguāng 日光；before daylight tiān-liàng qián 天亮前

dead /ded/ *adj* sǐ de 死的；he is dead tā sǐ le 他死了；(*more polite form*) qùshì de 去世的，shìshì de 逝世的；he is dead tā qùshì le 他去世了

deaf /def/ *adj* lóng de 聋的

deal /diːl/ *n* a deal (*in business*) yì bǐ mǎimai 一笔买卖；(*with a friend*) yí gè yuēdìng 一个约定；a great deal of [money | time | energy] dàliàng de [qián | shíjiān | jīnglì] 大量的 [钱 | 时间 | 精力] **2** *vb* to deal the cards fā pái 发牌；deal with chǔlǐ 处理，duìfu 对付；to deal with a problem chǔlǐ yí gè wèntí 处理一个问题

dear /dɪə(r)/ **1** *adj* (*in letters*) qīn'ài de 亲爱的；Dear Anne and Paul qīn'ài de Ānnī he Bǎoluó 亲爱的安妮和保罗；(*expensive*) guì de 贵的 **2** *exc* oh dear! a! tiān na! 啊！天哪！

death /deθ/ *n* sǐ 死，sǐwáng 死亡

death penalty /'deθ ˌpenəlti/ *n* sǐxíng 死刑

debate /dɪ'beɪt/ *n* a debate yí cì biànlùn 一次辩论

debt /det/ *n* a debt yì bǐ zhài 一笔债；to be in debt qiànzhài 欠债

decade /'dekeɪd/ *n* a decade shí nián 十年

decaffeinated /diːˈkæfɪneɪtɪd/ *adj* chúqù kāfēiyīn de 除去咖啡因的

deceive /dɪ'siːv/ *vb* qīpiàn 欺骗

December /dɪ'sembə(r)/ *n* shí'èryuè 十二月

decide /dɪ'saɪd/ *vb* juédìng 决定；he decided [to accept | to go | to get married...] tā juédìng [jiēshòu | qù | jiéhūn…] 他决定 [接受 | 去 | 结婚…]

decision /dɪˈsɪʒən/ n a decision yí xiàng juédìng 一项决定; to make a decision zuò yí gè juédìng 做一个决定

deck /dek/ n jiǎbǎn 甲板; on deck zài jiǎbǎn shang 在甲板上

deckchair /ˈdektʃeə(r)/ n a deckchair yì bǎ zhédiéshì tǎngyǐ 一把折叠式躺椅

decorate /ˈdekəreɪt/ vb zhuāngshì 装饰

decoration /ˌdekəˈreɪʃən/ n zhuāngshì 装饰

deep /diːp/ adj shēn de 深的; how deep is the lake? zhège hú yǒu duō shēn? 这个湖有多深?; the hole is three metres deep zhège dòng yǒu sān mǐ shēn 这个洞有 3 米深

deer /dɪə(r)/ n a deer yì tóu lù 一头鹿

defeat /dɪˈfiːt/ 1 vb to defeat an enemy zhànshèng dírén 战胜敌人; the team was defeated zhège duì bèi dǎbài le 这个队被打败了 2 n a defeat yí cì shībài 一次失败

defence /dɪˈfens/ (British English), **defense** (US English) n (protection) bǎohù 保护; (guarding against attack) bǎowèi 保卫

defend /dɪˈfend/ vb (to protect) bǎohù 保护; (to maintain against attack) bǎowèi 保卫

definite /ˈdefɪnɪt/ adj (describing an answer, a decision, a plan) míngquè de 明确的; (fixed) quèdìng de 确定的; nothing is definite shénme dōu méi quèdìng 什么都没确定; (obvious, visible) míngxiǎn de 明显的; a definite improvement míngxiǎn de gǎijìn 明显的改进

definitely /ˈdefɪnɪtlɪ/ adv kěndìng de 肯定的; they're definitely lying tāmen kěndìng zài shuōhuǎng 他们肯定在说谎; I'm definitely coming wǒ kěndìng lái 我肯定来

defy /dɪˈfaɪ/ vb mièshì 蔑视

degree /dɪˈgriː/ n (from a university) a degree yí gè xuéwèi 一个学位; (in measurements) dù 度; 5 degrees wǔ dù 5 度

delay /dɪˈleɪ/ 1 vb yánwù 延误, dānwù 耽误 2 n yánwù 延误, dānwù 耽误

deliberate /dɪ'lɪbərət/ *adj* gùyì de 故意的

deliberately /dɪ'lɪbərətlɪ/ *adv* gùyì de 故意地

delicious /dɪ'lɪʃəs/ *adj* hǎochī de 好吃的

delighted /dɪ'laɪtɪd/ *adj* gāoxìng de 高兴的; **to be delighted with a present** shōudào lǐwù hěn gāoxìng 收到礼物很高兴

deliver /dɪ'lɪvə(r)/ *vb* (*if it's something heavy*) (yùn) sòng (运)送; **to deliver goods** (yùn) sòng huòwù (运)送货物; (*if it's mail*) tóudì 投递; **to deliver mail** tóudì xìnjiàn 投递信件

demand /dɪ'mɑ:nd/ **1** *vb* yāoqiú 要求 **2** *n* yāoqiú 要求

demolish /dɪ'mɒlɪʃ/ *vb* chāihuǐ 拆毁

demonstration /ˌdemən'streɪʃən/ *n* (*a practical show or exhibition*) shìfàn 示范; **a demonstration** yí cì shìfàn 一次示范; (*a public procession or movement*) shìwēi 示威; **a demonstration** yí cì shìwēi 一次示威

denim jacket /'denɪm ˌdʒækɪt/ *n* **a denim jacket** yí jiàn láodòngbù jiákèshān 一件劳动布夹克衫

Denmark /'denmɑ:k/ *n* Dānmài 丹麦

dentist /'dentɪst/ *n* **a dentist** yí gè yáyī 一个牙医

deny /dɪ'naɪ/ *vb* fǒurèn 否认

department /dɪ'pɑ:tmənt/ *n* **a department**; (*in a firm*) yí gè bùmén 一个部门; (*in a university*) yí gè xì 一个系; (*in a large store*) a [food | clothes | furniture] department yí gè [shípǐn | fúzhuāng | jiājù] bù 一个 [食品 | 服装 | 家具] 部

department store /dɪ'pɑ:tmənt stɔ:(r)/ *n* **a department store** yí gè bǎihuò shāngdiàn 一个百货商店

depend /dɪ'pend/ *vb* (*to rely*) yīkào 依靠; **to depend on someone** yīkào mǒu rén 依靠某人; (*to be determined*) **it depends on you** zhè yào qǔjué yú nǐ 这要取决于你; **it depends** zhè děi kàn qíngkuàng (ér dìng) 这得看情况(而定)

depressed /dɪ'prest/ *adj* jǔsàng de 沮丧的, xiāochén de 消沉的

depressing /dɪ'presɪŋ/ *adj* lìng rén jǔsàng 令人沮丧

的，lìng rén xiāochén de 令人消沉的

deprive /dɪ'praɪv/ vb bōduó 剥夺

depth /depθ/ n shēnchù 深处，shēndù 深度

describe /dɪ'skraɪb/ vb (in writing) miáoxiě 描写；(in speaking) miáoshù 描述

description /dɪ'skrɪpʃən/ n (in writing) miáoxiě 描写；(in speaking) miáoshù 描述

desert /'dezət/ n a desert yí gè shāmò 一个沙漠

deserve /dɪ'zɜːv/ vb yīnggāi shòudào 应该受到；he deserves to be punished tā yīnggāi shòudào chéngfá 他应该受到惩罚

design /dɪ'zaɪn/ **1** vb (to contrive) shèjì 设计；to design clothes shèjì fúzhuāng 设计服装；that bridge was designed by him nà zuò qiáo shì tā shèjì de 那座桥是他设计的；(to plan) cèhuà 策划，jìhuà 计划；she designed the art exhibition zhè cì yìshù zhǎnlǎnhuì shì tā cèhuà de 这次艺术展览会是她策划的 **2** n (drawing or sketching) shèjì 设计；fashion design fúzhuāng shèjì 服装设计；(a pattern) tú'àn 图案；a design yí gè tú'àn 一个图案

desk /desk/ n a desk yì zhāng shūzhuō 一张书桌

desperate /'despərət/ adj (in a state of despair) juéwàng de 绝望的；(despairingly reckless) búgù-yíqiè de 不顾一切的

dessert /dɪ'zɜːt/ n tiánshí 甜食

destroy /dɪ'strɔɪ/ vb cuīhuǐ 摧毁，huǐhuài 毁坏

detail /'diːteɪl/ n a detail yí gè xìjié 一个细节；to go into detail xiángxì xùshù 详细叙述

detective /dɪ'tektɪv/ n a detective yí gè zhēntàn 一个侦探；a private detective yí gè sījiā zhēntàn 一个私家侦探

detective story /dɪ'tektɪv ˌstɔːrɪ/ n a detective story yí gè zhēntàn gùshi 一个侦探故事

determined /dɪ'tɜːmɪnd/ adj jiānjué de 坚决的，yǒu juéxīn de 有决心的；to be determined to go juéxīn yào qù 决心要去

develop /dɪˈveləp/ vb (to evolve) fāzhǎn 发展；to develop a friendly relationship fāzhǎn yǒuhǎo guānxì 发展友好关系；(to bring out what is latent or potential in) kāifā 开发；to develop a new market kāifā xīn shìchǎng 开发新市场

development /dɪˈveləpmənt/ n the rapid development of computer science jìsuànjī kēxué de xùnsù fāzhǎn 计算机科学的迅速发展；the development of natural resources zìrán zīyuán de kāifā 自然资源的开发

diagram /ˈdaɪəgræm/ n a diagram yì zhāng túbiǎo 一张图表

dial /ˈdaɪəl/ vb to dial a number bō yí gè hàomǎ 拨一个号码

dialling code /ˈdaɪəlɪŋ kəʊd/ n (British English) a dialling code yí gè qūhào 一个区号

dialling tone /ˈdaɪəlɪŋ təʊn/ (British English), **dial tone** /ˈdaɪəl təʊn/ (US English) n a dialling tone yí gè bōhàoyīn 一个拨号音

diamond /ˈdaɪəmənd/ n a diamond yì kē zuànshí 一颗钻石

diary /ˈdaɪərɪ/ n a diary yì běn rìjì 一本日记

dice /daɪs/ n a pair of dice yí duì tóuzi 一对骰子

dictionary /ˈdɪkʃənərɪ/ n a dictionary yì běn cídiǎn 一本词典，yì běn zìdiǎn 一本字典

die /daɪ/ vb (to die) sǐ 死；he died in the war tā zài zhànzhēng zhōng sǐ le 他在战争中死了；she is dying of cancer tā yīn déle áizhèng kuàiyào sǐ le 她因得了癌症快要死了；(to indicate extreme desire) I'm dying to go on holiday wǒ kěwàng qù dùjià 我渴望去度假

diet /ˈdaɪət/ n yǐnshí 饮食；to go on a diet jiéshí 节食

difference /ˈdɪfərəns/ n chābié 差别；I can't tell the difference wǒ kàn bù chū yǒu shénme chābié 我看不出有什么差别；it won't make any difference zhè bú huì yǒu shénme guānxì 这不会有什么关系；what difference does it make? zhè yǒu shénme guānxì? 这有什么关系？

different /'dɪfərənt/ *adj* bùtóng de 不同的

difficult /'dɪfɪkəlt/ *adj* nán de 难的；Chinese is not difficult to learn Zhōngwén bù nán xué 中文不难学；it is difficult to get along with someone gēn mǒu rén hěn nán xiāngchǔ 跟某人很难相处

difficulty /'dɪfɪkəltɪ/ *n* a difficulty yí gè kùnnan 一个困难；to have difficulty concentrating hěn nán jízhōng jīnglì 很难集中精力

dig /dɪg/ *vb* wā 挖；**dig up** (*when gardening*) wā chūlái 挖出来；(*to find what was buried*) wājué chūlái 挖掘出来

dim /dɪm/ *adj* (*describing a light*) àndàn de 暗淡的；(*describing a room*) hūn'àn de 昏暗的

diner /'daɪnə(r)/ (*US English*) *n* a diner yí gè kuàicāndiàn 一个快餐店

dining room /'daɪnɪŋ ˌrʊm/ *n* a dining room yí gè fàntīng 一个饭厅

dinner /'dɪnə(r)/ *n* a dinner (*the chief meal of the day*) yí dùn zhèngcān 一顿正餐；(*a feast*) yí cì yànhuì 一次宴会

dip /dɪp/ *vb* zhàn 蘸

direct /dɪ'rekt/ **1** *adj* zhíjiē de 直接的 **2** *vb* (*when talking about direction*) could you direct me to the station? nǐ néng gàosu wǒ qù chēzhàn zěnme zǒu ma? 你能告诉我去车站怎么走吗？；(*in cinema or theatre*) to direct [a film | a play] dǎoyǎn [yí bù diànyǐng | yì chū xì] 导演 [一部电影 | 一出戏]

direction /dɪ'rekʃən/ *n* a direction yí gè fāngxiàng 一个方向；is this the right direction? zhège fāngxiàng duì ma? 这个方向对吗？；they were walking in the other direction tāmen zài cháo lìng yí gè fāngxiàng zǒu 他们在朝另一个方向走

directions /'dɪrekʃənz/ *n* zhǐshì 指示；to give someone directions xiàng mǒu rén fāchū zhǐshì 向某人发出指示；to ask someone for directions xiàng mǒu rén qǐng (qiú zhǐ) shì 向某人请（求指）示；(*directions for use*) shǐyòng shuōmíng 使用说明

director /dɪˈrektə(r)/ n (of a film or play) dǎoyǎn 导演；a director yí gè dǎoyǎn 一个导演；a director (of a research institute or department) yí gè suǒzhǎng 一个所长，yí gè zhǔrèn 一个主任；(of a factory) yí gè chǎngzhǎng 一个厂长；(of a company) yí gè zǒngcái 一个总裁

dirt /dɜːt/ n zāng dōngxi 脏东西

dirty /ˈdɜːtɪ/ **1** adj zāng de 脏的 **2** vb nòngzāng 弄脏

disabled /dɪsˈeɪbld/ adj shāngcán de 伤残的，cánjí de 残疾的

disadvantage /ˌdɪsədˈvɑːntɪdʒ/ n a disadvantage yí gè búlì tiáojiàn 一个不利条件

disagree /ˌdɪsəˈgriː/ vb bù tóngyì 不同意；I disagree with you wǒ bù tóngyì nǐ de yìjiàn 我不同意你的意见

disappear /ˌdɪsəˈpɪə(r)/. vb bújiàn 不见，xiāoshī 消失

disappoint /ˌdɪsəˈpɔɪnt/ vb to disappoint someone shǐ mǒu rén shīwàng 使某人失望

disappointed /ˌdɪsəˈpɔɪntɪd/ adj shīwàng de 失望的

disappointing /ˌdɪsəˈpɔɪntɪŋ/ adj lìng rén shīwàng de 令人失望的

disappointment /ˌdɪsəˈpɔɪntmənt/ n shīwàng 失望

disapprove /ˌdɪsəˈpruːv/ vb to disapprove of someone bú zànchéng mǒu rén 不赞成某人

disaster /dɪˈzɑːstə(r)/ n a disaster yì chǎng zāinàn 一场灾难

discipline /ˈdɪsɪplɪn/ n jìlǜ 纪律

disco /ˈdɪskəʊ/ n (a party) dísīkē wǔhuì 迪斯科舞会；a disco yí gè dísīkē wǔhuì 一个迪斯科舞会；(the dance) dísīkē(wǔ) 迪斯科(舞)

disconnect /ˌdɪskəˈnekt/ vb (to cut off) qiēduàn 切断；(to separate) chāikāi 拆开

discourage /dɪsˈkʌrɪdʒ/ vb (dishearten) xièqì 泄气；to discourage someone shǐ mǒu rén xièqì 使某人泄气；he was discouraged by the difficulties he met tā yīnwèi yùdào kùnnan ér xièqì 他因为遇到困难而泄气；(*oppose by showing disfavour*) zǔzhǐ 阻止，quànzǔ 劝阻；to discourage someone zǔzhǐ mǒu rén 阻止某人

discover /dɪsˈkʌvə(r)/ *vb* fāxiàn 发现

discovery /dɪsˈkʌvərɪ/ *n* a discovery yí gè fāxiàn 一个发现

discreet /dɪsˈkriːt/ *adj* jǐnshèn de 谨慎的

discrimination /dɪsˌkrɪmɪˈneɪʃən/ *n* (*distinction*) qūbié 区别；(*different treatment of a group of people*) qíshì 歧视

discuss /dɪsˈkʌs/ *vb* tǎolùn 讨论；to discuss politics tǎolùn zhèngzhì 讨论政治

discussion /dɪsˈkʌʃən/ *n* a discussion yí cì tǎolùn 一次讨论

disease /dɪˈziːz/ *n* a disease yì zhǒng (jí)bìng 一种(疾)病

disguise /dɪsˈgaɪz/ **1** *n* wěizhuāng 伪装 **2** *vb* to disguise oneself as a woman bǎ zìjǐ zhuāngbàn chéng nǚ de 把自己装扮成女的

disgusting /dɪsˈgʌstɪŋ/ *adj* lìng rén ěxīn de 令人恶心的

dish /dɪʃ/ *n* (*food*) a dish yì pán cài 一盘菜；(*object on which to place food for eating*) yí gè pánzi 一个盘子；to wash the dishes xǐ pánzi 洗盘子

dishonest /dɪsˈɒnɪst/ *adj* bù chéngshí de 不诚实的

dishwasher /ˈdɪʃˌwɒʃə(r)/ *n* a dishwasher yì tái xǐwǎnjī 一台洗碗机

dislike /dɪsˈlaɪk/ *vb* bù xǐhuan 不喜欢；I dislike him wǒ bù xǐhuan tā 我不喜欢他

dismiss /dɪsˈmɪs/ *vb* (*to remove from office*) chè…de zhí 撤…的职；to dismiss someone from his post chè mǒu rén de zhí 撤某人的职；he was dismissed tā bèi chèzhí le 他被撤职了；(*to remove from employment*) jiěgù 解雇；to dismiss a worker jiěgù yí gè gōngrén 解雇一个工人；(*to send away*) the teacher didn't dismiss the class until 6 o'clock lǎoshī liù diǎn cái xiàkè 老师6点才下课

disobedient /ˌdɪsə'biːdjənt/ *adj* bù fúcóng de 不服从的；(*when talking about children*) bù tīnghuà de 不听话的；a disobedient child yí gè bù tīnghuà de háizi 一个不听话的孩子

disobey /ˌdɪsə'beɪ/ *vb* wéikàng 违抗，bù fúcóng 不服从；to disobey someone wéikàng mǒu rén 违抗某人

display /dɪs'pleɪ/ *n* zhǎnlǎn 展览，chénliè 陈列；a window display yí gè chúchuāng zhǎnlǎn 一个橱窗展览

dispute /dɪs'pjuːt/ *n* (*an argument or a debate*) zhēnglùn 争论，biànlùn 辩论；a dispute yí cì zhēnglùn 一次争论；(*a quarrel*) jiūfēn 纠纷，zhēngduān 争端；a dispute yí cì jiūfēn 一次纠纷

disqualify /dɪs'kwɒlɪfaɪ/ *vb* to disqualify someone qǔxiāo mǒu rén de zīgé 取消某人的资格

disrupt /dɪs'rʌpt/ *vb* (*to break up*) fēnliè 分裂；to disrupt a country fēnliè yí gè guójiā 分裂一个国家；(*to interrupt*) dǎluàn 打乱，rǎoluàn 扰乱；to disrupt the traffic rǎoluàn jiāotōng 扰乱交通

dissatisfied /ˌdɪs'sætɪsfaɪd/ *adj* bù mǎnyì de 不满意的

distance /'dɪstəns/ *n* jùlí 距离；in the distance zài yuǎnchù 在远处；to keep one's distance bǎochí shūyuǎn 保持疏远

distinct /dɪs'tɪŋkt/ *adj* (*distinguished*) dútè de 独特的；(*clear*) qīngchǔ de 清楚的

distinguish /dɪs'tɪŋgwɪʃ/ *vb* qūbié 区别；to distinguish between truth and lies qūbié zhēnlǐ yǔ huǎngyán 区别真理与谎言

distract /dɪs'trækt/ *vb* fēnsàn…de zhùyìlì 分散…的注意力；to distract someone from working fēnsàn mǒu rén de zhùyìlì shǐ tā bù néng gōngzuò 分散某人的注意力使他不能工作

distressed /dɪ'strest/ *adj* kǔnǎo de 苦恼的，tòngkǔ de 痛苦的

distribute /dɪ'strɪbjuːt/ *vb* (*to divide and deal out among several*) fēn 分；(*to spread out*) sànfā 散发

disturb /dɪˈstɜːb/ vb dǎrǎo 打扰

disturbing /dɪˈstɜːbɪŋ/ adj lìng rén bù'ān de 令人不安的

dive /daɪv/ vb tiàoshuǐ 跳水; to go diving qù tiàoshuǐ 去跳水

divide /dɪˈvaɪd/ vb (in arithmetic) chú 除; (to share) fēn 分

diving board /ˈdaɪvɪŋ ˌbɔːd/ n a diving board yí gè tiào-(shuǐ)tái 一个跳(水)台

divorce /dɪˈvɔːs/ **1** n líhūn 离婚 **2** vb she divorced him tā gēn tā líhūn le 她跟他离婚了

DIY /ˌdiː aɪ ˈwaɪ/, **Do-It-Yourself** n (British English) zìjǐ zhìzuò 自己制作

dizzy /ˈdɪzɪ/ adj tóuyūn de 头晕的; to feel dizzy gǎndào tóuyūn 感到头晕

do /强 duː;弱 du/ vb (to do) zuò 做, gàn 干; to do the cooking zuòfàn 做饭; to do one's homework zuò zuòyè 做作业; what is he doing? tā zài gàn shénme? 他在干什么?; as I told you ànzhào wǒ gàosu nǐ de nàyàng zuò 按照我告诉你的那样做; (in questions, negatives)! Note that in Chinese questions and negative, there is no auxiliary like the word do in English; when did you come? nǐ shénme shíhou lái de? 你什么时候来的?; do you like cats? nǐ xǐhuan māo ma? 你喜欢猫吗?; I didn't go wǒ méi qù 我没去; she doesn't live in Beijing tā bú zhù zài Běijīng 她不住在北京; (in imperatives) don't shout! bié hǎn! 别喊!; don't shut the door bié guānmén 别关门; do come on time yídìng yào zhǔnshí lái 一定要准时来; (in emphatic uses) quèshí quèshí, díquè 确实, 的确; I do like your dress wǒ quèshí xǐhuan nǐ de yīfu 我确实喜欢你的衣服; I do think you should go wǒ quèshí rènwéi nǐ yīnggāi qù 我确实认为你应该去; (in short answers)! Note that when do is used in English to refer to a previous verb, in Chinese the previous verb is normally repeated in short answers; 'Do you like strawberries?'— 'Yes, I do' "Nǐ xǐhuan cǎoméi ma?"—"(Duì, wǒ) xǐhuan" "你喜欢草莓吗?"—"(对, 我)喜欢"; 'I never said I liked him' — 'Yes, you did' "Wǒ cónglái méi shuōguo wǒ xǐhuan tā"—"Bù, nǐ shuōguo""我从来没说过我喜欢他"—"不, 你说过"; 'I love chocolate' — 'So do I' "Wǒ xǐhuan qiǎokèlì"— "Wǒ yě xǐhuan" "我喜欢巧克力"—"我也喜欢"; 'May I sit here?' — 'Of course, please do' "Wǒ kěyǐ zuò zài zhèr ma?"—"Dāngrán kěyǐ, qǐng zuò" "我可以坐在这儿吗?"—"当然可以, 请坐"; 'Who wrote it?' — 'I did'; "Shéi xiě de?"—"Wǒ xiě de" "谁写的?"—"我写的"; (in tag questions) ! Note that tag questions in English are usually translated as **shì bú shì 是不是** or **duì bú duì 对不对** in Chinese; **he is in London, doesn't he?** tā zhù zài Lúndūn, shì bú shì? 他住在伦敦, 是不是?; **you didn't phone, did you?** nǐ méi dǎ diànhuà, duì bú duì? 你没打电话, 对不对?; (to be enough) **ten pounds will do** shí bàng jiù gòu le 10 镑就够了; **that box will do** nàge hézi jiù xíng 那个盒子就行; (to perform) (when talking about a task, a project) **gàn 干**; **he did well** tā gàn de hěn hǎo 他干得很好; **he did badly** tā gàn de bù hǎo 他干得不好; (when talking about an exam) **kǎo 考**; **you did well** nǐ kǎo de hěn hǎo 你考得很好; (when talking about a performance, a show) **yǎn 演**; **she did well** tā yǎn de hěn hǎo 她演得很好; **do up** to do up one's buttons bǎ kòuzi kòuhǎo 把扣子扣好; **to do up a house** zhěngxiū fángzi 整修房子; **do with** it's got something to do with computers zhè yǔ jìsuànjī yǒuguān 这与计算机有关; **do without** méiyǒu…yě xíng 没有…也行; **I can do without a television** wǒ méiyǒu diànshìjī yě xíng 我没有电视机也行

dock /dɒk/ n **a dock** yí gè mǎtou 一个码头, yí gè chuánwù 一个船坞

doctor /'dɒktə(r)/ n **a doctor** (of medicine) yí gè yīshēng 一个医生, yí gè dàifu 一个大夫; (Ph. D) yí gè bóshì 一个博士

document /'dɒkjumənt/ n a document yí fèn wénjiàn 一份文件

documentary /ˌdɒkju'mentəri/ n a documentary yí bù jìlùpiàn 一部纪录片

dog /dɒg/ n a dog yì tiáo gǒu 一条狗

doll /dɒl/ n a doll yí gè (yáng) wáwa 一个(洋)娃娃

dollar /'dɒlə(r)/ n a [US|Canadian|Hong Kong] dollar yì [měiyuán|jiāyuán|gǎngbì] 一[美元|加元|港币]

dolphin /'dɒlfɪn/ n a dolphin yì tiáo hǎitún 一条海豚

dominoes /'dɒmɪnəʊz/ n duōmǐnuò gǔpái 多米诺骨牌

donkey /'dɒŋkɪ/ n a donkey yì tóu lǘ 一头驴

door /dɔ:(r)/ n a door yí gè mén 一个门

doorbell /'dɔ:bel/ n a doorbell yí gè ménlíng 一个门铃

dormitory /'dɔ:mɪtərɪ/ n a dormitory yí gè sùshè 一个宿舍

dose /dəʊz/ n a dose of medicine yí jì yào 一剂药；a dose of Chinese medicine yí fù zhōngyào 一服中药

double /'dʌbl/ **1** adj (for two people) shuāngrén de 双人的；a double bed yì zhāng shuāngrénchuáng 一张双人床；a double room yí gè shuāngrén fángjiān 一个双人房间；(twice as much) shuāng bèi de 双倍的，liǎng bèi de 两倍的；to pay double the money fù shuāng bèi de qián 付双倍的钱；(when spelling or giving a number) liǎng gè 两个；a double 'n' liǎng gè 'n' 两个'n'；three double five (British English) sān wǔ wǔ 三五五 **2** vb zēngjiā yí bèi 增加一倍；the number of students has been doubled xuésheng rénshù zēngjiāle yí bèi 学生人数增加了一倍

double bass /ˌdʌbl 'beɪs/ n a double bass yì bǎ dīyīn tíqín 一把低音提琴

double-decker /ˌdʌbl'dekə(r)/ n a double-decker yí liàng shuāngcéng qìchē 一辆双层汽车

doubt /daʊt/ **1** n huáiyí 怀疑，yíwèn 疑问；I have some doubt that it's true wǒ huáiyí zhè shì zhēn de 我怀疑这是真的；there is no doubt that he is innocent háowú yíwèn tā shì wúgū de 毫无疑问他是无辜的 **2** vb huáiyí 怀疑；I doubt if she'll come wǒ huáiyí tā huì lái 我怀疑她会来

dough /dəʊ/ n shēngmiàntuán 生面团

doughnut /'dəʊnʌt/, **donut** /'dəʊnət/ (US English) n a doughnut yí gè zhámiànbǐngquānr 一个炸面饼圈儿

down /daʊn/ ! Often down occurs in combination with verbs. For example calm down, let down, slow down, etc. To find the correct translations for this type of verb, look up the separate dictionary entries at calm, let, slow, etc. **1** prep to go down the street yánzhe mǎlù wǎng xià zǒu 沿着马路往下走；he walked down the corridor tā yánzhe zǒuláng zǒu qù 他沿着走廊走去；he ran down the hill tā pǎoxià shān qù 他跑下山去；the kitchen is down those stairs chúfáng zài lóutī xiàmian 厨房在楼梯下面 **2** adv she's down in the cellar tā zài xiàmian dìjiào lǐ tǎnzhe 她在下面地窖里；to go down xiàjiàng 下降；to fall down dǎoxià 倒下；down there zài xiàmian nàr 在下面那儿

downstairs /ˌdaʊn'steəz/ adv lóuxià 楼下；to go downstairs xià lóu 下楼；to bring the boxes downstairs bǎ hézi nádào lóuxià lái 把盒子拿到楼下来

dozen /'dʌzən/ n a dozen yì dá 一打；a dozen eggs yì dá jīdàn 一打鸡蛋；dozens of people jǐshí gè rén 几十个人

draft /drɑːft/ n a draft (a preliminary sketch, version, plan) yí fèn cǎogǎo 一份草稿；(an order for the payment of money) yì zhāng huìpiào 一张汇票

drag /dræg/ vb tuō 拖

drain /dreɪn/ vb (to discharge) páidiào 排掉；to drain away the water bǎ shuǐ páidiào 把水排掉；(to drink dry) hēwán guāng 喝完；he drained his glass of wine tā bǎ tā nà bēi jiǔ hēwán le 他把他那杯酒喝完了

drama /'drɑːmə/ n (a play) xì 戏；a drama yì chū xì 一出戏；(theatre) xìjù 戏剧

dramatic /drə'mætɪk/ n (belonging to the drama) xìjù de 戏剧的

戏剧的；(with the force and vividness of the drama) xìjùxìng de 戏剧性的

drapes /dreɪps/ n (US English) bùlián 布帘，chuānglián 窗帘

draught /drɑːft/ n (British English) a draught chuāntáng-fēng 穿堂风

draughts /drɑːfts/ n (British English) tiàoqí 跳棋

draw /drɔː/ **1** vb (with a pen or pencil) huà 画；to draw a rabbit huà yì zhī tùzi 画一只兔子；to draw a line huà yì tiáo xiàn 画一条线；(to pull) lā 拉；to draw the curtains lā chuānglián 拉窗帘；(to take out) to draw a knife chōuchū yì bǎ dāo 抽出一把刀；to draw a nail from the door cóng mén shang báchū yí gè dīngzi 从门上拔出一个钉子；(in a lottery) chōu 抽；to draw a ticket chōu yì zhāng cǎipiào 抽一张彩票；(to attract) xīyǐn 吸引；the circus drew a large crowd mǎxìtuán xīyǐnle hěn duō rén 马戏团吸引了很多人，(in sports) (British English) sàichéng píngjú 赛成平局；Christmas is drawing near Shèngdàn Jié kuài dào le 圣诞节快到了 **2** n (in sports) píngjú 平局；(in a lottery) chōujiǎng 抽奖；**draw aside** to draw someone aside bǎ mǒu rén lādào pángbiān 把某人拉到旁边；**draw back** to draw back the curtain bǎ chuānglián lā huílái 把窗帘拉回来；**draw up** to draw up a list lièchū yí gè míngdān 列出一个名单

drawer /drɔː(r)/ n a drawer yí gè chōuti 一个抽屉

drawing /'drɔːŋ/ n huàr 画儿

dread /dred/ vb jùpà 惧怕

dreadful /'dredfʊl/ adj (producing great fear) kěpà de 可怕的，hàipà de 害怕的；(very bad, unpleasant) jí huài de 极坏的，zāotòu de 糟透的

dream /driːm/ **1** n a dream yí gè mèng 一个梦；to have a dream zuò yí gè mèng 做一个梦 **2** vb to dream of going to Japan zuòmèng qù Rìběn 做梦去日本

dress /dres/ **1** n a dress yí jiàn nǚzhuāng 一件女装 **2** vb (to put one's own clothes on) chuān yīfu 穿衣服；to

dress someone gěi mǒu rén chuān yīfu 给某人穿衣服; **dress up** (*in good clothes*)dǎban 打扮; (*in a disguise*) zhuāngbàn 装扮

dressing gown /'dresɪŋ gaʊn/ n a dressing gown yí jiàn chényī 一件晨衣

drill /drɪl/ **1** n (*a training exercise*) cāoliàn 操练; a drill yí cì cāoliàn 一次操练; (*an instrument for boring hard substances*) zuàntóu 钻头; a drill yí gè zuàntóu 一个钻头 **2** vb to drill a hole zuān yí gè kǒng zuān 钻一个孔; to drill through the wall zuāntòu qiáng 钻透墙

drink /drɪŋk/ **1** vb hē 喝 **2** n yǐnliào 饮料; give me a drink of water gěi wǒ yìxiē shuǐ hē 给我一些水喝

drive /draɪv/ **1** vb (*in a car*) kāichē 开车; to learn to drive xué kāichē 学开车; he drives to work tā kāichē qù shàngbān 他开车去上班; to drive someone home kāichē sòng mǒu rén huíjiā 开车送某人回家; (*to make*) shǐ 使; to drive someone mad shǐ mǒu rén qì de fāfēng 使某人气得发疯 **2** n to go for a drive qù kāichē wányìwán 去开车玩一玩, qù dōufēng 去兜风; **drive away** (*in a car*) kāichē líkāi 开车离开; (*to chase away*) gǎnzǒu 赶走; **drive back** kāichē huílái 开车回来

driver /'draɪvə(r)/ n a driver yí gè sījī 一个司机, yí gè jiàshǐyuán 一个驾驶员

driver's license /'draɪvəz ˌlaɪsəns/ (*US English*), **driving licence** /'draɪvɪŋ ˌlaɪsəns/ (*British English*) n a driver's license yí gè jiàshǐ zhízhào 一个驾驶执照

drizzle /'drɪzl/ vb xià xiǎoyǔ 下小雨, xià máomaoyǔ 下毛毛雨

drop /drɒp/ **1** vb (*to come down*) xiàjiàng 下降; the temperature has dropped wēndù xiàjiàng le 温度下降了; (*to let fall*) rēngxià 扔下; she dropped her suitcase tā rēngxià xiāngzi 她扔下箱子; (*to fall*) diàoxia 掉下, luòxia 落下; the paper has dropped zhǐ diào xiàlái le 纸掉下来了; (*to fall in drops*) dīxia 滴下 **2** n (*a fall*) xiàjiàng 下降; a drop in temperature wēndù xiàjiàng 温

度下降；(of liquid) a drop yì dī 一滴；**drop in** shùnbiàn fǎngwèn 顺便访问；he dropped in to see me tā shùnbiàn lái kànkan wǒ 他顺便来看看我；**drop off** bǎ… fàngxia 把…放下；could you drop me off at the railway station? zài huǒchēzhàn bǎ wǒ fàngxia, hǎo ma? 在火车站把我放下，好吗？**drop out** tuìchū 退出；to drop out of school tuìxué 退学；to drop out of a race tuìchū bǐsài 退出比赛

drought /draut/ n a drought yì chǎng gānhàn 一场干旱

drown /draun/ vb yānsǐ 淹死

drug /drʌg/ **1** n dúpǐn 毒品；to be on drugs xīdú 吸毒；(for medical use) yào 药，yàopǐn 药品 **2** vb to drug someone shǐ mǒu rén xīdú 使某人吸毒！Note that Chinese uses the verb xī 吸, specifying the method by which the drugs are ingested, i. e. by smoking. However, xīdú 吸毒 generally means to take drugs, whether by smoking, injecting, or taking them as a pill.

drug addict /drʌg ˌədɪkt/ n a drug addict yí gè xīdú chéngyǐn de rén 一个吸毒成瘾的人

drum /drʌm/ n a drum yí gè gǔ 一个鼓；to play drums dǎ gǔ 打鼓，qiāo gǔ 敲鼓

drunk /drʌŋk/ adj (hē) zuì le (喝)醉的

dry /draɪ/ **1** adj gān de 干的，gānzào de 干燥的；the clothes are not dry yet yīfu hái bù gān 衣服还不干；a dry climate gānzào de qìhòu 干燥的气候 **2** vb (to dry in the sun) shàigān 晒干；(to dry by a heater or fire) kǎogān 烤干；(to dry with a towel or cloth) cāgān 擦干

duck /dʌk/ n a duck yì zhī yāzi 一只鸭子；a Peking roast duck yì zhī Běijīng kǎoyā 一只北京烤鸭

due /dju:/ **1** due to yīnwèi 因为，yóuyú 由于；the game was cancelled due to bad weather yóuyú tiānqì bù hǎo, bǐsài qǔxiāo le 由于天气不好，比赛取消了！Note that the phrase introduced by yóuyú 由于 or yīnwèi 因为 comes at the beginning of the sentence in Chinese. **2** adj (expected) the train is due (in) at two o'clock huǒchē yùdìng liǎng diǎn dào 火车预定两点到；(that ought to be paid or done) the amount of money due to someone yīnggāi fùgěi mǒu rén de qián 应该付给某人的钱；the rent is due tomorrow míngtiān yīnggāi jiāo fángzū le 明天应该交房租了；(proper) in due time zài shìdàng de shíhòu 在适当的时候；to pay due attention jǐyǔ yīngyǒu de zhùyì 给予应有的注意

dull /dʌl/ adj (describing a person) chídùn de 迟钝的, dāibèn de 呆笨的；a dull mind chídùn de tóunǎo 迟钝的头脑；(describing a colour) àndàn de 暗淡的；(describing the weather or a landscape) yīnchén de 阴沉的；(not interesting, boring) dāndiào fáwèi de 单调乏味的

dumb /dʌm/ adj (unable to speak) yǎ de 哑的；(stupid) bèn de 笨的

dump /dʌmp/ **1** vb (to unload) qīngdǎo 倾倒；(to get rid of) pāoqì 抛弃；(to sell at excessively low prices) qīngxiāo 倾销 **2** n a dump (a rubbish heap) yí gè lājīduī 一个垃圾堆；(an untidy place) (US English) her room is a dump tā de fángjiān luànqībāzāo 她的房间乱七八糟

during /'djuərɪŋ/ prep zài … qījiān 在 … 期间, zài … de shíhòu 在 … 的时候；during the examination zài kǎoshì qījiān 在考试期间

dust /dʌst/ **1** n huīchén 灰尘 **2** vb qùdiào … shang de huīchén 去掉 … 上的灰尘；to dust off one's clothes qùdiào yīfu shang de huīchén 去掉衣服上的灰尘

dustbin /'dʌstbɪn/ n (British English) a dustbin yí gè lājītǒng 一个垃圾桶

dustman /'dʌstmən/ n (British English) a dustman yí gè qīngjiégōng 一个清洁工

dustpan /'dʌstpæn/ n a dustpan yí gè bòji 一个簸箕, yí gè běnjī 一个畚箕

Dutch /dʌtʃ/ **1** adj Hélán de 荷兰的 **2** n (the language) Hélányǔ 荷兰语；(the people) Hélánrén 荷兰人

duty /'djuːtɪ/ n (a task, part of one's job) zhízé 职责；

a duty yí xiàng zhízé 一项职责；what are your duties? nǐ de zhízé shì shénme? 你的职责是什么?；(to be on duty) zhíbān 值班；(what one must do) yìwù 义务, zérèn 责任；it is our duty to protect the environment bǎohù huánjìng shì wǒmen de yìwù 保护环境是我们的义务；(a tax) shuì 税；customs duties guānshuì 关税；duty-free miǎnshuì de 免税的

dye /daɪ/ n rǎn 染；to dye one's hair rǎn tóufa 染头发

Ee

----

each /iːtʃ/ **1** det měi 每；each time I see him měi cì wǒ kànjiàn tā 每次我看见他 **2** pron！Note that when the pronoun each is translated into Chinese, it functions as a modifier rather than a pronoun；měi 每；each of the boys měi (yí) gè nánháir 每(一)个男孩儿；I wrote to each of them wǒ gěi tāmen měi (yí) gè rén dōu xiěle xìn 我给他们每(一)个人都写了信；each of the books měi (yì) běn shū 每(一)本书

each other /iːtʃ ˈʌðə(r)/ hùxiāng 互相, xiānghù 相互；they know each other already tāmen hùxiāng yǐjīng rènshi le 他们互相已经认识了；we write to each other every year wǒmen měi nián dōu hùxiāng tōngxìn 我们每年都互相通信

eager /ˈiːgə(r)/ adj kěwàng de 渴望的

ear /ɪə(r)/ n an ear yì zhī ěrduo 一只耳朵

early /ˈɜːlɪ/ adv zǎo 早；to get up early zǎo qǐchuáng 早起床；early in the afternoon xiàwǔ zǎoxiē shíhou 下午早些时候；early [last month | next month | last year | next year | this year] [shàngge yuè | xiàge yuè | qùnián | míngnián | jīnnián] chū [上个月 | 下个月 | 去年 | 明年 | 今年] 初

earn /ɜːn/ vb zhèng 挣, zhuàn 赚；to earn lots of

money zhèng hěn duō qián 挣很多钱

earring /ˈɪərɪŋ/ n an earring yí gè ěrhuán 一个耳环

earth /ɜːθ/ n (the planet) dìqiú 地球;(soil) tǔ 土;(land as opposed to sea) lùdì 陆地, dìmiàn 地面

easily /ˈiːzɪlɪ/ adv róngyì de 容易地

east /iːst/ 1 n (the eastern part of the heavens) dōngfāng 东方; the sun rises in the east tàiyáng cóng dōngfāng shēngqǐ 太阳从东方升起; the Far East Yuǎndōng 远东;(the eastern part of a region) dōngbù 东部; in the east of Asia zài Yàzhōu dōngbù 在亚洲东部 2 adv to go east wǎng dōng qù 往东去; to live east of Beijing zhù zài Běijīng dōngmian 住在北京东面 3 adj dōngbù de 东部的; to work in east London zài Lúndūn dōngbù gōngzuò 在东伦敦东部工作

Easter /ˈiːstə(r)/ n Fùhuó Jié 复活节; Happy Easter! Fùhuó Jié kuàilè! 复活节快乐!

Easter egg /ˈiːstər eg/ n an Easter egg yí gè Fùhuó Jié cǎidàn 一个复活节彩蛋

easy /ˈiːzɪ/ adj róngyì de 容易的, it's easy to fix hěn róngyì xiūlǐ 很容易修理; it's not easy to find work there zài nàr zhǎo gōngzuò bù róngyì 在那儿找工作不容易

eat /iːt/ vb chī 吃; eat out shàng fàndiàn chīfàn 上饭店吃饭

EC /iː ˈsiː/, **European Community** n the EC Ōuzhōu Gòngtóngtǐ 欧洲共同体

echo /ˈekəʊ/ n an echo yí gè huíshēng 一个回声, yí gè huíyīn 一个回音

economic /iːkəˈnɒmɪk/ adj jīngjì de 经济的

economics /iːkəˈnɒmɪks/ n jīngjìxué 经济学

economy /ɪˈkɒnəmɪ/ n jīngjì 经济

edge /edʒ/ n (of a road, table, forest, an object) biān 边; the edge of the lake húbiān 湖边; at the edge of the town zài chéngbiān 在城边;(of a blade or knife) dāokǒu 刀口, dāorèn 刀刃

educate /'edju:keɪt/ vb jiàoyù 教育；he was educated in America tā shì zài Měiguó shòu de jiàoyù 他是在美国受的教育

education /ˌedju:'keɪʃən/ n jiàoyù 教育

effect /ɪ'fekt/ n jiéguǒ 结果, xiàoguǒ 效果；an effect yí gè jiéguǒ 一个结果

effective /ɪ'fektɪv/ adj yǒuxiào de 有效的

efficient /ɪ'fɪʃənt/ adj gāo xiàolǜ de 高效率的

effort /'efət/ n nǔlì 努力；to make an effort zuòchū nǔlì 作出努力

egg /eg/ n an egg (a hen's egg) yí gè jīdàn 一个鸡蛋

eggcup /'egkʌp/ n an eggcup yí gè dànbēi 一个蛋杯

eight /eɪt/ num bā 八；eight apples bā gè píngguǒ 8 个苹果

eighteen /ˌeɪ'ti:n/ num shíbā 十八

eighteenth /ˌeɪ'ti:nθ/ num (in a series) dì-shíbā 第十八；(in dates) the eighteenth of August bāyuè shíbā hào 8 月 18 号

eighth /eɪtθ/ num (in a series) dì-bā 第八；(in dates) the eighth of August bāyuè bā hào 8 月 8 号

eighty /'eɪti/ num bāshí 八十

either /'aɪðə(r)/ **1** conj either... or...；(in the affirmative) huòzhě… huòzhě… 或者…或者…, yàome… yàome… 要么…要么…；they're coming on either Tuesday or Wednesday tāmen yàome xīngqī'èr lái, yàome xīngqīsān lái 他们要么星期二来，要么星期三来；(in the negative) yě… yě… 也…也…！Note that in the negative, the translation of either is sometimes optional and or is translated as yě 也；He didn't contact either Helen or Paul tā (yě) méi gēn Hǎilún liánxì yě méi gēn Bǎoluó liánxì 他 (也) 没跟海伦联系也没跟保罗联系 **2** pron (in the affirmative) rènhé yī… 任何一…；you can borrow either of the books zhè liǎng běn shū nǐ jiè rènhé yì běn dōu xíng 这两本书你借任何一本都行；(in the negative) dōu bù 都不；I don't know either of them tāmen liǎng gè rén wǒ dōu bú rènshi

他们两个人我都不认识 **3** det (in the affirmative) rènhé yī··· 任何一···；you can take either road nǐ kěyǐ zǒu rènhé yì tiáo lù 你可以走任何一条路；(in the negative) dōu bù 都不；I don't want to live in either country zhè liǎng gè guójiā wǒ dōu bù xiǎng zhù 这两个国家我都不想住 **4** adv yě bù 也不；she can't come either tā yě bù néng lái 她也不能来

elbow /ˈelbəʊ/ n gēbohzhǒu 胳膊肘

elder /ˈeldə(r)/ adj niánlíng jiào dà de 年龄较大的；his [elder brother|elder sister] tā [gēge|jiějie] 他 [哥哥|姐姐]

elderly /ˈeldəlɪ/ adj shàngle niánjì de 上了年纪的，lǎo de 老的

eldest /ˈeldɪst/ adj zuì niánzhǎng de 最年长的；the eldest [daughter|son|granddaughter|grandson] dà [nǚ'ér|érzi|sūnnǚ|sūnzi] 大 [女儿|儿子|孙女|孙子]

elect /ɪˈlekt/ vb xuǎnjǔ 选举

election /ɪˈlekʃən/ n an election yí cì xuǎnjǔ 一次选举；to win an election xuǎnjǔ zhōng huòshèng 选举中获胜

electric /ɪˈlektrɪk/ adj diàn de 电的

electrician /ˌɪlekˈtrɪʃən/ n an electrician yí gè diàngōng 一个电工

electricity /ˌɪlekˈtrɪsətɪ/ n diàn 电

electronic /ˌɪlekˈtrɒnɪk/ adj diànzǐ de 电子的

elegant /ˈelɪgənt/ adj yǎzhì de 雅致的，yōuyǎ de 优雅的

elephant /ˈelɪfənt/ n an elephant yì tóu dàxiàng 一头大象

elevator /ˈelɪveɪtə(r)/ n an elevator yí gè diàntī 一个电梯

eleven /ɪˈlevən/ num shíyī 十一；eleven apples shíyī gè píngguǒ 11 个苹果

eleventh /ɪˈlevənθ/ num (in a series) dì-shíyī 第十一；(in dates) the eleventh of May wǔyuè shíyī hào 5 月 11 号

else /els/ adj biéde 别的，qítā de 其他的；someone else bié(de) rén 别(的)人；there is nothing else méiyǒu biéde dōngxi 没有别的东西；what else did you say? nǐ hái shuō shénme le? 你还说什么了？；something else biéde dōngxi 别的东西；everything else qítā de suǒyǒu dōngxi 其他的所有东西；or else fǒuzé 否则，yàobù 要不；be quiet or else I'll get angry ānjìng yìdiǎnr, fǒuzé wǒ huì shēngqì de 安静一点儿，否则我会生气的

elsewhere /ˌelsˈhweə(r)/ *adv* zài biéchù 在别处

e-mail /ˈiːmeɪl/ *n* an e-mail yí gè diànzǐ yóujiàn 一个电子邮件

embarrassed /ɪmˈbærəst/ *adj* nánwéiqíng de 难为情的，bùhǎoyìsi de 不好意思的

embarrassing /ɪmˈbærəsɪŋ/ *adj* lìng rén nánwéiqíng de 令人难为情的

embassy /ˈembəsɪ/ *n* an embassy yí gè dàshǐguǎn 一个大使馆

emergency /ɪˈmɜːdʒənsɪ/ *n* an emergency yí gè jǐnjí qíngkuàng 一个紧急情况

emergency exit /ɪˈmɜːdʒənsɪ ˌeksɪt/ *n* an emergency exit yí gè jǐnjí chūkǒu 一个紧急出口

emigrate /ˈemɪgreɪt/ *vb* yíjū 移居

emotion /ɪˈməʊʃən/ *n* jīdòng 激动

emotional /ɪˈməʊʃənl/ *adj* (*describing a scene or moment*) dòngrén de 动人的；(*describing a person*) jīdòng de 激动的

emperor /ˈempərə(r)/ *n* an emperor yí gè huángdì 一个皇帝

employ /ɪmˈplɔɪ/ *vb* (*to give work to*) gùyòng 雇用，gù jiǔ 雇；(*to use as a means*) yòng 用，shǐyòng 使用

employed /ɪmˈplɔɪd/ *adj* to be employed by someone shòu gù yú mǒu rén 受雇于某人

employee /ˌemplɔɪˈiː/ *n* an employee yí gè gùyuán 一个雇员

employer /ɪmˈplɔɪə(r)/ *n* an employer yí gè gùzhǔ 一个雇主

employment /ɪmˈplɔɪmənt/ *n* (*the act of employing*) gùyòng 雇用；(*occupation*) gōngzuò 工作，zhíyè 职业

empty /'emptɪ/ **1** adj kōng de 空的 **2** vb to empty the dustbin bǎ lājītǒng dàokōng 把垃圾桶倒空; they emptied three bottles of wine tāmen hēguāngle sān píng jiǔ 他们喝光了 3 瓶酒

encourage /ɪn'kʌrɪdʒ/ vb gǔlì 鼓励

end /end/ **1** n (of a novel, film, play, speech) jiéwěi 结尾; the end of the book shū de jiéwěi 书的结尾; (of a month, year) dǐ 底; the end of next year míngnián dǐ 明年底; in the end zuìhòu 最后, zhōngyú 终于; (the furthest part) jìntóu 尽头; at the end of the street zài mǎlù jìntóu 在马路尽头 **2** vb (to come to an end) jiéshù 结束; (to put an end to, to finish) jiéshù 结束; to end the war jiéshù zhànzhēng 结束战争; to end a concert jiéshù yīnyuèhuì 结束音乐会

end up /'end ʌp/ he ended up in London tā zuìhòu dāizàile Lúndūn 他最后呆在了伦敦; to end up going abroad zuìhòu qùle guówài 最后去了国外

ending /'endɪŋ/ n jiéjú 结局, jiéwěi 结尾

enemy /'enəmɪ/ n an enemy yí gè dírén 一个敌人

energetic /ˌenə'dʒetɪk/ adj jīnglì wàngshèng de 精力旺盛的

energy /'enədʒɪ/ n (vigour) jīnglì 精力; (the power of doing work) néngliàng 能量

engaged /ɪn'geɪdʒd/ adj (to be married) dìnghūn de 订婚的; to be engaged (to someone) (yǔ mǒu rén) dìnghūn (与某人)订婚; (occupied) she is engaged in writing a new novel tā zhèng mángzhe xiě yí bù xīn xiǎoshuō 她正忙着写一部新小说; (British English) (describing a phone, a toilet) the line is engaged diànhuà zhànxiàn 电话占线; the toilet is engaged cèsuǒ yǒu rén 厕所有人

engine /'endʒɪn/ n an engine yì tái fādòngjī 一台发动机

engineer /ˌendʒɪ'nɪə(r)/ n an engineer yí gè gōngchéngshī 一个工程师

England /'ɪŋglənd/ n Yīnggélán 英格兰

English /ˈɪŋglɪʃ/ **1** adj Yīnggélán de 英格兰的 **2** n (the people) Yīnggélánrén 英格兰人；(the language) Yīngyǔ 英语

enjoy /ɪnˈdʒɔɪ/ vb (to like) xǐhuan 喜欢，xǐ'ài 喜爱；he enjoys fishing tā xǐhuan diàoyú 他喜欢钓鱼；did you enjoy your holiday？nǐ jiàqī guò de hǎo ma？你假期过得好吗？；(to use with delight) xiǎngshòu 享受；to enjoy social benefits xiǎngshòu shèhuì fúlì 享受社会福利；(to have a good time) enjoy yourself！zhù nǐ wán de kuàihuo！祝你玩得快活！

enjoyable /ɪnˈdʒɔɪəbl/ adj yúkuài de 愉快的，kuàilè de 快乐的

enormous /ɪˈnɔːməs/ adj jùdà de 巨大的，pángdà de 庞大的

enough /ɪˈnʌf/ **1** adj zúgòu de 足够的；I don't have enough [money｜time｜friends…] wǒ méiyǒu zúgòu de [qián｜shíjiān｜péngyou…] 我没有足够的 [钱｜时间｜朋友…]；there is enough wine for everyone yǒu zúgòu de jiǔ gōng dàjiā hē 有足够的酒供大家喝 **2** adv gòu 够，zúgòu 足够，is it big enough？zhè gòu dà ma？这够大吗？；you are not old enough nǐ de niánlíng hái bú gòu dà 你的年龄还不够大 **3** pron we have enough to eat wǒmen yǒu zúgòu de dōngxi chī 我们有足够的东西吃；I've had enough wǒ yǐjīng shòugòu le 我已经受够了；that's enough zúgòu le 足够了

enquire /ɪnˈkwaɪə(r)/ vb xúnwèn 询问；I'll enquire about the price wǒ xúnwèn yíxià jiàqian 我询问一下价钱

enter /ˈentə(r)/ vb (to go into) jìnrù 进入；(to take part in) cānjiā 参加；to enter a competition cānjiā bǐsài 参加比赛

entertain /ˌentəˈteɪn/ vb (to treat hospitably) kuǎndài 款待，zhāodài 招待；(to amuse) shǐ…gāoxìng 使…高兴；his performance entertained everyone tā de biǎoyǎn shǐ dàjiā dōu hěn gāoxìng 他的表演使大家都很高兴

entertaining /ˌentəˈteɪnɪŋ/ adj yǒuqù de 有趣的

entertainment /ˌentəˈteɪnmənt/ n (the act of entertaining guests) kuǎndài 款待, zhāodài 招待;(amusement) yúlè 娱乐, lèqù 乐趣

enthusiasm /ɪnˈθjuːzɪæzəm/ n rèqíng 热情

enthusiastic /ɪnˌθjuːzɪˈæstɪk/ adj rèqíng de 热情的

entrance /ˈentrəns/ n an entrance yí gè rùkǒu 一个入口; the entrance to the castle chéngbǎo de rùkǒu 城堡的入口

envelope /ˈenvələup/ n an envelope yí gè xìnfēng 一个信封

environment /ɪnˈvaɪərənmənt/ n huánjìng 环境

envy /ˈenvɪ/ 1 n (a feeling of chagrin at the fortune of another) jìdù 忌妒, dùjì 妒忌;(a person or an object being envied) jìdù de duìxiàng 忌妒的对象, jìdù de mùbiāo 忌妒的目标 2 vb jìdù 忌妒, dùjì 妒忌

episode /ˈepɪsəud/ n an episode (an event or an incident in a story, a novel, a film) yí gè qíngjié 一个情节;(an event) yí gè shìjiàn 一个事件

equal /ˈiːkwəl/ 1 adj (identical in quality, value, proportion, etc.) xiāngděng de 相等的, jūnděng de 均等的;(in social status) píngděng de 平等的; to fight for equal rights wèi píngděng quánlì ér dòuzhēng 为平等权利而斗争 2 vb děngyú 等于; six plus four equal ten liù jiā sì děngyú shí 6 加 4 等于 10

equality /iːˈkwɒlətɪ/ n píngděng 平等, tóngděng 同等

equator /ɪˈkweɪtə(r)/ n chìdào 赤道

equipment /ɪˈkwɪpmənt/ n (in a factory, laboratory, or office) shèbèi 设备;(in military forces) zhuāngbèi 装备

eraser /ɪˈreɪzə(r)/ n (for a blackboard) an eraser yí gè hēibǎncā 一个黑板擦;(a pencil rubber) (US English) an eraser yí kuài xiàngpí 一块橡皮

escalator /ˈeskəleɪtə(r)/ n an escalator yí gè zìdòng fútī 一个自动扶梯

escape /ɪˈskeɪp/ vb (to get away) táopǎo 逃跑; he escaped from prison tā cóng jiānyù li táopǎo le 他从监狱

里逃跑了；（ to avoid ）táobì 逃避，táotuō 逃脱；to escape punishment táobì chéngfá 逃避惩罚

especially /ɪˈspeʃəlɪ/ adv tèbié 特别，yóuqí 尤其

essay /ˈeseɪ/ n an essay yì piān wénzhāng 一篇文章

essential /ɪˈsenʃəl/ adj (relating to the essence) shízhì de 实质的，běnzhì de 本质的；(indispensable) bìyào de 必要的，bìbùkěshǎo de 必不可少的

ethnic /ˈeθnɪk/ adj zhǒngzú de 种族的

EU /iː ˈjuː/, **European Union** n Ōuzhōu Liánméng 欧洲联盟

euro /ˈjʊərəʊ/ n ōuyuán 欧元

Europe /ˈjʊərəp/ n Ōuzhōu 欧洲

European /ˌjʊərəˈpiːən/ adj Ōuzhōu de 欧洲的

evacuate /ɪˈvækjʊeɪt/ vb (to withdraw) chèlí 撤离；(to clear out inhabitants from) shūsàn 疏散

even[1] /ˈiːvən/ adv (when expressing surprise) shènzhì 甚至，lián…yě… 连…也…；he even works on weekends tā lián zhōumò yě gōngzuò 他连周末也工作；(in comparison) gèng 更，hái 还；it's even colder today jīntiān gèng lěng 今天更冷；(when used with the conjunction if or though) even if/though jíshǐ 即使，jíbiàn 即便；even if it rains tomorrow, you still have to go jíshǐ míngtiān xiàyǔ, nǐ yě děi qù 即使明天下雨，你也得去

even[2] /ˈiːvən/ adj (flat, smooth) píng de 平的，píngtǎn de 平坦的；(when talking about numbers) an even number yí gè shuāngshù 一个双数，yí gè ǒushù 一个偶数

evening /ˈiːvnɪŋ/ n an evening yí gè wǎnshang 一个晚上；at eight o'clock in the evening (zài) wǎnshang bā diǎn (在) 晚上 8 点

event /ɪˈvent/ n (an incident) shìjiàn 事件；an event yí gè shìjiàn 一个事件；(in a sports programme) xiàngmù 项目；an event yí gè xiàngmù 一个项目

eventually /ɪˈventʃʊəlɪ/ adv zhōngyú 终于，zuìhòu 最后

ever /ˈevə(r)/ adv (at any time) nothing ever happens

here zhèr cónglái bù fāshēng shénme shì 这儿从来不发生什么事；have you ever been to Thailand? nǐ qùguo Tàiguó ma? 你去过泰国吗？；I hardly ever go there wǒ jīhū cónglái bú qù nàr 我几乎从来不去那儿；for ever yǒngyuǎn 永远；We'll remember him for ever wǒmen jiāng yǒngyuǎn jìzhù tā 我们将永远记住他

every /'evrɪ/ det měi 每；every time I meet her měi cì wǒ jiàndào tā 每次我见到她；every [day | week | month | year] měi [tiān | zhōu | yuè | nián] 每 [天 | 周 | 月 | 年]；every other [day | week | month | year] měi gé [yì tiān | yì zhōu | yí gè yuè | yì nián] 每隔 [一天 | 一周 | 一个月 | 一年]；two out of every three people are men měi sān gè rén zhōng yǒu liǎng gè shì nánrén 每三个人中有两个是男人

everyone /'evrɪwʌn/, **everybody** /'evrɪˌbɒdɪ/ pron měi gè rén 每个人，dàjiā 大家；everyone else suǒyǒu qítā de rén 所有其他的人

everything /'evrɪθɪŋ/ pron (every single matter) měi jiàn shì 每件事，suǒyǒu de shì 所有的事；(every single thing) měi jiàn dōngxi 每件东西，suǒyǒu de dōngxi 所有的东西

everywhere /'evrɪweə(r)/ adv dàochù 到处；there are floweres everywhere dàochù dōu shì xiānhuā 到处都是鲜花；(when used to introduce a clause) everywhere I went, I would buy some souvenirs wǒ měi dào yí gè dìfang dōu yào mǎi yìxiē jìniànpǐn 我每到一个地方都要买一些纪念品

evidence /'evɪdəns/ n (support for a belief) zhèngjù 证据；a piece of evidence yí gè zhèngjù 一个证据；to give evidence tígōng zhèngjù 提供证据；(indications or signs)jixiàng 迹象

evil /'i:vəl/ n xié'è 邪恶，zuì'è 罪恶

exact /ɪg'zækt/ adj quèqiè de 确切的，jīngquè de 精确的

exactly /ɪg'zæktlɪ/ adv quèqiè de 确切地，jīngquè de 精确地

exaggerate /ɪg'zædʒəreɪt/ vb kuādà 夸大，kuāzhāng 夸张

exam /ɪgˈzæm/ *n* an exam yí cì kǎoshì 一次考试; to pass an exam kǎoshì jígé 考试及格; to take an exam cānjiā kǎoshì 参加考试

examine /ɪgˈzæmɪn/ *vb* (*to check*) jiǎnchá 检查; (*to test in schools or universities*) kǎo kǎo, kǎochá 考查

example /ɪgˈzɑːmpl/ *n* an example yí gè lìzi 一个例子; for example lìrú 例如, bǐrú 比如

excellent /ˈeksələnt/ *adj* yōuxiù de 优秀的, jiéchū de 杰出的; (*in an exclamation*) excellent! hǎo jí le! 好极了!

except /ɪkˈsept/ *prep* chúle…(yǐwài)…dōu 除了…(以外)…都

exchange /ɪksˈtʃeɪndʒ/ *vb* to exchange [books|students|gifts] jiāohuàn [shū|xuésheng|lǐwù] 交换 [书|学生|礼物]; to exchange [foreign currency | US dollars | British pounds] duìhuàn [wàibì|měiyuán|yīngbàng] 兑换 [外币|美元|英镑]; to exchange seats diàohuàn zuòwèi 调换座位

exchange rate /ɪksˈtʃeɪndʒ reɪt/ *n* huìlǜ 汇率

excited /ɪkˈsaɪtɪd/ *adj* jīdòng de 激动的, xīngfèn de 兴奋的

exciting /ɪkˈsaɪtɪŋ/ *adj* lìng rén jīdòng de 令人激动的, lìng rén xīngfèn de 令人兴奋的

exclude /ɪkˈskluːd/ *vb* (*hinder from participation*) I excluded him from the meeting wǒ méiyǒu ràng tā cānjiā zhège huì 我没有让他参加这个会; (*to rule out*) páichú 排除; I cannot exclude this possibility wǒ bù néng páichú zhè zhǒng kěnéngxìng 我不能排除这种可能性

excuse /ɪkˈskjuːs/ **1** *n* an excuse yí gè jièkǒu 一个借口; to make excuses zhìzào jièkǒu 制造借口 **2** /ɪkˈskjuːz/ *vb* yuánliàng 原谅; excuse me! duìbuqǐ! 对不起!, láojià! 劳驾!

exercise /ˈeksəsaɪz/ *n* (*physical exercise*) duànliàn 锻炼; to take exercise, to do exercise jìnxíng duànliàn 进行锻炼; (*a piece of work*) an exercise yí gè liànxí 一个练习

exercise book /'eksəsaɪz ˌbʊk/ *n* an exercise book yì gè liànxíběn 一个练习本

exhausted /ɪɡ'zɔːstɪd/ *adj* (*tired out*) jīnpí-lìjìn de 筋疲力尽的；(*consumed*) yòngwán de 用完的，hàojìn de 耗尽的

exhibition /ˌeksɪ'bɪʃən/ *n* an exhibition yí gè zhǎnlǎnhuì 一个展览会

exit /'eksɪt/ *n* an exit yí gè chūkǒu 一个出口

expect /ɪk'spekt/ *vb* (*to be prepared for*) qīdài 期待；to expect bad news qīdài huài xiāoxi 期待坏消息；they expect to win tāmen qīdàizhe yíng 他们期待着赢；(*to wait for*) děngdài 等待，děng 等；(*to want*) pànwàng 盼望，qīwàng 期望；they expect us to do the work tāmen qīwàng wǒmen zuò zhège gōngzuò 他们期望我们做这个工作

expenses /ɪk'spensɪz/ *n* huāfèi 花费，zhīchū 支出

expensive /ɪk'spensɪv/ *adj* guì de 贵的，ángguì de 昂贵的

experience /ɪk'spɪərɪəns/ *n* (*passing through an event or events*) jīnglì 经历；an experience yí cì jīnglì 一次经历；(*practical acquaintance with any matter*) jīngyàn 经验

experienced /ɪk'spɪərɪənst/ *adj* yǒu jīngyàn de 有经验的

experiment /ɪk'sperɪmənt/ **1** *n* an experiment yí cì shíyàn 一次实验，yí cì shìyàn 一次试验 **2** *vb* shíyàn 实验，shìyàn 试验

expert /'ekspɜːt/ *n* an expert yí gè zhuānjiā 一个专家

explain /ɪk'spleɪn/ *vb* jiěshì 解释，shuōmíng 说明；to explain a rule to someone xiàng mǒu rén jiěshì yí gè guīzé 向某人解释一个规则

explanation /ˌeksplə'neɪʃən/ *n* an explanation yí gè jiěshì 一个解释，yí gè shuōmíng 一个说明

explode /ɪk'spləʊd/ *vb* (*if it's a bomb*) bàozhà 爆炸；(*in personal emotion or feeling*) to explode with laughter hōngtáng-dàxiào 哄堂大笑

exploit /ɪk'splɔɪt/ *vb* (*to turn to use*) kāifā 开发，kāicǎi

开采；(to make gain at the expense of) bōxuē 剥削

explosion /ɪkˈspləʊʒən/ n an explosion yí cì bàozhà 一次爆炸

export /ɪkˈspɔːt/ vb chūkǒu 出口，shūchū 输出

express /ɪkˈspres/ **1** vb biǎoshì 表示，biǎodá 表达 **2** adj tèkuài de 特快的；an express train yí tàng kuàichē 一趟快车；an express letter yì fēng kuàixìn 一封快信

expression /ɪkˈspreʃən/ n a happy expression yí fù gāoxìng de biǎoqíng 一副高兴的表情；the expression of different opinions bùtóng yìjiàn de biǎodá 不同意见的表达

extinct /ɪkˈstɪŋkt/ adj (describing an animal or a plant) juézhǒng de 绝种的，mièjué de 灭绝的；(describing a volcano) xīmiè de 熄灭的，sǐ de 死的

extra /ˈekstrə/ **1** adj (beyond or more than the usual) éwài de 额外的；to pay an extra ten pounds éwài duō fù shí bàng qián 额外多付 10 镑钱；(additional) wàijiā de 外加的；an extra bed yì zhāng jiā chuáng 一张加床 **2** adv to pay extra for wine jiǔqián lìng fù 酒钱另付

extraordinary /ɪkˈstrɔːdənərɪ/ adj tèbié de 特别的，fēicháng de 非常的

extreme /ɪkˈstriːm/ adj (most remote) jìntóu de 尽头的；(highest in degree) jíduān de 极端的；(extraordinary in opinions or behaviour) jíjìn de 激进的，piānjí de 偏激的

extremely /ɪkˈstriːmlɪ/ adv jíduān de 极端地，fēicháng de 非常地

eye /aɪ/ n an eye yì zhī yǎnjing 一只眼睛

eyebrow /ˈaɪbraʊ/ n méimao 眉毛

eyelash /ˈaɪlæʃ/ n jiémáo 睫毛

eyelid /ˈaɪlɪd/ n yǎnjiǎn 眼睑，yǎnpí 眼皮

eye shadow /ˈaɪ ˌʃædəʊ/ n yǎnyǐng 眼影

eyesight /ˈaɪsaɪt/ n shìlì 视力

Ff

face /feɪs/ **1** n the face liǎn 脸, miànkǒng 面孔; to make a face zuò guǐliǎnr 做鬼脸儿 **2** vb (to be opposite) miànduì 面对; she was facing me tā miànduìzhe wǒ 她面对着我; (to have to deal with) zhèngshì 正视, duìfu 对付; we have to face these difficulties wǒmen bìxū zhèngshì zhèxiē kùnnan 我们必须正视这些困难; (to look toward(s)) cháo 朝, miànxiàng 面向; my room faces the sea wǒ de fángjiān cháo hǎi 我的房间朝海; face up to yǒnggǎn de duìdài 勇敢地对待

fact /fækt/ **1** n a fact yí gè shìshí 一个事实 **2** in fact qíshí 其实, shíjìshang 实际上

factory /'fæktəri/ n a factory yí gè gōngchǎng 一个工厂

fade /feɪd/ vb (if it's a flower or tree leaf) kūwěi 枯萎, diāoxiè 凋谢; (if it's a colour) tuìshǎi 褪色

fail /feɪl/ vb (in an examination) bù jígé 不及格; to fail an exam kǎoshì bù jígé 考试不及格; (miss an achievement) shībài 失败; his plan failed tā de jìhuà shībài le 他的计划失败了; (to prove deficient) the plane failed to arrive on time fēijī méiyǒu zhǔnshí dàodá 飞机没有准时到达; she never fails to remember my birthday tā cónglái méi wàngjì wǒ de shēngrì 她从来没忘记我的生日; (in health, sight or hearing) shuāituì 衰退, shuāiruò 衰弱

failure /'feɪljə(r)/ n a failure (an event, an attempt) yí cì shībài 一次失败; (a person in an exam) bù jígé 不及格

faint /feɪnt/ vb hūndǎo 昏倒, yūndǎo 晕倒

fair /feə(r)/ **1** adj (just) gōngpíng de 公平的, gōngzhèng de 公正的; it's not fair zhè bù gōngpíng 这不公平; (in colour) fair hair jīnhuángsè de tóufa 金黄色的头发; fair skin báinèn de pífū 白嫩的皮肤 **2** n (British English) (a funfair) a fair yí gè yóulèhuì 一个游乐会; (a display of goods) a (trade) fair yí gè shāngpǐn jiāoyìhuì 一个商品交易会

fairly /'feəlɪ/ adv (justly) gōngpíng de 公平地, gōngzhèng de 公正地; (quite)xiāngdāng 相当

faith /feɪθ/ n (trust or confidence) xìnrèn 信任, xiāngxìn 相信; **to have faith in someone** xìnrèn mǒu rén 信任某人; (in religion) xìnyǎng 信仰

faithful /'feɪθful/ adj zhōngchéng de 忠诚的, zhōngshí de 忠实的

fall /fɔːl/ **1** vb (if it's a person) shuāidǎo 摔倒, diēdǎo 跌倒; **she fell to the ground** tā shuāidǎo zài dì shang 她摔倒在地上; (to drop)luò 落, diào 掉; **an apple fell onto his head** yí gè píngguǒ diào zài tā de tóu shang 一个苹果掉在他的头上; (in price, temperature)xiàjiàng 下降, jiàngdī 降低; (other uses) **to fall asleep** shuìzháo 睡着; **to fall ill** bìng le 病了; **to fall in love with someone** àishang mǒu rén 爱上某人 **2** n (in price, temperature) xiàjiàng 下降, jiàngdī 降低; (US English) (autumn) qiūtiān 秋天; **fall down** (if it's a person)dǎoxià 倒下, shuāidǎo 摔倒; (if it's a building) dǎotā 倒塌, tāntā 坍塌; **fall off to fall off a chair** cóng yǐzi shang diē xiàlái 从椅子上跌下来; **fall out** (from somewhere) diào chūlái 掉出来; **the letter fell out of his pocket** xìn cóng tā kǒudài li diào chūlái 信从他口袋里掉出来; (to quarrel) chǎojià 吵架, nàofān 闹翻; **fall over** diējiāo 跌跤, diēdǎo 跌倒; **fall through** shībài 失败

false /fɔːls/ adj (untrue, not real) jiǎ de 假的; (wrong, erroneous) cuòwù de 错误的, miùwù de 谬误的

familiar /fə'mɪljə(r)/ adj shúxī de 熟悉的

family /'fæmɪlɪ/ n **a family** yí gè jiātíng 一个家庭

famous /'feɪməs/ adj zhùmíng de 著名的, yǒumíng de 有名的

fan /fæn/ n (of a pop star, an actor, a sport) mí 迷; a

football fan yí gè zúqiúmí 一个足球迷；(for cooling) a **fan** (electric) yì tái (diàn)fēngshàn 一台（电）风扇；(hand-held) yì bǎ shànzi 一把扇子

fancy dress party /ˌfænsɪ 'dres pɑːtɪ/ n (British English) a fancy dress party yí gè huàzhuāng wǔhuì 一个化装舞会

fantastic /fæn'tæstɪk/ adj (fanciful) huànxiǎng de 幻想的；(weird, odd) qíyì de 奇异的，gǔguài de 古怪的；**fantastic!** tài hǎo le! 太好了！

far /fɑː(r)/ 1 adv far (away) yuǎn 远；**how far is it to London?** dào Lúndūn yǒu duō yuǎn? 到伦敦有多远?；**how far is Oxford from London?** Niújīn lí Lúndūn yǒu duō yuǎn? 牛津离伦敦有多远?；**we went as far as the coast** wǒmen yìzhí zǒudàole hǎibiān 我们一直走到了海边；(in time) **as far back as 1950** yuǎn zài yījiǔwǔlíng nián 远在 1950 年；(very much) **you're eating far too much bread** miànbāo nǐ chī de tài duō le 面包你吃得太多了；**far** [better | colder | earlier...] [hǎo | lěng | zǎo...] de duō [好|冷|早...] 得多 2 adj (farther) nà yìbiān de 那一边的；**at the far side of the room** zài fángjiān de nà yìbiān 在房间的那一边；**the Far East** Yuǎndōng 远东 3 **so far** dào mùqián wéizhǐ 到目前为止

fare /feə(r)/ n the fare (on a bus, train, or underground) chēfèi 车费；(on a boat) chuánfèi 船费

farm /fɑːm/ n a farm (for cultivation) yí gè nóngchǎng 一个农场；(for pasture) yí gè xùmùchǎng 一个畜牧场

farmer /'fɑːmə(r)/ n a farmer yí gè nóngchǎngzhǔ 一个农场主

fascinating /'fæsɪneɪtɪŋ/ adj mírén de 迷人的

fashion /'fæʃən/ n (form or pattern) yàngzi 样子；(prevailing mode or shape of dress) liúxíng shìyàng 流行式样；**to be in fashion** zhèng shíxíng 正时兴；**to go out of fashion** guòshí 过时，bù shíxīng 不时兴

fashionable /'fæʃənəbl/ adj shímáo de 时髦的，liúxíng de 流行的

fast /fɑːst/ **1** adj (*rapid*) kuài de 快的，xùnsù de 迅速的；(*as a clock or watch*) kuài de 快的；my watch is ten minutes fast wǒ de shǒubiǎo kuài shí fēnzhōng 我的手表快 10 分钟 **2** adv kuài 快，xùnsù 迅速

fasten /'fɑːsən/ vb jìláo 系牢，jìhǎo 系好；to fasten a seatbelt jìhǎo ānquándài 系好安全带

fast-forward /ˌfɑːst'fɔːwəd/ vb to fast-forward a cassette kuàijìn cídài 快进磁带

fat /fæt/ adj (*describing a person*) pàng de 胖的；(*describing animals or meat*) féi de 肥的

fatal /'feɪtəl/ adj (*causing death*) zhìmìng de 致命的；(*decided by fate*) mìngzhōng-zhùdìng de 命中注定的；(*determining fate*) juédìng mìngyùn de 决定命运的；a fatal decision for me juédìng wǒ mìngyùn de juédìng 决定我命运的决定

father /'fɑːðə(r)/ n a father yí gè bàba 一个爸爸，yí gè fùqīn 一个父亲

Father Christmas /ˌfɑːðə'krɪsməs/ n (*British English*) Father Christmas Shèngdàn Lǎorén 圣诞老人

father-in-law /'fɑːðərɪnlɔː/ n(*husband's father*) gōnggong 公公；(*wife's father*) yuèfù 岳父

faucet /'fɔːsɪt/ n (*US English*) a faucet yí gè shuǐlóngtóu 一个水龙头

fault /fɔːlt/ n a fault (*a mistake made by someone*) yí gè guòcuò 一个过错；(*in a mechanical, electrical or electronic system*) yí gè gùzhàng 一个故障

favour /'feɪvə(r)/ (*British English*)，**favor** (*US English*) **1** n to do someone a favour bāng mǒu rén yí gè máng 帮某人一个忙；to ask someone a favour qǐng mǒu rén bāng gè máng 请某人帮个忙 **2** in favour of to be in favour of the new law zànchéng xīn de fǎlǜ 赞成新的法律

favourite /'feɪvərɪt/ (*British English*)，**favorite** (*US English*) adj tèbié xǐhuān de 特别喜欢的；it's my favourite film zhè shì wǒ tèbié xǐhuan de diànyǐng 这是我

特别喜欢的电影 .

fax /fæks/ n a fax yí fèn chuánzhēn 一份传真

fear /fɪə(r)/ n hàipà 害怕，kǒngjù 恐惧

feather /'feðə(r)/ n a feather yì gēn yǔmáo 一根羽毛

February /'februərɪ/ n èryuè 二月

fed up /,fed 'ʌp/ adj be fed up fēicháng yànjuàn 非常厌倦

fee /fi:/ n (for attending an event, a show) fèi 费；(for joining a club, a union) huìfèi 会费

feeble /'fi:bl/ adj xūruò de 虚弱的，wúlì de 无力的

feed /fi:d/ vb (if it's a person) wèi 喂；(if it's an animal) sìyǎng 饲养，wèi(yǎng) 喂(养)

feel /fi:l/ vb (referring to an emotion, an impression, or a physical feeling) juéde 觉得，gǎndào 感到；to feel happy gǎndào gāoxìng 感到高兴；he's feeling uncomfortable tā juéde bù shūfu 他觉得不舒服；to feel afraid juéde hàipà 觉得害怕；I feel as if I'm being followed wǒ gǎndào hǎoxiàng yǒu rén gēnzhe wǒ 我感到好像有人跟着我；to feel [hot | cold | sleepy] juéde [rè | lěng | kùn] 觉得 [热 | 冷 | 困]；to feel ill gǎnjué shēntǐ bù shūfu 感觉身体不舒服；I don't feel a thing wǒ shénme dōu gǎnjué bú dào 我什么都感觉不到；(describing how something seems) the box felt very heavy nàge hézi ná qǐlai hěn zhòng 那个盒子拿起来很重；the room feels very cold zhège fángjiān ràng rén juéde hěn lěng 这个房间让人觉得很冷；(to touch) mō 摸；the doctor felt her head dàifu mōle yíxià tā de tóu 大夫摸了一下她的头；to feel like [going out | eating | dancing...] xiǎngyào [chūqù | chī dōngxi | tiàowǔ...] 想要 [出去 | 吃东西 | 跳舞...]；I don't feel like it (if it's about going out) wǒ bù xiǎng (chū)qù 我不想(出)去；(if it's about eating) wǒ bù xiǎng chī 我不想吃；(if it's about doing something) wǒ bù xiǎng zuò 我不想做

feeling /'fi:lɪŋ/ n (emotional) gǎnqíng 感情；a feeling yì zhǒng gǎnqíng 一种感情；to hurt someone's

feelings shānghài mǒu rén de gǎnqíng 伤害某人的感情;
(*physical*) gǎnjué 感觉; a feeling yì zhǒng gǎnjué 一种感
觉; I have a feeling he's right wǒ juéde tā shì duì de 我
觉得他是对的

felt-tip pen /ˌfelttɪp 'pen/ *n* a felt-tip pen yì zhī
zhāntóubǐ 一支毡头笔

female /'fiːmeɪl/ *adj* (*in biology*) cíxìng de 雌性的;
(*relating to women*) nǚ de 女的, nǚxìng de 女性的;
(*relating to animals*) mǔ de 母的

feminine /'femɪnɪn/ *adj* (*female*) nǚxìng de 女性的;
(*effeminate*) nǚzǐqì de 女子气的, jiāoróu de 娇柔的

fence /fens/ *n* a fence yí gè líba 一个篱笆, yí gè wéilán
一个围栏

fencing /'fensɪŋ/ *n* jījiàn 击剑

festival /'festəvəl/ *n* a festival day yí gè jié(rì) 一个节
(日)

fetch /fetʃ/ *vb* ná 拿, qǔ 取; go and fetch some water
qù ná diǎn shuǐ lái 去拿点水来; fetch a doctor qǐng gè
dàifu lái 请个大夫来

fever /'fiːvə(r)/ *n* to have a fever fāshāo 发烧, fārè 发
热

few /fjuː/ **1** a few yìxiē 一些, jǐ gè 几个; a few [people|
houses|books...] yìxiē [rén|fángzi|shū...] 一些 [人|房子|
书...]; a few of them speak Cantonese tāmen
dāngzhōng de jǐ gè rén huì shuō Guǎngdōnghuà 他们当中
的几个人会说广东话 **2** *det* (*not many*) jīhū méiyǒu 几乎
没有, hěn shǎo 很少; few [people|letters|cars...] jīhū
méiyǒu [rén|xìn|chē...] 几乎没有 [人|信|车...]; (*several*) jǐ
gè 几个; the first few weeks kāishǐ de jǐ gè xīngqī 开始
的几个星期 **3** *pron* few of us succeeded wǒmen
dāngzhōng de jīhū méiyǒu rén chénggōng 我们当中几乎没有
人成功

field /fiːld/ *n* (*open country in general*) tiányě 田野,
tiándì 田地; a field yí kuài tiándì 一块田地; (*a piece of
ground enclosed for sports, construction, entertainment,*

etc.) **a field** yí gè chǎngdì 一个场地;(*an area of knowledge or speciality*) lǐngyù 领域;**a field** yí gè lǐngyù 一个领域

fifteen /ˌfɪfˈtiːn/ *num* shíwǔ 十五

fifteenth /ˌfɪfˈtiːnθ/ *num* (*in a series*) dì-shíwǔ 第十五;(*in dates*) **the fifteenth of May** wǔyuè shíwǔ hào 5 月 15 号

fifth /fɪfθ/ *num* (*in a series*) dì-wǔ 第五;(*in dates*) **the fifth of June** liùyuè wǔ hào 6 月 5 号

fifty /ˈfɪftɪ/ *num* wǔshí 五十

fight /faɪt/ **1** *vb* **to fight** (*against*) **prejudice** yǔ piānjiàn zuò dòuzhēng 与偏见作斗争;**to fight for justice** wèi zhèngyì ér fèndòu 为正义而奋斗;(*in war*) yǔ…zhàndòu 与…战斗,yǔ zuòzhàn 与…作战;**to fight** (*against*) **the enemy** yǔ dírén zhàndòu 与敌人战斗;(*physically*) yǔ…dǎzhàng 与…打仗,(*to quarrel*) yǔ…zhēngchǎo 与…争吵 **2** *n* (*a campaign*) dòuzhēng 斗争;**a fight** yì chǎng dòuzhēng 一场斗争;(*physical*) **a fight** yì chǎng zhàndòu 一场战斗,yì chǎng bódòu 一场搏斗;**fight back** huánjī 还击

figure /ˈfɪɡə(r)/ *n* (*a number*) shùzì 数字;**a figure** yí gè shùzì 一个数字;**to have a good figure** yǒu yí gè hǎo de tǐxíng 有一个好的体型

file /faɪl/ *n* **a file** (*for documents*) yí gè ànjuàn 一个案卷,yí gè juànzōng 一个卷宗;(*in a computer*) yí gè wénjiàn 一个文件

fill /fɪl/ *vb* (*to fill a container*) zhuāngmǎn 装满;(*if it's people filling a room or a hall*) jǐmǎn 挤满;**fill in** (*if it's a form*) tiánxiě 填写;(*if it's a hole or a sunken place*) tián 填

film /fɪlm/ **1** *n* (*in a cinema or on TV*) **a film** yí bù diànyǐng 一部电影;(*for a camera*) **a film** yì juǎn jiāojuǎn 一卷胶卷 **2** *vb* pāishè 拍摄

filthy /ˈfɪlθɪ/ *adj* āngzāng de 肮脏的

final /ˈfaɪnəl/ **1** *adj* zuìhòu de 最后的,zuìzhōng de 最终的

2 n a final (in sports) yì chǎng juésài 一次决赛;(an examination) qīzhōng kǎoshì 期终考试

finally /'faɪnəlɪ/ adv zuìhòu 最后,zuìzhōng 最终

find /faɪnd/ vb (to reach the thing or person one has looked for) zhǎodào 找到;(to discover) fāxiàn 发现;(to come to perceive) fājué 发觉,gǎnjué 感觉;**find out** to find out the truth cháming zhēnxiàng 查明真相;if he ever finds out he'll be furious rúguǒ tā fāxiàn le, tā huì dàfā-léitíng 如果他发现了,他会大发雷霆

fine /faɪn/ **1** adj (describing a person's character) yōuliáng de 优良的,yōuxiù de 优秀的;(describing the weather) qínglǎng de 晴朗的,búcuò de 不错的;(describing the appearance of a person, a building, or a scene) hǎokàn de 好看的,piàoliang de 漂亮的;(in good health) I feel fine wǒ gǎnjué hěn hǎo 我感觉很好;(expressing agreement) (that's) fine xíng 行 **2** n a fine yí fèn fákuǎn 一份罚款

finger /'fɪŋɡə(r)/ n shǒuzhǐ 手指

finish /'fɪnɪʃ/ **1** vb (to complete) wánchéng 完成;to finish one's [homework | task | experiment] wánchéng [zuòyè | rènwu | shíyàn] 完成 [作业 | 任务 | 实验];(used after a verb to indicate a result of an action) wán 完;to finish [cooking | eating] supper [zuò | chī] wán wǎnfàn [做 | 吃] 完晚饭;(to come to an end) jiéshù 结束;the film finishes at 8:00 diànyǐng bā diǎn jiéshù 电影8点结束 **2** n the finish (the last part in a film, a race, or a certain process) zuìhòu yí duàn 最后一段

fire /'faɪə(r)/ **1** n huǒ 火;a fire (for heat) lúhuǒ 炉火;(causing damage) yì chǎng huǒzāi 一场火灾;to catch fire zhǎohuǒ 着火,qǐhuǒ 起火;to be on fire zháohuǒ 着火,qǐhuǒ 起火 **2** vb (to shoot) kāiqiāng 开枪;(to dismiss) jiěgù 解雇,kāichú 开除

fire alarm /'faɪər əlɑːm/ n a fire alarm yí gè huǒjǐng bàojǐngqì 一个火警报警器

fire brigade /'faɪə brɪɡeɪd/ (British English), **fire**

department /'faɪə dɪˌpɑːtmənt/ （US English） n xiāofángduì 消防队

fire engine /'faɪə ˌendʒɪn/ n a fire engine yí liàng xiāofángchē 一辆消防车

fireman /'faɪəmən/ n a fireman yí gè xiāofáng duìyuán 一个消防队员

fire station /'faɪə ˌsteɪʃən/ n a fire station yí gè xiāofángzhàn 一个消防站

fireworks display /'faɪəwɜːks dɪsˌpleɪ/ n a fireworks display yì chǎng yānhuǒ wǎnhuì 一场烟火晚会

firm /fɜːm/ **1** n a firm yí gè gōngsī 一个公司 **2** adj （when describing a structure, foundation, or frame） jiēshí de 结实的，láogù de 牢固的；（when describing one's attitude, position） jiāndìng de 坚定的，jiānjué de 坚决的

first /fɜːst/ **1** adj the first [time|lesson|day] dì-yī [cì|kè|tiān] 第一 [次|课|天]；the first [three weeks|two months|few days] tóu [sān zhōu|liǎng gè yuè|jǐ tiān] 头 [三周|两个月|几天] **2** adv （to begin with） shǒuxiān 首先；first of all shǒuxiān 首先；（for the first time）dì-yī cì 第一次；to arrive first dì-yī gè dàodá 第一个到达 **3** n （in a series or group） the first dì-yī gè 第一个；he was the first to congratulate us tā shì dì-yī gè zhùhè wǒmen de rén 他是第一个祝贺我们的人；（in dates）the first of June liùyuè yī hào 6 月 1 日 **4** at first qǐchū 起初，kāishǐ de shíhou 开始的时候

first aid /ˌfɜːst 'eɪd/ n jíjiù 急救

first class /ˌfɜːst 'klɑːs/ adv to travel first class （in a boat or a plane） zuò tóuděngcāng lǚxíng 坐头等舱旅行；（in a train） zuò tóuděng chēxiāng lǚxíng 坐头等车厢旅行

first floor /ˌfɜːst 'flɔː(r)/ n （in Britain） èr lóu 二楼；（in the US） yī lóu 一楼

first name /'fɜːst neɪm/ n jiàomíng 教名，míng 名

fish /fɪʃ/ **1** n a fish yì tiáo yú 一条鱼 **2** vb to go fishing （with a rod） qù diàoyú 去钓鱼；（with a net） qù bǔyú 去捕鱼

fisherman /ˈfɪʃəmən/ n a fisherman yí gè yúmín 一个渔民

fishing /ˈfɪʃɪŋ/ n (with a rod) diàoyú 钓鱼;(with a net) bǔyú 捕鱼

fishing rod /ˈfɪʃɪŋ rɒd/ n a fishing rod yì gēn diàoyúgānr 一根钓鱼杆儿

fist /fɪst/ n quántou 拳头

fit /fɪt/ **1** vb the shoes don't fit me zhè shuāng xié wǒ chuān bù héshì 这双鞋我穿不合适;the photo won't fit into the envelope zhè zhāng zhàopiàn zhuāng bú jìn zhè gè xìnfēng li qù 这张照片装不进这个信封里去;will the table fit here? zhè zhāng zhuōzi fàng zài zhèr héshì ma? 这张桌子放在这儿合适吗? **2** adj (suitable) héshì de 合适的,shìhé de 适合的;the house isn't fit to live in zhè (zhuàng) fángzi bú shìhé jūzhù 这(幢)房子不适合居住;to be fit to drive shìhé kāichē 适合开车;he is not fit to be a leader tā bù shìhé zuò lǐngdǎo 他不适合做领导;(healthy) to be fit jiànkāng de 健康的;**fit in !** Note that the translation varies with the context, which determines the verb that is used;(in a car) can you all fit in? nǐmen dōu néng zuò jìnqù ma? 你们都能坐进去吗?;(in a group or team) can he fit in? tā néng gēn qítā rén hédelái ma? 他能跟其他人合得来吗?

fitness /ˈfɪtnɪs/ n (physical) fitness (shēntǐ) jiànkāng (身体)健康

five /faɪv/ num wǔ 五;five apples wǔ gè píngguǒ 5 个苹果

fix /fɪks/ vb (to decide on) quèdìng 确定,juédìng 决定;(to fasten or attach) gùdìng 固定,ānzhuāng 安装;(to repair) xiūlǐ 修理;(to prepare) zhǔnbèi 准备

flag /flæg/ n a flag yí miàn qí 一面旗

flame /fleɪm/ n huǒyàn 火焰

flash /flæʃ/ **1** n a flash (for a camera) yí gè shǎnguāngdēng 一个闪光灯 **2** vb to flash (on and off) shǎnliàng 闪亮,shǎnguāng 闪光

flashlight /ˈflæʃlaɪt/ *n* a flashlight yí gè shǎnguāngdēng 一个闪光灯

flat /flæt/ **1** *n* (*British English*) a flat yì jiān tàofáng 一间套房，yí tào dānyuán fángjiān 一套单元房间 **2** *adj* (*smooth and level*) píng de 平的，píngtǎn de 平坦的；to have a flat tyre chētāi biě le 车胎瘪了

flavour /ˈfleɪvə(r)/ (*British English*)，**flavor** (*US English*) *n* a flavour yì zhǒng wèidao 一种味道

flea /fliː/ *n* a flea yí gè tiàozao 一个跳蚤

flight /flaɪt/ *n* a flight (*a regular air journey, numbered and at a fixed time*) yí gè hángbān 一个航班，yí jià bānjī 一架班机；(*the act of flying*) fēi 飞，fēixíng 飞行

flight attendant /flaɪt əˈtendənt/ *n* a flight attendant yì míng kōngfúyuán 一名空服员

float /fləʊt/ *vb* (*in the air*) piāo 飘；to float up into the air piāodào kōngzhōng qù 飘到空中去；(*in the water*) piāo 漂；to float in the river zài hé lǐ piāo 在河里漂

flock /flɒk/ *n* a flock of [sheep | geese | birds...] yì qún [yáng | é | niǎo...] 一群 [羊 | 鹅 | 鸟...]

flood /flʌd/ *n* a flood yí cì hóngshuǐ 一次洪水，yí cì shuǐzāi 一次水灾

floor /flɔː(r)/ *n* (*a surface*) a floor dìbǎn 地板；to sit on the floor zuò zài dìbǎn shang 坐在地板上；(*a storey*) céng 层，lóu 楼；the ground floor (*British English*) yī céng 一层，yī lóu 一楼

florist /ˈflɒrɪst/ *n* a florist yí gè mài huā de rén 一个卖花的人，yí gè huāshāng 一个花商

flour /ˈflaʊə(r)/ *n* miàn 面，miànfěn 面粉

flow /fləʊ/ *vb* liú 流，liúdòng 流动

flower /ˈflaʊə(r)/ **1** *n* a flower (*if it's a single flower*) yì zhī huā 一枝花；(*if it's a plant*) yì kē huā 一棵花 **2** *vb* kāihuā 开花

flu /fluː/ *n* liúxíngxìng gǎnmào 流行性感冒，liúgǎn 流感

fluently /ˈfluːəntlɪ/ *adv* liúlì de 流利地

flush /flʌʃ/ *vb* to flush the toilet chōng cèsuǒ 冲厕所

flute /fluːt/ *n* a flute yì zhī chángdí 一支长笛

fly /flaɪ/ **1** *n* a fly yì zhī cāngying 一只苍蝇 **2** *vb* (*if it's a bird, plane*) fēi 飞; to fly from London to Beijing cóng Lúndūn fēidào Běijīng 从伦敦飞到北京; to fly a plane jiàshǐ yí jià fēijī 驾驶一架飞机; (*if it's a flag*) piāoyáng 飘扬; **fly away** fēizǒu 飞走

fog /fɒg/ *n* wù 雾

fold /fəʊld/ *vb* (*if it's a chair, bed, or table*) zhédié 折叠; (*if it's clothes, a handkerchief, a bed sheet*) dié 叠; to fold one's arms bǎ shuāngbì zài xiōngqián jiāochā qǐlai 把双臂在胸前交叉起来

folder /ˈfəʊldə(r)/ *n* a folder yí gè wénjiànjiā 一个文件夹

follow /ˈfɒləʊ/ *vb* (*to go or come after*) gēnsuí 跟随; (*to pursue*) zhuīgǎn 追赶, zhuīzōng 追踪; (*to understand*) dǒng/lǐjiě…de yìsi 懂/理解…的意思; (*to obey*) tīngcóng 听从, zūnxún 遵循; (*to imitate*) fǎngxiào 仿效; (*to keep an eye fixed on*) zhùshì 注视; (*to keep one's hearing fixed on*) qīngtīng 倾听; (*to keep one's attention fixed on*) zhùyì 注意

following /ˈfɒləʊɪŋ/ *adj* the following (*below*) xiàmian de 下面的; the following paragraph xiàmian yí duàn 下面一段; the following names xiàliè míngzi 下列名字; (*when talking about the day, the week, the month, the year*) dì-èr 第二; the following day dì-èr tiān 第 2 天

fond /fɒnd/ *adj* I'm very fond of you wǒ hěn xǐhuan nǐ 我很喜欢你

food /fuːd/ *n* shíwù 食物, shípǐn 食品

fool /fuːl/ **1** *vb* qīpiàn 欺骗, yúnòng 愚弄 **2** *n* a fool yí gè shǎzi 一个傻子, yí gè shǎguā 一个傻瓜

foot /fʊt/ *n* (*part of the leg*) jiǎo 脚; on foot bùxíng 步行; (*in measurements*) a foot yì yīngchǐ 一英尺

football /ˈfʊtbɔːl/ *n* (*soccer*) zúqiú 足球; (*American football*) gǎnlǎnqiú 橄榄球; (*a ball*) a football yí gè zúqiú 一个足球

footballer /ˈfutˌbɔːlə(r)/ (*British English*), **football player** /ˈfutbɔːl ˌpleɪə(r)/ (*US English*) *n* a footballer yí gè zúqiú yùndòngyuán 一个足球运动员

footprint /ˈfutprɪnt/ *n* a footprint yí gè jiǎoyìn 一个脚印

footstep /ˈfutstep/ *n* a footstep yí gè jiǎobù 一个脚步

for /fɔː(r); *弱* fə(r)/ *prep* (*indicating the purpose of*) wèile 为了, wèi 为; to fight for national interests wèile guójiā lìyì ér dòuzhēng 为了国家利益而斗争; (*indicating the beneficiary*) wèi 为, gěi 给; to work for a company wèi yí gè gōngsī gōngzuò 为一个公司工作; he cooked dinner for us tā gěi wǒmen zuòfàn 他给我们做饭; (*indicating time and distance*) ! *Note that when indicating time and distance*, for *is not translated into Chinese*: we've been living here for two years wǒmen zài zhèr zhùle liǎng nián le 我们在这儿住了两年了; he's going to Shanghai for a year tā yào qù Shànghǎi yì nián 他要去上海一年; we drove for 80 kilometres wǒmen kāile bāshí gōnglǐ 我们开了 80 公里; (*indicating the price of a purchase*) huā 花; he bought the bag for £50 tā huā wǔshí yīngbàng mǎile zhège bāo 他花 50 英镑买了这个包; (*indicating the selling price*) yǐ 以; he sold his bike for £40 tā yǐ sìshí yīngbàng màile tā de zìxíngchē 他以 40 英镑卖了他的自行车; (*in favour of*) zànchéng 赞成, yōnghù 拥护; are you for or against his suggestion? nǐ zànchéng háishì fǎnduì tā de jiànyì? 你赞成还是反对他的建议?; (*indicating to whom or what something or somebody is intended or destined*) ! *Note that in this use* for *is usually not translated into Chinese*; a letter for you nǐ de xìn 你的信; the Minister for Education jiàoyù bùzhǎng 教育部长; the money is for buying a new car zhè qián shì mǎi xīnchē yòng de 这钱是买新车用的; (*on behalf of*, *in place of*) tì 替, dài 代; let me do it for you ràng wǒ tì nǐ zuò ba 让我替你做吧; say hello to her for me dài wǒ xiàng tā wèn hǎo 代我向她问好; (*indicating the direction or the destination*) the plane for Beijing fēi wǎng Běijīng de fēijī 飞往北京的飞机；[the train | the bus | the boat] for London kāi wǎng Lúndūn de [huǒchē | qìchē | chuán] 开往伦敦的［火车｜汽车｜船］；(other uses) a cheque for £20 yì zhāng èrshí yīngbàng de zhīpiào 一张 20 英镑的支票；what is the Chinese for "badger"? Hànyǔ "badger" zěnme shuō? 汉语 "badger" 怎么说？；we went [for a swim | for a run | for a walk…] wǒmen qù [yóuyǒng | pǎobù | sànbù…] le 我们去［游泳｜跑步｜散步…］了

forbid /fə'bɪd/ vb jìnzhǐ 禁止，bùxǔ 不许；to forbid someone to go out bùxǔ mǒu rén chūqù 不许某人出去；smoking is forbidden jìnzhǐ xīyān 禁止吸烟

force /fɔːs/ **1** vb qiǎngpò 强迫，bī 逼；to force someone to leave qiǎngpò mǒu rén líkāi 强迫某人离开 **2** n (strength) lì 力，lìliàng 力量；(influence) shìlì 势力；by force tōngguò wǔlì 通过武力；[police | air] force [jǐngchá | kōngjūn] [警察｜空军]

forecast /'fɔːkɑːst/ n yùbào 预报；the forecast is for rain yùbào shuō yǒu yǔ 预报说有雨

forehead /'fɒrɪd/ n qián'é 前额

foreign /'fɒrən/ adj wàiguó de 外国的

foreigner /'fɒrənə(r)/ n a foreigner yí gè wàiguórén 一个外国人

forest /'fɒrɪst/ n a forest yí gè sēnlín 一个森林

forever /fər'evə(r)/, **for ever** adv yǒngyuǎn 永远

forget /fə'get/ vb wàng 忘，wàngjì 忘记；to forget about someone wàng le mǒu rén 忘了某人；to forget [to do the shopping | to eat | to call…] wàngle [mǎi dōngxi | chīfàn | dǎ diànhuà…] 忘了［买东西｜吃饭｜打电话…］

forgive /fə'gɪv/ vb yuánliàng 原谅

fork /fɔːk/ n a fork yì bǎ chāzi 一把叉子

form /fɔːm/ **1** n a form (a shape) yì zhǒng xíngzhuàng/yàngzi 一种形状/样子；(a style) yì zhǒng xíngshì/fāngshì 一种形式/方式；(a document) yì zhāng biǎogé 一张表格；(referring to mood or fitness) to be in good

form zhuàngtài liánghǎo 状态良好；(*British English*) (*a year in a school*) **a form** yí gè niánjí 一个年级；**to be in the sixth form** zài liù niánjí (zhōngxué) 六年级 **2** *vb* (*to create, to make*) xíngchéng 形成，gòuchéng 构成；**to form a circle** xíngchéng yí gè yuánquān 形成一个圆圈；(*to establish, set up*) zǔchéng 组成，jiànlì 建立

formal /ˈfɔːməl/ *adj* (*describing language*) guīfàn de 规范的；**to wear formal clothes** (*for the evening*) chuān wǎnlǐfú 穿晚礼服；(*official*) zhèngshì de 正式的

former /ˈfɔːmə(r)/ *adj* (*before in time, past*) yǐqián de 以前的，cóngqián de 从前的；(*the first of the two mentioned*) qiánmiàn de 前面的

fortnight /ˈfɔːtnaɪt/ *n* (*British English*) **a fortnight** liǎng gè xīngqī 两个星期

fortunately /ˈfɔːtʃənətlɪ/ *adv* xìngyùn de shì 幸运的是，xìngkuī 幸亏

fortune /ˈfɔːtʃən/ *n* **a fortune** yì bǐ cáichǎn 一笔财产；**to make a fortune** fā yì bǐ cái 发一笔财；**to tell someone's fortune** gěi mǒu rén suànmìng 给某人算命

forty /ˈfɔːtɪ/ *num* sìshí 四十

forward /ˈfɔːwəd/ **1** *adv* xiàngqián 向前；**to step forward** xiàngqián zǒu 向前走 **2** *vb* **to forward a letter to someone** bǎ yì fēng xìn zhuǎngěi mǒu rén 把一封信转给某人

found /faʊnd/ *vb* (*to found an organisation, a system, an institution*) jiànlì 建立，chuànglì 创立；(*to found a building, a city*) jiànshè 建设，jiànzhù 建筑

fountain /ˈfaʊntɪn/ *n* **a fountain** yí gè pēnquán 一个喷泉

four /fɔː(r)/ *num* sì 四

fourteen /ˈfɔːˈtiːn/ *num* shísì 十四

fourteenth /ˈfɔːˈtiːnθ/ *num* (*in a series*) dì-shísì 第十四；(*in dates*) **the fourteenth of July** qīyuè shísì hào 7 月 14 号

fourth /fɔːθ/ *num* (*in a series*) dì-sì 第四；(*in dates*) **the fourth of July** qīyuè sì hào 7 月 4 号

fox /fɒks/ *n* a fox yì zhī húli 一只狐狸

fragile /'frædʒaɪl/ *adj* (*easily broken*) yìsuì de 易碎的；(*delicate, frail*) cuìruò de 脆弱的

frame /freɪm/ *n* (*a structure*) yí gè gòujià 一个构架, yí gè jiégòu 一个结构；(*a case made to enclose, border, or support something*) yí gè kuàngzi 一个框子, yí gè kuàngjià 一个框架；(*the body*) yí gè shēnqū 一个身躯

France /frɑːns/ *n* Fǎguó 法国

frank /fræŋk/ *adj* tǎnshuài de 坦率的, zhíshuài de 直率的

freckle /'frekl/ *n* a freckle yí gè quèbān 一个雀斑

free /friː/ **1** *adj* (*costing nothing*) miǎnfèi de 免费的；he gets free medical treatment tā jiēshòu miǎnfèi zhìliáo 他接受免费治疗；(*independent, not bound by rules*) zìyóu de 自由的；free trade zìyóu màoyì 自由贸易；he is free to do what he likes tā kěyǐ zuò rènhé tā xiǎng zuò de shì 他可以做任何他想做的事；(*not occupied, available*) yǒukòngr de 有空儿的, kòngxián de 空闲的；are you free on Monday? nǐ xīngqīyī yǒukòngr ma? 你星期一有空儿吗? **2** *vb* to free the prisoners shìfàng qiúfàn 释放囚犯

freedom /'friːdəm/ *n* zìyóu 自由

freeway /'friːweɪ/ *n* (*US English*) a freeway yì tiáo (gāosù) gōnglù 一条(高速)公路

freeze /friːz/ *vb* (*if it is water, river*) jiébīng 结冰；the river froze hé jiébīng le 河结冰了；(*to freeze something*) dòng 冻；to freeze the chicken in the freezer bǎ jī fàng zài bīngxiāng li dòng qǐlái 把鸡放在冰箱里冻起来；the ground was frozen hard dì dòng de hěn yìng 地冻得很硬；(*to stop as if by cold*) dòngjié 冻结；to freeze the prices dòngjié wùjià 冻结物价；to freeze to death dòngsǐ 冻死

freezer /'friːzə(r)/ *n* a freezer yí gè lěngdòngguì 一个冷冻柜, yí gè lěngcángguì 一个冷藏柜

freezing /'friːzɪŋ/ *adj* hěn lěng de 很冷的, jí lěng de 极冷

的；it's freezing tiānqì hěn lěng 天气很冷

French /frentʃ/ **1** adj Fǎguó de 法国的 **2** n（the people）Fǎguórén 法国人；(the language）Fǎyǔ 法语，Fǎwén 法文

French fries /ˌfrentʃ 'fraɪz/ n（US English）yóuzhá tǔdòutiáo 油炸土豆条

fresh /freʃ/ adj（when describing food, vegetables, fruits, fish）xīnxiān de 新鲜的；(new）xīn de 新的；fresh paint xīn（shuā）de yóuqī 新（刷）的油漆

Friday /'fraɪdɪ/ n Friday xīngqīwǔ 星期五

fridge /frɪdʒ/ n a fridge yí gè bīngxiāng 一个冰箱

fried /fraɪd/ adj yóujiān de 油煎的，yóuzhá de 油炸的

fried egg /ˌfraɪd 'eɡ/ n a fried egg yí gè jiānjīdàn 一个煎鸡蛋

friend /frend/ n a friend yí gè péngyou 一个朋友；to make friends with someone hé mǒu rén jiāo péngyou 和某人交朋友

friendly /'frendlɪ/ adj yǒuhǎo de 友好的

fright /fraɪt/ n to get a fright chī yì jīng 吃一惊，xià yí tiào 吓一跳；to give someone a fright xià mǒu rén yí tiào 吓某人一跳，shǐ mǒu rén chī yì jīng 使某人吃一惊

frightened /'fraɪtənd/ adj to be frightened hàipà de 害怕的

fringe /frɪndʒ/ n（of the hair）(British English）liúhǎir 刘海儿；(border）biānyuán 边缘，biānyán 边沿

frog /frɒɡ/ n a frog yì zhī qīngwā 一只青蛙

from /强 frɒm；弱 frəm/ prep！There are many verbs which involve the use of from, like borrow from, escape from, etc. For translations, look up the entries at borrow, escape, etc.；(indicating a location, a place, a time, etc., which is the starting point of an activity, journey, period of time, etc.) cóng 从；the boy from London cóng Lúndūn lái de nánháir 从伦敦来的男孩儿；where did she come from？tā cóng nǎr lái？她从哪儿来？；to come back from the office cóng bàngōngshì huílái 从办公室回来；the shop is open from eight to six 这个商店从 8 点到 6 点开门；from Monday to Saturday cóng xīngqīyī dào xīngqīliù 从星期一到星期六；from April on cóng sìyuè qǐ 从 4 月起；(indicating a location, a place, an object from which distance is stated) lí 离；we live ten minutes from the city centre wǒmen zhù de dìfang lí shìzhōngxīn yǒu shí fēnzhōng de lù 我们住的地方离市中心有 10 分钟的路；my house is not very far from the seaside wǒ jiā lí hǎibiān bú tài yuǎn 我家离海边不太远；(indicating a basis on which a point of view, an assumption, an idea is formed) gēnjù 根据；from this information, I think we should let him go gēnjù zhège xìnxī, wǒ rènwéi wǒmen yīnggāi ràng tā qù 根据这个信息，我认为我们应该让他去；from his point of view gēnjù tā de guāndiǎn 根据他的观点

front /frʌnt/ **1** n (of a building) qiánmian 前面, zhèngmiàn 正面；my room is at the front of the house wǒde fángjiān zài fángzi de zhèngmiàn 我的房间在房子的正面；(of a car, a train or queue) qiánmian 前面；at the front of the bus zài qìchē qiánmian 在汽车前面 **2** in front of zài⋯⋯ qiánmian 在⋯⋯ 前面

front door /ˌfrʌnt 'dɔː(r)/ n qiánmén 前门

front page /ˌfrʌnt 'peɪdʒ/ n (of a newspaper) tóubǎn 头版；(of a book) biāotíyè 标题页

front seat /ˌfrʌnt 'siːt/ n qiánpái zuòwèi 前排座位

frost /frɒst/ n shuāngdòng 霜冻；shuāng 霜

frozen /'frəʊzən/ adj (turned solid by fall of temperature) bīngdòngle de 冰冻了的；(stopped as if by cold) dòngjié de 冻结的

fruit /fruːt/ n a piece of fruit yí kuài shuǐguǒ 一块水果；he likes fruit tā xǐhuan shuǐguǒ 他喜欢水果

frustrated /frʌ'streɪtɪd/ adj huīxīn de 灰心的，huīxīn-sàngqì de 灰心丧气的

fry /fraɪ/ vb (yóu)jiān (油)煎，(yóu)zhá (油)炸

frying pan /'fraɪŋ ˌpæn/ n a frying pan yí gè jiānguō 一个煎锅

full /fʊl/ adj (of people) jǐmǎn de 挤满的；the streets were full of people jiē shang jǐmǎnle rén 街上挤满了人；(describing a flight, a hotel, or maximum possible marks in an examination) mǎn de 满的；to get full marks dé mǎnfēn 得满分；(unable to eat any more) bǎo de 饱的；I'm full wǒ bǎo le 我饱了，wǒ chībǎo le 我吃饱了；(complete) quán de 全的；to pay the full fare fù quánfèi 付全费；his full name tā de quánmíng 他的全名；at full speed quánsù 全速

full-time /'fʊl'taɪm/ 1 adj zhuānzhí de 专职的，quánrì de 全日的；a full-time job yí gè zhuānzhí gōngzuò 一个专职工作 2 adv to work full-time quánrì gōngzuò 全日工作

fumes /fju:mz/ n (smoke) yān 烟；(of wine, chemicals) qì 气，qìwèi 气味

fun /fʌn/ n (amusement) hǎowánr 好玩儿，yǒuqù 有趣；it's fun zhè zhēn hǎowánr 这真好玩儿；skiing is fun huáxuě hěn yǒuqù 滑雪很有趣；she is fun tā hěn yǒuqù 她很有趣；to have fun wán de tòngkuai 玩得痛快

function /'fʌŋkʃən/ 1 n (the role played by a part in a system) yí gè gōngnéng 一个功能，yí gè zuòyòng 一个作用；(duty peculiar to any office) yí xiàng zhínéng 一项职能，yí xiàng zhízé 一项职责 2 vb (to work) gōngzuò 工作；(to perform a function) qǐ zuòyòng 起作用

funeral /'fju:nərəl/ n a funeral yí gè zànglǐ 一个葬礼

funfair /'fʌnfeə(r)/ n (British English) a funfair yí gè yóulèhuì 一个游乐会

funny /'fʌnɪ/ adj (amusing) hǎowánr de 好玩儿的，yǒuqù de 有趣的；(odd) gǔguài de 古怪的，qíguài de 奇怪的

fur /fɜ:(r)/ n (on an animal's coat) pímáo 皮毛；(on a garment) máopí 毛皮，pízi 皮子

furious /'fjʊərɪəs/ adj (describing a person) dànù de 大怒的，kuángnù de 狂怒的；(violent) měngliè de 猛烈的，

jùliè de 剧烈的

furniture /'fɜːnɪtʃə(r)/ *n* jiājù 家具；**a piece of furniture** yí jiàn jiājù 一件家具

further /'fɜːðə(r)/ *adv* (*when talking about distance*) gèng yuǎn de 更远地；**he lives further away from the school** tā zhù de lí xuéxiào gèng yuǎn 他住得离学校更远；(*in addition, to a greater degree*) jìnyíbù de 进一步地；**to improve quality further** jìnyíbù de tígāo zhìliàng 进一步地提高质量

fuss /fʌs/ *n* **to make a fuss about something** yīnwèi mǒu shì dàjīng-xiǎoguài 因为某事大惊小怪

future /'fjuːtʃə(r)/ **1** *n* (*prospects*) qiántú 前途；(*time to come*) jiānglái 将来，jīnhòu 今后；**in (the) future** jiānglái 将来，jīnhòu 今后 **2** *adj* jiānglái de 将来的，wèilái de 未来的；**my future wife** wǒ wèilái de tàitai 我未来的太太

Gg

gallery /'ɡælərɪ/ *n* (*a building for displaying works of art*) **a gallery** yí gè měishùguǎn 一个美术馆，yí gè huàláng 一个画廊；(*a long passage*) **a gallery** yì tiáo chángláng 一条长廊

game /ɡeɪm/ *n* (*a contest for recreation*) yóuxì 游戏；**a game** yí gè yóuxì 一个游戏；(*in sport*) bǐsài 比赛；**a game of** [football | tennis] yì chǎng [zúqiú | wǎngqiú] bǐsài 一场[足球|网球]比赛

games /ɡeɪmz/ *n* yùndònghuì 运动会；**the Olympic Games** Àolínpǐkè Yùndònghuì 奥林匹克运动会

gang /ɡæŋ/ *n* (*a group of friends, young people*) yì huǒ 一伙；(*of criminals*) yì bāng 一帮

gap /ɡæp/ *n* **a gap** (*in a fence or hedge*) yí gè quēkǒu 一

个缺口，yí gè huōkǒu 一个豁口；(between buildings, cars)yí duàn jiàngé 一段间隔，yí duàn jùlí 一段距离；(a period of time)yí duàn jiàngé 一段间隔

garage /'gærɑːdʒ/ n a garage (for keeping a car) yí gè chēkù 一个车库；(for fixing a car) yí gè qìchē xiūlǐchǎng 一个汽车修理厂

garbage /'gɑːbɪdʒ/ n (US English)lājī 垃圾

garden /'gɑːdən/ 1 n a garden yí gè huāyuán 一个花园 2 vb cóngshì yuányì 从事园艺

gardener /'gɑːdənə(r)/ n a gardener yí gè yuánlín gōngrén 一个园林工人

gardening /'gɑːdənɪŋ/ n yuányì 园艺

garlic /'gɑːlɪk/ n suàn 蒜，dàsuàn 大蒜

gas /gæs/ n (for cooking, heating) méiqì 煤气；(US English) (gasoline) qìyóu 汽油

gas station /gæs ˌsteɪʃən/ n (US English)a gas station yí gè jiāyóuzhàn 一个加油站

gate /geɪt/ n a gate yí gè mén 一个门，yí gè dàmén 一个大门

gather /'gæðə(r)/ vb(to come together) jíhé 集合，jùjí 聚集；(to collect) sōují 搜集，shōují 收集；to gather information sōují zīliào 搜集资料；(to pick up) cǎijí 采集；to gather fruit cǎijí shuǐguǒ 采集水果

gay /geɪ/ adj tóngxìngliàn de 同性恋的

gear /gɪə(r)/ n (in a car or bus, on a bike)a gear yí gè dǎng 一个挡；(equipment) yòngjù 用具；fishing gear diàoyú yòngjù 钓鱼用具；(clothes)my football gear wǒ de zúqiúfú 我的足球服；your swimming gear nǐ de yóuyǒngyī 你的游泳衣

general /'dʒenərəl/ 1 n a general yí gè jiāngjūn 一个将军 2 adj (common, not special) yìbān de 一般的，pǔtōng de 普通的；general knowledge yìbān zhīshi 一般知识，chángshí 常识；(whole or all) quántǐ de 全体的；a general meeting yí cì quántǐ dàhuì 一次全体大会；(vague) dàtǐ de 大体的，lǒngtǒng de 笼统的；a general idea yí gè dàtǐ de xiǎngfǎ 一个大体的想法；(*widespread*) pǔbiàn de 普遍的；a matter of general concern yí gè pǔbiàn guānxīn de wèntí 一个普遍关心的问题 **3 in general** dàtǐshang 大体上，yìbān shuōlái 一般说来

generation /ˌdʒenəˈreɪʃən/ n a generation yí dài rén 一代人

generous /ˈdʒenərəs/ adj kāngkǎi de 慷慨的，dàfang de 大方的

Geneva /dʒɪˈniːvə/ n Geneva Rìnèiwǎ 日内瓦

genius /ˈdʒiːnjəs/ n a genius yí gè tiāncái 一个天才

gentle /ˈdʒentl/ adj (*when describing manners or actions*) wényǎ de 文雅的，wēnróu de 温柔的；(*when describing a person's disposition*) wēnróu de 温柔的，(*amiable*) yǒushàn de 友善的

gentleman /ˈdʒentlmən/ n (*a polite term used for men in general*) a gentleman yí wèi xiānsheng 一位先生；(*a man of refined manners*) a gentleman yí wèi shēnshì 一位绅士

geography /dʒɪˈɒgrəfɪ/ n dìlǐ 地理

germ /dʒɜːm/ n xìjūn 细菌

German /ˈdʒɜːmən/ **1** adj Déguó de 德国的 **2** n (*the people*) Déguórén 德国人；(*the language*) Déyǔ 德语，Déwén 德文

Germany /ˈdʒɜːmənɪ/ n Déguó 德国

get /get/ vb get away (*to escape*) táotuō 逃脱；he won't get away with it tā zuò de zhè jiàn shì kěndìng huì bèi fājué 他做的这件事肯定会被发觉；get back (*to come back*) huílái 回来；(*to go back*) huíqù 回去；(*to have back after being stolen*) zhǎo huílái 找回来；I got my bike back wǒ bǎ zìxíngchē zhǎo huílái le 我把自行车找回来了；(*to have back after being borrowed*) huán huílái 还回来；he's got his book back tā de shū huán huílái le 他的书还回来了；get down (*to go down*) xiàqù 下去；(*to come down*) xiàlái 下来；can you get down from the tree? nǐ néng cóng shù shang xiàlái ma? 你能从树上下来吗？(*to take down*) ná xiàlái 拿下来；I got the box down from the shelf wǒ bǎ hézi cóng jiàzi shang ná xiàlái 我把盒子从架子上拿下来；(to be depressed over something) shǐ … jǔsàng 使 … 沮丧；it gets him down zhè shǐ tā hěn jǔsàng 这使他很沮丧；get in (to enter) jìnrù 进入；(to arrive) dàodá 到达；get off (to leave a bus or train) xià chē 下车；I'm getting off at the next stop wǒ xià yí zhàn xià chē 我下一站下车；he fell as he was getting off the train tā xià huǒchē de shíhou shuāidǎo le 他下火车的时候摔倒了；(to remove) bǎ … nòng xiàlái 把 … 弄下来；to get a stain out bǎ wūdiǎn nòng xiàlái 把污点弄下来；get on (to climb on board a bus or train) shàng chē 上车；to get on the bus shàngchē 上汽车；to get on well xiāngchǔ de hěn hǎo 相处得很好；I get on well with her wǒ gēn tā xiāngchǔ de hěn hǎo 我跟她相处得很好；(in polite enquiries) how did you get on? nǐ guò de zěnmeyàng? 你过得怎么样？how is she getting on at school? tā zài xuéxiào zěnmeyàng? 她在学校怎么样？get out she got out of the building tā cóng dàlóu li táo chūlái 她从大楼里逃出来；to get the furniture out of the house bǎ jiājù cóng fángzi li ná chūlái 把家具从房子里拿出来；get over to get over a shock cóng zhènjīng zhōng huīfù guòlái 从震惊中恢复过来；get through to get through to someone chuándào mǒu rén 传到某人；get together jùjí 聚集，jùhuì 聚会；get up when do you get up? nǐ shénme shíhou qǐchuáng? 你什么时候起床？

ghost /gəust/ n a ghost yí gè guǐ 一个鬼

gift /gɪft/ n (a present) yí jiàn lǐwù 一件礼物；(an ability) a gift tiānfù 天赋；to have a gift for languages yǒu yǔyán tiānfù 有语言天赋

ginger /ˈdʒɪndʒə(r)/ 1 n (a vegetable used for spices) jiāng 姜 2 adj jiānghuángsè de 姜黄色的；ginger hair (British English) jiānghuángsè de tóufa 姜黄色的头发

girl /gɜːl/ n a girl yí gè nǚhái(zi) 一个女孩(子)，yí gè gūniang 一个姑娘

girlfriend /'gɜːlfrend/ n a girlfriend yí gè nǚpéngyou 一个女朋友

give /gɪv/ vb ! For translations of expressions like to give someone a lift, to give someone an injection, to give someone a fright, etc., look up the entries lift, injection, fright ; to give gěi 给; to give someone a book gěi mǒu rén yì běn shū 给某人一本书; I gave him the photos wǒ bǎ nàxiē zhàopiàn gěile tā 我把那些照片给了他; (to offer as a gift) sònggěi 送给; to give someone a present sònggěi mǒu rén yí gè lǐwù 送给某人一个礼物; to give someone a message (dài) gěi mǒu rén yí gè kǒuxin (带)给某人一个口信(to make a present of ...) sònggěi biérén ... 送给别人…; to give away a secret xièlòu mìmì 泄漏秘密; give back huángěi 还给; give in ràngbù 让步, qūfú 屈服; give off to give off fumes màochū yān lái 冒出烟来; give out to give out the exercise books fēnfā liànxíběn 分发练习本; give up (to stop) to give up smoking jièyān 戒烟; to give up the idea of working abroad fàngqì qù guówài gōngzuò de xiǎngfǎ 放弃去国外工作的想法; to give oneself up to the police xiàng jǐngchá zìshǒu 向警察自首

glad /glæd/ adj gāoxìng de 高兴的

glass /glɑːs/ n a glass yí gè bōlibēi 一个玻璃杯; a glass of water yì bēi shuǐ 一杯水

glasses /'glɑːsɪz/ n yǎnjìng 眼镜

glove /glʌv/ n a pair of gloves yí fù shǒutào 一副手套

glow /gləʊ/ vb fāguāng 发光

glue /gluː/ **1** n jiāo 胶 **2** vb zhān 粘

go /gəʊ/ vb **go across** chuānguò 穿过; **go after** (physically) zhuī 追; (when talking about pursuing an abstract goal) zhuīqiú 追求; **go ahead** (if it's an event) zhàocháng jìnxíng 照常进行; the concert's going ahead yīnyuèhuì jiāng zhàocháng jìnxíng 音乐会将照常进行;(if it's a person) (when about to do something) gàn ba 干

吧；(when about to say something) shuō ba 说吧；(when about to walk somewhere) zǒu ba 走吧；**go away** zǒu 走，líkāi 离开；**go away!** nǐ zǒukāi! 你走开！gǔn! 滚 * !；**go back** huí 回，huíqù 回去；Gary went back to London Jiālǐ huí Lúndūn le 加里回伦敦了；to go back to school huíqù shàngxué 回去上学；to go back to work huíqù gōngzuò 回去工作；**go by** guòqù 过去；**go by...** lùguò... 路过...；**go down** (if it's a quality, a price, a salary) xiàjiàng 下降；(if it's a person) she went down to have a look tā xiàqù kànkan 她下去看看；they went down the hill tāmen xiàshān le 他们下山了；(if it's the sun or moon) luòxià 落下；(if it's a computer) huàile 坏了；**go in** jìnqù 进去；he didn't go in tā méi jìnqù 他没进去；**go off** (to explode) bàozhà 爆炸；(to ring) xiǎng 响；(to leave) líqù 离去，zǒudiào 走掉；(when talking about food becoming bad) biànzhì 变质；the milk will go off niúnǎi huì biànzhì 牛奶会变质；(to be switched off) guāndiào 关掉，tíngdiào 停掉；**go on** (to continue) jìxù 继续；to go on talking jìxù jiǎnghuà 继续讲话；(to happen) what's going on? fāshēngle shénme shì? 发生了什么事？；(to keep talking) he goes on (and on) about his work tā yígèjìnr de tán tā de gōngzuò 他一个劲儿地谈他的工作；(to be switched on) dǎkāi 打开；**go out** (to leave the house) chūqù 出去；are you going out this evening? jīntiān wǎnshang nǐ chūqù ma? 今天晚上你出去吗？；(as with a boyfriend, a girlfriend) tán péngyou 谈朋友；to go out with someone gēn mǒu rén tán péngyou 跟某人谈朋友；(to be switched off as a fire, to stop burning) xīmiè 熄灭；**go over** (to check) jiǎnchá 检查；to go over some grammar jiǎnchá yìxiē yǔfǎ 检查一些语法；(to revise) fùxí 复习；**go round** (British English) (to call on) shùnbiàn qù 顺便去；to go round to see someone shùnbiàn qù kànwàng mǒu rén 顺便去看望某人；

---

* in informal situations

(to walk around, to visit) guàng 逛; to go round the museums guàng bówùguǎn 逛博物馆; to go round the shops guàng shāngdiàn 逛商店; (to be enough) is there enough bread to go round? miànbāo gòu fēn de ma? 面包够分的吗?; **go round with** (British English) (to spend time with) to go round with someone gēn mǒu rén jiāowǎng 跟某人交往; **go through** (to have, to live through) to go through a difficult time jīnglì yí duàn kùnnan shíqí 经历一段困难时期; (to search) sōuchá sōuchá 搜查; (to check) jiǎnchá jiǎnchá 检查; **go together** xiāngpèi 相配; the skirt and blouse go well together qúnzi hé chènshān hěn xiāngpèi 裙子和衬衫很相配; **go up** (if it's a person) shàng 上; he went up the stairs tā shàng lóu le 他上楼了; to go up to the top of the hill shàng shāndǐng 上山顶; (if it's a price, a salary) zhǎng 涨; **go with** yǔ…xiāngpèi 与…相配; the trousers don't really go with the jacket kùzi yǔ jiākè bù xiāngpèi 裤子与夹克不相配

goal /gəʊl/ n (an end or aim) yí gè mùdì 一个目的, yí gè mùbiāo 一个目标; (a score in some ball games) yì fēn 一分; (in a football field) qiúmén 球门

goalkeeper /'gəʊlˌkiːpə(r)/ n a goalkeeper yí gè shǒuményuán 一个守门员

goat /gəʊt/ n a goat yì zhī shānyáng 一只山羊

god /gɒd/ n a god yí gè shén 一个神; God Shàngdì 上帝

goddaughter /'gɒdˌdɔːtə(r)/ n a goddaughter yí gè jiàonǚ 一个教女

godfather /'gɒdˌfɑːðə(r)/ n a godfather yí gè jiàofù 一个教父

godmother /'gɒdˌmʌðə(r)/ n a godmother yí gè jiàomǔ 一个教母

godson /'gɒdsʌn/ n a godson yí gè jiàozǐ 一个教子

going /'gəʊɪŋ/: to be going to zhǔnbèi 准备, dǎsuàn 打算; I'm going to [leave | go to Ireland | learn to drive...] wǒ zhǔnbèi [líkāi | qù Ài'ěrlán | xué kāichē…] 我准备 [离开 | 去爱尔兰 | 学开车…]

兰|学开车…]

gold /gəʊld/ **1** n gold jīn 金，huángjīn 黄金 **2** adj jīn de 金的；a gold ring yí gè jīn jièzhi 一个金戒指

goldfish /ˈgəʊldfɪʃ/ n a goldfish yì tiáo jīnyú 一条金鱼

golf /gɒlf/ n gāo'ěrfūqiú 高尔夫球

golf course /ˈgɒlf kɔːs/ n a golf course yí gè gāo'ěrfūqiúchǎng 一个高尔夫球场

good /gʊd/ **1** adj good hǎo de 好的；a good book yì běn hǎo shū 一本好书；to be good at [chemistry | drawing | chess…]shàncháng [huàxué | huà huà | xiàqí…] 擅长 [化学|画画|下棋…]；(beneficial) yǒuyì 有益，yǒu hǎochù 有好处；exercise is good for you duànliàn duì nǐ yǒuyì 锻炼对你有益；(pleasant) I had a good time wǒ guò de hěn yúkuài 我过得很愉快；(healthy) to look good kànshàngqù shēntǐ hěn hǎo 看上去身体很好；I don't feel too good wǒ gǎnjué shēntǐ bú tài hǎo 我感觉身体不太好；(talking about food) hǎochī de hǎo chī de 好吃的；(obedient) tīnghuà de 听话的；(when expressing gratitude) it's very good of you to let me know xièxiè nǐ gàosu wǒ 谢谢你告诉我 **2** n it's no good [shouting | crying | going there…] [hǎn | kū | qù nàr…] méiyǒu yòng [喊|哭|去那儿…] 没有用；he is no good at Latin tā de Lādīngyǔ hěn zāogāo 他的拉丁语很糟糕；the change will do you good zhège biànhuà huì duì nǐ yǒu hǎochù 这个变化会对你有好处 **3** exc Good heavens! tiān a! 天啊！；Good for you! gàn de hǎo! 干得好！ **4** for ever yǒngjiǔ 永久，yǒngyuǎn 永远

good afternoon /ˌgʊd ɑːftəˈnuːn/ n (also exc) (when meeting)xiàwǔ hǎo 下午好；(when leaving)zàijiàn 再见

goodbye /ˌgʊdˈbaɪ/ n (also exc) zàijiàn 再见

good evening /ˌgʊdˈiːvnɪŋ/ n (also exc) wǎnshang hǎo 晚上好

good-looking /ˌgʊdˈlʊkɪŋ/ adj hǎokàn de 好看的

good morning /ˌgʊdˈmɔːnɪŋ/ n (also exc) (when meeting)zǎoshang hǎo 早上好；(when leaving)zàijiàn 再见

goodnight /gʊdˈnaɪt/ *n* (*also exc*) wǎn'ān 晚安

goods /gʊdz/ *n* huòwù 货物

goose /guːs/ *n* a goose yì zhī é 一只鹅

gooseberry /ˈguːzbərɪ/ *n* a gooseberry yí gè cùlì 一个醋栗

gorilla /gəˈrɪlə/ *n* a gorilla yí zhī dà xīngxing 一大猩猩

gossip /ˈgɒsɪp/ *vb* (*to chat*) xiánliáo 闲聊;(*to talk in a harmful way*) sànbù liúyán-fēiyǔ 散布流言蜚语

got /gɒt/ *vb* (*to have*) yǒu *n*;I've got work to do wǒ yǒu gōngzuò yào zuò 我有工作要做;have you got a cold? nǐ gǎnmào le ma? 你感冒了吗?(*to be obliged to*)to have got to bìxū 必须, děi 得;I've got to [go|work|buy a new computer...]wǒ bìxū [zǒu|gōngzuò|mǎi yí tái xīn jìsuànjī...] 我必须 [走|工作|买一台新计算机...]

government /ˈgʌvənmənt/ *n* a government yí gè zhèngfǔ 一个政府

GP /ˌdʒiː ˈpiː/ **General Practitioner** (**medicine**) *n* a GP yí gè quánkē yīshēng 一个全科医生

grab /græb/ *vb* to grab someone by the arm zhuāzhù mǒu rén de gēbo 抓住某人的胳膊;he tried to grab my handbag tā shìtú qiǎng wǒ de shǒutíbāo 他试图抢我的手提包

grade /greɪd/ *n* (*a mark on an examination or in a class or course of study*) a grade yí gè fēnshù 一个分数;(*US English*) (*a class in school*) a grade yí gè niánjí 一个年级;he's in the eighth grade tā shàng bā niánjí 他上八年级

grade school /ˈgreɪd ˌskuːl/ *n* (*US English*) a grade school yì suǒ xiǎoxué 一所小学

gradually /ˈgrædʒʊəlɪ/ *adv* zhújiàn 逐渐, jiànjiàn 渐渐

gram(me) /græm/ *n* a gram yí kè 一克

grammar /ˈgræmə(r)/ *n* yǔfǎ 语法

grandchild /ˈgrændtʃaɪld/ *n* a grandchild (*a son's son*) yí gè sūnzi 一个孙子;(*a son's daughter*)yí gè sūnnǚ 一个孙女;(*a daughter's son*) yí gè wàisūn 一个外孙;(*a* *daughter's daughter*)yí gè wàisūnnǚ 一个外孙女

granddaughter /'grænˌdɔːtə(r)/ n **a granddaughter**(*a son's daughter*)yí gè sūnnǚ 一个孙女;(*a daughter's daughter*)yí gè wàisūnnǚ 一个外孙女

grandfather /'grændˌfɑːðə(r)/ n (*father's father*)yéye 爷爷,zǔfù 祖父;(*mother's father*)wàigōng 外公,lǎoye 姥爷,wàizǔfù 外祖父! *Note that* zǔfù 祖父 *and* wàizǔfù 外祖父 *cannot be used in direct address.*

grandmother /'grændˌmʌðə(r)/ n (*father's mother*)nǎinai 奶奶,zǔmǔ 祖母;(*mother's mother*)wàipó 外婆,lǎolao 姥姥,wàizǔmǔ 外祖母! *Note that* zǔmǔ 祖母 *and* wàizǔmǔ 外祖母 *cannot be used in direct address.*

grandparents /'grændˌpeərənts/ n (*father's parents*)yéye(hé)nǎinai 爷爷(和)奶奶;(*mother's parents*)lǎoyé(he)lǎolao 姥爷(和)姥姥,wàigōng(hé)wàipó 外公(和)外婆

grandson /'grændsʌn/ n **a grandson** (*a son's son*)yí gè sūnzi 一个孙子;(*a daughter's son*)yí gè wàisūn 一个外孙

grapefruit /'greipfruːt/ n pútáoyòu 葡萄柚;**a grapefruit** yí gè pútáoyòu 一个葡萄柚

grapes /greips/ n pútáo 葡萄;**a bunch of grapes** yí chuàn pútáo 一串葡萄

grass /grɑːs/ n cǎo 草;**to cut the grass** gē cǎo 割草

grasshopper /'grɑːsˌhɒpə(r)/ n **a grasshopper** yì zhī zhàměng 一只蚱蜢

grateful /'greitfʊl/ adj gǎnjī de 感激的,gǎnxiè de 感谢的;**I would be grateful if you could let me know** rúguǒ nǐ néng gàosu wǒ,wǒ huì hěn gǎnjī 如果你能告诉我,我会很感激

grave /greiv/ n **a grave** yí gè fénmù 一个坟墓

gray /grei/ (*US English*) ▶**grey**

grease /griːs/ n yóuzhī 油脂

greasy /'griːzɪ/ adj (yǒu)yóuzhī de (有)油脂的

great /greit/ adj (stressing size, amount) dà de 大的;**a great improvement** yí gè hěn dà de tígāo 一个很大的提

高；to have great difficulty reading yuèdú yǒu hěn dà de kùnnan 阅读有很大的困难；(when describing a country or an outstanding person) wěidà de 伟大的；your great country nǐmen wěidà de guójiā 你们伟大的国家；(showing enthusiasm) that's great！hǎo jí le！好极了！；I had a great time wǒ wán de fēicháng yúkuài 我玩得非常愉快

Great Britain /ˌgreɪt ˈbrɪtn/ n Dàbùlièdiān 大不列颠

great grandfather /ˌgreɪt ˈgrænfɑːðə(r)/ n (if it's on the father's side) zēngzǔfù 曾祖父；(if it's on the mother's side) wàizēngzǔfù 外曾祖父

great grandmother /ˌgreɪt ˈgrændmʌðə(r)/ n (if it's on the father's side) zēngzǔmǔ 曾祖母；(if it's on the mother's side) wàizēngzǔmǔ 外曾祖母

Greece /griːs/ n Xīlà 希腊

greedy /ˈgriːdɪ/ adj (having a voracious appetite) tānchī de 贪吃的，tānzuǐ de 贪嘴的；(inordinately desirous of increasing one's own share) tānlán de 贪婪的，tānxīn de 贪心的

Greek /griːk/ **1** adj Xīlà de 希腊的 **2** n (the people) Xīlàrén 希腊人；(the language) Xīlàyǔ 希腊语，Xīlàwén 希腊文

green /griːn/ adj lǜ de 绿的，lǜsè de 绿色的

greenhouse /ˈgriːnhaʊs/ n a greenhouse yí gè wēnshì 一个温室

grey /greɪ/ (British English)，**gray** (US English) adj huī de 灰的，huīsè de 灰色的；grey hair báitóufa 白头发

grill /grɪl/ vb zài kǎojià shang kǎo 在烤架上烤

grin /grɪn/ vb liěkāi zuǐ xiào 咧开嘴笑

grocer /ˈgrəʊsə(r)/ n a grocer yí gè záhuòshāng 一个杂货商

grocery /ˈgrəʊsərɪ/ n a grocery yí gè záhuòdiàn 一个杂货店

ground /graʊnd/ n dì 地；the ground is hard in winter dōngtiān dì hěn yìng 冬天地很硬；(land used for sports) a sports ground yí gè yùndòngchǎng 一个运动场

ground floor /ɡraʊd ˈflɔː(r)/ n (British English) the ground floor yī lóu 一楼，yī céng 一层

group /ɡruːp/ n (a number of persons or things put together in a certain way) zǔ 组；we are divided into 3 groups wǒmen bèi fēnchéng sān zǔ 我们被分成 3 组；(a crowd) qún 群；a group of children yì qún háizi 一群孩子；(a band) a rock group yí gè yáogǔn yuèduì 一个摇滚乐队

grow /ɡrəʊ/ vb (to get big, strong, long, tall) zhǎng 长，chéngzhǎng 成长；the tree grows fast shù zhǎng de hěn kuài 树长得很快；(as a gardener, a farmer) zhòng 种；to grow vegetables zhòng cài 种菜；(to let grow) to grow a beard liú húzi 留胡子；(to become) biàn de 变得！Note that it's often unnecessary to translate grow here；she's grown more cynical tā (biàn de) gèngjiā wánshì-bùgōng 她（变得）更加玩世不恭；he has grown old tā lǎo le 他老了；(to increase) zēngzhǎng 增长；the population will grow rénkǒu jiānghuì zēngzhǎng 人口将会增长；(to develop) fāzhǎn 发展；that place is growing into a city nàge dìfang zhèngzài fāzhǎn chéngwéi yí gè chéngshì 那个地方正在发展成为一个城市；grow up zhǎngdà 长大；when I grow up, I want to be a doctor wǒ zhǎngdà le yào dāng yīshēng 我长大了要当医生

grumble /ˈɡrʌmbl/ vb bàoyuàn 抱怨，fā láosāo 发牢骚

guard /ɡɑːd/ n a guard (in a prison) yí gè kānshǒu 一个看守；(in a bank or important institution) yí gè bǎowèi rényuán 一个保卫人员；(in the army) yí gè wèibīng 一个卫兵；to be on guard zhàngǎng 站岗

guard dog /ˈɡɑːd dɒɡ/ n a guard dog yì tiáo jǐngquǎn 一条警犬

guess /ɡes/ vb cāi 猜

guest /ɡest/ n a guest yí wèi kèrén 一位客人

guesthouse /ˈɡesthaʊs/ n a guesthouse yí gè zhāodàisuǒ 一个招待所

guide /gaɪd/ **1** *n* a guide (*for tourists*) yí gè dǎoyóu 一个导游;(*for travellers，mountaineers*) yí gè xiàngdǎo 一个向导 **2** *vb* yǐndǎo 引导

guide book /'gaɪd bʊk/ *n* a guide book yì běn lǚxíng zhǐnán 一本旅行指南

guided tour /ˌgaɪdɪd 'tʊə/ *n* a guided tour yí cì yǒu dǎoyóu de lǚxíng 一次有导游的旅行

guilty /'gɪltɪ/ *adj* (*having broken the law*) yǒuzuì de 有罪的；to feel guilty gǎndào nèijiù 感到内疚

guitar /gɪ'tɑː(r)/ *n* a guitar yì bǎ jítā 一把吉他

gum /gʌm/ *n* (*part of the mouth*) chǐyín 齿龈，yáchuáng 牙床;(*for chewing*) kǒuxiāngtáng 口香糖

gun /gʌn/ *n* a gun yì zhī qiāng 一支枪

gym /dʒɪm/，**gymnasium** /dʒɪm'neɪzɪəm/ *n* a gym/gymnasium yí gè tǐyùguǎn 一个体育馆

gymnastics /dʒɪm'næstɪks/ *n* tǐcāo 体操

Hh

habit /'hæbɪt/ *n* a habit yí gè xíguàn 一个习惯

hail /heɪl/ *n* bīngbáo 冰雹

hair /heə(r)/ *n* (*on the head*) tóufa 头发;(*on the body*) máo 毛

hairbrush /'heəbrʌʃ/ *n* a hairbrush yì bǎ fàshuā 一把发刷

hairdresser /'heəˌdresə(r)/ *n* a hairdresser yí gè lǐfàshī 一个理发师

hairdryer /'heəˌdraɪə(r)/ *n* a hairdryer yí gè chuīfēngjī 一个吹风机

hairstyle /'heəstaɪl/ *n* a hairstyle yì zhǒng fàxíng 一种发型

half /hɑːf/ **1** *n* a half yíbàn 一半；to cut a melon in half

half hour /hɑːf 'aʊə(r)/ n a half hour bàn gè xiǎoshí 半个小时

half term /hɑːf 'tɜːm/ n (British English) qīzhōngjià 期中假

hall /hɔːl/ n (in a house, an apartment) a hall yí gè tīng 一个厅, yí gè lǐtáng 一个礼堂

ham /hæm/ n huǒtuǐ 火腿

hamburger /'hæmbɜːgə(r)/ n a hamburger yí gè hànbǎobāo 一个汉堡包

hammer /'hæmə(r)/ n a hammer yì bǎ chuízi 一把锤子

hamster /'hæmstə(r)/ n a hamster yì zhī cāngshǔ 一只仓鼠

hand /hænd/ **1** n (the part of the body) shǒu 手; he had a pencil in his hand tā shǒu li názhe yì zhī qiānbǐ 他手里拿着一支铅笔; to hold someone's hand lāzhe mǒu rén de shǒu 拉着某人的手; (help) a hand bāngzhù 帮助; (on a clock or watch) a hand yì gēn zhǐzhēn 一根指针; (when judging a situation or subject) on the one hand... on the other... yì fāngmiàn…, lìng yì fāngmiàn… 一方面…, 另一方面… **2** vb (to pass with the hand) dì 递, gěi 给

handbag /'hændbæg/ *n* a handbag yí gè shǒutíbāo 一个手提包

handball /'hændbɔ:l/ *n* shǒuqiú 手球

handicapped /'hændɪkæpt/ *adj* cánjí de 残疾的

handkerchief /'hæŋkətʃɪf/ *n* a handkerchief yì tiáo shǒujuàn(r) 一条手绢(儿)

handle /'hændl/ *n* a handle yí gè bǎshǒu 一个把手

handsome /'hænsəm/ *adj* piàoliang de 漂亮的, yīngjùn de 英俊的; a handsome young man yí gè yīngjùn de niánqīngrén 一个英俊的年轻人

handwriting /'hænd,raɪtɪŋ/ *n* shūxiě 书写, bǐjì 笔迹

handy /'hændɪ/ *adj* (*convenient*) fāngbiàn de 方便的; (*near*) jìnbiàn de 近便的

hang /hæŋ/ *vb* (*on a hook, a coat hanger, a line*) guà 挂; to hang clothes (up) in a wardrobe bǎ yīfu guà zài yīguì li 把衣服挂在衣柜里; (*for drying*) liàng 晾; to hang clothes on a line bǎ yīfu liàng zài shéngzi shang 把衣服晾在绳子上; (*to suspend*) diào 吊; to hang the light above the table bǎ dēng diào zài zhuōzi shàng fāng 把灯吊在桌子上方; (*to kill*) diàosǐ 吊死, jiǎosǐ 绞死; **hang around** (*walking around doing nothing*) xiánguàng 闲逛; (*stay around out of affection or respect*) jù zài… pángbiān 聚在…旁边; the children hung around the old man háizimen jù zài lǎorén pángbiān 孩子们聚在老人旁边; **hang on to** jǐnjǐn wòzhù 紧紧握住; she was hanging on to the rope tā jǐnjǐn wòzhù shéngzi 她紧紧握住绳子; **hang up** (*on a hook, a coat hanger, a line*) guà 挂; to hang up one's coat guà yīfu 挂衣服; your coat's hanging up in the hall nǐ de wàiyī guà zài tīng li 你的外衣挂在厅里; (*for drying*) liàng 晾; drying clothes liàng yīfu 晾衣服; (*when phoning*) guàduàn 挂断

happen /'hæpən/ *vb* (*to occur*) fāshēng 发生; what happened? fāshēng shénme shì le? 发生什么事了?; the accident happened last week zhège shìgù shì shàng xīngqī fāshēng de 这个事故是上星期发生的；(to affect someone) **what happened to you?** nǐ zěnme le? 你怎么了？; **something odd happened to me** wǒ yùdàole yí jiàn qíguài de shì 我遇到了一件奇怪的事；(to chance) pèngqiǎo 碰巧；**I happened to be out when he came** tā lái de shíhou, wǒ pèngqiǎo chūqù le 他来的时候，我碰巧出去了

happy /'hæpɪ/ adj (delighted) gāoxìng de 高兴的；**to make someone happy** shǐ mǒu rén gāoxìng 使某人高兴；**they were happy to receive your letter** tāmen hěn gāoxìng shōudào nǐ de xìn 他们很高兴收到你的信；(content) mǎnyì de 满意的；**he's happy with the language course** tā duì yǔyánkè hěn mǎnyì 他对语言课很满意；(in greetings) kuàilè 快乐；**Happy Birthday!** Shēngrì kuàilè! 生日快乐!；**Happy New Year!** Xīnnián kuàilè! 新年快乐!

hard /hɑːd/ **1** adj (firm, stiff) yìng de 硬的；**the ground is hard** dì hěn yìng 地很硬；(difficult) nán de 难的；**a hard question** yí gè hěn nán de wèntí 一个很难的问题；**it's hard to explain this problem** hěn nán jiěshì zhège wèntí 很难解释这个问题；(harsh, tough) we were having a hard time during the war zhànzhēng qījiān wǒmen guòzhe jiānnán de rìzi 战争期间我们过着艰难的日子；(severe) **it's a hard blow to her** zhè duì tā shì ge chénzhòng de dǎjī 这对她是个沉重的打击 **2** adv (diligently) nǔlì de 努力地；**to work hard** nǔlì gōngzuò 努力工作；(severely) **it's raining hard** yǔ xià de hěn dà 雨下得很大

hardly /'hɑːdlɪ/ adv (not quite) bú tài 不太；**I hardly know them** wǒ bú tài rènshi tāmen 我不太认识他们；(scarcely) jīhū…bù jǐ hū 几乎…不, jiǎnzhí…bù 简直…不；**she could hardly recognize me** tā jīhū rèn bù chū wǒ lái le 她几乎认不出我来了

hardware /'hɑːdweə(r)/ n hardware (for computers) (jìsuànjī) yìngjiàn (计算机)硬件

hard-working /'hɑːdɪwɜːkɪŋ/ *adj* qínfèn de 勤奋的, nǔlì de 努力的

hare /heə(r)/ *n* a hare yì zhī yětù 一只野兔

harm /hɑːm/ *vb* to harm someone shānghài mǒu rén 伤害某人; to harm the environment sǔnhài huánjìng 损害环境

harmful /'hɑːmfʊl/ *adj* yǒuhài de 有害的

harmless /'hɑːmlɪs/ *adj* wúhài de 无害的

harp /hɑːp/ *n* a harp yí jià shùqín 一架竖琴

harvest /'hɑːvɪst/ *n* shōuhuò 收获, shōucheng 收成

hat /hæt/ *n* a hat yì dǐng màozi 一顶帽子

hate /heɪt/ *vb* (*to feel a strong dislike for*) bù xǐhuan 不喜欢; she hates pork tā bù xǐhuan zhūròu 她不喜欢猪肉; (*to feel hatred for*) hèn 恨; to hate somebody hèn mǒu rén 恨某人

hatred /'heɪtrɪd/ *n* (zēng)hèn (憎)恨

have /强 hæv;弱 həv/ **1** *vb* (*to possess or be in a special relation to*) yǒu 有; she doesn't have much money tā méiyǒu hěn duō qián 她没有很多钱; they have three children tāmen yǒu sān gè háizi 他们有 3 个孩子; (*to eat*) chī 吃; to have a sandwich chī yí kuài sānmíngzhì 吃一块三明治; to have dinner chīfàn 吃饭; (*to drink*) hē 喝; to have a glass of wine hē yì bēi jiǔ 喝一杯酒; (*to get*) I had a letter from Bob yesterday wǒ zuótiān shōudàole Bàobó de yì fēng xìn 我昨天收到了鲍勃的一封信; I'll let you have the money soon wǒ huì hěn kuài ràng nǐ nádào qián 我会很快让你拿到钱; (*to hold or organize*) jǔxíng 举行; to have a party jǔxíng yí gè jùhuì 举行一个聚会; to have a competition jǔxíng yí cì bǐsài 举行一次比赛; we had a nice day at the beach wǒmen zài hǎibiān dùguòle yúkuài de yì tiān 我们在海边度过了愉快的一天; I'll have a good time in Beijing wǒ huì zài Běijīng guò de hěn yúkuài 我会在北京过得很愉快; (*to suffer*) he had [a headache | a toothache | a stomachache...] tā [tóuténg | yáotòng | dùzi téng…] 他 [头疼 | 牙

痛│肚子疼…]！*Note that in this case*, **have** *is not translated into Chinese*；(*to catch a disease*) dé 得；**to have** [flu│cancer│heart disease...] dé [流感│癌症│心脏病…] 得；(*to get something done*) **to have the house painted** shuā fángzi 刷房子；**she had her hair cut** tā jiǎn tóufa le 她剪头发了 **2** *aux vb* **you've seen her, haven't you?** nǐ jiànguo tā, shì ba? 你见过她，是吧？；**they've already left, haven't they?** tāmen yǐjīng zǒu le, shì ba? 他们已经走了，是吧？ **3 to have to** bùdébù 不得不，bìxū 必须；**I have to** [study hard│go home│go to see a doctor] wǒ bùdébù [nǔlì xuéxí│huíjiā│qù kàn yīshēng] 我不得不 [努力学习│回家│去看医生]；**you have to come** nǐ bìxū lái 你必须来

hay /heɪ/ *n* gāncǎo 干草

hazel /'heɪzəl/ *adj* dànhèsè de 淡褐色的

hazelnut /'heɪzəlnʌt/ *n* **a hazelnut** yí gè zhēnzi 一个榛子

he /hiː/ *pron* tā 他

head /hed/ **1** *n* (*the part of the body*) tóu 头；(*the mind*) nǎozi 脑子；**he's got lots of ideas in his head** tā nǎozi li zhǔyì hěn duō 他脑子里主意很多；**a head of cabbage** yì kē juǎnxīncài 一棵卷心菜；**a head of lettuce** yì kē shēngcài 一棵生菜；(*the person in charge*) **the head of a delegation** dàibiǎotuán tuánzhǎng 代表团团长；**the head of the Chinese Department** zhōngwénxì xìzhǔrèn 中文系系主任；**a head of State** yí wèi guójiā yuánshǒu 一位国家元首 **2** *vb* (*to be in charge of*) **to head a team** shuàilǐng yí gè duì 率领一个队；(*in soccer*) **to head the ball** (yòng tóu) dǐng qiú (用头)顶球；**head for...** xiàng...qù 向…去；**the car headed for the city centre** qìchē xiàng shìzhōngxīn shǐqù 汽车向市中心驶去

headache /'hedeɪk/ *n* **he has a headache** tā tóuténg 他头疼 ！*Note that in* **have a headache**, **have** *is not translated into Chinese*；**my headache's gone** wǒ de tóuténg hǎo le 我的头疼好了

headlamp /'hedlæmp/, **headlight** /'hedlaɪt/ *n* a

headlamp /ˈhedlæm/ yí gè qiándēng 一个前灯

headline /ˈhedlaɪn/ n a headline yí gè biāotí 一个标题; to hit the headlines chéngwéi tóutiáo xīnwén 成为头条新闻; the news headlines xīnwén tíyào 新闻提要

headquarters /ˌhedˈkwɔːtəz/ n (of a company, an organization) zǒngbù 总部; (of an army) sīlìngbù 司令部

headteacher /ˈhedˈtiːtʃə(r)/ n a headteacher yí gè xiàozhǎng 一个校长

health /helθ/ n jiànkāng 健康

healthy /ˈhelθɪ/ adj (in good health) jiànkāng de 健康的; (good for the health) yǒuyìyú jiànkāng de 有益于健康的

hear /hɪə(r)/ vb to hear tīngjiàn 听见; he can't hear anything tā tīng bú jiàn rènhé shēngyīn 他听不见任何声音; I heard someone coming in wǒ tīngjiàn yǒu rén jìnlái 我听见有人进来; you can hear him practising the piano nǐ néng tīngjiàn tā liànxí gāngqín de shēngyīn 你能听见他练习钢琴的声音; (to learn, to discover) to hear the news tīngdào zhège xiāoxi 听到这个消息; I've heard about that school wǒ tīngshuōguo nàge xuéxiào 我听说过那个学校; he'd like to hear our opinions tā xiǎng tīng wǒmen de yìjian 他想听我们的意见; hear from... shōudào...de xìn 收到... 的信; have you heard from her? nǐ shōudàoguo tā de xìn ma? 你收到过她的信吗? hear of tīngshuōguo 听说过; I've never heard of the place wǒ cónglái méi tīngshuōguo nàge dìfang 我从来没听说过那个地方

heart /hɑːt/ n (part of the body) xīnzàng 心脏; (the centre) zhōngxīn 中心; right in the heart of London jiù zài Lúndūn zhōngxīn 就在伦敦中心; to learn... by heart jìzhù⋯ 记住⋯; to learn... by heart xiàlái⋯ 背下来⋯

heart attack /ˈhɑːt əˌtæk/ n a heart attack yí cì xīnzàngbìng fāzuò 一次心脏病发作

heat /hiːt/ **1** vb bǎ⋯jiārè 把⋯加热; to heat the water bǎ shuǐ jiārè 把水加热 **2** n (a high temperature, or hotness) gāowēn 高温, rè 热; I can't stand the heat in

Hong Kong wǒ shòubuliǎo Xiānggǎng de rè 我受不了香港的热；(*a degree of hotness*) rèdù 热度；the heat in the oven kǎoxiāng de rèdù 烤箱的热度；(*in a sporting contest*) a heat yí cì jìngsài 一次竞赛；heat up (*to cook*) shāorè 烧热；(*to warm up again*) chóngxīn jiārè 重新加热

heater /'hi:tə(r)/ *n* a heater yì tái jiārèqì 一台加热器

heating /'hi:tɪŋ/ *n* (*a system*) gōngnuǎn xìtǒng 供暖系统；(*providing the heat*) gōngrè 供热

heatwave /'hi:tweɪv/ *n* a heatwave yì gǔ rèlàng 一股热浪

heaven /'hevən/ *n* tiāntáng 天堂

heavy /'hevɪ/ *adj* (*in weight*) zhòng de 重的；(*in quantity, intensity*) the traffic is very heavy jiāotōng hěn yōngjǐ 交通很拥挤；a heavy smoker yí gè chōuyān hěn duō de rén 一个抽烟很多的人；to have a heavy cold dé zhòng gǎnmào 得重感冒；(*describing food*) nán xiāohuà de 难消化的；it's very heavy today jīntiān tiānqì hěn yīnchén 今天天气很阴沉；the air is heavy kōngqì hěn chènmèn 空气很沉闷

hedge /hedʒ/ *n* a hedge yì pái shùlí 一排树篱

hedgehog /'hedʒhɒg/ *n* a hedgehog yì zhī cìwei 一只刺猬

heel /hi:l/ *n* (*part of the foot*) jiǎohòugēn 脚后跟；(*part of the shoe*) hòugēn 后跟

height /haɪt/ *n* (*of a person*) shēngāo 身高；(*of a building, a tree*) gāodù 高度，gāo 高；to be afraid of heights hàipà dēnggāo 害怕登高

helicopter /'helɪkɒptə(r)/ *n* a helicopter yí jià zhíshēngjī 一架直升机

hell /hel/ *n* dìyù 地狱

hello /hə'ləʊ/ *n* hello!；(*when greeting someone*) nǐ hǎo! 你好！；(*on the phone*) wèi! 喂！

helmet /'helmɪt/ *n* a helmet yí gè tóukuī 一个头盔

help /help/ **1** *vb* to help bāngzhù 帮助；to help

someone [study | do the housework | escape...] bāngzhù mǒu rén [xuéxí | zuò jiāwù | táopǎo...] 帮助某人 [学习 | 做家务 | 逃跑...]; (to remedy) the medicine helps to cure the illness zhè zhǒng yào zhìliáo zhè zhǒng bìng 这种药治疗这种病; (at a meal) help yourselves! qǐng suíbiàn chī! 请随便吃!; I couldn't help laughing wǒ jīnbùzhù xiàole qǐlai 我禁不住笑了起来 **2** exc help! (when the speaker is in danger) jiùmìng a! 救命啊!; (when someone else is in danger) jiù rén a! 救人啊! **3** n (assistance) bāngzhù 帮助; to ask someone for help qǐng mǒu rén bāngzhù 请某人帮助; (one who assists) bāngshǒu 帮手, zhùshǒu 助手; she is quite a help to me tā shì wǒ de yí gè hǎo bāngshǒu 她是我的一个好帮手; **help out** help someone out bāngzhù mǒu rén bǎituō kùnjìng 帮助某人摆脱困境

helpful /'helpful/ adj (giving help) yǒu bāngzhù de 有帮助的; (useful) yǒuyòng de 有用的

helping /'helpɪŋ/ n a helping of food yí fèn fàn 一份饭

helpless /'helplɪs/ adj (having no one to help) méiyǒu rén bāngzhù de 没有人帮助的; she was left helpless tā bèi rēng zài nàr méiyǒu rén bāngzhù 她被扔在那儿没有人帮助; (because of weakness, ill health) gūruò de 孤弱的

hen /hen/ n a hen yì zhī mǔjī 一只母鸡

her /hɜː(r)/ **1** pron tā 她; I know her wǒ rènshi tā 我认识她 **2** det tā de 她的; I don't like her dog wǒ bù xǐhuan tā de gǒu 我不喜欢她的狗

herd /hɜːd/ n a herd of cattle yì qún niú 一群牛

here /hɪə(r)/ adv (when talking about location) zhèr 这儿, zhèli 这里; is your house far from here? nǐ de jiā lí zhèr yuǎn ma? 你的家离这儿远吗? he doesn't live here tā bú zài zhèlǐ zhù 他不在这里住; (when drawing attention) here's the post office zhè jiùshì yóujú 这就是邮局; here they are tāmen lái le 他们来了; here comes the train huǒchē lái le 火车来了; here's my telephone number zhè shì wǒ de diànhuà hàomǎ 这是我的电话号码

hers /hɜːz/ *pron* tā de 她的；the green pen is hers nà zhī lǜbǐ shì tā de 那支绿笔是她的；my room is smaller than hers wǒ de fángjiān bǐ tā de xiǎo 我的房间比她的小

herself /hɜː'self/ *pron* (*when used as a reflexive pronoun*) (tā)zìjǐ（她）自己 she's cut herself with a knife tā yòng dāo gēshāngle zìjǐ 她用刀割伤了自己；will she forgive herself? tā huì yuánliàng zìjǐ ma? 她会原谅自己吗?；(*when used for emphasis*) she said it herself tā qīnkǒu shuō de zhè jiàn shì 她亲口说的这件事；she did it all by herself zhè dōu shì tā yí gè rén zuò de 这都是她一个人做的

hesitate /'hezɪteɪt/ *vb* yóuyù 犹豫

hi /haɪ/ *exc* hi! nǐ hǎo! 你好!

hiccups /'hɪkʌps/ *n* to have hiccups dǎgér 打嗝儿

hidden /'hɪdən/ *adj* yǐncáng de 隐藏的

hide /haɪd/ *vb* (yǐn)cáng (隐)藏；she hid the money in her shoes tā bǎ qián cáng zài xié li 她把钱藏在鞋里

hi-fi /'haɪfaɪ/ *n* a hi-fi yí tào zǔhé yīnxiǎng 一套组合音响

high /haɪ/ **1** *adj* gāo de 高的；[the mountain | the price | the speed...] is high [shān | jiàgé | sùdù···] hěn gāo [山 | 价格 | 速度···] 很高；to get high grades dé gāofēn 得高分 **2** *adv* don't go any higher bié wǎng shàng qù le 别往上去了

high-rise block /haɪ raɪz 'blɒk/ *n* a high rise block yí zuò duōcéng gāolóu 一座多层高楼

high school /'haɪskuːl/ *n* a high school；(*in the US*) yì suǒ zhōngxué 一所中学；(*in Britain*) yì suǒ gāozhōng 一所高中

hijack /'haɪdʒæk/ *vb* jiéchí 劫持

hike /haɪk/ *vb* to go hiking qù túbù lǚxíng 去徒步旅行

hiking /'haɪkɪŋ/ *n* túbù lǚxíng 徒步旅行

hill /hɪl/ *n* a hill yí zuò xiǎo shān 一座小山；(*a rise in the road*) yí gè xiépō 一个斜坡

him /hɪm；弱 ɪm/ *pron* tā 他；I know him wǒ rènshi tā 我认识他

himself /hɪm'self/ *pron* (*when used as a reflexive*

pronoun）(tā) zìjǐ(他)自己；**he's cut himself with a knife** tā yòng dāo gēshāngle (tā)zìjǐ 他用刀割伤了(他)自己；**will he forgive himself?** tā huì yuánliàng zìjǐ ma? 他会原谅自己吗?；(*when used for emphasis*) **he said it himself** tā qīnkǒu shuō de zhè jiàn shì 他亲口说的这件事；**he did it all by himself** zhè dōu shì tā yí gè rén zuò de 这都是他一个人做的

hip /hɪp/ *n* túnbù 臀部

hire /'haɪə(r)/ *vb* (*to employ*) gù 雇；(*British English*) (*to rent*) zū 租；**to hire a car** zū yí liàng chē 租一辆车；(*to lend for a fee*) chūzū 出租；**they hire (out) bikes** tāmen chūzū zìxíngchē 他们出租自行车

his /hɪz/ **1** *det* tā de 他的；**I don't like his dog** wǒ bù xǐhuan tā de gǒu 我不喜欢他的狗 **2** *pron* tā de 他的；**the blue pen is his** lánsè de bǐ shì tā de 蓝色的笔是他的

history /'hɪstərɪ/ *n* lìshǐ 历史

hit /hɪt/ **1** *vb* (*to strike on purpose*) dǎ 打；**to hit someone on the head** dǎ mǒu rén de tóu 打某人的头；(*to strike accidentally*) pèng 碰；**she hit her head on a chair** tā de tóu pèng zài yì bǎ yǐzi shang 她的头碰在一把椅子上；(*to crash into*) zhuàng 撞；**to hit a wall** zhuàngdào qiáng shang 撞到墙上 **2** *n* **a hit**(*a song*) yì shǒu liúxíng gēqǔ 一首流行歌曲；(*a film or play*) yí bù fēngxíng-yìshí de zuòpǐn 一部风行一时的作品；(*in baseball*) défēn 得分；**hit back** huíjī 回击；**to hit someone back** huíjī mǒu rén 回击某人

hitchhike /'hɪtʃhaɪk/ *vb* (*to have a free lift in a vehicle*) miǎnfèi dā tārén de chē 免费搭他人的车；(*to request a free lift in a vehicle*) yāoqiú miǎnfèi dāchē 要求免费搭车

hitchhiker /'hɪtʃhaɪkə(r)/ *n* **a hitchhiker** yí gè yāoqiú miǎnfèi dāchē de rén 一个要求免费搭车的人

hoarse /hɔːs/ *adj* sīyǎ de 嘶哑的

hobby /'hɒbɪ/ *n* **a hobby** yí gè shìhào 一个嗜好

hockey /'hɒkɪ/ *n* qūgùnqiú 曲棍球

hold /həʊld/ **1** *vb* **to hold** názhe 拿着；**he held some**

keys in his hand tā shǒu li názhe yìxiē yàoshi 他手里拿着一些钥匙；to hold someone's hand wòzhe mǒu rén de shǒu 握着某人的手；(*when used to mean to have meetings, competitions, parties*) jǔxíng 举行；to hold a competition jǔxíng bǐsài 举行比赛；the party will be held in the school jùhuì jiāng zài xuéxiào jǔxíng 聚会将在学校举行；(*to detain*) kòuliú 扣留；hold someone hostage kòuliú mǒu rén zuò rénzhì 扣留某人作人质；(*to keep back*) (bǎo)liú (保)留；to hold a seat for someone wèi mǒu rén (bǎo)liú yí gè zuòwèi 为某人(保)留一个座位；(*other uses*) to hold the world record bǎochí shìjiè jìlù 保持世界纪录；to hold someone responsible yào mǒu rén fùzé 要某人负责；please hold the line! qǐng bié guàduàn (diànhuà)! 请别挂断(电话)! **2** *n* to get hold of the ball zhuāzhù qiú 抓住球；to get hold of someone zhǎodào mǒu rén 找到某人；**hold on** (*to wait*) děngyídeng 等一等；hold on tight! jǐnjǐn zhuāzhù! 紧紧抓住! hold on to the rope zhuāzhù shéngzi 抓住绳子；**hold up** (*to raise*) jǔqǐ 举起；to hold up one's hand jǔqǐ shǒu lái 举起手来；(*to delay*) to hold someone up tuōzhù mǒu rén 拖住某人；to hold up the traffic zǔsè jiāotōng 阻塞交通；(*to rob*) qiǎngjié 抢劫

hole /həʊl/ *n* a hole(*if it's a pit in the ground*) yí gè kēng 一个坑；(*if it's a round-shaped gap*) yí gè kǒng 一个孔，yí gè dòng 一个洞；(*in a wall, clothes*) yí gè kūlong 一个窟窿

holiday /ˈhɒlɪdɪ/ *n* (*British English*) (*a vacation*) a holiday yí gè jiàqī 一个假期；to go on holiday qù dùjià 去度假；(*a national or religious festival*) jiàrì 假日；a (public) holiday yí gè (gōngxiū) jiàrì 一个(公休)假日，(*British English*) (*time taken off work*) jià 假；to take two weeks' holiday xiū liǎng gè xīngqī de jià 休两个星期的假

Holland /ˈhɒlənd/ *n* Hélán 荷兰

home /həum/ **1** *n* a home (*a place to live*) yí gè jiā 一个家; (*a house*) yí gè zhùzhái 一个住宅; to leave home líkāi jiā 离开家; to work from home zài jiā shàngbān 在家上班; a home for elderly people yì suǒ yǎnglǎoyuàn 一所养老院; a home for handicapped children yí gè cánjí értóng zhī jiā 一个残疾儿童之家 **2** *adv* to go home (*to one's house*) huíjiā 回家; to one's home country huíguó 回国; on my way home zài wǒ huíjiā de lùshang 在我回家的路上; to be home (*from school, work*) dào jiā 到家; I can take you home wǒ kěyǐ sòng nǐ huíjiā 我可以送你回家 **3** at home (*in one's house*) zài jiā 在家; she's working at home tā zài jiā gōngzuò 她在家工作; he lives at home tā zài jiā zhù 他在家住; to feel at home bù jūshù 不拘束; make yourselves at home búyào jūshù 不要拘束; (*when talking about a sports team*) zài zhǔchǎng 在主场

homeless /'həumlɪs/ *adj* wújiā-kěguī de 无家可归的

homesick /'həumsɪk/ *adj* xiǎngjiā de 想家的

homework /'həumwɜ:k/ *n* zuòyè 作业

homosexual /ˌhəuməu'seksjuəl/ *n* a homosexual yí gè tóngxìngliànzhě 一个同性恋者

honest /'ɒnɪst/ *adj* chéngshí de 诚实的; (*frank, sincere*) tǎnshuài de 坦率的; to be honest, I'd rather stay here tǎnshuài de shuō, wǒ nìngyuàn dāi zài zhèr 坦率地说，我宁愿呆在这儿

honestly /'ɒnɪstlɪ/ *adv* chéngshí de 诚实地

honey /'hʌnɪ/ *n* fēngmì 蜂蜜

honeymoon /'hʌnɪmu:n/ *n* mìyuè 蜜月

hood /hud/ *n* (*to cover the head*) a hood yì dǐng dōumào 一顶兜帽; (*US English*) (*of a car*) the hood chēpéng 车篷

hoof /hu:f/ *n* a hoof yì zhī tízi 一只蹄子

hook /huk/ *n* (*for hanging clothes, pictures*) a hook yí gè gōu(zi) 一个钩(子); (*for fishing*) a hook yí gè yúgōu 一个渔钩

hooligan /'huːlɪgən/ n a hooligan yí gè liúmáng 一个流氓

hoover /'huːvə(r)/ vb (British English) to hoover the house gěi fángzi xī chén 给房子吸尘

hop /hɒp/ vb tiào 跳

hope /həʊp/ **1** vb xīwàng 希望；I hope you don't mind wǒ xīwàng nǐ bú jièyì 我希望你不介意；I hope so wǒ xīwàng rúcǐ 我希望如此 **2** n xīwàng 希望；she is my only hope tā shì wǒ de wéiyī xīwàng 她是我的唯一希望

hopeless /'həʊplɪs/ adj (without hope of success) méiyǒu xīwàng de 没有希望的；(without any ability) méiyǒu zàojiù de 没有造就的；to be hopeless at cooking zài zuòfàn fāngmiàn méiyǒu zàojiù 在做饭方面没有造就

horn /hɔːn/ n (on a car, a bus) lǎbā 喇叭；to blow a horn àn lǎbā 按喇叭；(of an animal) a horn yì zhī jiǎo 一只角；(an instrument) a horn yì bǎ hào 一把号

horoscope /'hɒrəskəʊp/ n zhànxīngshù 占星术

horrible /'hɒrəbl/ adj (exciting horror) kěpà de 可怕的，kǒngbù de 恐怖的；(very bad) zāogāo de 糟糕的，huài de 坏的

horror film /'hɒrə ˌfɪlm/ n a horror film yí bù kǒngbùpiàn 一部恐怖片

horse /hɔːs/ n a horse yì pǐ mǎ 一匹马

horseracing /'hɔːsˌreɪsɪŋ/ n sàimǎ 赛马

horseriding /'hɔːsraɪdɪŋ/ n qímǎ 骑马

hospital /'hɒspɪtl/ n a hospital yì jiā yīyuàn 一家医院；he's still in (the) hospital tā hái zài yīyuàn lǐ 他还在医院里；to be taken to (the) hospital bèi sòngjìn yīyuàn 被送进医院

host /həʊst/ n a host yí gè zhǔrén 一个主人

hostage /'hɒstɪdʒ/ n a hostage yì míng rénzhì 一名人质

hostel /'hɒstəl/ n a hostel yí gè zhāodàisuǒ 一个招待所

hostess /'həʊstɪs/ n a hostess (a female host) yí gè nǚzhǔrén 一个女主人；(in a plane) yí gè kōngzhōng xiǎojiě 一个空中小姐

hot /hɒt/ *adj* (*very warm*) rè de 热的; I'm very hot wǒ hěn rè 我很热; a hot meal yí dùn rè cān 一顿热餐; (*strong, with a lot of spices*) là de 辣的; a very hot dish yí dào hěn là de cài 一道很辣的菜

hot air balloon /ˌhɒt 'eə bəˈluːn/ *n* a hot air balloon yí gè rèqìqiú 一个热气球

hot dog /ˈhɒtˈdɒɡ/ *n* a hot dog yí gè hóngcháng miànbāo 一个红肠面包

hotel /həʊˈtel/ *n* a hotel yì jiā lǚguǎn 一家旅馆

hour /ˈaʊə(r)/ *n* an hour yí gè xiǎoshí 一个小时, yí gè zhōngtóu 一个钟头; I earn two pounds an hour wǒ yí gè xiǎoshí zhèng liǎng bàng qián 我一个小时挣两镑钱

house /haʊs/ *n* (*a building*) fángzi 房子; a house yí zuò fángzi 一座房子; (*a dwelling place*) jiā 家; to go to someone's house qù mǒu rén de jiā 去某人的家; the bike is at my house zìxíngchē zài wǒ jiālǐ 自行车在我家里

housewife /ˈhaʊswaɪf/ *n* a housewife yí gè jiātíng fùnǚ 一个家庭妇女

housework /ˈhaʊswɜːk/ *n* jiāwùhuór 家务活儿; to do the housework zuò jiāwùhuór 做家务活儿

housing estate /ˈhaʊzɪŋ ɪsˌteɪt/ (*British English*), **housing development** /ˈhaʊzɪŋ dɪˈveləpmənt/ (*US English*) *n* a housing estate yí gè zhùzháiqū 一个住宅区

hovercraft /ˈhɒvəkrɑːft/ *n* a hovercraft yì sōu qìdiànchuán 一艘气垫船

how /haʊ/ *adv* (*in what way*) zěnme 怎么, zěnyàng 怎样; how did you find us? nǐ zěnme zhǎodào wǒmen de? 你怎么找到我们的?; I know how [to swim | ride a horse | to cook a curry...] wǒ zhīdào zěnyàng [yóuyǒng | qímǎ | zuò gālí...] 我知道怎样 [游泳 | 骑马 | 做咖喱...]; (*in polite questions*) how are you? nǐ hǎo ma? 你好吗?; how is your mother? nǐ māma hǎo ma? 你妈妈好吗?; how was your holiday? nǐ jiàqī wánr de hǎo ma? 你假期玩儿得好吗?; (*in questions requiring specific information*) how long will it take? zhè yào huā duō cháng shíjiān? 这要花多长时间?; how tall are you? nǐ yǒu duō gāo? 你有多高?; how old is he? tā duōshào suì? 他多少岁? (when making a suggestion) how would you like to eat out? chūqù chīfàn zěnmeyàng? 出去吃饭怎么样?

however /hau'evə(r)/ adv (nevertheless) kěshì 可是，búguò 不过; however hard I try, I can't understand grammar bùguǎn zěnme nǔlì, wǒ yě nòng bù dǒng yǔfǎ 不管怎么努力,我也弄不懂语法

how many /hau 'meni/ 1 pron duōshào 多少; how many do you want? nǐ yào duōshǎo? 你要多少?; how many of you are there? nǐmen yǒu duōshǎo rén? 你们有多少人? 2 det duōshào 多少; how many children are going on the trip? yǒu duōshào háizi qù lǚxíng? 有多少孩子去旅行?

how much /hau 'mʌtʃ/ 1 pron duōshào 多少; how much does it come to? yígòng duōshǎo? 一共多少? 2 det duōshào 多少; how much money do you have left? nǐ hái shèng duōshǎo qián? 你还剩多少钱?

huge /hju:dʒ/ adj jùdà de 巨大的

human being /ˌhju:mən 'bi:ɪŋ/ n rén 人

humour /'hju:mə(r)/ (British English), **humor** (US English) n yōumò 幽默; to have a sense of humour yǒu yōumògǎn 有幽默感

hundred /'hʌndrəd/ num one hundred, a hundred yìbǎi 100; three hundred sānbǎi 300; five hundred and fifty dollars wǔbǎi wǔshí měiyuán 550 美元; about a hundred people dàyuē yìbǎi rén 大约一百人

hungry /'hʌŋgrɪ/ adj è de 饿的; I'm very hungry wǒ hěn è 我很饿

hunt /hʌnt/ vb dǎliè 打猎; to go hunting qù dǎliè 去打猎

hurdles /'hɜ:dlz/ n kuàlán 跨栏

hurrah /hʊ'rɑ:/, **hurray** /hʊ'reɪ/ n (also exc) hurrah! hǎo wa! 好哇!

hurry /'hʌrɪ/ **1** vb gǎnjǐn 赶紧；hurry home! gǎnjǐn huíjiā! 赶紧回家！；to hurry someone cuī mǒu rén 催某人 **2** n be in a hurry hěn cōngmáng 很匆忙；there's no hurry bú yòng zháojí 不用着急；hurry up gǎnjǐn 赶紧

hurt /hɜːt/ vb (to injure) I hurt myself wǒ shòule shāng 我受了伤；she hurt her leg tā de tuǐ shòule shāng 她的腿受了伤；(to be painful) téng 疼；my throat hurts wǒ de sǎngzi téng 我的嗓子疼；that hurts nà hěn téng 那很疼；(to upset) shānghài 伤害；to hurt someone's feelings shānghài mǒu rén de gǎnqíng 伤害某人的感情

husband /'hʌzbənd/ n zhàngfu 丈夫

Ii

I /aɪ/ pron wǒ 我；Mr. Li and I are going to Hong Kong tomorrow wǒ hé Lǐ xiānsheng míngtiān qù Xiānggǎng 我和李先生明天去香港

ice /aɪs/ n bīng 冰

ice cream /aɪs 'kriːm/ n an ice cream yí gè bīngqílín 一个冰淇淋

ice hockey /'aɪs ˌhɒkɪ/ n bīngqiú 冰球

ice rink /'aɪs rɪŋk/ n an ice rink yí gè huábīngchǎng 一个滑冰场

ice-skate /'aɪsskeɪt/ n a pair of ice-skates yì shuāng bīngxié 一双冰鞋

ice-skating /'aɪsskeɪtɪŋ/ n huábīng 滑冰

icing /'aɪsɪŋ/ n tángshuāng 糖霜

ID /aɪ 'diː/, **identity card** n an identity card yí gè shēnfènzhèng 一个身份证

idea /aɪ'dɪə/ n an idea (a thought) yì zhǒng sīxiǎng 一种思想；(a view) yì zhǒng kànfǎ 一种看法；(a plan) yí gè zhǔyi 一个主意；what a good idea! duōme hǎo de zhǔ yi a! 多么好的主意啊！

多么好的主意啊！；I've got no idea how much it costs
wǒ bù zhīdào zhè yào duōshǎo qián 我不知道这要多少钱

idiot /'ɪdɪət/ n an idiot yí gè báichī 一个白痴，yí gè shǎzi
一个傻子

if /ɪf/ conj (on condition that) rúguǒ 如果；you'll get
good marks if you study hard rúguǒ nǐ nǔlì xuéxí, nǐ huì
qǔdé hǎo chéngjì 如果你努力学习，你会取得好成绩；(in
case that) yàoshì 要是；we won't go if it rains yàoshì
xiàyǔ, wǒmen jiù bú qù 要是下雨，我们就不去；
(supposing that) jiǎrú 假如，yàoshì 要是；I would
travel if I were rich jiǎrú wǒ hěn yǒuqián, wǒ huì qù
lǚxíng 假如我很有钱，我会去旅行；I'd refuse if I were
you rúguǒ wǒ shì nǐ, wǒ jiù jùjué shì wǒ是你，我就拒
绝！Note that the conditional clause introduced by if
precedes the main clause in Chinese；(whether)shìfǒu 是
否；I don't know if they'll come wǒ bù zhīdào tāmen
shìfǒu huì lái 我不知道他们是否会来！Note that shìfǒu
是否 appears after the subject of the subordinate clause in
Chinese.

ignore /ɪɡ'nɔː(r)/ vb to ignore someone bù lǐ mǒu rén 不
理某人，to ignore a problem hūshì yí gè wèntí 忽视一个
问题

ill /ɪl/ adj bìng de 病的，yǒu bìng de 有病的；she is ill tā
bìng le 她病了

illegal /ɪ'liːɡəl/ adj fēifǎ de 非法的

illness /'ɪlnɪs/ n an illness yì zhǒng (jí)bìng 一种(疾)病

imagination /ɪˌmædʒɪ'neɪʃn/ n (the act of imagining)
xiǎngxiàng 想象；this is only my imagination zhè zhǐ
shì wǒ de xiǎngxiàng 这只是我的想象；(the ability to
imagine) xiǎngxiànglì 想象力；he has no imagination
tā méiyǒu xiǎngxiànglì 他没有想象力

imagine /ɪ'mædʒɪn/ vb (to form an image in one's mind)
xiǎngxiàng 想象；(to think vainly or falsely) shèxiǎng 设
想

imitate /'ɪmɪteɪt/ vb mófǎng 模仿，fǎngxiào 仿效

immediately /ɪˈmiːdɪətlɪ/ adv lìjí 立即，mǎshàng 马上

impatient /ɪmˈpeɪʃənt/ adj bú nàifán de 不耐烦的；to get impatient biàn de bú nàifán 变得不耐烦

import /ɪmˈpɔːt/ vb jìnkǒu 进口

important /ɪmˈpɔːtənt/ adj zhòngyào de 重要的；it is important to keep fit bǎochí jiànkāng hěn zhòngyào 保持健康很重要

impossible /ɪmˈpɒsəbl/ adj bù kěnéng de 不可能的；it's impossible to change this plan gǎibiàn zhège jìhuà shì bù kěnéng de 改变这个计划是不可能的

impress /ɪmˈpres/ vb I'm impressed by his speech tā de jiǎnghuà gěi wǒ liúxià hěn shēn de yìnxiàng 他的讲话给我留下了很深的印象

impression /ɪmˈpreʃən/ n yìnxiàng 印象；she made a good impression on me tā gěi wǒ liúxià hěn hǎo de yìnxiàng 她给我留下了很好的印象

improve /ɪmˈpruːv/ vb (to make better) tígāo 提高，gǎishàn 改善；to improve living conditions gǎishàn shēnghuó tiáojiàn 改善生活条件；to improve one's spoken Chinese tígāo zìjǐ de Hànyǔ kǒuyǔ shuǐpíng 提高自己的汉语口语水平；(to get better) hǎozhuǎn 好转；the economic situation is improving jīngjì xíngshì zhèngzài hǎozhuǎn 经济形势正在好转

improvement /ɪmˈpruːvmənt/ n gǎijìn 改进，gǎishàn 改善

in /ɪn/ ! Often in occurs in combination with verbs, for example; drop in, fit in, move in, etc. To find the correct translations for this type of verb, look up the separate dictionary entries at drop, fit, move, etc. **1** prep (inside) zài…li 在…里 ；in the house zài fángzi li 在房子里；there is a letter in the envelope (zài) xìnfēng li yǒu yì fēng xìn (在)信封里有一封信；(when talking about being in print) zài…shang 在…上；the woman in the photograph (zài) zhàopiàn shang de nǚrén (在)照片上的女人；I saw your picture in the newspaper wǒ zài bàozhǐ shang kàndào le nǐ de zhàopiàn 我在报纸上看到了你的照片；**in the world** zài shìjiè shang 在世界上！*Note that when* **zài 在** *appears at the beginning of a sentence or when a phrase introduced by* **zài 在** *is used to modify a noun phrase, the use of* **zài 在** *is optional；*（*at*）zài 在；**I am learning Japanese in school** wǒ zài xuéxiào xuéxí Rìyǔ 我在学校学习日语；**in the countryside** zài nóngcūn 在农村；（*when talking about countries or cities*）zài 在；**to live in** [America | Japan | Shanghai...] zhù zài [Měiguó | Rìběn | Shànghǎi...] 住在 [美国 | 日本 | 上海...]；（*dressed in*）chuānzhe 穿着；**in a skirt** chuānzhe qúnzi 穿着裙子；**to be dressed in black** chuānzhe hēisè de yīfu 穿着黑色的衣服；（*showing the way in which something is done*）yòng 用；**to write a letter in Chinese** yòng Zhōngwén xiěxìn 用中文写信；**we paid in cash** wǒmen yòng xiànjīn fùqián 我们用现金付钱；**in ink** yòng mòshuǐ 用墨水；（*during*）zài 在；**in October** zài shíyuè 在 10 月；**in the night** zài yèlǐ 在夜里；**in the morning** zài zǎochén 在早晨；（*within*）guò 过，zài...zhīnèi 在...之内；**I'll be ready in ten minutes** wǒ zài shí fēnzhōng zhīnèi huì zhǔnbèi hǎo 我在 10 分钟之内会准备好；**she'll be back in half an hour** tā guò bàn xiǎoshí huílái 她过半小时回来；（*other uses*）**to stay in the rain** dāi zài yǔ zhōng 呆在雨中；**she is in her twenties** tā èrshí jǐ suì 她二十几岁；**one in ten** shí gè dāngzhōng yǒu yí gè 10 个当中有一个；**to cut an apple in two** bǎ yí gè píngguǒ qiēchéng liǎng bàn 把一个苹果切成两半 **2** *adv*（*at home*）zài jiā 在家；（*available*）zài 在；**tell her I'm not in** gàosu tā wǒ bú zài 告诉她我不在；（*arrived*）**the train is in** huǒchē dào le 火车到了

inch /ɪntʃ/ *n* **an inch** yì yīngcùn 一英寸！*Note that an inch= 2.54 cm.*

include /ɪnˈkluːd/ *vb* bāokuò 包括；**service is included in the bill** zhàngdān li bāokuò fúwùfèi 账单里包括服务费

including /ɪnˈkluːdɪŋ/ *prep* bāokuò 包括；they were all invited,including the children tāmen dōu shòudào yāoqǐng,bāokuò háizi 他们都受到邀请，包括孩子

income /ˈɪŋkʌm/ *n* an income yí fèn shōurù 一份收入

income tax /ˈɪŋkʌm tæks/ *n* suǒdéshuì 所得税

inconvenient /ˌɪnkənˈviːnjənt/ *adj* bù fāngbiàn de 不方便的

increase /ɪnˈkriːs/ **1** *vb* zēngjiā 增加；to increase by 10% zēngjiā bǎi fēn zhī shí zēngjiā 10% **2** /ˈɪnkriːs/ *n* zēngjiā 增加

incredible /ɪnˈkredəbl/ *adj* nányǐzhìxìn de 难以置信的

independent /ˌɪndɪˈpendənt/ *adj* dúlì de 独立的

India /ˈɪndjə/ *n* Yìndù 印度

Indian /ˈɪndjən/ **1** *adj* Yìndù de 印度的 **2** *n* (*the people from India*) Yìndùrén 印度人；(*the indigenous people of America*) Yìndìānrén 印地安人

indicate /ˈɪndɪkeɪt/ *vb* (*to show*) biǎoshì 表示；(*to point out*) zhǐchū 指出

indifferent /ɪnˈdɪfərənt/ *adj* (*unconcerned*) bú zàihu de 不在乎的，bù guānxīn de 不关心的；(*of a middle quality*) zhìliàng bù gāo de 质量不高的

indigestion /ˌɪndɪˈdʒestʃən/ *n* to have indigestion xiāohuà bùliáng 消化不良

individual /ˌɪndɪˈvɪdjuəl/ **1** *adj* (*pertaining to one only or to each one separately*) gèrén de 个人的；(*separate*) gèbié de 个别的 **2** *n* an individual yí gè rén 一个人

indoor /ˈɪndɔː(r)/ *adj* shìnèi de 室内的；an indoor swimming pool yí gè shìnèi yóuyǒngchí 一个室内游泳池

indoors /ɪnˈdɔːz/ *adv* zài wū li 在屋里；go indoors jìn wū li 进屋里

industrial /ɪnˈdʌstriəl/ *adj* gōngyè de 工业的

industry /ˈɪndəstrɪ/ *n* gōngyè 工业

inevitable /ɪnˈevɪtəbl/ *adj* bùkě bìmiǎn de 不可避免的

infant school /ˈɪnfənt skuːl/ *n* (*British English*)；an infant school yí gè xuéqiánbān 一个学前班

infection /ɪnˈfekʃən/ n (the act of tainting) gǎnrǎn 感染; (the act of imparting some disease) chuánrǎn 传染; (an infectious disease) chuánrǎnbìng 传染病

influence /ˈɪnfluəns/ **1** n an influence yì zhǒng yǐngxiǎng 一种影响; to have influence over … yǒu yǐngxiǎng 对 … 有影响 **2** vb yǐngxiǎng 影响; to influence someone yǐngxiǎng mǒu rén 影响某人; to be influenced by someone shòudào mǒu rén de yǐngxiǎng 受到某人的影响

inform /ɪnˈfɔːm/ vb (to tell) gàosu 告诉; to inform them of the news gàosu tāmen zhège xiāoxi 告诉他们这个消息; (to impart knowledge) tōngzhī 通知; to inform the police of the accident bǎ zhège shìgù tōngzhī gěi jǐngchá 把这个事故通知给警察; to keep someone informed suíshí xiàng mǒu rén bàogào 随时向某人报告

informal /ɪnˈfɔːml/ adj (describing a person, a person's manner) suíbiàn de 随便的; (describing a word, a language) rìcháng shǐyòng de 日常使用的; (describing a discussion or an interview) fēi zhèngshì de 非正式的

information /ˌɪnfəˈmeɪʃən/ n a piece of information yì tiáo xiāoxi 一条消息; thank you for your information xièxie nǐ gàosù wǒ zhè tiáo xìnxī 谢谢你告诉我这条信息

information desk /ˌɪnfəˈmeɪʃən ˌdesk/ n wènxùnchù 问讯处

information technology /ˌɪnfəˈmeɪʃən tekˌnɒlədʒi/ n xìnxī jìshù 信息技术

ingredient /ɪnˈɡriːdjənt/ n an ingredient yì zhǒng pèiliào 一种配料

inhabitant /ɪnˈhæbɪtənt/ n an inhabitant yí gè jūmín 一个居民

injection /ɪnˈdʒekʃən/ n an injection yì zhī zhùshèjì 一支注射剂; to give someone an injection gěi mǒu rén dǎ yì zhēn 给某人打一针

injured /ˈɪndʒəd/ adj shòushāng de 受伤的

injury /ˈɪndʒəri/ n sǔnshāng 损伤, shāng 伤

ink /ɪŋk/ *n* mòshuǐ 墨水

innocent /'ɪnəsənt/ *adj* (*not legally guilty*) wúzuì de 无罪的; (*harmless*) wúhài de 无害的; (*naïve*) tiānzhēn de 天真的; (*ignorant of evil*) yòuzhì de 幼稚的

inquiry /ɪn'kwaɪərɪ/ *n* (*a question*) xúnwèn 询问, dǎting 打听; (*an investigation*) diàochá 调查; (*a search for knowledge*) tànjiū 探究

insect /'ɪnsekt/ *n* an insect yí gè kūnchóng 一个昆虫

inside /ɪn'saɪd/ **1** *prep* zài … lǐmiàn 在…里面; inside the house zài fángzi lǐmiàn 在房子里面 **2** *adv* lǐmiàn 里面; he's inside tā zài lǐmiàn 他在里面; I looked inside wǒ xiàng lǐmiàn kàn 我向里面看; let's bring the chairs inside wǒmen bǎ yǐzi nádào lǐmiàn qù ba 我们把椅子拿到里面去吧 **3** *n* lǐmiàn 里面; the inside of the house fángzi lǐmiàn 房子里面 **4** *adj* lǐmiàn de 里面的 **5** inside out to put one's shirt on inside out bǎ chènshān chuānfǎn le 把衬衫穿反了

inspect /ɪn'spekt/ *vb* (*to examine*) jiǎnchá 检查; (*to look at officially*) shìchá 视查; (*to look at ceremonially*) jiǎnyuè 检阅; the president inspected the guard of honour zǒngtǒng jiǎnyuèle yízhàngduì 总统检阅了仪仗队

inspector /ɪn'spektə(r)/ *n* an inspector (*an official officer*) yí gè jiǎncháyuán 一个检察员; (*one who inspects officially*) yí gè shìcháyuán 一个视察员; (*one who inspects ceremonially*) yí gè jiǎnyuèzhě 一个检阅者

instantly /'ɪnstəntlɪ/ *adv* lìjí 立即

instead /ɪn'sted/ **1** instead of (*rather than*) ér búshì 而不是; he hired a van instead of a car tā zūle yí liàng huòchē ér búshì yí liàng jiàochē 他租了一辆货车而不是一辆轿车; instead of working he watched TV tā kàn diànshì ér búshì gōngzuò 他看电视而不是工作; (*in place of*) dàitì 代替; use oil instead of butter yòng yóu dàitì huángyóu 用油代替黄油; his wife came instead of him tā tàitai dàitì tā lái le 他太太代替他来了 **2** *adv* I don't feel like going to the cinema—let's stay at home instead wǒ bù xiǎng qù kàn diànyǐng—zánmen dāi zài jiāli ba 我不想去看电影—咱们呆在家里吧

instruction /ɪn'strʌkʃən/ n an instruction yí xiàng zhǐshì 一项指示, yí xiàng mìnglìng 一项命令; to give someone instructions to check the baggage zhǐshì mǒu rén jiǎnchá xíngli 指示某人检查行李; instructions for use shǐyòng shuōmíng 使用说明

instrument /'ɪnstrumənt/ n an instrument (an indicating device) yí gè yíqì 一个仪器; (a tool) yí jiàn gōngjù 一件工具; (for hospital operations) yí jiàn qìxiè 一件器械; (for playing music) yí jiàn yuèqì 一件乐器

insult /ɪn'sʌlt/ vb wǔrǔ 侮辱

insurance /ɪn'ʃuərəns/ n bǎoxiǎn 保险

insure /ɪn'ʃuə(r)/ vb bǎoxiǎn 保险; is your car insured? nǐ de qìchē bǎoxiǎn le ma? 你的汽车保了险了吗?

intelligent /ɪn'telɪdʒənt/ adj cōngmíng de 聪明的

intend /ɪn'tend/ vb he intends to [leave|learn Cantonese| travel abroad...] tā dǎsuàn [zǒu| xué Guǎngdōnghuà| qù guówài lǚxíng...] 他打算 [走|学广东话|去国外旅行...]

intense /ɪn'tens/ adj (when describing a pain) jùliè de 剧烈的; (when describing feelings) qiángliè de 强烈的; (when describing an earnestly or deeply emotional person or manner) rèqiè de 热切的

intensive care /ɪn,tensɪv 'keə(r)/ n to be in intensive care jiēshòu tèbié jiānhù 接受特别监护

interest /'ɪntrɪst/ **1** n (enthusiasm) xìngqù 兴趣; to have an interest in music duì yīnyuè gǎn xìngqù 对音乐感兴趣; (premium paid for money borrowed from or saved in a bank) lìxī 利息; (benefit) lìyì 利益 **2** vb to interest somebody shǐ mǒu rén gǎn xìngqù 使某人感兴趣

interested /'ɪntrɪstɪd/ adj gǎn xìngqù de 感兴趣的; to be interested in [politics | sports | painting...] duì [zhèngzhì| tǐyù| huìhuà...] gǎn xìngqù 对 [政治|体育|绘画...] 感兴趣; are you interested? nǐ gǎn xìngqù ma? 你感兴趣

趣吗？

interesting /'ɪntrɪstɪŋ/ adj yǒuqù de 有趣的，yǒuyìsi de 有意思的

interfere /ɪntə'fɪə(r)/ vb (to get involved in) gānshè 干涉；to interfere in someone's business gānshè mǒu rén de shì 干涉某人的事；(to have a bad effect on) fáng'ài 妨碍；it's going to interfere with his work zhè huì fáng'ài tā de gōngzuò 这会妨碍他的工作

intermission /ɪntə'mɪʃn/ n jiànxiē 间歇，xiūxi 休息

international /ɪntə'næʃənəl/ adj guójì de 国际的

internet /'ɪntənet/ n the internet hùliánwǎng 互联网，yīntèwǎng 因特网

interpreter /ɪn'tɜːprɪtə(r)/ n an interpreter yí gè fānyì 一个翻译，yí gè kǒuyì 一个口译

interrupt /ɪntə'rʌpt/ vb (to break in upon someone's action, speech, etc.) dǎduàn 打断；(to disturb by breaking in upon) dǎrǎo 打扰；(to stop continuity in) zhōngduàn 中断

interval /'ɪntəvəl/ n (in time) jiàngé 间隔；at regular intervals měi gé yídìng shíjiān 每隔一定时间；(at a location)jiàngé 间隔；at regular intervals měi gé yídìng jùlí 每隔一定距离；(British English) (during a play, a show)mùjiān xiūxi 幕间休息

interview /'ɪntəvjuː/ **1** n an interview (for a job)yí cì miànshì 一次面试；(with a journalist) yí cì cǎifǎng 一次采访 **2** vb to interview someone (if it's an employer) miànshì mǒu rén 面试某人；(if it's a journalist) cǎifǎng mǒu rén 采访某人；(if it's the police) shěnwèn mǒu rén 审问某人

intimidate /ɪn'tɪmɪdeɪt/ vb dònghè 恫吓，kǒnghè 恐吓

into /'ɪntuː/ prep(when talking about a location) to walk into the garden zǒu jìn huāyuán 走进花园；to get into a car jìndào qìchē li 进到汽车里；to get into bed shàngchuáng 上床；(indicating a change) chéng 成；to translate a letter into French bǎ yì fēng xìn fānyì chéng Fǎwén 把一封信翻译成法文；to turn someone into a frog bǎ mǒu rén biànchéng yì zhī qīngwā 把某人变成一只青蛙

introduce /ˌɪntrəˈdjuːs/ vb (to bring in) to introduce a new technique yǐnjìn yí xiàng xīn jìshù 引进一项新技术；(when people meet , or on radio or television)jièshào 介绍；he introduced me to Peter tā bǎ wǒ jièshào gěi Bǐdé 他把我介绍给彼得；to introduce a programme jièshào yí gè jiémù 介绍一个节目

invade /ɪnˈveɪd/ vb qīnfàn 侵犯，qīnrù 侵入

invent /ɪnˈvent/ vb fāmíng 发明

invention /ɪnˈvenʃən/ n an invention yí xiàng fāmíng 一项发明

investigate /ɪnˈvestɪgeɪt/ vb diàochá 调查

investigation /ɪnˌvestɪˈgeɪʃən/ n an investigation yí xiàng diàochá 一项调查

invisible /ɪnˈvɪzəbl/ adj kàn bú jiàn de 看不见的

invitation /ˌɪnvɪˈteɪʃən/ n (the act of inviting) yāoqǐng 邀请；(a written form) qǐngtiě 请帖，qǐngjiǎn 请柬；an invitation yí fèn qǐngtiě 一份请帖，yí fèn qǐngjiǎn 一份请柬

invite /ɪnˈvaɪt/ vb yāoqǐng 邀请；to invite someone to dinner yāoqǐng mǒu rén chīfàn 邀请某人吃饭

involve /ɪnˈvɒlv/ vb to be involved in an accident juǎnrù yí cì shìgù 卷入一次事故；this activity involves both teachers and students zhè xiàng huódòng bāokuò lǎoshī hé xuésheng 这项活动包括老师和学生

Ireland /ˈaɪələnd/ n Ài'ěrlán 爱尔兰

Irish /ˈaɪrɪʃ/ **1** adj Ài'ěrlán de 爱尔兰的 **2** n (the people) Ài'ěrlánrén 爱尔兰人；(the language) Ài'ěrlányǔ 爱尔兰语

iron /ˈaɪən/ **1** n iron tiě 铁；an iron yí gè yùndǒu 一个熨斗 **2** vb yùn 熨

island /ˈaɪlənd/ n an island yí gè dǎo(yǔ) 一个岛(屿)

it /ɪt/ pron where is it? zài nǎr? 在哪儿?；who is it?

shéi (a)? 谁(啊)?; **it's me** (shì) wǒ (a) (是)我(啊); **it's a large school** zhè shì yí gè hěn dà de xuéxiào 这是一个很大的学校; **it is** [difficult | easy | interesting...] **to learn Chinese** xuéxí Zhōngwén [hěn nán | hěn róngyì | hěn yǒuyìsi...] 学习中文 [很难 | 很容易 | 很有意思...]; **it doesn't matter** méiguānxi 没关系; **it's** [cold | warm | mild...] (tiānqì) [hěn lěng | hěn rè | hěn nuǎnhuo...] (天气) [很冷 | 很热 | 很暖和...]; **I've heard about it** wǒ tīngshuōle zhè jiàn shì 我听说了这件事

Italian /ɪˈtæljən/ **1** adj Yìdàlì de 意大利的 **2** n (the people) Yìdàlìrén 意大利人; (the language) Yìdàlìyǔ 意大利语, Yìdàlìwén 意大利文

Italy /ˈɪtəlɪ/ n Yìdàlì 意大利

itchy /ˈɪtʃɪ/ adj **my leg is itchy** wǒ de tuǐ fāyǎng 我的腿发痒

its /ɪts/ det tā de 它的; **its** [nose | tail | eyes] tā de [bízi | wěiba | yǎnjīng] 它的 [鼻子 | 尾巴 | 眼睛]

itself /ɪtˈself/ pron (when used as a reflexive pronoun) (tā) zìjǐ (它)自己; **the dog is going to wash itself** zhè zhī gǒu yào gěi (tā) zìjǐ xǐzǎo 这只狗要给(它)自己洗澡; (when used for emphasis) **the car itself was not damaged** chē běnshēn méiyǒu sǔnhuài 车本身没有损坏; **the heating comes on by itself** nuǎnqì zìdòng kāi le 暖气自动开了

Jj

jacket /ˈdʒækɪt/ n **a jacket** yí jiàn duǎnshàngyī 一件短上衣; (gathered at the waist) yí jiàn jiákè 一件夹克

jail /dʒeɪl/ n **a jail** yì suǒ jiānyù 一所监狱

jam /dʒæm/ n guǒjiàng 果酱

January /ˈdʒænjʊərɪ/ n **January** yīyuè 一月

Japan /dʒə'pæn/ n Rìběn 日本

Japanese /ˌdʒæpə'niːz/ **1** adj Rìběn de 日本的 **2** n (the people) Rìběnrén 日本人；(the language) Rìwén 日文

jaw /dʒɔː/ n è 颚

jazz /dʒæz/ n juéshìyuè 爵士乐

jealous /'dʒeləs/ adj jìdu de 忌妒的；dùjì de 妒忌的；he is jealous of her tā jìdu tā 他忌妒她

jeans /dʒiːnz/ n niúzǎikù 牛仔裤

jeer /dʒɪə(r)/ vb to jeer someone cháoxiào mǒu rén 嘲笑某人

jelly /'dʒelɪ/ n (US English) (jam) guǒjiàng 果酱；(British English) (a gelatinized dessert) guǒdòng 果冻

Jesus /'dʒiːzəs/ n Yēsū 耶稣

jet /dʒet/ n a jet (an aircraft) yí jià pēnqìshì fēijī 一架喷气式飞机

jewellery /'dʒuːəlrɪ/ (British English), **jewelry** (US English) n zhūbǎo 珠宝；a piece of jewellery yí jiàn zhūbǎo 一件珠宝

Jewish /'dʒuːɪʃ/ adj Yóutàirén de 犹太人的

jigsaw puzzle /'dʒɪgsɔː ˌpʌzl/ n a jigsaw puzzle yí gè pīntú wánjù 一个拼图玩具

job /dʒɒb/ n (work) gōngzuò 工作；a job yí gè gōngzuò 一个工作；to look for a job zhǎo gōngzuò 找工作；(a task) rènwu 任务；a job yí xiàng rènwu 一项任务

jogging /'dʒɒgɪŋ/ n mànpǎo 慢跑

join /dʒɔɪn/ vb (become a member of) cānjiā 参加，jiārù 加入；to join a club cānjiā yí gè jùlèbù 参加一个俱乐部；to join a company jiārù yí gè gōngsī 加入一个公司；(meet up with) I'll join you for lunch tomorrow míngtiān wǒ hé nǐmen yìqǐ chī wǔfàn 明天我和你们一起吃午饭；to join the army cānjūn 参军；**join in** to join in a game cānjiā bǐsài 参加比赛

joke /dʒəʊk/ **1** n a joke yí gè wánxiào 一个玩笑，yí gè xiàohua 一个笑话 **2** vb kāi wánxiào 开玩笑

journalist /'dʒɜːnəlɪst/ n a journalist yí gè jìzhě 一个记者

journey /'dʒɜːnɪ/ n a journey yí cì lǚxíng 一次旅行；to go on a journey qù lǚxíng 去旅行

joy /dʒɔɪ/ n huānlè 欢乐，lèqù 乐趣

judge /dʒʌdʒ/ **1** n a judge (in a court) yí gè fǎguān 一个法官；(in competitions) yí gè cáipàn 一个裁判 **2** vb (in a court) shěnpàn 审判；(in competitions) píngpàn 评判；(to determine the truth) duàndìng 断定

judo /'dʒuːdəʊ/ n róudào 柔道

jug /dʒʌg/ n a jug yí gè guànzi 一个罐子

juice /dʒuːs/ n zhī 汁；fruit juice guǒzhī 果汁

July /dʒuˈlaɪ/ n qīyuè 七月

jump /dʒʌmp/ vb tiào 跳；the children were jumping on the bed háizimen zài chuáng shang tiào 孩子们在床上跳；to jump across the stream tiàoguò xiǎohé 跳过小河；to jump a rope tiàoshéng 跳绳；to jump out of the window tiàodào chuāng wài qù 跳到窗外去；to jump the queue (British English) chāduì 插队

jumper /'dʒʌmpə(r)/ n (British English) a jumper yí jiàn tàotóushān 一件套头衫

June /dʒuːn/ n liùyuè 六月

junior high school /ˌdʒuːnjə ˈhaɪ skuːl/ n (US English) a junior high school yì suǒ chūjí zhōngxué 一所初级中学

junior school /ˌdʒuːnjə ˈskuːl/ n (British English) a junior school yì suǒ xiǎoxué 一所小学

jury /'dʒʊərɪ/ n (in a court) péishěntuán 陪审团；(in a competition) píngwěihuì 评委会

just¹ /'dʒʌst/ adv (very recently) gāng 刚；I have just [arrived | seen | received the letter...] wǒ gāng [dào | kànjiàn tā | shōudào xìn...] 我刚 [到 | 看见他 | 收到信...]；I had just turned on the TV wǒ gāng dǎkāi diànshìjī 我刚打开电视机；(at this or that very moment) zhènghǎo 正好；I was just about to phone you wǒ zhènghǎo yào gěi nǐ dǎ diànhuà 我正好要给你打电话；I arrived just as he was leaving tā zhènghǎo yào zǒu de shíhou, wǒ dào le 他正好要走的时候，我到了；（only）jǐnjǐn 仅仅，zhǐbúguò 只不过；just two days ago jǐnjǐn liǎng tiān yǐqián 仅仅两天以前；he's just a child tā zhǐbúguò shì ge háizi 他只不过是个孩子；（barely）I got there just in time wǒ chàyìdiǎnr méi ànshí dào nàr 我差一点儿没按时到那儿；she's just 18 tā gānggāng shíbā suì 她刚刚18岁；（when comparing）she is just as intelligent as he is tā hé tā yíyàng cōngmíng 她和他一样聪明；（immediately）jiù 就；just before the weekend jiù zài zhōumò yǐqián 就在周末以前

just² /dʒʌst/ adj（righteous）zhèngyì de 正义的；（impartial, fair）gōngzhèng de 公正的，gōngpíng de 公平的

justice /'dʒʌstɪs/ n（rightness）zhèngyì 正义；（impartiality）gōngzhèng 公正，gōngpíng 公平

Kk

----

kangaroo /kæŋgə'ru:/ n a kangaroo yì zhī dàishǔ 一只袋鼠

karate /kə'rɑːti/ n Rìběn kōngshǒudào 日本空手道

keen /ki:n/ adj a keen teacher yí wèi rèxīn de lǎoshī 一位热心的老师；to be keen on swimming xǐhuan yóuyǒng 喜欢游泳

keep /ki:p/ vb（to maintain）bǎochí 保持；to keep a speed of 30 miles an hour bǎochí měi xiǎoshí sānshí yīnglǐ de sùdù 保持每小时30英里的速度；to keep bǎoliú 保留；could you keep this seat for me? qǐng nǐ gěi wǒ bǎoliú zhège zuòwèi, hǎo ma? 请你给我保留这个座位，好吗？；（to restrain from departure）liú 留；to keep someone in (the) hospital bǎ mǒu rén liú zài yīyuàn 把某人留在医院；（to preserve）（bǎo）cún 存（保）

存；we keep the wine in the cellar wǒmen bǎ jiǔ cún zài dìjiào li 我们把酒存在地窖里；(to cause to remain in a state or position) this sweater will keep you warm zhè jiàn máoyī huì shǐ nǐ nuǎnhuo 这件毛衣会使你暖和；to keep someone waiting ràng mǒu rén děnghòu 让某人等候；(to delay) dāng gē 耽搁；I won't keep you long wǒ bú huì dāng nǐ hěn jiǔ 我不会耽搁你很久；what kept you? shénme shì dāngele nǐ? 什么事耽搁了你？；(to put away) fàng 放；where do you keep the cups? nǐ bǎ chábēi fàng zài nǎr? 你把茶杯放在哪儿？；(not to break, not to reveal) to keep a promise lǚxíng nuòyán 履行诺言；to keep a secret bǎoshǒu mìmì 保守秘密，bǎomì 保密；(to continue) keep (on) bù tíng de 不停地；to keep (on) [walking | talking | running...] bù tíng de [zǒu | jiǎng | pǎo...] 不停地 [走 | 讲 | 跑...]；keep away bié kàojìn 别靠近；keep away from the fire! bié kàojìn huǒ! 别靠近火！；keep back liúxià 留下；he kept the children back after school fàngxué yǐhòu tā bǎ háizimen liúxià 放学以后他把孩子们留下；keep out to keep out of the sun búyào jiēchù yángguāng 不要接触阳光；to keep the rain out bú ràng yǔshuǐ liú jìnlái 不让雨水流进来；keep up gǎnshàng 赶上；to keep up with the other pupils gǎnshàng biédé xuésheng 赶上别的学生

kerb /kɜːb/ (British English) n lùyuán 路缘

kettle /ˈketl/ n a kettle yì bǎ shuǐhú 一把水壶

key /kiː/ n a key(of a lock) yì bǎ yàoshi 一把钥匙；(of a keyboard) yí gè jiàn 一个键

keyhole /ˈkiːhəʊl/ n a keyhole yí gè yàoshikǒng 一个钥匙孔

kick /kɪk/ vb tī 踢；to kick someone tī mǒu rén 踢某人；he didn't kick the ball tā méi tī qiú 他没踢球；kick off (in a football match) kāiqiú 开球；kick out to kick someone out bǎ mǒu rén gǎn chūqù 把某人赶出去

kid /kɪd/ n (a child) a kid yí gè xiǎoháir 一个小孩儿；(a young goat) a kid yì tóu xiǎo shānyáng 一头小山羊

kidnap /ˈkɪdnæp/ *vb* bǎngjià 绑架

kill /kɪl/ *vb* shāsǐ 杀死；kill [someone | a pig | a chicken...] shāsǐ [mǒu rén | yì tóu zhū | yì zhī jī...] 杀死 [某人 | 一头猪 | 一只鸡...]；(to kill in a certain way) sǐ …死；the poison killed lots of animals dúyào dúsǐle xǔduō dòngwù 毒药毒死了许多动物；the frost tonight will kill those plants jīnyè de yánshuāng huì dòngsǐ nàxiē zhíwù 今夜的严霜会冻死那些植物；(to kill oneself) zìshā 自杀

kilo /ˈkiːləʊ/, **kilogram(me)** /ˈkɪləʊgræm/ *n* a kilo yì gōngjīn 一公斤

kilometre /ˈkɪləʊmiːtə(r)/ (British English), **kilometer** (US English) *n* a kilometre yì gōnglǐ 一公里

kind /kaɪnd/ **1** *n* zhǒng 种；it's a kind of [fish | novel | hotel...] zhè shì yì zhǒng [yú | xiǎoshuō | lǚguǎn...] 这是一种 [鱼 | 小说 | 旅馆...]；this kind of film zhè zhǒng diànyǐng 这种电影 **2** *adj* shànliáng de 善良的, héʼǎi de 和蔼的

king /kɪŋ/ *n* a king yí gè guówáng 一个国王

kingdom /ˈkɪŋdəm/ *n* a kingdom yí gè wángguó 一个王国

kiss /kɪs/ **1** *vb* wěn 吻；to kiss someone wěn mǒu rén 吻某人 **2** *n* wěn 吻, jiēwěn 接吻

kitchen /ˈkɪtʃɪn/ *n* a kitchen yí gè chúfáng 一个厨房

kite /kaɪt/ *n* a kite yì zhī fēngzheng 一只风筝

kitten /ˈkɪtən/ *n* a kitten yì zhī xiǎomāo 一只小猫

knee /niː/ *n* xīgài 膝盖

kneel down /ˈniːl daʊn/ *vb* guìxià 跪下

knife /naɪf/ *n* a knife yì bǎ dāo 一把刀

knit /nɪt/ *vb* to knit a sweater out of wool zhī máoyī 织毛衣

knock /nɒk/ **1** *vb* qiāo 敲；to knock on the door qiāo mén 敲门 **2** *n* to get a knock on the head tóu bèi qiāole yí xià 头被敲了一下；**knock down** (in an accident) zhuàngdǎo 撞倒；(to demolish) chāichú 拆除；**knock out** (to make unconscious) dǎhūn 打昏；(in a contest) táotài 淘汰；**knock over** zhuàngdǎo 撞倒

knot /nɒt/ *n* a knot(*of a cord, a piece of ribbon or lace*) yí gè jié 一个结;(*of wood*) yí gè jiébā 一个节疤

know /nəʊ/ *vb* (*to be acquainted with*) rènshi 认识;do you know her? nǐ rènshi tā ma? 你认识她吗?(*when talking about languages*) dǒng 懂, huì 会;he knows five languages tā dǒng wǔ zhǒng yǔyán 他懂 5 种语言;(*to have the knowledge of*) zhīdào 知道;I know why he phoned wǒ zhīdao tā wèishénme dǎ diànhuà 我知道他为什么打电话;does he know about the party? tā zhīdào zhège jùhuì ma? 他知道这个聚会吗?;he knows how to [swim|ride a bike|play chess...] tā huì [yóuyǒng|qí zìxíngchē|xiàqí...] 他会 [游泳|骑自行车|下棋...];please let me know qǐng gàosu wǒ 请告诉我

knowledge /'nɒlɪdʒ/ *n* (*learning*) zhīshi 知识;(*that which is known*) zhīdào 知道, liǎojiě 了解

LI

laboratory /ləˈbɒrətərɪ/ *n* a laboratory yí gè shíyànshì 一个实验室

lace /leɪs/ *n* (*the material*) huābiānr 花边儿;(*for tying shoes*) xiédài 鞋带;to tie one's laces jì xiédài 系鞋带

lack /læk/ **1** *n* a lack of [food|money|air...] quēshǎo [shípǐn|qián|kōngqì...] 缺少 [食品|钱|空气...] **2** *vb* quēshǎo 缺少, quēfá 缺乏;he lacks confidence tā quēshǎo xìnxīn 他缺少信心

ladder /'lædə(r)/ *n* a ladder yí gè tīzi 一个梯子

lady /'leɪdɪ/ *n* a lady yí wèi nǚshì 一位女士

lake /leɪk/ *n* a lake yí gè hú 一个湖

lamb /læm/ *n* a lamb yì zhī yánggāo 一只羊羔

lamp /læmp/ *n* a lamp yì zhǎn dēng 一盏灯

lampshade /'læmpʃeɪd/ *n* a lampshade yí gè dēngzhào

一个灯罩

land /lænd/ **1** n (as opposed to the sea) lùdì 陆地; (for farming) tiándì 田地; (property) tǔdì 土地; **a piece of land** yí kuài tǔdì 一块土地; **to own land** yōngyǒu tǔdì 拥有土地 **2** vb (to fall) luò 落; (if it's a plane) jiàngluò 降落, zhuólù 着陆; (to set on shore) shàng'àn 上岸

landscape /'lændskeɪp/ n (scenery) fēngjǐng 风景, jǐngsè 景色; (a painting) fēngjǐnghuà 风景画

language /'læŋgwɪdʒ/ n **a language** yì zhǒng yǔyán 一种语言; **foreign languages** wàiyǔ 外语; **bad language** cūhuà 粗话, zānghuà 脏话

language laboratory /'læŋgwɪdʒ ləʊbɒrətərɪ/ n a language laboratory yí gè yǔyán shíyànshì 一个语言实验室

large /lɑːdʒ/ adj dà de 大的; **a large garden** yí gè dà huāyuán 一个大花园; **a large sum of money** yí dà bǐ qián 一大笔钱; **a large population** rénkǒu hěn duō 人口很多

last /lɑːst/ **1** adj (final) zuìhòu de 最后的; **the last month of the year** yì nián de zuìhòu yí gè yuè 一年的最后一个月; **the last person to leave** zuìhòu líkāi de nàge rén 最后离开的那个人; **that's the last time I saw her** nà shì wǒ zuìhòu yí cì kànjiàn tā 那是我最后一次看见她; (the most recent) **last** [time|week|month] shàng [yí cì|gè xīngqī|gè yuè] 上 [一次|个星期|个月]; **last year** qùnián 去年 **2** adv (most recently) shàng yí cì 上一次; **when I was last here** wǒ shàng yí cì lái zhèr de shíhou 我上一次来这儿的时候; (at the end) zuìhòu 最后; **I'll do the Chinese homework last** (of all) wǒ zuìhòu zuò Zhōngwén zuòyè 我最后做中文作业; **he came last in the race** tā bǐsài dé zuìhòu yìmíng 他比赛得最后一名 **3** pron (last to arrive) tāmen shì zuìhòu dào de 他们是最后到的; [the night|the day|the year] **before last** qián [tiān wǎnshang|tiān|nián] 前 [天晚上|天|年]; [the week|the month] **before last** dà shàngge [xīngqī|yuè] 大上个 [星期|月] **4** vb chíxù 持续; **the film lasts two hours**

diànyǐng chíxùle liǎng gè xiǎoshí 电影持续了两个小时

late /leɪt/ **1** adv (far into the day or night); late in the afternoon xiàwǔ wǎn xiē shíhou 下午晚些时候; late in the night shēnyè 深夜; (not on time) wǎn 晚, chí 迟; to arrive half an hour late wǎn dào bàn gè xiǎoshí 晚到半个小时 **2** adj wǎn de 晚的, chídào de 迟到的; to be late for work shàngbān chídào 上班迟到; the train was two hours late huǒchē wǎnle liǎng gè xiǎoshí 火车晚了两个小时; to make someone late shǐ mǒu rén chídào 使某人迟到

later /'leɪtə(r)/ adv I'll tell you later wǒ yǐhòu zài gàosu nǐ 我以后再告诉你; see you later huítóu jiàn 回头见, zàijiàn 再见

latest /'leɪtɪst/ adj (the most up-to-date) zuì xīn de 最新的; the latest news zuì xīn xiāoxi 最新消息; at the latest zuì chí 最迟

Latin /'lætɪn/ n Lādīngyǔ 拉丁语, Lādīngwén 拉丁文

laugh /lɑːf/ **1** vb xiào 笑; they laughed loudly tāmen dàshēng de xiào 他们大声地笑; to laugh at somebody xiàohua mǒu rén 笑话某人 **2** n xiào 笑

laundry /'lɔːndrɪ/ n (when referring to the place) xǐyīfáng 洗衣房; clean laundry xǐhǎo de yīfu 洗好的衣服; to do the laundry xǐ yīfu 洗衣服

law /lɔː/ n (a set of rules in a country) fǎlǜ 法律; to obey the law zūnshǒu fǎlǜ 遵守法律; it's against the law zhè shì wéifàn fǎlǜ de 这是违犯法律的; (physical or scientific law) dìnglǜ 定律; a law yì tiáo dìnglǜ 一条定律; (as a subject) fǎxué 法学

lawn /lɔːn/ n a lawn yí kuài cǎodì 一块草地

lawnmower /'lɔːnməʊə(r)/ n a lawnmower yí tái gēcǎojī 一台割草机

lawyer /'lɔːjə(r)/ n a lawyer yí gè lǜshī 一个律师

lay /leɪ/ vb (to put) fàng 放; to lay some newspapers on the floor bǎ yìxiē bàozhǐ fàng zài dì shang 把一些报纸放在地上; (when talking about setting the table for *dinner*) bǎi 摆；**to lay the table** bǎihǎo cānjù 摆好餐具；(*of a chicken*) xià 下；**to lay an egg** xià yí gè jīdàn 下一个鸡蛋；**lay down** fàngxià 放下；**he laid the tray down gently** tā bǎ pánzi qīngqīng fàngxià 他把盘子轻轻放下；**lay off** jiěgù 解雇

lazy /'leɪzɪ/ *adj* lǎn de 懒的，lǎnduò de 懒惰的

lead¹ /liːd/ *vb* (*to act as a head*) lǐngdǎo 领导；**to lead a political party** lǐngdǎo yí gè zhèngdǎng 领导一个政党；(*to guide*) **he led us through the forest** tā dàilǐng wǒmen chuānguò sēnlín 他带领我们穿过森林；(*in a match or a race*) lǐngxiān 领先；(*to live*) guò 过；**to lead a busy life** guò fánmáng de shēnghuó 过繁忙的生活；(*to have as a result*) dǎozhì 导致；**to lead to an accident** dǎozhì yì chǎng shìgù 导致一场事故

lead² /liːd/ *n* qiān 铅

leader /'liːdə(r)/ *n* a leader (*of a political party*) yí gè lǐngxiù 一个领袖；(*of a state*) yí gè lǐngdǎorén 一个领导人

leaf /liːf/ *n* a leaf yí piàn yèzi 一片叶子

leak /liːk/ *vb* lòu 漏；**the pipe leaks** guǎnzi lòu le 管子漏了

lean /liːn/ **1** *vb* (*to rest sideways against*) kào 靠；**to lean against the wall** kào zài qiáng shang 靠在墙上；**to lean a bicycle against the wall** bǎ zìxíngchē kào zài qiáng shang 把自行车靠在墙上；**to lean out of the window** bǎ shēnzi tànchū chuāng wài 把身子探出窗外 **2** *adj* (*not fat*) shòu de 瘦的；**lean on** yīkào 依靠

learn /lɜːn/ *vb* xué 学，xuéxí 学习；**to learn how to drive** xué kāichē 学开车

least /liːst/ **1** *adj* zuì shǎo de 最少的；**they have the least money** tāmen de zuì shǎo 他们的钱最少 **2** *pron* **it was the least I could do!** wǒ qǐmǎ kěyǐ zuò zhè jiàn shì! 我起码可以做这件事！**3** *adv* ! *Note that when the least is used to modify an adjective, the opposite of that adjective is used in Chinese, along with the word* **zuì**

最(＝ the most); the least expensive shop zuì piányi de shāngdiàn 最便宜的商店; the least difficult question zuì róngyì de wèntí 最容易的问题 **4 at least** zhìshǎo 至少; he's at least thirty tā zhìshǎo sānshí suì 他至少 30 岁

leather /'leðə(r)/ vb pí pí, pí gé 皮革

leave /li:v/ vb (to depart or go away from) líkāi 离开; she left the room tā líkāile fángjiān 她离开了房间; (to allow to remain) leave your coat here bǎ wàiyī fàng zài zhèr 把外衣放在这儿; she left the window open tā ràng chuānghu kāizhe 她让窗户开着; (to put, to give) liúxià 留下; he didn't leave a message tā méi liúxià shénme huà 他没留下什么话; she left him some money tā gěi tā liúxià yìxiē qián 她给他留下一些钱; (to put off) **leave the work until tomorrow** děngdào míngtiān zài zuò zhège gōngzuò 等到明天再做这个工作; (to forget) wàng 忘; I left my bag on the train wǒ bǎ wǒ de bāo wàng zài huǒchē shang le 我把我的包忘在火车上了; (to remain) shèngxia 剩下; **there's nothing left** shénme yě méi shèngxia le 什么也没剩下; **we've got only ten minutes left** wǒmen zhǐ shèngxia shí fēnzhōng le 我们只剩下 10 分钟了; (to let) ràng 让; I left them to clean the room wǒ ràng tāmen dǎsǎo fángjiān 我让他们打扫房间; **leave behind** liúxià 留下; he left his belongings behind tā bǎ xínglǐ liúxià le 他把行李留下了; **leave me alone** bié guǎn wǒ 别管我; **leave out** (not to show or talk about) (by accident) (deliberately) shěngqù 省去, lüèqù 略去; (to exclude) páichú 排除; **to leave out this possibility** páichú zhège kěnéngxìng 排除这个可能性; **leave over** shèngxia xià 剩下; **there is some food left over** shèngxia yìxiē fàn 剩下一些饭

lecture /'lektʃə(r)/ n a lecture (as part of the curriculum) yì táng kè 一堂课; (specially arranged) yí gè jiǎngzuò 一个讲座

left /left/ **1** n (when referring to the direction) zuǒ 左; **to**

turn to the left xiàng zuǒ zhuǎnwān 向左转弯；（ *when referring to the side* ）zuǒbian 左边；**she sat on my left** tā zuò zài wǒ de zuǒbian 她坐在我的左边 **2** *adj* zuǒ 左；**his left hand** tā de zuǒshǒu 他的左手 **3** *adv* xiàng zuǒ 向左；**to turn left** xiàng zuǒ guǎi 向左拐

leg /leg/ *noun* tuǐ 腿

legal /'liːgəl/ *adj* (*pertaining to law*) fǎlǜ de 法律的；(*lawful*) héfǎ de 合法的

leisure /'leʒə(r)/ *n* kòngxián 空闲

leisure centre /'leʒə ˌsentə(r)/ *n* **a leisure centre** yí gè yúlè zhōngxīn 一个娱乐中心

lemon /'lemən/ *n* **a lemon** yí gè níngméng 一个柠檬

lemonade /ˌlemə'neɪd/ *n* níngméngshuǐ 柠檬水

lend /lend/ *vb* jiègěi 借给；**to lend someone money** jiègěi mǒu rén qián 借给某人钱

length /leŋθ/ *n* (*in measurements*) chángdù 长度；(*of a book, a film, a list, an event*) chángdù 长度

leopard /'lepəd/ *n* **a leopard** yì zhī bào 一只豹

less /les/ **1** *det* shǎo 少；**drink less coffee** shǎo hē kāfēi 少喝咖啡；**I have less work than he does** wǒ de gōngzuò bǐ tā de shǎo 我的工作比他的少 **2** *pron* shǎo 少；**to pay less** shǎo fùqián 少付钱；**he has less than you** tā de bǐ nǐ de shǎo 他的比你的少 **3** *adv* **we travel less in winter** wǒmen dōngtiān lǚxíng bǐjiào shǎo 我们冬天旅行比较少 **4** *prep* (*minus*) jiǎnqù 减去 **5 less and less less and less often** yuèláiyuè bù jīngcháng 越来越不经常 **6 less than** bú dào 不到；**less than half an hour** bú dào bàn gè xiǎoshí 不到半个小时

lesson /'lesən/ *n* **a lesson** yì jié kè 一节课；**an English lesson** yì jié Yīngyǔkè 一节英语课

let /let/ *vb* (*when making suggestions*) **let's go home** zánmen huíjiā ba 咱们回家吧；**let's go!** zánmen zǒu ba! 咱们走吧!；(*to rent out*) (*British English*) chūzū 出租；(*to allow*) ràng 让；**he let me help him** tā ràng wǒ bāngzhù tā 他让我帮助他；**I let him use my computer**

wǒ ràng tā yòng wǒ de jìsuànjī 我让他用我的计算机；she
wouldn't let me go tā bú ràng wǒ zǒu 她不让我走；let
down let someone down shǐ mǒu rén shīwàng 使某人失
望；let go (to stop holding) fàngkāi 放开；he let go of
me tā fàngkāile wǒ 他放开了我；(to release) shìfàng 释
放；he let the prisoners go tā shìfàngle nàxiē fànrén 他
释放了那些犯人；let in (to a room or house) he didn't
let me in tā méi ràng wǒ jìn 他没让我进；to let in the
rain lòuyǔ 漏雨；let out (to allow to go out) fàng (…)
chūqù 放 (…) 出去；let me out! fàng wǒ chūqù! 放我出
去！；to let out a scream fāchū yì shēng jiānjiào 发出一
声尖叫；let through to let someone through ràng mǒu
rén guòqù 让某人过去

letter /ˈletə(r)/ n a letter yì fēng xìn 一封信

letter box /ˈletə bɒks/ n a letter box yí ge xìnxiāng 一
个信箱

lettuce /ˈletɪs/ n a head of lettuce yì kē shēngcài 一棵
生菜

level /ˈlevəl/ **1** n (a horizontal position) shuǐpíng 水平；
(a horizontal plane) shuǐpíngmiàn 水平面；(a horizontal
line) shuǐpíngxiàn 水平线 **2** adj píng de 平的

library /ˈlaɪbrərɪ/ n a library yí ge túshūguǎn 一个图书馆

licence /ˈlaɪsəns/ (British English), **license** (US English)
n a licence yí ge zhízhào 一个执照

license plate /ˈlaɪsəns pleɪt/ (US English) n a license
plate yí ge qìchē páizhào 一个汽车牌照

lick /lɪk/ vb tiǎn 舔

lid /lɪd/ n a lid yí ge gàizi 一个盖子

lie /laɪ/ **1** vb (on the ground, on a bed) tǎng 躺；he lay
down on the sofa tā tǎngdào shāfā shang 他躺到沙发
上；he was lying on the sofa tā tǎng zài shāfā shang 他
躺在沙发上；(to be situated) wèiyú 位于；(not to tell
the truth) shuōhuǎng 说谎，sāhuǎng 撒谎 **2** n huǎnghuà
谎话；to tell a lie shuō huǎnghuà 说谎话；lie around he
always leaves his keys lying around tā zǒngshì bǎ tā de

yàoshi dàochù luàn diū 他总是把他的钥匙到处乱丢；**lie down** tǎngxià 躺下

life /laɪf/ n (a living being) shēngmìng 生命；(the stretch of time between birth and death) shòumìng 寿命；(manner of living) shēnghuó 生活

lifestyle /'laɪfstaɪl/ n a lifestyle yì zhǒng shēnghuó fāngshì 一种生活方式

lift /lɪft/ **1** vb to lift one's arm táiqǐ gēbo 抬起胳膊；to lift a suitcase tíqǐ yí gè xiāngzi 提起一个箱子 **2** n (British English) (an elevator) a lift yí gè diàntī 一个电梯；(in a car) can you give me a lift to the station? wǒ néng dā nǐ de chē qù chēzhàn ma? 我能搭你的车去车站吗？

light /laɪt/ **1** n (from the sun, moon) guāng 光；(in a room, on a machine) dēng 灯；to switch on the light dǎkāi dēng 打开灯；traffic lights jiāotōngdēng 交通灯，hónglǜdēng 红绿灯；have you got a light? nǐ yǒu huǒ ma? 你有火吗？ **2** adj (not dark in colour) qiǎn de 浅的；a light blue dress yí jiàn qiǎnlánsè de yīfu 一件浅蓝色的衣服；(bright) míngliàng de 明亮的；a light room yì jiān míngliàng de fángjiān 一间明亮的房间；(not heavy) qīng de 轻的 **3** vb (to set fire to) diǎn 点，diǎnrán 点燃；he lit a cigarette tā diǎnle yì zhī yān 他点了一支烟；to light a fire diǎnhuǒ 点火；(to give light to) zhàoliàng 照亮；the lamp lit the room dēng zhàoliàng le fángjiān 灯照亮了房间

light bulb /'laɪt bʌlb/ n a light bulb yí gè dēngpào 一个灯泡

lighthouse /'laɪthaʊs/ n a lighthouse yí zuò dēngtǎ 一座灯塔

lightning /'laɪtnɪŋ/ n a lightning yí dào shǎndiàn 一道闪电

like¹ /laɪk/ prep (with a resemblance to) xiàng 像；he looks like a foreigner tā kànshàngqù xiàng ge wàiguórén 他看上去像个外国人；(in the same manner as) xiàng…

yíyàng 像…一样; **all his sons work like him** tā de érzimen dōu xiàng tā yíyàng gōngzuò 他的儿子们都像他一样工作

like² /laɪk/ vb (*when expressing an interest*) xǐhuan 喜欢; **I like** [**swimming** | **reading** | **dancing**...] wǒ xǐhuan [yóuyǒng | kànshū | tiàowǔ...] 我喜欢 [游泳 | 看书 | 跳舞...]; **how do you like America?** nǐ juéde Měiguó zěnmeyàng? 你觉得美国怎么样?; (*when expressing a wish*) xiǎng 想, xīwàng 希望; **I'd like coffee** wǒ xiǎng hē kāfēi 我想喝咖啡; **I'd like to live here** wǒ xīwàng zhù zài zhèr 我希望住在这儿

limit /'lɪmɪt/ n (*boundary*) jièxiàn 界限; (*that which may not be passed*) xiàndù 限度; (*restriction*) xiànzhì 限制

line /laɪn/ n xiàn 线; **a line** (*a thread, string, cord*) gēn xiàn 一根线; (*a long, mark*) yì tiáo xiàn 一条线; **a straight line** yì tiáo zhíxiàn 一条直线; (*US English*) (*a queue*) **to stand in line** páiduì 排队; (*a row*) pái pái 排排; **the line is engaged** diànhuà zhànxiàn 电话占线

link /lɪŋk/ vb (*physically*) liánjiē 连接; **to link London to Paris** bǎ Lúndūn gēn Bālí liánjiē qǐlai 把伦敦跟巴黎连接起来; (*to relate to*) liánxì 联系; **the two murders are linked** zhè liǎng cì móushā shì yǒu liánxì de 这两次谋杀是有联系的

lion /'laɪən/ n **a lion** yì tóu shīzi 一头狮子

lip /lɪp/ n chún 唇, zuǐchún 嘴唇

lipstick /'lɪpstɪk/ n kǒuhóng 口红

list /lɪst/ n **a list** (*a catalogue*) yí gè mùlù 一个目录; (*an enumeration*) yì zhāng biǎo 一张表, yìlánbiǎo 一览表; **a list of names** yí fèn míngdān 一份名单

listen /'lɪsən/ vb tīng 听; **to listen to music** tīng yīnyuè 听音乐

litre /'liːtə(r)/ (*British English*), **liter** (*US English*) n **a litre** yì shēng 一升

little /'lɪtl/ **1** adj (*in quantity*) **little** [**food** | **wine** |

money...] méiyǒu duōshǎo [fàn|jiǔ|qián...] 没有多少 [饭|酒|钱...]; there is very little time méiyǒu duōshǎo shíjiān le 没有多少时间了; (in size, age) xiǎo de 小的; a little girl yí gè xiǎo nǚhái 一个小女孩; the little finger xiǎozhǐ 小指 **2** pron a little yìdiǎnr 一点儿; I only ate a little wǒ zhǐ chīle yìdiǎnr 我只吃了一点儿 **3** adv he is little known hěn shǎo yǒu rén zhīdào tā 很少有人知道他 **4** a little(bit) yìxiē 一些，yìdiǎnr 一点儿; to add a little(bit of) sugar jiā yìxiē táng 加一些糖; I can speak a little(bit of) Chinese wǒ huì shuō yìdiǎnr Hànyǔ 我会说一点儿汉语 **5** little by little yìdiǎn yìdiǎn de 一点一点地，zhújiàn de 逐渐地

live¹ /lɪv/ vb (to have one's home) zhù 住; he lives in Beijing tā zhù zài Běijīng 他住在北京; (to be alive) huó 活; to live to be a hundred huódào yìbǎi suì 活到 100 岁; (to spend or pass) guò 过; to live a happy life guò xìngfú de shēnghuó 过幸福的生活

live² /laɪv/ adj (alive) huó de 活的; (of a broadcast) shíkuàng de 实况的，xiànchǎng de 现场的

lively /'laɪvlɪ/ adj (active) huóyuè de 活跃的; (vital) chōngmǎn huólì de 充满活力的; (vivacious) huópō de 活泼的; (vivid) shēngdòng de 生动的

living room /'lɪvɪŋ rʊm/ n a living room yì jiān qǐjūshì 一间起居室

load /ləʊd/ n (burden) fùdān 负担; (weight that can be carried) fùhè 负荷; loads of money dàliàng de qián 大量的钱

loaf /ləʊf/ n a loaf (of bread) yì tiáo (miànbāo) 一条(面包)

loan /ləʊn/ n (money lent) dàikuǎn 贷款; a loan yì bǐ dàikuǎn 一笔贷款; the book is on loan zhè běn shū jiè chūqù le 这本书借出去了

lobster /'lɒbstə(r)/ n a lobster yì zhī lóngxiā 一只龙虾

local /'ləʊkəl/ adj dāngdì de 当地的，běndì de 本地的; a local newspaper yí fèn dāngdì bàozhǐ 一份当地报纸;

the local people běndìrén 本地人

lock /lɒk/ **1** *vb* chǎng 锁; she locked the door tā suǒshangle mén 她锁上了门 **2** *n* a lock yì bǎ suǒ 一把锁; **lock in** bǎ mǒu rén suǒ zài lǐmian 把某人锁在里面; to lock oneself in bǎ zìjǐ guān zài lǐmian 把自己关在里面

locker /'lɒkə(r)/ *n* a locker yí gè yǒu suǒ de xiǎo chú 一个有锁的小橱

logical /'lɒdʒɪkəl/ *adj* fúhé luójí de 符合逻辑的

London /'lʌndən/ *n* Lúndūn 伦敦

lonely /'ləʊnlɪ/ *adj* gūdú de 孤独的

long /lɒŋ/ **1** *adj* cháng de 长的; a long letter yì fēng chángxìn 一封长信; long hair cháng tóufa 长头发; the film is two hours long zhè bù diànyǐng yǒu liǎng gè xiǎoshí cháng 这部电影有两个小时长; I haven't seen him for a long time wǒ hěn cháng shíjiān méi kànjiàn tā le 我很长时间没看见他了 **2** *adv* jiǔ 久; long ago hěn jiǔ yǐqián 很久以前; you can stay as long as you like nǐ yuànyì dāi duō jiǔ jiù dāi duō jiǔ 你愿意呆多久就呆多久 **3** as long as zhǐyào 只要; as long as the weather is nice zhǐyào tiānqì hǎo 只要天气好

look /lʊk/ **1** *vb* kàn 看; to look at a photograph kàn zhàopiàn 看照片; to look out of the window kàn chuāng wài 看窗外; (*to appear*) kànshàngqù 看上去; to look tired kànshàngqù hěn lèi 看上去很累; to look well kànshàngqù hěn hǎo 看上去很好; he looks young tā kànshàngqù hěn niánqīng 他看上去很年轻; she looks like her mother tā kànshàngqù xiàng tā māma 她看上去像她妈妈; what does he look like? tā (kànshàngqù) shénmeyàng? 他 (看上去) 什么样? **2** *n* have a look kàn (yi) kàn 看 (一) 看; let me have a look wǒ kàn (yi) kàn 让我看 (一) 看; **look after** zhàogù 照顾, zhàoliào 照料; to look after a child zhàogù yí gè háizi 照顾一个孩子; **look down on** kànbuqǐ 看不起; **look down on someone** kànbuqǐ mǒu rén 看不起某人; **look for** zhǎo 找

找; he is looking for a job tā zài zhǎo gōngzuò 他在找工作; **look forward to** qīdài 期待, pànwàng 盼望; I am looking forward to meeting her wǒ qīdàizhe gēn tā jiànmiàn 我期待着跟她见面; **look into** diàochá 调查, he has looked into this problem tā diàochále zhège wèntí 他调查了这个问题; **look out!** dāngxīn! 当心!, xiǎoxīn! 小心!; **look through** to look through a book cháyuè yìběn shū 查阅一本书; **look up** to look up a word in a dictionary zài cídiǎn lǐ chá yí gè cí 在词典里查一个词

loose /luːs/ adj (describing clothes) kuānsōng de 宽松的; (describing a screw, a tooth) sōng de 松的

lorry /'lɒrɪ/ n (British English) a lorry yí liàng kǎchē 一辆卡车

lose /luːz/ vb (when talking about a thing) diū(shī) 丢(失); to lose [a pen | a key | a bag...] diūshī [yì zhī bǐ | yì bǎ yàoshi | yí gè bāo···] 丢失 [一支笔 | 一把钥匙 | 一个包···]; (when talking about friendship or a psychological state) shīqù 失去; to lose [friends | interest | confidence] shīqù [péngyou | xìngqù | xìnxīn] 失去 [朋友 | 兴趣 | 信心]; (be defeated [in]) shū shū 输; we lost the game wǒmen shūle zhè chǎng bǐsài 我们输了这场比赛; to lose face diūliǎn, diūmiànzi 丢脸, 丢面子; to lose one's temper fāpíqì 发脾气

lost /lɒst/ adj to get lost mílù 迷路的

lot /lɒt/ pron a lot hěn duō 很多; he eats a lot tā chī de hěn duō 他吃得很多; a lot of [money | time | books...] hěn duō [qián | shíjiān | shū···] 很多 [钱 | 时间 | 书···]; there is not a lot left shèngxià de bù duō le 剩下的不多了

lottery /'lɒtərɪ/ n cǎijiǎng 彩奖; a lottery ticket yì zhāng cǎipiào 一张彩票

loud /laud/ adj dàshēng de 大声的; to talk in a loud voice dàshēng de jiǎnghuà 大声地讲话

loudspeaker /ˌlaud'spiːkə(r)/ n a loudspeaker yí gè lǎba 一个喇叭

lounge /laundʒ/ n a lounge yì jiān xiūxishì 一间休息室

love /lʌv/ **1** vb (when talking about people)ài 爱; do you love her? nǐ ài tā ma? 你爱她吗?(when talking about things, activities)àihào 爱好, xǐhuan 喜欢 **2** n to be in love zài tán liàn'ài 在谈恋爱; to make love zuò'ài 做爱

lovely /'lʌvlɪ/ adj (beautiful)měilì de 美丽的; a beautiful view měilì de jǐngsè 美丽的景色; you've got lovely eyes nǐ yǒu yì shuāng měilì de yǎnjīng 你有一双美丽的眼睛;(very nice)(lìng rén) yúkuài de (令人)愉快的; a lovely weekend yí gè (lìng rén) yúkuài de zhōumò 一个(令人)愉快的周末

low /ləʊ/ adj (when talking about temperature, voice, position)dī de 低的; to speak in a low voice dīshēng shuōhuà 低声说话;(when talking about heights)ǎi de 矮的; a low wall yì dǔ ǎiqiáng 一堵矮墙

lower /'ləʊə(r)/ vb to lower a flag bǎ qí jiàng xiàlái 把旗降下来; to lower the price jiàng/jiǎnjià 降/减价

loyal /'lɔɪəl/ adj zhōngchéng de 忠诚的, zhōngshí de 忠实的

luck /lʌk/ n yùnqì 运气; good luck! zhù nǐ hǎo yùnqì 祝你好运气!; to bring someone (good) luck gěi mǒu rén dàilái hǎo yùnqì 给某人带来好运气; to have poor luck bù zǒuyùn 不走运

lucky /'lʌkɪ/ adj xìngyùn de 幸运的, yùnqì hǎo de 运气好的; he is lucky tā hěn xìngyùn 他很幸运

lunch /lʌntʃ/ n wǔfàn 午饭

Luxembourg /'lʌksəmbɜːɡ/ n Lúsēnbǎo 卢森堡

luxury /'lʌkʃərɪ/ **1** n shēchǐ 奢侈 **2** adj a luxury hotel yì jiā háohuá lǚguǎn 一家豪华旅馆

Mm

machine /mə'ʃiːn/ n a machine yì tái jīqì 一台机器

mad /mæd/ adj (insane) fēng de 疯的; the dog went mad zhè tiáo gǒu fēng le 这条狗疯了; (infatuated) to be mad about [something| somebody] kuángrè de míliàn [mǒu shì| mǒu rén] 狂热地迷恋 [某事|某人]; (very angry) fēicháng shēngqì de 非常生气的

magazine /ˌmægə'ziːn/ n a magazine yì běn zázhì 一本杂志

magic /'mædʒɪk/ **1** adj yǒu mólì de 有魔力的 **2** n (referring to the magical arts) móshù 魔术, xìfǎ 戏法

maiden name /'meɪdən neɪm/ n niángjiā de xìng 娘家的姓

mail /meɪl/ **1** n (the postal system)yóudì 邮递, yóuzhèng xìtǒng 邮政系统; (letters)xìnjiàn 信件 **2** vb (US English) to mail a letter to someone gěi mǒu rén jì yì fēng xìn 给某人寄一封信

mailbox /'meɪlbɒks/ n (US English) a mailbox yí gè xìnxiāng 一个信箱

mailman /'meɪlmæn/ n a mailman yí gè yóudìyuán 一个邮递员

main /meɪn/ adj zhǔyào de 主要的

main course /'meɪn kɔːs/ n a main course yí dào zhǔcài 一道主菜

major /'meɪdʒə(r)/ **1** adj zhǔyào de 主要的; major industries zhǔyào gōngyè 主要工业 **2** n a major (a military rank) yí gè shàoxiào 一个少校; (in university or college) yì mén zhuānyè 一门专业; my major is mathematics wǒ de zhuānyè shì shùxué 我的专业是数学

majority /mə'dʒɒrətɪ/ n duōshù 多数, dàduōshù 大多数

make /meɪk/ vb! Note that the word make can be translated by zuò 做, zào 造, or shǐ 使, etc., depending on the meaning to be expressed. Very often the translation of the word make is decided by other words with which it is collocated, such as make a phone call or make friends. To find translations for other expressions like to make a mess, to make a mistake, to make sure, etc., *look up the entries at* **mess, mistake, sure,** *etc.* ; **to make** [breakfast|furniture|a dress...] zuò [zǎofàn|jiājù|yí jiàn yīfu...] 做 [早饭|家具|一件衣服...] ; (*to produce*) zào zào ; **to be made of** [gold|metal|wood...] shì [jīnzi|jīnshǔ|mùtou...] zào de 是 [金子|金属|木头...] 造的; (*to cause a particular reaction*) shǐ 使; **to make someone** [happy| angry|jealous...] shǐ mǒu rén [gāoxìng|shēngqì|jìdù...] 使某人 [高兴|生气|嫉妒...]; **to make someone wait** ràng mǒu rén děnghòu 让某人等候; **to make a bed** pūchuáng 铺床; **to make a film** shèzhì yí bù diànyǐng 摄制一部电影; **to make coffee** chōng kāfēi 冲咖啡; **to make room** téngchū dìfang 腾出地方; **to make a phone call** dǎ yí gè diànhuà 打一个电话; **to make friends** jiāo péngyou 交朋友; (*to earn*) **to make a lot of money** zhuàn hěn duō qián 赚很多钱; **to make a living** wéichí shēnghuó 维持生活; **to make a profit** huò(dé) lì(rùn) 获(得)利(润); **make do** còuhe 凑合; **make out** to make out a list of names liè yì zhāng míngdān 列一张名单; **to make a cheque out to someone** gěi mǒu rén kāi yì zhāng zhīpiào 给某人开一张支票; **make up** (*to be friends again*) héhǎo 和好, héjiě 和解; **to make up an excuse** biānzào yí gè jièkǒu 编造一个借口; **to make up a parcel** bāochéng yí gè bāoguǒ 包成一个包裹; **to make up for lost time** bǔshàng sǔnshī de shíjiān 补上损失的时间

make-up /'meɪkʌp/ *n* huàzhuāng 化妆; **she wears make-up** tā huàzhe zhuāng 她化着妆

male /meɪl/ *adj* (*in biology*) xióng de 雄的; (*relating to men*) nán de 男的

man /mæn/ *n* **a man** yí gè nánrén 一个男人; (*humankind*) rénlèi 人类

manage /'mænɪdʒ/ *vb* (*to run*) guǎnlǐ 管理; **to manage** [a school|a hospital|a factory] guǎnlǐ [yí gè xuéxiào|yí gè yīyuàn|yí gè gōngchǎng] 管理 [一个学校|一个医院|一个工厂]; **to manage to finish one's homework** shèfǎ zuòwán zuòyè 设法做完作业

manager /'mænɪdʒə(r)/ n a manager yí gè jīnglǐ 一个经理

mandarin /'mændərɪn/ n (standard Chinese) pǔtōnghuà 普通话；(the fruit) gānjú 柑橘；a mandarin yí gè gānjú 一个柑橘

manner /'mænə(r)/ n a manner (the way in which something is done) yì zhǒng fāngshì 一种方式；(method) yì zhǒng fāngfǎ 一种方法；(personal style of acting) yì zhǒng fēngdù 一种风度

manners /'mænəz/ n (good behaviour) lǐmào 礼貌；she has no manners tā méiyǒu lǐmào 她没有礼貌；(social conduct) guīju 规矩

manufacture /ˌmænjʊ'fæktʃə(r)/ vb zhìzào 制造

many /'menɪ/ **1** det (a lot of) xǔduō 许多，hěn duō 很多；were there many shops? yǒu xǔduō shāngdiàn ma? 有许多商店吗?；there weren't many people there nàr méiyǒu hěn duō rén 那儿没有很多人；(when used with how, and the anticipated number is above nine) how many? duōshǎo? 多少?；how many dictionaries do you have? nǐ yǒu duōshǎo běn cídiǎn?; 你有多少本词典?；(when used with how, and the anticipated number is below ten) how many? jǐ jǐ 几; how many elder brothers do you have? nǐ yǒu jǐ gè gēge? 你有几个哥哥?；too many tài duō 太多; so many zhème duō 这么多，nàme duō 那么多; as many as hé⋯yíyàng duō 和⋯一样多 **2** pron are there many left? shèngxia hěn duō ma? 剩下很多吗?；I've got too many wǒ dé tài duō le 我的太多了；take as many as you like nǐ yuànyì ná duōshǎo jiù ná duōshǎo 你愿意拿多少就拿多少; many of them speak English tāmen xǔduō rén huì shuō Yīngyǔ 他们许多人会说英语

map /mæp/ n a map yì zhāng dìtú 一张地图

marble /'mɑːbl/ n (a kind of stone) dàlǐshí 大理石；(a toy) dànzǐ 弹子；a marble yí gè dànzǐ 一个弹子

march /mɑːtʃ/ vb xíngjìn 行进

March /mɑːtʃ/ *n* sānyuè 三月

margarine /ˈmɑːdʒərɪn/ *n* rénzào huángyóu 人造黄油

mark /mɑːk/ *n* (*a symbol*) yí gè biāojì 一个标记, yí gè jìhào 一个记号; (*British English*) (*a grade*) chéngjì 成绩, fēnshù 分数; **to get good marks** dé hǎo chéngjì 得好成绩 **2** *vb* **to mark homework** pàn zuòyè 判作业; (*to indicate*) biāomíng 标明

marker /ˈmɑːkə(r)/ *n* **a marker** (*an examiner*) yí gè kǎoguān 一个考官; (*a pen*) yì zhī zhāntóubǐ 一支毡头笔; (*a bookmark*) yí gè shūqiān 一个书签

market /ˈmɑːkɪt/ *n* shìchǎng 市场; **a market** yí gè shìchǎng 一个市场; **a flea market** yí gè tiàozao shìchǎng 一个跳蚤市场; **the job market** láowù shìchǎng 劳务市场

marmalade /ˈmɑːməleɪd/ *n* júzijiàng 橘子酱; guǒjiàng 果酱

marriage /ˈmærɪdʒ/ *n* hūnyīn 婚姻, jiéhūn 结婚

married /ˈmærɪd/ *adj* jiéle hūn de 结了婚的, yǐhūn de 已婚的; **to be married to someone** gēn mǒu rén jiéhūn 跟某人结婚

marry /ˈmærɪ/ *vb* **to marry someone** gēn mǒu rén jiéhūn 跟某人结婚

marsh /mɑːʃ/ *n* **a marsh** yí kuài zhǎozédì 一块沼泽地

mashed potatoes /ˌmæʃt pəˈteɪtəʊz/ *n* tǔdóuní 土豆泥

mask /mɑːsk/ *n* **a mask** yí gè miànjù 一个面具

mat /mæt/ *n* **a mat** yí gè diànzi 一个垫子

match /mætʃ/ **1** *n* (*a game*) **a match** yì chǎng bǐsài 一场比赛, **a football match** (*British English*) yì chǎng zúqiú bǐsài 一场足球比赛; (*a matchstick*) **a match** yì gēn huǒchái 一根火柴 **2** *vb* **the shoes match the belt** xié hé pídài hěn xiāngpèi 鞋和皮带很相配

mate /meɪt/ *n* **a mate** (*a friend, good buddy, pal*) (*British English*) yí gè péngyou 一个朋友, yí gè huǒbàn 一个伙伴; (*a partner, husband, or wife*) yí gè duìxiàng 一个对象, yí gè bànlǚ 一个伴侣; (*for animals*) dòngwù de pèidui

动物的配对

material /mə'tɪərɪəl/ n a material(for making things) yì zhǒng cáiliào 一种材料; (in written form) yí fèn cáiliào 一份材料

math /mæθ/ (US English), **maths**/mæθs/(British English) n shùxué 数学

mathematics /ˌmæθə'mætɪks/ n shùxué 数学

matter /'mætə(r)/ **1** n what's the matter (with her)? (tā) zěnme le? (她) 怎么了? **2** vb does it really matter? zhè zhēn de hěn yàojǐn ma? 这真的很要紧吗?; it doesn't matter méiguānxi 没关系, búyàojǐn 不要紧

maximum /'mæksɪməm/ **1** adj (the highest) zuì gāo de 最高的; the maximum price zuì gāo jiàgé 最高价格; a maximum temperature zuì gāo wēndù 最高温度; (greatest in quantity) zuì dà de 最大的, zuì duō de 最多的; the maximum amount of work zuì dà de gōngzuòliàng 最大的工作量 **2** n the maximum (of quantity) zuì dà liàng 最大量; (of space) zuì dà kōngjiān 最大空间; (of speed) zuì gāo sùdù 最高速度 ! Note that the expression the maximum is translated into chinese as a modifier, which differs according to the noun it modifies.

may /meɪ/ vb (when talking about a possibility) kěnéng 可能, yěxǔ 也许; this may be true zhè kěnéng shì zhēn de 这可能是真的; he may have got lost tā yěxǔ mílù le 他也许迷路了; (when asking for or giving permission) kěyǐ 可以; may I come in? wǒ kěyǐ jìnlái ma? 我可以进来吗?; you may sit down nǐ kěyǐ zuòxià 你可以坐下

May /meɪ/ n wǔyuè 五月

maybe /'meɪbi:/ adv dàgài 大概, yěxǔ 也许

mayor /meə(r)/ n a mayor yí gè shìzhǎng 一个市长

me /强 mi:; 弱 mɪ/ pron wǒ 我; they know me tāmen rènshi wǒ 他们认识我

meal /mi:l/ n a meal yí dùn fàn 一顿饭

mean /mi:n/ **1** vb to mean shì… yìsi 是… 意思; what does it mean? zhè shì shénme yìsi? 这是什么意思?;

what does this word mean? zhège cí shì shénme yìsi? 这个词是什么意思？; what do you mean? nǐ shì shénme yìsi? 你是什么意思？; (*to have as a result*) yìwèizhe 意味着; it means giving up my job zhè yìwèizhe fàngqì wǒ de gōngzuò 这意味着放弃我的工作; (*to intend*) I meant to buy a new car wǒ yuánlái dǎsuàn mǎi yí liàng xīn qìchē 我原来打算买一辆新汽车; she didn't mean to upset you tā bú shì gùyì ràng nǐ bù gāoxìng 她不是故意让你不高兴; (*to be of much/ little importance*) her work means a lot to her tā de gōngzuò duì tā hěn zhòngyào 她的工作对她很重要; money doesn't mean much to him qián duì tā bìng bú zhòngyào 钱对他并不重要 **2** *adj* (*British English*) (*not generous*) lìnsè de 吝啬的，xiǎoqì de 小气的; (*unfriendly*) **to be mean to someone** duì mǒu rén bù yǒuhǎo 对某人不友好

meaning /'mi:nɪŋ/ *n* a meaning yì zhǒng yìsi 一种意思，yì zhǒng hányì 一种含义

means /mi:nz/ *n* (*an instrument*) gōngjù 工具; **a means of transport** yì zhǒng yùnshū gōngjù 一种运输工具; (*a way to an end*) fāngfǎ 方法; **a means of earning money** yì zhǒng zhuànqián de fāngfǎ 一种赚钱的方法

meanwhile /'mi:nhwaɪl/ *adv* tóngshí 同时

measles /'mi:zlz/ *n* mázhěn 麻疹

measure /'meʒə(r)/ *vb* liáng 量，cèliáng 测量

meat /mi:t/ *n* ròu 肉

mechanic /mɪ'kænɪk/ *n* a mechanic yí gè jìgōng 一个技工

medal /'medəl/ *n* a medal yí gè jiǎngzhāng 一个奖章，yí méi jiǎngpái 一枚奖牌; **a gold medal** yí kuài jīnpái 一块金牌，yí méi jīnzhì jiǎngzhāng 一枚金质奖章

media /'mi:dɪə/ *n* the media xīnwén méijiè 新闻媒介

medical /'medɪkəl/ *adj* yīxué de 医学的; **a medical college** yí gè yīxuéyuàn 一个医学院; **to have medical treatment** jiēshòu zhìliáo 接受治疗

medicine /'medəsən/ *n* (*the study*) yīxué 医学; (*a drug*)

药; a type of Chinese medicine yì zhǒng zhōngyào 一种中药

Mediterranean /ˌmedɪtəˈreɪnɪən/ n Dìzhōnghǎi 地中海

medium /ˈmiːdɪəm/ adj zhōngděng de 中等的

meet /miːt/ vb (by accident) yùjiàn 遇见, pèngshang 碰上; **she met him on the street** tā zài jiē shang yùjiànle tā 她在街上遇见了他; (by appointment) jiànmiàn 见面; **can we meet next week?** wǒmen xià xīngqī jiànmiàn, hǎo ma? 我们下星期见面, 好吗?; (to become acquainted with) rènshi 认识, jiéshí 结识; **she met him at a wedding** tā zài yí cì hūnlǐ shang rènshile tā 她在一次婚礼上认识了他; (to come face to face with) jiàn 见; **have you met Tom?** nǐ jiànguo Tāngmǔ ma? 你见过汤姆吗?; (to fetch) jiē 接; **I can come to the station to meet you** wǒ kěyǐ qù chēzhàn jiē nǐ 我可以去车站接你; (to satisfy) mǎnzú 满足; **can this meet your requirements?** zhè néng mǎnzú nǐ de yāoqiú ma? 这能满足你的要求吗?; (to have a meeting) kāihuì 开会; **the whole school will meet in the hall this afternoon** jīntiān xiàwǔ quánxiào zài lǐtáng kāihuì 今天下午全校在礼堂开会

meeting /ˈmiːtɪŋ/ n **a meeting** yí cì huì(yì) 一次会(议)

melon /ˈmelən/ n **a melon** yí gè guā 一个瓜

melt /melt/ vb rónghuà 融化; **the snow is starting to melt** xuě kāishǐ rónghuà le 雪开始融化了; (cause to melt) shǐ… rónghuà 使…溶化; **the salt will melt the ice** yán huì shǐ bīng rónghuà 盐会使冰融化

member /ˈmembə(r)/ n **a member** (of a party) yí gè dǎngyuán 一个党员; (of a team) yí gè duìyuán 一个队员; (of an association) yí gè huìyuán 一个会员; (of the Congress, Parliament) yí gè yìyuán 一个议员; **a member of staff** (in a school) yí gè jiàoyuán 一个教员; (in a bank, a firm) yí gè zhíyuán 一个职员

memory /ˈmemərɪ/ n jìyìlì 记忆力; **he's got a good memory** tā yǒu jìyìlì hěn hǎo 他的记忆力很好; (a *person , a place , or time*)huíyì 回忆；**a memory of one's childhood** duì tóngnián de huíyì 对童年的回忆

mend /mend/ *vb* (*to fix*)xiūlǐ 修理；(*by sewing*)féngbǔ 缝补

mental /'mentəl/ *adj* (*pertaining to the mind*)jīngshén de 精神的；(*done in the mind*)nǎolì de 脑力的；**mental labour** nǎolì láodòng 脑力劳动；(*relating to a disease of the mind*)jīngshénbìng de 精神病的；**a mental patient** yí gè jīngshénbìngrén 一个精神病人；**a mental hospital** yí gè jīngshénbìngyuàn 一个精神病院

menu /'menjuː/ *n* **a menu** yí fèn càidān 一份菜单，yí fèn càipǔ 一份菜谱

mess /mes/ *n* **a mess** yìtuánzāo 一团糟，luànqībāzāo 乱七八糟；**your room is** (**in**) **a mess** nǐ de fángjiān luànqībāzāo 你的房间乱七八糟；**to make a mess in the kitchen** bǎ chúfáng nòng de yìtuánzāo 把厨房弄得一团糟

message /'mesɪdʒ/ *n* **a message** (*if it's verbal*)yí gè kǒuxìn 一个口信；(*if it's written on a piece of paper*) yì zhāng tiáo 一张条；(*a piece of information*) yì tiáo xiāoxi 一条消息

metal /'metəl/ *n* **a type of metal** yì zhǒng jīnshǔ 一种金属

method /'meθəd/ *n* **a method** yì zhǒng fāngfǎ 一种方法

metre /'miːtə(r)/ (*British English*)，**meter**(*US English*) *n* **a metre** yì mǐ 一米

Mexico /'meksɪkəu/ *n* Mòxīgē 墨西哥

microphone /'maɪkrəfəun/ *n* **a microphone** yí gè màikèfēng 一个麦克风

microwave /'maɪkrəuweɪv/ *n* **a microwave** yí gè wēibōlú 一个微波炉

midday /'mɪddeɪ/ *n* zhèngwǔ 正午，zhōngwǔ 中午；**at midday** zài zhèngwǔ 在正午

middle /'mɪdl/ *n* zhōngjiān 中间；**in the middle of the road** zài mǎlù zhōngjiān 在马路中间；**to be in the**

middle of cooking a meal zhèngzài zuòfàn 正在做饭

middle-aged /'mɪdl'eɪdʒd/ adj zhōngnián de 中年的

midnight /'mɪdnaɪt/ n wǔyè 午夜；at midnight zài wǔyè 在午夜

might /maɪt/ vb (when talking about a possibility) yěxǔ 也许，kěnéng 可能；she might be right tā yěxǔ shì duì de 她也许是对的；he said he might not come tā shuō tā kěnéng bù lái 他说他可能不来；(when implying something didn't happen) you might have been late nǐ běnlái huì chídào de 你本来会来迟到的；she might have told us tā běnlái kěyǐ gàosu wǒmen 她本来可以告诉我们；(when making suggestions) you might like to phone him nǐ yěxǔ kěyǐ gěi tā dǎ gè diànhuà 你也许可以给他打个电话；it might be better to wait zuìhǎo děng yī děng 最好等一等

mild /maɪld/ adj (in temper and disposition) wēnhé de 温和的，(of weather) wēnnuǎn de 温暖的，nuǎnhuo de 暖和的；the weather's mild, it's mild tiānqì hěn nuǎnhuo 天气很暖和

mile /maɪl/ n a mile yì yīnglǐ 一英里！Note that one mile is 1609 metres.

military /'mɪlɪtərɪ/ adj jūnshì de 军事的

milk /mɪlk/ **1** n (of a cow) niúnǎi 牛奶，(of a mother) mǔrǔ 母乳 **2** vb jǐnǎi 挤奶

milkman /'mɪlkmən/ n a milkman yí gè sòng niúnǎi de rén 一个送牛奶的人

million /'mɪljən/ num one million, a million yìbǎi wàn 100 万；three million American dollars sānbǎi wàn měiyuán 300 万美元；a million inhabitants yìbǎi wàn jūmín 100 万居民

mind /maɪnd/ **1** n tóunǎo 头脑；to have a logical mind yǒu luójí tóunǎo 有逻辑头脑；to make up one's mind to change jobs xià juéxīn huàn gōngzuò 下决心换工作；to change one's mind gǎibiàn zhǔyì 改变主意 **2** vb (when expressing an opinion) 'where shall we go? '—'I don't mind' " **wǒmen qù nǎr?**" " **wǒ wúsuǒwèi**" "我们去哪儿?"—"我无所谓"; she doesn't mind the heat **tā bú zàihu rè** 她不在乎热; (in polite questions or requests) do you mind if I smoke? **wǒ chōuyān nǐ jièyì ma?** 我抽烟你介意吗?; would you mind turning on the light? **qǐng nǐ dǎkāi dēng, hǎo ma?** 请你打开灯,好吗?; (to be careful) **xiǎoxīn** 小心, **dāngxīn** 当心; mind the steps **xiǎoxīn lóutī** 小心楼梯; mind you don't break the plates **dāngxīn bié dǎpò pánzi** 当心别打破盘子; (to take care of) **zhàoliào** 照料, **zhàokàn** 照看; to mind a few children **zhàoliào jǐ gè háizi** 照料几个孩子; never mind, she'll get the next train **méiguānxi, tā huì zuò xià yí tàng huǒchē** 没关系,她会坐下一趟火车

mine¹ /maɪn/ pron **wǒ de** 我的; the green pen is mine **nà zhī lǜsè de bǐ shì wǒ de** 那支绿色的笔是我的

mine² /maɪn/ n (for extracting minerals from the ground) **yí gè kuàngjǐng** 一个矿井

miner /'maɪnə(r)/ n a miner **yí gè kuànggōng** 一个矿工

mineral water /'mɪnərəl ˌwɔːtə(r)/ n a bottle of mineral water **yì píng kuàngquánshuǐ** 一瓶矿泉水

minimum /'mɪnɪməm/ **1** adj (lowest) **zuì dī de** 最低的; the minimum price **zuì dī jiàgé** 最低价格; (smallest in quantity) **zuì xiǎo de** 最小的, **zuì shǎo de** 最少的; the minimum amount of work **zuì xiǎo gōngzuòliàng** 最小工作量 **2** n the minimum(of quantity) **zuì xiǎo liàng** 最小量, **zuì shǎo liàng** 最少量; (of space) **zuì xiǎo kōngjiān** 最小空间; (of speed) **zuì dī sùdù** 最低速度; Note that the expression the minimum is translated into Chinese as a modifier, which differs according to the noun it modifies.

minister /'mɪnɪstə(r)/ n (in government) **bùzhǎng** 部长; a minister **yí gè bùzhǎng** 一个部长; the minister for education **jiàoyù bùzhǎng** 教育部长; (in religion) **mùshī** 牧师; a minister **yí gè mùshī** 一个牧师

minor /'maɪnə(r)/ adj (small) **xiǎo de** 小的; a minor operation **yí gè xiǎo shǒushù** 一个小手术; (not serious) qīng de 轻的；a minor injury yí cì qīngshāng 一次轻伤

minority /maɪ'nɒrəti/ n (the smaller number) shǎoshù 少数；(in a population) shǎoshù mínzú 少数民族；a minority yí gè shǎoshù mínzú 一个少数民族

minus /'maɪnəs/ prep (in temperature) língxià 零下；it's minus four outside wàimian língxià sì dù 外面零下 4 度；(in calculation) jiǎn 减，10 minus 5 is 5 shí jiǎn wǔ děngyú wǔ 10 减 5 等于 5

minute /'mɪnɪt/ n (a minute) yì fēnzhōng 一分钟；wait a minute, please qǐng děng yíhuìr 请等一会儿

mirror /'mɪrə(r)/ n a mirror yí miàn jìngzi 一面镜子

miserable /'mɪzərəbl/ adj (extremely unhappy) tòngkǔ de 痛苦的；to feel miserable gǎndào tòngkǔ 感到痛苦，(extremely poor) pínkùn de 贫困的；to have a miserable life guò pínkùn de shēnghuó 过贫困的生活

miss /mɪs/ vb (to fail to hit) méi dǎzhòng 没打中，(to fail to see) you can't miss it nǐ bú huì kàn bú dào de 你不会看不到的；(to fail to take) cuòguò 错过；to miss an opportunity cuòguò yí gè jīhuì 错过一个机会，(to feel sad not to see) xiǎng(niàn) 想(念)；I miss you wǒ xiǎng nǐ 我想你，(other uses) don't miss this film bié cuòguò zhège diànyǐng 别错过这个电影；she missed her plane tā wùle fēijī 她误了飞机；to miss school quēkè 缺课

Miss /mɪs/ n xiǎojiě 小姐

missing /'mɪsɪŋ/ adj (not to be found) shīzōng de 失踪的；missing soldiers shīzōng de shìbīng 失踪的士兵，(lacking) quē(shǎo) 缺(少)；a dictionary with two pages missing yì běn quēle liǎng yè de cídiǎn 一本缺了两页的词典

mist /mɪst/ n wù 雾，wùqì 雾气

mistake /mɪ'steɪk/ n a mistake yí gè cuòwù 一个错误；to make a mistake fàn cuòwù 犯错误

mix /mɪks/ vb (to put together) hùn 混，huò 和；to mix blue paint with yellow paint bǎ lán yóuqī hé huáng yóuqī hùn zài yìqǐ 把蓝油漆和黄油漆混在一起；he mixed flour and water tā bǎ miàn hé shuǐ huò zài yìqǐ 他 把面和水和在一起; (to associate) láiwǎng 来往; **to mix with the other students** hé bié de xuésheng láiwǎng hé biéde xuésheng láiwǎng 和别的学生来往; **mix up** gǎohùn 搞混; **to get the two languages mixed up** bǎ liǎng zhǒng yǔyán gǎohùn le 把两种语言搞混了; **I'm always mixing him up with his brother** wǒ zǒngshì bǎ tā hé tā gēge gǎohùn 我总是把他和他哥哥搞混

mixture /'mɪkstʃə(r)/ n a mixture yì zhǒng hùnhéwù 一种混合物

model /'mɒdəl/ n (of a train, a car, a building) móxíng 模型; **a model** yí gè móxíng 一个模型; **a** (fashion) **model** yí gè (shízhuāng) mótèr 一个(时装)模特儿

modern /'mɒdən/ adj xiàndài de 现代的

mole /məʊl/ n a mole (if it's a small and round mark) yí gè hēizhì 一个黑痣; (if it's a large mark) yí kuài hēizhì 一块黑痣

moment /'məʊmənt/ n a moment yíhuìr 一会儿; **please wait a moment** qǐng děng yíhuìr 请等一会儿; **there's no-one there at the moment** xiànzài nàr méiyǒu rén 现在那儿没有人

Monday /'mʌndɪ/ n xīngqīyī 星期一, lǐbàiyī 礼拜一

money /'mʌnɪ/ n qián 钱

monkey /'mʌŋkɪ/ n a monkey yì zhī hóuzi 一只猴子

month /mʌnθ/ n a month yí gè yuè 一个月; **he'll be back in two months' time** tā liǎng gè yuè yǐhòu huílái 他两个月以后回来

monument /'mɒnjumənt/ n a monument (if it's a pillar, a stone) yí zuò jìniànbēi 一座纪念碑; (if it's an object) yí gè jìniànwù 一个纪念物

mood /muːd/ n (state of emotions) xīnqíng 心情, qíngxù 情绪; **to be in a good mood** qíngxù hěn hǎo 情绪很好; **I'm in a very bad mood** wǒ de qíngxù hěn bù hǎo 我的情绪很不好

moon /muːn/ n (the earth's satellite) yuèqiú 月球; (that *which gives moonlight*) yuèliàng 月亮；a moon cake yí kuài yuèbǐng 一块月饼；the Moon Festival Zhōngqiū Jié 中秋节

moonlight /'mu:nlaɪt/ *n* yuèguāng 月光

moral /'mɒrəl/ *adj* (*conforming to the right or the virtuous*) yǒu dàodé de 有道德的；(*relating to ethics*) dàodéshang de 道德上的

more /mɔː(r)/ **1** *det* gèngduō de 更多的；to have more [friends|money|time] yǒu gèngduō de [péngyou|qián|shíjiān] 有更多的 [朋友|钱|时间]；more...than someone bǐ mǒu rén duō … 比某人多；I have more work than he does wǒ de gōngzuò bǐ tā duō 我的工作比他多；he bought more books than I did tā mǎi de shū bǐ wǒ duō 他买的书比我多；there's no more [bread|milk|money] méiyǒu [miànbāo|niúnǎi|qián] le 没有 [面包|牛奶|钱] 了；there's more [bread|milk|money] hái yǒu [miànbāo|niúnǎi|qián] 还有 [面包|牛奶|钱]；would you like more [coffee|wine|vegetables]？nǐ hái yào [kāfēi|jiǔ|cài] ma？你还要 [咖啡|酒|菜] 吗?；he bought two more tickets tā yòu mǎile liǎng zhāng piào 他又买了两张票 **2** *pron* please give me a little more qǐng zài gěi wǒ yìxiē 请再给我一些；to cost more gènggùi 更贵；I did more than you wǒ zuò de bǐ nǐ duō 我做的比你多；she spends more of her time studying Chinese now xiànzài tā huā gèngduō de shíjiān xuéxí Hànyǔ 现在她花更多的时间学习汉语 **3** *adv* (*when comparing*) gèng 更；it's more complicated than that zhè bǐ nàge gèng fùzá 这比那个更复杂；(*when talking about time*) not...any more búzài… 不再…；he doesn't smoke any more tā búzài chōuyān le 他不再抽烟了 **4** more and more yuèláiyuè 越来越；more and more people can afford to buy cars yuèláiyuè duō de rén mǎi de qǐ qìchē le 越来越多的人买得起汽车了；more and more expensive yuèláiyuè gùi 越来越贵 **5** more or less huòduō - huòshǎo 或多或少 **6** more than duō 多；there were more than 20 people nàr yǒu èrshí duō gè rén 那儿有二十多个人

morning /ˈmɔːnɪŋ/ n a morning (*between dawn and 8 or 9 am*) yí gè zǎochén 一个早晨; (*between dawn and 12:00 noon*) yí gè shàngwǔ 一个上午; at three o'clock in the morning língchén sān diǎn zhōng 凌晨 3 点钟

mosquito /məsˈkiːtəʊ/ n a mosquito yí gè wénzi 一个蚊子

most /məʊst/ **1** det (*the majority of*) dàduōshù 大多数, dàbùfen 大部分; most schools start next week dàduōshù xuéxiào xiàge xīngqī kāixué 大多数学校下个星期开学; (*in quantity*) zuì duō 最多; who has the most money? shéi de qián zuì duō? 谁的钱最多? (*in degree*) zuì最; who has the most need of help? shéi zuì xūyào bāngzhù? 谁最需要帮助? **2** pron dàduōshù 大多数, dàbùfen 大部分; most of them are Chinese tāmen dāngzhōng dàduōshù shì Zhōngguórén 他们当中大多数是中国人; he did the most he could tā jìnle zuì dà de nǔlì 他尽了最大的努力 **3** adv zuì最; the most expensive shop in London Lúndūn zuì guì de shāngdiàn 伦敦最贵的商店; the most beautiful city in China Zhōngguó zuìměilì de chéngshì 中国最美丽的城市 **4** at (the) most zhìduō 至多, zuìduō 最多

mostly /ˈməʊstlɪ/ adv dàbùfen 大部分, duōbàn 多半

mother /ˈmʌðə(r)/ n a mother yí gè māma 一个妈妈; (*more formal*) yí wèi mǔqīn 一位母亲

mother-in-law /ˈmʌðərɪnlɔː/ n (*wife's mother*) yuèmǔ 岳母; (*husband's mother*) pópo 婆婆

motor /ˈməʊtə(r)/ n a motor (*a machine*) yì tái fādòngjī 一台发动机; (*a motor car*) yí liàng jīdòngchē 一辆机动车

motorbike /ˈməʊtəbaɪk/ n a motorbike yí liàng mótuōchē 一辆摩托车

motorcyclist /ˈməʊtəsaɪklɪst/ n a motorcyclist yí gè qí mótuōchē de rén 一个骑摩托车的人

motorist /ˈməʊtərɪst/ n a motorist yí gè kāi qìchē de rén 一个开汽车的人

motor racing /ˈməutə ˌreisiŋ/ n qìchē bǐsài 汽车比赛

motorway /ˈməutəwei/ n a motorway yì tiáo gāosù gōnglù 一条高速公路

mountain /ˈmauntin/ n a mountain yí zuò shān 一座山

mountain bike /ˈmauntin ˌbaik/ n a mountain bike yí liàng shāndì zìxíngchē 一辆山地自行车

mountain climbing /ˈmauntin ˌklaimiŋ/ n dēngshān 登山

mouse /maus/ n a mouse yì zhī lǎoshǔ 一只老鼠, yì zhī hàozi 一只耗子

moustache /məˈstɑːʃ/, **mustache** n a moustache yì zuǒ bāzìhú 一撮八字胡

mouth /mauθ/ n (of a person or an animal) zuǐ 嘴, kǒu 口; open your mouth bǎ kǒu zhāngkāi 把口张开; it has a big mouth tā de zuǐ hěn dà 它的嘴很大; (of a river or a volcano) kǒu 口; the mouth of [a river | a volcano] [hé | huǒshān] kǒu [河 | 火山] 口

move /muːv/ vb (to make a movement) don't move! bié dòng! 别动!; the train's starting to move huǒchē kāishǐ kāidòng le 火车开始开动了; (to make a movement with) to move the car yídòng qìchē 移动汽车; to move the chair (out of the way) bǎ yǐzi bānkāi 把椅子搬开; don't move the camera bié dòng zhàoxiàngjī 别动照相机; to move (house) bānjiā 搬家; (to live elsewhere) bānzǒu 搬走; (to make a movement away) líkāi 离开; to move away from the window líkāi chuānghu 离开窗户; move back (in house-moving) bānhuí 搬回; (to step back) hòutuì 后退; move forward qiánjìn 前进; move in bānjìn 搬进; he moved in yesterday tā zuótiān bān jìnqù le 他昨天搬进去了; move out bānchū 搬出

moved /muːvd/ adj to be moved to tears gǎndòng de liúlèi 感动得流泪

movement /ˈmuːvmənt/ n (a current of action) yùndòng 运动; a students' movement yí cì xuésheng yùndòng 一

次学生运动；(an act of moving) yídòng 移动，huódòng 活动

movie /'mu:vɪ/ (US English) n a movie yí bù diànyǐng 一部电影

movies /'mu:vɪz/ (US English) n the movies diànyǐng 电影

movie theatre /'mu:vɪ ˌθɪətə(r)/ (US English) n a movie theatre yí gè diànyǐngyuàn 一个电影院

moving /'mu:vɪŋ/ adj (affecting the feelings) dòngrén de 动人的，lìng rén gǎndòng de 令人感动的；(changing position) huódòng de 活动的

mow /məʊ/ vb gē 割；to mow the grass gē cǎo 割草；to mow the lawn xiūjiǎn cǎopíng 修剪草坪

MP /ˌem 'pi:/, **Member of Parliament** n an MP yí gè yìyuán 一个议员

Mr /'mɪstə(r)/ n xiānsheng 先生

Mrs /'mɪsɪz/ n fūrén 夫人，tàitai 太太

much /mʌtʃ/ **1** adv (in comparison) …duō …多；he is much taller than you tā bǐ nǐ gāo duō le 他比你高多了；her work is much more tiring tā de gōngzuò lèi duō le 她的工作累多了；(often) chángcháng 常常，jīngcháng 经常；they don't go out much tāmen bù jīngcháng chūqù 他们不经常出去；(when used with very or so) hěn 很，fēicháng 非常；he misses her very much tā hěn xiǎngniàn tā 他很想念她 **2** pron (in questions) hěn duō 很多；is there much to be done? yǒu hěn duō shì yào zuò ma? 有很多事要做吗？(in negative statements) he doesn't eat much tā chī de bù duō 他吃得不多 **3** det (a lot of) (in questions) hěn duō 很多；do you have much work? nǐ yǒu hěn duō gōngzuò ma? 你有很多工作吗？(in negative statements) duō 多；we haven't got much time wǒmen de shíjiān bù duō le 我们的时间不多了；(when used with how, very, too, so, or as) how much money have you got? nǐ yǒu duōshǎo qián? 你有多少钱？she doesn't eat very much meat tā chī ròu chī de bù duō 她吃肉吃得不多；I spent too much money wǒ huāqián huā de tài duō le 我花钱花得太多了；don't drink so much wine bié hē zhème duō jiǔ 别喝这么多酒；she has as much work as I do tā de gōngzuò hé wǒ de yíyàng duō 她的工作和我的一样多

mud /mʌd/ n ní 泥

mug /mʌg/ n a mug yí gè bēizi 一个杯子

multiply /'mʌltɪplaɪ/ vb (in arithmetic) chéng 乘；multiply three by five sān chéng wǔ 3 乘 5；(to increase) zēngjiā 增加；the population has multiplied there nàr rénkǒu zēngjiāle hěn duō 那儿人口增加了很多

mum, Mum /mʌm/ (British English) n māma 妈妈

murder /'mɜːdə(r)/ **1** n a murder yì qǐ móushā'àn 一起谋杀案 **2** vb móushā 谋杀

murderer /'mɜːdərə(r)/ n a murderer yí gè shārénfàn 一个杀人犯

muscle /'mʌsl/ n a muscle yí kuài jīròu 一块肌肉

museum /mjuːˈzɪəm/ n a museum yí gè bówùguǎn 一个博物馆

mushroom /'mʌʃruːm/ n a mushroom yí gè mógu 一个蘑菇

music /'mjuːzɪk/ n yīnyuè 音乐

musical instrument /ˌmjuːzɪkəl 'ɪnstrəmənt/ n a musical instrument yí jiàn yuèqì 一件乐器

musician /mjuːˈzɪʃən/ n a musician (a person who works with music) yí gè yīnyuè gōngzuòzhě 一个音乐工作者；(a person who is famed for working with music) yí gè yīnyuèjiā 一个音乐家

Muslim /'mʊzlɪm/ adj Mùsīlín de 穆斯林的

mussel /'mʌsəl/ n a mussel yí gè gébèi 一个蛤贝

must /mʌst/ vb (when indicating obligation) bìxū 必须，yídìng děi 一定得；you must come on time nǐ yídìng děi zhǔnshí lái 你一定得准时来；she must take the exam in June tā bìxū cānjiā liùyuè de kǎoshì 她必须参加 6 月的考试；(when indicating necessity) yídìng yào

一定要；you must go to the doctor nǐ yídìng yào qù kàn yīshēng 你一定要去看医生；we mustn't tell anyone wǒmen yídìng búyào gàosu rènhé rén 我们一定不要告诉任何人；(when assuming something is true) yídìng 一定，hěn kěnéng 很可能；he must be kidding tā yídìng shì zài kāi wánxiào 他一定是在开玩笑；they must have left tāmen hěn kěnéng yǐjīng zǒu le 他们很可能已经走了；(when indicating prohibition, with 'not') bùzhǔn 不准，jìnzhǐ 禁止；cars mustn't be parked in front of the gate ménqián bùzhǔn tíngchē 门前不准停车

mustard /'mʌstəd/ n jièmo 芥末

mutton /'mʌtən/ n yángròu 羊肉

my /maɪ/ det wǒ de 我的；this is my car zhè shì wǒ de chē 这是我的车；I broke my leg wǒ bǎ tuǐ shuāiduàn le 我把腿摔断了！Note that when talking about parts of the body，wǒ de 我的 is not used.

myself /maɪ'self/ pron(when used as a reflexive pronoun) zìjǐ 自己 I didn't hurt myself wǒ méiyǒu shānghe zìjǐ 我没有伤害自己；I bought myself a new watch wǒ gěi zìjǐ mǎile yí kuài xīn shǒubiǎo 我给自己买了一块新手表；(when used for emphasis) I told them myself shì wǒ qīnzì gàosu tāmen de 是我亲自告诉他们的；I did it all by myself zhè dōu shì wǒ yí gè rén zuò de 这都是我一个人做的

mystery /'mɪstərɪ/ n a mystery yí gè mí 一个谜

Nn

nail /neɪl/ n (for use in attaching, repairing) dīngzi 钉子；a nail yì kē dīngzi 一颗钉子；(on the fingers or toes) zhǐjiǎ 指甲；a nail yí gè zhǐjiǎ 一个指甲

nail polish /'neɪl pɒlɪʃ/ n zhǐjiǎyóu 指甲油

naked /'neɪkɪd/ adj (when describing the body) luǒtǐ de 裸体的，guāngzhe de 光着的；naked trees guāngtūtū de shù 光秃秃的树；a naked light yì zhǎn méiyǒu zhào de dēng 一盏没有罩的灯

name /neɪm/ n a name yí gè míngzi 一个名字；what's your name? nǐ jiào shénme míngzi? 你叫什么名字？my name is Louis wǒ (de míngzi) jiào Lùyìsī 我(的名字)叫路易斯

narrow /'nærəʊ/ adj zhǎi de 窄的，xiázhǎi de 狭窄的

nasty /'nɑːstɪ/ adj (when referring to a smell) nánwén de 难闻的，chòu de 臭的；(threatening, dangerous) xiōngxiǎn de 凶险的；(ill-natured) bēibì de 卑鄙的；nasty weather huài tiānqì 坏天气

national /'næʃənəl/ adj (of a country) guójiā de 国家的；the national team guójiāduì 国家队；(nation-wide) quánguóxìng de 全国性的；a national newspaper quánguóxìng de bàozhǐ 全国性的报纸；national income guómín shōurù 国民收入；national economy guómín jīngjì 国民经济；national anthem guógē 国歌；(referring to a group of people marked by common descent, language, culture, or historical tradition) mínzú de 民族的；national costume mínzú fúzhuāng 民族服装

native /'neɪtɪv/ adj a native language yì zhǒng mǔyǔ 一种母语；a native Chinese speaker mǔyǔ shì Hànyǔ de rén 母语是汉语的人

natural /'nætʃərəl/ adj (not made by humans) natural gas tiānránqì 天然气；natural resources zìrán zīyuán 自然资源；(happening in the usual course of things) zìrán de 自然的；a natural voice zìrán de shēngyīn 自然的声音；(normal) zhèngcháng de 正常的；a natural death zhèngcháng sǐwáng 正常死亡

naturally /'nætʃərəlɪ/ adv (in a natural manner) zìrán 自然；she acted very naturally tā biǎoyǎn de hěn zìrán 她表演得很自然；(of course) dāngrán 当然；he'll naturally be sad when he hears the news tā tīngdào xiāoxi hòu dāngrán huì nánguò 他听到消息后当然会难过

nature /'neɪtʃə(r)/ *n* (*the external world untouched by human beings*) zìránjiè 自然界；dàzìrán 大自然；(*inborn mind*) běnxìng 本性；(*disposition of a person*) gèxìng 个性；(*kind, sort*) zhǒng 种，lèi 类；mistakes of this nature zhè zhǒng cuòwù 这种错误；(*character of a certain matter*) xìngzhì 性质；this incident is quite serious in nature zhè jiàn shì de xìngzhì xiāngdāng yánzhòng 这件事的性质相当严重；the two questions are different in nature zhè liǎng gè wèntí de xìngzhì bù tóng 这两个问题的性质不同

naughty /'nɔːtɪ/ *adj* táoqì de 淘气的，tiáopí de 调皮的

navy /'neɪvɪ/ *n* hǎijūn 海军

navy blue /ˌneɪvɪ 'bluː/ *adj* zàngqīngsè de 藏青色的，hǎijūnlán de 海军蓝的

near /nɪə(r)/ **1** *prep* (*in proximity*) he lives near us tā zhù zài wǒmen fùjìn 他住在我们附近；(*with respect to a goal*) the new house is near completion zhè zuò xīn fángzi jiùyào wángōng le 这座新房子就要完工了 **2** *adv* (*close by*) they live quite near tāmen zhù de hěn jìn 他们住得很近；(*in time*) Christmas is drawing near Shèngdàn Jié kuài dào le 圣诞节快到了 **3** *adj* (*close*) jìn 近的；the school is quite near xuéxiào hěn jìn 学校很近；a near relative yí gè jìnqīn 一个近亲；in the near future bùjiǔ 不久，bùjiǔ de jiānglái 不久的将来

nearby /'nɪəˌbaɪ/ *adv* zài fùjìn 在附近

nearly /'nɪəlɪ/ *adv* chàbuduō 差不多，jīhū 几乎；I nearly [forgot | gave up | fell asleep] wǒ jīhū [wàng le | fàngqì le | shuìzháo le] 我几乎[忘了|放弃了|睡着了]；we're nearly there wǒmen kuài dào nàr le 我们快到那儿了

neat /niːt/ *adj* (*when describing a room, someone's clothing*) zhěngjié de 整洁的；(*when describing someone's handwriting*) gōngzhěng de 工整的；(*when describing objects that have been arranged*) zhěngqí de 整齐的

necessary /'nesɪsərɪ/ adj (when referring to something that must be or happen)bìxū de 必须的，yǒu bìyào de 有必要的；it's necessary to tell him immediately bìxū lìjí gàosu tā 必须立即告诉他；(when used with not)búbì 不必；it is not necessary for you to come nǐ búbì lái 你不必来；(indispensable)bìxū de 必需的；I'll only take the necessary tools wǒ zhǐ dài nàxiē bìxū de gōngjù 我只带那些必需的工具；(unavoidable)bìrán de 必然的；a necessary outcome yí gè bìrán jiéguǒ 一个必然结果；if necessary rúguǒ yǒu bìyào (de huà) 如果有必要(的话)；I'll phone you if necessary rúguǒ yǒu bìyào, wǒ huì gěi nǐ dǎ diànhuà 如果有必要，我会给你打电话

neck /nek/ n bózi 脖子

necklace /'neklɪs/ n a necklace yì tiáo xiàngliàn 一条项链

need /niːd/ vb (used with not to mean not have to)búbì 不必，bù xūyào 不需要；you don't need to ask him nǐ búbì wèn tā 你不必问他；the house doesn't need to be sold zhè zuò fángzi bù xūyào mài 这座房子不需要卖；(to have to or want)xūyào 需要；they need to leave early tāmen xūyào zǎo lái 他们需要早来；they need [money| help| friends...] tāmen xūyào [qián| bāngzhù| péngyou...] 他们需要[钱|帮助|朋友]；we need to see the doctor wǒmen xūyào kàn yīshēng 我们需要看医生

needle /'niːdl/ n a needle yì gēn zhēn 一根针

negative /'negətɪv/ **1** adj (expressing denial, refusal, or prohibition)fǒudìng de 否定的；a negative answer yí gè fǒudìng de huídá 一个否定的回答；(unconstructive)xiāojí de 消极的；(in mathematics and when referring to an electrical charge)fù de 负的 **2** n (a word that expresses denial)fǒudìngcí 否定词；a negative yí gè fǒudìngcí 一个否定词；(in photography)dǐpiàn 底片；a negative yì zhāng dǐpiàn 一张底片

neighbour /'neɪbə(r)/ (British English), **neighbor** (US

English) *n* a neighbour yí gè línjū 一个邻居

neither /'naɪðə(r)/ **1** *conj* (*in* neither...nor *sentences*) jì bù···yě bù 既不···也不···; jì méi···yě méi 既没···也没···; **she speaks neither Chinese nor Japanese** tā jì bú huì shuō Hànyǔ yě bú huì shuō Rìyǔ 她既不会说汉语也不会说日语; **I have neither the time nor the energy to argue with him** wǒ jì méiyǒu shíjiān yě méiyǒu jīnglì gēn tā zhēnglùn 我既没有时间也没有精力跟他争论; **I bought neither fruits nor vegetables** wǒ jì méi mǎi shuǐguǒ yě méi mǎi qīngcài 我既没买水果也没买青菜; (*nor*) yě bù 也不, yě méi 也没; 'I don't agree'—'neither do I' "wǒ bù tóngyì"—"wǒ yě bù tóngyì" "我不同意"—"我也不同意"; 'I didn't come'—'neither did she' "wǒ méi lái"—"tā yě méi lái" "我没来"—"她也没来"! *Note that in sentences using the verb* yǒu 有, *or sentences indicating past events,* (neither...) nor... *is translated as* (jì méi···) yě méi··· (既没···) 也没··· **2** *det* liǎng··· dōu bù/méi 两···都不/没; **neither book is mine** liǎng běn shū dōu bú shì wǒ de 两本书都不是我的; **neither girl came** liǎng gè nǚháir dōu méi lái 两个女孩儿都没来 **3** *pron* liǎng···dōu bù 两···都不, liǎng··· dōu méi 两···都没; **neither of them is coming** tāmen liǎng gè dōu bù lái 他们两个都不来; **neither of us has met her** wǒmen liǎng gè dōu méi jiànguò tā 我们两个都没见过她! *Note that in sentences with the verb* yǒu 有 *or sentences indicating past events, the determiner* **neither** *and the pronoun* **neither** *are translated as* liǎng···dōu méi 两···都没。

nephew /'nevju:/ *n* (*brother's son*) zhízi 侄子; **a nephew** yí gè zhízi 一个侄子; (*sister's son*) wàisheng 外甥; **a nephew** yí gè wàisheng 一个外甥

nerve /nɜːv/ *n* shénjīng 神经; **to get on someone's nerves** shǐ mǒu rén xīnfán 使某人心烦

nervous /'nɜːvəs/ *adj* (*frightened*) hàipà de 害怕的; (*anxious*) jǐnzhāng de 紧张的; **to feel nervous** gǎndào jǐnzhāng 感到紧张

nest /nest/ n a nest (for birds) yí gè cháo 一个巢, yí gè wō 一个窝; (for mice, wasps) yí gè wō 一个窝

net /net/ n (for fishing) yúwǎng 渔网; a net yì zhāng yúwǎng 一张渔网; (in sports) wǎng 网

Netherlands /'neðələndz/ n Hélán 荷兰

network /'netwɜːk/ n wǎng 网; a [radio | TV | railway...] network yí gè [guǎngbō | diànshì | tiělù...] wǎng 一个 [广播 | 电视 | 铁路...] 网

neutral /'njuːtrəl/ adj (not siding with either party) zhōnglì de 中立的; a neutral nation yí gè zhōnglìguó 一个中立国; (belonging to neither of two opposites in chemistry or electronics) zhōngxìng de 中性的

never /'nevə(r)/ adv (for future events or actions)jué bù 决不, yǒngyuǎn bù 永远不; I'll never go back again wǒ jué bú huì zài huíqù 我决不会再回去; she'll never forget that day tā yǒngyuǎn bú huì wàngjì nà yì tiān tā 永远不会忘记那一天; (for habitual events or actions) cónglái bù 从来不; they never come to see us tāmen cónglái bù lái kàn wǒmen 他们从来不来看我们; (for past events or actions) cónglái méi(yǒu) 从来没(有); she's never been to China tā cónglái méi(yǒu) qùguò Zhōngguó 她从来没(有)去过中国; never in my life have I read such a good novel wǒ cónglái méi(yǒu) kànguo zhème hǎo de xiǎoshuō 我从来没(有)看过这么好的小说

nevertheless /ˌnevəðə'les/ adv rán'ér 然而, búguò 不过

new /njuː/ adj xīn de 新的; a new bike yí liàng xīn zìxíngchē 一辆新自行车

newborn baby /ˈnjuːbɔːn ˌbeɪbɪ/ n a newborn baby yí gè xīnshēng yīng'ér 一个新生婴儿

news /njuːz/ n a piece of news yì tiáo xiāoxi 一条消息; have you heard the news? nǐ tīngdào zhè tiáo xiāoxi le ma? 你听到这条消息了吗?; (on radio, TV)xīnwén 新闻

newsagent's /ˈnjuːzˌeɪdʒənts/ n (British English) a

newsagent's yì jiā bàokān xiāoshòudiàn 一家报刊销售店

newspaper /ˈnjuːzˌpeɪpə(r)/ n a newspaper (a sheet) yì zhāng bàozhǐ 一张报纸；(if it consists of more than one sheet) yí fèn bàozhǐ 一份报纸

New Year /ˌnjuː ˈjɜː(r)/ n xīnnián 新年；Happy New Year! xīnnián kuàilè! 新年快乐!

New Year's Day /ˌnjuː jɜːz ˈdeɪ/, **New Year's** /ˌnjuː ˈjɜːz/ (US English) n Yuándàn 元旦

New Year's Eve /ˌnjuː jɜːz ˈiːv/ n chúxī 除夕

New Zealand /ˌnjuː ˈziːlənd/ n Xīnxīlán 新西兰

next /nekst/ **1** adj (when talking about what is still to come or what followed) xiàmiàn de 下面的；I'll take the next train to London wǒ zuò xià (yì) bān huǒchē qù Lúndūn 我坐下(一)班火车去伦敦；we chatted while waiting for the next bus wǒmen yìbiān liáotiān yìbiān děng xià (yí) tàng qìchē 我们一边聊天一边等下(一)趟汽车；'who's next?'—'I'm next' shéi shì xià yí gè?'—'wǒ shì xià yí gè' "谁是下一个?"—"我是下一个"；(when talking about future time) next [week│month│term] xiàge [xīngqī│yuè│xuéqí] 下个 [星期│月│学期]；next year míngnián 明年；next time xià yí cì 下一次；(when talking about the past) dì-èr 第二；the next [day│week│month│year], we went to Shanghai dì-èr [tiān│gè xīngqī│gè yuè│nián], wǒmen qùle Shànghǎi 第二 [天│个星期│个月│年], 我们去了上海 **2** adv (in the past) ránhòu 然后, jiēzhe 接着；what happened next? ránhòu fāshēngle shénme shì? 然后发生了什么事?；(now) xiàmiàn 下面, jiēxiàlái 接下来；what'll we do next? wǒmen xiàmiàn zuò shénme? 我们下面做什么?；(in the future) xià (yí) cì 下(一)次；when will you go to China next? nǐ xià (yī) cì shénme shíhou qù Zhōngguó? 你下(一)次什么时候去中国? **3** next to (adjacent to) jǐnʾāi 紧挨, jǐnkào 紧靠；(in rank) jǐn cìyú 仅次于

next door /ˌnekst ˈdɔː(r)/ adv gébì 隔壁

nice /naɪs/ adj (when talking about the weather) hǎo de 好

的；it's a nice day today jīntiān tiānqì hěn hǎo 今天天
气很好；(kind, friendly)hǎo de 好的；a nice girl yí gè
hǎo gūniang 一个好姑娘；to be nice to someone duì
mǒu rén hěn hǎo 对某人很好；(pleasant, delightful)lìng
rén yúkuài de 令人愉快的；we had a nice holiday
wǒmen dùguòle yí gè lìng rén yúkuài de jiàqī 我们度过了
一个令人愉快的假期

nickname /'nɪkneɪm/ n a nickname(given in contempt)
yí gè wàihào 一个外号，yí gè chuòhào 一个绰号；(given
to express affection) yí gè àichēng 一个爱称

niece /niːs/ n a niece(brother's daughter)yí gè zhínǚ 一
个侄女；(sister's daughter)yí gè wàishengnǚ 一个外甥女

night /naɪt/ n (as opposed to day)yè 夜；a night yí yè
一夜；I didn't sleep last night wǒ zuótiān yí yè méi shuì
我昨天一夜没睡；he stayed out all night tā yì zhěng yè
dōu zài wàimian 他一整夜都在外面；(evening)wǎnshang
晚上；a night yí gè wǎnshang 一个晚上；last night
zuótiān wǎnshang 昨天晚上；at night zài yèli 在夜里；
late at night zài shēnyè 在深夜

nightclub /'naɪtklʌb/ n a nightclub yí gè yèzǒnghuì 一个
夜总会

nightdress /'naɪtdres/ (British English), **nightgown**
/'naɪtgaun/ (US English) n a nightdress yí jiàn shuìyī 一
件睡衣

nightmare /'naɪtmeə(r)/ n a nightmare yí gè èmèng 一
个恶梦；to have a nightmare zuò yí gè èmèng 做一个恶
梦

nil /nɪl/ n líng 零

nine /naɪn/ num jiǔ 九

nineteen /ˌnaɪn'tiːn/ num shíjiǔ 十九

nineteenth /ˌnaɪn'tiːnθ/ num(in a series)dì-shíjiǔ 第十
九；(in dates) the nineteenth of July qīyuè shíjiǔ rì 7
月 19 日

ninety /'naɪntɪ/ num jiǔshí 九十

ninth /naɪnθ/ num(in a series)dì-jiǔ 第九；(in dates)

the ninth of December shí'èr yuè jiǔ rì 12 月 9 日

no /nəʊ/ **1** adv (in negative answers) bù 不; 'do you like it?'—'no, I don't' "nǐ xǐhuan ma?"—"bù, wǒ bù xǐhuan" "你喜欢吗?"—"不,我不喜欢"; (in a negative response to a negative statement or question) shì de 是的, duì 对; 'is he not coming?'—'no, he is not' "tā bù lái ma?"—"shìde, tā bù lái" "他不来吗?"—"是的,他不来"; 'you didn't go, did you?'—'no, I didn't' "nǐ méi qù, duì ma?"—"duì, wǒ méi qù" "你没去,对吗?"—"对,我没去"; no longer búzài 不再; he no longer smokes tā búzài chōuyān le 他不再抽烟了 **2** det (not any) méiyǒu 没有; we have no money wǒmen méiyǒu qián 我们没有钱; there are no trains méiyǒu huǒchē 没有火车; it's no problem méiyǒu wèntí 没有问题; (when refusing permission) bùxǔ 不许, jìnzhǐ 禁止; no smoking jìnzhǐ xīyān 禁止吸烟; no talking! bùxǔ jiǎnghuà! 不许讲话!

nobody /'nəʊbədɪ/ ▶ **no-one**

noise /nɔɪz/ n (sound of any kind) xiǎngshēng 响声; (excessively loud or disturbing sound) zàoshēng 噪声

noisy /'nɔɪzɪ/ adj cáoza de 嘈杂的, zàoshēng dà de 噪声大的

none /nʌn/ pron none of yí gè yě bù 一个也不, dōu bù 都不; none of [us | you | them...] can speak German [wǒmen | nǐmen | tāmen...] yí gè yě bú huì shuō Déyǔ [我们 | 你们 | 他们...] 一个也不会说德语; none of the [books | gifts | clothes...] is mine zhèxiē [shū | lǐwù | yīfu...] dōu bú shì wǒ de 这些 [书 | 礼物 | 衣服...] 都不是我的; (when used in sentences with the verb yǒu 有, or in sentences indicating past events or actions) yí gè yě méiyǒu 一个也没有, dōu méiyǒu 都没有; none of the girls went to the class nǚháizi yí gè yě méiyǒu qù shàngkè 女孩子一个也没有去上课; none of us has his telephone number wǒmen dōu méiyǒu tā de diànhuà hàomǎ 我们都没有他的电话号码; (when referring to something uncountable) yìdiǎnr yě méiyǒu 一点儿也没有；I wanted some bread but there was none left in the house wǒ xiǎng chī miànbāo, kěshì jiā li yìdiǎnr yě méiyǒu le 我想吃面包，可是家里一点儿也没有了！ Note that the measure word gè 个 in yí gè yě bù 一个也不 and yí gè yě méiyǒu 一个也没有 is replaced by a different measure word, such as jiàn 件 and běn 本, when certain nouns, such as yīfu 衣服 and shū 书, are used.

noodles /'nuːdlz/ n miàntiáo 面条

nonsense /'nɒnsəns/ n húshuō 胡说, fèihuà 废话

noon /nuːn/ n zhōngwǔ 中午

no-one /'nəʊwʌn/ pron (also **nobody**)！ Note that in sentences with the verb yǒu 有 or in sentences describing past events or actions, the negative méi 没 is used instead of bù 不；(when used as a subject) shéi yě bù 谁也不；méiyǒu rén 没有人；no-one has a Japanese dictionary shéi yě méiyǒu Rìwén cídiǎn 谁也没有日文词典；no-one tells me anything méiyǒu rén gàosu wǒ rènhé shìqing 没有人告诉我任何事情；no-one saw him méiyǒu rén kànjiàn tā 没有人看见他；(when used as an object) shéi yě bù 谁也不；I know no-one wǒ shéi yě bú rènshi 我谁也不认识；I saw no-one wǒ shéi yě méi kànjiàn 我谁也没看见

nor /nɔː(r)/ conj！ For translations of nor when used in combination with **neither**, look at the entry for **neither** in this dictionary；yě bù 也不；'I don't like him'—'nor do I'"wǒ bù xǐhuan tā"—"wǒ yě bù xǐhuan tā"“我不喜欢他”—“我也不喜欢他”；(when used with the verb yǒu 有 or to describe past events or actions) yě méi(yǒu) 也没(有)；I don't have any money and nor does he wǒ méiyǒu qián, tā yě méiyǒu qián 我没有钱,他也没有钱；he didn't come and nor did his wife tā méi(yǒu) lái, tā tàitai yě méi(yǒu) lái 他没(有)来,他太太也没(有)来

normal /'nɔːməl/ adj zhèngcháng de 正常的

normally /'nɔːməlɪ/ adv yìbān 一般，tōngcháng 通常

north /nɔːθ/ **1** n (when talking about the direction) běi 北，(when talking about the region) běifāng 北方，běibù 北部；in the north of China zài Zhōngguó de běifāng 在中国的北方 **2** adv (when talking about the direction) xiàng běi 向北，wǎng běi 往北；to drive north xiàng běi kāi 向北开；(when talking about the region) zài…běibiānr 在…北边儿；to live north of Beijing zhù zài Běijīng běibiānr 住在北京北边儿 **3** adj běi de 北的；to work in north London zài Lúndūn běibù gōngzuò 在伦敦北部工作

North America /ˌnɔːθ ə'merɪkə/ n Běi Měizhōu 北美洲

northeast /ˌnɔːθ'iːst/ n dōngběi 东北

Northern Ireland /ˌnɔːðən 'aɪələnd/ n Northern Ireland Běi Ài'ěrlán 北爱尔兰

northwest /ˌnɔːθ'west/ n the northwest xīběi 西北

Norway /'nɔːweɪ/ n Nuówēi 挪威

Norwegian /nɔː'wiːdʒən/ **1** adj Nuówēi de 挪威的 **2** n the Norwegians Nuówēirén 挪威人

nose /nəʊz/ n bízi 鼻子

not /nɒt/ **1** adv bù 不；this film is not bad zhè bù diànyǐng búcuò 这部电影不错；we are going to go out whether it rains or not bùguǎn xià bú xiàyǔ, wǒmen dōu yào chūqù 不管下不下雨，我们都要出去；he hasn't he phoned you? tā hái méi gěi nǐ dǎ diànhuà ma? 他还没给你打电话吗？ **2 not at all** (in no way) yìdiǎnr yě bù 一点也不；he's not at all worried tā yìdiǎnr yě bù dānxīn 他一点儿也不担心；'thanks a lot'—'not at all' "thanks a lot"—'not at all' "fēicháng gǎnxiè"—"búkèqi" "非常感谢"—"不客气"

note /nəʊt/ **1** n (to remind oneself) bǐjì 笔记，jìlù 记录；(a message) biàntiáo 便条；a note yì zhāng biàntiáo 一张便条；I left you a note wǒ gěi nǐ liúle yì zhāng biàntiáo 我给你留了一张便条；(an explanation attached to a text) zhùshì 注释；a note yì tiáo zhùshì 一条注释；(British English) (money) chāopiào 钞票，zhǐbì 纸币；a note yì zhāng chāopiào 一张钞票；a 50-pound note yì zhāng wǔshí yīngbàng de zhǐbì 一张 50 英镑的纸币 **2** vb (to make a note of) jìlù 记录，jìxià 记下；(to notice) zhùyì 注意

notebook /'nəutbuk/ n a notebook yì gè bǐjìběn 一个笔记本

nothing /'nʌθɪŋ/ pron ! Note that **shénme** 什么 often appears at the beginning of the sentence or after the subject；shénme (…) yě méiyǒu 什么(…) 也没有；**nothing has changed** shénme yě méiyǒu biàn 什么也没有变；**there's nothing left** shénme yě méiyǒu le 什么也没有了；**she said nothing** tā shénme yě méiyǒu shuō 她什么也没有说；(when used with verbs indicating the current state) shénme… shénme yě bù zhīdào 什么… 什么也不知道；**I know nothing** wǒ shénme yě bù zhīdào 我什么也不知道；**she is interested in nothing modern** xiàndài de dōngxi tā shénme yě bù gǎn xìngqù 现代的东西她什么也不感兴趣；**he likes nothing** tā shénme yě bù xǐhuan 他什么也不喜欢；**to have nothing to do with** hé … wúguān 和 … 无关；**I had nothing to do with it** wǒ hé zhè jiàn shì wúguān 我和这件事无关；**it's nothing to do with us** zhè jiàn shì hé wǒmen wúguān 这件事和我们无关

notice /'nəutɪs/ **1** vb (to observe) zhùyì 注意；(to write or publish a notice of) tōngzhī 通知 **2** n (an announcement circulated internally) tōngzhī 通知；**a notice** yí fèn tōngzhī 一份通知；(an announcement to the public) tōnggào 通告，bùgào 布告；**a notice** yì zhāng tōnggào 一张通告；(a warning) (yùxiān) … tōngzhī (预先) … 通知；**my landlord gave me a month's notice to move out** wǒ de fángdōng yùxiān yí gè yuè tōngzhī wǒ bān chūqù 我的房东预先一个月通知我搬出去；**the meeting was cancelled at short notice** huìyì línshí tōngzhī qǔxiāo le 会议临时通知取消了；**don't take any notice of this matter** bié lǐhuì zhè jiàn shì 别理会这件事

novel /'nɒvəl/ n a novel yì běn xiǎoshuō 一本小说

November /nəu'vembə(r)/ n shíyī yuè 十一月

now /nau/ **1** adv (at the present time) xiànzài 现在；he is in his office now tā xiànzài zài bàngōngshì li tā xiànzài zài 他现在在办公室里；from now on cóng xiànzài qǐ 从现在起；(immediately) mǎshàng 马上，lìkè 立刻；we have to do it now wǒmen bìxū mǎshàng zuò zhè jiàn shì 我们必须马上做这件事；do it right now xiànzài mǎshàng zuò 现在马上做 **2** now and again, now and then shícháng 时常，chángcháng 常常

nowhere /'nəuhweə(r)/ **1** adv (not to any place) nǎr dōu bù néng 哪儿都不，rènhé dìfang dōu bù 任何地方都不；I go nowhere without my dog méiyǒu wǒ de gǒu wǒ nǎr dōu bú qù 没有我的狗我哪儿都不去；(in sentences describing past actions) nǎr dōu méi 哪儿都没，rènhé dìfang dōu méi 任何地方都没；she went nowhere tā nǎr dōu méi qù 她哪儿都没去 **2** n méiyǒu dìfang 没有地方；there is nowhere to sit méiyǒu dìfang zuò 没有地方坐

nuclear /'nju:klɪə(r)/ adj (central) héxīn de 核心的，zhōngxīn de 中心的；(pertaining to the nucleus of an atom) a nuclear bomb yì kē yuánzǐdàn 一颗原子弹；a nuclear power-station yí zuò hédiànzhàn 一座核电站；a nuclear war yì chǎng hézhànzhēng 一场核战争；nuclear weapons héwǔqì 核武器

nuisance /'nju:sns/ n these flies are a nuisance zhèxiē cāngying zhēn tǎoyàn 这些苍蝇真讨厌；it's a nuisance having to pay in cash zhēn máfan, hái děi fù xiànjīn 真麻烦，还得付现金

numb /nʌm/ adj mámù de 麻木的；my hands are numb wǒ de shǒu mámù le 我的手麻木了；(anaesthetized) shīqù gǎnjué de 失去感觉的

number /'nʌmbə(r)/ **1** n a number (a figure) yí gè shù (-zì) 一个数(字)；(of a house, a bus, a telephone, a passport) yí gè hàomǎ 一个号码；(when talking about quantities) a number of yìxiē 一些；a number of people yìxiē rén 一些人；a small number of tourists wéishù bù duō de lǚyóuzhě 为数不多的旅游者；a large number of

new products dàliàng de xīn chǎnpǐn 大量的新产品 **2** vb (to give a number to) gěi…biānhào 给…编号；to number the documents gěi wénjiàn biānhào 给文件编号；(to amount to) zǒngjì 总计

number plate /'nʌmbə pleɪt/ n (British English) a number plate yí gè páizhào 一个牌照

nun /nʌn/ n a nun (Christian) yí gè xiūnǚ 一个修女；(Buddhist) yí gè nígū 一个尼姑

nurse /nɜːs/ n a nurse yí gè hùshi 一个护士

nursery /'nɜːsərɪ/ n a nursery yí gè tuō'érsuǒ 一个托儿所

nursery school /'nɜːsərɪ ˌskuːl/ n a nursery school yí gè yòu'éryuán 一个幼儿园

nut /nʌt/ n a nut (a walnut) yí gè hútáo 一个胡桃；(a chestnut) yí gè lìzi 一个栗子

nylon /'naɪlɒn/ n nílóng 尼龙

Oo

---

oak /əʊk/ n (a tree) xiàngshù 橡树；an oak yì kē xiàngshù 一棵橡树；(for making furniture, etc.) zuòmù 柞木，xiàngmù 橡木

oar /ɔː(r)/ n an oar yì gēn jiǎng 一根桨

obedient /əʊ'biːdɪənt/ adj shùncóng de 顺从的，gōngshùn de 恭顺的

obey /əʊ'beɪ/ vb fúcóng 服从，tīngcóng 听从；to obey someone fúcóng mǒu rén 服从某人；to obey the law zūnshǒu fǎlǜ 遵守法律

object /'ɒbdʒɪkt/ **1** n an object (a thing) yí gè dōngxi 一个东西；(something on which attention, interest, or emotion is fixed) yí gè duìxiàng 一个对象；(an end or goal) yí gè mùdì 一个目的；(part of a sentence) yí gè bīnyǔ 一个宾语 **2** vb fǎnduì 反对，bú zànchéng 不赞成；

object to this plan wǒ fǎnduì zhège jìhuà 我反对这个计划

oblige /əˈblaɪdʒ/ vb to be obliged to leave bèipò líkāi 被迫离开；to oblige someone to apologize qiǎngpò mǒu rén dàoqiàn 强迫某人道歉

observe /əbˈzɜːv/ vb (to watch attentively) guānchá 观察，kàn 看；(to notice) zhùyì 注意；(to act according to) zūnshǒu 遵守

obtain /əbˈteɪn/ vb dédào 得到，huòdé 获得

obvious /ˈɒbvɪəs/ adj míngxiǎn de 明显的，xiǎn'éryìjiàn de 显而易见的

obviously /ˈɒbvɪəslɪ/ adv xiǎnrán 显然

occasion /əˈkeɪʒən/ n (an event) an occasion yí gè chǎnghé 一个场合；on special occasions zài tèshū chǎnghé xià 在特殊场合下；(an opportunity) yí gè jīhuì 一个机会

occasionally /əˈkeɪʒənəlɪ/ adv ǒu'ěr 偶尔，ǒurán 偶然

occupy /ˈɒkjʊpaɪ/ vb (when talking about taking over a piece of land or a place) zhànlǐng 占领，zhànjù 占据；(when talking about taking up space or time) zhànyòng 占用，zhàn 占；she is occupied in writing a novel tā zhèng mángyú xiě xiǎoshuō 她正忙于写小说

occur /əˈkɜː(r)/ vb (to happen) fāshēng 发生；a traffic accident has occurred fāshēngle yì qǐ jiāotōng shìgù 发生了一起交通事故；(to come to mind) a good idea occurred to me wǒ xiǎngchūle yí gè hǎo zhǔyi 我想出了一个好主意；it suddenly occurred to him that he had to phone his wife tā tūrán xiǎngdào tā děi gěi tā tàitai dǎ diànhuà 他突然想到他得给他太太打电话

ocean /ˈəʊʃən/ n hǎiyáng 海洋

o'clock /əˈklɒk/ adv diǎn (zhōng) 点 (钟)；it's five o'clock now xiànzài wǔ diǎn (zhōng) 现在 5 点 (钟)

October /ɒkˈtəʊbə(r)/ n shíyuè 十月

octopus /ˈɒktəpəs/ n an octopus yì tiáo zhāngyú 一条章鱼

oculist /'ɒkjʊlɪst/ *n* an oculist (*an eye doctor*) yí gè yǎnkē yīshēng 一个眼科医生

odd /ɒd/ *adj* (*strange*) qíguài de 奇怪的，gǔguài de 古怪的；(*unpaired*) dānzhī de 单只的，bù chéngduì de 不成对的；(*when talking about numbers*) an odd number (*in mathematics*) yí gè jīshù 一个奇数；(*of a house, cinema seat or room*) yí gè dānhào 一个单号

odour /'əʊdə(r)/ (*British English*), **odor** (*US English*) *n* wèir 味儿，yì zhǒng wèir 一种味儿

of /强 ɒv; 弱 əv/ *prep* de 的；the sound of an engine fādòngjī de shēngyīn 发动机的声音；in the centre of Beijing zài Běijīng de shìzhōngxīn 在北京的市中心；the names of the pupils xuésheng de míngzi 学生的名字；(*when talking about quantities*)！Of is usually not translated in this use；a kilo of potatoes yì gōngjīn tǔdòu 一公斤土豆；a bottle of mineral water yì píng kuàngquánshuǐ 一瓶矿泉水；(*when talking about a smaller number out of a larger whole*) six of them tāmen dāngzhōng de liù gè rén 他们当中的 6 个人；only three of the students came xuésheng zhǐ láile sān gè 学生只来了 3 个；(*when the number or group mentioned is the entire whole*)！Of is usually not translated in this use；there were six of them tāmen yígòng liù gè rén 他们一共 6 个人；all of us agree wǒmen dōu tóngyì 我们都同意；(*when talking about cause*) he died of cancer tā sǐ yú áizhèng 他死于癌症；(*when talking about the material or substance used*) the bottle is made of plastic zhège píngzi shì sùliào zuò de 这个瓶子是塑料做的

off /ɒf/！Frequently off occurs in combinations with verbs, for example: get off, go off, take off, etc. To find the correct translations for this type of verb, look up the separate dictionary entries at get, go, take, etc. **1** *adv* (*leaving*) zǒu le 走了；I'm off wǒ yào zǒu le 我要走了；(*going*) qù 去；they are off to Japan tomorrow tāmen míngtiān yào qù Rìběn 他们明天要去日本；where are you off to? nǐ qù nǎr? 你去哪儿?;(*away*) the coast is a long way off hǎibiān lí zhèr hěn yuǎn 海边离这儿很远;Christmas is only a month off lí Shèngdàn Jié zhǐyǒu yí ge yuè le 离圣诞节只有一个月了;(*free*) to take a day off xiūjià yì tiān 休假一天;today's her day off jīntiān tā xiūxi 今天她休息;(*not working, switched off*) the lights are all off diàndēng quán miè le 电灯全灭了 **2** *adj* the milk is off niúnǎi huài le 牛奶坏了

offence /ə'fens/ (*British English*), **offense** (*US English*) *n* (*a crime*) fànzuì 犯罪,fànfǎ xíngwéi 犯法行为;an offence yì zhǒng fànzuì 一种犯罪;to take offence shēngqì 生气

offend /ə'fend/ *vb* (*to displease, to make angry*) dézuì 得罪,chùnù 触怒;offend against wéifàn 违犯;did he offend against the law? tā wéifàn fǎlǜ le ma? 他违犯法律了吗?

offer /'ɒfə(r)/ *vb* (*if what is offered is money, a job, an opportunity, a glass of wine, etc.*) tígōng 提供,gěi 给;to offer someone a job gěi mǒu rén tígōng yí ge gōngzuò jīhuì 给某人提供一个工作机会;to offer someone a cup of coffee gěi mǒu rén yì bēi kāfēi 给某人一杯咖啡;(*if what is offered is an opinion, an idea, a suggestion, a resignation, etc.*) tíchū 提出;to offer a suggestion tíchū yì tiáo jiànyì 提出一条建议;(*to propose a price*) chūjià 出价;he offered 1000 pounds for the car tā chūjià yìqiān bàng mǎi zhè liàng qìchē 他出价 1000 镑买这辆汽车;(*to express willingness*) biǎoshì yuànyì 表示愿意;to offer to help the children biǎoshì yuànyì bāngzhù háizi 表示愿意帮助孩子

office /'ɒfɪs/ *n* an office (*a room*) yí ge bàngōngshì 一个办公室;(*a department*) yí ge bànshìchù 一个办事处

office block /'ɒfɪs blɒk/ *n* (*British English*) an office block yí zuò bàngōnglóu 一座办公楼

officer /'ɒfɪsə(r)/ *n* an officer (*in the government*) yí ge guānyuán 一个官员;(*in the army or navy*) yí ge jūnguān 一个军官;(*in the police force*) yí ge jǐngguān 一个警官

office worker /ˈɒfɪs wɜːkə(r)/ n an office worker yí gè （gōngshāng qǐyè zhōng gùyòng de）zhíyuán，bànshìyuán 一个（工商企业中雇用的）职员，办事员

official /əˈfɪʃəl/ adj （issued or authorized by a public authority）guānfāng de 官方的；an official explanation guānfāng de jiěshì 官方的解释；（pertaining to an office）official duties gōngwù 公务

often /ˈɒfən/ adv jīngcháng 经常，chángcháng 常常

oil /ɔɪl/ n （in general）yóu 油；（from a mineral deposit）shíyóu 石油

okay, OK /ˌəʊˈkeɪ/ **1** adj （when asking or giving opinions）kěyǐ de 可以的；is it okay if I come later? wǒ wǎn diǎnr lái kěyǐ ma? 我晚点儿来可以吗?；it's okay to invite them kěyǐ yāoqǐng tāmen 可以邀请他们；（when talking about health）to feel okay gǎnjué búcuò 感觉不错；are you okay? nǐ méi shìr ba? 你没事儿吧? **2** adv okay hǎo 好，xíng 行；'please tell me'—'ok, I'll tell you' 'qǐng gàosu wǒ'—'hǎo，wǒ gàosu nǐ' "请告诉我"—"好，我告诉你"

old /əʊld/ adj （not new）jiù de 旧的；old clothes jiù yīfu 旧衣服；（not young）lǎo de 老的；old people lǎorén 老人；（with a long history）gǔlǎo de 古老的，lìshǐ yōujiǔ de 历史悠久的；an old church yí zuò gǔlǎo de jiàotáng 一座古老的教堂；（when talking about a person's age）how old are you? （to a child）nǐ jǐ suì le 你几岁了?；（to an older person）nǐ duō dà niánjì le 你多大年纪了?；（to others）nǐ duōshao suì le 你多少岁了?；a three-year old girl yí gè sānsuì de nǚháir 一个 3 岁的女孩儿；I'm as old as he is wǒ hé tā yíyàng dà 我和他一样大；she's eight years older than her brother tā bǐ tā dìdi dà bāsuì 她比她弟弟大 8 岁；he's the oldest tā de niánlíng zuì dà 他的年龄最大；（previous）that's my old address nà shì wǒ yǐqián de dìzhǐ 那是我以前的地址；in the old days zài guòqù 在过去

old-fashioned /ˌəʊldˈfæʃənd/ adj （when describing

attitudes, ideas, clothes) guòshí de 过时的;(*when describing people*) shǒujiù de 守旧的

olive /ˈɒlɪv/ **1** *n* an olive yí ge gǎnlǎn 一个橄榄 **2** *adj* gǎnlǎnsè de 橄榄色的

olive oil /ˌɒlɪv ˈɔɪl/ *n* gǎnlǎnyóu 橄榄油

Olympics /ɒˈlɪmpɪks/ *n* Àolínpǐkè Yùndònghuì 奥林匹克运动会

omelette /ˈɒmlɪt/ *n* an omelette yí ge jiāndànbǐng 一个煎蛋饼

on /ɒn/ ! *Frequently on occurs in combinations with verbs, for example:* count on, get on, keep on, *etc. To find the correct translations for this type of verb, look up the separate dictionary entries for* count, get, keep, *etc.* **1** *prep* (*when the prepositional phrase specifies a location*) (zài)⋯shang (在⋯上)! *Note that when* zài ⋯ shang 在 ⋯ 上 *occurs at the beginning of the sentence* zài 在 *is often omitted;* the book is on the table shū zài zhuōzi shang 书在桌子上; the hat is on top of the wardrobe màozi zài yīguì dǐng shang 帽子在衣柜顶上; on the shelf there are lots of dictionaries (zài) shūjià shang yǒu hěn duō cídiǎn (在) 书架上有很多词典; you've got a spot on your nose (zài) nǐ bízi shang yǒu ge hēidiǎnr (在)你鼻子上有个黑点儿;(*when the prepositional phrase is a modifier indicating a location*) ⋯shang ⋯上; I like the picture on the wall wǒ xǐhuan qiáng shang de nà zhāng huà 我喜欢墙上的那张画; the pen on the desk is not mine shūzhuō shang de gāngbǐ bú shì wǒ de 书桌上的钢笔不是我的;(*when followed by the name of a street*) zài 在; to live on Park Avenue zhù zài Gōngyuán Dàjiē 住在公园大街;(*when talking about transport*) to travel on the bus zuò gōnggòng qìchē lǚxíng 坐公共汽车旅行; I'm on my bike today wǒ jīntiān qí zìxíngchē 我今天骑自行车;(*about*) guānyú 关于; it's a book on Africa zhè shì yì běn guānyú Fēizhōu de shū 这是一本关于非洲的书; a TV programme on primary school pupils yí gè guānyú xiǎoxuéshēng de diànshì jiémù 一个关于小学生的电视节目;(when talking about time) ! Note that on is usually not translated in this use; she was born on the sixth of December tā shí'èr yuè liù hào chūshēng 她 12 月 6 号出生;I'll go there on Saturday wǒ xīngqīliù qù nàr 我星期六去那儿;(when talking about the media) on television zài diànshì shang 在电视上;I saw you on the news wǒ zài xīnwén jiémù li kàn jiàn nǐ le 我在新闻节目里看见你了;(when talking about an ongoing activity) zài 在; the workers are on strike gōngrénmen zài bàgōng 工人们在罢工; they are on holiday at the moment tāmen mùqián zài dùjià 他们目前在度假 2 adv (when talking about what one wears) to have a sweater on chuānshang yí jiàn máoyī 穿上一件毛衣;she has make-up on tā huàle zhuāng 她化了妆;(working, switched on) kāizhe 开着;why are all the lights on? wèishénme suǒyǒu de dēng dōu kāizhe? 为什么所有的灯都开着?;the radio was on all evening zhěnggè wǎnshang shōuyīnjī yìzhí kāizhe 整个晚上收音机一直开着;(showing) what's on? (on TV) diànshì shang yǎn shénme? 电视上演什么?;(in the cinema) diànyǐngyuàn yǎn shénme? 电影院演什么?;(when talking about a starting point) qǐ 起,kāishǐ 开始;from Tuesday on cóng xīngqī'èr qǐ 从星期二起;(continuously) go on jìxù xiàqù 继续下去;I kept on asking questions wǒ búduàn de wèn wèntí 我不断地问问题

once /wʌns/ **1** adv (one time) yí cì 一次;once a day yì tiān yí cì 一天一次;(formerly) cóngqián 从前,céngjīng 曾经;I once studied Japanese wǒ céng xuéguò Rìyǔ 我曾经学习过日语 **2** conj yídàn…jiù 一旦…; life will be easier once I've found a job wǒ yídàn zhǎodào gōngzuò,shēnghuó jiù róngyì le 我一旦找到工作,生活就容易了 **3** at once lìkè 立刻,mǎshàng 马上

one /wʌn/ **1** num yī 一;one child yí gè háizi 一个孩子;

one of my colleagues wǒ de yí gè tóngshì 我的一个同事；**one hundred** yìbǎi 一百 **2** det (the only) wéiyī 唯一；**she's the one person who can help you** tā shì wéiyī nénggòu bāngzhù nǐ de rén 她是唯一一能够帮助你的人；**it's the one thing that annoys me** zhè shì wéiyī shǐ wǒ fánnǎo de shì 这是唯一一使我烦恼的事；(the same) tóngyī 同一；**the two birds are flying in one direction** liǎng zhī niǎo zài cháo tóngyī fāngxiàng fēi 两只鸟在朝同一方向飞；(a certain) mǒu yī 某一；**one** [day|evening|morning] mǒu yì [tiān|tiān wǎnshang|tiān shàngwǔ] 某一[天|天晚上|天上午] **3** pron (when referring to something generally) ! Note that when one refers to something generally, it is often not translated；**I need an umbrella—have you got one?** wǒ xūyào yì bǎ yǔsǎn, nǐ yǒu ma? 我需要一把雨伞，你有吗?；(when referring to a specific person or thing) ! Note that when the one refers to a specific person or thing, the definite article the is often translated as zhè (yī) 这(一) or nà(yī) 那(一) followed by an appropriate measure word. One is often either not translated or is translated as the noun it refers to；**I like this new house but she prefers that old one** wǒ xǐhuan zhè zuò xīn fángzi, kěshì tā xǐhuan nà zuò jiù de 我喜欢这座新房子，可是她喜欢那座旧的；**he's the one who helped me** tā jiù shì bāngzhù wǒ de nàge rén 他就是帮助我的那个人；**which one?** (referring to a [book|bus|table]) nǎ [yì běn|yí liàng|yì zhāng]? 哪[一本|一辆|一张]?；**this one** (referring to a [book|bus|table]) zhè [yì běn|yí liàng|yì zhāng] 这[一本|一辆|一张]；(when used to mean you or people) **one must be honest** yí gè rén yídìng yào chéngshí 一个人一定要诚实；**in the room, one can see the sea** zài fángjiān li, nǐ kěyǐ kàndào dàhǎi 在房间里，你可以看到大海 **4** **one by one** yí gè yí gè de 一个一个地

one another /wʌn əˈnʌðə(r)/ pron hùxiāng 互相，bǐcǐ 彼此；**to help one another** hùxiāng bāngzhù 互相帮助

oneself /wʌnˈself/ pron zìjǐ 自己；**to hurt oneself**

shānghài zìjǐ 伤害自己

onion /'ʌnjən/ *n* an onion yí gè yángcōng 一个洋葱；a spring onion yì kē cōng 一棵葱

only /'əʊnlɪ/ **1** *adv* (*merely*) búguò 不过，jǐnjǐn 仅仅；it's only a game zhè búguò shì yì chǎng bǐsài 这不过是一场比赛；(*not more than*) zhǐ 只，cái 才；they've only met once tāmen zhǐ jiànguo yí cì (miàn) 他们只见过一次（面）**2** *adj* wéiyī 唯一；she was the only one who didn't speak French tā shì wéiyī bú huì jiǎng Fǎyǔ de rén 她是唯一不会讲法语的人；an only daughter yí gè dúshēngnǚ 一个独生女 **3** only just I've only just [arrived |heard the news|moved house...] wǒ gānggāng [dào|tīngdào zhège xiāoxi|bānjiā...] 我刚刚[到|听到这个消息|搬家...]

onto /'ɒntʊ/ *prep* dào…shang 到…上；to jump onto the table tiàodào zhuōzi shang 跳到桌子上

open /'əʊpən/ **1** *vb* to open dǎkāi 打开；to open a letter dǎkāi yì fēng xìn 打开一封信；the door opens very easily mén hěn róngyì dǎkāi 门很容易打开；(*when talking about the eyes*) zhēngkāi 睁开；to open one's eyes zhēngkāi yǎnjing 睁开眼睛；(*when talking about starting business for the day*) kāimén 开门；what time do you open? nǐmen jǐdiǎn kāimén? 你们几点开门？；(*when talking about beginning a film, a play*) kāiyǎn 开演；(*when talking about starting a new business*) kāi 开；she opened a Chinese restaurant here tā zài zhèr kāile yì jiā Zhōngguó cānguǎn 她在这儿开了一家中国餐馆 **2** *adj* (*not closed*) kāizhe de 开着的；leave the door open ràng mén kāizhe 让门开着；an open window kāizhe de chuāng 开着的窗；(*when talking about the eyes*) zhēngzhe de yǎnjing 睁着的眼睛；with open eyes zhēngzhe yǎnjing 睁着眼睛；(*public*) gōngkāi de 公开的；an open letter yì fēng gōngkāixìn 一封公开信；(*frank*) tǎnshuài de 坦率的 **3** *n* in the open (*outside the room*) zài shìwài 在室外；(*outside in the country or in a field*) zài yěwài 在野外

opener /'əʊpənə(r)/ *n* an opener yì bǎ qǐzi 一把起子

open-minded /ˈəupənˈmaɪndɪd/ adj (free from prejudice) méiyǒu piānjiàn de 没有偏见的；(ready to receive and consider new ideas) sīxiǎng kāifàng de 思想开放的

opera /ˈɒpərə/ n an opera yí bù gējù 一部歌剧

operate /ˈɒpəreɪt/ vb (to make something work) cāozuò 操作，kāidòng 开动；(to carry out an operation) zuò shǒushù 做手术；to operate on someone gěi mǒu rén zuò shǒushù 给某人做手术

operation /ɒpəˈreɪʃən/ n (when talking about a person running a machine) cāozuò 操作；(when talking about the machine working) yùnzhuǎn 运转；(when talking about a surgical procedure) shǒushù 手术；an operation yí gè shǒushù 一个手术；to have an operation zuò shǒushù 做手术，kāidāo 开刀

operator /ˈɒpəreɪtə(r)/ n an operator (a person running a machine) yí gè cāozuò rényuán 一个操作人员；(a person employed to connect calls) yí gè diànhuà jiēxiànyuán 一个电话接线员

opinion /əˈpɪnjən/ n an opinion yì zhǒng kànfǎ 一种看法；(when stating one's view) in my opinion yī wǒ kàn yī wǒ kàn 依我看，wǒ rènwéi 我认为；in my opinion, they're lying wǒ rènwéi tāmen zài sāhuǎng 我认为他们在撒谎

opponent /əˈpəunənt/ n an opponent (in a physical game or contest) yí gè duìshǒu 一个对手；(in an argument or debate) yí gè fǎnduìzhě 一个反对者

opportunity /ɒpəˈtjuːnətɪ/ n an opportunity yí gè jīhuì 一个机会；take the opportunity jiè zhège jīhuì 借这个机会，chèn zhège jīhuì 趁这个机会；to take the opportunity to visit Beijing jiè cǐ jīhuì fǎngwèn Běijīng 借此机会访问北京

oppose /əˈpəuz/ vb fǎnduì 反对；to oppose a plan fǎnduì yí gè jīhuì 反对一个计划；to be opposed to nuclear weapons fǎnduì héwǔqì 反对核武器

opposite /ˈɒpəzɪt/ **1** prep zài … duìmiàn 在 … 对面；she was sitting opposite me tā zuò zài wǒ duìmiàn 她坐在

我对面 **2** adj (directly contrary) xiāngfǎn de 相反的；the opposite direction xiāngfǎn de fāngxiàng 相反的方向；my answer is just the opposite wǒ de dá'àn zhènghǎo xiāngfǎn 我的答案正好相反；(facing, on the other side) duìmiàn de 对面的；he was on the opposite side of the street tā zài mǎlù de duìmiàn 他在马路的对面；the opposite sex yìxìng de 异性的 **3** n (that which is contrary) xiāngfǎn 相反；his view is completely the opposite tā de guāndiǎn wánquán xiāngfǎn 他的观点完全相反；(a word with an opposite meaning) fǎnyì cí 反义词；what is the opposite of 'big'? "dà" de fǎnyìcí shì shénme? "大"的反义词是什么？

optician /ˈɒptɪʃən/ n an optician (one who sells glasses) yí gè yǎnjìngshāng 一个眼镜商；(one who makes glasses) yí gè yǎnjìng zhìzhàozhě 一个眼镜制造者

optimist /ˈɒptɪmɪst/ n an optimist yí gè lèguānzhǔyìzhě 一个乐观主义者

optimistic /ˌɒptɪˈmɪstɪk/ adj lèguān de 乐观的，lèguānzhǔyì de 乐观主义的

or /ɔː(r)/ 弱 ə(r)/ conj huò (zhě) 或（者）；once or twice a week yí gè xīngqī yí cì huò(zhě) liǎng cì 一个星期一次或（者）两次；(when offering alternatives) háishi 还是；would you like tea or coffee? nǐ xiǎng hē chá háishì kāfēi? 你想喝茶还是咖啡？either... or... huòzhě...huòzhě... 或者...或者，yàome...yàome... 要么...要么；I'll come either on Saturday or on Sunday wǒ huòzhě xīngqīliù huòzhě xīngqītiān lái 我或者星期六或者星期天来；(otherwise) fǒuzé 否则，bùrán 不然；you have to come or she'll be angry nǐ yídìng děi lái，bùrán tā huì shēngqì de 你一定得来，不然她会生气的

oral /ˈɔːrəl/ adj (spoken, not written) kǒutóu de 口头的；(relating to the mouth) kǒubù de 口部的；(taken by mouth) kǒufú de 口服的

orange /ˈɒrɪndʒ/ **1** n an orange yí gè júzi 一个橘子，yí gè chéngzi 一个橙子 **2** adj júsè de 橘色的，chéngsè de 橙色的

orange juice /ˈɒrɪndʒ ˈdʒuːs/ n júzhī 橘汁，chéngzhī 橙汁

orchard /ˈɔːtʃəd/ n an orchard yí gè guǒyuán 一个果园

orchestra /ˈɔːkɪstrə/ n an orchestra yí gè guǎnxián yuèduì 一个管弦乐队

order /ˈɔːdə(r)/ **1** vb (to command) mìnglìng 命令；to order someone to leave mìnglìng mǒu rén líkāi 命令某人离开；(to request the supply of) dìnggòu 定购；to order goods from a shop xiàng yí gè shāngdiàn dìnggòu huòwù 向一个商店定购货物；(to ask for food in a restaurant) diǎncài 点菜 **2** n (a command) mìnglìng 命令；an order yí xiàng mìnglìng 一项命令；to give orders xià mìnglìng 下命令；(a sequence) shùnxù 顺序；in the right order àn zhèngquè shùnxù 按正确顺序 **3** in order to (when used at the beginning of a sentence) wèile 为了；in order to get a good seat, he arrived very early wèile dédào yí gè hǎo zuòwèi, tā hěn zǎo jiù dào le 为了得到一个好座位，他很早就到了；(when used in mid-sentence) yǐbiàn 以便；he arrived very early in order to get a good seat tā hěn zǎo jiù dào le, yǐbiàn dédào yí gè hǎo zuòwèi 他很早就到了，以便得到一个好座位

ordinary /ˈɔːdɪnərɪ/ adj pǔtōng de 普通的，yìbān de 一般的；an ordinary family yí gè pǔtōng de jiātíng 一个普通的家庭

organ /ˈɔːgən/ n (the musical instrument) fēngqín 风琴；an organ yí jià fēngqín 一架风琴；(a part of the body) qìguān 器官；an organ yí gè qìguān 一个器官

organization /ˌɔːgənaɪˈzeɪʃən/ n an organization yí gè zǔzhī 一个组织

organize /ˈɔːgənaɪz/ vb (to form into a whole) zǔzhī 组织；(to arrange) ānpái 安排

original /əˈrɪdʒənəl/ adj (first) zuì chū de 最初的，zuì zǎo de 最早的；(not copied or derived) yuán(lái) de 原(来)的；an original manuscript yí fèn yuángǎo 一份原稿；(new, fresh) xīnyíng de 新颖的，yǒu dúdào jiànjiě de 有独到见解的

ornament /ˈɔːnəmənt/ n an ornament yí gè zhuāngshìpǐn

一个装饰品

orphan /'ɔːfən/ n an orphan yí gè gū'ér 一个孤儿

other /'ʌðə(r)/ **1** adj lìng(wài) de 另(外)的，qítā de 其他的，biéde 别的！Note that qítā de 其他的 and bié de 别的 are used with plural nouns, and that lìng(wài) de 另(外)的 can be used with plural and singular nouns; not that dress, the other one bú shì nà jiàn yīfu, shì lìng(wài) yí jiàn 不是那件衣服，是另(外)一件；they sold the other three cars tāmen bǎ lìng(wài) sān liàng chē mài le 他们把另(外) 3 辆车卖了；to help the other pupils bāngzhù qítā de xuésheng 帮助其他的学生；every other day měi gé yì tiān 每隔一天 **2** pron he makes others angry tā shǐ biérén shēngqì 他使别人生气；this book is mine, the others are his zhè běn shū shì wǒ de, lìngwài de shū dōu shì tā de 这本书是我的，另外的书都是他的；they came in one after the other tāmen yí gè jiē yí gè de jìnlái 他们一个接一个地进来

otherwise /'ʌðəwaɪz/ conj fǒuzé 否则，bùrán 不然；it's not dangerous, otherwise I wouldn't go zhè bù wēixiǎn, fǒuzé wǒ bú luì qù 这不危险，否则我不会去

otter /'ɒtə(r)/ n an otter yí gè shuǐtǎ 一个水獭

ought /ɔːt/ vb (when saying what should be done or what may happen) yīngdāng 应当，yīnggāi 应该；you ought not to say things like that nǐ bù yīngdāng nàme jiǎnghuà 你不应当那么讲话；they ought to arrive tomorrow tāmen yīnggāi míngtiān dào 他们应该明天到；(when saying that something didn't happen) běn yīng(gāi) 本应(该)，běngāi 本该；he ought to have gone with them tā běn yīng(gāi) gēn tāmen yìqǐ qù 他本应(该)跟他们一起去

our /aʊə(r)/ det wǒmen de 我们的；what do you think of our house? nǐ juéde wǒmen de fángzi zěnmeyàng? 你觉得我们的房子怎么样？

ours /aʊəz/ pron wǒmen de 我们的；the grey car is ours nà liàng huīsè de chē shì wǒmen de 那辆灰色的车是我们的

ourselves /ˌauəˈselvz/ *pron* (*when used as a reflexive pronoun*) (wǒmen) zìjǐ (我们) 自己; we didn't hurt ourselves wǒmen méiyǒu shāngzhe zìjǐ 我们没有伤着自己; (*when used for emphasis*) we will go to buy the train tickets ourselves wǒmen zìjǐ qù mǎi huǒchēpiào 我们自己去买火车票; he wants us to solve the problem by ourselves tā yào wǒmen zìjǐ jiějué zhège wèntí 他要我们自己解决这个问题

out /aut/ ! Often out occurs in combinations with verbs, for example: blow out, come out, find out, give out, etc. To find the correct translations for this type of verb, look up the separate dictionary entries at blow, come, find, give, etc. **1** *adv* (*outside*) zài wàibian 在外边; to stay out in the rain dāi zài yǔ li 呆在雨里; she is out in the garden tā zài wàibian huāyuán li 她在外边花园里; (*away from the inside*) chū 出; to go out chūqù 出去; to come out chūlái 出来; (*absent*) bú zài 不在, chūqù 出去; he is out tā bú zài 他不在; someone phoned you while you were out nǐ chūqù de shíhou, yǒu rén gěi nǐ dǎ diànhuà 你出去的时候, 有人给你打电话; (*not lit, switched off*) (xī)miè (熄)灭; all the lights were out suǒyǒu de dēng dōu (xī) miè le 所有的灯都(熄)灭了 **2** out of to walk out of the building cóng dàlóu li zǒu chūlái 从大楼里走出来; please get out of this room qǐng líkāi zhège fángjiān 请离开这个房间

outdoor /ˈautdɔː(r)/ *adj* shìwài de 室外的; an outdoor swimming pool yí gè shìwài yóuyǒngchí 一个室外游泳池

outdoors /ˌautˈdɔːz/ *adv* (*outside the house or building*) zài shìwài 在室外; (*out in the field*) zài yěwài 在野外

outer space /ˌautə ˈspeis/ n wàicéng kōngjiān 外层空间

outside /ˌautˈsaid/ **1** *prep* zài...wàibian 在...外边; to wait outside the school zài xuéxiào wàibian děng 在学校外边等 **2** *adv* let's go outside zánmen chūqù ba 咱们出去吧; let's bring the chairs outside zánmen bǎ yǐzi bān chūlái ba 咱们把椅子搬出来吧 **3** n the outside wàibian 外边, wàimian 外面

the outside of the building dàlóu de wàibian 大楼的外边 4 *adj* wàibù de 外部的

oven /'ʌvən/ *n* an oven yí gè kǎoxiāng 一个烤箱

over /'əʊvə(r)/ ! *Often over occurs in combinations with verbs, for example*: get over, move over, *etc. To find the correct translations for this type of verb, look up the separate dictionary entries at* get, move, *etc.* **1** *prep* (*on*) zài…shang 在…上; to spread a cloth over the table bǎ yí kuài táibù pū zài zhuōzi shang 把一块台布铺在桌子上; to climb over a wall páguò yì dǔ qiáng 爬过一堵墙; come over here guòlái 过来; (*above*) zài…shàngfāng 在…上方; the picture is over the piano huà zài gāngqín de shàngfāng 画在钢琴的上方; (*above in age, value, quantity, number*) …yǐshàng …以上; young people over 18 shíbā suì yǐshàng de niánqīngrén 18 岁以上的年轻人; over 20 kilograms èrshí gōngjīn yǐshàng 20 公斤以上; (*during*) we saw them over the weekend wǒmen zhōumò kànjiàn tāmen le 我们周末看见他们了; (*everywhere*) I've looked all over the house for my keys zài zhè zuò fángzi li, wǒ dàochù dōu zhǎoguo wǒ de yàoshi 在这座房子里,我到处都找过我的钥匙; all over the world shìjiè gèdì 世界各地 **2** *adv* (*finished*) jiéshù 结束, wán 完; the term is over xuéqí jiéshù le 学期结束了; is the film over? diànyǐng wán le ma? 电影完了吗?; (*to one's home*) to ask someone over qǐng mǒu rén dào jiālǐ lái 请某人到家里来; to start all over again chóngxīn kāishǐ 重新开始

overdose /'əʊvədəʊs/ *n* guòliàng yòng yào 过量用药

overtake /əʊvə'teɪk/ *vb* (*when talking about driving*) chāochē 超车; (*to catch up with*) gǎnshàng 赶上

overweight /əʊvə'weɪt/ *adj* chāozhòng de 超重的

owe /əʊ/ *vb* (*to be indebted to*) qiàn 欠; to owe money to someone qiàn mǒu rén qián 欠某人钱

owl /aʊl/ *n* an owl yì zhī māotóuyīng 一只猫头鹰

own /əʊn/ **1** adj zìjǐ de 自己的；your own room nǐ zìjǐ de fángjiān 你自己的房间 **2** pron zìjǐ de 自己的；I didn't use his pencil—I've got my own wǒ méi yòng tā de qiānbǐ—wǒ yǒu wǒ zìjǐ de 我没用他的铅笔—我有我自己的；they have a house of their own tāmen yǒu tāmen zìjǐ de fángzi 他们有他们自己的房子 **3** vb (to possess) yǒu 有, yōngyǒu 拥有；he owns a shop in town tā zài chénglǐ yǒu yì jiā shāngdiàn 他在城里有一家商店 **4** on one's own dúzì de 独自地, dúlì de 独立地；own up tǎnbái 坦白, chéngrèn 承认；he owned up that he was wrong tā chéngrèn tā cuò le 他承认他错了

owner /ˈəʊnə(r)/ n an owner yí gè zhǔrén 一个主人

ox /ɒks/ n an ox yì tóu gōngniú 一头公牛

oxygen /ˈɒksɪdʒən/ n yǎngqì 氧气

oyster /ˈɔɪstə(r)/ n an oyster yí gè mǔlì 一个牡蛎

Pp

Pacific /pəˈsɪfɪk/ n the Pacific Ocean Tàipíngyáng 太平洋

pack /pæk/ **1** vb (to fill a space or container) zhuāng 装；he's packing his clothes into the suitcase tā zhèngzài bǎ tā de yīfu zhuāngjìn xiāngzi li 他正在把他的衣服装进箱子里；I've got to pack my suitcase wǒ děi zhuāng xiāngzi 我得装箱子；(to wrap up and bundle together) bāozhuāng 包装；to pack the china bāozhuāng cíqì 包装瓷器；(to get one's things together and ready to move) to pack up one's belongings shōushi zìjǐ de xíngli 收拾自己的行李 **2** n a pack yì bāo 一包, yì hé 一盒；a pack of cigarettes yì bāo xiāngyān 一包香烟；a pack of cards yì hé pūkèpái 一盒扑克牌

package /ˈpækɪdʒ/ n a package (a bundle) yì kǔn 一捆；(a parcel) yí jiàn bāoguǒ 一件包裹；(a packet) yì bāo 一包

packed /pækt/ adj (with people) jǐmǎn de 挤满的；the classroom was packed with students jiàoshì li jǐmǎnle xuésheng 教室里挤满了学生；(with things) zhuāngmǎn de 装满的；the box is packed with old newspapers hézi li zhuāngmǎnle jiù bàozhǐ 盒子里装满了旧报纸

packet /'pækɪt/ n a packet yì bāo 一包

page /peɪdʒ/ n a page yí yè 一页；on page six zài dì-liù yè 在第 6 页

pain /peɪn/ n téng 疼；I've got a pain in my back wǒ hòubèi téng 我后背疼；to be in pain tòngkǔ 痛苦

painful /'peɪnfʊl/ adj (full of pain) téngtòng de 疼痛的；(distressing) tòngkǔ de 痛苦的

paint /peɪnt/ 1 n (for furniture, doors, windows, etc.) yóuqī 油漆 2 vb (to produce a picture) huà 画；(to apply paint to furniture, doors, windows, etc.) yóu 油

paintbrush /'peɪntbrʌʃ/ n a paintbrush (for producing a picture) yì zhī huàbǐ 一支画笔；(for painting surfaces) yì bǎ shuāzi 一把刷子

painter /'peɪntə(r)/ n a painter (an artist) yí gè huàjiā 一个画家；(one whose job is painting surfaces) yí gè yóuqījiàng 一个油漆匠

painting /'peɪntɪŋ/ n (a picture) huà 画；a painting yì fú huà 一幅画；(the activity of painting pictures) huìhuà 绘画

pair /peə(r)/ n a pair of shoes yì shuāng xié 一双鞋；a pair of spectacles yí fù yǎnjìng 一副眼镜；a pair of vases yí duì huāpíng 一对花瓶

pajamas /pə'dʒɑːməz/ ▶ pyjamas

Pakistan /ˌpɑːkɪ'stɑːn/ n Bājīsītǎn 巴基斯坦

palace /'pælɪs/ n gōngdiàn 宫殿, gōng 宫；a palace yí zuò gōngdiàn 一座宫殿

pale /peɪl/ adj (when describing the face) cāngbái de 苍白的；(when describing the moon) àndàn de 暗淡的

pancake /'pænkeɪk/ n a pancake yí gè báo jiānbǐng 一个薄煎饼

panic /'pænɪk/ n kǒnghuāng 恐慌，jīnghuāng 惊慌

pants /pænts/ n (underwear) (British English) yì tiáo nèikù 一条内裤；(trousers) (US English) yì tiáo kùzi 一条裤子

pantyhose /'pæntɪhəʊz/ n (US English) jǐnshēnkù 紧身裤

paper /'peɪpə(r)/ n (for writing or drawing on) zhǐ 纸；a piece of paper yì zhāng zhǐ 一张纸；(a newspaper) bàozhǐ 报纸；a paper (a sheet) yì zhāng bàozhǐ 一张报纸；(consisting of more than one sheet) yí fèn bàozhǐ 一份报纸

parachuting /'pærəʃuːtɪŋ/ n tiàosǎn 跳伞

parade /pə'reɪd/ n a parade yí cì yóuxíng 一次游行

paralysed (British English), **paralyzed** (US English) adj tānhuàn de 瘫痪的

parcel /'pɑːsəl/ n a parcel yí gè bāoguǒ 一个包裹

parents /'peərənts/ n fùmǔ 父母

Paris /'pærɪs/ n Paris Bālí 巴黎

park /pɑːk/ 1 n a park yí gè gōngyuán 一个公园 2 vb to park a car tíngchē 停车；to park near the office zài bàngōngshì fùjìn tíngchē 在办公室附近停车

parking lot /'pɑːkɪŋ lɒt/ n (US English) a parking lot yí gè tíngchēchǎng 一个停车场

parking meter /'pɑːkɪŋ miːtə(r)/ n a parking meter yí gè tíngchē jìshíqì 一个停车计时器

parliament /'pɑːləmənt/ n guóhuì 国会，yìhuì 议会

parrot /'pærət/ n a parrot yì zhī yīngwǔ 一只鹦鹉

part /pɑːt/ n a part yí bùfen 一部分；part of the [book | programme | job] [shū | jiémù | gōngzuò] de yí bùfen [书 | 节目 | 工作] 的一部分；(region, area) dìqū 地区；in this part of China zài Zhōngguó de zhè yí dìqū 在中国的这一地区，(for a machine, a car, etc.) língjiàn 零件，bùjiàn 部件；a part yí gè língjiàn 一个零件；(a role) juésè 角色；to play the part of Tom bànyǎn Tāngmǔ de juésè 扮演汤姆的角色

participate /pɑː'tɪsɪpeɪt/ vb cānjiā 参加；to participate

in the discussion cānjiā tǎolùn 参加讨论

particular /pəˈtɪkjʊlə(r)/ **1** adj tèbié de 特别的，tèshū de 特殊的 **2** in particular tèbié 特别，yóuqí 尤其

partner /ˈpɑːtnə(r)/ n (in a love relationship) yí gè bànlǚ 一个伴侣；(in dancing) yí gè wǔbàn 一个舞伴；(in sports and games) yí gè dādàng 一个搭档；(in business) yí gè hézuòzhě 一个合作者

part-time /ˈpɑːtˈtaɪm/ adv fēi quánrì 非全日；to work part-time fēi quánrì gōngzuò 非全日工作

party /ˈpɑːtɪ/ n (a social event) jùhuì 聚会；a party yí cì jùhuì 一次聚会；(held in the evening) wǎnhuì 晚会；a birthday party yí cì shēngrì wǎnhuì 一次生日晚会；a political party yí gè zhèngdǎng 一个政党

pass /pɑːs/ vb (to go through) tōngguò 通过；to let someone pass ràng mǒu rén guòqù 让某人过去；(to go by) lùguò 路过，jīngguò 经过；to pass the school lùguò xuéxiào 路过学校；(to overtake) chāoguò 超过，chāoyuè 超越；to pass a car chāoguò yí liàng chē 超过一辆车；(to hand) dì 递；pass me the salt, please qǐng bǎ yán dìgěi wǒ 请把盐递给我；(to transfer to another person) chuán 传；to pass the ball to him bǎ qiú chuángěi tā 把球传给他；please pass the word to my mother qǐng bǎ zhège huà chuángěi wǒ māma 请把这个话传给我妈妈；(to spend) yòng 用；I pass my time [reading | painting | listening to the radio ...] wǒ bǎ wǒ de shíjiān yòng lái [dúshū | huàhuà | tīng shōuyīnjī ...] 我把我的时间用来[读书 | 画画 | 听收音机 ...]；(to succeed in an exam) tōngguò 通过；to pass an exam tōngguò yí cì kǎoshì 通过一次考试；(to succeed in an exam, just barely, and without honours) jígé 及格；he narrowly passed the test tā kǎoshì miǎnqiǎng jígé 他考试勉强及格；(to approve) tōngguò 通过，pīzhǔn 批准；the parliament has passed a new law yìhuì tōngguòle yí xiàng xīn de fǎlǜ 议会通过了一项新的法律

passage /ˈpæsɪdʒ/ n (a way or a route for going through) tōngdào 通道；a passage yì tiáo tōngdào 一条通道；(a piece of writing) duàn 段；a passage in a book shū zhōng de yí duàn 书中的一段

passenger /'pæsɪndʒə(r)/ n a passenger yí gè chéngkè 一个乘客

passport /'pɑːspɔːt/ n a passport yì běn hùzhào 一本护照

past /pɑːst/ **1** n the past guòqù 过去；in the past zài guòqù 在过去 **2** adj guòqù de 过去的；the past few days guòqù jǐ tiān 过去几天 **3** prep (when talking about time) guò 过！Note that when past means after the hour of, it is often not translated；it's five past four xiànzài sì diǎn (guò) wǔ fēn 现在 4 点(过) 5 分；it's past midnight yǐjīng guòle wǔyè le 已经过了午夜了；(by) to go past someone cóng mǒu rén pángbiān guòqù 从某人身边过去；she ran past me tā cóng wǒ pángbiān pǎo guòqù 她从我身旁边跑过去；(beyond) ... nàbiān 在···那边；it's just past the traffic lights jiù zài hónglǜdēng nàbiān 就在红绿灯那边 **4** adv to go past guòqù 过去；to walk past zǒu guòqù 走过去；to run past pǎo guòqù 跑过去

pasta /'pæstə/ n Yìdàlì miànshí 意大利面食

pastry /'peɪstrɪ/ n (for baking) miànhù 面糊；(a cake) gāodiǎn 糕点；a pastry yí kuài gāodiǎn 一块糕点

patch /pætʃ/ n (on a garment or a tyre) bǔdīng 补丁，a patch yí kuài bǔdīng 一块补丁；(a plaster for a cut or sore) gāoyào 膏药；a patch yí kuài gāoyào 一块膏药

path /pɑːθ/ n (a narrow way for pedestrians) xiǎodào 小道，lù 路；a path yì tiáo xiǎodào 一条小道；(a route for a thing to move along) guǐdào 轨道；a path yì tiáo guǐdào 一条轨道

patience /'peɪʃəns/ n nàixīn 耐心；to lose patience with someone duì mǒu rén shīqù nàixīn 对某人失去耐心

patient /'peɪʃənt/ **1** n a patient yí gè bìngrén 一个病人 **2** adj nàixīn de 耐心的

patrol /pə'trəʊl/ vb xúnluó 巡逻

patrol car /pə'trəʊl kɑ:(r)/ n a patrol car yí liàng xúnluóchē 一辆巡逻车

pattern /'pætn/ n a pattern (*a thing to be copied as in dressmaking, carpentry, etc.*) yí gè yàngbǎn 一个样板; (*a decorative design*) yí gè shìyàng 一个式样; (*a particular disposition of forms and colours*) yí gè tú'àn 一个图案

pavement /'peɪvmənt/ n (*British English*) the pavement rénxíngdào 人行道; (*US English*) the pavement (*a paved road*) pūguò de lùmiàn 铺过的路面, pūguò de dàolù 铺过的道路; (*a paved surface*) pūguò de dìmiàn 铺过的地面

paw /pɔ:/ n a paw yì zhī zhuǎzi 一只爪子

pay /peɪ/ **1** vb to pay fù tiǎn 付款; to pay the bills fùzhàng 付账; how much did you pay him? nǐ fùgěi tā duōshǎo qián? 你付给他多少钱?; to pay for; he paid for my meal tā fùle wǒ de fànqián 他付了我的饭钱; my father paid for her education wǒ bàba gōng tā shàngxué 我爸爸供她上学; (*when talking about wages*) the work doesn't pay very well zhè fèn gōngzuò gōngzī bù gāo 这份工作工资不高; I'm paid eight pounds an hour wǒ měi gè xiǎoshí zhèng bā bàng qián 我每个小时挣 8 镑钱; (*to give*) to pay attention to the teacher zhùyì lǎoshī 注意老师; to pay someone a visit bàifǎng mǒu rén 拜访某人; to pay someone a compliment zànyáng mǒu rén 赞扬某人 ! Note that when to pay means to give, it is usually not translated. In most cases, the object, such as attention, visit, or compliment, is translated by the verb in Chinese. **2** n gōngzī 工资, xīnshuǐ 薪水; the pay is very good gōngzī hěn hǎo 工资很好; **pay back** (*when in debt*) chánghuán 偿还; (*when in gratitude*) bàodá 报答

PE /ˌpiː'iː/, **physical education** n tǐyùkè education 体育课

pea /piː/ n a pea yí lì wāndòu 一粒豌豆; green peas qīngdòu 青豆

peace /piːs/ n (*freedom from war*) hépíng 和平; (*a state of quiet*) píngjìng 平静; (*freedom from disturbance*) ānníng 安宁

peach /piːtʃ/ n a peach yí gè táozi 一个桃子

peacock /'piːkɒk/ n a peacock yì zhī kǒngquè 一只孔雀

peanut /'piːnʌt/ n a peanut yí lì huāshēng 一粒花生

pear /peə(r)/ n a pear yí gè lí 一个梨

pearl /pɜːl/ n a pearl yì kē zhēnzhū 一颗珍珠

pebble /'pebl/ n a pebble yí gè shízǐ 一个石子，yí gè éluǎnshí 一个鹅卵石

pedestrian /pɪ'destrɪən/ n a pedestrian yí gè xíngrén 一个行人

pedestrian crossing /pɪ,destrɪən 'krɒsɪŋ/ n a pedestrian crossing yì tiáo rénxíng héngdào 一条人行横道

peel /piːl/ vb (to use one's hands to strip off an outer covering) bāo…pí 剥…皮；to peel an orange bāo júzi pí 剥橘子皮；(to use a knife to strip off an outer covering) xiāo…pí 削…皮；to peel an apple xiāo píngguǒ 削苹果

pen /pen/ n a pen yì zhī gāngbǐ 一支钢笔

penalty /'penltɪ/ n (punishment) chǔfá 处罚，chéngfá 惩罚；a penalty yí gè chǔfá 一个处罚；(in football) diǎnqiú 点球；a penalty yí cì diǎnqiú 一次点球

pencil /'pensl/ n a pencil yì zhī qiānbǐ 一支铅笔

pencil case /'pensl keɪs/ n a pencil case yí gè qiānbǐhé 一个铅笔盒

pencil sharpener /'pensl ˌʃɑːpənə(r)/ n a pencil sharpener yí gè qiānbǐdāo 一个铅笔刀

penfriend /'penfrend/ (British English), **penpal** /'penpæl/ (US English) n a penfriend yí gè bǐyǒu 一个笔友

penguin /'peŋgwɪn/ n a penguin yì zhī qǐ'é 一只企鹅

penknife /'pennaɪf/ n a penknife yì bǎ xiǎobiǎndāo 一把削笔刀

pensioner /'penʃənə(r)/ n a pensioner (a retired person entitled to a pension) yí gè tuìxiū de rén 一个退休的人；(a person receiving an allowance for being disabled, widowed, orphaned, etc.) yí gè língqǔ fǔxùjīn de rén 一

个领取抚恤金的人

people /'piːpl/ n (in general) rén 人；we met some very nice people wǒmen yùjiànle yìxiē hěn hǎo de rén 我们遇见了一些很好的人；most people don't know what's happened dàduōshù rén bù zhīdào fāshēngle shénme shì 大多数人不知道发生了什么事；(those from a city, from a nation, or of the world) rénmín 人民；the people of the world shìjiè rénmín 世界人民；(a nation, race, tribe, or ethnic group) mínzú 民族；a people yí gè mínzú 一个民族

pepper /'pepə(r)/ n (the spice) hújiāo 胡椒；(the general term for the vegetable, usually green) qīngjiāo 青椒；(when the colour is specified) a [green | red | yellow] pepper yí gè [qīng | hóng | huáng] jiāo 一个 [青 | 红 | 黄] 椒

per /强 pɜː(r); 弱 pə/ prep měi 每；per [person | hour | week...] měi gè [rén | xiǎoshí | xīngqī...] 每个 [人 | 小时 | 星期...]

per cent /pə 'sent/ n bǎi fēn zhī 百分之，%；30% bǎi fēn zhī sānshí 百分之三十

perfect /'pɜːfɪkt/ adj (extremely good) jí hǎo de 极好的；to speak perfect Chinese jiǎng yì kǒu jí hǎo de Hànyǔ 讲一口极好的汉语；(flawless) wánměi de 完美的，wúxiá de 无瑕的；nothing is perfect méi yǒu dōngxi shì wánměi de 没有东西是完美的

perform /pə'fɔːm/ vb (to do) to perform an operation zuò yí gè shǒushù 做一个手术；to perform a task wánchéng yí xiàng rènwu 完成一项任务；(to play an instrument in a performance) yǎnzòu 演奏；to perform a piece of music yǎnzòu yì zhī qǔzi 演奏一支曲子；(to act) biǎoyǎn 表演；to perform for the children wèi háizimen biǎoyǎn 为孩子们表演

perfume /'pɜːfjuːm/ n (if it's a liquid) xiāngshuǐ 香水；to spray perfume pēn xiāngshuǐ 喷香水；(if it's a fragrance) xiāngwèir 香味儿

perhaps /pə'hæps/ adv kěnéng 可能，yěxǔ 也许

period /'pɪərɪəd/ n a period of time yí duàn shíjiān 一段

时间；(*a stage or phase in history*) shíqī 时期；the period of the Cold War lěngzhàn shíqī 冷战时期；(*in the course of an event*) qījiān 期间；in the period of the experiment zài shíyàn qījiān 在实验期间；(*a full stop*) jùhào 句号；a period yí gè jùhào 一个句号；(*for women*) yuèjīngqī 月经期；a period yí cì yuèjīngqī 一次月经期；(*a school lesson*) kè 课；a period yì jié kè 一节课

permanent /'pɜːmənənt/ *adj* yǒngjiǔ de 永久的

permission /pə'mɪʃn/ *n* xǔkě 许可，yǔnxǔ 允许；to get permission to leave the hospital dédào chūyuàn de xǔkě 得到出院的许可

person /'pɜːsən/ *n* a person yí gè rén 一个人

personal /'pɜːsənəl/ *adj* (*one's own*) gèrén de 个人的；(*of private concerns*) sīrén de 私人的

personality /ˌpɜːsə'næləti/ *n* (*distinctive character*) xìnggé 性格，gèxìng 个性；a person with a strong personality yí gè xìnggé hěn qiáng de rén 一个性格很强的人

perspire /pə'spaɪə(r)/ *vb* chūhàn 出汗

persuade /pə'sweɪd/ *vb* quàn 劝，shuōfú 说服；to persuade someone to buy a car quàn mǒu rén mǎi yí liàng chē 劝某人买一辆车

pessimist /'pesɪmɪst/ *n* a pessimist yí gè bēiguānzhě 一个悲观者，yí gè bēiguān zhǔyìzhě 一个悲观主义者

pessimistic /ˌpesɪ'mɪstɪk/ *adj* bēiguān de 悲观的，bēiguānzhǔyì de 悲观主义的

pet /pet/ *n* a pet yí gè chǒngwù 一个宠物

petrol /'petrəl/ *n* (*British English*) qìyóu 汽油；to run out of petrol qìyóu yòngwán le 汽油用完了

petrol station /'petrəl ˌsteɪʃən/ *n* (*British English*) a petrol station yí gè jiāyóuzhàn 一个加油站

pet shop /ˌpet 'ʃɒp/ *n* a pet shop yí gè chǒngwù shāngdiàn 一个宠物商店

phone /fəʊn/ **1** *n* a phone yì tái diànhuà 一台电话；the phone's ringing diànhuà xiǎng le 电话响了；to answer the phone jiē diànhuà 接电话；he's on the phone tā zài dǎ diànhuà 他在打电话 **2** *vb* dǎ diànhuà 打电话；to phone someone gěi mǒu rén dǎ diànhuà 给人打电话

phone book /'fəun buk/ *n* a phone book yì běn diànhuàbù 一本电话簿

phone booth /'fəun buːð/ *n* a phone booth yí gè diànhuàtíng 一个电话亭

phone call /'fəun kɔːl/ *n* a phone call yí gè diànhuà 一个电话；to receive a phone call jiēdào yí gè diànhuà 接到一个电话

phone card /'fəun kɑːd/ *n* a phone card yì zhāng diànhuà cíkǎ 一张电话磁卡

phone number /'fəun nʌmbə(r)/ *n* a phone number yí gè diànhuà hàomǎ 一个电话号码

photo /'fəutəu/ *n* a photo yì zhāng zhàopiàn 一张照片，yì zhāng xiàngpiàn 一张像片

photocopier /'fəutəuˌkɒpɪə(r)/ *n* a photocopier yì tái fùyìnjī 一台复印机

photocopy /'fəutəuˌkɒpɪ/ **1** *n* a photocopy yí fèn fùyìnjiàn 一份复印件 **2** *vb* fùyìn 复印

photograph /'fəutəgrɑːf/ *n* a photograph yì zhāng zhàopiàn 一张照片，yì zhāng xiàngpiàn 一张像片；to take a photograph of someone gěi mǒu rén zhào yì zhāng xiàng 给某人照一张像

photographer /fə'tɒgrəfə(r)/ *n* a photographer yí gè shèyǐngshī 一个摄影师

physical /'fɪzɪkəl/ *adj* (*material*) wùzhì de 物质的；the physical world wùzhì shìjiè 物质世界；(*pertaining to natural science*) wùlǐ de 物理的；physical changes wùlǐ biànhuà 物理变化；(*bodily*) shēntǐ de 身体的；physical examinations shēntǐ jiǎnchá 身体检查

physics /'fɪzɪks/ *n* wùlǐxué 物理学，wùlǐ 物理

piano /pɪ'ænəu/ *n* a piano yí jià gāngqín 一架钢琴

pick /pɪk/ *vb* (*to choose*) tiāoxuǎn 挑选，xuǎnzé 选择；to pick a number tiāoxuǎn yí gè hàomǎ 挑选一个号码；

picnic

(to collect) zhāi 摘, cǎi 采; **to pick blackberries** zhāi hēiméi 摘黑莓; (to take) ná 拿; **to pick a book off the shelf** cóng shūjià shang náxià yì běn shū 从书架上拿下一本书; **pick on** (to find fault with) tiāotì 挑剔; (to single out for something unpleasant) tiāo chūlái pīpíng 挑出来批评; **he's always picking on me** tā zǒngshì bǎ wǒ tiāo chūlái pīpíng 他总是把我挑出来批评; **pick out** (to select) tiāoxuǎn chū 挑选出; (to make out, to distinguish) biànbié chū 辨别出; **pick up** (to lift) shíqǐ 拾起, jiǎnqǐ 捡起; **to pick the clothes up off the floor** bǎ yīfu cóng dì shang jiǎn qǐlai 把衣服从地上捡起来; **to pick a baby up** bǎ yí gè háizi bào qǐlai 把一个孩子抱起来; **to pick up the phone** náqǐ diànhuà lái 拿起电话来; (to collect) jiē 接; **to pick up passengers** jiē chéngkè 接乘客; **he's coming to pick me up** tā lái jiē wǒ 他来接我; (to buy) mǎi 买; **I stopped to pick up some milk** wǒ tíng xiàlái mǎi diǎnr niúnǎi 我停下来买点儿牛奶; (to learn) xuéhuì 学会; **to pick up a little German** xuéhuì yìdiǎnr Déyǔ 学会一点儿德语

picnic /ˈpɪknɪk/ n **a picnic** yí cì yěcān 一次野餐; **to go on a picnic** qù yěcān 去野餐

picture /ˈpɪktʃə(r)/ n **a picture** (a painting or a drawing) yì fú huà 一幅画; (a photograph) yì zhāng zhàopiàn 一张照片, yì zhāng xiàngpiàn 一张像片; (an image on a television screen) yí gè túxiàng 一个图像; **the pictures** (cinema) diànyǐng 电影

piece /piːs/ n **a piece of paper** yì zhāng zhǐ 一张纸; **a piece of cheese** yí kuài nǎilào 一块奶酪; **a piece of string** yì gēn xiànshéng 一根线绳; **a piece of furniture** yí jiàn jiājù 一件家具; **a piece of** [news | information ...] yì tiáo [xiāoxi | xìnxī ...] 一条 [消息 | 信息 ...]; (a part of a machine) bùjiàn 部件; **a piece** yí gè bùjiàn 一个部件; (a coin) yìngbì 硬币; **a 50-pence piece** yí gè wǔshí biànshì de yìngbì 一个 50 便士的硬币; (broken fragments of something thin) suìpiàn 碎片; **pieces of broken glass**

yìxiē suì bōlipiàn 一些碎玻璃片；(*portion of a solid object*) kuài 块；to cut an apple into four pieces bǎ píngguǒ qiēchéng sì kuài 把苹果切成四块

pierce /pɪəs/ *vb* (*to make a hole through*) chuānkǒng 穿孔, chuāndòng 穿洞；(*to thrust*) cìchuān 刺穿, cìpò 刺破

pig /pɪg/ *n* a pig yì tóu zhū 一头猪

pigeon /'pɪdʒɪn/ *n* a pigeon yì zhī gēzi 一只鸽子

pile /paɪl/ *n* a pile (*in a somewhat regular shape*) yí luò 一摞；a pile of books yí luò shū 一摞书；(*a heap*) yì duī 一堆；a pile of logs yì duī mùtou 一堆木头；(*a large amount, lots*) xǔduō 许多, dàliàng 大量；piles of [toys | records | money] xǔduō [wánjù | chàngpiàn | qián] 许多 [玩具 | 唱片 | 钱]

pill /pɪl/ *n* (*a tablet*) a pill yí piàn yào 一片药；(*a method of contraception*) the pill bìyùnyào 避孕药

pillow /'pɪləʊ/ *n* a pillow yí gè zhěntou 一个枕头

pilot /'paɪlət/ *n* a pilot (*of an aircraft*) yì míng fēixíngyuán 一名飞行员, yì míng fēijī jiàshǐyuán 一名飞机架驶员；(*of a ship*) yì míng lǐnghángyuán 一名领航员

pin /pɪn/ **1** *n* a pin yì méi biézhēn 一枚别针, yì méi dàtóuzhēn 一枚大头针 **2** *vb* yòng zhēn bié 用针别, yòng zhēn dìng 用针钉；to pin the flower to the dress bǎ huā yòng zhēn bié zài yīfu shang 把花用针别在衣服上

pinch /pɪntʃ/ *vb* to pinch níng 拧 niē 捏；he pinched my arm, he pinched me on the arm tā níng wǒ de gēbo 他拧我的胳膊；(*to hurt ... by being too tight*) jǐ...tòng 挤...痛；my shoes are pinching wǒ de xié jiājiǎo 我的鞋夹脚

pineapple /'paɪnæpl/ *n* a pineapple yí gè bōluó 一个菠萝

pine tree /'paɪn triː/ *n* a pine tree yì kē sōngshù 一棵松树

pink /pɪŋk/ *adj* fěnhóngsè de 粉红色的

pint /paɪnt/ *n* (*the quantity*) a pint yì pǐntuō 一品脱 ! Note that a pint is 0.57 l in Britain and 0.47 l in the

US；a pint of milk yì pǐntuō niúnǎi 一品脱牛奶；(*British English*)(*a drink*)**to go for a pint** qù hē yì bēi (jiǔ) 去喝一杯(酒)

pipe /paɪp/ *n*(*for gas*,*water*) guǎnzi 管子；**a pipe** yì gēn guǎnzi 一根管子；(*for smoking*) yāndǒu 烟斗；**a pipe** yí gè yāndǒu 一个烟斗

pirate /'paɪərət/ **1** *n* a pirate (*on the high seas*) yí gè hǎidào 一个海盗 **2** *vb*(*print or publish illegally*) dàoyìn 盗印；**a pirated edition** yí gè dàobǎn 一个盗版

pitch /pɪtʃ/ **1** *n*(*British English*) a pitch yí gè chǎngdì 一个场地；**a football pitch** yí gè zúqiúchǎng 一个足球场 **2** *vb*(*in baseball*) tóuzhì qiú 投掷球

pity /'pɪtɪ/ **1** *n* liánmǐn 怜悯，tóngqíng 同情；(*when expressing regret*) yíhàn 遗憾，kěxī 可惜；**what a pity!** zhēn yíhàn! 真遗憾！；**it's a pity you can't come** kěxī nǐ bù néng lái 可惜你不能来 **2** *vb* tóngqíng 同情，kělián 可怜

pizza /'pi:tsə/ *n* a pizza yí gè (Yìdàlì) bǐsàbǐng 一个(意大利)比萨饼

place /pleɪs/ **1** *n* a place yí gè dìfang 一个地方；**Oxford is a nice place** Niújīn shì yí gè hěn hǎo de dìfang 牛津是一个很好的地方；**this place is dirty** zhège dìfang hěn zāng 这个地方很脏；(*a home*) jiā 家；**at Alison's place** zài Àlìsēn de jiā 在阿利森的家；**I'd like a place of my own** wǒ xiǎng yǒu yí gè zìjǐ de jiā 我想有一个自己的家；(*on a bus*,*at a table*) wèizi 位子，zuòwèi 座位；**a place** yí gè zuòwèi 一个座位；**is this place free?** zhège wèizi yǒu rén ma? 这个位子有人吗？；**to take someone's place** zhànle mǒu rén de zuòwèi 占了某人的座位；(*in a car park*,*in a queue*) dìfang 地方，wèizhi 位置；**a place** yí gè wèizhi 一个位置；**to find a place to park** zhǎo yí gè wèizhi tíngchē 找一个位置停车；(*as an employee in a firm*,*university*,*hospital*) zhíwèi 职位，gōngzuò 工作；**a place** yí gè zhíwèi 一个职位；**to get a place at the university** zài dàxué zhǎodào yí gè zhíwèi 在大学找到一

个职位；(on a course, a team) wèizi 位子；a place yí gè wèizi 一个位子；to get a place in a Chinese course dédào yí gè shàng Zhōngwénkè de wèizi 得到一个上中文课的位子；(in a contest) a place yí gè míngcì 一个名次；to win first place dé dì-yī míng 得第 1 名 **2** vb (to put) fàng fàng 放，（ to arrange) ānpái 安置，ānfàng 安放

plain /pleɪn/ **1** adj (simple) jiǎndān de 简单的，pǔsù de 朴素的；a plain dress yí jiàn pǔsù de yīfu 一件朴素的衣服；(not good-looking) bù hǎo kàn de 不好看的；(ordinary) pǔtōng de 普通的，píngcháng de 平常的 **2** n a plain yí gè píngyuán 一个平原

plait /plæt/ n (British English) a plait yì gēn biànzi 一根辫子

plan /plæn/ **1** n (what one intends to do) jìhuà 计划，dǎsuàn 打算；a plan yí gè jìhuà 一个计划；we need a plan wǒmen xūyào yí gè jìhuà 我们需要一个计划；(what one has arranged to do) ānpái 安排；a plan yí gè ānpái 一个安排；I don't have any plans for tonight wǒ jīntiān wǎnshang méiyǒu shénme ānpái 我今天晚上没有什么安排 **2** vb (to prepare, to organize) ānpái 安排；to plan [a trip | a timetable | a meeting] ānpái [yí cì lǚxíng | yí gè shíjiānbiǎo | yí cì huìyì] 安排 [一次旅行 | 一个时间表 | 一次会议]；(to intend) jìhuà 计划，dǎsuàn 打算；I'm planning to visit Scotland wǒ jìhuà fǎngwèn Sūgélán 我计划访问苏格兰

plane /pleɪn/ n (aeroplane) fēijī 飞机；a plane yí jià fēijī 一架飞机；(flat or level surface) píngmiàn 平面；a plane yí gè píngmiàn 一个平面

planet /'plænɪt/ n a planet yí gè xíngxīng 一个行星

plant /plɑːnt/ **1** n (member of the vegetable kingdom) zhíwù 植物；a plant yì kē zhíwù 一棵植物；(factory) gōngchǎng 工厂；a plant yí gè gōngchǎng 一个工厂 **2** vb (to put into the ground for growth) zhòng 种，zǎi 栽；(to insert) chā 插，ānchā 安插

plaster /'plɑːstə(r)/ n (British English) a plaster yì tiē gāoyào 一贴膏药

plastic /ˈplæstɪk/ **1** *n* sùliào 塑料 **2** *adj* (made of plastic) sùliào de 塑料的；(flexible and malleable) kěsù de 可塑的，yǒu sùxìng de 有塑性的

plate /pleɪt/ *n* a plate yí gè pánzi 一个盘子

platform /ˈplætfɔːm/ *n* a platform (at a train station) yí gè zhàntái 一个站台；on platform 4 zài sì hào zhàntái 在 4 号站台；(a raised floor for speakers) yí gè jiǎngtái 一个讲台；(a raised floor for singers, dancers, musicians) yí gè wǔtái 一个舞台

play /pleɪ/ **1** *vb* (to have fun) wánr 玩儿；to play with friends gēn péngyoumen yìqǐ wánr 跟朋友们一起玩儿；to play a trick on someone zhuōnòng mǒu rén 捉弄某人；(when talking about sports) to play [football | cricket | basketball | tennis | cards | chess...] [tī zúqiú | dǎ bǎnqiú | dǎ lánqiú | dǎ wǎngqiú | dǎ pūkè | xiàqí...] [踢足球 | 打板球 | 打篮球 | 打网球 | 打扑克 | 下棋...]；England is playing (against) America Yīnggélánduì zài gēn Měiguóduì bǐsài 英格兰队在跟美国队比赛；(when talking about music) to play [the piano | the flute | the violin | to play drums] [tán gāngqín | chuī dízi | lā xiǎotíqín | qiāo gǔ...] [弹钢琴 | 吹笛子 | 拉小提琴 | 敲鼓...]；(to put on music, etc.) (bō)fàng (播)放；to play [a video | a CD | a record] fàng [lùxiàng | guāngpán | chàngpiàn] 放 [录像 | 光盘 | 唱片]；(to act in a role, a part, etc.) bànyǎn 扮演；to play the role of someone bànyǎn mǒu rén 扮演某人；(to be in a show in the theatre, cinema, etc.) shàngyǎn 上演；the film will soon be playing at this cinema zhè bù diànyǐng jiāng hěn kuài zài zhè jiā diànyǐngyuàn shàngyǎn 这部电影将很快在这家电影院上演 **2** *n* a play (a drama, a dramatic performance) yì chū xì 一出戏，yì chū jù 一出剧；(a script of a play) yí gè jùběn 一个剧本；**play back** to play back a tape dào cídài 倒磁带

player /ˈpleɪə(r)/ *n* a player (in sports) yí gè yùndòngyuán 一个运动员；(in a musical performance) yí gè yǎnzòuzhě 一个演奏者，yí gè yǎnyuán 一个演员

playground /'pleɪɡraʊnd/ n a playground (for children to play in) yí ge yóuxì chǎngdì 一个游戏场地；(a field at a school) yí ge cāochǎng 一个操场

please /pliːz/ adv qǐng 请；please come in qǐng jìn qǐng jìn 请进；'more cake?'—'yes please' nǐ hái yào dàngāo ma?"—"hǎo, qǐng zài gěi wǒ yìdiǎnr" 你还要蛋糕吗?"—"好，请再给我一点儿"

pleased /pliːzd/ adj (happy, delighted) gāoxìng de 高兴的, yúkuài de 愉快的；pleased to meet you hěn gāoxìng de 很高兴的；(content, satisfied) mǎnyì de 满意的；I was very pleased with myself wǒ duì zìjǐ hěn mǎnyì 我对自己很满意

plenty /'plentɪ/ pron to have plenty of [time | money | friends…] yǒu hěn duō [shíjiān | qián | péngyou…] 有很多 [时间 | 钱 | 朋友…]

plot /plɒt/ n (a secret plan) mìmì jìhuà 秘密计划, yīnmóu 阴谋；a plot yí ge yīnmóu 一个阴谋；(the story in a film, a novel, a play) qíngjié 情节；a plot yí ge qíngjié 一个情节

plug /plʌɡ/ n a plug (on an appliance) yí ge chātóu 一个插头；(in a sink or bath) yí ge sāizi 一个塞子；plug in bǎ chātóu chāshang 把插头插上

plum /plʌm/ n a plum yí ge lǐzi 一个李子

plumber /'plʌmə(r)/ n a plumber yí ge guǎnzigōng 一个管子工

plus /plʌs/ prep jiā 加；three plus three are six sān jiā sān děngyú liù 3 加 3 等于 6

pocket /'pɒkɪt/ n a pocket yí ge kǒudài 一个口袋, yí ge yīdōu 一个衣兜

pocketbook /'pɒkɪtbʊk/ n (US English) a pocketbook (for keeping money) yí ge qiánbāo 一个钱包；(for taking notes) yí ge xiǎo bǐjìběn 一个小笔记本

pocket money /'pɒkɪt ˌmʌnɪ/ n línghuāqián 零花钱, língyòngqián 零用钱

poem /'pəʊɪm/ n a poem yì shǒu shī 一首诗

point /pɔɪnt/ **1** n (a statement in a discussion) lùndiǎn 论点;a point yí gè lùndiǎn 一个论点;to make a point zhèngmíng yí gè lùndiǎn 证明一个论点;(the most important idea) yàodiǎn 要点;that's not the point nà bú shì yàodiǎn 那不是要点;(use, purpose) yòng 用;there's no point in shouting hǎn méiyǒu yòng 喊没有用;(when talking about time) to be on the point of [moving | leaving | selling the house] zhèngyào [dòngshēn | líkāi | mài fángzi] de shíhou 正要[动身|离开|卖房子]的时候;(the sharp end) jiān 尖;the point of a pencil qiānbǐjiān 铅笔尖;(in a contest, a game) fēn 分;a point yì fēn 一分 **2** vb (to indicate) zhǐ 指;to point (one's finger) at someone (yòng shǒu) zhǐxiàng mǒu rén 指向某人;to point at a house zhǐxiàng yí zuò fángzi 指向一座房子;to point the way to the station zhǐdiǎn qù chēzhàn de lù 指点去车站的路;to point a gun at someone bǎ qiāng duìzhǔn mǒu rén 把枪对准某人;point out zhǐchū 指出;to point out his mistakes zhǐchū tā de cuòwù 指出他的错误

poison /'pɔɪzən/ **1** n (drug) dúyào 毒药;(substance) dúwù 毒物 **2** vb (to kill with poison) dúsǐ 毒死;(to injure with poison) shǐ … zhòngdú 使…中毒;to poison someone shǐ mǒu rén zhòngdú 使某人中毒;she got food-poisoning tā shíwù zhòngdú le 她食物中毒了;(to corrupt) dúhài 毒害;to poison young people's minds dúhài niánqīngrén de sīxiǎng 毒害年轻人的思想

pole /pəul/ n (pole) gēn gān 一根杆

police /pə'liːs/ n the police jǐngchá 警察

policeman /pə'liːsmən/ n a policeman yí gè jǐngchá 一个警察

police station /pə'liːs ˌsteɪʃən/ n a police station yí gè jǐngchájú 一个警察局

policewoman /pə'liːswumən/ n a policewoman yí gè nǚjǐngchá 一个女警察

polish /'pɒlɪʃ/ vb to polish [shoes | the car | the

furniture...] cā [xié|qìchē|jiājù···] 擦 [鞋|汽车|家具···]

polite /pə'laɪt/ adj yǒu lǐmào de 有礼貌的, kèqi de 客气的

political /pə'lɪtɪkəl/ adj zhèngzhì de 政治的, zhèngzhì-shang de 政治上的

politician /ˌpɒlɪ'tɪʃən/ n a politician (in a neutral sense) yí gè zhèngzhìjiā 一个政治家; (in a negative sense) yí gè zhèngkè 一个政客

politics /'pɒlɪtɪks/ n zhèngzhì 政治

pollute /pə'ljuːt/ vb wūrǎn 污染

pollution /pə'ljuːʃən/ n wūrǎn 污染

pond /pɒnd/ n a pond yí gè chítáng 一个池塘

pony /'pəʊnɪ/ n a pony yì pǐ xiǎomǎ 一匹小马

ponytail /'pəʊnɪteɪl/ n a ponytail yì zhǒng mǎwěi fàxíng 一种马尾发型

pool /puːl/ n (a swimming pool) a pool yí gè yóuyǒngchí 一个游泳池; (on the ground, the floor) a pool of water yì tān shuǐ 一滩水; (the game) dànzǐxì 弹子戏

poor /pʊə(r)/ adj (not wealthy) qióng de 穷的, pínqióng de 贫穷的; (not satisfactory) chà de 差的, bù hǎo de 不好的; a poor memory bù hǎo de jìyìlì 不好的记忆力; (expressing sympathy) kělián de 可怜的; the poor boy is very ill zhè kělián de háizi bìng de hěn lìhai 这可怜的孩子病得很厉害

popular /'pɒpjʊlə(r)/ adj (prevailing among the people) liúxíng de 流行的; a popular hobby yì zhǒng hěn liúxíng de shìhào 一种很流行的嗜好; a popular song shòu liúxíng gēqǔ 一首流行歌曲; (enjoying the favour of) shòu···huānyíng de 受···欢迎的, shòu···xǐhuan de 受···喜欢的; a popular writer yí gè shòu (rén) huānyíng de zuòjiā 一个受 (人) 欢迎的作家; to be popular with the girls shòu nǚháizi xǐhuan 受女孩子喜欢

population /ˌpɒpjʊ'leɪʃən/ n rénkǒu 人口! Note that rénkǒu 人口 is uncountable and does not have a measure word; a population of one million yìbǎi wàn rénkǒu 100

万人口

pork /pɔːk/ n zhūròu 猪肉

port /pɔːt/ n a port yí gè gǎngkǒu 一个港口

portrait /'pɔːtrɪt/ n a portrait yì zhāng huàxiàng 一张画像, yì zhāng xiāoxiàng 一张肖像

Portugal /'pɔːtjugəl/ n Pútáoyá 葡萄牙

Portuguese /ˌpɔːtjuˈgiːz/ **1** adj Pútáoyá de 葡萄牙的 **2** n (the people) Pútáoyárén 葡萄牙人; (the language) Pútáoyáyǔ 葡萄牙语, Pútáoyáwén 葡萄牙文

position /pəˈzɪʃən/ n a position (place occupied) yí gè wèizhi 一个位置, yí gè fāngwèi 一个方位; (status or place in society) yí gè dìwèi 一个地位, yì zhǒng shēnfèn 一种身份; (post or appointment) yí gè zhíwèi 一个职位, yí gè zhíwù 一个职务; (attitude or ground taken in an argument) yì zhǒng tàidu 一种态度; (situation) yì zhǒng xíngshì 一种形势, yì zhǒng zhuàngkuàng 一种状况; (posture) yì zhǒng zīshì 一种姿势

positive /'pɒzɪtɪv/ adj (definitely and explicitly laid down) míngquè de 明确的, quèshí de 确实的; (beyond possibility of doubt) kěndìng de 肯定的; (fully convinced) quèxìn de 确信的; (having a good and constructive attitude) jījí de 积极的, jiànshèxìng de 建设性的

possibility /ˌpɒsəˈbɪlətɪ/ n a possibility yì zhǒng kěnéng (xìng) 一种可能(性)

possible /'pɒsəbl/ adj kěnéng de 可能的; it's possible that it'll rain tomorrow míngtiān kěnéng xiàyǔ 明天可能下雨; as quickly as possible jǐnkuài 尽快; please come as quickly as possible qǐng jǐnkuài lái 请尽快来

post /pəʊst/ (British English) **1** n the post (the system) yóuzhèng 邮政; (the letters) yóujiàn 邮件; has the post come yet? yóujiàn lái le ma? 邮件来了吗? **2** vb jì 寄, yóujì 邮寄; to post a letter jì yì fēng xìn 寄一封信

postbox /'pəʊstbɒks/ n (British English) a postbox yí gè xìnxiāng 一个信箱

postcard /'pəʊstkɑːd/ n a postcard yì zhāng míngxìnpiàn 一张明信片

张明信片

postcode /'pəʊstkəʊd/ n (British English) a postcode yí gè yóuzhèng biānmǎ 一个邮政编码

poster /'pəʊstə(r)/ n a poster (giving information) yì zhāng zhāotiě 一张招贴，yì zhāng guǎnggào 一张广告；(used as a picture) yì zhāng zhāotiěhuà 一张招贴画

postman /'pəʊstmən/ n (British English) a postman yí gè yóudìyuán 一个邮递员

post office /'pəʊst ˌɒfɪs/ n a post office yí gè yóujú 一个邮局

postpone /pəʊst'pəʊn/ vb tuīchí 推迟，yánqī 延期；let's postpone the party until next week zánmen bǎ jùhuì tuīchí dào xiàge xīngqī ba 咱们把聚会推迟到下个星期吧；the concert has been postponed yīnyuèhuì yánqī le 音乐会延期了

pot /pɒt/ n (a container for making coffee or tea) hú 壶，pot yí gè hú 一个壶；(a container for preserving something) guàn(zi) 罐(子)，a pot yí gè guànzi 一个罐子；(a saucepan) guō 锅，a pot yí gè guō 一个锅

potato /pə'teɪtəʊ/ n a potato yí gè tǔdòu 一个土豆

pottery /'pɒtəri/ n táoqì 陶器

pound /paʊnd/ n (the currency) yīngbàng 英镑；a pound yì (yīng) bàng 一(英)镑；(in weight) bàng 磅；a pound yí bàng 一磅；two pounds of apples liǎng bàng píngguǒ 两磅苹果

pour /pɔː(r)/ vb (from a container) dào 倒，pour milk into a bowl bǎ niúnǎi dàojìn wǎn li 把牛奶倒进碗里；to pour wine for someone gěi mǒu rén dào jiǔ 给某人倒酒；(to flow) liú 流，tǎng 淌；the water was pouring into the kitchen shuǐ liújìnle chúfáng 水流进了厨房；(to escape) mào 冒；there is smoke pouring out of the window yǒu yìxiē yān cóng chuānghu li mào chūlái 有一些烟从窗户里冒出来；(to rain) xià dàyǔ 下大雨；it's pouring (with rain) zhèngzài xià dàyǔ 正在下大雨；(to enter in large numbers) yǒngjìn 涌进；to pour into the city yǒngjìn chéngshì 涌进城市；(to leave in large numbers) yǒngchū 涌出；to pour out of the stadium yǒngchū tǐyùchǎng 涌出体育场

powder /'paʊdə(r)/ n fěn 粉

power /'paʊə(r)/ n(control) quánlì 权力；to be in power zhízhèng 执政，zhǎngquán 掌权；(influence) shìli 势力；to have great power yǒu hěn dà de shìli 有很大的势力；(electricity) diàn 电

practical /'præktɪkəl/ adj (given to action rather than theory) shíjiàn de 实践的；(relating to real existence or action) shíjì de 实际的；(workable) kěxíng de 可行的；(useful) shíyòng de 实用的

practically /'præktɪkəli/ adv shíjìshang 实际上，shìshíshang 事实上

practise /'præktɪs/ (British English)，**practice** (US English) vb (to work at improving a skill) liànxí 练习；to practise [the piano | one's Chinese | a song | playing basketball...] liànxí [gāngqín|Zhōngwén| yì shǒu gē| dǎ lánqiú···] 练习 [钢琴|中文|一首歌|打篮球···]；(to carry out) shíxíng 实行，shíshí 实施；to practise economy shíxíng jiéyuē 实行节约

praise /preɪz/ vb biǎoyáng 表扬，zànyáng 赞扬；to praise someone biǎoyáng mǒu rén 表扬某人

prawn /prɔːn/ n (British English) a prawn yì zhī duìxiā 一只对虾

pray /preɪ/ vb (in a religious sense) qídǎo 祈祷，dǎogào 祷告；(to hope) (yīnqiè) pànwàng (殷切) 盼望，qíqiú qǐngqiú 祈求；they are praying for rain tāmen pànwàngzhe xiàyǔ 他们盼望着下雨

prayer /preə(r)/ n dǎowén 祷文，dǎogào 祷告

precaution /prɪ'kɔːʃən/ n a precaution yí xiàng yùfáng cuòshī 一项预防措施

precious /'preʃəs/ adj bǎoguì de 宝贵的，zhēnguì de 珍贵的

precise /prɪ'saɪs/ adj jīngquè de 精确的，zhǔnquè de 准确的

predict /prɪˈdɪkt/ vb yùyán 预言, yùgào 预告

prediction /prɪˈdɪkʃən/ n yùyán 预言, yùgào 预告

prefer /prɪˈfɜː(r)/ vb xǐhuan 喜欢, yuànyì 愿意; to prefer Chinese food to English food xǐhuan Zhōngguófàn, bù xǐhuan Yīngguófàn 喜欢中国饭, 不喜欢英国饭。! *Note that in stating a preference for one thing over another, the thing that is less preferred is expressed in a negative phrase in Chinese, as in* bù xǐhuan Yīngguófàn 不喜欢英国饭 *above.* I'd prefer to phone wǒ yuànyì dǎ diànhuà 我愿意打电话

pregnant /ˈpregnənt/ adj huáiyùn de 怀孕的; she's become pregnant tā huáiyùn le 她怀孕了

prejudice /ˈpredʒudɪs/ n a prejudice (*against someone or something*) yì zhǒng piānjiàn 一种偏见; (*in favour of someone or something*) yì zhǒng piān'ài 一种偏爱; he has [a prejudice against | a prejudice in favour of] Japanese wine tā duì Rìběnjiǔ yǒu [yì zhǒng piānjiàn | yì zhǒng piān'ài] 他对日本酒有[一种偏见 | 一种偏爱]

prepare /prɪˈpeə(r)/ vb (*to get something or someone ready*) shǐ…zuòhǎo zhǔnbèi 使…做好准备; to prepare pupils for an exam shǐ xuésheng wèi kǎoshì zuòhǎo zhǔnbèi 使学生为考试做好准备; (*to get ready*) zhǔnbèi 准备; to prepare for [an exam | a trip | a party...] zhǔnbèi [yí cì kǎoshì | yí cì lǚxíng | yí cì jùhuì···] 准备[一次考试 | 一次旅行 | 一次聚会···]

prepared /prɪˈpeəd/ adj (*willing*) yuànyì de 愿意的; to be prepared to wait yuànyì děng 愿意等; (*ready*) zuòhǎo zhǔnbèi de 做好准备的; to be prepared for an exam wèi kǎoshì zuòhǎo zhǔnbèi 为考试做好准备

prescription /prɪˈskrɪpʃən/ n a prescription yí gè chǔfāng 一个处方

present /ˈprezənt/ **1** n (*a gift*) lǐwù 礼物, lǐpǐn 礼品; a present yí gè lǐwù 一个礼物; to give someone a present sònggěi mǒu rén yí gè lǐwù 送给某人一个礼物; (*now*) the present xiànzài 现在, mùqián 目前; I'm

staying here at present mùqián wǒ dǎi zài zhèr 目前我
呆在这儿 **2** adj (in a place) to be present (at a formal
event) chūxí de 出席的，dàochǎng de 到场的；to be
present at the meeting chūxí huìyì 出席会议；(in an
informal situation) zài 在；he was not present then
dāngshí tā bú zài 当时他不在；(now under consideration)
mùqián de 目前的，xiànzài de 现在的；the present
situation mùqián de xíngshì 目前的形势 **3** /prɪˈzent/ vb
(to give as a gift) zèngsòng 赠送；to present a book to
him zèngsòng gěi tā yì běn shū 赠送给他一本书；(to give
as an award) fāgěi 发给，jǐyǔ 给予；to present a gold
medal to someone fāgěi mǒu rén yí kuài jīnzhì jiǎngpái
发给某人一块金质奖牌；(to give to someone who is
one's senior) xiàngěi 献给；a girl presented the hero
with a bunch of flowers yí ge gūniang xiàngěi nàge
yīngxióng yí shù huā 一个姑娘献给那个英雄一束花；(to
introduce formally or to introduce on radio or TV) jièshào
介绍；may I present Mr. Wang to you? qǐng yǔnxǔ wǒ
bǎ Wáng xiānsheng jièshào gěi nín 请允许我把王先生介
绍给您；to present a programme jièshào yí ge jiémù 介绍
一个节目；(to hand something to someone formally) dìjiāo
递交；to present a report to the committee xiàng
wěiyuánhuì dìjiāo yí fèn bàogào 向委员会递交一份报告；
(to put forward) tíchū 提出；to present a proposal to
the government xiàng zhèngfǔ tíchū yí ge jiànyì 向政府
提出一个建议；(to put on a drama, a play) shàngyǎn 上
演；when will the play be presented? zhège huàjù
shénme shíhou shàngyǎn? 这个话剧什么时候上演？

president /ˈprezɪdənt/ n a president (of a country) yí ge
zǒngtǒng 一个总统；(of an association or a board) yí ge
huìzhǎng 一个会长；(of a university) yí ge xiàozhǎng 一
个校长；(of a college) yí ge yuànzhǎng 一个院长

press /pres/ **1** vb (with the hand) àn 按；to press the
button àn diànniǔ 按电钮；(to compress) yā 压；(to
urge strongly) dūncù 敦促；to press him to change his

mind dūncù tā gǎibiàn zhǔyi 敦促他改变主意 **2** *n* the press xīnwénjiè 新闻界

pressure / 'preʃə(r)/ *n* yālì 压力；to put pressure on someone xiàng mǒu rén shījiā yālì 向某人施加压力

pretend /prɪ'tend/ *vb* jiǎzhuāng 假装；he's pretending to be annoyed tā jiǎzhuāng shēngqì le 他假装生气了

pretty / 'prɪtɪ/ **1** *adj* piàoliang de 漂亮的，měilì de 美丽的；(*when talking about music or voice*) yōuměi de 优美的，hǎotīng de 好听的 **2** *adv* xiāngdāng 相当，tǐng tǐng 挺挺；that's pretty good nà hái tǐng hǎo 那还挺好

prevent /prɪ'vent/ *vb* (*to keep from happening*) fángzhǐ 防止，bìmiǎn 避免；to prevent a war fángzhǐ zhànzhēng 防止战争；(*to stop or hinder*) zǔzhǐ 阻止，zhìzhǐ 制止；to prevent someone from [working | smoking | going out...] zǔzhǐ mǒu rén [gōngzuò | xīyān | chūqù...] 阻止某人［工作 | 吸烟 | 出去...］；(*make unable*) shǐ… bù néng shǐ… 不能 使… 不能；the noise prevented him from sleeping zàoshēng shǐ tā bù néng shuìjiào 噪声使他不能睡觉

previous / 'priːvjəs/ *adj* the previous [night | year | headmaster] qián [yí gè wǎnshang | yì nián | yí gè xiàozhǎng] 前 ［一个晚上 | 一年 | 一个校长］；previous problems yǐqián de wèntí 以前的问题

price /praɪs/ *n* (*the amount for which a thing is bought or sold*) jiàqián 价钱，jiàgé 价格；(*the cost one suffers in order to gain something*) dàijià 代价

pride /praɪd/ *n* jiāo'ào 骄傲，zìháo 自豪；(*self-respect*) zìzūnxīn 自尊心

priest /priːst/ *n* a priest(*protestant*) yí gè mùshī 一个牧师；(*Roman Catholic*) yí gè shénfù 一个神父

primary school / 'praɪmərɪ ˌskuːl/ *n* a primary school yì suǒ xiǎoxué 一所小学

primary school teacher / 'praɪmərɪ ˌskuːl 'tiːtʃə(r)/ *n* a primary school teacher yí gè xiǎoxué jiàoshī 一个小学教师

prime minister /ˌpraɪm 'mɪnɪstə(r)/ *n* a prime minister yí wèi shǒuxiàng 一位首相

prince /prɪns/ n a prince yí gè wángzǐ 一个王子

princess /prɪn'ses/ n a princess yí gè gōngzhǔ 一个公主

principal /'prɪnsəpəl/ n a principal yí gè xiàozhǎng 一个校长

print /prɪnt/ **1** vb (to impress) yìn 印, yìnshuā 印刷；to print a book yìn yì běn shū 印一本书；(from a photographic negative) xǐ 洗, xǐyìn 洗印；to print photographs xǐ zhàopiàn 洗照片 **2** n (of a photo) a print yì zhāng zhàopiàn 一张照片；(of a finger) a print yí gè shǒuyìn 一个手印；(of a foot) a print yí gè jiǎoyìn 一个脚印

priority /praɪ'ɒrəti/ n a priority (something given special attention) yí gè zhòngdiǎn 一个重点；(the privilege of preferential treatment) yí gè yōuxiānquán 一个优先权

prison /'prɪzən/ n a prison yì suǒ jiānyù 一所监狱；to put someone in prison bǎ mǒu rén guānjìn jiānyù 把某人关进监狱

prisoner /'prɪzənə(r)/ n a prisoner (one confined in prison) yí gè fànrén 一个犯人, yí gè qiúfàn 一个囚犯；(a captive) yí gè fúlǔ 一个俘虏；to be taken prisoner bèi fúlǔ le 被俘虏了

private /'praɪvɪt/ **1** adj (personal) sīrén de 私人的, gèrén de 个人的；my private life wǒ de sīshēnghuó 我的私生活；(independent) sīlì de 私立的；a private school yì suǒ sīlì xuéxiào 一所私立学校；(not owned by the state) sīyǒu sīrén 私有私人；private property sīyǒu cáichǎn 私有财产；(not run by the state) sīyíng de 私营的；private industry sīyíng gōngyè 私营工业 **2** in private sīxià de 私下地, mìmì de 秘密地

prize /praɪz/ n a prize yí gè jiǎng(pǐn) 一个奖(品)

probably /'prɒbəbli/ adv hěn kěnéng 很可能, dàgài 大概

problem /'prɒbləm/ n a problem yí gè wèntí 一个问题

process /'prəʊses/ n a process yí gè guòchéng 一个过程；to be in the process of writing a letter zhèngzài xiě yì fēng xìn 正在写一封信

produce /prə'dju:s/ **1** vb (to make) shēngchǎn 生产，zhìzào 制造；(to bring about) chǎnshēng 产生，yǐnqǐ 引起；**to produce good results** chǎnshēng hǎo de jiéguǒ 产生好的结果；(to create) **to produce a film** shèzhì yí bù diànyǐng 摄制一部电影；**to produce a play** páiyǎn yì chū xì 排演一出戏 **2** n produce chǎnpǐn 产品

product /'prɒdʌkt/ n a product(a thing produced) yí gè chǎnpǐn 一个产品；(a result) yí gè jiéguǒ 一个结果

production /prə'dʌkʃən/ n (of food, clothes, etc.)shēngchǎn 生产；(of a film) shèzhì 摄制，pāishè 拍摄；(of a play) yǎnchū 演出

profession /prəu'feʃən/ n a profession yì zhǒng zhíyè 一种职业

professional /prəu'feʃənəl/ adj (pertaining to a profession) zhuānyè de 专业的；**professional knowledge** zhuānyè zhīshi 专业知识；(not amateur) zhíyè de 职业的；**a professional athlete** yí gè zhíyè yùndòngyuán 一个职业运动员

professor /prəu'fesə(r)/ n a professor yí wèi jiàoshòu 一位教授

profit /'prɒfɪt/ n a profit(benefit) yí gè yìchù 一个益处；(advantage) yí gè hǎochù 一个好处；(capital gain) yí fèn lìrùn 一份利润

program /'prəugræm/ **1** n (for a computer) chéngxù 程序；**a program** yí gè chéngxù 一个程序；(US English) ▶ **programme 2** vb (a computer) biān chéngxù 编程序；(a concert, a show, a radio or TV broadcast) ānpái jiémù 安排节目

programme /'prəugræm/ (British English), **program** (US English) n(on radio, TV) jiémù 节目；**a programme** yí gè jiémù 一个节目；**a programme about China** yí gè guānyú Zhōngguó de jiémù 一个关于中国的节目；(for a play, a concert) jiémùdān 节目单；**a programme** yì zhāng jiémùdān 一张节目单；(for a conference, a course) ānpái

安排；the programme of the conference huìyì de ānpái 会议的安排

progress /'prəʊgres/ n (forward movement) qiánjìn 前进；(advance to something better or higher in development) jìnbù 进步；to make progress jìnbù 进步

project /'prɒdʒekt/ n a project (for study or research) yí gè kètí 一个课题；(in construction) yí xiàng gōngchéng 一项工程；(a scheme) yí xiàng guīhuà 一项规划，yí gè jìhuà 一个计划

promise /'prɒmɪs/ **1** vb dāying 答应，yǔnnuò 允诺；to promise to [come | repay a loan | say nothing] dāying [lái | huán dàikuǎn | shénme yě bù shuō] 答应 [来 | 还贷款 | 什么也不说] **2** n a promise yí gè nuòyán 一个诺言，yí gè yǔnnuò 一个允诺；[to keep | to break] one's promise [zūnshǒu | bù zūnshǒu] nuòyán [遵守 | 不遵守] 诺言

pronounce /prə'naʊns/ vb (to articulate) fā···de yīn 发···的音，niàn 念；how do you pronounce this character? nǐ zěnme fā zhège zì de yīn? 你怎么发这个字的音？

proof /pruːf/ n zhèngmíng 证明，zhèngjù 证据

properly /'prɒpəlɪ/ adv (in an appropriate manner) shìdàng de 适当地，qiàdàng de 恰当地；(strictly) yángé de 严格地

property /'prɒpətɪ/ n (something that is owned) cáichǎn 财产；(house that is owned) fángchǎn 房产；(land that is owned) dìchǎn 地产

protect /prə'tekt/ vb (to guard) bǎohù 保护；to protect oneself bǎohù zìjǐ 保护自己；(to defend) bǎowèi 保卫

protest /prə'test/ vb (to make a declaration against) kàngyì 抗议，fǎnduì 反对；(assert formally) duànyán 断言，biǎoshì 表示；he protested his innocence tā duànyán zìjǐ wúzuì 他断言自己无罪

protester /prə'testə(r)/ n a protester yí gè kàngyìzhě 一个抗议者

proud /praʊd/ adj jiāo'ào de 骄傲的，zìháo de 自豪的；

she's proud of herself tā wèi zìjǐ gǎndào jiāo'ào 她为自己感到骄傲

prove /pruːv/ vb zhèngmíng 证明，zhèngshí 证实

provide /prəʊ'vaɪd/ vb tígōng 提供；to provide meals tígōng fàn 提供饭；to provide a transport service tígōng jiāotōng fúwù 提供交通服务

provided /prəʊ'vaɪdɪd/ conj jiǎrú 假如；I'll lend you my car provided you pay me jiǎrú nǐ fùgěi wǒ qián，wǒ jiù bǎ chē jiègěi nǐ 假如你付给我钱，我就把车借给你！Note that the clause introduced by jiǎrú 假如 comes before the main clause and jiù 就 is often used after the subject in the main clause.

psychiatrist /psaɪ'kaɪətrɪst/ n a psychiatrist yí gè jīngshénbìng yīshēng 一个精神病医生

psychologist /psaɪ'kɒlədʒɪst/ n a psychologist (one who does research) yí gè xīnlǐxuéjiā 一个心理学家；(one who sees patients) yí gè xīnlǐyīshēng 一个心理医生

pub /pʌb/ n (British English) a pub yí gè jiǔguǎn(r) 一个酒馆(儿)

public /'pʌblɪk/ **1** n the public gōngzhòng 公众，mínzhòng 民众 **2** adj (open to all) gōnggòng de 公共的；a public library yí gè gōnggòng túshūguǎn 一个公共图书馆；(used by all) gōngyòng de 公用的；a public telephone yí gè gōngyòng diànhuà 一个公用电话；(known to all) gōngkāi de 公开的；to make their relationship public bǎ tāmen de guānxì gōngkāi 把他们的关系公开 **3** in public dāngzhòng 当众

public holiday /'pʌblɪk 'hɒlədɪ/ n a public holiday yí gè gōngdìng jiàrì 一个公定假日

public transport /'pʌblɪk 'trænspɔːt/ n gōnggòng jiāotōng 公共交通

pudding /'pʊdɪŋ/ n a pudding yí gè bùdīng 一个布丁；(general term for a dessert) (British English) yí dào tiándiǎn 一道甜点

puddle /'pʌdl/ n a puddle yí gè shuǐkēng 一个水坑

pull /pʊl/ vb (to move something toward oneself) lā 拉；
to pull on a rope lā yì gēn shéngzi 拉一根绳子；(if there
is a means to facilitate the action, such as wheels or
rollers, or if it's a person walking) lā 拉；to pull the
piano into the sitting room bǎ gāngqín lā dào kètīng li
把钢琴拉到客厅里；to pull someone away from the
door bǎ mǒu rén cóng ménkǒu lāzǒu 把某人从门口拉走；
(if there is no means to facilitate the pulling action) tuō
拖；to pull the dead body out of the river bǎ shītǐ cóng
hé li tuō chūlái 把尸体从河里拖出来；the
demonstrators were pulled away by the policeman
shìwēizhě bèi jǐngchá tuōzǒu le 示威者被警察拖走了；(to
extract something that is fixed) bá 拔；to pull [a tooth |
a nail | the weeds] bá [yì kē yá | yí gè dīngzi | cǎo] 拔 [一颗牙|一个
钉子|草]；to pull a face(British English) zuò guǐliǎnr 做鬼
脸儿，**pull down** (to knock down) chāidiào 拆掉；(to
lower) jiàngdī 降低，**pull out** to pull a tooth out báchū
yì kē yá 拔出一颗牙，**pull up** (to stop) tíngxià 停下；(to
remove) to pull up the weeds bá cǎo 拔草；to pull up
one's socks bǎ wàizi lā qǐlai 把袜子拉起来

pullover /'pʊl,əʊvə(r)/ n a pullover yí jiàn tàotóushān 一
件套头衫

pump /pʌmp/ n (for moving or raising fluids) bèng 泵；a
pump yí gè bèng 一个泵；(for transferring air) a bicycle
pump yí gè dǎqìtǒng 一个打气筒；**pump up** dǎqì 打气

pumpkin /'pʌmpkɪn/ n a pumpkin yí gè nánguā 一个南
瓜

punch /pʌntʃ/ vb yòng quán dǎ 用拳打；she punched
him in the face tā yòng quán dǎ tā de liǎn 她用拳打他的
脸

puncture /'pʌŋktʃə(r)/ n a puncture yí gè cìkǒng 一个
刺孔

punish /'pʌnɪʃ/ vb chǔfá 处罚，chéngfá 惩罚

pupil /'pjuːpəl/ n a pupil yí gè xuésheng 一个学生

puppet /'pʌprt/ n a puppet yí gè mù'ǒu 一个木偶

puppy /'pʌpɪ/ *n* a puppy yì zhī xiǎogǒu 一只小狗

pure /pjuə(r)/ *adj* (*unmixed and untainted*) chún de 纯的；**pure gold** chúnjīn 纯金；(*clean*) chúnjìng de 纯净的；jiéjìng de 洁净的；**pure air** chúnjìng de kōngqì 纯净的空气；(*free from bad taste，bad ideas，evil thinking*) chúnjié de 纯洁的；**pure love** chúnjié de àiqíng 纯洁的爱情；(*sheer*) wánquán de 完全的，chúncuì de 纯粹的；**it's pure nonsense** zhè wánquán shì húshuō-bādào 这完全是胡说八道；(*when talking about the use of a language*) chúnzhèng de 纯正的；**a pure Beijing accent** chúnzhèng de Běijīng kǒuyīn 纯正的北京口音

purple /'pɜːpl/ *adj* zǐsè de 紫色的

purpose /'pɜːpəs/ *n* **1** *n* purpose (*intention*) yí gè yìtú 一个意图；(*aim*) yí gè mùdì 一个目的；(*a useful function*) yí gè yòngchù 一个用处 **2 on purpose** gùyì de 故意地；**you did it on purpose!** nǐ shì gùyì zhèyàng zuò de! 你是故意这样做的!

purse /pɜːs/ *n* (*for money*) qiánbāo 钱包；**a purse** yí gè qiánbāo 一个钱包；(*US English*) (*a handbag*) shǒutíbāo 手提包；**a purse** yí gè shǒutíbāo 一个手提包

push /puʃ/ *vb* (*press or move forward by pressure*) tuī 推；**to push a car** tuī chē 推车；**to push someone down the stairs** bǎ mǒu rén tuīxià lóutī 把某人推下楼梯；(*urge*) cuī(cù) 催(促)；**don't push her too hard** tài jǐn jìn cuī tā tài jǐn 别催她太紧；(*sell*) fànmài 贩卖；**to push drugs** fànmài dúpǐn 贩卖毒品

pushchair /'puʃtʃeə(r)/ *n* (*British English*) a pushchair yí gè yīng'ér tuīchē 一个婴儿推车

pusher /'puʃə(r)/ *n* a pusher (*a drug seller*) yí gè fàndú de rén 一个贩毒的人

put /put/ *vb* (*to place or to add*) fàng 放；**to put the book on the table** bǎ shū fàng zài zhuōzi shang 把书放在桌子上；**don't put sugar in my coffee** bié wǎng wǒ de kāfēi li fàng táng 别往我的咖啡里放糖；(*to raise*) tíchū 提出；**to put a question to him** xiàng tā tíchū yí gè wèntí

向他提出一个问题；(*to cause to be in a position or state*)**to put someone in prison** 把某人关进监狱；**to put someone in a bad mood** 使某人心情不好；**put away** (*to pack up*) 收起来；**put your tools away** 把你的工具收起来；(*to put into a proper or desirable place*) 放好 放好；**to put the money away** 把钱放好；**put back** (*to return to its place*) 放回；**to put the book back on the shelf** 把书放回书架；(*to change the time*) **to put the clock back** 把钟表往回拨；**put down** (*to lay down*) 放下；**put the knife down!** 把刀放下吧！把刀放下！；(*when phoning*) 挂断；**put the phone down** 挂断电话；(*British English*) (*to give a lethal injection to*) 给…注射药品使它安乐死去；**our dog had to be put down** 只好给我们的狗注射药品使它安乐死去；(*to write down*) 写下；**please put your name down on this paper** 请在这张纸上写下你的名字；**put forward** (*to propose*) 提出；**to put forward a suggestion** 提出一个建议；(*to change the time*) **to put the clocks forward** 把表往前拨；**put off** (*to delay*) 推迟；**to put off the meeting till next week** 把会议推迟到下个星期；(*to switch off*) 关上；**put on** (*if it's clothes, shoes, socks*) 穿上；**to put jeans on** 穿上牛仔裤；(*if it's a hat, gloves, glasses, a scarf*) 戴上；**to put on one's watch** 戴上手表；(*to switch on*) 打开；**to put the heating on** 把暖气打开；**to put a CD on** 放上一张光盘；**to put on weight** 增加

tǐzhòng 增加体重；(*to organize，to produce*) shàngyǎn 上演；**to put on a play** shàngyǎn yì chū xì 上演一出戏；**put out to put out a cigarette** mièdiào 灭掉烟卷儿；(*to switch off*) guāndiào 关掉；**to put out the lights** bǎ dēng guāndiào 把灯关掉；**put up** (*to raise*) jǔqǐ 举起；táiqǐ 抬起；**to put up one's hand** jǔqǐ shǒu 举起手；**to put a sign up** guàqǐ yí gè zhāopai 挂起一个招牌；(*to erect*) dāqǐ 搭起；**to put up a tent** dāqǐ yí gè zhàngpeng 搭起一个帐篷；(*British English*) (*to raise*) tígāo 提高；**to put the rent up** tígāo fángzū 提高房租；(*to give someone a place to stay*) **to put someone up** gěi mǒu rén tígōng zhùchù 给某人提供住处；**put up with** rěnshòu 忍受，róngrěn 容忍

puzzle /ˈpʌzl/ *n* **a puzzle** (*a riddle*) yí gè míyǔ 一个谜语；(*a question*) yí gè nántí 一个难题；(*a bewildering situation*) yí gè mí 一个谜；(*a jigsaw puzzle*) yí gè pīnbǎn wánjù 一个拼板玩具

pyjamas /pəˈdʒɑːməz/ *n* shuìyī 睡衣；(*if it's trousers only*) shuìkù 睡裤

qualified /ˈkwɒlɪfaɪd/ *adj* (*having the right qualifications*) yǒu zīgé de 有资格的；(*competent and fit*) shèngrèn de 胜任的

quality /ˈkwɒlɪtɪ/ *n* (*grade of goodness*) zhìliàng 质量；(*attribute*) pǐnzhì 品质；(*characteristic*) tèxìng 特性

quantity /ˈkwɒntɪtɪ/ *n* liàng 量，shùliàng 数量；**a [small| large] quantity of oil** [shǎo|dà] liàng de yóu [少|大] 量的油；**large quantity of bananas** dàliàng de xiāngjiāo 大量的香蕉

quarrel /ˈkwɒrəl/ **1** *n* **a quarrel** yí cì zhēngchǎo 一次争

吵，yí cì chǎojià 一次吵架 **2** *vb* zhēngchǎo 争吵，chǎojià 吵架；to quarrel with someone gēn mǒu rén zhēngchǎo 跟某人争吵

quarter /'kwɔːtə(r)/ **1** *n* a quarter of an hour yí kè zhōng 一刻钟；to divide the tomatoes in quarters bǎ xīhóngshì fēnchéng sì fèn 把西红柿分成 4 份 **2** *pron* (*when talking about quantities, numbers*) a quarter sì fēn zhī yī 四分之一；a quarter of the population can't read sì fēn zhī yī de rénkǒu bù shízì 四分之一的人口不识字；(*when talking about time*) a quarter yí kè (zhōng) 一刻 (钟)，shíwǔ fēn (zhōng) 15 分 (钟)；an hour and a quarter yì xiǎoshí (líng) yí kè zhōng 一小时(零)一刻钟；it's a quarter past five wǔ diǎn shíwǔ (fēn) 5 点 15 (分)! Note that when talking about a point of time, zhōng 钟 is not used.

quay /kiː/ *n* a quay yí gè mǎtou 一个码头

queen /kwiːn/ *n* a queen yí gè nǚwáng 一个女王

question /'kwestʃən/ **1** *n* a question yí gè wèntí 一个问题；to ask someone a question wèn mǒu rén yí gè wèntí 问某人一个问题；to answer a question huídá yí gè wèntí 回答一个问题 **2** *vb* (*to put questions to*) xúnwèn 询问，xùnwèn 讯问；(*when handling a suspect or a criminal*) shěnwèn 审问

queue /kjuː/ (*British English*) **1** *n* a queue yì gè duì 一个队；to join the queue cānjiā páiduì 参加排队；to jump the queue chāduì 插队，bú àn cìxù páiduì 不按次序排队，jiāsāir 加塞儿 *vb* páiduì 排队

quick /kwɪk/ *adj* kuài de 快的，xùnsù de 迅速的；a quick answer yí gè hěn kuài de dáfù 一个很快的答复；it's quicker to go by train zuò huǒchē qù gèng kuài 坐火车去更快；it's the quickest way [to get to London | to save money | to make friends] zhè shì [qù Lúndūn | shěngqián | jiāo péngyou] de zuì kuài fāngfǎ 这是 [去伦敦|省钱|交朋友] 的最快方法

quickly /'kwɪklɪ/ *adv* kuài 快，hěn kuài de 很快地

quiet /'kwaɪət/ **1** adj (silent) jìng de 静的，ānjìng de 安静的；to keep quiet bǎochí ānjìng 保持安静；be quiet! ānjìng! 安静!；(not talkative) wénjìng de 文静的，(calm) píngjìng de 平静的，níngjìng de 宁静的；a quiet little village yí gè níngjìng de xiǎo cūnzhuāng 一个宁静的小村庄 **2** n ānjìng 安静，píngjìng 平静；quiet please! qǐng ānjìng! 请安静!

quietly /'kwaɪətlɪ/ adv to speak quietly qīngshēng de jiǎnghuà 轻声地讲话；[to sit there | to read newspapers | to drink tea] quietly jìngjìng de [zuò zài nàr | kàn bào | hē chá] 静静地 [坐在那儿 | 看报 | 喝茶]

quit /'kwɪt/ vb (to resign) cízhí 辞职；(US English) (to give up) to quit [smoking | drinking | taking drugs] jiè [yān | jiǔ | dú] 戒 [烟 | 酒 | 毒]；to quit school tuìxué 退学

quite /kwaɪt/ adv (rather) xiāngdāng 相当，tǐng 挺；I quite like Chinese food wǒ tǐng xǐhuan zhōngcān 我挺喜欢中餐；she earns quite a lot of money tā zhèng de qián xiāngdāng duō 她挣的钱相当多；(completely) wánquán 完全，shífēn 十分；I'm not quite ready yet wǒ hái méi wánquán zhǔnbèi hǎo 我还没完全准备好；you're quite right nǐ wánquán zhèngquè 你完全正确；I'm not quite sure what he does wǒ bù shífēn qīngchǔ tā zuò shénme 我不十分清楚他做什么

quiz /kwɪz/ n a quiz yí cì wèndá bǐsài 一次问答比赛

Rr

---

rabbit /'ræbɪt/ n a rabbit yì zhī tùzi 一只兔子

rabies /'reɪbiːz/ n kuángquǎnbìng 狂犬病

race /reɪs/ **1** n (a contest) bǐsài 比赛；a race yí cì bǐsài 一次比赛；to have a race jìnxíng yí cì bǐsài 进行一次比赛；(for horse-racing) the races sàimǎ 赛马；(a group of *people*) rénzhǒng 人种，zhǒngzú 种族；**a race** yí ge rénzhǒng 一个人种 **2** *vb* (*to compete with*) gēn…bǐsài 跟…比赛；**to race** (*against*) **someone** gēn mǒu rén bǐsài 跟某人比赛；**I'll race you to the car** wǒ gēn nǐ bǐsài，kàn shéi xiān pǎodào nà liàng qìchē nàli 我跟你比赛，看谁先跑到那辆汽车那里；(*to take part in a contest*) cānjiā bǐsài 参加比赛

racehorse /'reɪshɔːs/ *n* **a racehorse** yì pǐ bǐsài yòng de mǎ 一匹比赛用的马

racetrack /'reɪstræk/ *n* **a racetrack** yì tiáo pǎodào 一条跑道；yì tiáo (sài)chēdào 一条(赛)车道

racism /'reɪsɪzəm/ *n* zhǒngzúzhǔyì 种族主义，zhǒngzú qíshì 种族歧视

racket，racquet /'rækɪt/ *n* **a racket** yí ge pāizi 一个拍子，yí ge qiúpāi 一个球拍

radiator /'reɪdieɪtə(r)/ *n* **a radiator** (*for heating*) yí ge nuǎnqìpiàn 一个暖气片

radio /'reɪdiəʊ/ *n* **a radio** yì tái shōuyīnjī 一台收音机；**on the radio** zài guǎngbō li 在广播里

radio station /'reɪdiəʊ ˌsteɪʃən/ *n* **a radio station** yí ge (guǎngbō) diàntái 一个(广播) 电台

rage /reɪdʒ/ *n* kuángnù 狂怒，dànù 大怒；**to fly into a rage** bórán-dànù 勃然大怒

raid /reɪd/ *vb* xíjī 袭击；**to raid a bank** xíjī yì jiā yínháng 袭击一家银行；**the police raided the building** jǐngchá xíjīle nà zuò dàlóu 警察袭击了那座大楼

rail /reɪl/ *n* (*for holding on to*) fúshǒu 扶手，lángān 栏杆；**a rail** yí ge fúshǒu 一个扶手；(*for trains*) **rails** tiěguǐ 铁轨，tiělù 铁路

railway /'reɪlweɪ/ (*British English*)，**railroad** /'reɪlrəʊd/ (*US English*) *n* (*a track*) tiělù 铁路，tiědào 铁道；**a railway** yì tiáo tiělù 一条铁路；(*the rail system*) **the railway** tiělù xìtǒng 铁路系统

railway line /'reɪlweɪ ˌlaɪn/ *n* (*British English*) **a railway line** yì tiáo tiělùxiàn 一条铁路线

railway station /ˈreɪlweɪ ˌsteɪʃən/ n (British English) a railway station yí gè huǒchēzhàn 一个火车站

rain /reɪn/ **1** n yǔ 雨;to stand in the rain zhànzài yǔ zhōng 站在雨中 **2** vb xiàyǔ 下雨;it's raining zhèngzài xiàyǔ 正在下雨

rainbow /ˈreɪnbəʊ/ n a rainbow yí dào cǎihóng 一道彩虹

raincoat /ˈreɪnkəʊt/ n a raincoat yí jiàn yǔyī 一件雨衣

raise /reɪz/ vb (to lift) jǔqǐ 举起,táiqǐ 抬起;(to increase) tígāo 提高;to raise prices tígāo jiàqian 提高价钱;to raise one's voice tígāo shēngyīn 提高声音;(to bring up, as an issue or question) tíchū 提出;to raise a question tíchū yí gè wèntí 提出一个问题;(to bring up, as a child) fǔyǎng 抚养;to raise children fǔyǎng háizi 抚养孩子

range /reɪndʒ/ n (variation between limits) fúdù 幅度;a range yí gè fúdù 一个幅度;the range of increase in temperature qìwēn shēnggāo de fúdù 气温升高的幅度;(scope) fànwéi 范围;a range yí gè fànwéi 一个范围;your range of choices nǐ kěyǐ xuǎnzé de fànwéi 你可以选择的范围;(of mountains) shānmài 山脉;a mountain range yí dào shānmài 一道山脉;(US English) (for cooking) a range yí gè lúzào 一个炉灶

rare /reə(r)/ adj (not common) hǎnjiàn de 罕见的,xīyǒu de 稀有的;(very slightly cooked) bàn shú de 半熟的

rarely /ˈreəlɪ/ adv hěn shǎo 很少,nándé 难得

rasher /ˈræʃə(r)/ n (British English) a rasher (of bacon) yí piàn xiánròu 一片咸肉

raspberry /ˈrɑːzbərɪ/ n a raspberry yí gè mùméi 一个木莓

rat /ræt/ n a rat yì zhī lǎoshǔ 一只老鼠,yì zhī hàozi 一只耗子

rather /ˈrɑːðə(r)/ adv (when saying what one would prefer) I'd rather [leave | stay here | read the paper…] wǒ nìngyuàn [zǒu | dāi zài zhèr | kàn bàozhǐ…] 我宁愿 [走 | 呆在这儿 | 看报纸…];I'd rather you go with me wǒ dào xīwàng nǐ hé wǒ yìqǐ qù 我倒希望你和我一起去；**I'd rather go than stay here** wǒ xiǎng zǒu,bù xiǎng dāi zài zhèr 我想走，不想呆在这儿；(quite) xiāngdāng 相当，挺；**I think he's rather nice** wǒ rènwéi tā xiāngdāng hǎo 我认为他相当好

raw /rɔ:/ adj (uncooked) shēng de 生的；**raw fish** shēngyú 生鱼；(not manufactured) **raw materials** yuáncáiliào 原材料

razor /'reɪzə(r)/ n **a razor** yì bǎ guāliǎndāo 一把刮脸刀，yì bǎ guāhúdāo 一把刮胡刀

razor blade /'reɪzə bleɪd/ n **a razor blade** yí gè dāopiàn 一个刀片

reach /ri:tʃ/ vb (to arrive at) dàodá 到达；**they reached the school at midnight** tāmen bànyè dàodá xuéxiào 他们半夜到达学校；(to be delivered to) **the letter never reached me** wǒ cónglái jiù méi shōudào nà fēng xìn 我从来就没收到那封信；(by stretching) **I can't reach the shelf** wǒ gòu bù zháo shūjià 我够不着书架；(to come to) **to reach an agreement** dáchéng yí gè xiéyì 达成一个协议；(to contact) gēn ··· liánxì 跟 ··· 联系；**you can reach me at this number** nǐ kěyǐ dǎ zhège diànhuà hàomǎ gēn wǒ liánxì 你可以打这个电话号码跟我联系；**reach out** shēnchū 伸出；**to reach out one's hand** shēnchū shǒu 伸出手

react /rɪ'ækt/ vb fǎnyìng 反应；**the audience reacted warmly to his speech** tīngzhòng duì tā de jiǎnghuà fǎnyìng rèliè 听众对他的讲话反应热烈

read /ri:d/ vb (to look at and comprehend) kàn 看，dú 读；**to read the newspaper** kàn bào 看报；(to read aloud) niàn 念，dú 读；**she is reading a story to her children** tā zài gěi tā de háizi niàn yí gè gùshi 她在给她的孩子念一个故事；(to study) xuéxí 学习；**she's reading medicine at a university** tā zài yì suǒ dàxué xuéxí yīxué 她在一所大学学习医学；(understand by reading) kàndǒng 看懂；**can you read Chinese?** nǐ kàn de dǒng

Zhōngwén ma? 你看得懂中文吗?；**read out** to read out the names niàn míngzi 念名字；**read through** tōngdú 通读，cóngtóu dúdào wěi 从头读到尾

reading /'ri:dɪŋ/ n (the action of reading) yuèdú 阅读，dúshū 读书；(material for reading) yuèdú cáiliào 阅读材料

ready /'redɪ/ adj (prepared) zhǔnbèi hǎo de 准备好的；are you ready? nǐ zhǔnbèi hǎo le ma? 你准备好了吗?；to get the meal ready bǎ fàn zhǔnbèi hǎo 把饭准备好；(happy) lèyì de 乐意的，yuànyì de 愿意的；I'm ready to help you wǒ hěn lèyì bāngzhù nǐ 我很乐意帮助你

real /'rɪəl/ adj (genuine) zhēn de 真的，zhēnzhèng de 真正的；**real diamonds** zhēn zuànshí 真钻石；(actual) xiànshí de 现实的，zhēnshí de 真实的；**real life** xiànshí shēnghuó 现实生活；it's a real shame zhè zhēn kěxī 这真可惜

reality /rɪ'æləti/ n xiànshí 现实，shíjì cúnzài 实际存在

realize /'rɪəlaɪz/ vb (make real) shíxiàn 实现；he has realized his goal tā shíxiànle tā de mùbiāo 他实现了他的目标；(to comprehend completely) rènshi dào 认识到；he didn't realize that he was wrong tā méiyǒu rènshi dào tā cuò le 他没有认识到他错了

really /'rɪəlɪ/ adv (truly, actually) quèshí 确实；it's really easy to make zhè quèshí hěn róngyì zuò 这确实很容易做；really? zhēn de ma? 真的吗?

rear /rɪə(r)/ **1** n (back part) hòubù 后部，hòumiàn 后面 **2** vb (to care for and educate) fǔyǎng 抚养，yǎngyù 养育；to rear the children fǔyǎng háizi 抚养孩子；(to breed) sìyǎng 饲养；to rear pigs sìyǎng zhū 饲养猪

reason /'ri:zən/ n (ground or cause) yuányīn 原因，lǐyóu 理由；a reason yí gè yuányīn 一个原因；the reason for being late chídào de yuányīn 迟到的原因；(sensible or logical thought or view) dàoli 道理；there is reason in what he said tā shuō de yǒu dàoli 他说的有道理

reassure /ˌri:ə'ʃʊə(r)/ vb the policeman reassured me about my daughter's safety jǐngchá ràng wǒ búyào wèi wǒ nǚ'ér de ānquán dānyōu 警察让我不要为我女儿的安全担忧；this letter reassured me zhè fēng xìn shǐ wǒ fàngxīn le 这封信使我放心了

receipt /rɪ'siːt/ n a receipt yì zhāng shōujù 一张收据

receive /rɪ'siːv/ vb (to obtain from someone by delivery) shōudào 收到，jiēdào 接到；we received a letter from the teacher wǒmen shōudào lǎoshī de yì fēng xìn 我们收到老师的一封信；(to get) dédào 得到；to receive help from someone dédào mǒu rén de bāngzhù 得到某人的帮助；(meet and welcome) jiēdài 接待；the delegation was well received dàibiǎotuán shòudàole hěn hǎo de jiēdài 代表团受到了很好的接待

recent /'riːsənt/ adj zuìjìn de 最近的，jìnlái de 近来的

recently /'riːsəntlɪ/ adv zuìjìn 最近，jìnlái 近来

reception /rɪ'sepʃən/ n (in a hotel, a hospital, a company) the reception (area) jiēdàichù 接待处；ask at reception zài jiēdàichù xúnwèn 在接待处询问；(a formal event) a reception yí gè zhāodàihuì 一个招待会；(the act of receiving or being received) jiēdài 接待

receptionist /rɪ'sepʃənɪst/ n a receptionist yí gè jiēdàiyuán 一个接待员

recipe /'resɪpɪ/ n a recipe (instructions for cooking a dish) yì zhǒng pēngtiáo fāngfǎ 一种烹调方法；(medical prescription) yí gè yàofāng 一个药方

recognize /'rekəgnaɪz/ vb (to identify as known) rènchū 认出；(to acknowledge) chéngrèn 承认

recommend /ˌrekə'mend/ vb (to command or introduce as suitable) tuījiàn 推荐；(to advise) quàngào 劝告，jiànyì 建议

record /'rekɔːd/ **1** n (details about a fact or proceeding) jìlù 纪录；(information about a person's past) lǚlì 履历，jīnglì 经历；(the best recorded achievement) a record yí xiàng jìlù 一项纪录；to break the world record dǎpò shìjiè jìlù 打破世界纪录；(for playing music) a record yì zhāng chàngpiàn 一张唱片 **2** /rɪ'kɔːd/ vb (to put in *writing*)jìlù 记录;(*to make a recording of music , speech , etc.*) lùyīn 录音

recorder /rɪˈkɔːdə(r)/ *n* a recorder (*a musical instrument*) yì zhī dízi 一支笛子;(*a machine for recording sounds*) yì tái lùyīnjī 一台录音机

record player /ˈrekɔːd ˌpleɪə(r)/ *n* a record player yì tái diànchàngjī 一台电唱机,yì tái liúshēngjī 一台留声机

recover /rɪˈkʌvə(r)/ *vb* (*to regain one's health*) huīfù 恢复;the patient has completely recovered from his illness bìngrén yǐjīng wánquán huīfù le 病人已经完全恢复了;(*get back or find again*) zhǎohuí 找回;I have recovered the money I lost wǒ bǎ wǒ diū de qián zhǎo huílái le 我把我丢的钱找回来了

recycle /ˌriːˈsaɪkl/ *vb* (*to reprocess and reuse*) huíshōu chǔlǐ 回收处理,xúnhuán shǐyòng 循环使用;to recycle newspapers huíshōu chǔlǐ bàozhǐ 回收处理报纸;to recycle these bottles xúnhuán shǐyòng zhèxiē píngzi 循环使用这些瓶子

red /red/ *adj* hóng de 红的,hóngsè de 红色的;to go red, to turn red biàn hóng 变红

red-haired /ˌredˈheəd/ *adj* hóng tóufa de 红头发的

reduce /rɪˈdjuːs/ *vb* (*to lower*) jiǎn shǎo 减少;to reduce prices jiǎnjià 减价;(*to diminish in weight, pain, pressure*) jiǎnqīng 减轻;to reduce one's weight jiǎnqīng tǐzhòng 减轻体重;(*to slow down*) jiǎndī 减低,jiǎnmàn 减慢;to reduce speed jiǎndī sùdù 减低速度

reduction /rɪˈdʌkʃən/ *n* jiǎnshǎo 减少,suōjiǎn 缩减

redundant /rɪˈdʌndənt/ *adj* (*British English*) (*of worker, no longer needed and therefore dismissed*) bèi cáijiǎn de 被裁减的;to be made redundant bèi cáijiǎn 被裁减;(*superfluous*) guòshèng de 过剩的,duōyú de 多余的

referee /ˌrefəˈriː/ *n* a referee (*in matches and games*) yì míng cáipàn 一名裁判;(*one who testifies to someone's character, knowledge, etc.*) yì míng jiàndìngrén 一名鉴定人,yì míng shěnchárén 一名审查人;(*an arbitrator*) yì míng zhòngcáirén 一名仲裁人

reflection /rɪˈflekʃən/ n a reflection (a conscious thought) yì zhǒng xiǎngfǎ 一种想法，yì zhǒng jiànjiě 一种见解；(an image reflected in water, etc.) yí gè dàoyǐng 一个倒影；(an expression) yì zhǒng fǎnyìng 一种反映，yì zhǒng biǎoxiàn 一种表现；a reflection of the living standards in this country zhège guójiā shēnghuó shuǐpíng de yì zhǒng fǎnyìng 这个国家生活水平的一种反映

refreshing /rɪˈfreʃɪŋ/ adj (pleasantly cooling) qīngshuǎng de 清爽的，liángshuǎng de 凉爽的；(invigorating) shǐ rén zhènzuò de 使人振作的

refrigerator /rɪˈfrɪdʒəreɪtə(r)/ n a refrigerator yì tái (diàn)bīngxiāng 一台(电)冰箱

refugee /ˌrefjʊˈdʒiː/ n a refugee yí gè bìnànzhě 一个避难者，yí gè nànmín 一个难民

refuse¹ /rɪˈfjuːz/ vb jùjué 拒绝，bùkěn 不肯；to refuse [to listen｜to accept a gift｜to pay the money...] jùjué [tīng｜jiēshòu lǐwù｜fùqián…]拒绝[听｜接受礼物｜付钱…]

refuse² /ˈrefjuːs/ n lājī 垃圾，fèiwù 废物

regards /rɪˈɡɑːdz/ n wènhòu 问候，zhìyì 致意；give her my regards dài wǒ xiàng tā wènhòu 代我向她问候

region /ˈriːdʒən/ n a region (area, district) yí gè dìqū 一个地区，(part of the body) yí gè bùwèi 一个部位

regional /ˈriːdʒənəl/ adj dìqū de 地区的，júbù de 局部的

register /ˈredʒɪstə(r)/ n a register (a written record regularly kept) yì běn dēngjìbù 一本登记簿；to take the register dēngjì 登记

regret /rɪˈɡret/ vb (to wish something had not happened) hòuhuǐ 后悔，àohuǐ 懊悔；I regret changing my mind wǒ hòuhuǐ gǎibiànle zhǔyì 我后悔改变了主意，(feel sorry) yíhàn 遗憾；he regrets that he can't come tā hěn yíhàn tā bù néng lái 他很遗憾他不能来

regular /ˈreɡjʊlə(r)/ adj (habitual or according to rule) yǒu guīlǜ de 有规律的，guīzé de 规则的；(periodical) dìngqī de 定期的；(*normal*) zhèngcháng de 正常的

regularly /'regjʊləli/ *adv* (*habitually, by rule*) yǒu guīlù de 有规律的，guīzé de 规则地；(*periodically*) dìngqī de 定期地

rehearsal /rɪ'hɜːsəl/ *n* a rehearsal (*a trial or practise performance*) yí cì páiliàn 一次排练，yí cì páiyǎn 一次排演

rehearse /rɪ'hɜːs/ *vb* (*to perform privately for trial or practice*) páiliàn 排练，páiyǎn 排演

reject /rɪ'dʒekt/ *vb* (*to refuse to accept*) jùjué (jiēshòu) 拒绝(接受)；to reject someone's advice jùjué (jiēshòu) mǒu rén de quàngào 拒绝(接受)某人的劝告；(*to refuse to pass, as a bill, proposal, etc.*) fǒujué 否决；to reject a candidate fǒujué yì míng hòuxuǎnrén 否决一名候选人

relationship /rɪ'leɪʃənʃɪp/ *n* guānxì 关系；she has a good relationship with her parents tā gēn tā de fùmǔ guānxì hěn hǎo 她跟她的父母关系很好！Note that the indefinite article a in this sentence is not translated.

relative /'relətɪv/ *n* a relative yí gè qīnqi 一个亲戚

relax /rɪ'læks/ *vb* (*to make less rigid or strict*) fāngkuān 放宽，fàngsōng 放松；to relax a rule fàngkuān yí xiàng guīdìng 放宽一项规定；(*to make less tense*) fàngsōng 放松；to relax [one's grip | one's muscles | one's efforts] [sōngshǒu | fàngsōng jīròu | sōngjìn(r)] [松手 | 放松肌肉 | 松劲(儿)]；(*to become loose or slack*) fàngsōng 放松；you can relax now nǐ xiànzài kěyǐ fàngsōng le 你现在可以放松了；(*to become less tense*) sōngxiè 松懈，fàngsōng 放松；their efforts have started to relax tāmen de nǔlì kāishǐ sōngxiè le 他们的努力开始松懈了；(*to have a rest*) xiūxi 休息；let's stop and relax for a while zánmen tíng xiàlái xiūxi yíhuìr ba 咱们停下来休息一会儿吧

relaxed /rɪ'lækst/ *adj* (*loosened, slackened*) fàngsōng de 放松的；(*becoming less tense, severe*) huǎnhé de 缓和的

relay race /'riːleɪ ˌreɪs/ vb **a relay race** yì chǎng jiēlì bǐsài 一场接力比赛

release /rɪ'liːs/ (*to set free*) shìfàng 释放; he was released tā bèi shìfàng le 他被释放了; (*to relieve*) jiěchú 解除; **to release him from his pain** jiěchú tā de téngtòng 解除他的疼痛; (*to make available or known widely*); (*if it's a film, a CD, a video*) fāxíng 发行; **to release a Chinese film** fāxíng yí bù Zhōngguó diànyǐng 发行一部中国电影; (*if it's an announcement, a piece of news*) fābiǎo 发表, fābù 发布; **the government is going to release a piece of important news** zhèngfǔ zhǔnbèi fābù yì tiáo zhòngyào xiāoxi 政府准备发布一条重要消息

reliable /rɪ'laɪəbl/ adj (*dependable*) kěkào de 可靠的; **is this news reliable?** zhè xiāoxi kěkào ma? 这消息可靠吗?; (*trustworthy*) kěyǐ xìnlài de 可以信赖的; **a reliable lawyer** yí wèi kěyǐ xìnlài de lǜshī 一位可以信赖的律师

relieved /rɪ'liːvd/ adj kuānwèi de 宽慰的; **my mother was relieved to receive my letter** wǒ māma shōudào wǒ de xìn gǎndào hěn kuānwèi 我妈妈收到我的信感到很宽慰

religion /rɪ'lɪdʒən/ n zōngjiào 宗教

religious education /rɪ'lɪdʒəs edjuˈkeɪʃən/, **RE** (*British English*) n zōngjiàokè 宗教课

rely /rɪ'laɪ/ vb (*to lean on as a support*) yīkào 依靠; (*to count on*) yīlài 依赖, zhǐwàng 指望; **can we rely on you?** wǒmen kěyǐ zhǐwàng nǐ ma? 我们可以指望你吗?

remain /rɪ'meɪn/ vb (*to stay or be left behind*) liúxià 留下; **only I remained** zhǐyǒu wǒ yí gè rén liúxià le 只有我一个人留下了; (*to be left over*) shèngxia 剩下; **you can take all those things that remain** nǐ kěyǐ bǎ shèngxia de dōngxi dōu názǒu 你可以把剩下的东西都拿走; (*to continue in the same place*) hái zài 还在, réngrán cúnzài 仍然存在; **that old building remains** nà zuò gǔlǎo jiànzhù hái zài 那座古老建筑还在; (*to dwell or abide*) dāi dāi/dài 呆/待, dòuliú 逗留; **I'll remain in Shanghai for a**

week wǒ yào zài Shànghǎi dāi yí gè xīngqī 我要在上海呆一个星期;(to continue to be) réngrán 仍然; **she remained unhappy** tā réngrán bù gāoxìng 她仍然不高兴

remark /rɪ'mɑːk/ n a remark(a comment) yí piān pínglùn 一篇评论;(a statement) yí duàn chénshù 一段陈述;(something said on a subject) yí duàn huà 一段话

remarkable /rɪ'mɑːkəbl/ adj fēifán de 非凡的, zhuóyuè de 卓越的

remember /rɪ'membə(r)/ vb (to have in mind) jìde 记得;**do you remember her?** nǐ jìde tā ma? 你记得她吗?;(to recall) xiǎngqǐ 想起;**now I remember** xiànzài wǒ xiǎng qǐlai le 现在我想起来了;(to retain in one's memory) jìzhù 记住;(to remember to turn off the lights jìzhù bǎ dēng guānshang 记住把灯关上

remind /rɪ'maɪnd/ vb (to put in mind of) tíxǐng 提醒;**to remind someone to buy milk** tíxǐng mǒu rén mǎi niúnǎi 提醒某人买牛奶;(to cause to remember) shǐ … xiǎngqǐ 使… 想起;**she reminds me of my younger sister** tā shǐ wǒ xiǎngqǐ wǒ de mèimei 她使我想起我的妹妹

remote control /rɪ'məut kən'trəul/ n a remote control yí gè yáokòngqì 一个遥控器

remove /rɪ'muːv/ vb (to take or put away by hand) nákāi 拿开, bānzǒu 搬走;**to remove these books** bǎ zhèxiē shū nákāi 把这些书拿开;(to clean off) qùdiào 去掉, nòngdiào 弄掉;**to remove stains from a carpet** bǎ wūjì cóng dìtǎn shang nòngdiào 把污迹从地毯上弄掉;**to remove someone from his post** chèdiào mǒu rén de zhíwù 撤掉某人的职务;**to remove this wall** bǎ zhè dǔ qiáng chāichú 把这堵墙拆除

rent / 1 vb zū 租, zūyòng 租用;**to rent a house** yí dòng fángzi 租一栋房子 **2** n a rental payment yí fèn zūjīn 一份租金, **rent out** chūzū 出租

repair /rɪ'peə(r)/ vb (if it's something mechanical, electrical, electronic, or a piece of furniture) xiūlǐ 修理; **to repair** [a bicycle | a TV set | a bed...] xiūlǐ [yí liàng zìxíngchē| yì tái diànshìjī| yì zhāng chuáng…]修理［一辆自行车|一台电视机|一张床…]；(to patch) bǔ 补，xiūbǔ 修补；to repair the damage míbǔ sǔnshī 弥补损失

repeat /rɪˈpiːt/ vb (to say again) chóngfù 重复，chóngshuō 重说；(to do again) chóngzuò 重做；don't repeat this mistake bié zài fàn zhè zhǒng cuòwù le 别再犯这种错误了

replace /rɪˈpleɪs/ vb (put back) fànghuí yuánchù 放回原处；please replace the magazine after reading zázhì kànwán hòu qǐng fànghuí yuánchù 杂志看完后请放回原处；(substitute for) dàitì 代替，tìhuàn 替换；can computers replace human beings? jìsuànjī néng dàitì rén ma? 计算机能代替人吗?；they replaced the fence with a wall tāmen bǎ líba chāi le, qìle yì dǔ qiáng 他们把篱笆拆了，砌了一堵墙

reply /rɪˈplaɪ/ 1 vb huídá 回答；to reply to [someone | a question] huídá [mǒu rén | yí gè wèntí] 回答 [某人 | 一个问题]；to reply to [a letter | a fax] huí [xìn | chuánzhēn] 回 [信 | 传真] 2 n a reply yí gè huídá 一个回答，yí gè dáfù 一个答复

report /rɪˈpɔːt/ 1 vb (to tell about) bàogào 报告；to report an accident bàogào yí cì shìgù 报告一次事故；(in the news) bàodǎo 报导；to report on a demonstration bàodǎo yí cì shìwēi yóuxíng 报导一次示威游行；(to lay a charge against) gàofā 告发，jiēfā 揭发；to report someone to the police xiàng jǐngchá gàofā mǒu rén 向警察告发某人 2 n (in the news) a report yì tiáo bàodào 一条报道，(an official document) yì fèn bàogào 一份报告，(British English) (from school) a (school) report yí fèn xuéxiào chéngjì bàogào 一份学校成绩报告

report card /rɪˈpɔːt kɑːd/ n (US English) a report card yí fèn xuéshēng chéngjì bàogào 一份学生成绩报告

reporter /rɪˈpɔːtə(r)/ n a reporter (a journalist) yí gè jìzhě 一个记者；(a person who reports) yí gè bàogàorén 一个报告人

represent /ˌreprɪˈzent/ vb (to act on behalf of) dàibiǎo 代表

代表；would you like her to represent you? nǐ yuànyì tā dàibiǎo nǐ ma? 你愿意她代表你吗?；(stand for, symbolize) biǎoshì 表示，xiàngzhēng 象征；this gift represents our friendship zhège lǐwù xiàngzhēng wǒmen de yǒuyì 这个礼物象征我们的友谊

republic /rɪ'pʌblɪk/ n a republic yí gè gònghéguó 一个共和国

request /rɪ'kwest/ n a request yí gè qǐngqiú 一个请求

rescue /'reskju:/ vb (from danger) yuánjiù 援救，yíngjiù 营救

resemble /rɪ'zembl/ vb xiàng 像；the two brothers resemble each other xiōngdìliǎ zhǎng de hěn xiàng 兄弟俩长得很像

resent /rɪ'zent/ vb duì ··· bùmǎn 对 ··· 不满，duì ··· bù gāoxìng 对 ··· 不高兴；to resent someone duì mǒu rén bùmǎn 对某人不满；he resents me for winning tā duì wǒ yíng le bù gāoxìng 他对我赢了不高兴

reservation /ˌrezə'veɪʃən/ n a reservation (a booking at a restaurant , theatre , etc.) yùdìng 预订；to make a reservation for two people yùdìng liǎng gè rén de zuòwèi 预订两个人的座位；(an uncertainty about something) yí gè bǎoliú yìjiàn 一个保留意见，yì zhǒng bǎoliú tàidu 一种保留态度；I have serious reservations about this contract wǒ duì zhège hétong chí yánsù de bǎoliú yìjiàn 我对这个合同持严肃的保留意见；(limiting condition) yí xiàng bǎoliú 一项保留；we accept your proposal with some reservations wǒmen yǒu bǎoliú de jiēshòu nǐ de tíyì 我们有保留地接受你的提议

reserve /rɪ'zɜːv/ vb (to book) dìng 订，yùdìng 预订；I've reserved rooms for my whole family in that hotel wǒ yǐjīng zài nà jiā lǚguǎn wèi wǒ quánjiā yùdìng le fángjiān 我已经在那家旅馆为我全家预订了房间；(to hold back or set aside) bǎoliú 保留，liúchū 留出；we've reserved ten seats for the delegation wǒmen wèi dàibiǎotuán liúchū shí gè zuòwèi 我们为代表团留出了 10 个座位；

(to save up for a future occasion) chǔbèi 储备，chǔcún 储存

resign /rɪ'zaɪn/ vb (to give up) cíqù 辞去；I've resigned my position as head of department wǒ yǐjīng cíqùle xìzhǔrèn de gōngzuò 我已经辞去了系主任的工作；(to give up office, employment) cízhí 辞职；are you going to resign? nǐ yào cízhí ma? 你要辞职吗?

resist /rɪ'zɪst/ vb (to strive against) dǐkàng 抵抗，fǎnkàng 反抗；to resist violence fǎnkàng bàolì 反抗暴力；(to withstand) kàng 抗，nài 耐；does this kind of material resist heat? zhè zhǒng cáiliào nàirè ma? 这种材料耐热吗?；(to hinder the action of) rěnzhù 忍住。Note that the negative form of **rěnzhù 忍住** is **rěnbuzhù 忍不住**；she could not resist laughing tā rěnbuzhù xiào le 她忍不住笑了

respect /rɪ'spekt/ 1 vb zūnzhòng 尊重，zūnjìng 尊敬 2 n (deferential esteem) zūnzhòng 尊重，zūnjìng 尊敬；out of respect chūyú zūnzhòng 出于尊重；(point, aspect) fāngmiàn 方面；in this respect zài zhège fāngmiàn 在这个方面

responsibility /rɪ,spɒnsə'bɪlətɪ/ n (a duty on a job, a task) zhízé 职责；(obligation) zérèn 责任

responsible /rɪ'spɒnsəbl/ adj (personally accountable for) fùzé de 负责的；to be responsible for the damage duì zàochéng de sǔnhuài fùzé 对造成的损坏负责；(in charge) fùzé de 负责的；to be responsible for organizing a trip fùzé zǔzhī lǚxíng 负责组织旅行

rest /rest/ 1 n (a break, time to recover) xiūxi 休息；to need rest xūyào xiūxi 需要休息；to have a rest xiūxi yíhuìr 休息一会儿；(what is left) the rest shèngxià de 剩下的，qíyú de 其余的；we spent the rest of the day in the garden zhè yì tiān shèngxià de shíjiān wǒmen shì zài huāyuán lǐ dùguò de 这一天剩下的时间我们是在花园里度过的 2 vb xiūxi 休息

restaurant /'restərɒŋ/ n a restaurant yì jiā fànguǎn 一

家饭馆，yì jiā fàndiàn 一家饭店

result /rɪ'zʌlt/ n (*effect, consequence*) jiéguǒ 结果；a good result yí gè hǎo de jiéguǒ 一个好的结果；(*outcome of an exam, a race, a competition*) chéngjì 成绩，fēnshù 分数；the results of the competition bǐsài chéngjì 比赛成绩；the examination results kǎoshì fēnshù 考试分数；as a result of an accident yīnwèi yí cì shìgù 因为一次事故，yóuyú yí cì shìgù 由于一次事故

résumé /'rezju:meɪ/ n (*US English*) a résumé yí fèn jiǎnlì 一份简历

retire /rɪ'taɪə(r)/ vb (*to give up office or work because of old age*) tuìxiū 退休；my father retired at the age of 60 wǒ bàba liùshí suì tuìxiū 我爸爸 60 岁退休；(*to go away*) líkāi 离开了；after dinner, all the ladies retired chīwán fàn hòu, nǚshìmen dōu líkāi le 吃完饭后，女士们都离开了；(*to go to bed*) shuìjiào 睡觉，jiùqǐn 就寝

return /rɪ'tɜ:n/ vb (*to go back*) huí 回，huíqù 回去；(*to come back*) huí 回，huílái 回来；(*from abroad, to one's home country*) huíguó 回国；(*to give back*) huán 还，can you return my book? nǐ bǎ wǒ de shū huángěi wǒ hǎo ma? 你把我的书还给我好吗？；(*to send back*) tuìhuán 退还；to return goods tuìhuán huòwù 退还货物；(*to start again*) to return to work huīfù gōngzuò 恢复工作；to return to school fùkè 复课

return ticket /rɪ'tɜ:n ˌtɪkɪt/ n (*British English*) a return ticket yì zhāng wǎngfǎnpiào 一张往返票，yì zhāng láihuípiào 一张来回票

reveal /rɪ'vi:l/ vb to reveal a secret xièlòu yí gè mìmì 泄露一个秘密

revenge /rɪ'vendʒ/ n bàochóu 报仇，bàofù 报复；to have one's revenge on someone for something wèi mǒu shì xiàng mǒu rén bàochóu 为某事向某人报仇

revolution /ˌrevə'lju:ʃən/ n a revolution yì chǎng gémìng 一场革命

reward /rɪ'wɔ:d/ **1** n a reward yì bǐ chóujīn 一笔酬金，yì

bǐ bàochou 一笔报酬 **2** vb (to give a reward in return for a deed or service rendered) chóuxiè 酬谢;(to give as a reward) jiǎngshǎng 奖赏，jiǎnglì 奖励

rewind /riː'waɪnd/ n jiézòu 节奏，jiépāi 节拍

rhythm /'rɪðəm/ n jiézòu 节奏，jiépāi 节拍

rib /rɪb/ n a rib (in the human body) yì gēn lèigǔ 一根肋骨;(as in spare rib) yì gēn páigǔ 一根排骨

rice /raɪs/ n (raw) dàmǐ 大米;(cooked) mǐfàn 米饭

rich /rɪtʃ/ adj fù de 富有的，fùyù de 富裕的，yǒuqián de 有钱的;to get rich fù qǐlai 富起来，zhìfù 致富

rid /rɪd/:to get rid of vb qùdiào 去掉，chúqù 除去

ride /raɪd/ **1** vb (on a horse or a bicycle) qí 骑;to ride a horse qímǎ 骑马，to go riding qù qímǎ 去骑马;he is riding a bike tā zài qí zìxíngchē 他在骑自行车;(in a plane, a train, or on a bus) chéng 乘，zuò 坐;to ride [on a train|in a plane|in a bus] zuò [huǒchē|feijī|qìchē] 坐 [火车|飞机|汽车] **2** n to go for a ride (in a car) qù kāi yíhuìr chē 去开一会儿车，qù dōufēng 去兜风;(on a bike) qù qí yíhuìr zìxíngchē 去骑一会儿自行车;(on a horse) qù qí yíhuìr mǎ 去骑一会儿马

ridiculous /rɪ'dɪkjuləs/ adj huāngmiù de 荒谬的，huāngtáng de 荒唐的

rifle /'raɪfl/ n a rifle yì zhī bùqiāng 一支步枪

right /raɪt/ **1** adj (not left) yòu de 右的，yòubiān de 右边的;his right hand tā de yòushǒu 他的右手;(proper) héshì de 合适的，qiàdàng de 恰当的;is she the right person for this job? tā zuò zhège gōngzuò héshì ma? 她做这个工作合适吗?;(correct) duì de 对的，zhèngquè de 正确的;the right answer zhèngquè de dá'àn 正确的答案;is this the right direction? zhège fāngxiàng duì ma? 这个方向对吗?;what's the right time? xiànzài zhǔnquè de shíjiān shì jǐdiǎn? 现在准确的时间是几点?;you're right nǐ shì duì de 你是对的;that's right duì 对 **2** n (the direction) the right yòu 右，yòubiān 右边;the first road on the right yòubian dì-yī tiáo mǎlù 右边第 1 条马路；(what one is entitled to) a right yí xiàng quánlì 一项权利；to have a right to education yǒu quánlì shòu jiàoyù 有权利受教育；human rights rénquán 人权 **3** adv (correctly) duì 对；did I do it right? wǒ zuò de duì ma? 我做得对吗？；(to the right side) xiàng yòu 向右；to turn right xiàng yòu zhuǎn 向右转；(for emphasis) right now mǎshàng 马上，lìkè 立刻；she stood right in the centre of the garden tā zhàn zài huāyuán zhèng zhōngyāng 她站在花园正中央

ring /rɪŋ/ **1** vb (British English) (to phone) dǎ diànhuà 打电话；to ring for a taxi dǎ diànhuà jiào chūzūchē 打电话叫出租车；(to make a sound) xiǎng 响；the telephone rang diànhuàlíng xiǎng le 电话铃响了；(to activate a door or bicycle bell) àn líng 按铃；to ring the doorbell àn ménlíng 按门铃；(to sound a church bell) qiāo zhōng 敲钟 **2** n (a piece of jewellery) a ring yì méi jièzhi 一枚戒指；a wedding ring yì méi jiéhūn jièzhi 一枚结婚戒指；(a circle) a ring yí gè yuánquān 一个圆圈，yí gè huán 一个环；(in a circus) the ring yuánxíng chǎngdì 圆形场地；**ring up** (British English) dǎ diànhuà 打电话

rinse /rɪns/ vb chōngxǐ 冲洗，qīngxǐ 清洗

ripe /raɪp/ adj shú de 熟的，chéngshú de 成熟的

rise /raɪz/ vb (if it's the sun or moon) shēngqǐ 升起；(if it's smoke, a balloon, a plane) shàngshēng 上升；(if it's a price, a water level) shàngzhǎng 上涨；(if it's temperature) shēnggāo 升高

risk /rɪsk/ **1** n wēixiǎn 危险 **2** vb mào…wēixiǎn 冒…危险；to risk losing one's job mào shīqù gōngzuò de wēixiǎn 冒失去工作的危险

river /'rɪvə(r)/ n a river yì tiáo hé 一条河

riverbank /'rɪvəbæŋk/ n a riverbank yì tiáo hé'àn 一条河岸

road /rəʊd/ n a road yì tiáo (dào) lù 一条（道）路；the road to London qù Lúndūn de lù 去伦敦的路

road sign /'rəʊd saɪn/ n a road sign yí gè lùbiāo 一个路标

roadworks /'rəʊdwɜːks/ n xiūlù gōngchéng 修路工程

roar /rɔː(r)/ vb (if it's a lion) hǒu 吼, hǒujiào 吼叫;(if it's a person) hūhǎn 呼喊, dàhǎn-dàjiào 大喊大叫;(if it's an engine) hōngmíng 轰鸣;(if it's the wind) hūxiào 呼啸

roast /rəʊst/ 1 vb kǎo 烤 2 adj kǎo 烤;to eat Peking duck chī Běijīng kǎoyā 吃北京烤鸭 3 n a roast yí kuài kǎoròu 一块烤肉

rob /rɒb/ vb qiǎng 抢, qiǎngjié 抢劫;to rob someone of his money qiǎng mǒu rén de qián 抢某人的钱;to rob a bank qiǎngjié yínháng 抢劫银行

robbery /'rɒbərɪ/ n yí gè qiǎngjié'àn 一个抢案

robin /'rɒbɪn/ n yì zhī zhīgēngniǎo 一只知更鸟

robot /'rəʊbɒt/ n a robot yí gè jīqìrén 一个机器人

rock /rɒk/ n (a large stone) a rock yí kuài shítou 一块石头, yí kuài yánshí 一块岩石;(as a material for construction) yánshí 岩石, shítou 石头;(a type of music) yáogǔnyuè 摇滚乐

rock climbing /'rɒk ˌklaɪmɪŋ/ n pānyán yùndòng 攀岩运动

rocket /'rɒkɪt/ n a rocket yì méi huǒjiàn 一枚火箭

role /rəʊl/ n (an actor's part) juésè 角色;a role yí gè juésè 一个角色;(a function) zuòyòng 作用;he played an important role in organizing this conference tā zài zǔzhī zhè cì huìyì zhōng qǐle zhòngyào de zuòyòng 他在组织这次会议中起了重要的作用

roll /rəʊl/ 1 vb (to move by turning over and over) gǔn (dòng) 滚(动);the ball rolled under a car qiú gǔndàole yí liàng qìchē xiàmian 球滚到了一辆汽车下面;to roll the pastry into a ball bǎ miàn gǔnchéng yí gè qiú 把面滚成一个球 2 n (of paper, cloth, plastic) juǎn 卷;a roll of film yì juǎn jiāojuǎn 一卷胶卷;(bread) a roll gè miànbāojuǎn 一个面包卷；(US English) (at school) to call the roll diǎnmíng 点名；**roll about, roll around** (if it's an object) dàochù gǔn tā dì chù xíng 到处滚；**roll over** fān fān 翻；**roll up** juǎn 卷；to roll up a newspaper juǎnqǐ bàozhǐ 卷起报纸

roller coaster /ˈrəʊlə ˈkəʊstə(r)/ n a roller coaster yí liè guòshānchē 一列过山车

roller-skate /ˈrəʊləskeɪt/ n hànbīngxié；a pair of roller-skates yì shuāng hànbīngxié 一双旱冰鞋

roller-skating /ˈrəʊləˌskeɪtɪŋ/ n huá hànbīng 滑旱冰

romantic /rəʊˈmæntɪk/ adj (characterized by romance) luómàndìkè de 罗曼蒂克的，làngmàn de 浪漫的；(passionate and imaginative) fùyǔ huànxiǎng de 富于幻想的，xiǎngrùfēifēi de 想入非非的

roof /ruːf/ n a roof yí gè wūdǐng 一个屋顶，yí gè fángdǐng 一个房顶

room /ruːm/ n a room yí gè fángjiān 一个房间 (space) kōngjiān 空间，dìfāng 地方；to make room kòngchū dìfāng 空出地方；is there room? hái yǒu kōngjiān ma? 还有空间吗？；(scope) yúdì 余地；there is still room for improvement hái yǒu gǎijìn de yúdì 还有改进的余地

root /ruːt/ n (of a plant) a root yí gè gēn 一个根；(source, origin, cause) yí gè gēnyuán 一个根源

rope /rəʊp/ n a rope yì gēn shéngzi 一根绳子

rose /rəʊz/ n a rose (a plant) yì zhū méiguì 一株玫瑰；(a flower) yì zhī méiguīhuā 一枝玫瑰花

rosy /ˈrəʊzɪ/ adj (rose-red) méiguìsè de 玫瑰色的；rosy cheeks hóngrùn de liǎnjiá 红润的脸颊

rotten /ˈrɒtən/ adj fǔlàn de 腐烂的，fǔxiǔ de 腐朽的

rough /rʌf/ adj (not smooth) bù píng de 不平的，bù guānghuá de 不光滑的；(when talking about the skin, paper) cūcāo de 粗糙的；rough skin cūcāo de pífū 粗糙的皮肤；(when talking about roads) qíqū-bùpíng de 崎岖不平的；the road is rough zhè tiáo lù qíqū-bùpíng 这条路崎岖不平；(not gentle) cūbào de 粗暴的，cūlǔ de 粗鲁的

(*tough*) **to live in a rough area** zhù zài yí gè zhì'ān chà de dìqū 住在一个治安差的地区;(*not exact, precise*) cūlüè de 粗略的;**a rough figure** yí gè cūlüè de shùzì 一个粗略的数字;(*difficult*) jiānnán de 艰难的;**he had a rough time there** tā zài nàr guòle yí duàn hěn jiānnán de rìzi 他在那儿过了一段很艰难的日子;(*caused by bad weather*) **a rough sea** bōtāo-xiōngyǒng de hǎimiàn 波涛汹涌的海面

round /raʊnd/ *!* *often round occurs in combinations with verbs. For more information see the note at around.* **1** *prep* (*on every side of*) wéizhe 围着;**to sit round a table** wéizhe zhuōzi zuò 围着桌子坐;(*to complete a circuit*) rào zhe... wéirào 围绕;**to sail round the world** wéirào dìqiú hángxíng 围绕地球航行;(*all over*) zài... gèchù 在…各处,zài... dàochù 在…到处;**we walked round Oxford** wǒmen zài Niújīn gèchù zǒu le zǒu 我们在牛津各处走了走 **2** *adv* (*on a circular or circuitous course*) zhuànquān 转圈;**to run round the track on the sports ground** zài cāochǎng shang zhuànquān pǎo 在操场上转圈跑;**to go round to John's** ràodào qù Yuēhàn jiā 绕道去约翰家;**to invite someone round** yāoqǐng mǒu rén dào jiā li lái 邀请某人到家里来 **3** *n* **a round** (*in a quiz show or showjumping*) yì chǎng 一场,yì chǎng 一场;(*in boxing*) yí gè huíhé 一个回合;(*in an election, a negotiation, a tournament*) yì lún 一轮 **4** *adj* (*circular*) yuán de 圆的,yuánxíng de 圆形的;(*spherical*) qiúxíng de 球形的;(*plump*) fēngmǎn de 丰满的

roundabout /'raʊndəbaʊt/ *n* (*British English*) (*in a playground or at a fair*) **a roundabout** yí gè xuánzhuǎn mùmǎ 一个旋转木马;(*for traffic*) **a roundabout** yí gè huánxíng lùkǒu 一个环形路口

route /ruːt/ *n* (*on land*) lùxiàn 路线;**a route** yì tiáo lùxiàn 一条路线;**a [bus | train] route** yì tiáo [qìchē | huǒchē] lùxiàn 一条[汽车|火车]路线;(*for planes and ships*) hángxiàn 航线;**a route** yì tiáo hángxiàn 一条航线

routine /ruːˈtiːn/ n chángguī 常规，guànlì 惯例

row¹ /rəʊ/ **1** n (*a line of persons or things*) pái 排；a row of [people|seats|cars...] yì pái [rén|zuòwèi|qìchē...] 一排 [人|座位|汽车...]；the pupils were sitting in rows xuéshengmen yì pái yì pái de zuòzhe 学生们一排一排地坐 着；in a row liánxù 连续，yìlián 一连；to arrive late five days in a row liánxù wǔ tiān chídào 连续五天迟到 **2** vb (*to propel with an oar*) huá 划；to row a boat huá chuán 划船；(*to transport by rowing*) huáchuán sòng 划船送；I can row you across the river wǒ kěyǐ huá chuán sòng nǐ guò hé 我可以划船送你过河；(*as a sport*) huáchuán bǐsài 划船比赛；Oxford University rowed against Cambridge University on the river Thames Niújīn Dàxué gēn Jiànqiáo Dàxué zài Tàiwùshì Hé shang jìnxíngle huáchuán bǐsài 牛津大学跟剑桥大学在泰晤士河上进行 了划船比赛

row² /raʊ/ n (*British English*) a row yí cì chǎojià 一次吵 架，yí cì chǎozuǐ 一次吵嘴；to have a row with someone gēn mǒu rén chǎojià 跟某人吵架

rowing /ˈrəʊɪŋ/ n huáchuán 划船

rowing boat /ˈraʊɪŋ bəʊt/,（ *British English* ）, **rowboat** /ˈrəʊbəʊt/ (*US English*) n a rowing boat yì tiáo huátǐng 一条划艇

royal /ˈrɔɪəl/ adj the Royal Family wángshì 王室，huángjiā 皇家；the Royal Navy Huángjiā Hǎijūn 皇家海 军；[Your|His|Her] Royal Highness diànxià 殿下；a royal palace (*for a queen*) yí zuò huánggōng 一座王宫；(*for a king*) yí zuò huánggōng 一座王宫

rub /rʌb/ vb (*to apply pressure to with a circular or backward and forward movement*) róu 揉；to rub one's eyes róu yǎnjīng 揉眼睛；**rub out** (*British English*) cādiào 擦掉；to rub out that character cādiào nàge zì 擦掉那个字

rubber /ˈrʌbə(r)/ n (*the material*) xiàngjiāo 橡胶；(*British English*) (*an eraser*) a rubber yí kuài xiàngpí 一块橡皮

rubbish /'rʌbɪʃ/ n (refuse) lājī 垃圾；(anything worthless) fèiwù 废物；(nonsense) fèihuà 废话

rubbish bin /'rʌbɪʃ bɪn/ n (British English) a rubbish bin yí gè lājītǒng 一个垃圾桶

rucksack /'rʌksæk/ n a rucksack yí gè bèibāo 一个背包

rude /ruːd/ adj (not polite) cūlǔ de 粗鲁的, wúlǐ de 无礼的；to be rude to someone duì mǒu rén hěn wúlǐ 对某人很无礼；(vulgar) dījí de 低级的；xiàliú de 下流的；a rude story yí gè xiàliú gùshi 一个下流故事

rug /rʌg/ n a rug (a floor mat) yí kuài xiǎo dìtǎn 一块小地毯；(a thick covering or wrap) yì tiáo máotǎn 一条毛毯

rugby /'rʌgbɪ/ n gǎnlǎnqiú 橄榄球

ruin /'ruːɪn/ 1 vb (spoil) gǎozāo 搞糟；he's ruined this meal tā bǎ zhè dùn fàn gǎozāo le 他把这顿饭搞糟了；(damage) huǐhuài 毁坏；you'll ruin your shoes nǐ huì huǐle nǐ de xié 你会毁了你的鞋；(to destroy completely) huǐmiè 毁灭；his hope was ruined tā de xīwàng (bèi) huǐmiè le 他的希望（被）毁灭了 2 n (destruction) huǐmiè 毁灭；(a fallen or broken state) fèixū 废墟；the whole school is now in ruins zhěnggè xuéxiào xiànzài chéngle yí piàn fèixū 整个学校现在成了一片废墟

rule /ruːl/ 1 n a rule (of a game, a language) yì tiáo guīzé 一条规则；(in a school, an organization) yì tiáo guīdìng 一条规定 it's against the rules zhè wéifǎn guīdìng 这违反规定 2 vb (to govern) tǒngzhì 统治；to rule a country tǒngzhì yí gè guójiā 统治一个国家；(to control) kòngzhì 控制；he ruled his family with an iron hand tā jǐnjǐn de kòngzhìzhe quánjiā 他紧紧地控制着全家；(to determine or decree) cáijué 裁决，cáidìng 裁定；the court ruled that he was guilty fǎyuàn cáijué tā yǒu zuì 法院裁决他有罪

ruler /'ruːlə(r)/ n a ruler (for measuring or ruling lines) yì bǎ chǐzi 一把尺子；(a person who governs) yí gè tǒngzhìzhě 一个统治者

rumour /'ruːmə(r)/ (British English), **rumor** (US English) n a rumour (a statement of doubtful accuracy) yí gè yáoyán 一个谣言；(hearsay) yí gè chuánwén 一个传闻

run /rʌn/ **1** vb (to run) pǎo 跑；to run across the street pǎoguò mǎlù 跑过马路；(compete in a race) sàipǎo 赛跑；to run a race cānjiā sàipǎo 参加赛跑；(from danger) táopǎo 逃跑；(to manage) guǎnlǐ 管理；to run a school guǎnlǐ yí gè xuéxiào 管理一个学校；(to work, to operate) yùnzhuǎn 运转, yùnxíng 运行；the machine is running well jīqì yùnzhuǎn liánghǎo 机器运转良好；(if it's a vehicle) xíngshǐ 行驶；the car is running at 80 kilometres per hour qìchē zài yǐ měi xiǎoshí bāshí gōnglǐ de sùdù xíngshǐ 汽车在以每小时 80 公里的速度行驶；(to organize) bàn 办；to run a competition bàn yí gè bǐsài 办一个比赛；(to flow) liú 流；to run a bath wǎng zǎopén li fàng shuǐ 往澡盆里放水；(to come off, as stains or make-up) diào 掉；the rain has made her make-up run yǔshuǐ bǎ tā liǎn shang de zhuāng chōngdiào le 雨水把她脸上的妆冲掉了；(in an election) jìngxuǎn 竞选；to run for president jìngxuǎn zǒngtǒng 竞选总统；(other uses) it is running late shíjiān bù duō le 时间不多了；he is running a temperature tā zài fāshāo 他在发烧 **2** n to go for a run qù pǎobù 去跑步；**run about, run around** dàochù pǎo 到处跑, sìchù pǎo 四处跑；**run away** (to escape) táopǎo 逃跑, qiántáo 潜逃；(to gallop away uncontrollably) shīqù kòngzhì 失去控制；**run off** (to escape) táopǎo 逃跑

runner /'rʌnə(r)/ n a runner (one who runs) yí gè pǎobù de rén 一个跑步的人；(one who runs in a race) yì míng sàipǎo yùndòngyuán 一名赛跑运动员

rush /rʌʃ/ **1** vb (to hurry) jímáng 急忙, cōngcōng 匆匆, cōngmáng 匆忙！Note that in this sense, the force of the word rush is often carried by such adverbs as those in the *translations above*. *Where necessary*, *another verb functions as the predicate*; to rush to finish one's homework jímáng zuòwán zuòyè 急忙做完作业; he rushed into a shop tā cōngcōng de jìnle yì jiā shāngdiàn 他匆匆地进了一家商店; to rush out of the house cōngmáng chōngchū fángzi 匆忙冲出房子; to be rushed to the hospital bèi jísù sòngjìn yīyuàn 被急速送进医院; (*to put pressure on*) cuī 催, cuīcù 催促; please don't rush me qǐng búyào cuī wǒ 请不要催我 **2** *n* to be in a rush cōngmáng 匆忙, mánglù 忙碌; to do one's homework in a rush cōngmáng de zuò zuòyè 匆忙地做作业

rush hour /'rʌʃ aʊə(r)/ *n* the rush hour jiāotōng gāofēng shíjiān 交通高峰时间

Russia /'rʌʃə/ *n* Éguó 俄国, Éluósī 俄罗斯

Russian /'rʌʃən/ **1** *adj* Éguó de 俄国的, Éluósī de 俄罗斯的 **2** *n* (*the people*) the Russians Éguórén 俄国人, Éluósīrén 俄罗斯人; (*the language*) Éyǔ 俄语, Éwén 俄文

rusty /'rʌsti/ *adj* (*shēng*)xiù de (生)锈的

Ss

---

sad /sæd/ *adj* (*sorrowful*) nánguò de 难过的, bēishāng de 悲伤的; he feels sad tā gǎndào nánguò 他感到难过; (*grave*, *saddening*) lìng rén nánguò de 令人难过的, lìng rén bēishāng de 令人悲伤的; sad news lìng rén nánguò de xiāoxi 令人难过的消息; (*regrettable*) yíhàn de 遗憾的, kěxī de 可惜的; it's sad that you didn't get a scholarship hěn yíhàn, nǐ méiyǒu dédào jiǎngxuéjīn 很遗憾,你没有得到奖学金

saddle /'sædl/ *n* a saddle yí gè ānzi 一个鞍子, yí gè mǎ'ān 一个马鞍

safe /seɪf/ **1** adj (free from danger, without risk) ānquán de 安全的；a safe place yí gè ānquán de dìfang 一个安全的地方；is it safe to go there? qù nàr ānquán ma? 去那儿安全吗？；to feel safe gǎndào ānquán 感到安全；(sure, reliable) yǒu bǎwò de 有把握的，yídìng de 一定的；it is safe to say that she will get the scholarship tā yídìng huì dédào jiǎngxuéjīn 她一定会得到奖学金 **2** a safe yí gè bǎoxiǎnxiāng 一个保险箱

safety /'seɪftɪ/ n ānquán 安全

sail /seɪl/ **1** n a sail yí gè fān 一个帆；to set sail kāiháng 开航，chūháng 出航 **2** vb (chéngchuán) hángxíng (乘船)航行；to sail around the world huánrào shìjiè hángxíng 环绕世界航行；to go sailing qù chéngchuán hángxíng 去乘船航行

sailing /'seɪlɪŋ/ n (in sports) hánghǎi yùndòng 航海运动；(travelling by boat) chéngchuán lǚxíng 乘船旅行

sailing boat /'seɪlɪŋ bəʊt/ (British English), **sailboat** /'seɪlbəʊt/ (US English) n a sailing boat yì sōu fānchuán 一艘帆船

sailor /'seɪlə(r)/ n a sailor yì míng shuǐshǒu 一名水手，yì míng hǎiyuán 一名海员

saint /seɪnt/ n a saint yí gè shèngrén 一个圣人，yí gè shèngtú 一个圣徒

salad /'sæləd/ n a salad yí fèn sèlā 一份色拉，xīcān liángbàncài 西餐凉拌菜

salary /'sælərɪ/ n a salary yí fèn gōngzī 一份工资，yí fèn xīnshuǐ 一份薪水

sale /seɪl/ n to be on sale at a reduced price jiǎnjià chūshòu 减价出售；for sale chūshòu 出售，dàishòu 待售；the total sales of this year quánnián xiāoshòu'é 全年销售额

sales assistant /'seɪlz əsɪstənt/ n (British English) a sales assistant yí gè tuīxiāoyuán 一个推销员，yí gè xiāoshòuyuán 一个销售员

salmon /'sæmən/ n a salmon yì tiáo sānwényú 一条三文鱼，yì tiáo guīyú 一条鲑鱼

salt /sɔːlt/ *n* yán 盐

same /seɪm/ **1** *adj* (*identical*) tóngyī de 同一的; they go to the same school tāmen zài tóng yí gè xuéxiào shàngxué 他们在同一个学校上学; (*similar in style or type*) tóngyàng de 同样的, yíyàng de 一样的; she has the same coat as I do tā de shàngyī gēn wǒ de yíyàng 她的上衣跟我的一样; I made the same mistake as he did wǒ hé tā fànle tóngyàng de cuòwù 我和他犯了同样的错误; the houses all look the same zhèxiē fángzi kànshàngqù dōu yíyàng 这些房子看上去都一样 **2** *pron* ! Note that in this sense, the meaning conveyed by same in English has to be stated overtly in Chinese; I bought my girlfriend a bottle of perfume, and he did the same wǒ gěi wǒ nǚpéngyou mǎile yì píng xiāngshuǐ, tā yě gěi tā nǚpéngyou mǎile yì píng 我给我女朋友买了一瓶香水, 他也给他女朋友买了一瓶; to do the same as the others xiàng biérén yíyàng zuò 像别人那样做; 'Happy New Year!'—'the same to you!' "xīnnián kuàilè!"—"yě zhù nǐ xīnnián kuàilè!" "新年快乐!"—"也祝你新年快乐!"

sand /sænd/ *n* shāzi 沙子, shā 沙

sandal /ˈsændəl/ *n* a sandal yì zhī liángxié 一只凉鞋; a pair of sandals yì shuāng liángxié 一双凉鞋

sandwich /ˈsænwɪdʒ/ *n* a sandwich yí gè sānmíngzhì 一个三明治; a ham sandwich yí gè huǒtuǐ sānmíngzhì 一个火腿三明治

Santa (Claus) /ˈsæntə (ˌklɔːz)/ *n* Shèngdàn lǎorén 圣诞老人

sardine /sɑːˈdiːn/ *n* a sardine yì tiáo shādīngyú 一条沙丁鱼

satellite TV /ˌsætəlaɪt tiː ˈviː/ *n* wèixīng diànshì 卫星电视

satisfactory /ˌsætɪsˈfæktəri/ *adj* lìng rén mǎnyì de 令人满意的

satisfied /ˈsætɪsfaɪd/ *adj* mǎnyì de 满意的

Saturday /'sætədɪ/ n xīngqīliù 星期六, lǐbàiliù 礼拜六

sauce /sɔːs/ n a sauce yì zhǒng jiàngzhī 一种酱汁, yì zhǒng tiáowèizhī 一种调味汁

saucepan /'sɔːspən/ n a saucepan yí gè (chángbǐng) píngdǐguō 一个（长柄）平底锅

saucer /'sɔːsə(r)/ n a saucer yí gè chábēidié 一个茶杯碟

sausage /'sɒsɪdʒ/ n a sausage yì gēn xiāngcháng 一根香肠

save /seɪv/ vb (to rescue) jiù 救; they saved his life tāmen jiùle tā de mìng 他们救了他的命; (to avoid spending) chǔxù 储蓄, zǎn zǎn 攒; to save money zǎnqián 攒钱; (to avoid wasting) jiéshěng 节省, jiéyuē 节约; to save [time | energy | money...] jiéshěng [shíjiān | jīnglì | jīnqián] 节省 [时间 | 精力 | 钱...]; (to keep) liú 留; to save a piece of cake for someone gěi mǒu rén liú yí kuài dàngāo 给某人留一块蛋糕; (to preserve in the computer) cún 存, chǔcún 储存; to save a file cún yí gè wénjiàn 存一个文件; (to spare) to save someone a lot of work jiéshěng mǒu rén hěn duō gōngzuò 节省某人很多工作; it will save us from having to write to him again zhè kěyǐ shǐ wǒmen miǎnde zài gěi tā xiěxìn 这可以使我们免得再给他写信

savings /'seɪvɪŋz/ n chǔxù 储蓄, cúnkuǎn 存款

saw /sɔː/ n a saw yì bǎ jù 一把锯

saxophone /'sæksəfəʊn/ n a saxophone yì gēn sàkèsīguǎn 一根萨克斯管

say /seɪ/ vb (to utter in words) shuō 说; to say goodbye shuō zàijiàn 说再见; she says (that) she can't go out tonight tā shuō jīnwǎn tā bù néng chūqù 她说今晚她不能出去; he said to wait here tā shuō zài zhèr děng 他说在这儿等; (to express) shuōmíng 说明, biǎomíng 表明; what do these figures say? zhèxiē shùzì shuōmíng shénme? 这些数字说明什么?; (to report in the newspaper, on the radio, TV) bàodǎo shuō 报导说, bàogào shuō 报告说; the radio said the Queen was

going to visit China shōuyīnjī bàodǎo shuō nǚwáng yào
fǎngwèn Zhōngguó 收音机报导说女王要访问中国;(to
suppose) jiǎdìng 假定，jiǎshè 假设；let's say there will
be twenty people at the party zánmen jiǎdìng yǒu èrshí
gè rén cānjiā zhège jùhuì 咱们假定有 20 个人参加这个聚
会

scandal /ˈskændəl/ n a scandal yí jiàn chǒuwén 一件丑
闻，yí jiàn chǒushì 一件丑事

scare /skeə(r)/ vb xià xià 吓，jīngxià 惊吓；you scared me!
nǐ xiàle wǒ yí tiào! 你吓了我一跳!；scare away bǎ ⋯
xiàpǎo 把⋯吓跑；to scare someone away bǎ mǒu rén
xiàpǎo 把某人吓跑

scared /skeəd/ adj I am scared wǒ hàipà 我害怕

scarf /skɑːf/ n a scarf yì tiáo wéijīn 一条围巾

scenery /ˈsiːnərɪ/ n fēngjǐng 风景，jǐngsè 景色

school /skuːl/ n a school yì suǒ xuéxiào 一所学校；to be
a student at school zài shàngxué 在上学；a school bus
yí liàng xiàochē 一辆校车

schoolbag /ˈskuːlbæg/ n a schoolbag yí gè shūbāo 一个
书包

schoolboy /ˈskuːlbɔɪ/ n a schoolboy yí gè nánxuéshēng
一个男学生

schoolgirl /ˈskuːlgɜːl/ n a schoolgirl yí gè nǚxuéshēng 一
个女学生

schoolwork /ˈskuːlwɜːk/ n gōngkè 功课，zuòyè 作业

science /ˈsaɪəns/ n kēxué 科学；to study science xuéxí
kēxué 学习科学

scientist /ˈsaɪəntɪst/ n a scientist yì míng kēxuéjiā 一名
科学家

scissors /ˈsɪzəz/ n jiǎnzi 剪子，jiǎndāo 剪刀；a pair of
scissors yì bǎ jiǎnzi 一把剪子

score /skɔː(r)/ **1** vb to score a goal jìn yí gè qiú 进一个
球；to score a point dé yì fēn 得一分 **2** n (points gained
in a game or competition) bǐfēn 比分；the final score of
the football match zúqiú bǐsài de zuìhòu bǐfēn 足球比赛

的最后比分；(result of a test or examination) a score yí xiàng chéngjì 一项成绩

Scotland /ˈskɒtlənd/ n Sūgélán 苏格兰

Scottish /ˈskɒtɪʃ/ adj Sūgélán(rén) de 苏格兰(人)的

scratch /skrætʃ/ vb (when itchy) náo 挠，sāo 搔；to scratch one's arm náo gēbo 挠胳膊；(if it's a person or an animal) zhuā 抓；(if it's a knife, a thorn) guā 刮，huá 划；(to mark with a knife or something hard) kè 刻

scream /skriːm/ vb jiānjiào 尖叫，dàjiào 大叫

screen /skriːn/ n (of a TV set or a computer) yí gè píngmù 一个屏幕；(of a cinema) yí gè yínmù 一个银幕

screw /skruː/ n a screw yì kē luósī(dīng) 一颗螺丝(钉)

sea /siː/ n hǎi 海，hǎiyáng 海洋；beside the sea, by the sea zài hǎibiān 在海边

seagull /ˈsiːgʌl/ n a seagull yì zhī hǎi'ōu 一只海鸥

seal /siːl/ **1** n a seal (the animal) yì zhī hǎibāo 一只海豹；(a tool used to impress) yì méi túzhāng 一枚图章 **2** vb (to close up) fēng 封；to seal the envelope bǎ xìnfēng fēng qǐlai 把信封封起来；to seal up mìfēng 密封；(to stamp) gàizhāng 盖章；to seal a document zài wénjiàn shang gàizhāng 在文件上盖章

search /sɜːtʃ/ vb to search xúnzhǎo 寻找；to search for someone xúnzhǎo mǒu rén 寻找某人；(to examine a place, a person) sōuchá 搜查；they searched my luggage at the airport tāmen zài fēijīchǎng sōuchále wǒ de xíngli 他们在飞机场搜查了我的行李

seashell /ˈsiːʃel/ n a seashell yí gè bèiké 一个贝壳

seasick /ˈsiːsɪk/ adj to be seasick, to get seasick yūnchuán 晕船

seaside /ˈsiːsaɪd/ n hǎibiān 海边；at the seaside zài hǎibiān 在海边

season /ˈsiːzən/ n (one of the four divisions of the year) jì 季，jìjié 季节；a season yí jì 一季，yí gè jìjié 一个季节；strawberries are in season xiànzài shì cǎoméi wàngjì 现

在是草莓旺季

seat /siːt/ *n* a seat(*something to sit on*) yí gè zuòwèi 一个座位；(*a right to sit in a council or committee*) yí gè xíwèi 一个席位

seatbelt /'siːtbelt/ *n* a seatbelt yí gè ānquándài 一个安全带

second /'sekənd/ **1** *adj* dì-èr 第二；it's the second time I've called her zhè shì wǒ dì-èrcì gěi tā dǎ diànhuà 这是我第 2 次给她打电话；(*of lower quality*) èrděng de 二等的；a second class cabin èrděng cāng 二等舱 **2** *n* (*in a series*) the second dì-èr 第二；(*in time*) a second yì miǎo 一秒，yì miǎo zhōng 一秒钟；(*a very short time*) yíhuìr 一会儿，piànkè 片刻；(*in dates*) èr rì 2 日，èr hào 2 号；the second of May wǔyuè èr rì 5 月 2 日 **3** *adv* dì-èr 第二；to come second in the race zài sàipǎo zhōng dé dì-èr 在赛跑中得第 2

secondary school /'sekəndərɪ ˌskuːl/ *n* a secondary school yì suǒ zhōngxué 一所中学

second-hand /'sekənd'hænd/ *adj* (biérén) yòngguo de (别人) 用过的，èrshǒu de 二手的；a second-hand table yì zhāng yòngguo de zhuōzi 一张用过的桌子；a second-hand car yí liàng èrshǒuchē 一辆二手车；a second-hand coat yí jiàn biérén chuānguo de wàiyī 一件别人穿过的外衣

secret /'siːkrɪt/ **1** *n* mìmì 秘密 **2** *n* a secret yí gè mìmì 一个秘密；to tell someone a secret gàosu mǒu rén yí gè mìmì 告诉某人一个秘密 **3** *in secret* mìmì de 秘密地

secretary /'sekrətərɪ/ *n* a secretary (*in an office, dealing with papers, keeping records, etc.*) yí gè mìshū 一个秘书；(*of a political party or party organization*) yí gè shūjì 一个书记；(*a government minister*) yí gè dàchén 一个大臣

see /siː/ *vb* to see kànjiàn 看见，kàndào 看到；what can you see? nǐ néng kànjiàn shénme? 你能看见什么？；I didn't see them wǒ méi jiàndào tāmen 我没见到他们；

she can't see the words on the blackboard tā kàn bú jiàn hēibǎn shang de zì 她看不见黑板上的字! Note that to negate to see kànjiàn 看见, the negative bù 不 comes between kàn 看 and jiàn 见；(to meet) jiànmiàn 见面；do you see each other often? nǐmen jīngcháng jiànmiàn ma? 你们经常见面吗？see you tomorrow! míngtiān jiàn! 明天见！；(to look at) kàn 看；please let me see your ticket qǐng ràng wǒ kàn yíxià nǐ de piào 请让我看一下你的票；(to visit) kàn 看；I'm going to see a doctor 我要去看医生 wǒ yào qù kàn yīshēng；he came to see me yesterday tā zuótiān lái kàn wǒ le 他昨天来看我了；(to watch) kàn 看；to see [a film | a play | an exhibition] kàn [diànyǐng | xì | zhǎnlǎnhuì] 看 [电影 | 戏 | 展览会]；(to understand, apprehend) dǒng 懂、lǐjiě 理解、míngbai 明白；do you see what I mean? nǐ dǒng wǒ de yìsi ma? 你懂我的意思吗？；(to accompany) péi 陪；I'll see you home wǒ péi nǐ huíjiā 我陪你回家

seem /siːm/ vb (to appear) hǎoxiàng 好像、sìhu 似乎；she seems [happy | annoyed | tired...] tā hǎoxiàng [hěn gāoxìng | hěn nǎohuǒ | hěn lèi...] 她好像 [很高兴 | 很恼火 | 很累...]；(when talking about one's impressions) kànlái 看来、kànyàngzi 看样子；it seems (that) there are many problems kànlái yǒu hěn duō wèntí 看来有很多问题

seldom /'seldəm/ adv hěn shǎo 很少、bù cháng 不常

self-confident /ˌself'kɒnfɪdənt/ adj yǒu zìxìnxīn de 有自信心的

selfish /'selfɪʃ/ adj zìsī de 自私的

sell /sel/ vb mài 卖、chūshòu 出售；to sell books to the students mài shū gěi xuésheng 卖书给学生；he sold me his car tā bǎ tā de chē màigěile wǒ 他把他的车卖给了我；water is sold in bottles shuǐ àn píng chūshòu 水按瓶出售

send /send/ vb (to direct someone to go on a mission) pài 派、pàiqiǎn 派遣；to send someone to post a letter pài mǒu rén qù jì xìn 派某人去寄信；(to cause to be *conveyed by post*) jì 寄;**to send a package to someone** jìgěi mǒu rén yí gè bāoguǒ 寄给某人一个包裹;**he sent her a letter** tā jìgěi tā yì fēng xìn 他寄给她一封信;(*to cause to be conveyed by electronic means*) fā 发;**to send an e-mail message to someone** gěi mǒu rén fā yí gè diànzǐ yóujiàn 给某人发一个电子邮件;**to send a pupil home from school** bǎ yí gè xuésheng cóng xuéxiào dǎfā huí jiā 把一个学生从学校打发回家;**send away**(*to dismiss*) jiěgù 解雇;(*to expel*) qūzhú 驱逐;**send back** tuìhuán 退还,sònghuílái 送还来;**send for** qù jiào 去叫;**to send for the doctor** qù jiào yīshēng 去叫医生;**send off to send a player off** bǎ yì míng duìyuán fá xiàchǎng 把一名队员罚下场;**send on to send on baggage** tíqián yùnsòng xínglǐ 提前运送行李;**to send on post** zhuǎnsòng xìnjiàn 转送信件

senior high school /ˌsiːnjə ˈhaɪ skuːl/ (*US English*),
senior school /ˈsiːnjə ˌskuːl/ (*British English*) n a
senior (high) school yì suǒ gāozhōng 一所高中

sense /sens/ n (*the body's capacity for perception*) **the sense of** [sight|hearing|taste|smell|touch] [shì tīng|wèi|xiù|chù]jué [视|听|味|嗅|触]觉 ;(*meaning, significance*) yìyì 意义,yìsi 意思;**it doesn't make sense** zhè méiyǒu yìyì 这没有意义;(*reasonableness*) dàolǐ 道理;**it makes sense to check first** xiān jiǎnchá yíxià shì yǒu dàolǐ de 先检查一下是有道理;**to have the sense not to go** bú qù shì yǒu dàolǐ de 不去是有道理的;**common sense** chángshí 常识,chánglǐ 常理;(*mental attitude*) **a sense of** [honour|justice|humour|beauty] yì zhǒng [róngyù|zhèngyì|yōumò|měi] gǎn 一种 [荣誉|正义|幽默|美] 感;(*consciousness*) zhījué 知觉;**he is still in hospital but has recovered his senses** tā hái zài yīyuàn li,dàn yǐjīng huīfù zhījué le 他还在医院里,但已经恢复知觉了;(*feeling for what is appropriate*) lǐzhì 理智,lǐxìng 理性;**he has obviously lost his senses** tā xiǎnrán shīqùle lǐzhì 他显然失去了理智

sensible /'sensəbl/ adj (when describing a person) dǒngshì de 懂事的, míngzhì de 明智的;(when describing a decision, a plan) qièhé shíjì de 切合实际的; hélǐ de 合理的;(when describing clothes) shíyòng de 实用的

sensitive /'sensɪtɪv/ adj (easily affected) mǐngǎn de 敏感的; he is very sensitive to criticism tā duì pīpíng fēicháng mǐngǎn 他对批评非常敏感; a sensitive market yí gè mǐngǎn de shìchǎng 一个敏感的市场

sentence /'sentəns/ **1** n (in language) jùzi 句子; a sentence yí gè jùzi 一个句子; yí jù huà 一句话;(for a crime) pànjué 判决; pànxíng 判刑; a (prison) sentence yí xiàng pànjué 一项判决 **2** vb pàn 判, pànjué 判决; to sentence someone to one year in prison pàn mǒu rén yì nián túxíng 判某人一年徒刑

separate /'sepəreɪt/ **1** adj (individual) dāndú de 单独的; the children have separate rooms háizimen yǒu dāndú de fángjiān 孩子们有单独的房间;(distinct) bù tóng de 不同的; there are two separate problems yǒu liǎng gè bù tóng de wèntí 有两个不同的问题 **2** vb (if it's a couple) fēnjū 分居; her parents separated two years ago tā fùmǔ liǎng nián qián fēnjū le 她父母两年前分居了; to separate the meat from the fish bǎ ròu gēn yú fēnkāi 把肉跟鱼分开

separated /'sepəreɪtɪd/ adj fēnkāi de 分开的, gékāi de 隔开的

separately /'sepərətlɪ/ adv (apart) fēnkāi de 分开地;(individually) fēnbié de 分别地

September /sep'tembə(r)/ n jiǔyuè 九月

serial /'sɪərɪəl/ n a serial (if it's a novel) yí bù liánzǎi xiǎoshuō 一部连载小说;(if it's a periodical publication) yí fèn qīkān 一份期刊;(if it's a TV play) yí bù diànshì liánxùjù 一部电视连续剧

series /'sɪərɪːz/ n (sequence) xìliè 系列; a series of problems yí xìliè wèntí 一系列问题;(set) a series of stamps yí tào yóupiào 一套邮票; a new series of

Chinese language textbooks yí tào xīn de Zhōngwén jiàokēshū 一套新的中文教科书

serious /'sɪərɪəs/ adj (causing worry) yánzhòng de 严重的；a serious accident yí cì yánzhòng shìgù 一次严重事故；(when describing a personality) rènzhēn de 认真的；to be serious about [football | going to college] duì [zúqiú | shàng dàxué]hěn zhòngshì 对 [足球 | 上大学]很重视

serve /sɜːv/ vb (in a shop) are you being served? yǒu rén jiēdài nín ma? 有人接待您吗?；(at table) to serve the soup shàng tāng 上汤；he served the guest a cup of Chinese tea tā gěi kèrén duānshàng yì bēi Zhōngguóchá 他给客人端上一杯中国茶；(to work for) wèi…fúwù …服务；can computers serve agriculture? jìsuànjī kěyǐ wèi nóngyè fúwù ma? 计算机可以为农业服务吗?；(in tennis, badminton, etc.) fāqiú 发球

service /'sɜːvɪs/ n (the act of serving) fúwù 服务；(the act of helping or assisting) bāngzhù 帮助；(in a church) yíshì 仪式；(other uses) military service bīngyì 兵役；public services gōnggòng shìyè 公共事业；there are eight bus services to Beijing everyday měi tiān yǒu bā bān gōnggòng qìchē qù Běijīng 每天有 8 班公共汽车去北京

service station /'sɜːvɪs ‚steɪʃən/ n a service station yí gè jiāyóuzhàn 一个加油站

set /set/ **1** n (a collection) tào 套；a set of [keys | stamps | plates] yí tào [yàoshi | yóupiào | pánzi] 一套 [钥匙 | 邮票 | 盘子]；(in tennis) pán 盘；a set yì pán 一盘 **2** vb (to decide on) (guī)dìng (规) 定；to set [a date | a price | a goal…] (guī)dìng [yí gè rìqī | yí gè jiàgé | yí gè mùbiāo…](规) 定 [一个日期 | 一个价格 | 一个目标…]；(to adjust for a specific time or condition) tiáo 调；to set [an alarm clock | a video | a camera lens] tiáo [nàozhōng | lùxiàngjī | zhàoxiàngjī jìngtóu]调 [闹钟 | 录像机 | 照相机镜头]；(for assignments or exams) to set homework bùzhì zuòyè 布置作业；to set an exam chū kǎojuàn 出考卷；(to create) chuàngzào 创造；to set a new world record chuàngzào yí xiàng xīn de shìjiè jìlù 创造一项新的世界纪录；(to establish) shùlì 树立；**to set a good example for someone** wèi mǒu rén shùlì yí gè hǎo bǎngyàng 为某人树立一个好榜样；(when talking about a story, a film, or the physical stage for a play) yǐ…wéi bèijǐng 以…为背景；**the film is set in Shanghai** zhè bù diànyǐng yǐ Shànghǎi wéi bèijǐng 这部电影以上海为背景；(when talking about the sun) luòshān 落山；(other uses) **to set the table** bǎi cānzhuō 摆餐桌；**to set fire to a house** fànghuǒ shāo yí zuò fángzi 放火烧一座房子；**to set someone free** shìfàng mǒu rén 释放某人；**set off** (to leave) chūfā 出发, dòngshēn 动身；(to cause to go off) **to set off fireworks** ránfàng yānhuǒ 燃放烟火；**to set off a bomb** shǐ yì kē zhàdàn bàozhà 使一颗炸弹爆炸；**to set off a burglar alarm** nòngxiǎng fángdào bàojǐngqì 弄响防盗报警器；**set up** (establish) jiànlì 建立, shèlì 设立；**to set up an organization** jiànlì yí gè zǔzhī 建立一个组织；(to start and manage) kāibàn 开办；**to set up a company** kāibàn yì jiā gōngsī 开办一家公司；(to place in position) shùqǐ 竖起, dāqǐ 搭起；**to set up a tent** dāqǐ yí gè zhàngpeng 搭起一个帐篷

settle /ˈsetl/ vb (to end) jiějué 解决；tiáotíng 调停；**to settle** [an argument | a dispute | a problem] jiějué [yì chǎng zhēnglùn | yí gè jiūfēn | yí gè wèntí] 解决 [一场争论 | 一个纠纷 | 一个问题]；(to decide on) dìng 定, juédìng 决定；**nothing is settled yet** yíqiè dōu hái méi dìng 一切都还没定；(to make one's home) dìngjū 定居；**settle down** (to live comfortably in one's new home) ānjū 安居；(to calm down) píngjìng xiàlái 平静下来, ānxià xīn lái 安下心来；**she settled down to her homework** tā ānxià xīn lái zuò zuòyè 她安下心来做作业；**settle in** āndùn 安顿

seven /ˈsevən/ num qī 七

seventeen /ˌsevənˈtiːn/ num shíqī 十七

seventeenth /ˌsevənˈtiːnθ/ num (in a series) dì-shíqī 第十七；(in dates) **the seventeenth of May** wǔyuè shíqī rì

5 月 17 日，wǔyuè shíqī hào 5 月 17 号

seventh /'sevənθ/ *num* (*in a series*) dì-qī 第七；(*in dates*) **the seventh of July** qīyuè qī rì 7 月 7 日，qīyuè qī hào 7 月 7 号

seventy /'sevəntɪ/ *num* qīshí 七十

several /'sevərəl/ *det* jǐ gè 几个；**several tables** jǐ zhāng zhuōzi 几张桌子；**several books** jǐ běn shū 几本书！ *Note that in* jǐ gè 几个，gè 个 *is a measure word that may be replaced by a different measure word, depending on the noun that follows.*

severe /sɪ'vɪə(r)/ *adj* (*harsh*) yánlì de 严厉的；(*giving cause for concern*) yánzhòng de 严重的；(*strict*) yángé de 严格的

sew /səʊ/ *vb* féng 缝，féngzhì 缝制

sewing /'səʊɪŋ/ *n* féngrèn 缝纫

sewing machine /'səʊɪŋ məʃiːn/ *n* **a sewing machine** yì tái féngrènjī 一台缝纫机

sex /seks/ *n* (*state of being male or female*) xìngbié 性别；(*sexual intercourse*) xìngjiāo 性交；**to have sex with someone** hé mǒu rén fāshēng xìngguānxi 和某人发生性关系，hé mǒu rén xìngjiāo 和某人性交

shade /ʃeɪd/ *n* (*out of the sun*) yīn 阴，yīnliángchù 阴凉处；**to sit in the shade of a tree** zuò zài shùyīn xià 坐在树阴下；(*a colour*) nóngdàn 浓淡；**a shade** yì zhǒng sèdiào 一种色调；(*for a lamp*) dēngzhào 灯罩；**a shade** yí gè dēngzhào 一个灯罩

shadow /'ʃædəʊ/ *n* **a shadow** yí gè yǐngzi 一个影子

shake /ʃeɪk/ *vb* (*to move with quick vibrations*) yáo (huàng) 摇(晃)，yáo(dòng) 摇(动)；**to shake a bottle** yáohuàng yí gè píngzi 摇晃一个瓶子；**to grasp the hand of another in greeting** wò 握；**to shake hands with someone** hé mǒu rén wòshǒu 和某人握手；(*when saying no*) yáo 摇；**to shake one's head** yáotóu 摇头；(*with cold, fear, shock*) fādǒu 发抖；**he was shaking with fear** tā xià de fādǒu 他吓得发抖；(*during an explosion* an earthquake) zhèndòng 震动；the earthquake shook the building dìzhèn bǎ zhěnggè dàlóu dōu zhèndòng le 地震把整个大楼都震动了

shall /ʃæl/强/ʃəl/ vb (when talking about the future) huì 会，jiāng(yào) 将要；I shall see you next Tuesday xiàge xīngqī'èr wǒ huì jiàndào nǐ 下个星期二我会见到你；we shall arrive there on time wǒmen jiāng ànshí dàodá nàr 我们将按时到达那儿；(when making suggestions) hǎo ma… 好吗，yào bú yào… 要不要…；shall I set the table? yào bú yào wǒ bǎi cānzhuō? 要不要我摆餐桌？shall we go to the cinema? wǒmen qù kàn diànyǐng hǎo ma? 我们去看电影好吗？

shame /ʃeɪm/ n (emotion caused by a humiliating feeling) xiūkuì 羞愧，xiūchǐ 羞耻；she felt shame at having failed the exam tā yīn kǎoshì bù jígé ér gǎndào xiūkuì 她因考试不及格而感到羞愧；(disgrace or dishonour) chǐrǔ 耻辱；to bring shame on someone gěi mǒu rén dàilái chǐrǔ 给某人带来耻辱；shame on you! nǐ zhēn diūrén! 你真丢人！；(when expressing regret) yíhàn 遗憾，kěxī 可惜；that's a shame zhēn yíhàn 真遗憾

shampoo /ʃæm'puː/ n xǐfàjì 洗发剂，xiāngbō 香波

shape /ʃeɪp/ n (a form) xíng 形，xíngzhuàng 形状；a square shape yí gè xíngzhuàng 一个形状；a square shape yí gè fāngxíng 一个方形；in the shape of an apple chéng píngguǒ (de) xíngzhuàng 呈苹果(的)形状；(when talking about health) qíngkuàng 情况，zhuàngtài 状态；she is in good shape after the operation tā shǒushù hòu shēntǐ zhuàngkuàng hěn hǎo 她手术后身体状况很好；to get in shape chǔyú liánghǎo zhuàngtài 处于良好状态

share /ʃeə(r)/ **1** vb (to join with others in using) héyòng 合用；to share a house héyòng/hézhù yí dòng fángzi 合用/合住一栋房子；(when talking about dividing costs, rent, work) fēndān 分担；to share [the cost | the petrol | the work] (with someone) (hé mǒu rén) fēndān [fèiyòng | qìyóu fèi | zhè xiàng gōngzuò] (和某人) 分担 [费用 | 汽油费 | 这项

工作；(to take a share of) fēnxiǎng 分享；he shared [the profit|the money|her joy] (with his sister) tā (hé tā mèimei) fēnxiǎng [lìrùn|qián|tā de huānxǐ] 他(和他妹妹)分享[利润|钱|她的欢乐] 2 n (portion) fēnr 份儿；a share yí fènr 一份儿；to pay one's fair share fù yīng fù de nà yí fènr 付应付的那一份儿；(unit of ownership in a public company) gǔpiào 股票；a share yì gǔ 一股；share out (British English) (amongst others) fēn 分

shark /ʃɑːk/ n a shark yì tiáo shāyú 一条鲨鱼

sharp /ʃɑːp/ adj (when speaking of knives, blades, etc.) kuài de 快的；(pointed) jiān de 尖的；(sudden, extreme) jí de 急的；a sharp bend yí ge jí zhuǎnwān 一个急转弯；(intelligent) jīngmíng de 精明的；(aggressive) jiānkè de 尖刻的，kēkè de 苛刻的；(when talking about a pain) jùliè de 剧烈的

shave /ʃeɪv/ vb guāliǎn 刮脸，tìxū 剃须

she /ʃiː/ pron tā 她

sheep /ʃiːp/ n a sheep yì zhī yáng 一只羊

sheet /ʃiːt/ n (for a bed) chuángdān 床单；a sheet yì tiáo chuángdān 一条床单；(a piece) a sheet (of paper) yì zhāng zhǐ 一张纸；(of glass) yí kuài bōli 一块玻璃

shelf /ʃelf/ n a shelf yí ge jiàzi 一个架子；a book shelf yí ge shūjià 一个书架

shell /ʃel/ n a shell yí ge ké 一个壳

shelter /'ʃeltə(r)/ 1 n (from rain, danger) a shelter yí ge duǒbìchù 一个躲避处；(for homeless people) a shelter yí ge qīshēn zhī dì 一个栖身之处；a bus shelter yí ge gōnggòng qìchē hòuchētíng 一个公共汽车候车亭 2 vb (to take shelter) duǒbì 躲避；(to give protection to) bìhù 庇护，bǎohù 保护

shin /ʃɪn/ n the shin xiǎotuǐ 小腿

shine /ʃaɪn/ vb (if it's the sun) zhàoyào 照耀；the sun is shining yángguāng zhàoyào 阳光照耀；(to give off light) fāguāng 发光；the light in the lighthouse is shining dēngtǎ li de dēng zài shǎnshǎn-fāguāng 灯塔里的灯在闪

闪发光;(to reflect light) fāliàng 发亮，fāguāng 发光；the ring on her hand shone in the sun tā shǒu shang de jièzhi zài yángguāng xià shǎnshǎn-fāliàng 她手上的戒指在阳光下闪闪发光；(to point a light at) to shine a torch at someone yòng shǒudiàntǒng zhào mǒu rén 用手电筒照某人

ship /ʃɪp/ n a ship yì sōu chuán 一艘船；a passenger ship yì sōu kèlún 一艘客轮

shirt /ʃɜːt/ n a shirt yí jiàn chènshān 一件衬衫，yí jiàn chènyī 一件衬衣

shiver /'ʃɪvə(r)/ vb fādǒu 发抖，duōsuo 哆嗦

shock /ʃɒk/ **1** n (an upsetting experience) zhènjīng 震惊，dǎjī 打击，a shock yí gè zhènjīng 一个震惊，yí gè dǎjī 一个打击；to get a shock shòudào zhènjīng 受到震惊；to give someone a shock gěi mǒu rén yí gè dǎjī 给某人一个打击；(the medical state) xiūkè 休克，zhòngfēng 中风；to be in shock chǔyú xiūkè zhuàngtài 处于休克状态；(from electricity) a shock yí cì diànjī 一次电击；to get a shock chùdiàn 触电 **2** vb (to upset) shǐ…zhènjīng 使…震惊；to shock someone shǐ mǒu rén zhènjīng 使某人震惊；we were shocked by the news duì zhège xiāoxi wǒmen dōu gǎndào zhènjīng 对这个消息我们都感到震惊；(to cause a scandal) shǐ…fènkǎi 使…愤慨；to shock someone shǐ mǒu rén gǎndào fènkǎi 使某人感到愤慨

shoe /ʃuː/ n (for a person) xié 鞋；a shoe yì zhī xié 一只鞋；a pair of shoes yì shuāng xié 一双鞋；(for a horse) tiětí 蹄铁；a shoe yí gè tiětí 一个蹄铁

shoot /ʃuːt/ vb (to aim and fire a weapon) shèjī 射击，kāi qiāng 开枪；to shoot at someone xiàng mǒu rén shèjī 向某人射击；(to hit with a missile from a weapon) jīzhòng 击中，shèzhòng 射中；they shot him in the leg tāmen jīzhòngle tā de tuǐ 他们击中了他的腿；to shoot someone dead kāi qiāng dǎsǐ mǒu rén 开枪打死某人；(to move very fast) his car shot past me tā de chē cóng wǒ pángbiān fēisù kāi guòqu 他的车从我旁边飞速开过去；

(when talking about film production) pāishè 拍摄；to shoot a film pāishè yí bù diànyǐng 拍摄一部电影

shop /ʃɒp/ **1** n a shop yì jiā shāngdiàn 一家商店 **2** vb to go shopping qù mǎi dōngxi 去买东西

shop assistant /'ʃɒp əˌsɪstənt/ n (British English) a shop assistant yì míng shòuhuòyuán 一名售货员

shopkeeper /'ʃɒpˌkiːpə(r)/ n a shopkeeper yí gè diànzhǔ 一个店主

shopping /'ʃɒpɪŋ/ n a mǎi dōngxi 买东西；to do the shopping mǎi dōngxi 买东西

shopping cart /'ʃɒpɪŋ kɑːt/ n (US English) a shopping cart yí liàng gòuwù shǒutuīchē 一辆购物手推车

shopping centre /'ʃɒpɪŋ ˌsentə(r)/ (British English), **shopping center** (US English) n a shopping centre, a shopping mall yí gè gòuwù zhōngxīn 一个购物中心

shopping trolley /'ʃɒpɪŋ ˌtrɒlɪ/ n (British English) a shopping trolley yí liàng gòuwù shǒutuīchē 一辆购物手推车

shop window /ʃɒp 'wɪndəu/ n a shop window yí gè chúchuāng 一个橱窗

shore /ʃɔː(r)/ n (the edge of the sea) hǎi'àn 海岸；(dry land) hǎibīn 海滨

short /ʃɔːt/ **1** adj (not long) duǎn de 短的；the days are getting shorter tiān yuèláiyuè duǎn le 天越来越短了；a short skirt yì tiáo duǎnqún 一条短裙；he has short hair tā shì duǎn tóufa 他是短头发；(not tall) ǎi de 矮的；he's shorter than I tā bǐ wǒ ǎi 他比我矮；(not long) jiǎnduǎn de 简短的；a short speech yí gè jiǎnduǎn de jiǎnghuà 一个简短的讲话；(lacking, wanting) quē(shǎo) de 缺(少)的；to be short of [money | food | ideas . . .] quēshǎo [qián | shíwù | zhǔyi . . .] 缺少 [钱 | 食物 | 主意 . . .] **2 in short** zǒngzhī 总之

short cut /ˈʃɔːt kʌt/ n a short cut yí tiáo jiéjìng 一条捷径

shortly /'ʃɔːtlɪ/ adv (soon) lìkè 立刻，mǎshàng 马上；(not long) bùjiǔ 不久；shortly before we left wǒmen líkāi qián bùjiǔ 我们离开前不久

shorts /ʃɔːts/ n duǎnkù 短裤;a pair of shorts yì tiáo duǎnkù 一条短裤

shot /ʃɒt/ n (from a gun) a shot (kāi) yì qiāng (开) 一枪,yí cì shèjí 一次射击;to fire a shot at someone xiàng mǒu rén kāi yì qiāng 向某人开一枪;(in sports) a shot (in football) yí cì shèmén 一次射门

should /ʃud/弱 ʃəd/ vb (when talking about what is right, what one ought to do) yīnggāi 应该,yīngdāng 应当;she should learn to drive tā yīnggāi xué kāichē 她应该学开车;you shouldn't be late nǐ bù yīngdāng chídào 你不应当迟到;(when saying something may happen) yīnggāi huì 应该会,kěnéng huì 可能会;we should be there by midday zhōngwǔ yǐqián wǒmen yīnggāi huì dàodá nàr 中午以前我们应该会到达那儿;it shouldn't be too difficult zhè kěnéng bú huì tài nán 这可能不会太难;(when implying that something, though likely, didn't happen) běnlái (yīnggāi) 本来(应该);the letter should have arrived yesterday zhè fēng xìn běnlái yīnggāi zuótiān dào 这封信本来应该昨天到;(when implying that something happened though it ought not to have) běnlái bù (yīng)gāi 本来不(应)该;you shouldn't have said that nǐ běnlái bù yīnggāi nàme shuō 你本来不应该那么说;(when used in a conditional clause to express a hypothetical condition) wànyī 万一;if it should rain tomorrow,we shall have to change our plans míngtiān wànyī xiàyǔ,wǒmen jiù děi gǎibiàn jìhuà 明天万一下雨,我们就得改变计划;(when asking for permission) kě(yǐ) bù kěyǐ 可(以)不可以;should I call him? wǒ kě bù kěyǐ gěi tā dǎ diànhuà? 我可不可以给他打电话?(when asking for advice) yīng(gāi) bù yīnggāi 应(该)不应该,hǎo ma 好吗;should I call the doctor? wǒ yīng bù yīnggāi jiào yīshēng? 我应不应该叫医生?(when expressing a past expectation of a future event) jiāng 将,huì 会;they didn't expect that I should come and attend the meeting tāmen méi xiǎngdào wǒ huì lái cānjiā huìyì 他们没想到我会来参加会议；(when expressing surprise at something unexpected) huì zǒu (huì) 竟 (会)；it is surprising that he should be so foolish tā jìng huì zhème shǎ, zhēn ràng rén chījīng 他竟会这么傻，真让人吃惊；(when used after such verbs as propose, suggest, or such adjectives as necessary, important)! Note that in these cases, should is often not translated; I suggest that he should discuss this matter with you wǒ jiànyì tā hé nǐ tǎolùn zhège wèntí 我建议他和你讨论这个问题

shoulder /'ʃəʊldə(r)/ n jiān bǎng, jiānbǎng 肩膀；to wear a sweater over one's shoulders bǎ yí jiàn máoyī pī zài jiān shang 把一件毛衣披在肩上；he has strong shoulders tā de jiānbǎng hěn jiēshi 他的肩膀很结实

shout /ʃaʊt/ 1 vb hǎn, jiào 喊，叫；to shout at someone duì mǒu rén hǎn 对某人喊 2 n hūhǎn 呼喊，hǎnjiào 喊叫；a shout yì shēng hūhǎn 一声呼喊；shout out hǎn chūlái 喊出来，dàshēng shuō chūlái 大声说出来

shovel /'ʃʌvəl/ n a shovel yì bǎ tiěxiān 一把铁锨，yì bǎ tiěchǎn 一把铁铲

show /ʃəʊ/ 1 vb (to let someone see) gěi…kàn 给…看；to show someone a photo gěi mǒu rén kàn yì zhāng zhàopiàn 给某人看一张照片；(to guide) dài dài 带，dài lǐng (带)领；I'll show you to your room wǒ dài nǐ qù nǐ de fángjiān 我带你去你的房间；(to point to) to show someone where to go gàosu mǒu rén wǎng nǎr zǒu 告诉某人往哪儿走；there's a sign showing the way to the swimming pool yǒu yí gè lùbiāo gàosu nǐ qù yóuyǒngchí de lù zěnme zǒu 有一个路标告诉你去游泳池的路怎么走；(to be on TV, at the cinema) fàngyìng 放映；the film is showing at that cinema zhè bù diànyǐng zhèngzài nà jiā diànyǐngyuàn fàngyìng 这部电影正在那家电影院放映；to be shown on TV zài diànshì shang fàngyìng/bōfàng 在电视上放映/播放；(to indicate) biǎomíng 表

明，shuōmíng 说明；this shows that he doesn't agree with our plan zhè biǎomíng tā bù tóngyì wǒmen de jìhuà 这表明他不同意我们的计划；(to demonstrate) gěi … shìfàn 给…示范，zuògěi… kàn 做给…看；let me show you how to use this computer wǒ lái gěi nǐ shìfàn zěnme shǐyòng zhè tái jìsuànjī 我来给你示范怎么用这台计算机 2 n a show (on a stage) yì chǎng yǎnchū 一场演出；(on TV) yí gè diànshì jiémù 一个电视节目；(on radio) yí gè guǎngbō jiémù 一个广播节目；(at a cinema) yì chǎng diànyǐng 一场电影；(an exhibition) a show yí gè zhǎnlǎn 一个展览；show off màinòng 卖弄，xuànyào 炫耀；show round to show someone round the town dài mǒu rén cānguān chéngqū 带某人参观城区；show up (to be present) dàochǎng 到场；(to appear) xiǎnlù 显露，xiǎnchū 显出；(to expose) jiēlù 揭露，jiēchuān 揭穿

shower /ˈʃaʊə(r)/ n (for washing) línyù 淋浴；a shower yí gè línyù 一个淋浴；to have a shower xǐ línyù 洗淋浴；(rain) zhènyǔ 阵雨；a shower yì chǎng zhènyǔ 一场阵雨

showjumping /ˈʃəʊ,dʒʌmpɪŋ/ n qímǎ yuè zhàng yùndòng 骑马越障运动

shrimp /ʃrɪmp/ n a shrimp yì zhī xiā 一只虾

shrink /ʃrɪŋk/ vb (when talking about clothing) shōusuō 收缩；the shirt shrank after washing zhè jiàn chènshān xǐ hòu suōshuǐ le 这件衬衫洗后缩水了；(when talking about an economy, etc.) suōxiǎo 缩小，jiǎnshǎo 减少

shut /ʃʌt/ 1 adj (when referring to a book) héshang de 合上的；the book was shut shū shì héshang de 书是合上的；(when describing the eyes, the mouth) bìshang de 闭上的；my eyes were shut wǒ bìzhe yǎnjīng 我闭着眼睛；(when describing a door, a shop) guān(mén) de 关(门)的；all the shops are shut suǒyǒu de shāngdiàn dōu guānmén le 所有的商店都关门了 2 vb (if it's a window, a door) guān 关；to shut [the window | the door] guān [chuānghu | mén]关 [窗户 |门]；the door does not shut properly zhè mén guān bú shàng 这门关不上；(if it's a book，a dictionary，a magazine to be closed) héshang 合上；to shut [the book | the dictionary] héshang [shū | cídiǎn] 合上 [书 | 词典]；(if the eyes，the mouth to be closed) bìshang 闭上；to shut [one's eyes | one's mouth] bìshang [yǎnjing | zuǐ] 闭上 [眼睛 | 嘴]；**shut down** (to close) guānbì 关闭；**the factory shut down in May last year** zhè jiā gōngchǎng qùnián wǔyuè guānbì le 这家工厂去年 5 月关闭了；**shut out** to shut someone out bǎ mǒu rén guān zài wàimian 把某人关在外面；**shut up** (to be quiet) zhùzuǐ 住嘴，zhùkǒu 住口；(to lock inside) to shut someone up bǎ mǒu rén guān qǐlai 把某人关起来；to shut something up bǎ mǒu wù shōucáng qǐlai 把某物收藏起来

shy /ʃaɪ/ adj (bashful) hàixiū de 害羞的，miǎntiǎn de 腼腆的；(easily frightened) dǎnqiè de 胆怯的

sick /sɪk/ adj (ill) bìng de 病的，shēngbìng de 生病的；**he got sick** tā bìng le 他病了；**she felt sick** tā juéde bù shūfu 她觉得不舒服；**to be sick** (British English) (to vomit) ěxīn 恶心，yào ǒutù 要呕吐；(fed up) fán le 烦了，yànjuàn le 厌倦了；**he's sick of his neighbours** tā duì tā de línjū yànjuàn le 他对他的邻居厌倦了

sickness /'sɪknɪs/ n a sickness yì zhǒng jíbìng 一种疾病

side /saɪd/ n (a line forming part of a boundary or the part near the boundary) biān 边；a side yì biān 一边；**there are shops on either side of the road** mǎlù liǎng biān dōu yǒu shāngdiàn 马路两边都有商店；**by the side of the river** zài hébiān 在河边；**the north side of Beijing** Běijīng de běibiān 北京的北边；(of a person's body) cè cè 侧；**to be lying on one's side** cèzhe shēnzi tǎngzhe 侧着身子躺着；**on my right side** wǒ shēntǐ de yòucè 我身体的右侧；(a surface of something flat) miàn 面；a side yí miàn 一面；**please read the other side of the page** qǐng kàn zhè yí yè de lìng yí miàn 请看这一页的另一面；(aspect) fāngmiàn 方面；a side yí gè fāngmiàn 一个方面；**to consider all sides of the problem** kǎolǜ zhège wèntí de gè gè fāngmiàn 考虑这个问题的各个方面；(in a conflict, a contest) pài 派，fāng 方；**a side** yí pài 一派，yì fāng 一方；(a team) duì 队，fāng 方；**a side** yì duì 一队；**side with** zhàn zài…de yì biān 站在…的一边，zhīchí 支持

sidewalk /'saidwɔ:k/ n (US English) **a sidewalk** yì tiáo rénxíngdào 一条人行道

sigh /sai/ vb tànxì 叹息，tànqì 叹气

sight /sait/ n (faculty of seeing) shìlì 视力，shìjué 视觉；**to have good sight** shìlì hǎo 视力好；**to be** [long/short] **sighted** huàn [yuǎn/jìn] shì 患 [远/近] 视；(view) **to catch sight of someone** kànjiàn mǒu rén 看见某人，**to be out of sight** kàn bú jiàn 看不见

sightseeing /'saitsi:iŋ/ n guānguāng 观光，yóulǎn 游览

sign /sain/ **1** n (a mark, symbol) **a sign** yí gè fúhào 一个符号，yí gè jìhào 一个记号；**the US dollar sign** měiyuán de fúhào 美元的符号；(for traffic) **a sign** yí gè biāozhì 一个标志；(for shops, advertising) **a sign** yí gè zhāopái 一个招牌；(a notice) **a sign** yí gè páizi 一个牌子；(evidence, indication) **a sign** yí gè zhēngzhào 一个征兆，yì zhǒng jìxiàng 一种迹象 **2** vb (to put one's signature to) zài … shang qiānzì/míng 在 … 上签字/名；**to sign (one's name on) a cheque** zài zhīpiào shang qiānzì 在支票上签字；**sign on** (British English) (to record one's arrival at work) qiāndào 签到；(to begin a new job) **to sign on** kāishǐ yí xiàng xīn gōngzuò 开始一项新工作

signal /'signl/ **1** n **a signal** yí gè xìnhào 一个信号 **2** vb (using lights, flags, a coding system) fā xìnhào 发信号；**to signal to turn left** fāchū xiàng zuǒ guǎi de xìnhào 发出向左拐的信号；(using one's hands) dǎ shǒushì 打手势；**to signal someone to come** dǎ shǒushì ràng mǒu rén lái 打手势让某人来

signature /'signitʃə(r)/ n **a signature** yí gè qiānmíng 一个签名

signpost /'sainpəust/ n **a signpost** yí gè lùbiāo 一个路标

silence /'saɪləns/ n (*absence of noise*) jìjìng 寂静, wúshēng 无声;(*refraining from speech*) chénmò 沉默, mòbúzuòshēng 默不作声

silent /'saɪlənt/ adj (*quiet*) jìjìng de 寂静的,(*not speaking or making any sound*) chénmò de 沉默的, mòbúzuòshēng de 默不作声

silk /sɪlk/ n 丝 sī, sīchóu 丝绸

silly /'sɪlɪ/ adj shǎ de 傻的, yúchǔn de 愚蠢的, hútu de 糊涂的

silver /'sɪlvə(r)/ **1** n (*the metal*) yín de 银的, yínzi 银子;(*silver coins*) yínbì 银币 **2** adj yín de 银的;a silver ring yì zhī yín jièzhi 一只银戒指

simple /'sɪmpl/ adj (*not complicated*) jiǎndān de 简单的;(*plain*) pǔsù de 朴素的;(*unsuspecting*) dānchún de 单纯的;(*ordinary*) pǔtōng de 普通的, píngcháng de 平常的

since /sɪns/ **1** prep! *Note that the phrase or clause beginning with* since *appears at the beginning of the sentence in Chinese*; cóng…yǐlái 从…以来, zìcóng 自从; I haven't been feeling well since Monday cóng xīngqīyī yǐlái, wǒ yìzhí gǎnjué shēntǐ bù shūfu 从星期一以来,我一直感觉身体不舒服;she has been living in China since 1988 zìcóng yìjiǔbābā nián, tā yìzhí zhù zài Zhōngguó 自从1988年,她一直住在中国;I haven't seen him since last week wǒ zìcóng shàng xīngqī yìzhí méi jiànguo tā 我自从上星期一直没见过他 **2** conj (*from the time when*) cóng…yǐlái 从…以来, …yǐhòu …以后;I haven't heard from her since she left tā líkāi yǐhòu, wǒ hái méi shōudàoguo tā de xìn 她离开以后,我还没收到过她的信;I've lived here since wǒ cóng shí suì yǐlái yìzhí zhù zài zhèr 我从10岁以来一直住在这儿;it's ten years since she died tā sǐle shí nián le 她死了10年了;(*because*) yīnwèi 因为, jìrán 既然;since she was ill, she couldn't go yīnwèi tā bìng le, suǒyǐ tā bù néng qù 因为她病了,所以她不能去 **3** adv (*from that time*) cóng nà yǐhòu 从那以后，hòulái 后来；I have been living here ever since cóng nà yǐhòu wǒ yìzhí zhù zài zhèlǐ 从那以后我一直住在这里

sincere /sɪn'sɪə(r)/ adj zhēnchéng de 真诚的，chéngkěn de 诚恳的

sincerely /sɪn'sɪəlɪ/ adv zhēnchéng de 真诚地，chéngkěn de 诚恳地；Yours sincerely (British English) , Sincerely yours (US English) nín de zhēnchéng de 您的真诚的；I sincerely hope that... wǒ zhōngxīn xīwàng… 我衷心希望…

sing /sɪŋ/ vb chàng 唱，chànggē 唱歌

singer /'sɪŋə(r)/ n a singer (one who sings as a profession) yì míng gēshǒu 一名歌手；(one whose fame for singing is widely recognized) yì míng gēchàngjiā 一名歌唱家

singing /'sɪŋɪŋ/ n chànggē 唱歌，gēchàng 歌唱

single /'sɪŋgl/ adj (one) yī 一；we visited three towns in a single day wǒmen yì tiān fǎngwènle sān gè chéngzhèn 我们一天访问了3个城镇；I didn't see a single person wǒ méiyǒu kànjiàn yí gè rén 我没有看见一个人；(without a partner) dúshēn de 独身的；(for one person) dānrén de 单人的；a single bed yì zhāng dānrénchuáng 一张单人床；(denoting ticket for transport valid for outward journey only) (British English) dānchéng de 单程的；a single ticket yì zhāng dānchéngpiào 一张单程票

sink /sɪŋk/ **1** n a sink (in a kitchen) yí gè shuǐchí 一个水池，yí gè xǐdícáo 一个洗涤槽 **2** vb (to become submerged in water) chénmò 沉没，chén 沉；the boat sank in five minutes nà tiáo chuán bú dào wǔ fēnzhōng biàn chénmò le 那条船不到5分钟便沉没了；(subside) xiàxiàn 下陷；(to cause to sink) to sink a ship shǐ yì sōu chuán chénmò 使一艘船沉没

sister /'sɪstə(r)/ n a sister (elder) yí gè jiějie 一个姐姐；(younger) yí gè mèimei 一个妹妹

sister-in-law /'sɪstərɪnlɔː/ n a sister-in-law (elder

brother's wife) yí ge sǎozi 一个嫂子；(*younger brother's wife*) yí ge dìmèi 一个弟妹/弟媳；(*husband's elder sister*) yí ge dàgūzi 一个大姑子；(*husband's younger sister*) yí ge xiǎogūzi 一个小姑子；(*wife's elder sister*) yí ge dàyízi 一个大姨子；(*wife's younger sister*) yí ge xiǎoyízi 一个小姨子

sit /sɪt/ vb (*to take a seat*) zuò 坐；**to be sitting on the floor** zuò zài dìshang 坐在地上；(*British English*) (*to take*) **to sit an exam** cānjiā kǎoshì 参加考试；**sit down** zuòxià 坐下；**sit up** (*to rise to a sitting position*) zuò qǐlai 坐起来

sitting room /'sɪtɪŋ rʊm/ n **a sitting room** yì jiān qǐjūshì 一间起居室

situated /'sɪtjʊeɪtɪd/ adj wèiyú…de 位于…的，zuòluò zài…de 坐落在…的；**situated near the town centre** wèiyú shìzhōngxīn fùjìn 位于市中心附近

situation /ˌsɪtjʊ'eɪʃən/ n (*location*) wèizhi 位置，dìdiǎn 地点；**a situation** yí ge wèizhi 一个位置；(*momentary state*) chǔjìng 处境，jìngkuàng 境况；**to be in a dangerous situation** chǔjìng wēixiǎn 处境危险；(*a set of circumstances*) xíngshì 形势，júshì 局势；[international | domestic | economic] **situation** [guójì | guónèi | jīngjì] xíngshì 国际 | 国内 | 经济] 形势

six /sɪks/ num liù 六

sixteen /'sɪks'tiːn/ num shíliù 十六

sixteenth /'sɪks'tiːnθ/ num(*in a series*) dì-shíliù 第十六；(*in dates*) **the sixteenth of July** qīyuè shíliù rì 7 月 16 日，qīyuè shíliù hào 7 月 16 号

sixth /sɪksθ/ num(*in a series*) dì-liù 第六；(*in dates*) **the sixth of February** èryuè liù rì 2 月 6 日，èryuè liù hào 2 月 6 号

sixty /'sɪkstɪ/ num liùshí 六十

size /saɪz/ n(*when talking about a person*) shēncái 身材；**she's about your size** tā de shēncái gēn nǐ chàbuduō 她的身材跟你差不多；(*when talking about hats, socks,* *shoes*) hào 号；**a size** yí gè hào 一个号；**what size shoes do you wear?** nǐ chuān jǐ hào de xié? 你穿几号的鞋?；(*when talking about clothes*) chǐcun 尺寸；**do you have trousers of this size?** nǐmen yǒu zhège chǐcun de kùzi ma? 你们有这个尺寸的裤子吗?；(*when talking about how big something is*) **what is the size of** [*your house* | *England* | *that school* | *the apple*]? [nǐ de fángzi | Yīnggélán | nà suǒ xuéxiào | píngguǒ]yǒu duō dà? [你的房子 | 英格兰 | 那所学校 | 苹果]有多大?；**I like a garden of this size** wǒ xǐhuan zhème zhème dàxiǎo de huāyuán 我喜欢这么大小的花园；**the size of the window** chuānghu de dàxiǎo 窗户的大小，chuānghu de chǐcun 窗户的尺寸

skateboard /'skeɪtbɔːd/ *n* **a skateboard** yí gè (sìlún) huábǎn 一个(四轮)滑板

skating /'skeɪtɪŋ/ *n* **ice-skating** huábīng 滑冰；**roller-skating** liūbīng 溜冰

skating rink /'skeɪtʃ rɪŋk/ *n* **a skating rink** (*for ice-skating*) yí gè huábīngchǎng 一个滑冰场；(*for roller-skating*) yí gè liūbīngchǎng 一个溜冰场

sketch /sketʃ/ *n* (*a drawing*) cǎotú 草图，sùmiáo 素描；**a sketch** yì zhāng cǎotú 一张草图；(*a funny scene*) xiǎopǐn 小品；**a sketch** yí gè xiǎopǐn 一个小品

ski /skiː/ **1** *n* **a ski** yì zhī huáxuěbǎn 一只滑雪板；**a pair of skis** yí fù huáxuěbǎn 一副滑雪板 **2** *vb* **to go skiing** qù huáxuě 去滑雪

skiing /'skiːɪŋ/ *n* huáxuě 滑雪

skilful /'skɪlfʊl/ (*British English*)，**skillful** (*US English*) *adj* shúliàn de 熟练的，língqiǎo de 灵巧的

skill /skɪl/ *n* (*the quality*) jìyì 技艺，jìqiǎo 技巧；(*a particular ability*) jìnéng 技能，jìshù 技术

skin /skɪn/ *n* pífū 皮肤，pí 皮

skinny /'skɪnɪ/ *adj* (*thin*) jí shòu de 极瘦的，pí bāogǔ de 皮包骨的

skip /skɪp/ *vb* (*to give little jumps*) bèng 蹦；(*with a rope*) tiàoshéng 跳绳；**to skip classes** táoxué 逃学，táokè

逃课

ski resort /'ski: rɪˌzɔːt/ n a ski resort yí gè huáxuě shèngdì 一个滑雪胜地

skirt /skɜːt/ n a skirt yì tiáo qúnzi 一条裙子

sky /skaɪ/ n the sky tiān 天, tiānkōng 天空；a clear sky qínglǎng de tiānkōng 晴朗的天空

skydiving /'skaɪˌdaɪvɪŋ/ n tiàosǎn yùndòng 跳伞运动

slap /slæp/ vb to slap someone's face dǎ mǒu rén ěrguāng 打某人耳光；to slap someone on the back zài mǒu rén bèi shang pāi yí xià 在某人背上拍一下

sled /sled/ n, **sledge** /sledʒ/ (British English) **1** a sled yí gè xuěqiāo 一个雪橇 **2** vb to go sledging (British English) qù chéng xuěqiāo 去乘雪橇

sleep /sliːp/ n **1** shuìjiào 睡觉, shuìmián 睡眠；to go to sleep shuìzháo 睡着, rùshuì 入睡；I cannot go to sleep wǒ shuì bù zháo 我睡不着；to go back to sleep chóngxīn shuìzháo 重新睡着；to put someone to sleep shǐ mǒu rén rùshuì 使某人入睡 **2** vb (to be asleep) shuì 睡, shuìjiào 睡觉；to sleep with someone hé mǒu rén fāshēng xìngguānxì 和某人发生性关系, hé mǒu rén shuìjiào 和某人睡觉；sleep in (to let oneself sleep longer than usual) wǎn qǐchuáng 晚起床, shuì lǎnjiào 睡懒觉

sleeping bag /'sliːpɪŋ bæg/ n a sleeping bag yí gè shuìdài 一个睡袋

sleepy /'sliːpɪ/ adj to be sleepy, to feel sleepy xiǎng shuìjiào de 想睡觉的, gǎnjué kùn de 感觉困的

sleet /sliːt/ n yǔ jiā xuě 雨夹雪

sleeve /sliːv/ n a sleeve yì zhī xiùzi 一只袖子；to roll up one's sleeves juǎnqǐ xiùzi 卷起袖子

slice /slaɪs/ **1** n a slice of [bread|meat|lemon|cucumber] yí piàn [miànbāo|ròu|níngméng|huángguā] 一片 [面包|肉|柠檬|黄瓜] **2** vb to slice bread bǎ miànbāo qiēchéng piàn 把面包切成片

slide /slaɪd/ **1** vb (to slip or slide) huá 滑, huádòng 滑动；to slide on ice huábīng 滑冰；(to slip off) huáluò 滑落

落；the plates slid off the table pánzi cóng zhuōzi shang huáluò xiàqù 盘子从桌子上滑落下去 **2** *n* (*an image from a photograph*) **a slide** yì zhāng huàndēngpiàn 一张幻灯片；(*in a playground*) **a slide** yí gè huátī 一个滑梯

slim /slɪm/ **1** *adj* miáotiáo de 苗条的，xìcháng de 细长的 **2** *vb* (*British English*) jiǎnféi 减肥

slip /slɪp/ *vb* (*to glide or slide*) huá 滑，huádòng 滑动；(*to fall down by sliding*) huádǎo 滑倒；she slipped when coming down the mountain tā xiàshān de shíhou huádǎo le 她下山的时候滑倒了；(*to fall off by sliding*) huáluò 滑落；the glass slipped out of my hands bōlíbēi cóng wǒ shǒu zhōng huáluò xiàqù 玻璃杯从我手中滑落下去

slipper /'slɪpə(r)/ *n* **a slipper** yì zhī tuōxié 一只拖鞋；a pair of slippers yì shuāng tuōxié 一双拖鞋

slippery /'slɪpərɪ/ *adj* huá de 滑的

slot machine /'slɒt məˌʃiːn/ *n* **a slot machine** yì tái tóubì dǔbójī 一台投币赌博机

slow /sləʊ/ *adj* (*not fast*) màn de 慢的，huǎnmàn de 缓慢的；to make slow progress jìnbù hěn màn 进步很慢；(*not bright*) chídùn de 迟钝的，bèn de 笨的；(*describing a watch, a clock*) màn de 慢的；the clock is 20 minutes slow zhège zhōngbiǎo màn èrshí fēnzhōng 这个钟表慢 20 分钟；slow down fàngmàn sùdù 放慢速度，màn xiàlái 慢下来

slowly /'sləʊlɪ/ *adv* mànmàn de 慢慢地，huǎnmàn de 缓慢地

sly /slaɪ/ *adj* jiǎohuá de 狡猾的，jiǎozhà de 狡诈的

small /smɔːl/ *adj* xiǎo de 小的；a small car yí liàng xiǎoqìchē 一辆小汽车；a small quantity shǎoliàng 少量

small ad /'smɔːl æd/ *n* (*British English*) **a small ad** yí gè xiǎoguǎnggào 一个小广告

smart /smɑːt/ *adj* (*British English*) (*elegant*) xiāosǎ de 潇洒的，piàoliang de 漂亮的；(*intelligent*) cōngmíng de 聪明的，jīngmíng de 精明的

smash /smæʃ/ *vb* (*to break*) dǎsuì 打碎，dǎpò 打破；(*to*

get broken）pò pò，suì suì；**smash up** dǎohuǐ 搗毀，dǎpò 打破

smell /smel/ **1** n（*an odour*）a smell yì zhǒng qìwèi 一种气味；（*the sense*）the sense of smell xiùjué 嗅觉 **2** vb（*to perceive by nose*）wén 闻；I can smell burning wǒ néng wéndào húwèir 我能闻到糊味儿；（*to give off an odour*）this smells nice zhè wén qǐlai wén qǐlai hěn hǎowén 这闻起来很好闻

smile /smaɪl/ **1** vb xiào 笑，wēixiào 微笑；to smile at someone xiàng mǒu rén（wēi）xiào 向某人（微）笑 **2** n a smile xiào 笑，wēixiào 微笑

smoke /sməʊk/ **1** n yān 烟，yānqì 烟气 **2** vb（*to give off smoke*）màoyān 冒烟；（*to inhale and expel tobacco smoke*）chōuyān 抽烟，xīyān 吸烟；do you smoke? nǐ xīyān ma? 你吸烟吗?；（*to inhale and expel smoke from*）xī 吸，chōu 抽；to smoke a pipe chōu yāndǒu 抽烟斗

smooth /smuːð/ adj（*when describing a road, the ground*）píngtǎn de 平坦的；a smooth road yì tiáo píngtǎn de dàolù 一条平坦的道路；（*when describing the surface of paper, glass, a table, a floor*）guānghuá de 光滑的；the floor is very smooth dìmiàn hěn guānghuá 地面很光滑；（*when describing an action*）píngwěn de 平稳的；the flight was not very smooth fēixíng bú tài píngwěn 飞行不太平稳；（*when describing a writing style*）tōngshùn de 通顺的，liúchàng de 流畅的

smother /'smʌðə(r)/ vb（*to suffocate by excluding air*）shǐ…zhìxī 使…窒息，shǐ…tòu bú guò qì lái 使…透不过气来；to smother someone shǐ mǒu rén zhìxī 使某人窒息

snack /snæk/ n xiǎochī 小吃，kuàicān 快餐

snail /sneɪl/ n a snail yì zhī wōniú 一只蜗牛

snake /sneɪk/ n a snake yì tiáo shé 一条蛇

snapshot /'snæpʃɒt/ n a snapshot yì zhāng kuàizhào 一张快照

sneaker /'sniːkə(r)/ n（*US English*）a sneaker（*a shoe*）yì zhī yùndòngxié 一只运动鞋；a pair of sneakers yì shuāng yùndòngxié 一双运动鞋

sneeze /sniːz/ vb dǎ pēntì 打喷嚏

snobbish /'snɒbɪʃ/ adj shìlì de 势利的, chǎnshàng-qīxià de 谄上欺下的

snooker /'snuːkə(r)/ n táiqiú 台球

snore /snɔː(r)/ vb dǎhān 打鼾, dǎ hūlu 打呼噜

snow /snəʊ/ **1** n xuě 雪 **2** vb xiàxuě 下雪; it's snowing zhèngzài xiàxuě 正在下雪

snowball /'snəʊbɔːl/ n a snowball yí gè xuěqiú 一个雪球

snowman /'snəʊmæn/ n a snowman yí gè xuěrén 一个雪人

so /səʊ/ 弱 sə/ **1** adv (to such an extent) zhème 这么, nàme 那么; he's so [happy | stupid | smart...] tā nàme [gāoxìng | bèn | cōngmíng] 他那么 [高兴 | 笨 | 聪明…]; they speak so fast tāmen shuō de zhème kuài 他们说得这么快; I have so much work to do wǒ yǒu zhème duō gōngzuò yào zuò 我有这么多工作要做; (also) yě 也! Note that in this sense, the meaning conveyed by so in English has to be stated overtly in Chinese; I'm fifteen and so is he wǒ shíwǔ suì, tā yě shíwǔ suì 我 15 岁,他也 15 岁; if you go, so will I rúguǒ nǐ qù, wǒ yě qù 如果你去,我也去; (very) fēicháng 非常, hěn 很; I'm so pleased to hear the news tīngdào zhège xiāoxi, wǒ fēicháng gāoxìng 听到这个消息,我非常高兴; (other uses) I think so wǒ xiǎng shì zhèyàng 我想是这样; I'm afraid so kǒngpà shì zhèyàng 恐怕是这样; who says so? shéi shuō de? 谁说的?; so what? nà yòu zěnyàng ne? 那又怎样呢?; and so on děngděng 等等 **2** conj (therefore) suǒyǐ 所以, yīncǐ 因此; she was sick, so I went to see her tā bìngle, suǒyǐ wǒ qù kàn tā 她病了,所以我去看她; so (that) yǐbiàn 以便, wèi de shì 为的是; he moved to a house near his mother, so that he could look after her better tā bāndào lí tā mā hěn jìn de yì suǒ fángzi, yǐbiàn néng gèng hǎo de zhàogù tā 他搬到离他妈很近的一所房子,以便他能更好地照顾她; (then, in that case) nàme

那么，zhèyàng kànlái 这样看来；so you are going to study Chinese nàme nǐ dǎsuàn xué Zhōngwén le 那么你打算学中文了 3 so as yǐbiàn 以便，wèi de shì 为的是；we left early so as not to miss the train wǒmen hěn zǎo jiù líkāi le，wèi de shì bú wù huǒchē 我们很早就离开了，为的是不误火车

soap /səup/ n (for washing) féizào 肥皂；(on TV) a soap yí bù féizàojù 一部肥皂剧

soccer /'sɒkə(r)/ n zúqiú 足球

social /'səuʃəl/ adj (relating to society) shèhuì de 社会的；(sociable) xǐhuan jiāojì de 喜欢交际的

social studies /'səuʃəl ˌstʌdiz/ n shèhuì yánjiū 社会研究，shèhuìxué 社会学

social worker /'səuʃəl wɜːkə(r)/ n a social worker yí gè shèhuìgōngzuòzhě 一个社会工作者

sock /sɒk/ n a sock yì zhī duǎnwà 一只短袜；a pair of socks yì shuāng duǎnwà 一双短袜

sofa /'səufə/ n a sofa yí gè shāfā 一个沙发

soft /sɒft/ adj (not hard or tough) ruǎn de 软的；the ground is soft here zhèr de dì hěn ruǎn 这儿的地很软，a soft toffee yí kuài ruǎn nǎitáng 一块软奶糖；(when describing colours, lights, voice) róuhé de 柔和的；soft lights róuhé de dēngguāng 柔和的灯光；(when describing a manner, an action) wēnhé de 温和的；a soft answer yí gè wēnhé de dáfù 一个温和的答复；(yielding easily to pressure) ruǎnruò de 软弱的，shùncóng de 顺从的；you are too soft with him nǐ duì tā tài ruǎnruò 你对他太软弱；soft drinks ruǎnyǐnliào 软饮料

software /'sɒftweə(r)/ n ruǎnjiàn 软件

soldier /'səuldʒə(r)/ n a soldier yí gè shìbīng 一个士兵，yí gè zhànshì 一个战士

sole /səul/ n the sole (of the foot) jiǎodǐ 脚底；(of a shoe) a sole yí gè xiédǐ 一个鞋底

solicitor /sə'lɪsɪtə(r)/ n (British English) a solicitor yí gè lǜshī 一个律师

solution /sə'lju:ʃən/ n a solution yí gè jiějué bànfǎ 一个解决办法

solve /sɒlv/ vb jiě 解，jiějué 解决；to solve a problem jiějué yí gè wèntí 解决一个问题

some /sʌm/ **1** det (an amount or number of)；(when used in mid-sentence) yìxiē 一些；I have to buy some bread wǒ děi mǎi yìxiē miànbāo 我得买一些面包；she ate some strawberries tā chīle yìxiē cǎoméi 她吃了一些草莓；we visited some beautiful towns wǒmen fǎngwènle yìxiē měilì de chéngzhèn 我们访问了一些美丽的城镇；(when used at the beginning of a sentence) yǒuxiē 有些；some shops don't open on Sunday yǒuxiē shāngdiàn xīngqītiān bù kāimén 有些商店星期天不开门；(certain) mǒu (yī) 某（一）；she is studying at some university in Beijing tā zài Běijīng de mǒu (yì) suǒ dàxué xuéxí 她在北京的某（一）所大学学习；some people don't like travelling by plane mǒu (yì) xiē rén bù xǐhuan zuò fēijī lǚxíng 某（一）些人不喜欢坐飞机旅行 **2** pron (an amount or number of)，(when used in mid-sentence) yìxiē 一些；I know where you can find some wǒ zhīdào zài nǎr nǐ néng zhǎodào yìxiē 我知道在哪儿你能找到一些；(when used at the beginning of a sentence) yǒu yìxiē 有一些；some are useful yǒu yìxiē hěn yǒuyòng 有一些很有用；(certain people) yǒu (yì) xiē rén 有（一）些人；some (of them) are Chinese (tāmen dāngzhōng) yǒu yìxiē rén shì Zhōngguórén （他们当中）有一些人是中国人；(certain things) yǒu (yì) xiē dōngxi 有（一）些东西；some are quite expensive yǒu yìxiē dōngxi xiāngdāng guì 有一些东西相当贵

someone /'sʌmwʌn/ pron (also somebody) mǒu rén 某人，mǒu (yí) gè rén 某（一）个人；someone famous mǒu yí gè yǒumíng de rén 某一个有名的人

something /'sʌmθɪŋ/ pron (an undefined thing) yí gè dōngxi 一个东西，mǒu wù 某物；I saw something interesting wǒ kàndào yí gè yǒuqù de dōngxi 我看到一个

有趣的东西；(an undefined matter) yí jiàn shì 一件事，mǒu shì 某事；I'd like to discuss something with you wǒ xiǎng gēn nǐ tǎolùn yí jiàn shì 我想跟你讨论一件事

sometimes /'sʌmtaɪmz/ adv yǒushíhou 有时候，yǒushí 有时

somewhere /'sʌmhweə(r)/ adv zài mǒu (yí) ge dìfang 在某(一)个地方，zài shénme dìfang 在什么地方；they live somewhere in Scotland tāmen zhù zài Sūgélán de mǒu ge dìfang 他们住在苏格兰的某个地方；let's go somewhere else zánmen qù lìngwài yí ge dìfang ba 咱们去另外一个地方吧

son /sʌn/ n a son yí ge érzi 一个儿子

song /sɒŋ/ n a song yì shǒu gē 一首歌，yì zhī gē 一支歌

son-in-law /'sʌnɪnlɔ:/ n a son-in-law yí ge nǚxu 一个女婿

soon /su:n/ adv (before long, in a short time) hěn kuài 很快，bùjiǔ 不久；he'll go to China soon tā hěn kuài jiùyào qù Zhōngguó le 他很快就要去中国了；(in a moment) yìhuǐr 一会儿；I'll come back soon wǒ yíhuǐr jiù huílái 我一会儿就回来；(early) zǎo 早，the sooner the better yuè zǎo yuè hǎo 越早越好；as soon as possible jínzǎo 尽早，(quickly) kuài 快；as soon as possible jínkuài 尽快；come as soon as you can nǐ jínkěnéng kuài lái 你尽可能快来

sore /sɔ:(r)/ adj to have a sore [throat | leg | back...] [sǎngzi | tuǐ | hòubèi...]téng [嗓子 | 腿 | 后背...]疼；my arm is very sore wǒ de gēbo hěn téng 我的胳膊很疼

sorry /'sɒrɪ/ adj (when apologizing) duìbuqǐ de 对不起的，bàoqiàn de 抱歉的；sorry! duìbuqǐ! 对不起!；I'm sorry I'm late duìbuqǐ, wǒ lái wǎn le 对不起，我来晚了；to say sorry shuō duìbuqǐ 说对不起；(when expressing regret) yíhàn de 遗憾的；I'm sorry you can't come hěn yíhàn nǐ bù néng lái 很遗憾你不能来；(when expressing regret for what one did in the past) hòuhuǐ de 后悔的，àohuǐ de 懊悔的；I feel very sorry for what I did wǒ duì wǒ suǒ zuò de shì gǎndào hěn hòuhuǐ 我对我所做的事感到很后悔;(when expressing pity or sympathy) nánguò de 难过的，wǎnxī de 惋惜的;to feel sorry for someone wèi mǒu rén nánguò 为某人难过

sort /sɔːt/ **1** n zhǒng 种，lèi 类;it's a sort of [bird | computer | loan...] zhè shì yì zhǒng [niǎo | jìsuànjī | dàikuǎn...]这是一种 [鸟|计算机|贷款...];he's not that sort of person tā bú shì nà lèi rén 他不是那类人 **2** vb (to classify) bǎ…fēnlèi 把…分类;to sort files bǎ dàng'àn fēnlèi 把档案分类;(to arrange) zhěnglǐ 整理;to sort the books into piles bǎ shū zhěnglǐ chéng yí luò yí luò de 把书整理成一摞一摞的;**sort out** (to solve) jiějué 解决;to sort out a problem jiějué yí gè wèntí 解决一个问题;(to deal with) chǔlǐ 处理;I'll sort it out wǒ huì chǔlǐ zhè jiàn shì 我会处理这件事;(to arrange and organize) zhěnglǐ 整理;to sort out these documents zhěnglǐ zhèxiē wénjiàn 整理这些文件;(to classify) bǎ…fēnlèi 把…分类;to sort out the photos bǎ zhàopiàn fēnlèi 把照片分类;to sort out the old clothes from the new bǎ yīfu àn xīn-jiù fēnlèi 把衣服按新旧分类

sound /saʊnd/ **1** n shēng 声，shēngyīn 声音;a sound yí gè shēngyīn 一个声音;I heard the sound of voices wǒ tīngjiàn shuōhuàshēng le 我听见说话声了;to turn up the sound of the television bǎ diànshìjī de shēngyīn tiáodà 把电视机的声音调大;the sound of a piano gāngqínshēng 钢琴声 **2** vb (to give out a sound) xiǎng 响;the alarm clock sounded at 7 o'clock nàozhōng qī diǎn xiǎng le 闹钟 7 点响了;(to give an impression on hearing) tīng qǐlai 听起来;it sounds [dangerous | odd | interesting...] zhè tīng qǐlai [hěn wēixiǎn | hěn qíguài | hěn yǒuyìsi...]这听起来 [很危险|很奇怪|很有意思...];it sounds like a piano zhè tīng qǐlai xiàng gāngqín 这听起来像钢琴

soup /suːp/ n a soup yí gè tāng 一个汤

sour /saʊə(r)/ adj suān de 酸的;the milk has gone sour niúnǎi suān le 牛奶酸了

south /saʊθ/ **1** n the south nánfāng 南方，nánbù 南部；in the south of China zài Zhōngguó de nánfāng 在中国的南方 **2** adv to go south qù nánfāng 去南方；to live south of Beijing zhù zài Běijīng de nánbù 住在北京的南部 **3** adj nánbù de 南部的；to work in south London zài Lúndūn nánbù gōngzuò 在伦敦南部工作

South Africa /ˌsaʊθ ˈæfrɪkə/ n Nánfēi 南非

South America /ˌsaʊθ əˈmerɪkə/ n Nánměizhōu 南美洲

southeast /ˌsaʊθˈiːst/ n the southeast dōngnán 东南

southwest /ˌsaʊθˈwest/ n the southwest xīnán 西南

souvenir /ˌsuːvəˈnɪə(r)/ n a souvenir yí gè jìniànpǐn 一个纪念品

space /speɪs/ n (room) kōngjiān 空间；to take up space zhàn kōngjiān 占空间；(an area of land or a place) kòng-dì 空地，dìfang 地方；an open space yí kuài kòng-dì 一块空地；(outer space) tàikōng 太空；(a gap) kòng 空，kòngbái 空白；a space yí gè kòng 一个空；fill the spaces with verbs yòng dòngcí tiánkòng 用动词填空

Spain /speɪn/ n Xībānyá 西班牙

Spanish /ˈspænɪʃ/ **1** adj Xībānyá de 西班牙的，Xībānyárén de 西班牙人的 **2** n xībānyáyǔ 西班牙语，Xībānyáwén 西班牙文

spare /speə(r)/ adj (extra) duōyú de 多余的；I've got a spare ticket wǒ yǒu yì zhāng duōyú de piào 我有一张多余的票；(not in actual use) kòng de 空的；are there any spare seats? hái yǒu kòng zuòwèi ma? 还有空座位吗？

spare part /ˌspeə ˈpɑːt/ n a spare part yí gè bèijiàn 一个备件

spare room /ˌspeə ˈruːm/ n a spare room yì jiān kōng fángjiān 一间空房间

spare time /ˌspeə ˈtaɪm/ n kòngyú shíjiān 空余时间

speak /spiːk/ vb (utter words) shuōhuà 说话，jiǎnghuà 讲话；to speak to a friend gēn yí gè péngyou shuōhuà 跟一个朋友说话；who's speaking, please? qǐng wèn, nín shì nǎ wèi? 请问，您是哪位？；generally speaking yìbān shuōlái 一般说来；(to utter) shuō 说，jiǎng 讲；to speak Japanese shuō Rìyǔ 说日语；speak up (to speak boldly) dàdǎn de shuō 大胆地说；(to speak so as to be heard easily) qīngchǔ xiǎngliàng de shuō 清楚响亮地说

special /'speʃəl/ adj (exceptional) tèshū de 特殊的，tèbié de 特别的；a special purpose yí gè tèshū de mùdì 一个特殊的目的；(designed for a particular purpose) zhuānmén de 专门的；a special school yì suǒ zhuānmén de xuéxiào 一所专门的学校；(intimate) tèbié qīnmì de 特别亲密的；she's a special friend of mine tā shì wǒ tèbié qīnmì de péngyou 她是我特别亲密的朋友

speciality /ˌspeʃɪ'ælətɪ/ (British English)，**specialty** /'speʃəltɪ/ (US English) n (an occupation or area of study) yì mén zhuānyè 一门专业；(a skill) yí gè tècháng 一个特长，yí gè zhuāncháng 一个专长；(a product) yí gè tèchǎn 一个特产

specially /'speʃəlɪ/ adv tèyì de 特意地，tèdì 特地

spectator /spek'teɪtə(r)/ n a spectator yí gè guānzhòng 一个观众

speech /spiːtʃ/ n a speech yí gè jiǎnghuà 一个讲话，yí gè fāyán 一个发言

speed /spiːd/ 1 n (rate of progress) sùdù 速度 2 vb to speed away kuàisù kāizǒu 快速开走，kuàisù shǐqù 快速驶去；(to drive too fast) chāosù xíngshǐ 超速行驶；speed up jiāsù 加速，zēngsù 增速

speed limit /'spiːd ˌlɪmɪt/ n sùdù jíxiàn 速度极限

spell /spel/ vb (to give letters of a word in order)；(when speaking) pīn 拼，pīndú 拼读；(when writing) pīn 拼，pīnxiě 拼写；how do you spell this word? zhège cí (nǐ) zěnme pīn? 这个词(你)怎么拼?

spelling /'spelɪŋ/ n pīnfǎ 拼法

spend /spend/ vb (to pay out) huā 花；how much money have you spent? nǐ huāle duōshao qián? 你花了多少钱?；(to give or bestow for any purpose) huā 花，huāfèi 花费，yòng 用；she spent lots of her time and energy in helping me tā huāfèile hěn duō shíjiān hé jīnglì lái bāngzhù wǒ 她花费了很多时间和精力来帮助我；he spent an hour writing a letter to his girlfriend tā huàle yí gè xiǎoshí gěi tā de nǚpéngyou xiě xin 他花了一个小时给他的女朋友写信；(to pass, as time) guò 过，dùguò 度过；I shall spend my Christmas in China wǒ jiāng zài Zhōngguó guò Shèngdàn Jié 我将在中国过圣诞节

spider /'spaɪdə(r)/ n a spider yì zhī zhīzhū 一只蜘蛛

spill /spɪl/ vb (to cause to pour or flow over) shǐ/bǎ…sǎ 使/把…洒；don't spill the milk bié bǎ niúnǎi sǎ chūlái 别把牛奶洒出来；(to flow over or fall out) yìchū 溢出，jiànchū 溅出

spinach /'spɪnɪdʒ/ n bōcài 菠菜

spit /spɪt/ vb (to eject from mouth) tǔ 吐；(to eject saliva) tǔtán 吐痰

spite /spaɪt/; in spite of prep jǐnguǎn 尽管；we went out in spite of the rain jǐnguǎn xiàyǔ, wǒmen háishì chūqù le 尽管下雨，我们还是出去了！Note that the phrase introduced by jǐnguǎn 尽管 must be at the beginning of the sentence.

spiteful /'spaɪtful/ adj yǒu èyì de 有恶意的，yǒu yuànhèn de 有怨恨的

spoil /spɔɪl/ vb (to mar) huǐle 毁了，nòngzāo 弄糟，gǎozāo 搞糟；the rain spoilt [the party | the football match | the picnic] yǔ bǎ [jùhuì | zúqiú bǐsài | yěcān] huǐle 雨把 [聚会 | 足球比赛 | 野餐] 毁了；(to ruin, to damage) sǔnhuài 损坏，(as a parent) jiāoguàn 娇惯，guànhuài 惯坏；to spoil a child jiāoguàn háizi 娇惯孩子

sponge /spʌndʒ/ n a sponge yí kuài hǎimián 一块海绵

spoon /spuːn/ n a spoon yì bǎ sháozi 一把勺子，yì bǎ chízi 一把匙子

sport /spɔːt/ n a sport yì zhǒng yùndòng 一种运动，yì zhǒng tǐyù 一种体育；to be good at sports shàncháng tǐyù yùndòng 擅长体育运动

sports centre /ˈspɔːts sentə(r)/ (British English), **sports center** (US English) n a sports centre yí gè tǐyù (yùndòng) zhōngxīn 一个体育(运动)中心

sports club /ˈspɔːts klʌb/ n a sports club yí gè tǐyù jùlèbù 一个体育俱乐部

spot /spɒt/ 1 n (on an animal) a spot yí gè bāndiǎn 一个斑点; (British English) (on the face or body) a spot yí gè bāndiǎn 一个斑点, yí gè hēidiǎn 一个黑点; (dirt mark or stain) a spot yí gè wūdiǎn 一个污点; (a place) a spot yí gè dìdiǎn 一个地点; on the spot dāngchǎng 当场, xiànchǎng 现场 2 vb (to detect) fāxiàn 发现; (to see someone you recognize) rènchū 认出

sprain /sprein/ vb niǔshāng 扭伤; to sprain one's wrist niǔshāng shǒuwàn 扭伤手腕

spring /sprɪŋ/ n chūntiān 春天, chūnjì 春季; the Spring Festival (the Chinese New Year) Chūn Jié 春节

spy /spai/ n a spy yí gè jiàndié 一个间谍, yí gè mìtàn 一个密探, yí gè tèwù 一个特务

square /skweə(r)/ 1 n (the shape) a square yí gè zhèngfāngxíng 一个正方形; (in a town) a square yí gè guǎngchǎng 一个广场 2 adj (having the geometrical form) zhèngfāngxíng de 正方形的, fāng de 方的

squash /skwɒʃ/ 1 n (the sport) bìqiú 壁球 2 vb (to crush flat) bǎ…yābiǎn 把…压扁; be careful not to squash the tomatoes xiǎoxīn bié bǎ xīhóngshì yābiǎn le 小心别把西红柿压扁了; (to crowd) jǐ(rù) 挤(入), jǐ (jìn) 挤(进); they managed to squash into the lift tāmen shèfǎ jǐjìnle diàntī 他们设法挤进了电梯

squeak /skwiːk/ vb zhīzhī de jiào 吱吱地叫

squeeze /skwiːz/ vb (for the purpose of getting juice) zhà 榨; to squeeze [oranges | lemons | apples…] zhà [júzi | níngméng | píngguǒ…] zhī 榨 [橘子 | 柠檬 | 苹果…] 汁; (to injure) jǐshāng 挤伤; to squeeze one's fingers jǐshāng shǒuzhǐ 挤伤手指; (showing affection or friendship) to squeeze someone's hand jǐnwò mǒu rén de shǒu 紧握某

人的手；to squeeze something into a bag 往一个包里塞某件东西 往一个包里塞某件东西 wǎng yí gè bāo li sāi mǒu jiàn dōngxi；all six people were squeezed into a small car 6 个人都挤在一辆小汽车里 liù gè rén dōu jǐ zài yí liàng xiǎoqìchē li

squirrel /'skwɪrəl/ n a squirrel yì zhī sōngshǔ 一只松鼠

stable /'steɪbl/ **1** n a stable yí gè mǎjiù 一个马厩；a stable yí gè mǎpéng 一个马棚 **2** adj（constant and not ready to change）wěndìng de 稳定的；（firmly fixed）láogù de 牢固的，jiāngù de 坚固的

stadium /'steɪdɪəm/ n a stadium yí gè tǐyùchǎng 一个体育场，yí gè yùndòngchǎng 一个运动场

staff /stɑːf/ n the staff（of a company, a bank）quántǐ zhíyuán 全体职员；（of a school, a college）quántǐ jiàozhíyuán 全体教职员

stage /steɪdʒ/ n（a step in development）jiēduàn 阶段；a stage yí gè jiēduàn 一个阶段；a stage（for a performance）yí gè wǔtái 一个舞台；（for a speech）yí gè jiǎngtái 一个讲台

stain /steɪn/ **1** n a stain yí gè wūdiǎn 一个污点 **2** vb（to soil or change the colour of）zhānwū 沾污；（to bring disgrace upon）diànwū 玷污

stairs /steəz/ n lóutī 楼梯；to fall down the stairs cóng lóutī shang shuāi xiàlái 从楼梯上摔下来

stamp /stæmp/ n（for postage）a stamp yì zhāng yóupiào 一张邮票；（an imprinted mark）a stamp yí gè chuō 一个戳，yí gè yìn 一个印；（a tool for marking）a stamp yì méi túzhāng 一枚图章

stamp-collecting /'stæmp kəlektɪŋ/ n jíyóu 集邮

stand /stænd/ vb zhàn 站；he stood by the window tā zhàn zài chuānghu pángbiān 他站在窗户旁边；to stay standing, to remain standing zhànzhe bú dòng 站着不动；（to be situated）zuòluò 坐落，wèiyú 位于；the house stands by a river nà zuò fángzi zuòluò zài yì tiáo hébiān 那座房子坐落在一条河边；（to put）to stand a vase on a table bǎ yí gè huāpíng fàng zài zhuōzi shang 把一个花

瓶放在桌子上；(to step) to stand on a nail cǎi zài yí gè dīngzi shang 踩在一个钉子上；(to bear) rěnshòu 忍受；can you stand the hot weather there? nǐ néng shòudeliǎo nàr de rè tiānqì ma? 你能受得了那儿的热天气吗？；he can't stand playing football tī zúqiú tā shòubuliǎo 踢足球他受不了；(other uses) to stand in someone's way fáng'ài mǒu rén 妨碍某人, dǎng mǒu rén de dào 挡某人的道；to stand for election (British English) cānjiā jìngxuǎn 参加竞选；to stand trial shòushěn 受审；**stand back** wǎng hòu zhàn 往后站, tuìhòu 退后；**stand for** (to represent) dàibiǎo 代表；(to mean) yìsi shì 意思是, yìwèizhe 意味着；**stand out** (to be prominent) tūchū 突出, chūsè 出色；**stand up** to stand up zhàn qǐlái 站起来；(given as an order in the classroom or the army) stand up! qǐlì! 起立！；to stand someone up (fail to keep an appointment) gēn mǒu rén shīyuē 跟某人失约；**stand up for** (to support) zhīchí 支持；(to defend) hànwèi 捍卫；to stand up for one's rights hànwèi zìjǐ de quánlì 捍卫自己的权利；**stand up to** (to meet face to face) yǒnggǎn de miànduì 勇敢地面对；to stand up to the hooligans yǒnggǎn de miànduì liúmáng 勇敢地面对流氓；(to show resistance to) dǐkàng 抵抗

star /stɑ:(r)/ n (in space) a star yì kē xīng 一颗星；(a famous person) a star yí gè míngxīng 一个明星

stare /steə(r)/ vb dīngzhe kàn 盯着看, mùbùzhuǎnjīng de kàn 目不转睛地看；to stare at someone dīngzhe kàn mǒu rén 盯着看某人

start /stɑ:t/ **1** vb (to begin) kāishǐ 开始；to start [working/writing letters/running...] kāishǐ [gōngzuò/xiěxìn/pǎo...] 开始 [工作/写信/跑...]；you should start by phoning them nǐ yīnggāi kāishǐ xiān gěi tāmen dǎ diànhuà 你应该开始先给他们打电话；(to begin one's working life) to start (out) as a teacher kāishǐ dāng lǎoshī 开始当老师；(to set out) chūfā 出发, dòngshēn 动身；when will you start for China? nǐ shénme shíhou chūfā qù Zhōngguó? 你什么时候出发去中国?；(to cause) fādòng 发动；to start a war fādòng yì chǎng zhànzhēng 发动一场战争；(to begin working) fādòng 发动, qǐdòng 起动；the car won't start qìchē fādòng bù qǐlái 汽车发动不起来；(to put into action) kāi(dòng) 开(动)；to start [a car | a machine] kāidòng [qìchē|jīqì] 开动 [汽车|机器]；(to set up and run) kāibàn 开办, chuàngbàn 创办；they've decided to start a new school in the village tāmen juédìng zài cūn li kāibàn yì suǒ xīn xuéxiào 他们决定村里开办一所新学校 **2** n a start yí gè kāishǐ 一个开始, yí gè kāiduān 一个开端；at the start of [the race | the meeting | the week] [bǐsài|huìyì|zhège xīngqí] kāishǐ de shíhou [比赛|会议|这个星期]开始的时候；**start off** (to set out) chūfā 出发, dòngshēn 动身；(to begin) kāishǐ 开始；**start over** (US English) chóngxīn kāishǐ 重新开始

starter /'stɑːtə(r)/ n (British English) (of a meal) tóupán 头盘；a starter yí gè tóupán 一个头盘

state /steɪt/ n (a country) guójiā 国家；a state yí gè guójiā 一个国家；(a constituent member of a federation) zhōu 州；a state yí gè zhōu 一个州；(a government) the State zhèngfǔ 政府；(a condition) zhuàngtài 状态, zhuàngkuàng 状况；the state of her health is worrying tā de jiànkāng zhuàngkuàng hěn lìng rén dānyōu 她的健康状况很令人担忧；to be in a bad state of repair xūyào xiūlǐ 需要修理

statement /'steɪtmənt/ n a statement (an account) yí gè chénshù 一个陈述；(a formal declaration or account) yí xiàng shēngmíng 一项声明

station /'steɪʃən/ n (for trains or coaches) zhàn 站；a [train|coach] station yí gè [huǒchē|qìchē] zhàn 一个 [火车|汽车]站；(on TV or radio) tái 台；a [TV|radio] station yí gè [diànshì|guǎngbō diàn]tái 一个 [电视|广播电]台

statue /'stætʃuː/ n a statue yí zuò diāoxiàng 一座雕像, yí zuò sùxiàng 一座塑像

stay /steɪ/ **1** vb (to remain) dāi 呆/待，tíngliú 停留；we stayed there for a week wǒmen zài nàr dāile yí gè xīngqī 我们在那儿呆了一个星期；(to have accommodation) zhù 住；to stay with friends yǔ péngyou zhù zài yìqǐ 与朋友住在一起 **2** n she enjoyed her stay in Shanghai tā zài Shànghǎi guò de hěn yúkuài 她在上海过得很愉快；to make a short stay here zài zhèr duǎnqī zhù yí duàn shíjiān 在这儿短期住一段时间；**stay away from** bú qù 不去；to stay away from school bú qù shàngxué 不去上学；**stay in** dāi zài jiā lǐ 呆在家里，bù chūmén 不出门；**stay out** dāi zài wàimian 呆在外面，bù huíjiā 不回家；to stay out late dāi zài wàimian hěn wǎn (bù huíjiā) 呆在外面很晚（不回家）；**stay up** (to keep late hours) bú shuìjiào 不睡觉

steady /'stedɪ/ adj (constant, stable) wěndìng de 稳定的，bú biàn de 不变的；to keep up a steady speed bǎochí wěndìng de sùdù 保持稳定的速度；(not likely to move) wěngù de 稳固的

steak /steɪk/ n a steak(beef) yí kuài niúpái 一块牛排；(fish) yí kuài yú 一块鱼

steal /stiːl/ vb (to practise theft) tōu dōngxi 偷东西；to steal from someone cóng mǒu rén nàr tōu dōngxi 从某人那儿偷东西；(to take by theft) tōu 偷；to steal money from someone cóng mǒu rén nàr tōu qián 从某人那儿偷钱

steam /stiːm/ n zhēngqì 蒸汽，shuǐzhēngqì 水蒸气

steel /stiːl/ n gāng 钢，gāngtiě 钢铁

steep /stiːp/ adj (when describing a rise or decline in price, living standards) jíjù de 急剧的；(when describing a road or a mountain) dǒu 陡，dǒuqiào de 陡峭的

steering wheel /'stɪərɪŋ hwiːl/ n a steering wheel(of a car or lorry) yí gè fāngxiàngpán 一个方向盘

step /step/ **1** n (when walking) bù 步；a step yí bù 一步；to take a step mài/zǒu yí bù 迈/走一步；(in a flight of stairs) tījí 梯级；a step yí gè tījí 一个梯级；(in front of a

door, a doorstep) táijiē 台阶；a step yí gè táijiē 一个台
阶；(*one of a series of actions*) bùzhòu 步骤；to take
steps cǎiqǔ bùzhòu 采取步骤 **2** *vb* (*to walk*) zǒu 走；to
step into the house zǒujìn fángzi 走进房子；(*to
advance by taking a step or steps*) màibù 迈步；to step
on a nail cǎi zài dīngzi shang 踩在钉子上；step aside
zǒudào pángbiān qù 走到旁边去，kào biān zhàn 靠边站

stepbrother /'stepˌbrʌðə(r)/ *n* a stepbrother (*elder
brother by a stepmother*) yí gè yìmǔ gēge 一个异母哥哥；
(*younger brother by a stepmother*) yí gè yìmǔ dìdi 一个异
母弟弟；(*elder brother by a stepfather*) yí gè yìfù gēge 一
个异父哥哥；(*younger brother by a stepfather*) yí gè yìfù
dìdi 一个异父弟弟

stepfather /'stepfɑːðə(r)/ *n* a stepfather yí gè jìfù 一个
继父，yí gè yìfù 一个异父

stepmother /'stepmʌðə(r)/ *n* a stepmother yí gè jìmǔ
一个继母，yí gè yìmǔ 一个异母

stepsister /'stepsɪstə(r)/ *n* a stepsister (*elder sister by
a stepfather*) yí gè yìfù jiějie 一个异父姐姐，(*younger
sister by a stepfather*) yí gè yìfù mèimei 一个异父妹妹；
(*elder sister by a stepmother*) yí gè yìmǔ jiějie 一个异母
姐姐；(*younger sister by a stepmother*) yí gè yìmǔ mèimei
一个异母妹妹

stereo /'steriəʊ/ *n* a stereo yì tái lìtǐshēng shōulùjī 一台
立体声收录机

stewardess /'stjʊədɪs/ *n* a stewardess(*on a plane*) yí
gè kōng(zhōng xiǎo)jiě 一个空(中小)姐；(*on a ship*) yí
gè nǚfúwùyuán 一个女服务员

stick /stɪk/ **1** *vb* (*using glue or tape*) tiē 贴，zhān 粘；to
stick a stamp on an envelope zài xìnfēng shang tiē
yóupiào 在信封上贴邮票；(*to attach by a pin or clip*) bié
别；she stuck her badge onto her coat tā bǎ tā de páizi
bié zài wàiyī shang 她把她的牌子别在外衣上；(*when
something pointed is pushed into or through something
else*) cì 刺，chā 插；he stuck the fork into the meat tā

bǎ chāzi chājìn ròu lǐ 他把叉子插进肉里；(to become unmovable) qiǎzhù 卡住；the door is stuck mén qiǎzhù le 门卡住了；(to reach an obstacle, to be stumped) nánzhù 难住；I'm stuck by this problem wǒ bèi zhège wèntí nánzhù le 我被这个问题难住了 **2** n (a piece of wood) a stick yì gēn zhītiáo 一根枝条；(for walking) shǒuzhàng 手杖；a stick yì gēn shǒuzhàng 一根手杖；**stick at** to stick at one's work jiānchí gōngzuò 坚持工作；**stick out** shēnchū 伸出，tūchū 凸出；there's a nail sticking out yǒu yí gè dīngzi shēn chūlái 有一个钉子伸出来

sticky tape /'stɪkɪ teɪp/ n (British English) jiāodài 胶带

stiff /stɪf/ adj (not soft, not supple) jiāngyìng de 僵硬的，jiāngzhí de 僵直的；I had stiff legs wǒ de tuǐ gǎndào jiāngyìng 我的腿感到僵硬；(not easy to move) bù línghuó de 不灵活的；(rigid and hard) yìng de 硬的；this pair of shoes is too stiff zhè shuāng xié tài yìng le 这双鞋太硬了

still[1] /stɪl/ adv (when indicating no change) hái 还，réngrán 仍然；does she still play the piano? tā hái tán gāngqín ma? 她还弹钢琴吗?；I still don't understand why you left wǒ réngrán bù míngbai nǐ wèishénme líkāi 我仍然不明白你为什么离开；she could still win tā hái néng yíng 她还能赢；(used in comparisons) gèng(jiā) 更(加)，háiyào 还要；it is hot today, but it'll be still hotter tomorrow jīntiān hěn rè，dànshì míngtiān huì gèng rè 今天很热,但是明天会更热

still[2] /stɪl/ adj (quiet) jìjìng de 寂静的，ānjìng de 安静的；(motionless) jìngzhǐ de 静止的，bú dòng de 不动的；to sit still zuòzhe bú dòng 坐着不动

sting /stɪŋ/ vb to sting someone (if it's a wasp or an insect) zhē mǒu rén 蜇某人，(if it's a mosquito) dīng mǒu rén 叮某人，yǎo mǒu rén 咬某人；(feel sharp pain) gǎndào cìtòng 感到刺痛

stir /stɜː(r)/ vb (to use an implement to mix something) jiǎodòng 搅动，jiǎohuo 搅和；**to stir the coffee with a spoon** yòng sháozi jiǎodòng kāfēi 用勺子搅动咖啡；(*to cause a sensation in*) hōngdòng 轰动；**the news stirred the whole school** zhè tiáo xiāoxi hōngdòngle quánxiào 这条消息轰动了全校；**stir up hatred** shāndòng chóuhèn 煽动仇恨，tiǎoqǐ chóuhèn 挑起仇恨；**stir up patriotism** jīqǐ àiguózhǔyì 激起爱国主义

stomach /'stʌmək/ *n* the stomach wèi 胃，dùzi 肚子；**to have a pain in one's stomach** wèi téng 胃疼，dùzi téng 肚子疼

stone /stəʊn/ *n* a stone(*a piece of rock*) yí kuài shítou 一块石头；(*a gem*) yí kuài bǎoshí 一块宝石，yí kuài zuànshí 一块钻石；(*the hard seed of a fruit*) hé 核；**an apricot stone** yí gè xìnghé 一个杏核

stop /stɒp/ **1** *vb* (*to put an end to*) tíngzhǐ 停止；**to stop** [laughing | working | learning Chinese] tíngzhǐ [xiào | gōngzuò | xué Zhōngwén]停止 [笑 | 工作 | 学中文]；**to stop smoking** jièyān 戒烟；(*when giving an order*) bié 别，búyào 不要！ Note that when **bié 别** or **búyào 不要** is used to stop what is going on, **le 了** is required at the end of the sentence；**to stop** [talking | writing | playing football]! bié [shuōhuà | xiě | tī zúqiú] le! 别 [说话 | 写 | 踢足球]了！；(*to prevent*) zǔzhǐ 阻止；**to stop someone from** [leaving | playing the violin | talking] zǔzhǐ mǒu rén [líkāi | lā xiǎotíqín | jiǎnghuà] 阻止某人 [离开 | 拉小提琴 | 讲话]；(*to come to a halt*) tíng 停；**the bus didn't stop** qìchē méi tíng 汽车没停；(*when talking about noise, weather, music*) tíng 停，tíngzhǐ 停止；**suddenly the noise stopped** tūrán zàoshēng tíng(zhǐ) le 突然噪声停(止)了；**it's stopped raining** yǔ tíng le 雨停了 **2** *n* a (*bus*) stop yí gè qìchēzhàn 一个汽车站；**to miss one's stop** zuòguòle zhàn 坐过了站

store /stɔː(r)/ *n* a store(*a shop*) yí gè shāngdiàn 一个商店；(*a place for keeping goods*) yí gè cāngkù 一个仓库

storey /'stɔːrɪ/ (*British English*)，**story** (*US English*) *n* a storey yì céng 一层

storm /stɔːm/ n a storm yì chǎng fēngbào 一场风暴（with rain）yì chǎng bàofēngyǔ 一场暴风雨；（with snow）yì chǎng bàofēngxuě 一场暴风雪

story /'stɔːrɪ/ n (a tale) a story yí gè gùshi 一个故事；(a literary genre) a (short) story yí bù (duǎnpiān) xiǎoshuō 一部（短篇）小说；(in a newspaper) a story yì tiáo bàodào 一条报道；(a rumour) a story yí gè yáochuán 一个谣传；(US English) ▶**storey**

stove /stəʊv/ n (US English) a stove yí gè lúzi 一个炉子

straight /streɪt/ **1** adj zhí de 直的；a straight line yì tiáo zhíxiàn 一条直线；she had straight hair tā de tóufa shì zhí de 她的头发是直的；(in the right position) zhèng de 正的；the picture isn't straight zhè zhāng huà bú zhèng 这张画不正；(honest) chéngshí de 诚实的，zhèngzhí de 正直的 **2** adv zhí de 直的；to stand up straight zhànzhí 站直；to go straight ahead yìzhí wǎng qián zǒu 一直往前走；(without delay) lìkè 立刻，mǎshàng 马上；to go straight home lìkè huíjiā 立刻回家

strange /streɪndʒ/ adj (odd) qíguài de 奇怪的；it's strange that she didn't come tā méi lái hěn qíguài 她没来很奇怪；(unknown) mòshēng de 陌生的，bù shúxi de 不熟悉的

stranger /'streɪndʒə(r)/ n a stranger yí gè (mò)shēngrén 一个（陌）生人；(someone from another region) yí gè yìxiāngrén 一个异乡人

straw /strɔː/ n (for feeding animals) dàocǎo 稻草，màigǎn 麦秆；(for drinking) a straw yì gēn xīguǎn 一根吸管

strawberry /'strɔːbərɪ/ n a strawberry yí gè cǎoméi 一个草莓

stream /striːm/ n a stream yì tiáo xiǎohé 一条小河，yì tiáo xiǎoxī 一条小溪

street /striːt/ n a street yì tiáo jiē(dào) 一条街（道），yì tiáo mǎlù 一条马路

streetlamp /'striːtlæmp/ (British English), **streetlight** /'striːtlaɪt/ (US English) n a streetlamp yí gè jiēdēng 一

个街灯

strength /streŋθ/ n (quality of being strong) lìliang 力量，lì (qì) 力（气）；(capacity for exertion or endurance) qiángdù 强度

stressful /'stresfʊl/ adj jǐnzhāng de 紧张的，yālì dà de 压力大的

stretch /stretʃ/ vb (to extend in space) shēnkāi 伸开，shēnchū 伸出；to stretch one's arms shēnkāi gēbo 伸开胳膊；(to make straight by tension) bǎ···lāzhí 把···拉直；to stretch the wire bǎ diànxiàn lāzhí 把电线拉直

strict /strɪkt/ adj (stern) yángé de 严格的，yánlì de 严厉的；(observing exact rules) yánjǐn de 严谨的

strike /straɪk/ n (an attack) a strike yí cì dǎjī 一次打击，yí cì gōngjī 一次攻击；(a cessation of work) a strike yí cì bàgōng 一次罢工；to go on strike jǔxíng bàgōng 举行罢工

string /strɪŋ/ n (thin cord) a piece of string yì gēn xiànshéng 一根绳绳

striped /straɪpt/ adj yǒu tiáowén de 有条纹的

stroke /strəʊk/ vb (to touch lightly in an affectionate way) fǔmó 抚摩，lǚ 捋

stroller /'strəʊlə(r)/ n (US English) (a push-chair) a stroller yí gè yīng'ér tuīchē 一个婴儿推车

strong /strɒŋ/ adj (having physical strength) qiángzhuàng de 强壮的，qiángjiàn de 强健的；she's strong tā hěn qiángzhuàng 她很强壮；(having mental strength) jiānqiáng de 坚强的，jiānjué de 坚决的；(intense) qiángliè de 强烈的；strong [feeling | contrast | protests] qiángliè de [gǎnqíng | duìbǐ | kàngyì] 强烈的 [感情 | 对比 | 抗议]；(not easily damaged) jiēshi de 结实的；láogù de 牢固的；(when describing one's attitude, standpoint, determination) jiāndìng de 坚定的；(having force, power) a strong wind yì chǎng dàfēng 一场大风；strong tea nóngchá 浓茶；a strong wine yì zhǒng lièjiǔ 一种烈酒；(obvious, noticeable) a strong German accent yì kǒu hěn zhòng de Déyǔ kǒuyīn 一口很重的德语口音；a strong smell of garlic yì gǔ hěn nóng de dàsuàn wèi 一股很浓的大蒜味；(having military power) qiángdà de 强大的

stubborn /'stʌbən/ adj wángù de 顽固的，gùzhí de 固执的

student /'stjuːdənt/ n a student yí gè xuésheng 一个学生

study /'stʌdɪ/ 1 vb (to be engaged in learning) xuéxí 学习；she is studying for an exam tā zài xuéxí zhǔnbèi kǎoshì 她在学习准备考试；(to make study of) xuéxí 学习，xué 学；to study history xué(xí) lìshǐ 学(习)历史；(to scrutinize) zǐxì kàn 仔细看 2 n (a room) a study yì jiān shūfáng 一间书房；(act of studying) xuéxí 学习

stuff /stʌf/ 1 n (things) dōngxi 东西，(material) cáiliào 材料 2 vb (to pack, to fill) zhuāng 装，sāi 塞；to stuff a suitcase with clothes wǎng xiāngzi li zhuāng yīfu 往箱子里装衣服；(to feed) to stuff the children with cakes yòng dàngāo tiánbǎo háizimen de dùzi 用蛋糕填饱孩子们的肚子

stuffing /'stʌfɪŋ/ n tián(sāi)liào 填(塞)料

stupid /'stjuːpɪd/ adj bèn de 笨的，yúchǔn de 愚蠢的

style /staɪl/ n (a way of dressing, behaviour) her way of dressing always has style tā chuān de zǒngshì hěn rùshí 她穿得总是很入时；(a manner of doing things) a style yì zhǒng zuòfēng 一种作风，yì zhǒng fēnggé 一种风格；his working style tā de gōngzuò zuòfēng 他的工作作风；(a way of writing) a style yì zhǒng wéntǐ 一种文体；(a distinctive characteristic) a style (of architecture) yì zhǒng (jiànzhù) fēnggé 一种(建筑)风格；(a design, a type) a style yì zhǒng shìyàng 一种式样，yì zhǒng yàngshì 一种样式；the style of a car qìchē de shìyàng 汽车的式样；a hair style yì zhǒng fàxíng 一种发型；(a way of life) a life style yì zhǒng shēnghuó fāngshì 一种生活方式；to live in (grand) style shēnghuó háohuá 生活豪华；(a fashion) a style yì zhǒng shímáo 一种时髦

stylish /'staɪlɪʃ/ *adj* shímáo de 时髦的, piàoliang de 漂亮的

subject /'sʌbdʒɪkt/ *n* (*of a conversation*) huàtí 话题; a subject yí gè huàtí 一个话题; (*being studied*) kēmù 科目, kèchéng 课程; a subject yí gè kèchéng 一个课程; (*topic*) tímù 题目; a subject yí gè tímù 一个题目

suburb /'sʌbɜːb/ *n* the suburbs jiāoqū 郊区, jiāowài 郊外

subway /'sʌbweɪ/ *n* (*US English*) (*the underground*) the subway dìtiě 地铁; (*British English*) (*an underground passage*) a subway yì tiáo dìxià tōngdào 一条地下通道

succeed /sək'siːd/ *vb* (*to accomplish what is attempted*) chénggōng 成功; (*follow, take the place of*) jìchéng 继承, jiētì 接替

success /sək'ses/ *n* chénggōng 成功

successful /sək'sesfʊl/ *adj* chénggōng de 成功的

such /sʌtʃ/ **1** *det* zhèyàng 这样; there's no such thing méiyǒu zhèyàng de dōngxi 没有这样的东西 **2** *adv* nàme 那么; they have such a lot of money tāmen yǒu nàme duō qián 他们有那么多钱; she's such a strange person tā shì nàme qíguài de yí gè rén 她是那么奇怪的一个人

suddenly /'sʌdənlɪ/ *adv* tūrán 突然, hūrán 忽然

suffer /'sʌfə(r)/ *vb* (*to be affected by*) zāoshòu 遭受, zāodào 遭到; to suffer [heavy casualties | enormous economic losses] zāoshòu [yánzhòng shāngwáng | jùdà jīngjì sǔnshī] 遭受 [严重伤亡 | 巨大经济损失]; (*to feel pain*) shòu (tòng) kǔ shòu (痛) 苦; to suffer from [TB | heart failure | a cold] déle [fèijiéhé | xīnlì shuāijié | gǎnmào] 得了 [肺结核 | 心力衰竭 | 感冒]

sugar /'ʃʊgə(r)/ *n* táng 糖

suggestion /səg'dʒestʃən/ *n* a suggestion yì tiáo jiànyì 一条建议

suicide /'sjuːɪsaɪd/ *n* to commit suicide zìshā 自杀

suit /sjuːt/ **1** *n* a suit (*a man's*) yí tào nánshì xīfú 一套男式西服; (*a woman's*) yí tào nǚshì xīfú 一套女式西服

2 vb (to be convenient, to fit) héshì 合适, shìhé 适合；
to suit someone duì mǒu rén héshì 对某人合适；does
Friday suit you? xīngqīwǔ duì nǐ héshì ma? 星期五对你
合适吗?；the hat suits you zhè dǐng màozi nǐ dài hěn
shìhé 这顶帽子你戴很适合

suitable /ˈsjuːtəbl/ adj héshì de 合适的, shìyí de 适宜的；
a suitable present yí gè héshì de lǐwù 一个合适的礼物；
these books are suitable for children zhèxiē shū shìyí
értóng kàn 这些书适宜儿童看

suitcase /ˈsjuːtkeɪs/ n a suitcase yí gè shǒutíxiāng 一个
手提箱

sum /sʌm/ n a sum of money yì bǐ qián 一笔钱；(a
problem in arithmetic) a sum yí dào suànshùtí 一道算术
题；to be good at sums suànshù hěn hǎo 算术很好；sum
up zǒngjié 总结，gàikuò 概括

summer /ˈsʌmə(r)/ n xiàtiān 夏天，xiàjì 夏季

summer holiday /ˌsʌmə ˈhɒlədɪ/ (British English) ,
summer vacation /ˌsʌmə vəˈkeɪʃən/ (US English) n
shǔjià 暑假

sun /sʌn/ n the sun tàiyáng 太阳，(sunshine) yángguāng
阳光；to sit in the sun zuò zài yángguāng xià 坐在阳光
下

sunbathe /ˈsʌnbeɪð/ vb jìnxíng rìguāngyù 进行日光浴，
shài tàiyáng 晒太阳

sunburn /ˈsʌnbɜːn/ n shàishāng 晒伤

sunburned /ˈsʌnbɜːnd/ adj she got sunburned tā
shàishāng le 她晒伤了

Sunday /ˈsʌndɪ/ n xīngqīrì 星期日，xīngqītiān 星期天，
lǐbàitiān 礼拜天

sunglasses /ˈsʌnˌɡlɑːsɪz/ n tàiyángjìng 太阳镜，mòjìng
墨镜

sunny /ˈsʌnɪ/ adj qínglǎng de 晴朗的，yángguāng
míngmèi de 阳光明媚的；a sunny day yí gè qíngtiān 一个
晴天

sunset /ˈsʌnset/ n rìluò 日落

sunshade /'sʌnʃeɪd/ *n* a sunshade yì bǎ yángsǎn 一把阳伞

sunshine /'sʌnʃaɪn/ *n* yángguāng 阳光

suntan /'sʌntæn/ *n* shàihēi 晒黑；you've got a suntan nǐ shàihēi le 你晒黑了

suntan oil /'sʌntæn ˌɔɪl/ *n* a suntan oil yì zhǒng fángshàiyóu 一种防晒油

supermarket /'sjuːpəˌmɑːkɪt/ *n* a supermarket yì jiā chāojí shìchǎng 一家超级市场，yì jiā chāoshì 一家超市

supper /'sʌpə(r)/ *n* a supper yí dùn wǎnfàn 一顿晚饭，yí dùn wǎncān 一顿晚餐

support /sə'pɔːt/ *vb* (*to agree with*, *to help*) zhīchí 支持，zhīyuán 支援；to support the strike zhīchí bàgōng 支持罢工；(*to keep*) to support a family yǎngjiā 养家；to support oneself yǎnghuó zìjǐ 养活自己；(*to hold up or bear the weight of*) zhīchēng 支撑；what are we going to use to support the roof? wǒmen yòng shénme lái zhīchēng wūdǐng? 我们用什么来支撑屋顶?

supporter /sə'pɔːtə(r)/ *n* a supporter (*of a team*, *a party*) yí gè zhīchízhě 一个支持者；(*one who supports a view*, *a policy*) yí gè yōnghùzhě 一个拥护者

suppose /sə'pəʊz/ *vb* (*to posit a hypothetical situation*) jiǎdìng 假定，jiǎrú 假如；suppose you can't come, please give us a call jiǎdìng nǐ bù néng lái, qǐng gěi wǒmen dǎ gè diànhuà 假定你不能来，请给我们打个电话；(*to incline to believe*, *guess*) xiǎng 想，cāixiǎng 猜想！ Note that while in English the verb suppose is negated in the main clause, the negation is shifted to the subordinate clause in Chinese；I don't suppose you know yet? wǒ xiǎng nǐ hái bù zhīdào ba? 我想你还不知道吧？（ *to be supposed to*) to be supposed to yīnggāi 应该，yīngdāng 应当；I'm supposed to arrive there at 10 wǒ yīnggāi shí diǎn dào nàr 我应该 10 点到那儿

sure /ʃʊə(r)/ *adj* (*certain*) gǎn kěndìng de 敢肯定的，yǒu bǎwò de 有把握的；I'm sure he said nine o'clock wǒ gǎn kěndìng tā shuō de shì jiǔ diǎn 我敢肯定他说的是 9 点;**are you sure?** nǐ yǒu bǎwò ma? 你有把握吗?;**she is not sure if she can come** tā bù gǎn kěndìng tā néng lái 她不敢肯定她能来;(*bound*) yídìng huì 一定会,kěndìng huì 肯定会;**he is sure to win** tā yídìng huì yíng 他一定会赢;**sure of oneself** yǒu xìnxīn 有信心;**she's sure of herself** tā hěn yǒu xìnxīn 她很有信心;**to make sure that...** yídìng yào... 一定要···,bǎozhèng··· 保证···;**to make sure that the door is closed** yídìng yào bǎ mén guānhǎo 一定要把门关好

surf /sɜːf/ *vb* **to go surfing** qù chōnglàng 去冲浪

surface /'sɜːfɪs/ **1** *n* **a surface** yí gè biǎomiàn 一个表面 **2** *vb* (*to rise to the surface of the water*) lùchū shuǐmiàn 露出水面

surfboard /'sɜːfbɔːd/ *n* **a surfboard** yí gè chōnglàngbǎn 一个冲浪板

surgeon /'sɜːdʒən/ *n* **a surgeon** yí gè wàikē yīshēng 一个外科医生

surgery /'sɜːdʒərɪ/ *n* **to have surgery** zuò/dòng shǒushù 做/动手术,(*British English*) (*the place*) **a surgery** yí gè zhěnsuǒ 一个诊所

surname /'sɜːneɪm/ *n* **a surname** yí gè xìng 一个姓

surprise /sə'praɪz/ **1** *n* **a surprise** (*an event*) yí jiàn yìxiǎngbúdào de shìqing 一件意想不到的事情,(*a gift*) yí gè yìxiǎngbúdào de lǐwù 一个意想不到的礼物,(*an item of news*) yì tiáo yìxiǎngbúdào de xiāoxi 一条意想不到的消息 **!** *Note that when a surprise is translated into Chinese, it is often necessary to categorize the thing that is surprising by using an appropriate noun, and to modify it by* yìxiǎngbúdào de 意想不到的, *which means unexpected or surprising*;(*the state of being amazed*) jīngqí 惊奇,jīngyà 惊讶;**to take someone by surprise** shǐ mǒu rén hěn jīngqí 使某人很惊奇;**to someone's surprise** shǐ mǒu rén jīngyà de shì 使某人惊讶的是;**he looked up in surprise** tā jīngqí de táiqǐ tóu lái 他惊奇地

抬起头来 **2** *vb* to surprise someone shǐ mǒu rén jīngqí
使某人惊奇，shǐ mǒu rén jīngyà 使某人惊讶

surprised /sə'praɪzd/ *adj* gǎndào chījīng de 感到吃惊的，
gǎndào yìwài de 感到意外的；I'm not surprised wǒ bù
gǎndào chījīng 我不感到吃惊；to be surprised at
something duì mǒu shì gǎndào chījīng 对某事感到吃惊；
I'm surprised that he didn't come tā méi lái, wǒ gǎndào
hěn yìwài 他没来，我感到很意外

surrender /sə'rendə(r)/ *vb* (*to give oneself up to the
police, the authorities, etc.*) zìshǒu 自首；(*to give up in
a fight, battle, or war*) tóuxiáng 投降；(*to give
something up to an enemy, the police, etc.*) jiāochū 交
出；(*to give something up as a result of pressure or
necessity*) fàngqì 放弃

surround /sə'raʊnd/ *vb* wéi wéi 围，bāowéi 包围；the police
surrounded the house jǐngchá bāowéile nà zuò fángzi 警
察包围了那座房子；the house is surrounded by trees
fángzi zhōuwéi dōu shì shù 房子周围都是树

surroundings /sə'raʊndɪŋz/ *n* zhōuwéi 周围，huánjìng 环
境

survey /'sɜːveɪ/ *n* a survey yí xiàng diàochá 一项调查

survive /sə'vaɪv/ *vb* xìngmiǎn yú 幸免于，huó xiàlai 活
下来；to survive an accident xìngmiǎn yú yì cháng shìgù
幸免于一场事故；to survive the winter huóguo
dōngtiān 活过冬天

suspect /sə'spekt/ **1** *vb* (*to imagine that someone is
guilty of*) huáiyí 怀疑；she's suspected of stealing
money rénmen huáiyí tā tōu qián 人们怀疑她偷钱；(*to be
inclined to believe*) cāixiǎng 猜想，rènwéi 认为；I
suspect that this may be true wǒ cāixiǎng zhè kěnéng
shì zhēn de 我猜想这可能是真的 **2** *n* a suspect yí gè
xiányífàn 一个嫌疑犯，yí gè kěyí fènzǐ 一个可疑分子

suspicious /sə'spɪʃəs/ *adj* (*inclined to suspect*) huáiyí de
怀疑的，cāiyí de 猜疑的；to be suspicious of someone
huáiyí mǒu rén 怀疑某人；(*giving ground for suspicion*)

kěyí de 可疑的

swan /swɒn/ *n* a swan yì zhī tiān'é 一只天鹅

swap /swɒp/ *vb* jiāohuàn 交换，jiāoliú 交流

sweat /swet/ *vb* chūhàn 出汗

sweater /'swetə(r)/ *n* (US English) a sweater(usually woolen) yí jiàn máoyī 一件毛衣；(worn before or after physical exercise) yí jiàn yùndòngyī 一件运动衣

sweatshirt /'swetʃɜːt/ *n* a sweatshirt yí jiàn yùndòngshān 一件运动衫；yí jiàn xiūxiánshān 一件休闲衫

Sweden /'swiːdən/ *n* Ruìdiǎn 瑞典

Swedish /'swiːdɪʃ/ **1** *adj* Ruìdiǎn de 瑞典的 **2** *n* (the people) Ruìdiǎnrén 瑞典人；(the language) Ruìdiǎnyǔ 瑞典语

sweep /swiːp/ *vb* sǎo 扫，dǎsǎo 打扫

sweet /swiːt/ **1** *adj* (tasting of sugar) tián de 甜的，tiánwèi de 甜味的；the wine is too sweet zhè jiǔ tài tián le 这酒太甜了；to have a sweet tooth xǐhuan chī tiánshí 喜欢吃甜食；(fragrant) fāngxiāng de 芳香的；(kind, gentle) qīnqiè de 亲切的，hé'ǎi de 和蔼的；to be sweet to someone duì mǒu rén qīnqiè 对某人亲切；(cute) kě'ài de 可爱的 **2** *n* (British English) a sweet yí kuài táng 一块糖

swim /swɪm/ **1** *vb* (to propel oneself in water) yóuyǒng 游泳；(to travel by propelling oneself in water) yóu 游；to swim across the lake yóuguò hú qù 游过湖去 **2** *n* a swim yóuyǒng 游泳；to go for a swim qù yóuyǒng 去游泳

swimming /'swɪmɪŋ/ *n* yóuyǒng 游泳

swimming pool /'swɪmɪŋ puːl/ *n* a swimming pool yí gè yóuyǒngchí 一个游泳池

swimsuit /'swɪmsjuːt/ *n* a swimsuit yí jiàn yóuyǒngyī 一件游泳衣

swing /swɪŋ/ **1** *vb* (to move back and forth) bǎidòng 摆动，yáobǎi 摇摆；to swing on a gate zài mén shang bǎidòng 在门上摆动；(to move something back and forth) bǎidòng 摆动，huàngdòng 晃动；to swing one's legs

huàngdòng tuǐ 晃动腿 **2** n a swing (for children) yí gè
qiūqiān 一个秋千

Swiss /swɪs/ **1**adj Ruìshì de 瑞士的 **2** n the Swiss
Ruìshìrén 瑞士人

switch /swɪtʃ/ **1** n a switch yí gè kāiguān 一个开关 **2**
vb (zhuǎn)huàn (转)换，gǎibiàn 改变；to switch seats
huàn zuòwèi 换座位；to switch from English to
Chinese cóng Yīngyǔ huànchéng yòng Hànyǔ 从英语换成
用汉语；**switch off** guān 关；to switch off the light
guān diàndēng 关电灯；**switch on** dǎkāi 打开；to switch the
radio on dǎkāi shōuyīnjī 打开收音机

Switzerland /'swɪtsələnd/ n Ruìshì 瑞士

sympathetic /ˌsɪmpə'θetɪk/ adj (showing pity) tóngqíng
de 同情的；(showing understanding) zànchéng de 赞成的，
yǒu tónggǎn 有同感的

syringe /'sɪrɪndʒ/ n a syringe yí gè zhùshèqì 一个注射器

system /'sɪstəm/ n(a complex whole, an organization)
a system yí gè tǐxì 一个体系，yí gè xìtǒng 一个系统；(of a
society or a political organization) a system yí gè zhìdù
一个制度，yí gè tǐxì 一个体系；(of a political organization) a system yí
gè tǐzhì 一个体制；a democratic system yí
gè mínzhǔ zhìdù 一个民主制度；(a method) a system yí
tào fāngfǎ 一套方法

Tt

table /'teɪbl/ n a table yì zhāng zhuōzi 一张桌子

tablet /'tæblɪt/ n (when talking about medicine) a tablet
yí piàn yào 一片药

table tennis /'teɪbl ˌtenɪs/ n table tennis pīngpāngqiú 乒
乓球

tail /teɪl/ n a tail (of an animal) yí tiáo wěiba 一条尾巴；
(of other things) yí gè wěibù 一个尾部

take /teɪk/ vb (to take hold of in the hand) ná 拿 | let me take your raincoat wó gěi nǐ názhe yǔyī 我给你拿着雨衣 ; (to take hold of in one's arms) bào 抱 | I took the baby in my arms wǒ bǎ yīng'ér bào zài huái li 我把婴儿抱在怀里 ; (to take someone by the hand) lā 拉 | she took me by the hand tā lāzhe wǒ de shǒu 她拉着我的手 ; (to carry) dài 带 | I took my umbrella wǒ dàizhe yǔsǎn 我带着雨伞 ; I'll take the letters to her wǒ gěi tā dàiqù zhèxiē xìn 我给她带去这些信 ; (to accompany, lead, guide) lǐng 领, dài(lǐng) 带(领) ; to take the children for a walk lǐng háizi qù sànbù 领孩子去散步 ; to take someone home dài mǒu rén huíjiā 带某人回家 ; (to cause to go) názǒu 拿走 ; who's taken my dictionary? shéi názǒule wǒ de cídiǎn? 谁拿走了我的词典? ; (to remove) to take a book off the shelf cóng shūjià shang náxià yì běn shū 从书架上拿下一本书 ; (to steal) tōu 偷 ; (to cope with, to bear) shòubuliǎo 受不了 | he can't take the pain tā shòubuliǎo téng 他受不了疼 ; (when talking about what is necessary) xūyào 需要 ; it takes [time | courage | patience...] xūyào [shíjiān | yǒngqì | nàixīn...] 需要 [时间 | 勇气 | 耐心...] ; it takes two hours to get to London dào Lúndūn xūyào liǎng gè xiǎoshí 到伦敦需要两个小时 ; to take a long time to do one's homework zuò zuòyè xūyào hěn cháng shíjiān 做作业需要很长时间 ; it won't take long búyào hěn cháng shíjiān 不要很长时间 ; (to accept) jiēshòu 接受 ; to take someone's advice jiēshòu mǒu rén de zhōngqào 接受某人的忠告 ; (to eat, to swallow) chī 吃 ; to take medicine chī yào 吃药 | I don't take sugar in my tea wǒ hē chá bú fàng táng 我喝茶不放糖 ; (when talking about travelling) zuò 坐, chéng 乘 ; to take [a taxi | the bus | the underground] zuò [chūzūchē | gōnggòng qìchē | dìtiě] 坐 [出租车 | 公共汽车 | 地铁] ; to take exams kǎoshì 考试 ; (when talking about selecting courses) xué 学, xuéxí 学习 ; to take [Chinese history | computer studies | driving lessons] xué [zhōngguó lìshǐ |

jìsuànjī|kāichē|学〔中国历史|计算机|开车〕;(to wear) chuān
穿;to take a size 10 chuān shí hào de 穿 10 号的;
(when used with various nouns) to take〔a bath| a rest| a
walk| a photograph| a look〕〔xǐ gè zǎo|xiūxi yíhuìr|sànbù|zhào
zhāng xiàng|kànyìkàn〕〔洗个澡|休息一会儿|散步|照张相|看一
看〕;take apart chāikāi 拆开;take away to take away
the rubbish bǎ lājī nòngzǒu 把垃圾弄走;the meeting
took him away early yīnwèi kāihuì tā děi zǎo yìdiǎnr líkāi
因为开会他得早一点儿离开;to take back náhuí 拿回;
I had to take the dress back wǒ bùdébù bǎ yīfu ná huíqù
我不得不把衣服拿回去;take down (to remove) náxià
拿下, qǔxià 取下;to take the painting down bǎ huà ná
xiàlái 把画拿下来;(to write down) jìxià 记下;I took
down his address wǒ jìxià tā de dìzhǐ 我记下他的地址;
take hold of názhe 拿着, zhuāzhe 抓着;take off (from
an airport) qǐfēi 起飞;(to remove) to take off one's
〔coat| shirt| skirt| trousers| shoes...〕tuōxià〔wàiyī|chènshān
|qúnzi|kùzi|xié...〕脱下〔外衣|衬衫|裙子|裤子|鞋...〕;to take
off one's〔hat| glasses| gloves| ring| necklace...〕zhāixià
〔màozi|yǎnjìng|shǒutào|jièzhi|xiàngliàn...〕摘下〔帽子|眼镜|手套
|戒指|项链...〕;take out (from a box, a pocket, a bag)
náchū 拿出;he took a pen out of his pocket tā cóng
kǒudai lǐ náchū yì zhī gāngbǐ 他从口袋里拿出一支钢笔;
(from a bank account) qǔ qián, tí qián;to take money out
qǔqián 取钱;(to release one's anger at) to take
something out on someone yīnwèi mǒu shì xiàng mǒu
rén fāxiè 因为某事向某人发泄;take part cānjiā 参加;to
take part in a game cānjiā yí xiàng bǐsài 参加一项比赛;
take place (if it's an unexpected incident or accident)
fāshēng 发生;(if it's an organized event) jǔxíng 举行;
take up (as a hobby) kāishǐ (cóngshì) 开始 (从事);to
take up sailing kāishǐ fānchuán yùndòng 开始帆船运动;
(to use up) zhàn 占;to take up space zhàn kōngjiān 占
空间

talented /ˈtæləntɪd/ adj yǒu cáinéng de 有才能的, yǒu

cáihuá de 有才华的

talk /tɔːk/ **1** vb (to speak) jiǎnghuà 讲话；tánhuà 谈话；to talk in Chinese yòng Hànyǔ jiǎnghuà 用汉语讲话；to talk to someone hé mǒu rén jiǎnghuà 和某人讲话；I talked to them about the trip wǒ gēn tāmen tánle zhè cì lǚxíng de qíngkuàng 我跟他们谈了这次旅行的情况；they were talking about you tāmen zài tánlùn nǐ 他们在谈论你；to talk on the phone dǎ diànhuà 打电话；(to speak at a meeting or a conference) yǎnjiǎng 演讲，jiǎnghuà 讲话；he is going to talk to the students and teachers at Peking University tā yào zài Běijīng Dàxué xiàng shīshēngmen yǎnjiǎng 他要在北京大学向师生们演讲；(to chat) xiánliáo 闲聊 **2** n (a conversation) a talk yí cì tánhuà 一次谈话，yí cì jiāotán 一次交谈；(a lecture) a talk (in class) yí cì jiǎngzuò 一次讲座；(to a club, a group, a meeting) yí gè bàogào 一个报告，yí cì yǎnjiǎng 一次演讲；(discussions) huìtán 会谈；the two leaders had friendly talks yesterday liǎng wèi lǐngdǎorén zuótiān jǔxíngle yǒuhǎo de huìtán 两位领导人昨天举行了友好的会谈

talkative /ˈtɔːkətɪv/ adj jiàntán de 健谈的，xǐhuan jiǎnghuà de 喜欢讲话的

tall /tɔːl/ adj gāo de 高的；to be six feet tall liù yīngchǐ gāo 6 英尺高

tan /tæn/ n a tan rìshài hòu de fūsè 日晒后的肤色；to get a tan shài de hēihēi de 晒得黑黑的

tanned /tænd/ adj shàihēile de 晒黑了的

tap /tæp/ **1** n (British English) a tap yí gè shuǐlóng (tóu) 一个水龙 (头)；to turn the tap off bǎ shuǐlóng (tóu) guānshang 把水龙 (头) 关上 **2** vb to tap on the door qiāo mén 敲门

tape /teɪp/ **1** n a tape (for a tape recorder) yì pán lùyīndài 一盘录音带；(for a video) yì pán lùxiàngdài 一盘录像带；(for sticking) jiāodài 胶带 **2** vb (to record) bǎ …lù xiàlái 把…录下来；she's taped that film tā bǎ nà bù diànyǐng lù xiàlái le 她把那部电影录下来了

tape recorder /'teɪp rɪ,kɔːdə(r)/ *n* a tape recorder yì tái lùyīnjī 一台录音机

target /'tɑːgɪt/ *n* a target (*in shooting*) yí gè bǎizi 一个靶子;(*what is aimed at*) yí gè mùbiāo 一个目标;(*an object of criticism*) yí gè duìxiàng 一个对象

tart /tɑːt/ *n* (*British English*) a tart yí gè xiànrbǐng 一个馅儿饼;an apple tart yí gè píngguǒ xiànrbǐng 一个苹果馅儿饼

task /tɑːsk/ *n* a task yí gè rènwu 一个任务,yí xiàng gōngzuò 一项工作

taste /teɪst/ **1** *n* (*when eating, drinking*) a taste yì zhǒng wèidao 一种味道,yì zhǒng zīwèi 一种滋味;(*power of discerning and judging*) taste jiànshǎng (néng)lì 鉴赏 (能)力;she has good taste tā jùyǒu liánghǎo de jiànshǎng nénglì 她具有良好的鉴赏能力 **2** *vb* (*when describing a flavour*) cháng qǐlai 尝起来,chī qǐlai 吃起来;to taste good cháng qǐlai wèidao hěn hǎo 尝起来味道很好;to taste awful cháng qǐlai wèidao hěn zāogāo 尝起来味道很糟糕;it tastes like cabbage chī qǐlai wèidao xiàng juǎnxīncài 吃起来味道像卷心菜;(*when eating, drinking*) cháng 尝,pǐncháng 品尝

tax /tæks/ *n* shuì 税

taxi /'tæksi/ *n* a taxi yí liàng chūzūchē 一辆出租车

taxi rank /'tæksi ræŋk/ (*British English*), **taxi stand** /'tæksi stænd/ (*US English*) *n* a taxi rank yí gè chūzū-qìchēzhàn 一个出租汽车站

tea /tiː/ *n* (*the product*) tea chá 茶;a cup of tea yì bēi chá 一杯茶;(*British English*) (*a meal*) fàn 饭,chádiǎn 茶点

teach /tiːtʃ/ *vb* (*to train, educate, or impart knowledge*) jiāo 教;to teach someone [to read | to drive | to ride a horse] jiāo mǒu rén [niànshū | kāichē | qímǎ] 教某人 [念书 | 开车 | 骑马];to teach Chinese to adults jiāo chéngrén Zhōngwén 教成人中文;(*to work as a teacher*) jiāoshū 教

书,jiāoxué 教学; where does she teach? tā zài nǎr jiāoshū? 她在哪儿教书?

teacher /'tiːtʃə(r)/ n a teacher yì míng jiàoshī 一名教师, yí wèi lǎoshī 一位老师

team /tiːm/ n a team yí gè duì 一个队; a football team yì zhī zúqiúduì 一支足球队

teapot /'tiːpɒt/ n a teapot yí gè cháhú 一个茶壶

tear¹ /teə(r)/ vb (to pull apart, to rend) sī 撕, chě 扯; to tear a page out of a book cóng shū shang sīxià yí yè zhǐ 从书上撕下一页纸; (to become torn) sīpò 撕破, chěpò 扯破; this kind of paper tears easily zhè zhǒng zhǐ hěn róngyì sīpò 这种纸很容易撕破; tear off (to remove by tearing) chědiào 扯掉; (to depart hurriedly) xùnsù zǒudiào 迅速走掉, páodiào 跑掉; tear up to tear up a letter bǎ yì fēng xìn sī de fěnsuì 把一封信撕得粉碎; the wind tore up many houses dàfēng cuīhuǐle hěn duō fángzi 大风摧毁了很多房子

tear² /tɪə(r)/ n a tear yì dī yǎnlèi 一滴眼泪; to burst into tears dàkū qǐlai 大哭起来

tease /tiːz/ vb dòunòng 逗弄, xìnòng 戏弄

teaspoon /'tiːspuːn/ n a teaspoon yì bǎ cháchí 一把茶匙

technical /'teknɪkəl/ adj jìshù de 技术的, zhuānyèxìng de 专业性的

teenager /'tiːneɪdʒə(r)/ n a teenager yí gè shíjǐ suì de háizi 一个十几岁的孩子

telephone /'telɪfəʊn/ n a telephone yí bù diànhuà 一部电话

telephone directory /'telɪfəʊn dɪˌrektərɪ/ n a telephone directory yì běn diànhuàbù 一本电话簿

telescope /'telɪskəʊp/ n a telescope yí jià wàngyuǎnjìng 一架望远镜

television /'telɪˌvɪʒən/ n a television yì tái diànshìjī 一台电视机; I saw the film on television wǒ shì zài diànshì shang kàn de zhè bù diànyǐng 我是在电视上看的这部电影

tell /tel/ vb (to say to) gàosu 告诉;did you tell your parents? nǐ gàosu nǐ fùmǔ le ma? 你告诉你父母了吗?; to tell someone about a problem gàosu mǒu rén yí gè wèntí 告诉某人一个问题;don't tell anyone bié gàosu biérén 别告诉别人;(for telling a story, a joke) jiǎng 讲; to tell jokes jiǎng xiàohua 讲笑话;(for telling a lie, a joke) shuō 说;to tell a lie shuōhuǎng 说谎;(when giving orders or instructions) ràng 让, jiào 叫, mìnglìng 命令; to tell someone to leave the classroom ràng mǒu rén líkāi jiàoshì 让某人离开教室;to tell someone not to smoke jiào mǒu rén búyào chōuyān 叫某人不要抽烟;(to work out, to know) kànchū 看出, zhīdào 知道, duàndìng 断定;I can tell (that) she's disappointed wǒ néng kàn chūlái tā hěn shīwàng 我能看出来她很失望;you can tell he's lying nǐ néng kànchū tā zài shuōhuǎng 你能看出他在说谎;(when making distinctions) fēnbiàn 分辨, biànbié 辨别;to tell him from his twin brother fēnbiàn tā hé tā de luánshēng xiōngdì 分辨他和他的孪生兄弟;I can't tell which is which wǒ biànbié bù chū nǎge shì nǎge 我辨别不出哪个是哪个;tell off to tell someone off zébèi mǒu rén 责备某人

temper /ˈtempə(r)/ n (temperament, disposition) píqi 脾气;she has a rather bad temper tā píqi hěn huài 她脾气很坏;to lose one's temper fā píqi 发脾气;(mood) xīnqíng 心情;to be in a good temper xīnqíng hǎo 心情好

temperature /ˈtemprətʃə(r)/ n (of the body) tǐwēn 体温;to have a temperature fāshāo 发烧;(degree of heat or cold) wēndù 温度;(about the weather) qìwēn 气温

temple /ˈtempl/ n a temple yí zuò (sì)miào 一座(寺)庙

temporary /ˈtemprərɪ/ adj línshí de 临时的, zànshí de 暂时的

ten /ten/ num shí 十

tennis /ˈtenɪs/ n wǎngqiú 网球

tennis court /ˈtenɪs kɔːt/ n a tennis court yí gè

wǎngqiúchǎng 一个网球场

tense /tens/ adj jǐnzhāng de 紧张的

tent /tent/ n a tent yì dǐng zhàngpeng 一顶帐篷

tenth /tenθ/ num (in a series) dì-shí 第十；(in dates) rì shí 日，shí hào 十号；the tenth of October shíyuè shí hào 10 月 10 号

term /tɜːm/ n a term (in schools or universities) yí gè xuéqī 一个学期；(of office or appointment) yí gè rènqī 一个任期；(a limited period of time) yí gè qīxiàn 一个期限；(a word or expression) shùyǔ 术语，cíyǔ 词语；a term yí gè shùyǔ 一个术语；(conditions) tiáojiàn 条件

terrible /'terəbl/ adj (expressing shock) kěpà de 可怕的，xiàrén de 吓人的；(used for emphasis) jídù de 极度的，lìhài de 厉害的；(awful, very bad) zāogāo de 糟糕的

terrified /'terɪfaɪd/ adj hàipà de 害怕的，xià de yàomìng de 吓得要命的

terror /'terə(r)/ n terror kǒngbù 恐怖，kǒngjù 恐惧

terrorist /'terərɪst/ n a terrorist yì míng kǒngbù fènzǐ 一名恐怖分子

test /test/ n **1** vb (to put to the proof) jiǎnyàn 检验；(to try out) shìyàn 试验 **2** n a test (means of trial) yí cì shìyàn 一次试验；(in school, college) yí cì cèyàn 一次测验；(written) yí cì bǐshì 一次笔试；(oral) yí cì kǒushì 一次口试；a driving test yí cì jiàshǐ kǎoshì 一次驾驶考试；to have an eye test zuò yí cì yǎnjīng jiǎnchá 做一次眼睛检查

than /ðæn/ **1** prep (in comparisons) bǐ 比；to be [stronger| more intelligent| faster...] than someone bǐ mǒu rén [qiángzhuàng| cōngmíng| kuài···]bǐ某人 [强壮| 聪明| 快···]；I've got more money than you wǒ de qián bǐ nǐ de duō 我的钱比你的多；(when talking about quantities) more than yǐshàng 以上；more than half of the pupils are absent yíbàn yǐshàng de xuésheng méi lái 一半以上的学生没来；less than bú dào 不到；it's worth less than £ 100 tā de jiàzhí bú dào yìbǎi yīngbàng 它的价值不到

100 英镑 **2** *conj* bǐ 比；he's older than I am tā bǐ wǒ dà 他比我大

thank /θæŋk/ *vb* xièxie 谢谢，gǎnxiè 感谢

thanks /θæŋks/ **1** *adv* gǎnxiè 感谢，gǎnjī 感激；many thanks，thanks a lot duōxiè 多谢 **2** thanks to xìngkuī 幸亏，yóuyú 由于

thank you /'θæŋk juː/ *adv* xièxie 谢谢，xièxie nín 谢谢您；thank you for coming xièxie nín guānglín 谢谢您光临；'more wine?'—'thank you' zài jiā diǎnr jiǔ ma?'—'xièxie，qǐng zài jiā diǎnr' "再加点儿酒吗?"—"谢谢，请再加点儿"

that /ðæt/ 弱 ðət/! Note that as a determiner or a pronoun, that is often translated as **nàge** 那个，where **gè** 个 is a measure word and varies with the noun that follows or with the noun to which it refers. **1** *det* nà 那，nàge 那个；at that time nà shíhou 那时候，who is that person? nàge rén shì shéi? 那个人是谁?；I don't like that novel wǒ bù xǐhuan nà běn xiǎoshuō 我不喜欢那本小说 **2** *pron* nà 那，nàge 那个！ Note that sometimes that is translated as **nàge rén** 那个人，and in the latter, **nàge dōngxi** 那个东西；what's that? nà(ge dōngxi) shì shénme? 那(个东西)是什么?；who's that? nà(ge rén) shì shéi? 那(个人)是谁?；who put that on the table? shì shéi bǎ nàge fàng zài zhuōzi shang de? 是谁把那个放在桌子上的?；is that Tom? shì Tāngmǔ ma? 是汤姆吗?；(when used as a relative pronoun)！ Note that when used as a relative pronoun, that is not translated；the girl that I met is his sister wǒ jiàndào de nàge gūniang shì tā mèimei 我见到的那个姑娘是他妹妹；do you know the person that I was talking to just now? nǐ rènshi wǒ gāngcái gēn tā jiǎnghuà de nàge rén ma? 你认识我刚才跟他讲话的那个人吗? **3** *conj*！ Note that when used as a conjunction, that is usually not translated；she said that she would come tā shuō tā huì lái 她说她会来 **4** *adv* nàme 那么，nàyàng 那样；the question is not that difficult zhège wèntí méiyǒu nàme nán 这个问题没有那么难

the /ðiː/ 弱 ðə/ det (when referring to a person or thing mentioned here or previously) zhè zhège ...: nà 那; the student you want to meet is not here today nǐ yào jiàn de nàge xuésheng jīntiān bú zài 你要见的那个学生今天不在; if you like the book, I can lend it to you yàoshì nǐ xǐhuan zhè běn shū, wǒ kěyǐ jiègěi nǐ 要是你喜欢这本书, 我可以借给你; (when referring to something understood, something unique)! Note that in this sense, the is not translated; **please switch off** [the radio | the TV | the light...] qǐng bǎ [shōuyīnjī | diànshìjī | dēng...] guānshang 请把[收音机 | 电视机 | 灯...]关上; the sun has come out tàiyáng chūlai le 太阳出来了; (when referring to a particular type, class, or group of people or objects)! Note that in this sense, the is not translated; the Japanese like to eat raw fish Rìběnrén xǐhuan chī shēngyú 日本人喜欢吃生鱼; the rich should help the poor fùrén yīnggāi bāngzhù qióngrén 富人应该帮助穷人; the horse is a useful animal mǎ shì yǒuyòng de dòngwù 马是有用的动物; (when used with the comparative or superlative)! Note that in this sense, the is not translated; you've made it all the worse nǐ bǎ tā gǎo de gèng zāo le 你把它搞得更糟了; she's the most hardworking student in the class tā shì bān lǐ zuì nǔlì de xuésheng 她是班里最努力的学生

theatre /ˈθɪətə(r)/ (British English), **theater** (US English) n a theatre (a place where plays are performed) yí gè jùyuàn 一个剧院, yí gè xìyuàn 一个戏院; (a surgical operating room) yí gè shǒushùshì 一个手术室; a lecture theatre yí gè jiētī jiàoshì 一个阶梯教室

their /ðeə(r)/ 弱 ðə(r)/ det (for men, or men and women together) tāmen de 他们的; I don't like their house wǒ bù xǐhuan tāmen de fángzi 我不喜欢他们的房子; (for women) tāmen de 她们的; (for non-human and inanimate beings) tāmen de 它们的

theirs /ðeəz/ pron (for men, or men and women together) tāmen de 他们的;which car is theirs? nǎ liàng chē shì tāmen de? 哪辆车是他们的?;(for women) tāmen de 她们的;(for non-human and inanimate beings) tāmen de 它们的

them /ðem; 弱 ðəm/ pron (for men, or men and women together) tāmen 他们;I don't know them wǒ bú rènshi tāmen 我不认识他们;(for women) tāmen 她们;(for non-human and inanimate beings) tāmen 它们! Note that in this sense, them is usually not translated if it is an object following a verb;please put them on the table qǐng fàng zài zhuōzi shang 请放在桌子上;when you finish reading these magazines, please remember to return them nǐ kànwán zhèxiē zázhìhòu, qǐng jìzhù huán huílái 你看完这些杂志后,请记住还回来;I bought two gifts for my parents and they like them very much wǒ gěi wǒ fùmǔ mǎile liǎng jiàn lǐwù,tāmen hěn xǐhuan 我给我父母买了两件礼物,他们很喜欢

themselves /ðəm'selvz/ pron (when used as a reflexive pronoun) themselves (for men, or men and women together) (tāmen) zìjǐ (他们)自己;they didn't hurt themselves tāmen méiyǒu shāngzhe zìjǐ 他们没有伤着自己;(for women) (tāmen) zìjǐ (她们)自己;(for emphasis) zìjǐ 自己;qīnzì 亲自;they said it themselves tāmen zìjǐ shuō de 他们自己说的;they didn't attend the meeting themselves tāmen méiyǒu qīnzì cānjiā huìyì 他们没有亲自参加会议

then /ðen/ adv (at that point in time) nàshí 那时,dāngshí 当时;I was living in Taiwan then dāngshí wǒ zhù zài Táiwān 当时我住在台湾;from then on cóng nàshí qǐ 从那时起;(after, next) ránhòu 然后,jiēzhe 接着;I went to Beijing and then to Shanghai wǒ qùle Běijīng,ránhòu yòu qùle Shànghǎi 我去了北京,然后又去了上海

there /ðeə(r)/ 弱 ðə(r)/ **1** pron (when followed by the verb to be) yǒu 有! Note that the negative form of yǒu 有

is méiyǒu 没有；there is a problem yǒu yí gè wèntí 有
一个问题；there aren't any shops méiyǒu rènhé
shāngdiàn 没有任何商店；(*when used with verbs like to
exist, to appear, etc.*)！*Note that in this case, there
is not translated*）there exist many problems cúnzài hěn
duō wèntí 存在很多问题；there appears some hope
chūxiànle yìxiē xīwàng 出现了一些希望 **2** *adv* (*when
talking about location*) nàr 那儿，nàli 那里；who's there?
shéi zài nàr? 谁在那儿？the train wasn't there huǒchē
bú zài nàli 火车不在那里；when will we get there?
wǒmen shénme shíhou dào nàr? 我们什么时候到那儿？；
they don't go there very often tāmen bù cháng qù nàli
他们不常去那里；(*when drawing attention*) there's [the
sea｜my watch｜your mother] [dàhǎi｜wǒ de biǎo｜nǐ māma]zài nàr
[大海｜我的表｜你妈妈]在那儿；there you are, there you
go gěi (nǐ) 给(你)

therefore /'ðeəfɔː(r)/ *adv* yīncǐ 因此，suǒyǐ 所以

these /ðiːz/ **1** *det* zhèxiē 这些；these books aren't mine
zhèxiē shū bú shì wǒ de 这些书不是我的 **2** *pron* zhèxiē 这
些；these are your things zhèxiē shì nǐ de dōngxi 这些是
你的东西；these are my friends zhèxiē shì wǒ de péngyou
这些是我的朋友

they /ðeɪ/ *pron* (*for men, or men and women together*)
tāmen 他们；they'll be there too tāmen yě huì zài nàr
他们也会在那儿；(*for women*) tāmen 她们；they're
intelligent girls tāmen shì hěn cōngmíng de gūniang 她
们是很聪明的姑娘；(*for non-human and inanimate
beings*) tāmen 它们

thick /θɪk/ *adj* (*having a large distance between
surfaces*) hòu de 厚的，(*great in diameter*) cū de 粗的，
(*dense*) mì de 密的，nóngmì de 浓密的；(*when
describing a liquid*) chóu de 稠的，nóng de 浓的；(*when
describing smoke*) nóng de 浓的

thief /θiːf/ *n* a thief yí gè xiǎotōu 一个小偷

thigh /θaɪ/ *n* the thigh dàtuǐ 大腿

thin /θɪn/ adj (slim , lean) shòu de 瘦的；(having little distance between surfaces) báo de 薄的；(small in diameter) xì de 细的；(of little density) xīshǎo de 稀少的；(watery) xībó de 稀薄的

thing /θɪŋ/ n (a material object) **a thing** yí gè dōngxi 一个东西，yí jiàn dōngxi 一件东西；**what's the thing on the table?** zhuōzi shang de dōngxi shì shénme? 桌子上的东西是什么？；(a matter , an affair) **a thing** yí jiàn shì (qíng) 一件事 (情)；**I've got things to do** wǒ yǒu shìqing yào zuò 我有事情要做；(belongings) **things** yòngpǐn 用品，suǒyǒuwù 所有物

think /θɪŋk/ vb (when talking about opinions) rènwéi 认为，juédé 觉得；**what do you think of it?** nǐ rènwéi zhège zěnmeyàng? 你认为这个怎么样？；**I think it's unfair** wǒ juédé zhè bù gōngpíng 我觉得这不公平；'**will they come?**'—'**I don't think so**' "tāmen huì lái ma?"—"wǒ rènwéi bú huì" "他们会来吗？"—"我认为不会"；**who do you think will win?** nǐ juédé shéi huì yíng? 你觉得谁会赢？；(to concentrate on an idea) xiǎng 想，kǎolǜ 考虑；**think hard before answering** xiǎnghǎole zài huídá 想好了再回答；(to remember) xiǎngqǐ 想起；**I can't think of his name** wǒ xiǎng bù qǐ tā de míngzi 我想不起他的名字；**can you think of where we met him?** nǐ néng xiǎngqǐ wǒmen zài nǎr jiànguo tā ma? 你能想起我们在哪儿见过他吗？；(to have in mind) xiǎngdào 想到，xiǎngqǐ 想起；**I thought of him when I saw the address** wǒ kàndào zhège dìzhǐ jiù xiǎngdàole nǐ 我看到这个地址就想到了你；(to have vague plans to) dǎsuàn 打算，jìhuà 计划；**to be thinking of changing jobs** dǎsuàn huàn gōngzuò 打算换工作；(to solve by a process of thought) xiǎngchū 想出；**to think of a solution** xiǎngchū yí gè jiějué bànfǎ 想出一个解决办法；**he couldn't think of a better idea** tā xiǎng bù chū yí gè gèng hǎo de zhǔyi 他想不出一个更好的主意！Note that when **bù 不** is used to negate **xiǎngqǐ 想起**，**xiǎngdào 想到**，or **xiǎngchū 想出**

bù 不 *comes between the verb* xiǎng 想 *and its complement as in* xiǎng bù qǐ 想不起，xiǎng bú dào 想不到 *and* xiǎng bù chū 想不出

third /θɜːd/ **1** *adj* dì-sān de 第三的 **2** *n* (*in a series*) the third dì-sān 第三；(*in dates*) sān hào 三号，sān rì 三日；the third of June liùyuè sān hào 6 月 3 号；(*when talking about quantities*) a third of the population sān fēn zhī yī de rénkǒu 三分之一的人口 **3** *adv* dì-sān 第三；to come third in a race zài bǐsài zhōng dé dì-sān 在比赛中得第 3

thirsty /'θɜːstɪ/ *adj* kě de 渴的，kǒukě de 口渴的；I'm very thirsty wǒ hěn kě 我很渴

thirteen /'θɜː'tiːn/ *num* shísān 十三

thirteenth /'θɜː'tiːnθ/ *num* (*in a series*) dì-shísān 第十三；(*in dates*) shísān hào 13 号，shísān rì 13 日；Friday the thirteenth shísān hào xīngqīwǔ 13 号星期五

thirty /'θɜːtɪ/ *num* sānshí 三十

this /ðɪs/ 弱 ðəs/ ! *Note that as a determiner or a pronoun, this is often translated as* zhège 这个 *where* gè 个 *is a measure word that varies with the noun to which it refers.*
1 *det* zhè 这，zhège 这个；I like [this garden｜this book｜this shop...] wǒ xǐhuan [zhège huāyuán｜zhè běn shū｜zhè jiā shāngdiàn...] 我喜欢 [这个花园｜这本书｜这家商店...]；(*when referring to today*) jīntiān 今天；this [morning｜afternoon｜evening] jīntiān [shàngwǔ｜xiàwǔ｜wǎnshang] 今天 [上午｜下午｜晚上]；this year jīnnián 今年 **2** *pron* zhè 这，zhège 这个；what's this? zhè shì shénme? 这是什么?；who's this? zhè shì shéi? 这是谁?；this is the kitchen zhè shì chúfáng 这是厨房 **3** *adv* zhème 这么，zhèyàng 这样；he is about this tall tā chàbuduō yǒu zhème gāo 他差不多有这么高

thorn /θɔːn/ *n* a thorn yì gēn cì 一根刺

those /ðəʊz/ **1** *det* those nàxiē 那些；those books are yours nàxiē shū shì nǐ de 那些书是你的 **2** *pron* those nàxiē 那些；what are those? nàxiē shì shénme? 那些是什么?；those are my friends nàxiē shì wǒ de péngyou 那些

是我的朋友

though /ðəʊ/ *conj* suīrán 虽然, jǐnguǎn 尽管; though he can speak good Chinese, he can't write in Chinese suīrán tā Hànyǔ shuō de hěn hǎo, dàn(shì) tā bú huì xiě hànzì 虽然他汉语说得很好, 但(是)他不会写汉字 ! *Note that in Chinese the use of* suīrán 虽然 *or* jǐnguǎn 尽管 *does not exclude the use of* kěshì 可是 (= but) *or* dànshì 但是 (= but).

thought /θɔːt/ *n* a thought (*an idea*) yì zhǒng xiǎngfǎ 一种想法; (*a school of thought*) yì zhǒng sīxiǎng 一种思想

thousand /'θaʊzənd/ *num* qiān 千; one thousand, a thousand yìqiān 一千; four thousand pounds sìqiān yīngbàng 4000 英镑

thread /θred/ *n* a thread yì gēn xiàn 一根线

threat /θret/ *n* wēixié 威胁, kǒnghè 恐吓

threaten /'θretən/ *vb* wēixié 威胁, kǒnghè 恐吓

three /θriː/ *num* three sān 三; three schools sān suǒ xuéxiào 3 所学校

throat /θrəʊt/ *n* the throat sǎngzi 嗓子, hóulóng 喉咙

through /θruː/ *!* Often through occurs in combinations with verbs, for example: go through, let through, read through, etc. To find the correct translations for this type of verb, look up the separate dictionary entries at go, let, read, etc.; *prep* (*from one side to the other*) chuānguò 穿过, tōngguò 通过; to drive through the desert kāichē chuānguò shāmò 开车穿过沙漠; to go through the town centre chuānguò shìzhōngxīn 穿过市中心; to look out through a window tōngguò chuānghu xiàng wài kàn 通过窗户向外看; to go through customs tōngguò tōngguò hǎiguān 通过海关; to go through a red light chuǎng hóngdēng 闯红灯; (*from the beginning to the end*) cóngtóu-dàowěi 从头到尾; he didn't read through all these letters tā méiyǒu cóngtóu-dàowěi kànwán zhèxiē xìn 他没有从头到尾看完这些信; (*by way of*) tōngguò 通过; I came to know her through a friend wǒ tōngguò yí gè péngyou

rènshile tā 我通过一个朋友认识了她；she found a new
job through the newspaper tā tōngguò bàozhǐ zhǎodàole
yí gè xīn gōngzuò 她通过看报纸找到了一个新工作；(when
talking about time) right through the day zhěngzhěng yì
tiān 整整一天；from Friday through to Sunday cóng
xīngqīwǔ dào xīngqīrì 从星期五到星期日；open April
through September (US English) cóng sìyuè dào jiǔyuè
kāifàng 从 4 月到 9 月开放

throw /θrəʊ/ vb (to fling, cast) rēng 扔；to throw
stones at someone xiàng mǒu rén rēng shítou 向某人扔
石头；throw me the ball bǎ qiú rēnggěi wǒ 把球扔给我；
to throw a book to the floor bǎ yì běn shū rēng zài dì
shang 把一本书扔在地上；(to cause to fall) to
throw someone to the ground bǎ mǒu rén shuāidǎo zài
dì shang 把某人摔倒在地上；throw away, throw out
rēngdiào 扔掉

thumb /θʌm/ n the thumb dàmǔzhǐ 大拇指

thunder /'θʌndə(r)/ n léi 雷，léishēng 雷声

thunderstorm /'θʌndəstɔːm/ n a thunderstorm yì chǎng
léibàoyǔ 一场雷暴雨

Thursday /'θɜːzdɪ/ n Thursday xīngqīsì 星期四，lǐbàisì 礼
拜四

ticket /'tɪkɪt/ n a ticket yì zhāng piào 一张票

tickle /'tɪkl/ vb (to itch) fāyǎng 发痒；(to cause to
produce laughter) to tickle someone dòu mǒu rén xiào
逗某人笑

tide /taɪd/ n the tide cháo 潮，cháoshuǐ 潮水；the tide is
out tuìcháo le 退潮了；the tide is coming in zhǎngcháo
le 涨潮了

tidy /'taɪdɪ/ adj zhěngjié de 整洁的，zhěngqí de 整齐的；
tidy up zhěnglǐ 整理，shōushí 收拾

tie /taɪ/ **1** vb (to fasten, tether) shuān 拴；to tie a dog
to a tree bǎ yì zhī gǒu shuān zài yì kē shù shang 把一只
狗拴在一棵树上；(to bind) kǔn 捆，zā 扎；to tie the
parcel (up) with string yòng shéngzi bǎ bāoguǒ kǔn

qǐlai 用绳子把包裹捆起来；(*to make a knot*) jì 系；**to tie one's shoelaces** jì xiédài 系鞋带；**to tie one's tie** dǎ lǐngdài 打领带 *n* (*worn with a shirt*) **a tie** yì tiáo lǐngdài 一条领带；(*in sport*) **a tie** yí gè píngjú 一个平局，**tie up** (*to parcel up*) kǔnzā 捆扎；(*to tether*) shuān 拴

tiger /'taɪɡə(r)/ *n* **a tiger** yì zhī lǎohǔ 一只老虎

tight /taɪt/ *adj* (*firmly fixed*) láogù de 牢固的，jǐn de 紧的；(*taut, tense*) lājǐn de 拉紧的，bēngjǐn de 绷紧的；(*closely fitting*) jǐn de 紧的；**are the shoes too tight for you?** zhè shuāng xié nǐ chuān tài jǐn le ma? 这双鞋你穿太紧了吗？；(*air-tight, water-tight*) mìfēng de 密封的

tights /taɪts/ *n* jǐnshēnkù 紧身裤

till¹ /tɪl/ ▶ **until**

till² /tɪl/ *n* **a till** yí gè fàng qián de chōuti 一个放钱的抽屉

timber /'tɪmbə(r)/ *n* mùcái 木材，mùliào 木料

time /taɪm/ *n* shíjiān 时间；**I don't have time to go there** wǒ méiyǒu shíjiān qù nàr 我没有时间去那儿；**we haven't seen them for a long time** wǒmen hěn cháng shíjiān méiyǒu kànjian tāmen le 我们很长时间没有看见他们了；**there is no time for you to argue** méiyǒu shíjiān ràng nǐmen zhēnglùn 没有时间让你们争论；**a long time ago** hěnjiǔ yǐqián 很久以前；(*when talking about a specific hour or period of time*) **what's the time? what time is it?** jǐ diǎn le? 几点了？；**what time does the film start?** diànyǐng jǐ diǎn kāiyǎn? 电影几点开演？，diànyǐng shénme shíhou kāiyǎn? 电影什么时候开演？；**on time** ànshí yídào 按时到达；**to arrive on time** ànshí dàodá ànshí dàodá 按时到达；**in** [**five days'** | **a week's** | **six months'**] **time** guò [wǔ tiān | yí gè xīngqī | liù gè yuè] 过［5天 | 一个星期 | 6个月］；**this time last year** qùnián zhège shíhou 去年这个时候；**by this time next week** xiàge xīngqī zhège shíhou (zhīqián) 下个星期这个时候（之前）；**it's time we left** wǒmen gāi zǒu le 我们该走了；(*a moment*) **at times** yǒushí 有时，bùshí 不时；**from time to time** yǒushí 有时，bùshí 不时；**at the right time** zài shìdàng de shíhou 在适当的时候；

any time now cóng xiànzài qǐ suíshí 从现在起随时；he may arrive at any time now cóng xiànzài qǐ tā suíshí dōu huì dàodá 从现在起他随时都会到达；for the time being zànshí 暂时；(a period in the past) we didn't know each other at the time nà shí(hou) wǒmen hùxiāng bú rènshi 那时(候)，我们互相不认识；(an experience) to have a good time guò de hěn yúkuài 过得很愉快；to have a hard time concentrating wúfǎ jízhōng jīnglì 无法集中精力；(an occasion) cì 次，huí 回：[this | last | next | first | second | the last] time [zhè | shàng | xià | dì-èr | zuìhòu] cì [这 | 上 | 下] 第 1 [第 2 | 最后] 次；[five | several | many] times [wǔ | jǐ | xǔduō] cì [5 | 几 | 许多]次；the first time we met wǒmen dì-yī cì jiànmiàn de shíhou 我们第 1 次见面的时候；(-fold) bèi 倍：three times more expensive guì sān bèi 贵 3 倍；ten times quicker kuài shí bèi 快 10 倍。

timetable /'taɪmˌteɪbl/ n (for trains, buses) a timetable yí gè shíkèbiǎo 一个时刻表；(in school, at work) a timetable yí gè shíjiānbiǎo 一个时间表

tin /tɪn/ n (the metal) tin xī 锡；(British English) (a tin can) a tin yì tǒng (guàntou) 一筒(罐头)；a tin of beans yì tǒng dòuzi guàntou 一筒豆子罐头

tin opener /'tɪn ˌəʊpənə(r)/ n (British English) a tin opener yì bǎ guàntou qǐzi 一把罐头起子，yì bǎ kāiguàntoudāo 一把开罐头刀

tiny /'taɪni/ adj jí xiǎo de 极小的，wēixiǎo de 微小的

tip /tɪp/ n (the point) the tip of [a pen | the finger | the nose | the tongue] [bǐ | shǒuzhǐ | bízi | shétou]jiān [笔 | 手指 | 鼻子 | 舌头]尖；(an extra sum of money given to reward good service) a tip yí fèn xiǎofèi 一份小费；(a piece of advice) a tip yí gè gàojiè 一个告诫；(a hint) a tip yí gè tíshì 一个提示，yí gè ànshì 一个暗示

tire /'taɪə(r)/ n (US English) a tire yí gè lúntāi 一个轮胎，yí gè chētāi 一个车胎

tired /'taɪəd/ adj (needing rest) lèi de 累的，pílao de 疲劳的，píjuàn de 疲倦的；he is tired tā lèi le 他累了；

(*needing a change*) **to be tired of** yànfán 厌烦，yànjuàn 厌倦；**I'm tired of being a waitress** wǒ duì dāng nǚfúwùyuán yànfán le 我对当女服务员厌烦了

tiring /'taɪərɪŋ/ *adj* lèi rén de 累人的，lìng rén píláo de 令人疲劳的

tissue /'tɪʃjuː/ *n* **a tissue** yì zhāng wèishēngzhǐ 一张卫生纸，yì zhāng miánzhǐ 一张棉纸

to /强 tuː; 弱 tʊ/ *prep* ! *There are many adjectives like* mean, rice, rude, *etc.*, *and verbs like* belong, write, *etc.*, *which involve the use of* to. *For translations*, *look up the adjective entres at* mean, nice, rude *or the verb entries at* belong, write.

toast /təʊst/ *n* kǎomiànbāo 烤面包；**a piece of toast** yí piàn kǎomiànbāo 一片烤面包

toaster /'təʊstə(r)/ *n* **a toaster** yí gè kǎomiànbāoxiāng 一个烤面包箱

today /tə'deɪ/ *adv* jīntiān 今天，jīnrì 今日

toe /təʊ/ *n* jiǎozhǐ 脚趾，jiǎojiān 脚尖

toffee /'tɒfɪ/ *n* nǎitáng 奶糖，tàifēitáng 太妃糖

together /tə'geðə(r)/ *adv* yìqǐ 一起，yíkuàir 一块儿

toilet /'tɔɪlɪt/ *n* **a toilet** yí gè cèsuǒ 一个厕所

toilet paper /'tɔɪlɪt ˌpeɪpə(r)/ *n* wèishēngzhǐ 卫生纸

tomato /tə'mɑːtəʊ/ *n* **a tomato** yí gè xīhóngshì 一个西红柿，yí gè fānqié 一个番茄

tomorrow /tə'mɒrəʊ/ *adv* míngtiān 明天，míngrì 明日

tongue /tʌŋ/ *n* shétou 舌头，shé 舌

tonight /tə'naɪt/ *adv* (*this evening*) jīntiān wǎnshang 今天晚上，jīnwǎn 今晚；(*during the night*) jīntiān yèlǐ 今天夜里，jīnyè 今夜

too /tuː/ *adv* (*also*) yè 也；**I'm going too** wǒ yě qù 我也去；(*more than is necessary or desirable*) tài 太；**it's too** [big|expensive|far] tài [dà|guì|yuǎn] le 太 [大|贵|远] 了；**there were too many people** rén tài duō le 人太多了；**I ate too much** wǒ chī de tài duō le 我吃得太多了

tool /tuːl/ *n* **a tool** yí gè gōngjù 一个工具

tooth /tu:θ/ n a tooth yì kē yá 一颗牙；a set of false teeth yí tào jiǎyá 一套假牙

toothache /'tu:θeɪk/ n he has a toothache tā yá tòng 他牙痛

toothbrush /'tu:θbrʌʃ/ n a toothbrush yì bǎ yáshuā 一把牙刷

toothpaste /'tu:θpeɪst/ n yágāo 牙膏

top /tɒp/ **1** n (the highest part) dǐng 顶, dǐngbù 顶部；at the top of [the hill | the tree | the tower | the stairs] (zài) [shān | shù | tǎ | lóutī] dǐng (shang) (在) [山 | 树 | 塔 | 楼梯] 顶 (上)；the fourth line from the top cóng shàngmian shǔ dì-sì háng 从上面数第 4 行；(a cover, a lid) a top (on a bottle, pot, pan) yí gè gàir 一个盖儿, yí gè gàizi 一个盖子；(on a pen) yí gè bǐmào 一个笔帽；(the highest level) to get to the top in the competition zài bǐsài zhōng huòdé dì-yī 在比赛中获得第1；to be at the top of the class zài bān li míngliè dì-yī 在班里名列第一 **2** adj the top [shelf | drawer | button] dǐngshang de [jiàzi | chōuti | kòuzi] 顶上的 [架子 | 抽屉 | 扣子]

torch /tɔːtʃ/ n (a flashlight) (British English) a torch yí gè shǒudiàn (tǒng) 一个手电 (筒)；(a portable stick of inflammable material for producing a flame) a torch yí gè huǒjù 一个火炬, yí gè huǒbǎ 一个火把

torn /tɔːn/ adj sīpòle de 撕破了的, chěpòle de 扯破了的

tortoise /'tɔːtəs/ n a tortoise yì zhī (wū) guī 一只 (乌) 龟

total /'təʊtəl/ **1** n a total zǒngshù 总数；(if it's money) zǒng'é 总额 **2** adj zǒng de 总的, quánbù de 全部的

touch /tʌtʃ/ **1** vb (with one's hand) mō 摸, chùmō 触摸；(come into contact with) pèng 碰, jiēchù 接触；(affect one's feelings) shǐ … gǎndòng 使 … 感动；the story touched us all zhège gùshi shǐ wǒmen dōu hěn gǎndòng 这个故事使我们都很感动 **2** n to get in touch with someone yǔ mǒu rén liánxì 与某人联系；to keep/stay in touch with someone yǔ mǒu rén bǎochí liánxì 与某人保

持联系

tough /tʌf/ adj (strong, resilient, not brittle) jiānrèn de 坚韧的，jiēshi de 结实的；(sturdy) jiànzhuàng de 健壮的；(unyielding, as a policy, attitude, or view) qiángyìng de 强硬的；(when describing a person) wánqiáng de 顽强的，jiānqiáng de 坚强的；(difficult) kùnnan de 困难的，nánbàn de 难办的；(rough) a tough **area** yí gè hěn luàn de dìqū 一个很乱的地区

tour /tʊə(r)/ **1** n (by a singer, a band, a theatre group) a tour yí cì xúnhuí yǎnchū 一次巡回演出；on tour zhèngzài xúnhuí yǎnchū 正在巡回演出；(by a sports person, a sports team) a tour yí cì xúnhuí bǐsài 一次巡回比赛；(by tourists, pupils, visitors) a tour (when travelling from place to place) yí cì lǚxíng 一次旅行，yí cì lǚyóu 一次旅游；(visiting a single area) yí cì yóulǎn 一次游览，yí cì cānguān 一次参观；to go on a tour of the castle qù yóulǎn chéngbǎo 去游览城堡 **2** vb to go touring qù lǚxíng 去旅行；to tour the United States zhōuyóu Měiguó 周游美国

tourism /'tʊərizəm/ n lǚyóuyè 旅游业

tourist /'tʊərɪst/ n a tourist yí wèi yóukè 一位游客，yì míng lǚxíngzhě 一名旅行者

tourist information office /ˌtʊərɪst ɪnfə'meɪʃən ˌɒfɪs/ n a tourist information office yí gè lǚyóu xìnxī fúwùchù 一个旅游信息服务处

toward /tə'wɔːd/ prep (in the direction of) xiàng 向，cháo 朝；towards the east xiàng dōngbian cháo 东边，朝东边；(shortly before) jiāngjìn 将近，jiējìn 接近；towards evening jiāngjìn wǎnshang 将近晚上；(when talking about attitudes, feelings) duì 对，duìyú 对于；to be friendly towards someone duì mǒu rén hěn yǒuhǎo 对某人很友好

towel /'taʊəl/ n a towel yì tiáo máojīn 一条毛巾

tower /'taʊə(r)/ n a tower yí zuò tǎ 一座塔

tower block /'taʊə blɒk/ n (British English) a tower

block yí zuò gāolóu 一座高楼

town /taʊn/ n a town yí gè chéng(zhèn) 一个城(镇)，yí gè zhèn 一个镇；to go into town jìn chéng 进城

town hall /ˌtaʊn ˈhɔːl/ n a town hall yí gè shìzhèngtīng 一个市政厅

toy /tɔɪ/ n a toy yí gè wánjù 一个玩具

track /træk/ n (a path) a track yì tiáo lù 一条路，yì tiáo xiǎodào 一条小道；(in sports) a track yì tiáo pǎodào 一条跑道；(rails) the track(s) tiěguǐ 铁轨，guǐdào 轨道；(left by a person, an animal, a car) tracks xíngzōng 行踪，zōngjì 踪迹

tracksuit /ˈtræksjuːt/ n a tracksuit yí tào yùndòngfú 一套运动服

trade /treɪd/ n màoyì 贸易，jiāoyì 交易；a trade yì zhǒng zhíyè 一种职业，yì zhǒng hángyè 一种行业

tradition /trəˈdɪʃən/ n a tradition yí gè chuántǒng 一个传统

traffic /ˈtræfɪk/ n jiāotōng 交通

traffic jam /ˈtræfɪk dʒæm/ n a traffic jam jiāotōng dǔsè 交通堵塞

traffic lights /ˈtræfɪk laɪts/ n jiāotōng xìnhàodēng 交通信号灯，hónglùdēng 红绿灯

train /treɪn/ **1** n a train yí liè huǒchē 一列火车；the train to Shanghai qù Shànghǎi de huǒchē 去上海的火车 **2** vb (to teach, to prepare) péixùn 培训，xùnliàn 训练；to train employees péixùn gùyuán 培训雇员；to train athletes xùnliàn yùndòngyuán 训练运动员；(to learn a job) to train as a doctor jiēshòu zuò yīshēng de xùnliàn 接受做医生的训练；(for a sporting event) xùnliàn 训练，duànliàn 锻炼；to train for a better result in the sports meet wèi zài yùndònghuì shang qǔdé gèng hǎo de chéngjì ér xùnliàn 为在运动会上取得更好的成绩而训练

trainer /ˈtreɪnə(r)/ n (a shoe) (British English) yùndòngxié 运动鞋；a pair of trainers yì shuāng yùndòngxié 一双运动鞋；(a person in sports) a trainer yí wèi jiàoliànyuán 一位教练员

training course /'treɪnɪŋ ˌkɔːs/ *n* a training course yí gè péixùnbān 一个培训班

tramp /træmp/ *n* a tramp yí gè liúlàngzhě 一个流浪者

translate /træns'leɪt/ *vb* (to turn from one language into another) fānyì 翻译 翻译;(to interpret, to explain) jiěshì 解释,shuōmíng 说明

translator /træns'leɪtə(r)/ *n* a translator yì míng fānyì 一名翻译

transport /træn'spɔːt/, **transportation** /ˌtrænspə'teɪʃən/ (US English) *n* yùnshū 运输,jiāotōng 交通;a means of transport yì zhǒng yùnshū gōngjù 一种运输工具,yì zhǒng jiāotōng gōngjù 一种交通工具;public transport gōnggòng jiāotōng 公共交通;gōnggòng yùnshū 公共运输

trap /træp/ *n* a trap (a device for catching) yí gè xiànjǐng 一个陷阱;(a plan to deceive, betray, etc.) yí gè quāntào 一个圈套;to set a trap for someone wèi mǒu rén shè yí gè quāntào 为某人设一个圈套

trash /træʃ/ *n* (US English) fèiwù 废物,lājī 垃圾

trash can /'træʃ ˌkæn/ *n* (US English) a trash can yí gè lājīxiāng 一个垃圾桶

travel /'trævəl/ *vb* lǚxíng 旅行;to travel [abroad | to China | by bike] [qù guówài | qù Zhōngguó | qí zìxíngchē] lǚxíng [去国外 | 去中国 | 骑自行车] 旅行

travel agency /'trævəl ˌeɪdʒənsɪ/ *n* a travel agency yì jiā lǚxíngshè 一家旅行社

traveller /'trævələ(r)/ (British English), **traveler** (US English) *n* a traveller yí gè lǚxíngzhě 一个旅行者,yí gè yóukè 一个游客

traveller's cheque /'trævələz ˌtʃek/ (British English), **traveler's check** (US English) *n* a traveller's cheque yì zhāng lǚxíng zhīpiào 一张旅行支票

tray /treɪ/ *n* a tray yí gè pánzi 一个盘子,yí gè tuōpán 一个托盘

treat /triːt/ *vb* (to behave towards) duìdài 对待;to

treat someone [badly|nicely|politely] duìdài mǒu rén [hěn bù hǎo|hěn hǎo|hěn yǒu lǐmào]对待某人 [很不好|很好|很有礼貌];(*to deal with, to handle*) chǔlǐ 处理;**we have to treat this carefully** wǒmen děi xiǎoxīn chǔlǐ zhè jiàn shì 我们得小心处理这件事;(*to give medical treatment to*) yīzhì 医治, zhìliáo 治疗;**to treat someone for flu** gěi mǒu rén yīzhì liúgǎn 给某人医治流感;(*to pay for*) **to treat someone to Peking duck** qǐng mǒu rén chī Běijīng kǎoyā 请某人吃北京烤鸭

treatment /ˈtriːtmənt/ *n* (*behaviour towards someone*) dàiyù 待遇, kuǎndài 款待;**to receive warm and friendly treatment from someone** shòudào mǒu rén rèqíng yǒuhǎo de kuǎndài 受到某人热情友好的款待;(*by a doctor*) zhìliáo 治疗;**free treatment** miǎnfèi zhìliáo 免费治疗

tree /triː/ *n* **a tree** yì kē shù 一棵树

tremble /ˈtrembl/ *vb* fādǒu 发抖, duōsuo 哆嗦;**they were trembling with fear** tāmen xià de fādǒu 他们吓得发抖

trendy /ˈtrendɪ/ *adj* shímáo de 时髦的, suí cháoliú de 随潮流的

trial /ˈtraɪəl/ *n* (*a test or an experiment*) **a trial** yí cì shìyàn 一次试验;(*in court*) **a trial** yí cì shěnwèn/shěnpàn 一次审问/审判;**to go on trial** shòu shěn(pàn) 受审(判)

triangle /ˈtraɪæŋgl/ *n* **a triangle** yí gè sānjiǎo(xíng) 一个三角(形)

trick /trɪk/ **1** *n* (*a joke*) **a trick** yí gè èzuòjù 一个恶作剧;**to play a trick on someone** zhuōnòng mǒu rén 捉弄某人;(*a means of deceiving*) **a trick** yí gè guǐjì 一个诡计, yí gè piànjú 一个骗局;(*to entertain*) **a trick** yí gè xìfǎ 一个戏法, yí gè bǎxì 一个把戏 **2** *vb* qīpiàn 欺骗, hǒngpiàn 哄骗

trip /trɪp/ **1** *n* (*a journey*) **a trip** yí cì lǚxíng 一次旅行;**to be on a business trip** chūchāi 出差, zuò yí cì gōngwù lǚxíng 做一次公务旅行 **2** *vb* (*to stumble*) bàn(dǎo) 绊

(倒)；I tripped over the step at the gate wǒ ràng ménkǒu de táijiē bànle yíxià 我让门口的台阶绊了一下；to trip someone (up) bǎ mǒu rén bàndǎo 把某人绊倒

trouble /'trʌbl/ n (difficulties) kùnnan 困难；he has trouble using this computer tā yòng zhè tái jìsuànjī yǒu kùnnan 他用这台计算机有困难；(a scrape) kùnjìng 困境；to be in trouble chǔyú kùnjìng 处于困境；to get someone into trouble shǐ mǒu rén xiànrù kùnjìng 使某人陷入困境；(disturbance) máfan 麻烦；to make trouble zhìzào máfan 制造麻烦，nàoshì 闹事；I'm sorry to have given you so much trouble duìbuqǐ, wǒ gěi nǐmen tiānle zhème duō máfan 对不起，我给你们添了这么多麻烦；(an effort) tā bùcí-láokǔ wèi měi gè bìngrén dōu zuòle jiǎnchá 他不辞劳苦为每个病人都做了检查；to go to a lot of trouble helping others bùcí-láokǔ bāngzhù biérén 不辞劳苦帮助别人

trousers /'trauzəz/ n kùzi 裤子；a pair of trousers yì tiáo kùzi 一条裤子

trout /traut/ n a trout yì tiáo zūnyú 一条鳟鱼，yì tiáo guīyú 一条鲑鱼

truck /trʌk/ n a truck yí liàng kǎchē 一辆卡车

truck driver /'trʌk ˌdraɪvə(r)/ n a truck driver yí wèi kǎchē sījī 一位卡车司机

true /tru:/ adj (genuine) zhēn de 真的；(in accordance with facts) zhēnshí de 真实的，zhēn de 真的；is it true that he's leaving? tā yào zǒu shì zhēn de ma? 他要走是真的吗？；a true story yí gè zhēnshí de gùshi 一个真实的故事；to come true shíxiàn 实现；(faithful) zhōngshí de 忠实的；a true friend yí gè zhōngshí de péngyou 一个忠实的朋友

trumpet /'trʌmpɪt/ n a trumpet yí gè (xiǎo)hào 一个(小)号

trunk /trʌŋk/ n (of a tree) a trunk yí gè shùgàn 一个树干；(of an elephant) a trunk yí gè xiàng bízi 一个象鼻子；(US English) (of a car) the trunk xínglixiāng 行李箱

trust /trʌst/ vb (believe in) xìnrèn 信任，xiāngxìn 相信；
I don't trust them wǒ bú xìnrèn tāmen 我不信任他们；
(to rely on) xìnlài 信赖；you can't trust them nǐ bù
néng xìnlài tāmen 你不能信赖他们

truth /truːθ/ n (a proposition that agrees with actuality) a
truth yì tiáo zhēnlǐ 一条真理；(the actual fact, the real
situation) the truth zhēnxiàng 真相，zhēnshí qíngkuàng
真实情况

try /traɪ/ **1** vb (to endeavour) jìnlì 尽力，jǐnliàng 尽量，
lìtú 力图；to try to [learn Chinese well | come early | forget
that matter...] lìtú [xuéhǎo Hànyǔ | zǎo lái | wàngjì nà jiàn shì...]
力图[学好汉语 | 早来 | 忘记那件事...]；(to attempt) shì shì，
chángshì 尝试；try phoning him shìzhe gěi tā dǎ diànhuà
试着给他打电话；let me try ràng wǒ shì yíxià 让我试一
下；(to test) shì shì，shìyòng 试用；to try (out) a new
method shìyòng yì zhǒng xīn de fāngfǎ 试用一种新的方
法；to try (on) a pair of jeans shì (chuān) yì tiáo
niúzǎikù 试(穿)一条牛仔裤；(to taste) (pǐn) cháng (品)
尝；(in court) shěnxùn 审讯，shěnpàn 审判 **2** n let me
have a try ràng wǒ shì yíxià 让我试一下

T-shirt /ˈtiːʃɜːt/ n a T-shirt yí jiàn tìxùshān 一件T恤衫

tube /tjuːb/ n a tube yì gēn guǎnzi 一根管子；(for a
wheel) a tube yí gè nèitāi 一个内胎；(British English)
(the underground) the tube dìtiě 地铁，dìxià tiědào 地下
铁道

Tuesday /ˈtjuːzdɪ/ n xīngqī'èr 星期二，lǐbài'èr 礼拜二

tuna /ˈtjuːnə/ n jīnqiāngyú 金枪鱼

tunnel /ˈtʌnəl/ n a tunnel yì tiáo suìdào 一条隧道

turkey /ˈtɜːkɪ/ n a turkey yì zhī huǒjī 一只火鸡

turn /tɜːn/ **1** vb (to rotate) zhuàn 转，zhuàndòng 转动；
the wheel is turning fast lúnzi zài hěn kuài de
zhuàndòng 轮子在很快地转动；to turn the handle
zhuàndòng bǎshǒu 转动把手；(to move one's body)
zhuǎnshēn 转身；she turned and walked away tā
zhuǎnshēn zǒu le 她转身走了；(to change direction) zhuǎn

转；to turn right xiàng yòu zhuǎn 向右转；she turned her face towards the sun tā bǎ liǎn zhuǎnxiàng tàiyáng 她把脸转向太阳；(when talking about a page) fān 翻；please turn to page 10 qǐng fāndào dì-shí yè 请翻到第 10 页；(to change) bǎ…biànchéng 把…变成；to turn the bedroom into an office bǎ wòshì biànchéng yì jiān bàngōngshì 把卧室变成一间办公室；(to become) biànchéng 变成；to turn into a butterfly biànchéng yì zhī húdié 变成一只蝴蝶；to turn red biàn(chéng) hóng (de) 变(成)红(的)；(on the road, in the corridor) guǎi 拐；don't turn left bié wǎng zuǒ guǎi 别往左拐 **2** n (a bend) a turn yí gè zhuǎnwān 一个转弯，yí gè guǎiwān 一 个拐弯；(when talking about taking turns) whose turn is it? lúndào shéi le? 轮到谁了？；it's your turn now xiànzài lúndào nǐ le 现在轮到你了；**turn around, turn round** (to face the other way) (if it's a person) zhuǎnguò shēn (qù) 转过身(去)；(if it's a car) diàotóu 调头；(to go round and round) zhuànquān 转圈；**turn away** (to turn or look in a different direction) zhuǎnguò shēn/liǎn qù 转 过身/脸去；she turned away embarrassed tā bùhǎoyìsi de zhuǎnguò shēn qù 她不好意思地转过身去；(to dismiss from service) jiěgù 解雇；(to cause to leave) dǎfā zǒu 打 发走，niǎnzǒu 撵走；the police turned the students away jǐngchá bǎ nàxiē xuéshēng dǎfā zǒu le 警察把那些 学生打发走了；**turn back** (to return) zhéhuí 折回，wǎng huí zǒu 往回走；he found this was the wrong road and then turned back tā fāxiàn zhè tiáo lù bú duì, jiù wǎng huí zǒu le 他发现这条路不对，就往回走了；(when dealing with pages) fān huídào 翻回到；please turn back to page 5 qǐng fān huídào dì-wǔ yè 请翻回到第 5 页，**turn down** (to lower) guānxiǎo 关小，tiáodī 调低；to turn down the radio bǎ shōuyīnjī guānxiǎo 把收音机关 小；(to reject) jùjué 拒绝；to turn someone down jùjué mǒu rén 拒绝某人，**turn off** guānshang 关上；to turn off [the oven | the light | the tap…] bǎ [kǎoxiāng | dēng |

shuǐlóngtóu…]guānshang 把 [烤箱|灯|水龙头…]关上；**turn on dǎkāi** 打开，**kāi** 开；**to turn on** [the TV | the radio | the tap…] bǎ [diànshìjī|shōuyīnjī|shuǐlóngtóu…]dǎkāi 把 [电视机|收音机|水龙头…]打开；**turn out to turn out all right** (**in the end**) (zuìhòu) jiéguǒ búcuò (最后) 结果不错；**to turn out to be easy** yuánlái hěn róngyì 原来很容易；**turn over** (*to roll over*) dǎfān 打翻；**he turned the vase over** tā bǎ huāpíng dǎfān le 他把花瓶打翻了；**to turn over the page** fāndào xià yí yè 翻到下一页；**turn up** (*to arrive*) lái, dào 来，到；(*to increase*) to turn up [the heating | the music | the TV] bǎ [nuǎnqì|yīnyuè|diànshì]kāidà 把 [暖气|音乐|电视]开大

turtle /ˈtɜːtl/ *n* a (**sea**) **turtle** yí zhī (hǎi)guī 一只(海)龟；(*US English*) (*a tortoise*) **a turtle** yí zhī wūguī 一只乌龟

TV /ˌtiːˈviː/ *n* **a TV** yì tái diànshìjī 一台电视机

twelfth /twelfθ/ *num* (*in a series*) dì-shí'èr 第十二；(*in dates*) shí'èr rì 十二日，shí'èr hào 十二号；**the twelfth of July** qīyuè shí'èr hào 7 月 12 号

twelve /twelv/ *num* **twelve** shí'èr 十二

twenty /ˈtwentɪ/ *num* **twenty** èrshí 二十

twice /twaɪs/ *adv* (*when talking about the number of times*) liǎng cì 两次；**I met him twice** wǒ jiànguo tā liǎng cì 我见过他两次；(*two-fold*) liǎng bèi 两倍；**twice** [as many people | as much time] liǎngbèi [duō de rén | duō de shíjiān] 两倍 [多的人|多的时间]

twin /twɪn/ **1** *n* **a twin** yí duì shuāngbāotāi 一对双胞胎 **2** *adj* shuāngbāotāi de 双胞胎的，luánshēng de 孪生的；**a twin** [brother | sister] (*younger*) yí gè shuāngbāotāi de [dìdi | mèimei] 一个双胞胎的 [弟弟|妹妹]；(*older*) yí gè shuāngbāotāi de [gēge | jiějie] 一个双胞胎的 [哥哥|姐姐]；**twin** [brothers | sisters] luánshēng [xiōngdì|jiěmèi] 孪生 [兄弟|姐妹]

twist /twɪst/ *vb* (*to form a spiral*) níng/nǐng 拧，niǔ 扭；**to twist a rope** níng yì gēn shéngzi 拧一根绳子；(*to injure*) niǔshāng 扭伤；**he twisted his ankle** tā niǔshāngle jiǎobózi 他扭伤了脚脖子

two /tuː/ num (in counting , in numbers , digits) èr 二；
(the year) 2002 èrlínglíng'èr nián 2002 年；(when used
with a measure word) liǎng 两；**two brothers** liǎng gè
xiōngdi 两个兄弟

type /taɪp/ **1** n a type (a sort , a kind) yì zhǒng (lèixíng)
一种（类型）；**this type of** [person | book | building...] zhè
zhǒng [rén | shū | lóu...]这种 [人 | 书 | 楼...]；**he's not my type**
tā bú shì wǒ xǐhuan de nà zhǒng rén 他不是我喜欢的那种
人 **2** vb dǎzì 打字

typewriter /'taɪpˌraɪtə(r)/ n a typewriter yì tái dǎzìjī
一台打字机

typical /'tɪpɪkəl/ adj diǎnxíng de 典型的

typist /'taɪpɪst/ n a typist yì míng dǎzìyuán 一名打字员

tyre /taɪə(r)/ n (British English) **a tyre** yí gè lúntāi 一个
轮胎，yí gè chētāi 一个车胎

Uu

---

ugly /'ʌɡlɪ/ adj (unpleasant to the sight) chǒu(lòu) de 丑
陋(的)，nánkàn de 难看的

umbrella /ʌm'brelə/ n an umbrella yì bǎ (yǔ)sǎn 一把雨
伞

unbelievable /ˌʌnbɪ'liːvəbl/ adj nányǐ-zhìxìn de 难以置
信的，wúfǎ xiāngxìn de 无法相信的

uncle /'ʌŋkl/ n an uncle (father's elder brother) yí gè
bófù 一个伯父，yí gè bóbo 一个伯伯；(father's younger
brother) yígè shūshu 一个叔叔；(mother's younger or elder
brother) yí gè jiùjiu 一个舅舅；(husband of father's
sister) yí gè gūfu 一个姑父；(husband of mother's sister)
yí gè yífu 一个姨父；(not a relation) **an uncle** (a man
younger than one's father) yí gè shūshu 一个叔叔；(a man
older than one's father) yí gè bóbo 一个伯伯

uncomfortable /ˌʌnˈkʌmfətəbl/ adj (awkward and uneasy) bú zìzài de 不自在的, bù'ān de 不安的；to make someone (feel) uncomfortable shǐ mǒu rén (gǎndào) bú zìzài 使某人感到不自在；(describing a physical feeling) bù shūfu de 不舒服的；I felt uncomfortable sitting in that chair wǒ zuò zài nà bǎ yǐzi shang gǎnjué bù shūfu 我坐在那把椅子上感觉不舒服；(describing the physical condition of something) bù shūfu de 不舒服的, bù shūshì de 不舒适的；an uncomfortable bed yì zhāng bù shūfu de chuáng 一张不舒服的床

unconscious /ˌʌnˈkɒnʃəs/ adj (not knowing) bù zhīdào de 不知道的；I was unconscious of his presence wǒ bù zhīdào tā zàichǎng 我不知道他在场；(lose consciousness) shīqù zhījué de 失去知觉的, búxìng-rénshì de 不省人事的；to knock someone unconscious bǎ mǒu rén zhuàng de shīqù zhījué 把某人撞得失去知觉；(not aware) wúyìshi de 无意识的；an unconscious act yí gè wúyìshi de dòngzuò 一个无意识的动作

under /ˈʌndə(r)/ prep under zài…xiàmian 在…下面, zài …dǐxia 在…底下；to hide under the bed cáng zài chuáng xiàmian 藏在床下面；I found the newspaper under the table wǒ zài zhuōzi dǐxia zhǎodàole bàozhǐ 我在桌子底下找到了报纸；(less than) to earn under three pounds an hour měi xiǎoshí zhèng bú dào sān yīngbàng 每小时挣不到 3 英镑；children under five wǔ suì yǐxià de háizi 5 岁以下的孩子, bù mǎn wǔ suì de háizi 不满 5 岁的孩子

underground /ˈʌndəɡraʊnd/ n (British English) the underground dìtiě 地铁

underline /ˌʌndəˈlaɪn/ vb (to put a line under) zài…xiàmian huà xiàn 在…下面划线；to underline all the names zài suǒyǒu de míngzi xiàmian huà xiàn 在所有的名字下面划线；(to emphasise) qiángdiào 强调；to underline the importance of this meeting qiángdiào zhè cì huìyì de zhòngyàoxìng 强调这次会议的重要性

underneath /ˌʌndə'niːθ/ **1** adv（zài）xiàmian（在）下面，（zài）dǐxià（在）底下／I want to see what's underneath wǒ xiǎng kàn yíxià xiàmian yǒu shénme 我想看一下下面有什么 **2** prep 在…xiàmian 在…下面，zài…xiàbian 在…下边；underneath the building zài dàlóu xiàmian 在大楼下面

underpants /'ʌndəpænts/ n nèikù 内裤

understand /ˌʌndə'stænd/ vb（to comprehend）dǒng懂；I can't understand what they're saying wǒ bù dǒng tāmen shuō de huà 我不懂他们说的话；do you understand Japanese? nǐ dǒng Rìyǔ ma? 你懂日语吗？；to make oneself understood biǎodá qīngchǔ zìjǐ de yìsi 表达清楚自己的意思；(to be able to follow the working, logic, or meaning of) lǐjiě 理解／I can understand why he wants to learn Chinese wǒ kěyǐ lǐjiě tā wèishénme xiǎng xué Zhōngwén 我可以理解他为什么想学中文；(to know) liǎojiě 了解／he doesn't understand the difficult situation I'm in tā bù liǎojiě wǒ suǒ chǔ de kùnjìng 他不了解我所处的困境

understanding /ˌʌndə'stændɪŋ/ adj（sympathetic）néng liàngjiě rén de 能谅解人的；(discerning) an understanding smile huìxīn de wēixiào 会心的微笑；an understanding person yí gè shànjiě-rényì de rén 一个善解人意的人

underwater /'ʌndə'wɔːtə(r)/ adv zài shuǐ xià 在水下

underwear /'ʌndəweə(r)/ n nèiyī 内衣

undo /ʌn'duː/ vb（for buttons, knots）jiěkāi 解开；to undo a button jiěkāi yí gè kòuzi 解开一个扣子；(for parcels, boxes) dǎkāi 打开；(to cancel, to annul) qǔxiāo 取消

undress /ʌn'dres/ vb gěi…tuōxia yīfu 给…脱下衣服；she undressed her daughter tā gěi tā nǚ'ér tuōxia yīfu 她给她女儿脱下衣服；I undressed and went to bed wǒ tuōxia yīfu shàngchuáng shuìjiào 我脱下衣服上床睡觉

uneasy /ʌn'iːzɪ/ adj（anxious）(xīnshén-) bù'ān de（心

神）不安的，yōulǜ de 忧虑的；(uncomfortable) jūshù de 拘束的，bú zìzai de 不自在的

unemployed /ˌʌnɪmˈplɔɪd/ adj (out of work) shīyè de 失业的；he is **unemployed** tā shīyè le 他失业了；**unemployed workers** shīyè de gōngrén 失业的工人

unemployment /ˌʌnɪmˈplɔɪmənt/ n shīyè 失业

unfair /ˌʌnˈfeə(r)/ adj bù gōngpíng de 不公平的，bù gōngzhèng de 不公正的

unfortunately /ˌʌnˈfɔːtʃənətlɪ/ adv búxìng de shì 不幸的是，yíhàn de shì 遗憾的是

unfriendly /ˌʌnˈfrendlɪ/ adj bù yǒuhǎo de 不友好的，lěngmò de 冷漠的

ungrateful /ˌʌnˈgreɪtfʊl/ adj wàng'ēn-fùyì de 忘恩负义的，bù lǐngqíng de 不领情的

unhappy /ˌʌnˈhæpɪ/ adj (not glad) bù gāoxìng de 不高兴的，bù yúkuài de 不愉快的；(not satisfied) bù mǎnyì de 不满意的；**are you unhappy with your new job?** nǐ duì nǐ de xīn gōngzuò bù mǎnyì ma? 你对你的新工作不满意吗?；(without happiness) bú xìngfú de 不幸福的；**he had an unhappy life there** tā zài nàr de shēnghuó hěn bú xìngfú 他在那儿的生活很不幸福

unhealthy /ˌʌnˈhelθɪ/ adj (describing a person) bú jiànkāng de 不健康的，yǒubìng de 有病的；(describing a way of life, food) duì jiànkāng yǒuhài de 对健康有害的；(not morally or spiritually wholesome) bùliáng 不良

uniform /ˈjuːnɪfɔːm/ n a uniform yí tào zhìfú 一套制服；**a school uniform** yí tào xiàofú 一套校服；**a police uniform** yí tào jǐngfú 一套警服；**an army uniform** yí tào jūnzhuāng 一套军装

union /ˈjuːnjən/ n a union (a trade union) yí gè gōnghuì 一个工会；(a federation) yí gè liánhéhuì 一个联合会

unique /juːˈniːk/ adj (being the only one of its kind) wéiyī de 唯一的，dúyī-wú'èr de 独一无二的；(unusual) dútè de 独特的

United Kingdom /juːˌnaɪtɪd ˈkɪŋdəm/ n Liánhé Wángguó 联合王国

联合王国，Yīngguó 英国

United States（of America） /juːˌnaɪtɪd ˈsteɪts（əv əˈmerɪkə）/ n Měilìjiān Hézhòngguó 美利坚合众国，Měiguó 美国

universe /ˈjuːnɪvɜːs/ n（the whole system of things）yǔzhòu 宇宙，tiāndì wànwù 天地万物；（the world）shìjiè 世界

university /juːnɪˈvɜːsəti/ n a university yì suǒ dàxué 一所大学

unkind /ˌʌnˈkaɪnd/ adj（when describing a person, an action）bù réncí de 不仁慈的，bù héshàn de 不和善的；（when describing a remark）kēkè de 苛刻的，kèbó de 刻薄的

unknown /ˌʌnˈnəʊn/ adj his telephone number is unknown to me tā de diànhuà hàomǎ wǒ bù zhīdào 他的电话号码我不知道；an unknown number yí gè wèizhīshù 一个未知数；an unknown hero yí gè wúmíng yīngxióng 一个无名英雄

unless /ənˈles/ conj rúguǒ（…）bù 如果（…）不，chúfēi…fǒuzé 除非…否则！Note that the clause introduced by rúguǒ bù 如果不 must precede the main clause. Note also that rúguǒ 如果 and bù 不 can be separated by the subject or put together after the subject；she won't come unless you phone her rúguǒ nǐ bù gěi tā dǎ diànhuà，tā bú huì lái 如果你不给她打电话，她不会来；you wouldn't understand this book unless you know Chinese history nǐ rúguǒ bù liǎojiě Zhōngguó lìshǐ，nǐ jiù huì kàn bù dǒng zhè běn shū 你如果不了解中国历史，你就会看不懂这本书；I'll cancel the meeting unless he can come chúfēi tā néng lái，fǒuzé wǒ jiù qǔxiāo zhè cì huìyì 除非他能来，否则我就取消这次会议

unlock /ˌʌnˈlɒk/ vb bǎ…（de）suǒ dǎkāi 把…（的）锁打开，to unlock the door bǎ ménsuǒ dǎkāi 把门锁打开

unlucky /ˌʌnˈlʌki/ adj（unfortunate）bú xìngyùn de 不幸运的，dǎoméi de 倒霉的；you were unlucky nǐ běn bú xìngyùn

你很不幸运;(ill-omened) bù jíxiáng de 不吉祥的

unpack /ˌʌn'pæk/ vb to unpack a suitcase dǎkāi xiāngzi bǎ dōngxi ná chūlái 打开箱子把东西拿出来

unsuitable /ˌʌn'sjuːtəbl/ adj bù héshì de 不合适的, bù shìyì de 不适宜的

untidy /ˌʌn'taɪdɪ/ adj (describing a place) bù zhěngqí de 不整齐的, língluàn de 凌乱的;(describing a person) lātà de 邋遢的, bùxiū-biānfú de 不修边幅的

until /ən'tɪl/ **1** prep dào 到, (zhí) dào… (wéizhǐ) (直)到…(为止);I'm staying until Thursday wǒ dāi dào xīngqīsì 我呆到星期四;until now zhídào xiànzài 直到现在;I'm going to wait until after Christmas wǒ dǎsuàn děng dào Shèngdàn Jié yǐhòu 我打算等到圣诞节以后;(when used in a negative sentence) ! Note that when until is used in a negative sentence, the pattern not… until is often translated as (zhí) dào… cái…(直)到…才… or (zài)… yǐqián… bù/méi (在)…以前…不/没;she won't get an answer until next week xiàgè xīngqī yǐqián tā bú huì dédào dáfù 下个星期以前她不会得到答复;not until yesterday did I meet him wǒ zhídào zuótiān cái jiàndào tā 我直到昨天才见到他 **2** conj (zhí) dào (直)到;I'll wait until he gets back home wǒ yào děng dào tā huí jiā 我要等到他回家;we'll stay here until they come back wǒmen yào zài zhèr dāi dào tāmen huílái 我们要在这儿呆到他们回来;(when used with a negative main clause) ! Note that when until is used with a negative main clause, the pattern not… until is often translated as (zhí) dào… cái…(直)到…才… or (zài)… yǐqián… bù/méi (在)…以前…不/没;she didn't go to see the doctor she was very ill tā zhídào bìng de hěn lìhai cái qù kàn yīshēng 她直到病得很厉害才去看医生;she won't go to London until her friend has found her a language school there tā péngyou gěi tā zhǎodào yǔyán xuéxiào yǐqián,tā bú huì qù Lúndūn 在她的朋友给她找到语言学校以前,她不会去伦敦

unusual /ʌnˈjuːʒʊəl/ adj (rare) hǎnjiàn de 罕见的，shǎoyǒu de 少有的；such a strong wind is quite unusual in this area zhème dà de fēng zài zhège dìqū shì shǎoyǒu de 这么大的风在这个地区是少有的；(not ordinary) bù xúncháng de 不寻常的，bù píngcháng de 不平常的；it's an unusual day for her today duì tā lái shuō, jīntiān shì gè bù xúncháng de rìzi 对她来说，今天是个不寻常的日子

up /ʌp/ ! often up occurs in combinations with verbs, for example: blow up, give up, own up, etc. To find the correct translations for this type of verb, look up the separeate dictionary entries at blow, give, own, etc. **1** prep the cat's up the tree māo zài shù shang 猫在树上；to go up the street yánzhe mǎlù wǎng qián zǒu 沿着马路往前走；she ran up the stairs tā pǎoshang lóutī 她跑上楼梯；the library is up those stairs túshūguǎn zài nàge lóutī shàngmian 图书馆在那个楼梯上面 **2** adv up in the sky zài tiānshang 在天上；up on (top of) the wardrobe zài yīguì shàngmian 在衣柜上面；to go up to Scotland shàngqù 上去；to go up to Scotland Sūgélán 上苏格兰；up there zài nàr 在那儿；put the painting a bit further up bǎ huà zài wǎng shàng fàng yìdiǎnr 把画再往上放一点儿；to climb up [a hill|a ladder|a tree] pá [shān|tīzi|shù] 爬[山|梯子|树] **3** adj (out of bed) is he up yet? tā qǐchuáng le ma? 他起床了吗？; he was up all night tā yí yè méi shuì 他一夜没睡；(higher in amount, level) the price of fish is up by 20% yújià shàngzhǎngle bǎi fēn zhī èrshí 鱼价上涨了 20% **4** up to (well enough) he is not up to going out yet tā hái bù néng chūqù 他还不能出去；(capable of) is she up to this translation work? tā néng shèngrèn zhège fānyì gōngzuò ma? 她能胜任这个翻译工作吗？;(when talking about who is responsible) it's up to [me|you|them] to decide yóu [wǒ|nǐ|tāmen] (lái) juédìng 由[我|你|他们](来)决定；(until) zhídào 直到；up to [now|1996|yesterday] zhídào [xiànzài|yījiǔjiǔliù nián] zuótiān]直到 [现在 | 1996 年 | 昨天]

upset /ʌp'set/ **1** adj to be/get upset (annoyed) 烦恼 de 烦恼的，恼火 de 恼火的；he got very upset when his car broke down on the way tā de chē zài lùshang huàile de shíhou, tā fēicháng nǎohuǒ 他的车在路上坏了的时候，他非常恼火；(distressed) 苦恼 de 苦恼的，yōushāng de 忧伤的；she was very upset to hear the news of the accident tīngdào zhège shìgù de xiāoxi, tā fēicháng yōushāng 听到这个事故的消息，她非常忧伤 **2** vb (to make someone unhappy) shǐ…yōushāng/kǔnǎo 使…忧伤/苦恼；to upset someone shǐ mǒu rén yōushāng/kǔnǎo 使某人忧伤/苦恼；(to annoy) shǐ…fánnǎo/nǎohuǒ 使…烦恼/恼火；to upset someone shǐ mǒu rén fánnǎo/nǎohuǒ 使某人烦恼/恼火

upside down /ˌʌpsaɪd 'daʊn/ adv (turned over completely) dào 倒，diāndǎo 颠倒；you're holding the book upside down nǐ bǎ shū ná dào le 你把书拿倒了；(in disorder or chaos) luànqībāzāo 乱七八糟；they turned everything in the room upside down tāmen bǎ wū li de dōngxi nòng de luànqībāzāo 他们把屋里的东西弄得乱七八糟

upstairs /ˌʌp'steəz/ adv lóushàng 楼上；to go upstairs shàng lóu 上楼；to bring the cases upstairs bǎ xiāngzi nádào lóushàng lái 把箱子拿到楼上来

urgent /'ɜːdʒənt/ adj jínjí de 紧急的，jíqiè de 急切的

us /ʌs/ 弱 əs/ pron wǒmen 我们；they don't know us tāmen bú rènshi wǒmen 他们不认识我们

USA /ˌju es 'eɪ/ n Měiguó 美国

use /juːz/ **1** vb (to make use of) yòng 用，shǐyòng 使用；I use this car to go to work wǒ kāi zhè liàng chē shàngbān 我开这辆车上班；he uses this room as an office tā bǎ zhège fángjiān yòngzuò bàngōngshì 他把这个房间用做办公室；what is it used for? zhè shì yònglái zuò shénme de? 这是用来做什么的?；to use [water|petrol|electricity] (shǐ) yòng [shuǐ|qìyóu|diàn] (使) 用 [水 | 汽油 | 电]

电]；(to take advantage of) 利用 lìyòng；to use [someone] this opportunity] 利用 lìyòng [某人 | 这个机会] **2** n to make use of a room 利用一个房间 lìyòng yí gè fángjiān；he has the use of a car 有汽车供他使用 yǒu qìchē gōng tā shǐyòng；she's lost the use of her legs 她的两条腿不能走路了 tā de liǎng tiáo tuǐ bù néng zǒulù le；(when talking about what is useful) to be of use to someone 对某人有用 duì mǒu rén yǒuyòng；to be (of) no use 没用 méi yòng；this bike is no use any more 这辆自行车没用了 zhè liàng zìxíngchē méi yòng le；what's the use of complaining? 抱怨有什么用？bàoyuàn yǒu shénme yòng? ；use up he's used up all the money 他把钱都花完了 tā bǎ qián dōu huāwán le；have you used up the milk? 你把牛奶用完了吗？nǐ bǎ niúnǎi yòngwán le ma?

used /juːst/ **1** vb (did so frequently or regularly) 过去常常 guòqù chángcháng；I used to go there by bike 我过去常常骑自行车去那儿 wǒ guòqù chángcháng qí zìxíngchē qù nàr；(did so formerly) 过去 guòqù；I used not to smoke 我过去不抽烟 wǒ guòqù bù chōuyān；there used to be a castle here 过去这儿过去有个城堡 zhèr guòqù yǒu gè chéngbǎo **2** adj to be/get used to 习惯 xíguàn；he's not used to living on his own 他不习惯一个人生活 tā bù xíguàn yí gè rén shēnghuó；to get used to a new job 习惯新的工作 xíguàn xīn de gōngzuò；(not new) 使用过的 shǐyòngguo de, 旧的 jiù de；used cars 使用过的汽车 shǐyòngguo de qìchē；used furniture 旧家具 jiùjù

useful /ˈjuːsfʊl/ adj (of use) 有用的 yǒuyòng de；(helpful) 有帮助的 yǒu bāngzhù de

useless /ˈjuːslɪs/ adj (having no use, point, or purpose) 没(有)用的 méi(yǒu) yòng de, 无用的 wúyòng de；it's useless complaining 抱怨没有用 bàoyuàn méiyǒu yòng；(describing a person) 无能的 wúnéng de；I'm useless at chemistry 我的化学很差 wǒ de huàxué hěn chà

usually /ˈjuːʒʊəlɪ/ adv 通常 tōngcháng, 一般 yìbān

Vv

vacant /'veɪkənt/ adj (unoccupied) kòng de 空的, kòngxiánzhe de 空闲着的; is there a vacant room in the house? fángzi li yǒu kòng fángjiān ma? 房子里有空房间吗?; (when describing a post or a position) kòngquē de 空缺的; a vacant post yí gè kòngquē de zhíwèi 一个空缺的职位

vacation /və'keɪʃən/ n (US English) a vacation yí gè jiàqī 一个假期; to take a vacation xiūjià 休假; the [summer|winter|Christmas] vacation [shǔ|hán|Shèngdàn]jià [暑|寒|圣诞]假

vacuum /'vækjʊəm/ vb to vacuum a room yòng xīchénqì dǎsǎo fángjiān 用吸尘器打扫房间

vacuum cleaner /'vækjʊəm ˌkliːnə(r)/ n a vacuum cleaner yí gè xīchénqì 一个吸尘器

vague /veɪg/ adj (indefinite, uncertain) hánhu de 含糊的, bù quèqiè de 不确切的; a vague answer yí gè hánhu de huídá 一个含糊的回答; (indistinct) móhu de 模糊的, bù qīngxī de 不清晰的; (not clearly expressed) biǎodá (de) bù qīngchu de 表达(得)不清楚的

vain /veɪn/ adj (pettily self-complacent) zìfù de 自负的; he is vain about his learning tā duì zìjǐ de xuéwèn hěn zìfù 他对自己的学问很自负; (valuing oneself inordinately on some trivial personal distinction) ài xūróng de 爱虚荣的; is he a vain person? tā shì yí gè ài xūróng de rén ma? 他是一个爱虚荣的人吗?; (futile) túláo de 徒劳的, báifèi de 白费的; in vain túláo 徒劳, báifèi 白费; all my efforts were in vain wǒ de suǒyǒu nǔlì dōu báifèi le 我的所有努力都白费了

valid /'vælɪd/ adj (legally adequate) yǒuxiào de 有效的; -

is this ticket still **valid**? zhè zhāng piào hái yǒuxiào ma? 这张票还有效吗?;(*capable of being justified*) zhèngdàng de 正当的;a **valid reason** yí gè zhèngdàng de lǐyóu 一个正当的理由;(*well based*) quèzáo de 确凿的,yǒu gēnjù de 有根据的;**valid evidence** quèzáo de zhèngjù 确凿的证据

valley /'vælɪ/ n a **valley** (*a low area between hills*) yí gè shāngǔ 一个山谷;(*the basin in which a river flows*) yí gè liúyù 一个流域

valuable /'væljubəl/ adj (*very useful*) bǎoguì de 宝贵的,yǒujiàzhí de 有价值的;(*worth a lot of money*) zhíqián de 值钱的 guìzhòng de 贵重的;**this watch is rather valuable** zhè kuài biǎo xiāngdāng zhíqián 这块表相当值钱

van /væn/ n a **van** yí liàng yùnhuòchē 一辆运货车

vandalize /'vændəlaɪz/ vb pòhuài 破坏,huǐhuài 毁坏

vanilla /və'nɪlə/ n xiāngzǐlán 香子兰,xiāngcǎo 香草

various /'veərɪəs/ adj (*diverse*) gèzhǒng-gèyàng de 各种各样的,bù tóng de 不同的;**there are various ways of saying it** yǒu gèzhǒng-gèyàng de shuōfǎ 有各种各样的说法;(*several*) jǐ gè 几个;**they visited several schools** tāmen fǎngwènle jǐ gè xuéxiào 他们访问了几个学校

vary /'veərɪ/ vb (*to differ, be different*) bù tóng 不同,bù yíyàng 不一样;**food prices vary from town to town** shípǐn de jiàgé měi gè chéngzhèn dōu bù tóng 食品的价格每个城镇都不同;(*to change intentionally*) gǎibiàn 改变,gēnggǎi 更改;**to vary one's working style** gǎibiàn gōngzuò fāngshì 改变工作方式

vase /vɑːz/ n a **vase** yí gè huāpíng 一个花瓶

veal /viːl/ n xiǎoniúròu 小牛肉

vegetable /'vedʒɪtəbl/ n (*shū*) cài (蔬)菜;a **vegetable** yì kē cài 一棵菜

vegetarian /ˌvedʒɪ'teərɪən/ n a **vegetarian** yí gè sùshízhǔyìzhě 一个素食主义者

vein /veɪn/ n a **vein** (*for carrying blood in the body*) yì gēn xuèguǎn 一根血管

velvet /'velvɪt/ n tiān'éróng 天鹅绒，sīróng 丝绒

versus /'vɜːsəs/ prep duì 对

very /'verɪ/ **1** adv hěn 很，fēicháng 非常；I don't know him very well wǒ bù hěn liǎojiě tā 我不很了解他；we like them very much wǒmen fēicháng xǐhuan tāmen 我们非常喜欢他们；not (...) very bù hěn 不很，bú tài 不太；it is not very hot today jīntiān bú tài rè 今天不太热；(for emphasis)！Note that in this case, very is usually not translated；for the very first time dì-yī cì 第 1 次；they called me the very next day tāmen dì-èr tiān jiù gěi wǒ dǎ diànhuà le 他们第 2 天就给我打电话了 **2** adj！Note that when very is used as an adjective, it is often translated as jiù 就 or zhèng 正；she studied in that very school tā jiù zài nà suǒ xuéxiào xuéxí 她就在那所学校学习；you are the very person I need nǐ zhèng shì wǒ suǒ xūyào de rén 你正是我所需要的人；at the very beginning gāng kāishǐ de shíhou 刚开始的时候；to stay to the very end dāi dào zuìhòu 呆到最后

vest /vest/ n (British English) (a piece of underwear) a vest yí jiàn hànshān 一件汗衫，yí jiàn bèixīn 一件背心；(US English) (a waistcoat) a vest yí jiàn bèixīn 一件背心，yí jiàn mǎjiǎ 一件马甲

vet /vet/ n a vet yí gè shòuyī 一个兽医

via /'vaɪə/ prep (when talking about a route) jīngyóu 经由，jīngguò 经过，lùjīng 路经；to go to Japan via Beijing jīngyóu Běijīng qù Rìběn 经由北京去日本；(when talking about a means) tōngguò 通过，lìyòng 利用；I returned the book to him via a student of his wǒ tōngguò tā de yí gè xuésheng bǎ shū huángěile tā 我通过他的一个学生把书还给了他

vicious /'vɪʃəs/ adj (ferocious) xiōng'è de 凶恶的，xiōngcán de 凶残的；(nasty, meant to hurt) èyì de 恶意的，èdú de 恶毒的；(addicted to vice or bad habits) duòluò de 堕落的

victory /ˈvɪktərɪ/ n a victory yí cì shènglì 一次胜利；to win a victory yíngdé shènglì 赢得胜利

video /ˈvɪdɪəʊ/ 1 n (a recorded film, programme, event) a video yì pán lùxiàngdài 一盘录像带 ▶ video cassette, video recorder 2 vb (to record) lù xiàng 录像；(to film) to video a wedding gěi yí gè hūnlǐ shèxiàng 给一个婚礼摄像

video camera /ˈvɪdɪəʊ ˌkæmərə/ n a video camera yì tái shèxiàngjī 一台摄像机

video cassette /ˈvɪdɪəʊ kəˈset/ n a video cassette yì pán lùxiàngdài 一盘录像带

video game /ˈvɪdɪəʊ ˌgeɪm/ n a video game yì pán diànzǐ yóuxì 一盘电子游戏

video recorder /ˈvɪdɪəʊ rɪˈkɔːdə(r)/ n a video recorder yì tái lùxiàngjī 一台录像机

view /vjuː/ n (a scene viewed by the eyes) kàn 看，guānkàn 观看；if you want to get a better view, you'd better come here yàoshì nǐ xiǎng kàn de qīngchǔ, zuìhǎo dào zhèr lái 要是你想看得清楚，最好到这儿来；(a line of vision) shìxiàn 视线；you're blocking my view nǐ dǎngzhùle wǒ de shìxiàn 你挡住了我的视线；(an opinion) a view yí gè guāndiǎn 一个观点，yí gè yìjiàn 一个意见；point of view yí gè guāndiǎn 一个观点；I'd like to know your views on this matter wǒ xiǎng zhīdào nǐ duì zhè jiàn shì de yìjiàn 我想知道你对这件事的意见

village /ˈvɪlɪdʒ/ n a village yí gè cūnzhuāng 一个村庄

vinegar /ˈvɪnɪgə(r)/ n cù 醋

vineyard /ˈvɪnjəd/ n a vineyard yí gè pútáoyuán 一个葡萄园

violent /ˈvaɪələnt/ adj (of great force) měngliè de 猛烈的，qiángliè de 强烈的，jīliè de 激烈的；(vicious) xiōngcán de 凶残的，cánbào de 残暴的；(marked by extreme force or fierceness) bàolì de 暴力的

violin /ˌvaɪəˈlɪn/ n a violin yì bǎ xiǎotíqín 一把小提琴

visit /ˈvɪzɪt/ 1 vb (to pay an official call upon) fǎngwèn 访

问；the British delegation is visiting China Yīngguó dàibiǎotuán zhèngzài fǎngwèn Zhōngguó 英国代表团正在访问中国；(to come or go to see formally) cānguān 参观，fǎngwèn 访问；they visited some hospitals and schools tāmen cānguānle yìxiē yīyuàn hé xuéxiào 他们参观了一些医院和学校；(for sightseeing and pleasure) cānguān 参观，yóulǎn 游览；are you going to visit the Great Wall? nǐmen yào qù yóulǎn Chángchéng ma? 你们要去游览长城吗?；(out of affection) kàn 看，kànwàng 看望；to go to visit [a patient | my grandmother | my old friend...] qù kàn [yí gè bìngrén | wǒ de nǎinai | wǒ de lǎopéngyou···] 去看[一个病人|我的奶奶|我的老朋友···]；(to stay with) we visited my parents for a week wǒmen zài wǒ fùmǔ nàr zhùle yí gè xīngqī 我们在我父母那儿住了一个星期 **2** n a visit (an official call) yí cì fǎngwèn 一次访问；(when talking about visits to institutions, museums, exhibitions, etc.) yí cì cānguān 一次参观；(a sightseeing excursion) yí cì yóulǎn 一次游览；(a call at someone's home) yí cì bàifǎng 一次拜访；yí cì tànwàng 一次探望；(a stay) I paid my elder brother a visit for two days wǒ zài wǒ gēge nàr dāile liǎng tiān 我在我哥哥那儿呆了两天

visitor /'vɪzɪtə(r)/ n (a guest) a visitor yí gè kèrén 一个客人；to have visitors yǒu kèrén 有客人；(a tourist) a visitor yí gè yóukè 一个游客

vocabulary /vəʊˈkæbjʊlərɪ/ n cíhuì 词汇

voice /vɔɪs/ n (the sound of a person speaking, singing, etc.) a voice yí gè shēngyīn 一个说话声音；to speak [in a low voice | in a loud voice] [xiǎoshēng de | dàshēng de] shuōhuà [小声地|大声地]说话；(the quality of the sound one makes while singing or speaking) sǎngzi 嗓子，sǎngyīn 嗓音；she has a good voice tā de sǎngzi hěn hǎo 她的嗓子很好

volleyball /'vɒlɪbɔːl/ n páiqiú 排球

vomit /'vɒmɪt/ vb ǒutù 呕吐，tù 吐

vote /vəʊt/ vb (to express one's choice by vote) tóupiào 投票

投票; to vote [for | against] someone tóupiào [xuǎn | bù xuǎn]mǒu rén 投票 [选|不选]某人; to vote [for | against] a plan tóupiào [zànchéng | fǎnduì]yí gè jìhuà 投票 [赞成|反对] 一个计划; (to determine by vote) tóupiào juédìng 投票决定; to vote in a new policy tóupiào juédìng yí xiàng xīn zhèngcè 投票决定一项新政策

Ww

wages /'weɪdʒɪz/ n gōngzī 工资
waist /weɪst/ n the waist yāo 腰, yāobù 腰部
waistcoat /'weɪstkəʊt/ n (British English) a waistcoat yí jiàn bèixīn 一件背心, yí jiàn mǎjiǎ 一件马甲
wait /weɪt/ vb to wait děng(hòu) 等(候); to wait for someone děng mǒu rén 等某人; I'm waiting to use the phone wǒ zài děngzhe yòng diànhuà 我在等着用电话; I can't wait to see them wǒ jíqiè de xiǎng jiàndào tāmen 我急切地想见到他们; (in a restaurant) to wait on tables, to wait tables (US English) fúshì kèrén chīfàn 服侍客人吃饭; wait up děng(hòu) zhe bú shuìjiào 等(候) 着不睡觉; to wait up for someone wèi děnghòu mǒu rén ér bú shuìjiào 为等候某人而不睡觉
waiter /'weɪtə(r)/ n a waiter yí gè fúwùyuán 一个服务员
waiting room /'weɪtɪŋ ruːm/ n a waiting room (at a train or a bus station) yí gè hòuchēshì 一个候车室; (at an airport) yí gè hòujīshì 一个候机室; (at a port) yí gè hòuchuánshì 一个候船室; (in a hospital) yí gè hòuzhěnshì 一个候诊室
waitress /'weɪtrɪs/ n a waitress yí gè nǚzhāodài 一个女招待
wake /weɪk/ vb (to be roused from sleep) xǐng 醒,

xǐnglái 醒来；has she woken（up）? tā xǐngle ma? 她醒了吗?；(to rouse from sleep) jiàoxǐng 叫醒，nòngxǐng 弄醒；to wake someone（up）bǎ mǒu rén jiàoxǐng 把某人叫醒

Wales /weɪlz/ n Wēi'ěrshì 威尔士

walk /wɔːk/ **1** vb (to go on foot) zǒu 走，zǒulù 走路；are you walking to the station? nǐ yào zǒulù qù chēzhàn ma? 你要走路去车站吗?；(for pleasure) sànbù 散步；to walk in the park zài gōngyuán sànbù 在公园散步；(to take an animal out on a leash, etc.) liù 遛；to walk the dog liù gǒu 遛狗；(to escort by walking) péi（zhe）…zǒu 陪（着）… 走，sòng 送；I'll walk you to the bus stop wǒ péi（zhe）nǐ zǒu dào chēzhàn 我陪（着）你走到车站 **2** n a walk sànbù 散步；(to go for a walk) qù sànbù 去散步；(act of walking) zǒu 走，zǒulù 走路；my school is five minutes' walk from here wǒ de xuéxiào lí zhèr zǒulù yào wǔ fēnzhōng 我的学校离这儿走路要 5 分钟；**walk around** sànbù 散步；to walk around town zài chéng li sànbù 在城里散步；to walk around the lake zài hú zhōuwéi sànbù 在湖周围散步；**walk away** zǒukāi 走开；**walk back** zǒuhuí 走回；to walk back home zǒu huí jiā 走回家；**walk by** zǒuguò 走过；**walk in**（to）zǒujìn 走进；**walk out** zǒuchū 走出；to walk out of the room zǒuchū fángjiān 走出房间；**walk up to** zǒujìn 走进，zǒuxiàng 走向

walkman® /'wɔːkmən/ n a walkman yì tái suíshēntīng 一台随身听

wall /wɔːl/ n a wall yì dǔ qiáng 一堵墙；the Great Wall Chángchéng 长城

wallet /'wɒlɪt/ n a wallet yí gè qiánbāo 一个钱包，yí gè píjiāzi 一个皮夹子

wallpaper /'wɔːlˌpeɪpə(r)/ n qiángzhǐ 墙纸

walnut /'wɔːlnʌt/ n a walnut yí gè hétao 一个核桃

wander /'wɒndə(r)/ vb (to ramble, to roam) xiánguàng 闲逛，mànbù 漫步；to wander around town zài chéng li xiánguàng 在城里闲逛；**wander away, wander off**

mànman de zǒukāi 慢慢地走开

want /wɒnt/ vb (to desire something or someone) (xiǎng) yào (想) 要；do you want another coffee? nǐ hái (xiǎng) yào yì bēi kāfēi ma? 你还(想)要一杯咖啡吗?；do you want me to go with you? nǐ (xiǎng) yào wǒ hé nǐ yìqǐ qù ma? 你(想)要我和你一起去吗?；(to desire to do something) (xiǎng) yào (想) 要；he wants [to go out | to go home | to play basketball ...] tā xiǎng [chūqù | huíjiā | dǎ lánqiú···] 他想 [出去 | 回家 | 打篮球···]；she didn't want to stay there tā bù xiǎng dāi zài nàr 她不想呆在那儿；(to need) xūyào 需要；the house wants repairs zhè dòng fángzi xūyào xiūlǐ le 这栋房子需要修理了

war /wɔː(r)/ n a war yì chǎng zhànzhēng 一场战争

wardrobe /'wɔːdrəʊb/ n a wardrobe yí gè yīguì 一个衣柜, yí gè yīchú 一个衣橱

warm /wɔːm/ **1** adj (moderately hot) nuǎnhuo de 暖和的, wēnnuǎn de 温暖的；I'm very warm wǒ hěn nuǎnhuo 我很暖和；he doesn't feel warm tā gǎnjué bù nuǎnhuo 他感觉不暖和；the weather is getting warm tiānqì nuǎnhuo qǐlai le 天气暖和起来了；(ardent, enthusiastic) rèqíng de 热情的, rèliè de 热烈的；they gave us a warm reception tāmen rèqíng de jiēdàile wǒmen 他们热情地接待了我们；a warm welcome rèliè de huānyíng 热烈地欢迎；(hearty) rèxīn de 热心的, rèqíng de 热情的；a warm person yí gè rèxīn de rén 一个热心的人 **2** vb to warm the plates bǎ pánzi rè yíxià 把盘子热一下；to warm one's hands bǎ shǒu nuǎnhuo yíxià 把手暖和一下；warm up (to get warm) nuǎnhuo qǐlai 暖和起来；the room is warming up fángjiān nuǎnhuo qǐlai le 房间暖和起来了；(for a sport event) zuò zhǔnbèi huódòng 做准备活动；(to make warm) rè 热, jiārè 加热；to warm up the food bǎ fàn rè yíxià 把饭热一下

warn /wɔːn/ vb jǐnggào 警告, gàojiè 告诫；to warn someone about the risks jǐnggào mǒu rén yǒu wēixiǎn

警告某人有危险；to warn someone to be careful gàojiè mǒu rén yào xiǎoxīn 告诫某人要小心

wash /wɒʃ/ vb (to clean) xǐ 洗；to wash one's clothes xǐ yīfu 洗衣服；to wash one's face xǐliǎn 洗脸；(to get clean) xǐ 洗；this sheet doesn't wash easily zhè tiáo chuángdān bù hǎo xǐ 这条床单不好洗；wash out (to remove by washing) xǐdiào 洗掉，xǐqù 洗去；to wash a stain out bǎ wūdiǎn xǐdiào 把污点洗掉；wash up (British English) (to do the dishes) xǐ wǎn 洗碗，xǐ cānjù 洗餐具；(US English) (to clean one's hands) xǐ shǒu 洗手；(to clean one's face) xǐ liǎn 洗脸

washbasin /'wɒʃˌbeɪsən/ (British English) n a washbasin yí gè xǐliǎnpén 一个洗脸盆，yí gè xǐshǒupén 一个洗手盆

washing /'wɒʃɪŋ/ n the washing (to be washed) yào xǐ de yīfu 要洗的衣服；(being washed) zhèngzài xǐ de yīfu 正在洗的衣服；(washed) xǐhǎole de yīfu 洗好了的衣服；to do the washing xǐ yīfu 洗衣服

washing machine /'wɒʃɪŋ məˌʃiːn/ n a washing machine yì tái xǐyījī 一台洗衣机

washing-up /ˌwɒʃɪŋˈʌp/ n (British English) the washing-up (to be washed) yào xǐ de cānjù 要洗的餐具；(being washed) zhèngzài xǐ de cānjù 正在洗的餐具；(washed) xǐhǎole de cānjù 洗好了的餐具；to do the washing-up xǐ wǎn 洗碗，xǐ cānjù 洗餐具

wasp /wɒsp/ n a wasp yì zhī huángfēng 一只黄蜂，yì zhī mǎfēng 一只马蜂

waste /weɪst/ **1** vb làngfèi 浪费；to waste [money | time | energy...] làngfèi [qián | shíjiān | jīnglì...] 浪费 [钱 | 时间 | 精力...] **2** n làngfèi 浪费；it's a waste of [money | time | energy...] zhè shì làngfèi [qián | shíjiān | jīnglì...] 这是浪费 [钱 | 时间 | 精力...]；it's a waste of time going there qù nàr shì làngfèi shíjiān 去那儿是浪费时间；(an uncultivated region) huāngdì 荒地，huāngyě 荒野；a waste yí piàn huāngdì 一片荒地；(refuse or rejected material) lājī 垃

坂，fèiwù 废物

watch /wɒtʃ/ **1** vb (to look at) kàn 看；to watch [television | a football match | a Peking opera] kàn [diànshì | zúqiúsài | jīngjù] 看 [电视 | 足球赛 | 京剧]；she watched me making the meal tā kàn wǒ zuòfàn 她看我做饭；(to observe, to follow) jiānshì 监视；I feel I'm being watched wǒ juéde yǒu rén zài jiānshì wǒ 我觉得有人在监视我；(to pay attention to) zhùyì 注意；please watch your spelling qǐng zhùyì nǐ de pīnxiě 请注意你的拼写；(to tend) zhàokàn 照看，zhàoliào 照料；watch out zhùyì 注意，dāngxīn 当心 **2** n a watch (a timepiece) yí kuài shǒubiǎo 一块手表

water /wɔːtə(r)/ **1** n shuǐ 水；drinking water yǐnyòngshuǐ 饮用水 **2** vb to water [the flowers | the tree | the garden] gěi [huā | shù | huāyuán] jiāoshuǐ 给 [花 | 树 | 花园] 浇水；(to irrigate with water) guàngài 灌溉；(to salivate) liú kǒushuǐ 流口水

waterfall /wɔːtəfɔːl/ n a waterfall yí gè pùbù 一个瀑布

water-skiing /wɔːtəˌskiːɪŋ/ n huáshuǐ 滑水

wave /weɪv/ **1** vb (to greet or call someone) zhāoshǒu 招手；to wave to someone xiàng mǒu rén zhāoshǒu 向某人招手；(to say farewell or send signals) huīshǒu 挥手；to wave goodbye huīshǒu gàobié 挥手告别；to wave red flags huīwǔ/huīdòng hóngqí 挥舞/挥动红旗 **2** n a wave (on the surface of the sea, river, etc.) yí gè (bō) làng 一个（波）浪；(in physics) yí gè bō 一个波

way /weɪ/ n a way (a means, a method) yì zhǒng fāngfǎ 一种方法；it's a way of earning money zhè shì yì zhǒng zhuànqián de fāngfǎ 这是一种赚钱的方法；it's a good way to make friends zhè shì yì zhǒng jiāo péngyou de hǎo fāngfǎ 这是一种交朋友的好方法；he does it the wrong way tā zuò de fāngfǎ bú duì 他做的方法不对；(when referring to the manner of doing something) a way yì zhǒng fāngshì 一种方式；I like their way of life wǒ xǐhuan tāmen de shēnghuó fāngshì 我喜欢他们的生活方

式；I don't like this way of educating children wǒ bù xǐhuan zhè zhǒng jiàoyù háizi de fāngshì 我不喜欢这种教育孩子的方式；(a route, a road) lù 路，dàolù 道路；a way yì tiáo lù 一条路；I can't remember the way to the station wǒ bú jìde qù chēzhàn de lù le 我不记得去车站的路了；we can buy something to eat along the way wǒmen kěyǐ mǎi yìdiǎn dōngxi zài lùshang chī 我们可以买一点东西在路上吃；on the way back (going back) zài huíqù de lùshang 在回去的路上；(coming back) zài huílái de lùshang 在回来的路上；I met them on the way back from town wǒ zài cóng chéng li huílái de lùshang yùjiànle tāmen 我在从城里回来的路上遇见了他们；on the way to Shanghai zài qù Shànghǎi de lùshang 在去上海的路上；where's the way out? cóng nǎr kěyǐ chūqù? 从哪儿可以出去？；can you tell me the way to the underground? qǐng wèn qù dìtiě zěnme zǒu? 请问去地铁怎么走？；to lose one's way mílù 迷路；(a direction) fāngxiàng 方向；which way are you going? nǐ qù nǎge fāngxiàng? 你去哪个方向？；they went that way tāmen qùle nàge fāngxiàng 他们去了那个方向；come this way zhèbiān lái 这边来；(someone's route) to be in someone's way dǎng mǒu rén de dào/lù 挡某人的道/路；to be in the way dǎngdào 挡道，àishì 碍事；Get out of the way! gǔnkāi! 滚开！*；(when talking about distances) the airport is a long way from here fēijīchǎng lí zhèr hěn yuǎn 飞机场离这儿很远；to come all the way from Tibet cóng Xīzàng yuǎndào ér lái 从西藏远道而来；(what one wants) she always wants her own way tā zǒngshì wǒxíng-wǒsù 她总是我行我素；if I had my own way, I'd go alone jiǎrú wǒ néng shuōlesuàn, wǒ jiù yí gè rén qù 假如我能说了算，我就一个人去 **2 by the way** (when used with a question) shùnbiàn wèn yíxià 顺便问一下；what's his name, by the way? shùnbiàn

* in infomal situations

wèn yíxià, tā jiào shénme míngzi? 顺便问一下,他叫什么名字?;(when used with a statement) shùnbiàn shuō yíxià 顺便说一下;by the way, I've bought the train tickets shùnbiàn shuō yíxià, wǒ yǐjīng mǎile huǒchēpiào le 顺便说一下,我已经买了火车票了

we /wiː/ 弱 wɪ/ *pron* wǒmen 我们;**we didn't agree** wǒmen méi tóngyì 我们没同意

weak /wiːk/ *adj* (*having very little power*) ruǎnruò de 软弱的, wúlì de 无力的;**a weak government** yí gè ruǎnruò (-wúlì) de zhèngfǔ 一个软弱(无力)的政府;(*not healthy*) ruò de 弱的, xūruò de 虚弱的;**she has a weak heart** tā de xīnzàng hěn xūruò 她的心脏很虚弱;(*not good or able*) chà de 差的, bóruò de 薄弱的;**I'm weak at foreign languages** wǒ de wàiyǔ hěn chà 我的外语很差;(*describing tea or coffee*) dàn de 淡的

wealthy /'welθɪ/ *adj* fù(yǒu) de 富(有)的, yǒuqián de 有钱的

wear /weə(r)/ *vb* (*when talking about wearing coats, shirts, dresses, trousers, socks, shoes*) chuān 穿;**she's wearing jeans** tā chuānzhe niúzǎikù 她穿着牛仔裤;**to wear black** chuān hēisè de yīfu 穿黑色的衣服;(*when talking about wearing hats, scarves, glasses, or accessories such as rings, necklaces, etc.*) dài 戴;**he's wearing a red tie today** jīntiān tā dàizhe yì tiáo hóngsè de lǐngdài 今天他戴着一条红色的领带;(*to damage, as clothes*) mópò 磨破, chuānpò 穿破;**the trousers are all worn** kùzi dōu chuānpò le 裤子都穿破了;**wear out** (*to damage by wearing*) chuānpò 穿破;**to wear one's shoes out** bǎ xié chuānpò 把鞋穿破;(*to damage through use*) yònghuài 用坏;**the toothbrush is worn out** yáshuā yǐjīng yònghuài le 牙刷已经用坏了;(*to make tired and exhausted*) **the work has worn everyone out** zhège gōngzuò bǎ měi gè rén dōu lèi de jīngpí-lìjìn 这个工作把每个人都累得精疲力尽;**I feel worn out** wǒ gǎndào hěn pífá 我感到很疲乏

weather /'weðə(r)/ *n* the weather tiānqì 天气；what's the weather like? tiānqì zěnmeyàng? 天气怎么样？；[fine|cloudy|wet] weather [qíng|yīn|yǔ] tiān [晴|阴|雨]天

weather forecast /'weðə ˌfɔːkɑːst/ *n* the weather forecast tiānqì yùbào 天气预报

webpage /'webpeɪdʒ/ *n* a webpage yì gè wǎngyè 一个网页

website /'websaɪt/ *n* a website yí gè wǎngzhǐ 一个网址

wedding /'wedɪŋ/ *n* a wedding yí gè hūnlǐ 一个婚礼；to attend a wedding cānjiā yí gè hūnlǐ 参加一个婚礼

Wednesday /'wenzdeɪ/ *n* xīngqīsān 星期三，lǐbàisān 礼拜三

week /wiːk/ *n* a week yí gè xīngqī 一个星期，yì zhōu 一周；[this|last|next] week [zhège|shàng(ge)|xià(ge)] xīngqī [这个|上(个)|下(个)] 星期

weekend /ˌwiːk'end/ *n* a weekend yí gè zhōumò 一个周末

weigh /weɪ/ *vb* (to find the weight of) chēng 称；to weigh the luggage chēng xíngli 称行李；to weigh oneself chēng zìjǐ de tǐzhòng 称自己的体重；(to have the weight of) zhòng 重，zhòngliàng shì 重量是；how much do you weigh? nǐ yǒu duō zhòng? 你有多重？；my luggage weighs 20 kilos wǒ de xíngli zhòng èrshí gōngjīn 我的行李重 20 公斤

weight /weɪt/ *n* (the heaviness of a thing) zhòngliàng 重量；(the heaviness of one's body) tǐzhòng 体重；[to lose|to gain] weight [jiǎnqīng|zēngjiā] tǐzhòng [减轻|增加] 体重

weird /wɪəd/ *adj* (strange, bizarre) qíguài de 奇怪的，bùkě-sīyì de 不可思议的

welcome /'welkəm/ **1** *vb* huānyíng 欢迎；to welcome someone huānyíng mǒu rén 欢迎某人 **2** *adj* (when receiving people) huānyíng 欢迎；welcome to the united States huānyíng (nǐmen) dào Měiguó lái 欢迎(你们) 到美国来；suggestions are welcome huānyíng dàjiā tíchū jiànyì 欢迎大家提出建议；a welcome guest yí wèi shòu huānyíng de kèrén 一位受欢迎的客人；（when acknowledging thanks）'thanks'—'you're welcome' "xièxie"—"bú yòng kèqi" "谢谢"—"不用客气" **3** *n* a welcome huānyíng 欢迎

well /wel/ **1** *adv*（in good manner or degree）! Note that in this sense well is often translated as hǎo 好. However, it can also be expressed as búcuò 不错, shùnlì 顺利 etc.；well hǎo 好；she speaks Chinese well tā Hànyǔ shuō de hěn hǎo 她汉语说得很好；well done gàn de hǎo 干得好；he's not eating well（because of a poor appetite）tā chīfàn bú tài hǎo 他吃饭不太好，ta shíyù bú zhèn 他食欲不振；did everything go well? yíqiè shùnlì ma? 一切顺利吗；he treated us well tā duì wǒmen búcuò 他对我们不错；she was dressed well tā chuān de hěn piàoliang 她穿得很漂亮；（fully, thoroughly）I understand her feeling wǒ wánquán lǐjiě tā de xīnqíng 我完全理解她的心情；please clean the room well before you leave qǐng nǐ líkāi qián bǎ fángjiān chèdǐ dǎsǎo yíxià 请你离开前把房间彻底打扫一下；（very possibly）hěn kěnéng 很可能；you may well be right nǐ hěn kěnéng shì duì de 你很可能是对的；he may well come to see you tā hěn kěnéng lái kàn nǐ 他很可能来看你；（to a considerable degree）this is well beyond her ability zhè dàdà chāochūle tā de nénglì 这大大超出了她的能力；it's well worth considering zhè hěn zhídé kǎolǜ 这很值得考虑；his exam result is well above the average tā de kǎoshì chéngjì gāochū píngjūnfēn hěn duō 他的考试成绩高出平均分很多 **2** *adj* he's not feeling well tā juéde bù shūfu 他觉得不舒服；everyone is well dàjiā dōu hěn hǎo 大家都很好；I very well wǒ hěn hǎo 我很好；you don't look very well nǐ（kànshàngqù）liǎnsè bú tài hǎo 你（看上去）脸色不太好；I hope you'll get well soon wǒ xīwàng nǐ zǎorì huīfù jiànkāng 我希望你早日恢复健康 **3** as well yě 也；he speaks Japanese as well tā yě huì shuō Rìyǔ 他也会说日语 **4** as well as bùjǐn…érqiě… 不仅… 而且…，jì…yòu… 既… 又…；he bought a Japanese dictionary as well as a Chinese dictionary tā bùjǐn mǎile yì běn Zhōngwén cídiǎn, érqiě hái mǎile yì běn Rìwén cídiǎn 他不仅买了一本中文词典，而且还买了一本日文词典

well-known /'wel'nəun/ adj (celebrated) zhùmíng de 著名的，(fully and widely known) chūmíng de 出名的；(fully and widely known) zhòngsuǒzhōuzhī de 众所周知的

Welsh /welʃ/ **1** adj Wēiěrshì de 威尔士的 **2** n (the people) the Welsh Wēiěrshìrén 威尔士人；(the language) Welsh Wēiěrshìyǔ 威尔士语

west /west/ **1** n xībù 西部，xībian 西边；in the west of China zài Zhōngguó de xībù 在中国的西部；the West Xīfāng 西方 **2** adv to go west wǎng xī(bian) qù 往西(边)去；to live west of Beijing zhù zài Běijīng xībù 住在北京西部 **3** adj xī bù de 西部的；to work in west London zài Lúndūn xībù gōngzuò 在伦敦西部工作

wet /wet/ **1** adj (saturated with water) shī de 湿的；your hair is wet nǐ de tóufa shīle 你的头发湿了；(damp) cháo de 潮的，(rainy) wet weather duōyǔ de tiānqì 多雨的天气；a wet day yí gè yǔtiān 一个雨天；(not yet dry) bù gān de 不干的；the paint is still wet yóuqī hái méi gān 油漆还没干 **2** vb (to make wet) nòngshī 弄湿

what /hwɒt; 弱hwət/ **1** pron (used in questions) shénme 什么；what's that box? nàge hézi shì shénme? 那个盒子是什么？；what does he look like? tā zhǎng de shénme yàngr? 他长得什么样儿？；I don't know what he's doing wǒ bù zhīdào tā zài zuò shénme 我不知道他在做什么；what's your name? nǐ jiào shénme míngzi? 你叫什么名字？；what's the time? jǐ diǎn le? 几点了？；what's the Chinese for 'boring'? Zhōngwén "boring" zěnme shuō? 中文 "boring" 怎么说？；what's her phone number? tā de diànhuà hàomǎ shì duōshǎo? 她的电话号码是多少？；(used as a relative pronoun) what he [bought|sold|asked for...]was a computer tā (suǒ) [mǎi|mài|yào...]de shì yì tái jìsuànjī 他(所)[买|卖|要...]的是一台计算机；is this what he [said|needed|wrote...]? zhè shì tā (suǒ) [shuō|xūyào|xiě...]de ma? 这是他(所)[说|需要|写...]的吗？；do what you want nǐ xiǎng zuò shénme jiù zuò shénme 你想做什么就做什么 2 det shénme 什么；what [books|colours|food...] do you like? nǐ xǐhuan shénme [shū|yánsè|shíwù...]? 你喜欢什么[书|颜色|食物...]?；what time is it? jǐ diǎn le? 几点了？；(in exclamations) duōme 多么；what [a good idea|cold weather|a pretty girl]! duōme [hǎo de zhǔyì|lěng de tiānqì|měilì de gūniang] a! 多么[好的主意|冷的天气|美丽的姑娘]啊！3 adv what do you think of him? nǐ juéde tā zěnmeyàng? 你觉得他怎么样？；what does it matter to him? zhè gēn tā yǒu shénme guānxi? 这跟他有什么关系？4 what if (what would happen if) rúguǒ...zěnme bàn 如果...怎么办；what if I can't get there on time? rúguǒ wǒ bù néng ànshí dàodá nàr, zěnme bàn ne? 如果我不能按时到达那儿，怎么办呢？；(what would it matter if) jíshǐ...yòu yǒu shénme guānxi 即使...又有什么关系；what if I don't get there on time? jíshǐ wǒ bú ànshí dàodá nàr, yòu yǒu shénme guānxi ne? 即使我不按时到达那儿，又有什么关系呢？

whatever /hwɒt'evə(r)/ pron (when anything is possible) take whatever you want nǐ yào shénme jiù ná shénme ba 你要什么就拿什么吧；whatever you think is useful fánshì nǐ xiǎng de dōu hěn yǒuyòng 凡是你想的都很有用；(when it doesn't matter) whatever [happens|they do|you say...], I won't change my mind bùguǎn [fāshēng|tāmen zuò|nǐ shuō...]shénme, wǒ dōu bú huì gǎibiàn zhǔyì 不管[发生|他们做|你说...]什么，我都不会改变主意

wheat /hwiːt/ n xiǎomài 小麦, màizi 麦子

wheel /hwiːl/ n a wheel yí gè lúnzi 一个轮子

wheelchair /'hwiːltʃeə(r)/ n a wheelchair yí gè lúnyǐ 一个轮椅

when /'hwen/ 1 adv shénme shíhou 什么时候；when did

she leave? tā shì shénme shíhou líkāi de? 她是什么时候离开的？；when is your birthday? nǐ shénme shíhou guò shēngrì? 你什么时候过生日？；I don't know when the film starts wǒ bù zhīdào diànyǐng shénme shíhou kāiyǎn 我不知道电影什么时候开演 **2** conj (dāng/zài) …de shíhou (当/在) …的时候；he didn't study any Chinese when he was at school tā zài zhōngxué de shíhou méi xué Zhōngwén 他在中学的时候没学中文；when I'm 18, I'll have my own car wǒ shíbā suì de shíhou, wǒ yào yǒu yí liàng zìjǐ de qìchē 我 18 岁的时候，我要有一辆自己的汽车；(when talking about something unexpected happening in the midst of another action) I was asleep when the phone rang wǒ zhèngzài shuìjiào, tūrán diànhuàlíng xiǎng le 我正在睡觉，突然电话铃响了；we were playing basketball when it started to rain wǒmen zhèngzài dǎ lánqiú, tūrán tiān xiàqǐ yǔ lái 我们正在打篮球，突然天下起雨来 **3** pron (used as a relative pronoun)！Note that in this case, **when** is usually not translated；in the days when there was no TV zài méiyǒu diànshì de rìzi li 在没有电视的日子里；(used in questions) shénme shíhou 什么时候；until when did you work last night? zuótiān yèli nǐ yìzhí gōngzuò dào shénme shíhou? 昨天夜里你一直工作到什么时候？

where /hweə(r)/ **1** adv nǎli 哪里, nǎr 哪儿；where are you going? nǐ shàng nǎr? 你上哪儿？；where do they work? tāmen zài nǎli gōngzuò? 他们在哪里工作？；do you know where [he is | Tom is | we're…] going? nǐ zhīdào [tā yào | Tāngmǔ yào | wǒmen yào…]qù nǎr ma? 你知道 [他要 | 汤姆要 | 我们要…] 去哪儿吗？；I wonder where he lives wǒ xiǎng zhīdào tā zhù zài nǎli 我想知道他住在哪里 **2** conj …de dìfang …的地方；that's where she fell nà jiùshì tā diēdǎo de dìfang 那就是她跌倒的地方；I'll leave the key where you can see it wǒ huì bǎ yàoshi fàng zài nǐ néng kànjiàn de dìfang 我会把钥匙放在你能看见的地方 **3** pron (used as a relative pronoun in a defining relative *clause*）！*Note that in this case*，**where** *is usually not translated*；**the village where we live** wǒmen zhù de cūnzi 我们住的村子；（*used as a relative pronoun in a non-defining relative clause*）**zài nàli** 在那里，**zài nàr** 在那儿；**I went to Shanghai last year, where I visited some Chinese families** qùnián wǒ qùle Shànghǎi, zài nàli wǒ fǎngwènle yìxiē Zhōngguó jiātíng 去年我去了上海，在那里我访问了一些中国家庭；（*used in questions*）**nǎli** 哪里，**nǎr** 哪儿；**where do you come from?** nǐ cóng nǎli lái? 你从哪里来？

whether /'hweðə(r)/ *conj*（*if*）**shìfǒu** 是否，**shì bú shì** 是不是；**I don't know whether or not to accept her invitation** wǒ bù zhīdào shìfǒu yīnggāi jiēshòu tā de yāoqǐng 我不知道是否应该接受她的邀请；**whether... or...**（*when introducing two alternatives*）…**háishì**… 还是…；**I wonder whether I should go to Beijing or Shanghai** wǒ bù zhīdào (wǒ) yīnggāi qù Běijīng háishì qù Shànghǎi 我不知道（我）应该去北京还是去上海；（*in any case, in any event*）**bùguǎn/búlùn**…**háishì**… 不管/不论…还是…；**whether you come to me or I go to you, we must find time to discuss this problem this week** bùguǎn nǐ lái wǒ zhèr háishì wǒ qù nǐ nàr, zhège xīngqī wǒmen bìxū zhǎo shíjiān tǎolùn zhège wèntí 不管你来我这儿是我去你那儿，这个星期我们必须找时间讨论这个问题

which /hwɪtʃ/ **1** *pron*（*used as a relative pronoun in a defining relative clause*）！*Note that in this case*，**which** *is usually not translated*；**the house which I told you about** wǒ gàosu nǐ de nà zuò fángzi 我告诉你的那座房子；**the book which is on the table**（zài）zhuōzi shang de shū（在）桌子上的书；（*used as a relative pronoun in a non-defining relative clause*）！*Note that in this case*，**which** *is often translated as the noun it refers to*, *or as the pronouns*，**zhè** 这 *or* **nà** 那；**he was teaching at Peking university, which was very far from the city centre**

tā zài Běijīng Dàxué jiāoshū, nàr lí shìzhōngxīn hěn yuǎn 他在北京大学教书,那儿离市中心很远;he has given up smoking, which makes his wife very pleased tā jièyān le,zhè shǐ tā tàitai fēicháng gāoxìng 他戒烟了,这使他太太非常高兴;(in questions)which…? ! Note that in questions, **which** as a pronoun is usually translated as **nǎxiē 哪些** if it refers to a plural noun, and as **nǎ(yí)gè 哪(一)个** if it refers to a singular noun. In **nǎ(yí)gè 哪(一)个**, the measure word **gè 个** may be replaced with a different measure word depending on the noun being referred to;(when the noun is plural)nǎxiē 哪些;**which of these books are yours?** zhèxiē shū zhōng nǎxiē shì nǐ de? 这些书中哪些是你的?;(when the noun is singular)nǎ(yí)gè 哪(一)个;**of these parks, which is the largest?** zhèxiē gōngyuán nǎ yí gè zuì dà? 这些公园哪一个最大?;**of these books, which is most useful?** zhèxiē shū nǎ yì běn zuì yǒuyòng? 这些书哪一本最有用?;**there are three computers; which do you want to buy?** yǒu sān tái jìsuànjī,nǐ xiǎng mǎi nǎ yì tái? 有3台计算机,你想买哪一台? **2** det (when the noun that follows is plural)nǎxiē 哪些;**which books did he borrow?** tā jiè le nǎxiē shū? 他借了哪些书?;(when the noun that follows is singular)nǎ(yí)gè 哪(一)个;! Note that in **nǎ(yí)gè 哪(一)个**, the measure word **gè 个** may be replaced by a different measure word depending on the noun being referred to;**which one of the nurses speaks Chinese?** nǎ yí gè hùshi huì shuō Hànyǔ? 哪一个护士会说汉语?;**which car is yours?** nǎ yí liàng chē shì nǐ de? 哪一辆车是你的?;**he asked me which shirt I liked** tā wèn wǒ xǐhuan nǎ yí jiàn chènshān 他问我喜欢哪一件衬衫

while /hwaɪl/ conj (in the time that)(dāng)…de shíhou (当)…的时候;**I was ill while I was on holiday in Japan** wǒ zài Rìběn dùjià de shíhou bìng le 我在日本度假的时候病了;**she fell asleep while watching TV** tā kàn diànshì de shíhou shuìzháo le 她看电视的时候睡着了,tā kànzhe diànshì shuìzháo le 她看着电视睡着了

whisper /'hwɪspə(r)/ vb (to say in soft, hushed tones) xiǎoshēng de shuō 小声地说；dīshēng de shuō 低声地说

whistle /'hwɪsl/ **1** vb (with the mouth) chuī kǒushào 吹口哨；(with a whistle) chuī shàozi 吹哨子；(when referring to a train) míngdí 鸣笛 **2** n a whistle (blown with the mouth) yí gè shàozi 一个哨子；(sounded by escaping steam) yí gè qìdí 一个汽笛

white /hwaɪt/ adj bái de 白的, báisè de 白色的

who /huː/ pron (used in questions) shéi/shuí 谁；who told you? shéi gàosu nǐ de? 谁告诉你的?；who did you invite? nǐ qǐngle shéi? 你请了谁?；who did he buy the book for? tā gěi shéi mǎi de shū? 他给谁买的书?；(used as a relative pronoun in a defining relative clause)! Note that in this case, who is usually not translated; those who can't come by bike nàxiē bù néng qí zìxíngchē lái de rén 那些不能骑自行车来的人；the man who you want to see nǐ xiǎng jiàn de nàge rén 你想见的那个人；(used as a relative pronoun in a non-defining relative clause)! Note that in this case, who is translated as tā 他 if it refers to a man, as tā 她 if it refers to a woman, and as tāmen 他们 if it refers to a plural noun; I went to see my mother, who had just come back from China wǒ qù kàn wǒ māma le, tā gāng cóng Zhōngguó huílái 我去看我妈妈了, 她刚从中国回来；he is waiting for his friends, who are coming to celebrate his birthday tā zài děng tā de péngyou, tāmen yào lái gěi tā guò shēngrì 他在等他的朋友, 他们要来给他过生日

whole /həʊl/ **1** n the whole of [the country | London | August...] zhěnggè [guójiā|Lúndūn|bāyuè…] 整个[国家|伦敦|8 月…] **2** adj a whole day yì zhěng tiān 一整天；three whole weeks zhěngzhěng sān gè xīngqī 整整三个星期；the whole world quánshìjiè 全世界；I don't want to spend my whole life here wǒ bù xiǎng zài zhèlǐ dùguò wǒ de zhěnggè yìshēng 我不想在这里度过我的整个一生

whom /huːm/弱 hʊm/ *pron*(*used in questions*) shéi/shuí 谁; **whom did you meet**? nǐ yùjiàn shéi? 你遇见了谁?; (*used as a relative pronoun in a defining clause*)！*Note that in this case, whom is usually not translated*; **the person who you met yesterday** zuótiān nǐ jiàn de nàge rén 昨天你见的那个人;(*used as a relative pronoun in a non-defining clause*) tā 他, tā 她, tāmen 他们！*Note that in this case, whom is translated as tā 他 if it refers to a man, as tā 她 if it refers to a woman, and as tāmen 他们 if it refers to a plural noun*; **my younger brother, whom you met in my house, is going to China to study Chinese** wǒ dìdi yào qù Zhōngguó xuéxí Hànyǔ, nǐ zài wǒ jiā jiànguo tā 我弟弟要去中国学习汉语,你在我家见过他; **these students, for whom I have to arrange accommodation, came from China** zhèxiē xuésheng láizì Zhōngguó, wǒ děi gěi tāmen ānpái zhùsù 这些学生来自中国,我得给他们安排住宿

whose /huːz/ **1** *pron*(*used in questions*) shéi de/shuí de 谁的; **whose is this nice hat**? zhè dǐng piàoliang de màozi shì shéi de? 这顶漂亮的帽子是谁的?;(*used as a relative pronoun*)！*Note that in this case, whose is often translated as tā de 他的 if it refers to a masculine singular noun, as tā de 她的 if it refers to a feminine singular noun, as tā de 它的 if it refers to a non-human singular noun, as tāmen de 他们的 if it refers to a human plural noun, and as tāmen de 它们的 if it refers to a non-human plural noun. Sometimes, whose is not translated at all in a defining relative clause*; **the boy whose bike was stolen** (tā de) zìxíngchē bèi rén tōuzǒule de nàge nánháir (他的) 自行车被人偷走了的那个男孩儿; **the woman whose house I'm buying** wǒ yào mǎi tā de fángzi de nàge nǚ de 我要买她的房子的那个女的; **they are Mr. and Mrs. Brown, whose son used to be a student of mine** tāmen shì Bùlǎng xiānsheng hé Bùlǎng tàitai, tāmen de érzi yǐqián shì wǒ de xuésheng 他们是布朗先生和布朗太太,他们的儿子以前是我的学生;the chair whose leg is broken duànle tuǐ de nà bǎ yǐzi 断了腿的那把椅子 2 det shéi de/shuí de 谁的;whose car is that? nà shì shéi de chē? 那是谁的车?;whose pen did you borrow? nǐ jiè shéi de bǐ? 你借谁的笔?

why /hwaɪ/ **1** adv wèishénme 为什么;why did you tell him? nǐ wèishénme gàosu tā? 你为什么告诉他?;why aren't they coming? tāmen wèishénme bù lái? 他们为什么不来?;why not wèishénme bù 为什么不?;why don't we eat out tonight? jīntiān wǎnshang wǒmen wèishénme bù chūqù chī ne? 今天晚上我们为什么不出去吃呢? **2** conj …de yuányīn …的原因;that's (the reason) why I can't stand him zhè jiù shì wǒ bù néng rěnshòu tā de yuányīn 这就是我不能忍受他的原因;please tell me why you want to learn Chinese qǐng nǐ gàosu wǒ nǐ yào xué Zhōngwén de yuányīn 请你告诉我你要学中文的原因, qǐng nǐ gàosu wǒ nǐ wèishénme yào xué Zhōngwén 请你告诉我你为什么要学中文

wide /waɪd/ adj (in size) kuān de 宽的;a wide garden yí gè hěn kuān de huāyuán 一个很宽的花园;the room is ten metres wide zhège fángjiān shí mǐ kuān 这个房间10米宽;(in range) a wide range of choices guǎngfàn de xuǎnzé fànwéi 广泛的选择范围;a person with wide interests yí gè xìngqù guǎngfàn de rén 一个兴趣广泛的人;a wide range of games zhǒnglèi fánduō de yóuxì 种类繁多的游戏

width /wɪdθ/ n (the distance between) kuāndù 宽度;(being wide) kuānkuò 宽阔;a road of great width yì tiáo kuānkuò de mǎlù 一条宽阔的马路

wife /waɪf/ n (less formal) qīzi 妻子, àiren 爱人;(more formal) fūrén 夫人, tàitai 太太;a wife yí wèi fūrén 一位夫人

wild /waɪld/ adj (describing animals, plants) yěshēng de 野生的;wild plants yěshēng zhíwù 野生植物;wild animals yěshēng dòngwù 野生动物;(*noisy, out of control*) fāfēng de 发疯的, fākuáng de 发狂的;he's gone **wild** tā fāfēng le 他发疯了;(*not cultivated*) huāngwú de 荒芜的, huāngliáng de 荒凉的

wildlife /'waɪldlaɪf/ *n* yěshēng dòngwù 野生动物

will /wɪl/ *vb* (*when talking about the future*) (*in positive statements and questions*) huì 会, jiāng(yào) 将(要);**will she agree?** tā huì tóngyì ma? 她会同意吗?;**it will rain tomorrow** míngtiān yào xiàyǔ 明天要下雨;**we will discuss this problem** wǒmen jiāng tǎolùn zhège wèntí 我们将讨论这个问题;(*in negative sentences*) **will not** (jiāng) bú huì (将)不会;**she won't agree** tā bú huì tóngyì 她不会同意;**I won't forget** wǒ bú huì wàngjì 我不会忘记;(*when talking about willingness*) yuànyì 愿意;**I will do my best to help this child** wǒ yuànyì jìn zuì dà nǔlì bāngzhù zhège háizi 我愿意尽最大努力帮助这个孩子;**she won't come** tā bú yuànyì lái 她不愿意来;(*when talking about intentions*) xiǎng, yào 想, 要;**will you visit the Great Wall?** nǐ yào qù cānguān Chángchéng ma? 你要去参观长城吗?;**we won't stay too long** wǒmen bú huì dai hěn cháng shíjiān 我们不会呆很长时间;(*in invitations and requests*) (qǐng) …hǎo ma? (请) … 好吗?;**will you have some coffee?** nín hē diǎnr kāfēi, hǎo ma? 您喝点儿咖啡, 好吗?;**will you pass me the salt, please?** qǐng nǐ bǎ yán dìgěi wǒ, hǎo ma? 请你把盐递给我, 好吗?;(*when making an assumption about the future*) huì 会;**they won't know what's happened** tāmen bú huì zhīdào fāshēngle shénme shì 他们不会知道发生了什么事

win /wɪn/ *vb* (*be victorious*) yíng 赢, huòshèng 获胜;(*to gain in a battle, match, contest*) yíngdé 赢得, huòdé 获得;**to win a gold medal** huòdé yì méi jīnpái 获得一枚金牌

wind /wɪnd/ *n* a wind fēng 风

window /'wɪndəʊ/ *n* a window (*in a house, a car, a*

plane) yí gè chuānghu 一个窗户；(in a shop) yí gè chúchuāng 一个橱窗

windsurfing /'wɪndsɜːfɪŋ/ n fānbǎn yùndòng 帆板运动

windy /'wɪndɪ/ adj guā (dà) fēng de 刮(大)风的，fēng dà de 风大的；it's very windy outside wàimian guā dàfēng 外面刮大风

wine /waɪn/ n pútáojiǔ 葡萄酒

wing /wɪŋ/ n a wing (of a bird) yì zhī chìbǎng 一只翅膀，(for a plane) yí gè jīyì 一个机翼

winter /'wɪntə(r)/ n dōngtiān 冬天，dōngjì 冬季

wipe /waɪp/ vb cā 擦；to wipe [one's nose|one's tears|the table...] cā [bízi|yǎnlèi|zhuōzi...]擦[鼻子|眼泪|桌子...]

wise /waɪz/ adj (when describing a person) cōngming de 聪明的；(when describing a decision, a choice, or a leader) yīngmíng de 英明的，míngzhì de 明智的

wish /wɪʃ/ **1** n (a hope) a wish yí gè yuànwàng 一个愿望；best wishes (in greetings) zuì měihǎo de zhùyuàn 最美好的祝愿；to give one's best wishes to someone xiàng mǒu rén zhìyì 向某人致意；(in a letter) with best wishes zhù hǎo 祝好 **2** vb (to want, to be inclined) xiǎng 想，yào 要；how long do they wish to stay here for? tāmen xiǎng zài zhèr dāi duōjiǔ? 他们想在这儿呆多久?；(to long, to hope) kěwàng 渴望；I wish to visit Shanghai wǒ kěwàng qù Shànghǎi fǎngwèn 我渴望去上海访问；(expressing what one would like to happen or to have happened) yàoshi...jiù hǎo le yàoshi... jiù hǎo le 要是... 就好了；I wish they could come yàoshi tāmen néng lái jiù hǎo le 要是他们能来就好了；she wished she hadn't lied tā xiǎng yàoshi tā méi sāhuǎng jiù hǎo le 她想要是她没撒谎就好了；(in greetings) zhù 祝，zhùyuàn 祝愿；to wish someone a happy birthday zhù mǒu rén shēngrì kuàilè 祝某人生日快乐

with /wɪð/ prep (in the company of) hé...(yìqǐ) 和...(一起)，gēn...(yìqǐ) 跟...(一起)；he went away with his friends tā hé tā de péngyou (yìqǐ) zǒu le 他和他的朋友

（一起）走了；I'm living with my parents wǒ gēn wǒ fùmǔ zhù zài yìqǐ 我跟我父母住在一起；(by means of) yòng 用；she's wiping her tears with her hands tā zài yòng shǒu cā yǎnlèi 她在用手擦眼泪；(in the possession of)！Note that in this case, with is often not translated；a girl with black hair yí gè hēi tóufa de nǚháir 一个黑头发的女孩儿；the boy with the broken leg nàge duànle tuǐ de nánháir 那个断了腿的男孩儿；a man with a great sense of humour yí gè hěn yōumò de rén 一个很幽默的人；he left with a smile tā xiàozhe zǒu le 他笑着走了；she's married with two children tā jiéhūn le, yǒu liǎng gè háizi 她结婚了，有两个孩子；(denoting support) zàntóng 赞同，zhīchí 支持；most people are with this proposal dàduōshù rén dōu zàntóng zhège tíyì 大多数人都赞同这个提议；(denoting understanding) dǒng 懂，míngbai 明白，lǐjiě 理解；I'm with you wǒ dǒng nǐ de yìsi 我懂你的意思；(because of)！Note that in this case, with is often not translated；she jumped with joy tā gāoxìng de tiàole qǐlai 她高兴地跳了起来；she shivered with fear tā xià de fādǒu 她吓得发抖；(at hand) I haven't got any money with me wǒ (shēnshang) méi dài qián 我（身上）没带钱；you'd better take a dictionary with you nǐ zuìhǎo suíshēn dài yì běn cídiǎn 你最好随身带一本词典；(at the same time as) suízhe 随着；the living standard improves with the increase in the people's income shēnghuó shuǐpíng suízhe rénmen shōurù de zēngjiā ér tígáo 生活水平随着人们收入的增加而提高

without /wɪˈðaut/ prep méiyǒu 没有；we got in without paying wǒmen méiyǒu fùqián jiù jìnqù le 我们没有付钱就进去了

wolf /wʊlf/ n a wolf yì tiáo láng 一条狼

woman /ˈwʊmən/ n a woman yí wèi fùnǚ 一位妇女；a single woman yí gè dānshēn fùnǚ 一个单身妇女

wonder /ˈwʌndə(r)/ vb (to ask oneself) xiǎng zhīdào 想

知道；I wonder [how he came|why he came|who came…] wǒ xiǎng zhīdào [tā shì zěnme lái de|tā wèishénme lái|shéí lái le…] 我想知道[他是怎么来的|他是为什么来|谁来了…]；I was wondering when you'd arrive wǒ xiǎng zhīdào nín shénme shíhou dào 我想知道您什么时候到；(in polite requests) I wonder if you could help me? bù zhī nǐ néng bù néng bāng wǒ ge máng? 不知你能不能帮我个忙？

wonderful /'wʌndəful/ adj (when describing a performance, a match) jīngcǎi de 精彩的；(when describing someone's courage, memory) jīngrén de 惊人的；(when describing the weather, an idea, a plan, etc.) jí hǎo de 极好的，jí miào de 极妙的；the weather is wonderful tiānqì hǎo jí le 天气好极了；what a wonderful idea! zhège zhǔyi miào jí le! 这个主意妙极了！；wonderful! tài hǎo le! 太好了！

wood /wud/ n (timber) mùtou 木头；the table is made of wood zhè zhāng zhuōzi shì mùtou zuò de 这张桌子是木头做的；(a small forest) a wood yí piàn shùlín 一片树林

wool /wul/ n (soft hair of a sheep, goat, etc.) yángmáo 羊毛，máo 毛；(yarn spun from sheep or goat hair) máoxiàn 毛线，róngxiàn 绒线

word /wɜːd/ n (the smallest meaningful unit in a language) yí gè (dān) cí 一个(单)词；what's the Chinese word for 'break'? 'break' de Zhōngwén dāncí shì shénme? 'break' 的中文单词是什么？；(utterance) huà huà 话；I didn't say a word wǒ yí jù huà yě méi shuō 我一句话也没说；in other words huàn jù huà shuō 换句话说；(a brief conversation) can I have a word with you? wǒ kěyǐ gēn nǐ tán yíxià ma? 我可以跟你谈一下吗？

work /wɜːk/ **1** vb (to do a job) gōngzuò 工作；to work at home zài jiā li gōngzuò 在家里工作；(to have a job) to work as [a doctor|a teacher|an actor…] dāng [yīshēng|lǎoshī|yǎnyuán…] 当 [医生|老师|演员…]；(to operate properly) gōngzuò 工作；the TV isn't working diànshìjī huài le 电视机坏了；(to be successful) (if it's an idea, a *plan*, *a trick*) xíngdetōng 行得通；! *Note that the negative form is* xíngbutōng 行不通；the plan doesn't work zhège jìhuà xíngbutōng 这个计划行不通；(*if it's a medicine, a treatment*) qǐ zuòyòng 起作用；(*to use, to operate*) shǐyòng 使用，cāozuò 操作；do you know how to work the computer? nǐ zhīdào zěnme shǐyòng zhè tái jìsuànjī ma? 你知道怎么使用这台计算机吗? **2** *n* work gōngzuò 工作，huór 活儿；I've got a lot of work to do wǒ yǒu hěn duō gōngzuò yào zuò 我有很多工作要做；(*employment*) have you found work yet? nǐ zhǎodào gōngzuò le ma? 你找到工作了吗? she is out of work tā shīyè le 她失业了；(*students' work*) zuòyè 作业；(*for building, for repairs*) gōngchéng 工程；there are road-works outside at the moment wàimian zhèngzài jìnxíng xiūlù gōngchéng 外面正在进行修路工程；(*by a writer, an artist, a musician*) a work yí gè zuòpǐn 一个作品；(*a book*) works zhùzuò 著作；work out (*to find*) zhǎochū 找出；to work out the answer zhǎochū dá'àn 找出答案；(*to understand*) nòng míngbai 弄明白，nòng qīngchu 弄清楚；(*with figures*) suànchū 算出；(*to take exercise*) duànliàn 锻炼；(*to devise*) shèjì chū 设计出；(*to formulate, to make*) zhìdìng chū 制订出；to work out a plan zhìdìng chū yí xiàng jìhuà 制订出一项计划；work up (*when talking about getting excited*) to get worked up jīdòng qǐlái 激动起来；(*to rouse*) huànqǐ 唤起，jīqǐ 激起；to work up enthusiasm for learning Chinese huànqǐ xuéxí Zhōngwén de rèqíng 唤起学习中文的热情

worker /'wɜːkə(r)/ *n* a worker (*in a factory*) yí gè gōngrén 一个工人；(*in an office, a bank*) yí gè gōngzuò rényuán 一个工作人员

world /wɜːld/ *n* the world shìjiè 世界；all over the world quánshìjiè 全世界；the biggest city in the world shìjièshang zuì dà de chéngshì 世界上最大的城市

World Cup /ˌwɜːld 'kʌp/ *n* the World Cup Shìjièbēi 世界杯

World Wide Web /ˈwɜːld waɪd ˌweb/ , **WWW** n the World Wide Web wànwéiwǎng 万维网

worm /wɜːm/ n a worm yì tiáo chóngzi 一条虫子

worried /ˈwʌrɪd/ adj dānxīn de 担心的，bú fàngxīn de 不放心的；to be worried about someone dānxīn mǒu rén 担心某人

worry /ˈwʌrɪ/ vb (to be worried) dānxīn 担心，bú fàngxīn 不放心；there's nothing to worry about méiyǒu shénme kě dānxīn de 没有什么可担心的；(to make someone worried) shǐ… dānxīn 使…担心，shǐ… bù'ān 使…不安；it's worrying me zhè shǐ wǒ hěn dānxīn 这使我很担心

worse /wɜːs/ adj (evil in a higher degree) gèng huài de 更坏的；this idea is worse than that one zhège zhǔyi bǐ nàge gèng huài 这个主意比那个更坏；(when describing a standard, the weather, a condition) gèng chà de 更差的，gèng zāo de 更糟的；she's worse than me at sports zài tǐyù fāngmiàn tā bǐ wǒ gèng chà 在体育方面她比我更差；the weather is going to get worse tiānqì huì biàn de gèng zāo 天气会变得更糟；(when describing an illness) gèng zhòng de 更重的；he is getting worse tā de bìng gèng zhòng le 他的病更重了

worst /wɜːst/ **1** n the worst (when talking about a wicked person) zuì huài de rén 最坏的人；(when talking about an ability, a condition, a standard, the weather) zuì chà de 最差的，zuì zāo(gāo) de 最糟(糕)的；I'm the worst at Chinese zài xuéxí Zhōngwén fāngmiàn, wǒ shì zuì chà de 在学习中文方面，我是最差的 **2** adj (most wicked or evil) zuì huài de 最坏的；(when talking about an ability, a condition, a standard, the weather) zuì chà de 最差的，zuì zāo(gāo) de 最糟(糕)的；the worst hotel in town chéng li zuì chà de lǚguǎn 城里最差的旅馆；the worst film I've ever seen wǒ suǒ kànguo de zuì zāo(gāo) de diànyǐng 我所看过的最糟(糕)的电影；his worst enemy tā zuì xiōng'è de dírén 他最凶恶的敌人；

(*the most severe or serious*) zuì yánzhòng de 最严重的; **the worst accident** zuì yánzhòng de shìgù 最严重的事故

worth /wɜːθ/ *adj* (*equal in value to*) zhí 值; **to be worth 100** zhí yìbǎi yīngbàng 值 100 英镑; (*deserving of*) zhíde 值得; **the exhibition is not worth visiting** zhège zhǎnlǎnhuì bù zhíde cānguān 这个展览会不值得参观

would /wud/弱 wəd/ *vb* (*when talking about hypothetical rather than real situations*) huì 会, jiù huì 就会; **if I had more money, I would buy a car** wǒ yàoshi yǒu gèng duō de qián, wǒ huì mǎi yí liàng qìchē 我要是有更多的钱,我会买一辆汽车; **we would have missed the train if we'd left later** rúguǒ wǒmen zài wǎn diǎnr zǒu, wǒmen jiù wǔle huǒchē le 如果我们再晚点儿走,我们就误了火车了; (*when used as the past tense of will*) jiāng 将, (jiāng)huì (将)会! Note that in this sense, *the negative form is* (jiāng) bú huì (将)不会; **I thought you'd forget to come** wǒ yǐwéi nǐ huì wàngle lái 我以为你会忘了来; **we knew she wouldn't like it** wǒmen zhīdào tā bú huì xǐhuan 我们知道她不会喜欢; (*when talking about probability or likelihood*) dàgài 大概, yěxǔ 也许; **she'd be 30 now** tā xiànzài dàgài sānshí suì le 她现在大概 30 岁了; **he would be in the library now** xiànzài tā yěxǔ zài túshūguǎn 现在他也许在图书馆; (*to be willing to*) yuànyì 愿意, yào 要; **he wouldn't listen to me** tā bú yuànyì tīng wǒ de huà 他不愿意听我的话; (*when talking about one's wishes*) xiǎng 想; **I'd like a beer** wǒ xiǎng yào yì bēi píjiǔ 我想要一杯啤酒; **we would like to stay another night** wǒmen xiǎng zài dāi yí gè wǎnshang 我们想再呆一个晚上; (*when making a polite request*) qǐng… hǎo ma 请…好吗, qǐng…kěyǐ ma 请…可以吗; **would you turn the TV off, please**? qǐng bǎ diànshì guānshang, hǎo ma? 请把电视关上,好吗?; **would you pass the book to me, please**? qǐng bǎ nà běn shū dìgěi wǒ, kěyǐ ma? 请把那本书递给我,可以吗?; (*when* *talking about a habitual action in the past*) zǒngshì 总是 , zǒnghuì 总会 ; *she would sit beside me* tā zǒngshì zuò zài wǒ de pángbiān 她总是坐在我的旁边

wrap /ræp/ *vb* (*to cover by putting something all over*) bāo 包 ; *to wrap* (*up*) *a present* bāo yí gè lǐwù 包一个礼物 ; (*to cover by putting something from the middle*) guǒ 裹 , bāo 包 ; *to wrap the child in a blanket* yòng tǎnzi bǎ háizi guǒ qǐlai 用毯子把孩子裹起来

wreck /rek/ **1** *vb* (*to destroy, to ruin*) pòhuài 破坏 , sǔnhài 损害 ; *be wrecked* (*if it's a ship, a train, or a plane*) shīshì 失事 ; *the ship was wrecked* nà sōu chuán shīshì le 那艘船失事了 **2** *n* (*if it's damaged but might be fixed*) *a wreck* (*of a ship*) yì sōu shīshì de chuán 一艘失事的船 ; (*of a car*) yí liàng shīshì de qìchē 一辆失事的汽车 ; (*if it's completely in ruins*) cánhái 残骸 ; *the wreck of* [*a ship | a car | a plane*] de cánhái [一艘船 | 一辆汽车 | 一架飞机] 的残骸

wrestling /'reslɪŋ/ *n* shuāijiāo yùndòng 摔跤运动

wrist /rɪst/ *n* the wrist shǒuwàn 手腕 , wànzi 腕子

write /raɪt/ *vb* write xiě 写 [*an essay | a cheque | a letter...*] xiě [yì piān wénzhāng | yì zhāng zhīpiào | yì fēng xìn···] 写 [一篇文章 | 一张支票 | 一封信···] ; (*to write a letter*) xiěxìn 写信 ; *to write to someone* (*US English*) gěi mǒu rén xiěxìn 给某人写信 ; *write back* huíxìn 回信 ; *write down* jìxià 记下 , xiěxià 写下 ; *write out* (*to transcribe*) xiěchū 写出 ; (*to write in full*) quánbù xiěchū 全部写出

writing /'raɪtɪŋ/ *n* (*the act of one who writes*) xiě 写 ; (*a literary production or composition*) xiězuò 写作 ; (*handwriting*) bǐjì 笔迹 , zìjì 字迹

writing pad /'raɪtɪŋ pæd/ *n* a writing pad yí gè biànjiānběn 一个便笺本

wrong /rɒŋ/ *adj* (*not as it should be*) there's something wrong with the TV diànshìjī yǒu diǎnr bú zhèngcháng 电视机有点儿不正常 ; *what's wrong* (*with you*)? (nǐ) zěnme le? (你)怎么了? ; *what's wrong with that?* nà yǒu shénme búduì? 那有什么不对?；there isn't anything wrong with him tā méi yǒu shénme wèntí 他没有什么问题；(not proper or suitable) bù héshì de 不合适的；I'm sorry I've said the wrong thing duìbuqǐ, wǒ shuōle bù héshì de huà 对不起, 我说了不合适的话；that's the wrong thing to do nàyàng zuò bù héshì 那样做不合适；(not correct) cuò de 错的, bú duì de 不对的；that's wrong nà shì bú duì de 那是不对的；to dial the wrong number bōcuò hàomǎ 拨错号码；it's the wrong answer zhège dá'àn shì cuò de 这个答案是错的；you are wrong nǐ cuò le 你错了；I took the wrong key wǒ nácuòle yàoshi 我拿错了钥匙；they went the wrong way tāmen zǒucuòle lù 他们走错了路；(immoral) bú dàodé de 不道德的, bú duì de 不对的；it's wrong to steal tōu dōngxi shì bú dàodé de 偷东西是不道德的；she hasn't done anything wrong tā méiyǒu zuò shénme bú duì de shì 她没有做什么不对的事

Xx

xerox /ˈzɪərɒks/ **1** n fùyìn 复印 **2** vb fùyìn 复印

X-ray /ˈeksˌreɪ/ **1** n an X-ray yì zhāng àikèsīguāngpiàn 一张 X 光片；to have an X-ray jìnxíng àikèsīguāng jiǎnchá 进行 X 光检查 **2** vb yòng àikèsīguāng jiǎnchá 用 X 光检查

Yy

yacht /jɒt/ n a yacht；(for pleasure) (US English) yì sōu yóutǐng 一艘游艇；(for racing) yì sōu sàitǐng 一艘赛艇；

(for sailing) yì sōu fānchuán 一艘帆船

yard /jɑːd/ *n* (*a measurement of length*) **a yard** yì mǎ 一码;(*area around a building*) **a yard** yí gè yuànzi 一个院子;(*US English*) (*a garden*) **a yard** yí gè huāyuán 一个花园

yawn /jɔːn/ *vb* dǎ hāqiàn 打哈欠

year /jɜː(r)/ *n* (*when talking about time*) **a year** yì nián 一年; [last|this|next] **year** [qù|jīn|míng]nián [去|今|明]年; **the year** [before last|after next] nián [前|后]年; **two years ago** liǎng nián (yǐ)qián 两年(以)前; **to work all year round** quánnián gōngzuò 全年工作; **he's lived there for years** tā zài nàli zhùle hěn duō nián le 他在那里住了很多年了;(*when talking about age*) **a year** yí suì 一岁; **he is 15 years old, he is 15 years of age** tā shíwǔ suì (le) 他 15 岁(了);**a four-year old** yí gè sì suì de háizi 一个 4 岁的孩子;(*in a school system*) niánjí 年级; **first year, year one** yī niánjí 一年级; **she is in second year, she is in year two** tā zài èr niánjí 她在二年级

yell /jel/ **1** *vb* (jiào) hǎn (叫)喊; **to yell at someone** chòngzhe mǒu rén hǎn 冲着某人喊 **2** *n* **a yell** yì shēng dàhǎn 一声大喊

yellow /ˈjeləʊ/ *adj* huáng de 黄的, huángsè de 黄色的; **the leaves have gone yellow** yèzi biànhuáng le 叶子变黄了

yes /jes/ *adv* shì (de) 是(的), duì 对;'are you going with us?'—'yes, I am' "nǐ gēn wǒmen yìqǐ qù ma?"—"shì de, wǒ gēn nǐmen yìqǐ qù" "你跟我们一起去吗?"—"是的,我跟你们一起去";(*when providing a positive response to a negative statement or question*) bù 不;'they don't know each other'—'yes, they do' "tāmen hùxiāng bú rènshi"—"bù, tāmen hùxiāng rènshi" "他们互相不认识"—"不,他们互相认识";'didn't he tell you?'—'yes, he did' "tā méi gàosu nǐ ma?"—"bù, tā gàosu wǒ le" "他没告诉你吗?"—"不,他告诉我了"

yesterday /ˈjestədɪ/ *adv* zuótiān 昨天; **the day before**

yesterday qiántiān 前天

yet /jet/ **1** adv (in a negative sentence) hái 还；not yet hái méiyǒu 还没有；it's not ready yet hái méi zhǔnbèi hǎo 还没准备好；I haven't told him yet wǒ hái méiyǒu gàosu tā 我还没有告诉他；(in a question) yǐjīng 已经！Note that in this case, yet is often not translated；have they arrived yet? tāmen (yǐjīng) dào le ma? 他们（已经）到了吗？；has she met them yet? tā (yǐjīng) jiàndào tāmen le ma? 她（已经）见到他们了吗？ **2** conj rán'ér 然而，dànshì 但是

yogurt /'jogət/ n suānnǎi 酸奶

you /ju；弱 jʊ/ pron (singular) nǐ 你；do you speak Chinese? nǐ huì shuō Hànyǔ ma? 你会说汉语吗？；he will help you tā huì bāngzhù nǐ 他会帮助你；(plural) nǐmen 你们；are you students? nǐmen shì xuésheng ma? 你们是学生吗？；(the polite form, singular) nín 您；may I ask you a question? wǒ kěyǐ wèn nín yí gè wèntí ma? 我可以问您一个问题吗？；(when used impersonally) nǐ 你，rénmen 人们；you can buy anything here zài zhèlǐ shénme nǐ dōu néng mǎidào 在这里什么你都能买到；you never know what will happen shéi yě bù zhīdào huì fāshēng shénme shì 谁也不知道会发生什么事；these mushrooms can make you ill zhèxiē mógu néng shǐ rén débìng 这些蘑菇能使人得病

young /jʌŋ/ **1** adj niánqīng de 年轻的，niánqīng de 年青的；a young lady yí wèi niánqīng de nǚshì 一位年轻的女士；young people niánqīngrén 年轻人，qīngnián 青年；she is a year younger than I tā bǐ wǒ xiǎo yí suì 她比我小 1 岁；to look young xiǎn de niánqīng 显得年轻；a younger brother yí gè dìdi 一个弟弟；a younger sister yí gè mèimei 一个妹妹；(when describing children, babies, animals) yòuxiǎo 幼小；a young [baby|animal] yí gè yòuxiǎo de [yīng'ér|dòngwù]一个幼小的［婴儿|动物］；a young child yí gè yòutóng 一个幼童 **2** n the young (of people) qīngnián 青年，

niánqīngrén 年轻人；(of animals) yòuzǎi 幼崽；(of birds) yòuniǎo 幼鸟，chúniǎo 雏鸟

your /jɔː(r)/ 弱 jə(r)/ det (singular) nǐ de 你的；is this your book? zhè shì nǐ de shū ma? 这是你的书吗?；(plural) nǐmen de 你们的；(the polite form, singular) nín de 您的；here is your room zhè shì nín de fángjiān 这是您的房间；(when used impersonally)! Note that in this case, your is usually not translated；smoking is bad for your health xīyān duì shēntǐ yǒuhài 吸烟对身体有害

yours /jɔːz/ pron (singular) nǐ de 你的；the red car is yours nà liàng hóng chē shì nǐ de 那辆红车是你的；(plural) nǐmen de 你们的；our garden is bigger than yours wǒmen de huāyuán bǐ nǐmen de dà 我们的花园比你们的大；(polite form, singular) nín de 您的；is this suitcase yours? zhège xiāngzi shì nín de ma? 这个箱子是您的吗?

yourself /jɔːˈself/ pron (when used as a reflexive pronoun) yourself (nǐ) zìjǐ (你) 自己；you should trust yourself nǐ yīnggāi xiāngxìn (nǐ) zìjǐ 你应该相信(你)自己；(polite form) (nín) zìjǐ (您) 自己；you haven't poured any wine for yourself nín hái méiyǒu gěi (nín) zìjǐ dàojiǔ ne 您还没有给(您)自己倒酒呢；(when used for emphasis) qīnzì 亲自，běnrén 本人，zìjǐ 自己；you don't have to go yourself nǐ búbì qīnzì qù 你不必亲自去

yourselves /jɔːˈselvz/ pron (when used as a reflexive pronoun) (nǐmen) zìjǐ (你们) 自己；what have you bought for yourselves? nǐmen gěi (nǐmen) zìjǐ mǎile xiē shénme? 你们给(你们)自己买了些什么?；(when used for emphasis) qīnzì 亲自，zìjǐ 自己；are you going to organize it yourselves? nǐmen dǎsuàn zìjǐ zǔzhī ma? 你们打算自己组织吗?

youth /juːθ/ n (a young man) a youth yí gè nánqīngnián 一个男青年，yí gè xiǎohuǒzi 一个小伙子；(young people) the youth niánqīngrén 年轻人，niánqīngrén 年

青人

youth club /ˈjuːθ klʌb/ *n* a youth club yí gè qīngnián jùlèbù 一个青年俱乐部

youth hostel /ˈjuːθ ˌhɒstəl/ *n* a youth hostel yí gè qīngnián lǚguǎn 一个青年旅馆

youth worker /ˈjuːθ ˌwɜːkə(r)/ *n* a youth worker yí wèi qīngshàonián gōngzuòzhě 一位青少年工作者

Zz

zap /zæp/ *vb* (*to destroy*) huǐdiào 毁掉，cuīhuǐ 摧毁；(*British English*) (*to switch channels*)(zhuǎn)huàn píndào (转)换频道；to zap from channel to channel bùtíng de (zhuǎn)huàn píndào 不停地(转)换频道

zapper /ˈzæpə(r)/ *n* (*British English*) a zapper (*a remote control*) yí gè yáokòngqì 一个遥控器

zebra /ˈziːbrə/ *n* a zebra yì pǐ bānmǎ 一匹斑马

zebra crossing /ˈziːbrə krɒsɪŋ/ *n* (*British English*) a zebra crossing yì tiáo rénxíng héngdào 一条人行横道

zero /ˈzɪərəu/ *num* líng 零

zip /zɪp/ (*British English*), **zipper** /ˈzɪpə(r)/ (*US English*) **1** *n* a zip yì tiáo lāliàn 一条拉链，yì tiáo lāsuǒ 一条拉锁；to undo a zip lākāi lāliàn 拉开拉链 **2** *vb* lāshang…de lāliàn 拉上…的拉链；to zip up[one's trousers | one's jacket | the bag…] bǎ [kùzi|jiākè|bāo…]de lāliàn lāshang 把 [裤子|夹克|包…]的拉链拉上

zip code /ˈzɪp kəud/ *n* (*US English*) a zip code yí gè yóuzhèng biānmǎ 一个邮政编码

zone /zəun/ *n* a zone yí gè dìdài 一个地带，yí gè dìqū 一个地区

zoo /zuː/ *n* a zoo yí gè dòngwùyuán 一个动物园

Aa

阿 **ā** *prf* (*informal name prefix especially in Yangtze Delta region*) 阿 Q 阿 Q Ah Q

阿拉伯 **Ālābó** *n* Arabia

阿姨 **āyí** *n* (*term of address for a woman of one's her mother's generation*) auntie; (*term of address for a childminder*) nanny, baby-sitter

啊 **ā** **1** *exc* (*to express surprise*) oh! ah!; ā, nǐ lái le! 啊, 你来了! ah, here you are! **2** *pt* (*placed at the end of a sentence to express admiration, warning, or request*) duō hǎo de tiānr a! 多好的天儿啊! what a beautiful day!; bié chídào a! 别迟到啊! don't be late!; nǐ kuài lái a! 你快来啊! come here quickly!

哎 **āi** *exc* (*to express surprise or discontent*) āi, nǐ bǎ qián fàng zài nǎli le? 哎, 你把钱放在哪里了? but where did you put the money?

哎呀 **āiyā** *exc* (*expressing surprise*) my goodness!; āiyā, wǒ de qiánbāo diū le! 哎呀, 我的钱包丢了! oh dear, I've lost my wallet!

挨 **āi** *vb* ▶ See also 挨 ái . get close to, be next to or near tā jiā āizhe xuéxiào 他家挨着学校 his house is next to the school; (*in sequence, by turns*) shénme shíhou néng āidào wǒ? 什么时候能挨到我? when can it be my turn?

挨 **ái** *vb* ▶ See also 挨 āi . suffer, endure; áidòng 挨冻 suffer from the freezing cold; áimà 挨骂 get a scolding; áidǎ 挨打 get a beating, come under attack

癌 **ái** *n* cancer; áizhèng 癌症 cancer

矮 **ǎi** *adj* (*in stature*) short; (*of inanimate objects*) low

爱 **ài** *vb* (*if the object is a person*) love, be fond of; wǒ ài nǐ 我

爱你 I love you;(*if the object is an activity*) like,love;**wǒ ài tīng nàge gùshi** 我爱听那个故事 I like to hear that story

爱好 àihào 1 *vb* be keen on;**àihào dǎ wǎngqiú** 爱好打网球 be keen on tennis **2** *n* hobby;**qí mǎ shì tā de àihào** 骑马是她的爱好 horse-riding is her hobby!Note that **hào** 好 in this essentially verbal usage is fourth tone.

爱护 àihù *vb* cherish,treasure,protect;**àihù zìjǐ de shēntǐ** 爱护自己的身体 take good care of one's own health

爱情 àiqíng *n* (*between lovers*) love,affection

爱人 àiren *n* husband or wife,lover,spouse;**wǒ de àiren shì lǎoshī** 我的爱人是老师 my wife/husband is a teacher

爱惜 àixī *vb* cherish,treasure,use sparingly

安 ān 1 *adj* peaceful,secure,content;**xīnli bù'ān** 心里不安 feel worried **2** *vb* install;settle down;**ānjiā** 安家 settle a family down in a place

安定 āndìng 1 *vb* (*for a family,system,etc.*) settle down in peace;**xíngshì yǐjīng āndìng xiàlái le** 形势已经安定下来了 the situation has calmed down;stabilize **2** *adj* settled,stable,secure;**yí gè āndìng de shèhuì huánjìng** 一个安定的社会环境 a stable social environment

安静 ānjìng *adj* peaceful,quiet;**qǐng ānjìng!** 请安静!please be quiet!

安排 ānpái 1 *vb* arrange,plan,fix up;**ānpái shísù** 安排食宿 arrange room and board **2** *n* arrangements

安全 ānquán 1 *adj* safe,secure;**zhèli bù ānquán** 这里不安全 this place is not safe;**ānquándài** 安全带 safety belt **2** *n* safety,security;**bǎohù tāmen de ānquán** 保护他们的安全 preserve their safety

安慰 ānwèi 1 *vb* comfort,console **2** *n* comfort,reassurance

安心 ānxīn *vb* feel at ease,be relieved;**shǐ tā ānxīn** 使她make her feel at ease

安装 ānzhuāng *vb* install;**ānzhuāng jìsuànjī** 安装计算

机 have a computer installed

岸 àn *n* bank, shore, coast; [海|湖|河]岸 [seashore|lake shore|river bank]; **shàng'àn** 上岸 go ashore

按 àn 1 *prep* according to, by; **qǐng nǐ àn wǒ shuō de zuò** 请你按我说的做 please do it the way I told you; **àn yuè suàn** 按月算 calculate by the month **2** *vb* press, push down; **ànxià diànniǔ** 按下电钮 press down the button; restrain, control; **tā àn bú zhù zìjǐ de fènnù** 他按不住自己的愤怒 he cannot restrain his anger

按时 ànshí *adv* on time, on schedule; **huǒchē huì ànshí dào ma?** 火车会按时到吗? will the train arrive on time?

按照 ànzhào *prep* according to, based on; **ànzhào tāmen de xǐhào, wǒ gěi tāmen měi gè rén mǎile yí jiàn lǐwù** 按照他们的喜好，我给他们每个人买了一件礼物 I bought each of them a present according to their hobbies

暗 àn *adj* dark, dim, dull; **nà jiān wūzi hěn àn** 那间屋子很暗 that room is very dark; hidden, secret; **wǒmen zài ànchù guānchá dírén de xíngdòng** 我们在暗处观察敌人的行动 we were observing the enemy's actions from a hidden position

肮脏 āngzāng *adj* dirty, filthy

奥林匹克运动会 Àolínpǐkè Yùndònghuì *n* the Olympic Games

傲慢 àomàn *adj* arrogant, haughty

澳大利亚 Àodàlìyà *n* Australia

懊悔 àohuǐ *adj* regretful, repentful

懊恼 àonǎo *adj* annoyed, upset, vexed

Bb

八 bā *num* eight

八月 bāyuè *n* August

拔 bá *vb* pull, pull out, uproot; **báyá 拔牙** extract a tooth or have a tooth extracted; (*for people of talent*) choose, select; **xuǎnbá 选拔** select from a number of candidates; capture, seize

把 bǎ 1 *mw* ▶ **623** (*for objects with a handle or with something a person can hold*); (*for things that can be grouped in bunches or bundles*) bunch, bundle; handful **2** *prep*! As a preposition, **bǎ 把** acts as a structural device that brings the object from the post-verbal position to the pre-verbal position. The object of the preposition **bǎ 把** is also the object of the verb; **wǒ xiǎng bǎ tā mài le 我想把它卖了** I want to sell it; **háizimen bǎ táng dōu chīwán le 孩子们把糖都吃完了** the children ate all the sweets; **xiān bǎ liànxí zuòwán 先把练习做完** finish the exercises first; **tā bǎ wǒ qìhuài le 他把我气坏了** he made me very angry; **bǎ quánjiā jiào qǐlai 把全家叫起来** awaken the whole family

爸爸 bàba *n* father, dad, papa

吧 ba *pt* (*used to make a mild imperative sentence*) **zánmen zǒu ba 咱们走吧** let's go; **gěi wǒ shū ba 给我书吧** give me the book; **gěi nǐ ba 给你吧** here, you take it; **chī bǐnggān ba? 吃饼干吧?** how about having a biscuit?; **bié gàosu tā ba 别告诉他吧** better not tell him; (*used to imply agreement*) **jiù zhèyàng ba 就这样吧** OK, let's leave it like that; (*used to imply a degree of certainty*) **tā jīntiān lái ba? 他今天来吧?** he is coming today, isn't he?; (*to express unwillingness, reluctance, or hesitation*) **nǐ quèshí xiǎng mǎi, nà nǐ jiù qù mǎi ba 你确实想买,那你就去买吧** if you really want to buy it, go and buy it then

白 bái 1 *adj* white, pure, plain, blank; **báifàn 白饭** plain rice; **kòngbái 空白** blank; **báihuà 白话** vernacular Chinese **2** *adv* in vain, to no effect; **bái pǎo yí tàng 白跑一趟** make a trip for nothing; **báifèijìn 白费劲** waste one's effort；**bái sòng** 白送 give as a gift；free of charge；**qīngbái** 清白 clean，pure

白菜 báicài *n* Chinese cabbage

白天 báitiān *n* daytime，day

百 bǎi *num* hundred，unit of a hundred

摆 bǎi *vb* put，place，arrange；sway，wave；**xiàng mǒu rén bǎishǒu** 向某人摆手 wave one's hand at someone

败 bài *vb* be defeated in a battle or contest；**tāmen bài de hěn cǎn** 他们败得很惨 they suffered a heavy defeat；(*of an enemy or opponent*) defeat；**dǎbài** 打败 defeat；spoil，ruin；**bàihuài míngyù** 败坏名誉 to spoil one's reputation；wither

班 bān 1 *n* class；**èr niánjí yǒu sān gè bān** 二年级有三个班 there are three classes in second grade；shift，duty；**shàngbān** 上班 go to work；[zǎo|zhōng|yè]**bān** [早|中|夜]班 [morning|afternoon|night] shift；squad **2** *mw* ▶ **623** (*for scheduled services of public transportation*)

班长 bānzhǎng *n* head of a class，squad，or team

搬 bān *vb* take away，move，remove；move house；**tā bānzǒu le** 他搬走了 he moved away

板 bǎn *n* board，plank，plate

办 bàn *vb* handle，manage，attend to；**méiyǒu qián，zěnme bàn?** 没有钱，怎么办? what will we do if we have no money？**zhè jiàn shì tā bàn bù wán** 这件事他办不完 he can't finish this；set up，run；**bàn xuéxiào** 办学校 run a school；**bàn gōngsī** 办公司 set up a company，found，have；**bàn yí cì zuòwén bǐsài** 办一次作文比赛 hold a writing competition；**bàn zhǎnlǎnhuì** 办展览会 hold an exhibition

办法 bànfǎ *n* way，method，way to handle a problem

办公 bàngōng *vb* handle official business

办公室 bàngōngshì *n* office

办事 bànshì *vb* handle affairs，handle a matter，work

半 bàn *adj* half；**bàn gè píngguǒ** 半个苹果 half an apple；

yí gè bàn yuè 一个半月 one and a half months; partly, about half; tā chīle yíbàn jiù zǒu le 他吃了一半就走了 he ate about half his meal and then left

半导体 bàndǎotǐ n semi-conductor, transistor

半天 bàntiān n half a day; for a long time, quite a while; tā yǐjīng shuōle bàntiān le 他已经说了半天了 he has already been talking for a long time

半夜 bànyè n midnight; in the middle of the night; half a night; qiánbànyè 前半夜 first half of the night; hòubànyè 后半夜 second half of the night

帮 bāng vb help, assist; wǒ kěyǐ bāng nǐ 我可以帮你 I can help you

帮忙 bāngmáng，帮…忙 bāng…máng vb help, lend a hand, do a favour; tā bú yuànyì bāngmáng 他不愿意帮忙 he is not willing to help; tā xǐhuan bāng biéren de máng 她喜欢帮别人的忙 she likes to help other people

帮助 bāngzhù vb help, assist; wǒ yuànyì bāngzhù nǐ 我愿意帮助你 I am willing to help you

榜样 bǎngyàng n good example, model; wèi dàjiā zuòchū yí gè bǎngyàng 为大家做出一个榜样 set an example for everyone

傍晚 bàngwǎn n at dusk, toward evening or nightfall

包 bāo 1 n parcel, package, bundle bag **2** mw ▶ 623 package, packet, bundle **3** vb wrap with paper, cloth, or some other material; bǎ dōngxi bāo qǐlai 把东西包起来 wrap things up; bāo jiǎozi 包饺子 make jiaozi (Chinese dumplings); assure, guarantee; bāo nǐ gāoxìng 包你高兴 you'll be happy, I assure you; hire, charter; bāo yí liàng chūzūchē 包一辆出租车 hire a taxi; bāojī 包机 charter a plane

包括 bāokuò vb include, consist of, comprise

包子 bāozi n steamed stuffed bun

薄 báo adj thin, slight, insubstantial; (how a person is *treated*) coldly, shabbily；**dài tā bù báo** 待他不薄 treat him generously

饱 bǎo *adj* (*to describe a person after eating*) full, replete；**wǒ chībǎo le** 我吃饱了 I have eaten my fill；(*to describe a thing*) full, plump

宝贵 bǎoguì *adj* valuable, precious

保 bǎo *vb* protect, defend, safeguard；keep, maintain, preserve；**bǎoxiān 保鲜** keep something fresh；guarantee, ensure；**bǎozhì-bǎoliàng 保质保量** ensure both quality and quantity

保持 bǎochí *vb* keep, maintain；**bǎochí ānjìng 保持安静** keep quiet

保存 bǎocún *vb* preserve, conserve, keep；**bǎocún de hěn wánzhěng 保存得很完整** be well preserved, be intact

保护 bǎohù 1 *vb* protect, safeguard **2** *n* protection

保护人 bǎohùrén *n* guardian

保留 bǎoliú *vb* retain, keep；**réngjiù bǎoliú yǐqián de tàidu 仍旧保留以前的态度** still retain one's former attitude；hold or keep back, reserve；**bǎoliú (…de) quánlì 保留(…的)权利** reserve the right (to...)

保守 bǎoshǒu *adj* conservative

保卫 bǎowèi *vb* defend, protect, safeguard

保险 bǎoxiǎn *n* insurance

保证 bǎozhèng 1 *vb* pledge, guarantee, assure；**bǎozhèng fùkuǎn 保证付款** pledge or guarantee to pay **2** *n* guarantee

报 bào *n* newspaper；[**rì | wǎn | zǎo**] **bào** [**日 | 晚 | 早**]**报** [daily | evening | morning] paper；periodical, journal；**yuèbào 月报** monthly journal；**zhōubào 周报** weekly；bulletin, report；**jǐngbào 警报** alarm, warning；**xǐbào 喜报** good news

报仇 bàochóu *vb* revenge

报到 bàodào *vb* report for work, check in, register

报道 bàodào, 报导 bàodǎo 1 *vb* report or cover the

news **2** *n* news reporting, story；**guānyú dìzhèn de bàodào** 关于地震的报道 reports about the earthquake

报告 bàogào 1 *vb* report, make known；**yīnggāi xiàng jīnglǐ bàogào** 应该向经理报告 should report it to the manager **2** *n* report, speech, lecture；**zuò bàogào** 做报告 make a speech

报名 bàomíng *vb* register, sign up

报纸 bàozhǐ *n* newspaper, newsprint

抱 bào *vb* embrace, enfold, carry in the arms；(*when referring to a child*) adopt；cherish, harbour；**tā duì zhè jiàn shì bào hěn dà de xīwàng** 他对这件事抱很大的希望 he has a lot of hope for that matter

抱歉 bàoqiàn 1 *adj* sorry；**hěn bàoqiàn** 很抱歉 I'm sorry **2** *vb* apologize

杯 bēi *n* cup, glass, tumbler；**yì bēi chá** 一杯茶 a cup of tea；(*as a prize*) cup, trophy；**Shìjièbēi** 世界杯 the World Cup

杯子 bēizi *n* cup, glass, mug

背 bēi *vb* carry on one's back；bear, shoulder；**tā bēizhe chénzhòng de jīngshén fùdān** 他背着沉重的精神负担 he has a heavy load on his mind

悲痛 bēitòng *adj* grieved, feeling melancholy

碑 bēi *n* large stone tablet or stele used for commemorative purposes；**jìniànbēi** 纪念碑 commemorative monument；**mùbēi** 墓碑 tombstone

北 běi *n* north；**Huáběi** 华北 North China；**běijí** 北极 North Pole

北边 běibian *n* the North, the north side, on the north！ *This term can also be used to refer either to the northern border or what is north of the border*；**Měiguó de běibian shì Jiānádà** 美国的北边是加拿大 north of the United States of America is Canada

北部 běibù *n* the north, northern section or part; **Sūgélán zài Yīngguó de běibù** 苏格兰在英国的北部 Scotland is in the north of Britain

北方 běifāng *n* the north; the northern part of China, the area north of the Yangtze River

北京 Běijīng *n* Beijing, the capital of China; **Běijīng kǎoyā** 北京烤鸭 Peking duck

背 bèi *n* the back of the body, the back of an object; **zài mǎbèi shang** 在马背上 on the back of the horse

背后 bèihòu *n* behind, at the back, to the rear; **tā duǒ zài mǔqīn bèihòu** 他躲在母亲背后 he hid behind his mother; behind someone's back **tā cháng zài rénjia de bèihòu luàn shuō** 她常在人家的背后乱说 she often gossips behind people's backs

背面 bèimiàn *n* reverse side; **xiàngpiàn de bèimiàn** 像片的背面 the back of the photograph

倍 bèi *n* times,-fold; **shíbèi** 10 倍 ten times; **X bǐ Y zhòng shíjǐ bèi X** 比 Y 重十几倍 X is more than ten times heavier than Y

被 bèi *prep by* ! *The preposition* **bèi** 被 *is used in passive sentence and usually marks the agent in a passive construction;* **wǒ de háizi bèi tā dǎ le** 我的孩子被他打了 my child was hit by him; **tā zuìjìn bèi cítuì le** 他最近被辞退了 he was recently discharged from his job

被子 bèizi *n* quilt, duvet

本 běn 1 *n* edition of a book; **Yīngwén bǎnběn** 英文版本 English edition **2** *mw* ▶ **623** *(for things that are bound, such as books, magazines, etc.)* **3** *adj* one's own, oneself, personally; **wǒ běnshēn bù zhīdào** 我本身不知道 I personally don't know; **tā běnrén méiyǒu qù** 他本人没有去 he didn't go himself; this, current, present; **běnxiào** 本校 our school; **běnnián** 本年 this year; *(when referring to a place)* native; **běndìrén** 本地人 a native of this place **4** *adv* originally; wǒ běn xiǎng qù, kěshì hòulái méi qù 我本想去，可是后来没去 originally I wanted to go, but in the end I didn't go

本来 běnlái 1 *adv* originally, at first; wǒ běnlái xiǎng zài cānguǎn chīfàn, kěshì tài wǎn le 我本来想在餐馆吃饭，可是太晚了 I originally wanted to eat at a restaurant, but it was too late **2** *adj* original; wǒ běnlái de xiǎngfǎ 我本来的想法 my original idea

本领 běnlǐng *n* skill, ability, capability

本事 běnshi *n* ability

本质 běnzhì *n* essence, true nature

本子 běnzi *n* notebook, exercise book

笨 bèn *adj* (*of a person's mental ability*) slow, stupid, dull; (*of a person's physical ability*) clumsy, awkward; tiàowǔ wǒ xué bú huì; wǒ tài bèn! 跳舞我学不会；我太笨! I can't learn how to dance; I'm too clumsy!

逼 bī *vb* force, compel, press; press for, extort; bīgòng 逼供 extort a confession; bīsǐ 逼死 hound to death; bīzū 逼租 press for payment of rent; press on towards, press up to, bījìn 逼近 draw close to, press hard upon(*as an army to a city*)

鼻子 bízi *n* nose

比 bǐ 1 *prep* compared with, than; tā bǐ wǒ gāo he is taller than I am; nǐ fùqīn bǐ nǐ mǔqīn dà jǐ suì? 你父亲比你母亲大几岁? How many years older than your mother is your father?; (*comparison over time*) tā yì tiān bǐ yì tiān jiēshi 他一天比一天结实 he gets stronger every day; (*indicating a score of a match or game*) wǔ bǐ sān 5 比 3 five to three **2** *vb* compare, emulate; bǎ hóng de gēn lán de bǐyìbǐ 把红的跟蓝的比一比 make a comparison between the red one and the blue one **3** bǐfāng(shuō) 比方(说) for example, such as **4** bǐrú(shuō) 比如(说) for example, such as

比较 bǐjiào 1 adv quite, relatively, rather；wǒ bǐjiào xǐhuan dúshū 我比较喜欢读书 I rather enjoy reading **2** vb compare, contrast；bǐjiào liǎng jiàn yīfu de zhìliàng 比较两件衣服的质量 compare the qualities of the two items of clothing

比例 bǐlì n ratio, proportion；nán-nǚ xìngbié bǐlì 男女性别比例 the ratio of males to females

比赛 bǐsài 1 vb compete；gēn Yīnggélánduì bǐsài 跟英格兰队比赛 have a match against the English team **2** n match, competition

笔 bǐ 1 n pen, brush；stroke, touch of the brush；zhège hànzì de bǐhuà 这个汉字的笔画 the strokes that make up this Chinese character；zhège zì de dì-yī bǐ 这个字的第1笔 the first stroke of the character **2** mw ▶ 623 (for sums of money)；(for deals in business or trade)

笔记 bǐjì n notes；bǐjìběn 笔记本 notebook

必然 bìrán adj inevitable, certain；yí gè bìrán de guīlǜ 一个必然的规律 an inexorable law

必须 bìxū vb must, have to；nǐ bìxū lái 你必须来 you must come

必要 bìyào adj necessary

毕业 bìyè vb graduate, finish school

闭 bì vb shut, close；bìshang yǎnjing 闭上眼睛 close one's eyes；bìzuǐ！闭嘴！hold your tongue！, shut up！

避 bì vb avoid, stay away from, hide；bì fēngyǔ 避风雨 get out of the wind and rain；bìnàn 避难 run away from trouble, escape calamity；prevent, keep away, repel；bìyùn 避孕 prevent contraception

避免 bìmiǎn vb avoid, refrain from, avert

边 biān n side；[nà|zhèi|běi|shàng|xià] bian [那|这|北|上|下] 边 [over there | over here | the north | above | below] frontier, border；biānjiāng 边疆 border；biānjiè 边界 border, limit, edge；

shùlín biān 树林边 the edge of a forest; close by; zhàn zài chuāng biān 站在窗边 stand by the window

边…biān… *conj*！Biān 边 is used before two different verbs to indicate simultaneous actions. It is sometimes expressed as yìbiān… yìbiān… 一边…一边…; (yì)biān chī (yì)biān tán(一)边吃(一)边谈 eat and talk at the same time; yìbiān tīng yīnyuè yìbiān kànshū 一边听音乐一边看书 read while listening to music

编 biān *vb* edit, arrange in order, compile; biān cídiǎn 编词典 edit or compile a dictionary; weave, plait

扁 biǎn *adj* flat; lúntāi biǎn le 轮胎扁了 the tyre has become flat

变 biàn *vb* change, become different; xiànzài Zhōngguó biàn le 现在中国变了 China has changed now; transform, change, turn; biàn huàishì wéi hǎoshì 变坏事为好事 turn a bad thing into a good thing

变成 biànchéng *vb* change into; bǎ hēizì biànchéng hóngzì 把黑字变成红字 turn the black characters into red ones

变化 biànhuà 1 *vb* change, vary **2** *n* change

便 biàn ▶ See also 便 pián. **1** *adv* then; tiān yí liàng tā biàn shàngbān qù le 天一亮她便上班去了 she left for work as soon as it was light **2** *adj* convenient; biànlì 便利 convenient

便条 biàntiáo *n* informal note

遍 biàn 1 *mw* **▶ 623**(to indicate the number of times an action or state occurs) time！Note that biàn 遍 is different from cì 次 in that it emphasizes the whole process from the beginning to the end. **2** *adv* everywhere, all over; yóu biàn quánshìjiè 游遍全世界 travel all over the world

标点 biāodiǎn *n* punctuation; biāodiǎn fúhào 标点符号 punctuation mark

标准 biāozhǔn 1 n standard；**biāozhǔnhuà 标准化** standardization **2** adj standard；**nǐ de zhōngguóhuà hěn biāozhǔn 你的中国话很标准** your Chinese is very good

表 biǎo n table，form，list；**shíjiānbiǎo 时间表** timetable，schedule；**shēnqǐngbiǎo 申请表** application form；meter，gauge；watch；**shǒubiǎo 手表** wristwatch；the relationship between children with two common grandparents but without sharing the same paternal grandfather；**biǎogē 表哥** elder male cousin；**biǎodì 表弟** younger male cousin；**biǎojiě 表姐** elder female cousin；**biǎomèi 表妹** younger female cousin

表达 biǎodá vb（thoughts and feelings，ideas）express

表面 biǎomiàn n surface，face，outside appearance

表明 biǎomíng vb make known，make clear，state clearly

表示 biǎoshì 1 vb show，express，indicate **2** n gesture，manifestation

表现 biǎoxiàn 1 vb show，display，manifest；show off；**tā xǐhuan biǎoxiàn zìjǐ 他喜欢表现自己** he likes to show off；behave **2** n expression，manifestation；behaviour

表演 biǎoyǎn 1 vb perform，act，play **2** n performance

表扬 biǎoyáng vb praise

别 bié 1 adv（negative imperative）not；**bié ［qù／zǒu／chī］别 ［去／走／吃］** don't ［go／leave／eat］；**wǒ ràng tā bié lái 我让他别来** I told him not to come **2** adj other，another；**biéchù 别处** elsewhere，another place；**nǐ hái yào bié de （dōngxi） ma？ 你还要别的（东西）吗？** do you want anything else？

别人 biérén n others，other people；**biérén dōu shuō yǒu yìsi 别人都说有意思** other people all say it's interesting

宾馆 bīnguǎn n hotel，guesthouse

冰 bīng n ice

冰球 bīngqiú n ice hockey

兵 **bīng** *n* soldier, troops

饼干 **bǐnggān** *n* biscuit, cracker, cookie

并 **bìng 1** *adv* (*used before a negative for emphasis*) actually, in reality, in fact; tā bìng méi qù 他并没去 he actually didn't go **2** *conj* and, also

并且 **bìngqiě** *conj* and ! Often used in a pattern with búdàn 不但 *to mean* not only...but also...; tā búdàn hěn cōngmíng bìngqiě hěn hǎokàn 他不但很聪明并且很好看 he is not only intelligent but also very handsome; moreover, besides

病 **bìng 1** *vb* be ill, become ill; tā bìng le 他病了 he is ill **2** *n* disease, ailment; tā yǒubìng 他有病 he has an illness; tā shēngbìng le 他生病了 he has become ill; kànbìng 看病 examine someone who is ill; be examined by a doctor, see a doctor

病房 **bìngfáng** *n* hospital ward, hospital room

病菌 **bìngjūn** *n* bacteria, germs

病人 **bìngrén** *n* ill person, patient

玻璃 **bōli** *n* glass; bōlibēi 玻璃杯 a glass

伯父 **bófù**, 伯伯 **bóbo** *n* father's elder brother, uncle

伯母 **bómǔ** *n* aunt, wife of father's elder brother

脖子 **bózi** *n* neck

补 **bǔ** *vb* mend, patch, repair; fill, supply, make up for; bǔ kòngquē 补空缺 fill a vacancy; nourish; bǔ shēntǐ 补身体 build up health; bǔxuè 补血 enrich the blood

补充 **bǔchōng 1** *vb* replenish, supplement **2** *adj* supplementary; bǔchōng cáiliào 补充材料 supplementary materials

补课 **bǔkè** *vb* make up for a missed lesson; gěi xuésheng bǔkè 给学生补课 give tutorials to students who have missed classes

补习 **bǔxí** *vb* take lessons after school or work, have

remedial lessons; **bǔxíbān** 补习班 special class for supplementary learning

捕 bǔ vb catch, seize, arrest

不 bú, or **bù** ! As is true of yī 一, the tone on bù 不 changes depending on the tone of the word that follows it. It is pronounced bù before words in first, second, and third tone, but bú before the fourth tone. Because the tone changes for bù 不 do not indicate any difference in meaning, but only of pronounciation, combinations beginning with bù 不 are listed in alphabetical order below, regardless of tone; adv (vsed to form a negative) no, not; wǒ bùkěn qù 我不肯去 I'm not willing to go; (used to indicate negative potentiality) tā bā diǎn yǐqián zuò bù wán zuòyè 他 8 点以前做不完作业 he won't be able to finish his homework by 8 o'clock

不必 búbì vb need not, be unnecessary; wǒmen jīntiān búbì shàngkè 我们今天不必上课 we don't have to attend class today

不错 búcuò adj correct, right; nǐ de jìsuàn yìdiǎnr dōu búcuò 你的计算一点儿都不错 your calculations were completely correct; (to indicate that what has been said is right) búcuò, tā míngtiān yào lái 不错, 他明天要来 yes, he will come tomorrow; (colloquial) not bad, pretty good; tā de zuòwén búcuò 他的作文不错 his essay was pretty good

不大 búdà adv not very, not too; jiàqián búdà piányi 价钱不大便宜 the prices are not very cheap; not often; tā wǎnshang búdà niànshū 他晚上不大念书 he doesn't study in the evening very often

不但 búdàn conj ! Usually used in a sentence pattern with érqiě 而且 or bìngqiě 并且 in the form bùdàn··· érqiě/ bìngqiě··· 不但···而且/并且··· to mean not only...but also .... not only; tā búdàn yǎnjing bù hǎo, érqiě jìxing yě bù kěkào 他不但眼睛不好，而且记性也不可靠 not only is his eyesight bad but his memory is also unreliable

不得不 bùdébù *vb* have no choice or option but to, cannot but, have to; tā bùdébù qù 他不得不去 he has to go

不得了 bùdéliǎo 1 *adj* extremely serious, important, extreme; zhè bú shì shénme bùdéliǎo de wèntí 这不是什么不得了的问题 this is not such a desperate matter **2** *adv* (*used after* de *得 as a complement*) extremely, exceedingly; tā gāoxìng de bùdéliǎo 她高兴得不得了 she is overjoyed

不断 búduàn *adv* unceasingly, continuously, in an uninterrupted fashion; búduàn de késou 不断地咳嗽 cough continuously

不敢当 bùgǎndāng ! *This is a polite expression in reply to a compliment*; thank you! you're flattering me! I don't deserve it

不管 bùguǎn *conj* no matter what or how; bùguǎn dào shénme dìfang qù dōu xíng 不管到什么地方去都行 it doesn't matter where we go, it will be fine with me

不过 búguò 1 *conj* but; dàxiǎo kěyǐ, búguò yánsè bùxíng 大小可以，不过颜色不行 the size is fine, but the colour won't do **2** *adv* only, merely; tā búguò shì gè háizi 他不过是个孩子 he's only a child **3** *superlative emphatic* zài [hǎo | jiǎndān | xìngyùn] búguò le 再 [好 | 简单 | 幸运] 不过了 [better | simpler | luckier]

不好意思 bùhǎoyìsi *vb* feel embarrassed, be ill at ease, find embarrassing

不仅 bùjǐn *adv* not only; zhè bùjǐn shì tā zìjǐ de kànfǎ 这不仅是他自己的看法 this not only is his personal view; bùjǐn rúcǐ 不仅如此 not only that, moreover

不久 bùjiǔ *adv* soon, before long; nǐmen bùjiǔ jiùyào bìyè le 你们不久就要毕业了 soon you will graduate; not long after, soon after; xiàlè kè bùjiǔ jiù kāishǐ xiàyǔ le

下了课不久就开始下雨了 not long after class ended it began to rain

不论 búlùn *conj* no matter what, it doesn't matter；búlùn nǐ zuò shénme shì, dōu yào zuò hǎo 不论你做什么事，都要做好 it doesn't matter what you do, you must do it well

不平 bùpíng *adj* indignant, resentful；unjust

不然 bùrán *conj* or else, otherwise, if not；nǐ děi fùxí shēngcí, bùrán huì dōu wàng le 你得复习生词，不然会都忘了 you must revise the new words or else you'll forget them all

不如 bùrú *vb* (*before a noun*) not as... as, not measure up to, compare unfavourably with；wǒ Hànyǔ shuō de bùrú tā liúlì 我汉语说得不如她流利 my spoken Chinese is not as fluent as hers；(*before a clause*) had better；nǐ bùrú jīntiān niànshū 你不如今天念书 you had better study today

不少 bùshǎo *adj* quite a bit, quite a few；bùshǎo qián 不少钱 quite a large amount of money

不同 bùtóng *adj* different, distinct

不行 bùxíng *vb* it's out of the question, it's not allowed；be no good, won't work

不幸 búxíng 1 *adj* unfortunate, unlucky, sad **2** *n* misfortune

不许 bùxǔ *vb* not allow；wǒ de mǔqīn bùxǔ wǒ chūmén 我的母亲不许我出门 my mother doesn't allow me to leave the house；must not, be forbidden；nǐ bùxǔ chōuyān 你不许抽烟 you mustn't smoke

不要 búyào *vb* don't；búyào nàyàng wúlǐ 不要那样无礼 don't be so rude

不要紧 búyàojǐn 1 *adj* not important, not serious；wǒ de shāng búyàojǐn 我的伤不要紧 my injury is not serious **2** búyàojǐn 不要紧 it doesn't matter

不一定 bùyídìng *adv* not necessarily；wǒ bùyídìng néng

qù 我不一定能去 I won't necessarily be able to go

不用 búyòng *vb* need not; **búyòng jǐnzhāng 不用紧张** you needn't be nervous

布 bù *n* cloth, cotton cloth

布置 bùzhì *vb* fix up, arrange, decorate; **bùzhì bàngōngshì 布置办公室** decorate the office; assign, arrange; **bùzhì zuòyè 布置作业** assign homework

步 bù *n* step, pace; stage, step, procedure, condition, situation, state; **nǐ zěnme luòdào zhè yí bù? 你怎么落到这一步?** how could you get yourself into such a situation?

部 bù 1 *n* part, area, section; **xībù 西部** the western part; unit, ministry, department; **wàijiāobù 外交部** Ministry of Foreign Affairs; **biānjíbù 编辑部** editorial board or office **2** *mw* ▶ 623 (for novels, films, etc.)

部队 bùduì *n* army; troops, unit in a military force

部分 bùfen *n* part, section, portion; **dì-yī bùfen 第 1 部分** Part One

部门 bùmén *n* department or branch in a government, company, etc.

部长 bùzhǎng *n* minister, head of a department; **wàijiāobù bùzhǎng 外交部部长** Minister of Foreign Affairs

----

Cc

擦 cā *vb* wipe, clean; (spread on) **zài liǎn shang cā xuěhuāgāo 在脸上擦雪花膏** put cream on one's face

猜 cāi *vb* guess, conjecture, speculate

猜想 cāixiǎng *vb* suppose, guess, suspect

才 cái 1 *n* ability, talent, gift **2** *adv* just; **diànyǐng cái kāishǐ 电影才开始** the film has just started; so late; **nǐ**

zěnme cái lái 你怎么才来 why are you so late?; only; tā cái shísān suì 他才 13 岁 he is only 13 years old; then and only then; wǒmen děi děng tā huílái yǐhòu, cái néng zǒu 我们得等他回来以后，才能走 we have to wait until he comes back; then we can go

才能 cáinéng n ability, talent

才子 cáizǐ n talented scholar

材料 cáiliào n material, data

财产 cáichǎn n property

财富 cáifù n wealth

财政 cáizhèng n finance

裁缝 cáifeng n tailor, dressmaker

裁判 cáipàn n referee, umpire, judge

采 cǎi vb pick, gather

采访 cǎifǎng vb (by a news reporter) gather material, cover news, interview

采购 cǎigòu vb purchase, buy

采取 cǎiqǔ vb adopt, take; cǎiqǔ jǐnjí cuòshī 采取紧急措施 take emergency steps

采用 cǎiyòng vb adopt for use, use; cǎiyòng xīn jìshù 采用新技术 adopt new techniques

彩色 cǎisè n colour, multicolour; cǎisè diànshì 彩色电视 colour television

踩 cǎi vb step on

菜 cài n vegetable; (food in general) food; mǎicài 买菜 shop for food; dish; course

菜单 càidān n menu

参观 cānguān vb visit, look around

参加 cānjiā vb join, take part in; attend; cānjiā huìyì 参加会议 attend meetings

参考 cānkǎo 1 vb consult, refer to **2** n cānkǎoshū 参考书 reference book

参谋 cānmóu 1 *n* adviser，staff officer；**cānmóuzhǎng 参谋长** chief of staff **2** *vb* give advice

餐 cān *n* food，meal；[xī|zhōng|wǔ|yě]cān [西|中|午|野]餐 [Western food|Chinese food|lunch|picnic]

餐车 cānchē *n* dining car，restaurant car

餐厅 cāntīng *n* dining room，dining hall

残废 cánfèi *adj* disabled，physically handicapped

残酷 cánkù *adj* cruel，ruthless，brutal

惭愧 cánkuì *adj* ashamed

惨 cǎn *adj* miserable，pitiful，tragic

灿烂 cànlàn *adj* magnificent，splendid，bright

仓库 cāngkù *n* warehouse，storehouse

苍白 cāngbái *adj* pale

苍蝇 cāngyíng *n* fly

舱 cāng *n* cabin；**kècāng 客舱** passenger cabin；**huòcāng 货舱** a (ship's)hold

藏 cáng *vb* hide，store，put by

操场 cāochǎng *n* playground，sports ground，drill ground

草 cǎo *n* grass，straw

草地 cǎodì *n* grassland，meadow，lawn

草原 cǎoyuán *n* steppe，grasslands，prairie

册 cè *mw* ▶ 623 (*for books or volumes of books*) volume，book；(*for copies of books*) copy

厕所 cèsuǒ *n* lavatory，toilet，loo

测验 cèyàn 1 *vb* test **2** *n* test

策略 cèlüè *n* tactics，strategy

层 céng 1 *mw* ▶ 623 storey，floor；(*for a layer, coat, sheet*) **2** *n* floor；**wǒ de fángjiān zài sān céng 我的房间在 3 层** my room is on the third floor！Note that Chinese is similar to US usage where the 1st floor is the ground floor，whereas in British English the storey above the *ground floor is called the 1st floor*.

曾 céng *adv* once, formerly, sometime ago; **tā céng zuòguo zhè zhǒng gōngzuò** 他曾做过这种工作 he did this kind of work once before

曾经 céngjīng *adv* once, formerly; **tāmen céngjīng shì hǎo péngyou** 他们曾经是好朋友 they were once good friends

叉子 chāzi *n* fork

插 chā *vb* stick in, insert; interpolate; insert; **tā bàn jù huà yě chā bú jìnqu** 他半句话也插不进去 he couldn't get a word in edgeways

茶 chá *n* tea

茶杯 chábēi *n* teacup

茶点 chádiǎn *n* tea and snacks, tea and biscuits

茶馆 cháguǎn *n* teahouse

茶壶 cháhú *n* teapot

茶叶 cháyè *n* tea leaves

查 chá *vb* check, examine, inspect; look into, investigate, find out; look up, consult; **chá zìdiǎn** 查字典 consult a dictionary

差 chà 1 *vb* differ from, fall short of; **chà de yuǎn** 差得远 differ substantially **2** *adj* wanting, short of; **hái chà liǎng kuài qián** 还差两块钱 still two yuan short; **chà wǔ fēn qī diǎn** 差 5 分 7 点 five minutes to seven

差不多 chàbuduō *adv* almost, nearly; **tā líkāi chàbuduō liǎng nián le** 他离开差不多两年了 he's been gone nearly two years now; about the same, similar

差点儿 chàdiǎnr *adv* almost, nearly, on the verge of; **tā chàdiǎnr shībài** 她差点儿失败 she very nearly failed

拆 chāi *vb* take apart, tear open; pull down, demolish; unravel; **bǎ yí jiàn jiù máoyī chāi le** 把一件旧毛衣拆了 unravel an old jumper

产量 chǎnliàng *n* output, yield

产品 chǎnpǐn *n* product, produce

产生 chǎnshēng *vb* produce, engender, bring about; emerge, come into being

长 cháng *adj* long

长城 Chángchéng *n* the Great Wall

长处 chángchù *n* good qualities, strong points

长度 chángdù *n* length

长江 Cháng Jiāng *n* Yangtze River, Yangtse River

长久 chángjiǔ *adj* long-lasting, long-term

长期 chángqī *n* a long period of time, long term

长途 chángtú *n* long distance; **chángtú diànhuà 长途电话** long-distance telephone call

尝 cháng *vb* taste, try the flavour of

常 cháng, 常常 chángcháng *adv* frequently, often

场 chǎng 1 *mw* ▶ 623 (for the whole process of being ill); (for a natural disturbance, war, disaster, etc.); (for a show, performance, game, or debate); (to indicate the occasion on which a state or an action occurs) **2** *n* site, spot, place where people gather; (for ballgames) court, field, ground; [**lánqiú|páiqiú|zúqiú|wǎngqiú**]**chǎng** [**篮球|排球|足球|网球**]**场** [basketball court | volleyball court | football field | tennis court]; stage; **dēngchǎng 登场** come on stage

唱 chàng *vb* sing

唱歌 chànggē *vb* sing songs

抄 chāo *vb* copy, transcribe; plagiarize

抄写 chāoxiě *vb* make a clear copy

超 chāo *vb* exceed, surpass, overtake

超过 chāoguò *vb* outstrip, surpass, exceed

超级市场 chāojí shìchǎng *n* supermarket

朝 cháo 1 *prep* facing, towards; **cháo Lúndūn kāi 朝伦敦**

开 drive towards London **2** vb face, towards; zhè fángzi cháo nán 这房子朝南 this house faces south **3** n dynasty or period; Hàncháo 汉朝 the Han Dynasty

朝鲜 cháoxiǎn n North Korea

巢 cháo n nest

吵 chǎo 1 vb quarrel, wrangle, squabble; wèi yìxiē xiǎoshì chǎojià 为一些小事吵架 bicker over small matters **2** adj noisy

吵架 chǎojià vb quarrel, have an argument

吵闹 chǎonào vb make a fuss, make trouble

吵嘴 chǎozuǐ vb quarrel, bicker

炒 chǎo vb stir-fry

车 chē n vehicle, car, bus

车带 chēdài n tyre on a car or bicycle

车间 chējiān n workshop

车票 chēpiào n bus ticket, train ticket

车站 chēzhàn n station, stop

彻底 chèdǐ adj thorough

沉 chén 1 vb sink, sink down, lower **2** adj shuì de hěn chén 睡得很沉 sleep soundly, sleep deeply; heavy

沉默 chénmò adj reticent, uncommunicative; silent

沉重 chénzhòng adj heavy

陈列 chénliè vb display, exhibit

衬衫 chènshān n shirt

衬衣 chènyī n underclothes, shirt

趁 chèn vb take advantage of, avail oneself of; chèn zhège jīhuì xiūxi yíxià 趁这个机会休息一下 take this opportunity to have a rest

称 chēng vb name, call; wǒmen dōu chēng tā shūshu 我们都称他叔叔 we all call him Uncle; weigh; state, say

称赞 chēngzàn vb praise, acclaim, commend

成 chéng vb become, change to, develop into; tā chéngle

yì míng dàifu 他成了一名大夫 he became a doctor; accomplish, succeed; zhè bǐ jiāoyì méi chéng 这笔交易 没成 the deal did not succeed

成分 chéngfèn *n* composition, component part, ingredient; one's class status or family background

成功 chénggōng 1 *vb* succeed **2** *n* success

成果 chéngguǒ *n* accomplishment, achievement

成绩 chéngjì *n* achievement, success

成家 chéngjiā *vb* (*referring to a man*) get married

成就 chéngjiù *n* achievement, accomplishment, attainment

成立 chénglì *vb* set up, found, establish

成年 chéngnián *vb* grow up, come of age

成人 chéngrén *n* adult

成熟 chéngshú 1 *vb* ripen, mature **2** *adj* ripe, mature

成为 chéngwéi *vb* become, change to, develop into

成长 chéngzhǎng *vb* grow up

承认 chéngrèn *vb* admit, acknowledge, recognize; give diplomatic recognition to, recognize

承受 chéngshòu *vb* bear, endure

诚恳 chéngkěn *adj* sincere

诚实 chéngshí *adj* honest

城 chéng *n* city, town; city wall, wall

城市 chéngshì *n* town, city

城镇 chéngzhèn *n* cities and towns, town

乘 chéng *vb* ride; chéng [huǒchē | fēijī | gōnggòng qìchē] lǚxíng 乘 [火车 | 飞机 | 公共汽车] 旅行 travel by [train | plane | bus]; take advantage of; (*in mathematical operations*) multiply; wǔ chéng sān děngyú shíwǔ 5 乘 3 等于 15 five times three equals fifteen

乘务员 chéngwùyuán *n* train attendant, conductor, ticket collector

程度 chéngdù *n* level, degree, extent

吃 chī *vb* eat

吃醋 chīcù *vb* be jealous

吃惊 chījīng *vb* be startled, be shocked, be amazed; **dàchīyìjīng 大吃一惊** *vb* be greatly surprised

迟到 chídào *vb* be late

尺 chǐ *n* (*unit of length*, 1/3 *metre*) *chi*

尺寸 chǐcùn *n* size, measurement, dimension

尺子 chǐzi *n* (*to measure length*) ruler

赤道 chìdào *n* equator

翅膀 chìbǎng *n* wing

充分 chōngfèn *adj* full, ample, abundant

充满 chōngmǎn *vb* be full of, be brimming with

充足 chōngzú *adj* adequate, ample, abundant

冲 chōng *vb* pour boiling water on; **chōng chá 冲茶** make tea; rinse, flush, wash away; **chōng cèsuǒ 冲厕所** flush the toilet; charge, rush, dash; **chōng jìn fángzi 冲进房子** rush into the house; (*for film*) develop; **chōng jiāojuǎn 冲胶卷** develop a roll of film

冲突 chōngtū *n* conflict, clash

虫子 chóngzi *n* insect, worm

重 chóng *adv* ▶ See also **重 zhòng**. over again; **chóng fǎng Yīngguó 重访英国** revisit the U.K.

重叠 chóngdié *vb* overlap, pile on top of one another

重复 chóngfù *vb* repeat, duplicate

重新 chóngxīn *adv* again, anew, afresh

崇高 chónggāo *adj* lofty, high

宠爱 chǒng'ài *vb* dote on, make a pet of someone

抽 chōu *vb* take out (*from in between*); **cóng shūjià shang chōuchū yì běn shū 从书架上抽出一本书** take a book from the shelf; (*cigarette, pipe*) smoke; (*water*) draw; **chōushuǐ 抽**

水 draw water(*from a well*, *etc*.);lash,whip,thrash

抽象 **chōuxiàng** *adj* abstract

抽烟 **chōuyān** *vb* smoke (a cigarette or a pipe)

愁 **chóu** *vb* worry,be anxious; **bié chóu 别愁** don't worry

丑 **chǒu** *adj* ugly,disgraceful

臭 **chòu** *adj* smelly,stinking,foul; **chòu jīdàn 臭鸡蛋** rotten egg; **chòu dòufu 臭豆腐** fermented beancurd

出 **chū** *vb* go or come outissue,put forth;produce,turn out; publish; **chū xīnshū 出新书** publish new books;arise,happen, occur; **chū shìgù 出事故** there was an accident;exceed,go beyond; **bù chū sān nián 不出 3 年** within three years;vent; **chūqì 出气**,vent one's spleen,express one's anger

出版 **chūbǎn** *vb* publish

出版社 **chūbǎnshè** *n* publishing company,publishing house

出发 **chūfā** *vb* set out,start off;start,proceed

出发点 **chūfādiǎn** *n* starting point,point of departure

出国 **chūguó** *vb* go abroad,leave the country

出口 **chūkǒu 1** *n* export **2** *n* export;exit

出来 **chūlái** *vb* come out;(*after a verb to indicate movement in an outward direction or a completed action*) **bǎ qián ná chūlái 把钱拿出来** take out the money; **xiàngpiàn xǐ chūlái le 像片洗出来了** the photographs have been developed; **tā xiǎng chūláile yí gè hǎo bànfǎ 他想出来了一个好办法** he thought of a good solution

出路 **chūlù** *n* a way out,a solution to a problem

出名 **chūmíng** *adj* famous,well-known

出去 **chūqù** *vb* go out,get out;(*after a verb to indicate movement in an outward direction*) **cóng wū li pǎo chūqù 从屋里跑出去** run out from the room

出色 **chūsè** *adj* excellent,outstanding,remarkable

出生 **chūshēng** *vb* be born

出席 **chūxí** *vb* (*when speaking of a meeting,banquet,etc*.)

attend, be present

出现 chūxiàn *vb* appear, emerge, come to light

出院 chūyuàn *vb* leave hospital, be discharged from hospital after recovery

出租汽车 chūzū qìchē *n* taxi

初 chū 1 *adj* early; chū [dōng|chūn|xià|qiū] 初 [冬|春|夏|秋] early [winter | spring | summer | autumn]; elementary, rudimentary; chūzhōng 初中 (abbreviation of chūjí zhōngxué 初级中学) junior middle school, junior high school; (*used to enumerate days of the lunar month up to ten*) chū [yī|èr|sān|sì···] 初 [一|二|三 四···] the [first | second | third | fourth···] day of a lunar month **2** *n* beginning; [zhège yuè|míngnián|shàngge shìjì] chū [这个月|明年| 上个世纪] 初 the beginning of [this month | next year | the last century]

初步 chūbù *adj* initial, preliminary, tentative

初级 chūjí *adj* elementary, primary

除 chú *vb* get rid of, do away with, remove; chúdiào [huài xíguàn |jiù sīxiǎng] 除掉 [坏习惯 |旧思想] get rid of [bad habits|old ways of thinking]; divide; sān chú liù dé èr 3 除 6 得 2 six divided by three equals two

除非 chúfēi *conj* ! When chúfēi 除非 is used, it is often necessary to use fǒuzé 否则 or bùrán 不然 at the beginning of the main clause to indicate the necessary consequence of the clause introduced by chúfēi 除非; only if, unless; chúfēi tiānqì bù hǎo, fǒuzé wǒmen míngtiān qù hǎibiān wánr 除非天气不 好,否则我们明天去海边玩儿 we'll go to the seashore tomorrow unless the weather isn't good

除了···(以外)chúle···(yǐwài) *prep* ! Note that the use of yǐwài 以外 is optional; (*used with* dōu 都 *or* yě 也) except; chúle tā (yǐwài) ,biérén dōu bú huì chàng zhè shǒu gē 除了 她(以外),别人都不会唱这首歌 no one can sing this song except her; (*used with* hái 还) apart from, besides, in addition to...; tā chúle kànshū yǐwài, hái xiězuò 她除了看书以外, 还写作 in addition to reading she also does some writing

厨房 chúfáng *n* kitchen

处 chǔ *vb* deal with, handle; **chǔshì 处事** handle affairs, manage matters; be in a certain position (*literal or figurative*); **chǔyú 处于** (*literal or figurative*) to be located in a place or position; **tā chǔyú búlì dìwèi 他处于不利地位** he is in a disadvantageous position

处分 chǔfèn 1 *n* disciplinary action, punishment **2** *vb* take disciplinary action against

处理 chǔlǐ 1 *vb* handle, deal with, dispose of; **chǔlǐ jiāwù 处理家务** do household chores; **chǔlǐ jiàgé 处理价格** reduced price, bargain price; **chǔlǐpǐn 处理品** goods sold at reduced or sale prices **2** *n* handling, treatment, disposal

处 chù *n* place; **tíngchēchù 停车处** car park, parking lot; point, feature; **gòngtóng zhī chù 共同之处** common feature; department, office; **mìshūchù 秘书处** secretariat

穿 chuān *vb* wear, put on, be dressed in; pierce through, penetrate; **chuāntòu 穿透** penetrate; pass through, cross; **chuānguò mǎlù 穿过马路** cross the road; **chuānshang 穿上** put on; **chuānshang nǐ de dàyī 穿上你的大衣** put on your coat

传 chuán *vb* pass, pass on; (*for news, rumours, etc.*) spread, transmit; hand down; (*for heat, electricity, etc.*) transmit, conduct

传播 chuánbō *vb* propagate, disseminate, spread

传染 chuánrǎn *vb* infect, catch; **wǒ bǎ gǎnmào chuánrǎn gěile tā 我把感冒传染给了他** he caught my cold

传说 chuánshuō *n* rumour, legend

传统 chuántǒng *n* tradition, conventions

传真 chuánzhēn *n* facsimile, fax

船 chuán *n* boat, ship

窗(户) chuāng(hu) *n* window

床 chuáng 1 *n* bed; **shàngchuáng shuìjiào 上床睡觉** go to bed, get into bed **2** *mw* ▶ **623** (*for quilt, blanket, sheet*)

床单 **chuángdān** *n* (bed)sheet

闯 **chuǎng** *vb* rush, force one's way in or out

创 **chuàng** *vb* initiate, achieve for the first time, innovate; **chuàng jìlù 创纪录** set a record

创造 **chuàngzào 1** *vb* create, produce, bring about **2** *n* creation

创作 **chuàngzuò 1** *vb* (*works of art or literature*) create, write, produce **2** *n* literary or artistic creation

吹 **chuī** *vb* blow, exhale; **chuī yì kǒu qì 吹一口气** blow out a puff of air; (*wind instruments*) play; **chuī dízi 吹笛子** play the flute; (*colloquial*) brag, boast; (*colloquial, referring to a relationship*) break off, break up, fall through; **tāmen liǎ chuī le 他们俩吹了** they have broken up; **chuīmiè 吹灭** blow out; **bǎ làzhú chuīmiè 把蜡烛吹灭** blow out the candle

吹牛 **chuīniú** *vb* brag, boast

吹嘘 **chuīxū** *vb* brag, boast

春 **chūn** *n* (*the season*) spring; **chūnjì 春季** spring season

春节 **Chūn Jié** *n* Spring Festival, the Chinese New Year

春天 **chūntiān** *n* spring, springtime

纯粹 **chúncuì** *adj* pure, simple

唇 **chún** *n* lip

词 **cí** *n* word, term; speech, statement; **kāimùcí 开幕词** opening speech

词典 **cídiǎn** *n* dictionary, lexicon

词汇 **cíhuì** *n* vocabulary

辞职 **cízhí** *vb* leave or quit a job, resign

磁带 **cídài** *n* (magnetic) tape

此 **cǐ** *det* this; **cǐ** [**chù**|**rén**] 此[处|人]this [place|person]

此外 **cǐwài** *adv* besides, moreover, in addition

次 **cì** *mw* ▶ 623 (for events such as examinations, accidents, experiments, etc.); (to indicate the number of times an action or state occurs) time

刺 cì 1 vb prick, stab; irritate, criticize **2** n thorn

刺杀 cìshā vb assassinate

匆忙 cōngmáng adv hurriedly, hastily

聪明 cōngmíng adj intelligent, bright, clever

从 cóng prep (used to indicate the starting point) from; cóng Běijīng chūfā 从北京出发 start off from Beijing; cóng lǐlùnshang jiǎng 从理论上讲 theoretically speaking

从不/没 cóng bù/méi adv never; wǒ cóng bù hējiǔ 我从不喝酒 I never drink wine; wǒ cóng méi qùguo Yìdàlì 我从没去过意大利 I've never been to Italy

从此 cóngcǐ adv from now on, henceforth

从…到… cóng…dào… prep from…to… cóng zǎoshàng jiǔ diǎn dào wǎnshàng bā diǎn 从早上9点到晚上8点 from 9:00 am to 8:00 pm

从而 cóng'ér conj thus, and then, and then proceed to

从来 cónglái adv always, all along! Note that cónglái normally precedes the negative word bù 不 or méi 没; wǒ cónglái méi jiànguo tā 我从来没见过他 I have never seen him before; tā cónglái bù hējiǔ 他从来不喝酒 he never drinks wine

从…起 cóng…qǐ prep from…on, from…forward; cóng xiànzài qǐ… 从现在起… from now on…

从前 cóngqián adv before, in the past, formerly

从事 cóngshì vb go in for, be engaged in

凑合 còuhe vb gather together; get together; tāmen měi gè zhōumò dōu còuhe zài yìqǐ hēchá liáotiān 他们每个周末都凑合在一起喝茶聊天 every weekend they get together for tea and have a chat; make do; tā yìzhí zài còuhezhe yòng nà tái jiù jìsuànjī 他一直在凑合着用那台旧计算机 he has been making do with that old computer all along; do in a pinch, be OK, be not too bad; "nà bù Měiguó diànyǐng zěnmeyàng?"—"hái còuhe" "那部美国电影怎么样?"—"还凑合" 'how was that American film?'—'it wasn't too bad'

凑巧 còuqiǎo *adv* luckily, by coincidence

粗 cū *adj* thick; careless, negligent

粗心 cūxīn *adj* careless, thoughtless

促进 cùjìn *vb* promote, advance, accelerate

醋 cù *n* vinegar;(*in love affairs*) jealousy

催 cuī *vb* hurry, urge, speed up

村 cūn *n* village

村庄 cūnzhuāng *n* village

村子 cūnzi *n* village

存 cún *vb* store, keep, preserve; place something for safe keeping, deposit; **bǎ qián cún zài yínháng li 把钱存在银行里** save money in a bank; exist, live, survive

存放 cúnfàng *vb* leave in someone's care

存款 cúnkuǎn *n* deposit account, bank savings

存在 cúnzài *vb* exist

寸 cùn *n* (*a unit of length*, 1/30 metre) cun

措施 cuòshī *n* measure, step, suitable action

错 cuò 1 *adj* wrong, mistaken, erroneous; **cuòzì 错字** wrong Chinese character **2** *n* mistake, error, fault; **zhè bú shì nǐ de cuò 这不是你的错** it's not your fault **2** *adv* by mistake, in the wrong way; **zuòcuòle 做错了** made a mistake; **zuòcuòle chē 坐错了车** took the wrong bus

错过 cuòguò *vb* miss, let slip; **bié cuòguò zhège hǎo jīhuì 别错过这个好机会** don't miss this good opportunity

错误 cuòwù *n* mistake, error

Dd

搭 dā *vb* put up, put together, construct; **dā yí gè xiǎo péng 搭一个小棚** put up a shed/arbour; join up with, establish contact;

dāhuǒ 搭伙 join a group; **dāshang guānxì** 搭上关系 establish contact; (*a ship, train, plane, etc.*) go by, go aboard; **dā** [chuán|huǒchē|chē] 搭 [船|火车|车] go by [ship|train|car]

答应 dāying vb respond, reply; **méi rén dāying** 没人答应 no one answered; agree, promise; **tā dāying qù** 他答应去 he agreed to go

达到 dádào vb attain, reach; **dádào mùdì** 达到目的 attain a goal

答 dá vb answer, reciprocate

答案 dá'àn n answer, solution

答复 dáfù vb (*in a formal way*) reply, answer

答卷 dájuàn n answer booklet, answer sheet

打 dǎ vb hit, strike, beat; **dǎrén 打人** hit a person; fight, make (war); (*when talking about an object*) break, smash, destroy; **dǎpò jìngzi 打破镜子** break a mirror; (*when talking about prejudice, tradition, record, relationship, etc.*) **dǎpò** [piānjiàn|jiù chuántǒng|jìlù] 打破 [偏见|旧传统|纪录] [dispel a prejudice| break an old tradition| break a record]; (*for games played with the hands, some musical instruments*) play; **dǎqiú 打球** play a (ball) game; **dǎ tàijíquán 打太极拳** practice taiji boxing; **dǎpái 打牌** play cards; **dǎgǔ 打鼓** play a drum/drumstype on a typewriter, use a keyboard on a computer; **dǎzì 打字** type, typing; send, dispatch; **dǎbào** [diànbào|diànhuà] 打 [电报|电话] [send a telegram| make a phone call]; (*other uses*) **dǎchái 打柴** gather firewood; **dǎgōng 打工** do odd jobs; **dǎliè 打猎** go hunting; **dǎ máoyī 打毛衣** knit a sweater; **dǎqì 打气** (*for tyres*) inflate with air; (*for people*) encourage, boost morale; **dǎqiāng 打枪** fire a gun; **dǎshuǐ 打水** fetch water; **dǎyóu 打油** buy oil; **dǎyú 打鱼** catch fish

打败 dǎbài vb defeat

打扮 dǎbàn vb dress up, deck out, make up

打倒 dǎdǎo vb down with..., overthrow

打击 dǎjī vb attack, hit, strike

打架 dǎjià vb fight, come to blows

打开 dǎkāi vb open(something)

打喷嚏 dǎ pēntì vb sneeze

打扰 dǎrǎo vb bother, disturb, trouble

打扫 dǎsǎo vb (when referring to housework) clean, sweep

打算 dǎsuàn 1 vb intend to, plan to **2** n intention, plan

打听 dǎtīng vb ask about, inquire about

打仗 dǎzhàng vb fight, make war

打招呼 dǎ zhāohu vb greet politely, make a sign of greeting politely

打针 dǎzhēn vb inject, give or have an injection

打字 dǎzì vb type, word-process, key in

打字机 dǎzìjī n typewriter

大 dà 1 adj big, large, major, heavy, strong; **fēng hěn dà 风很大** the wind is strong; (when referring to sound) loud; (when referring to age) old, elder; **háizi duō dà le? 孩子多大了?** how old is the child?; **dàjiě 大姐** elder sister **2** adv (to a great extent, to an extreme) **dà nào 大闹** create a major disturbance; (after a negative) not very, not often; **bú dà hǎo 不大好** not very good; **bú dà huì 不大会** cannot (do something) very well

大胆 dàdǎn adj bold, daring, audacious

大多数 dàduōshù n the great majority

大概 dàgài 1 adj general, approximate; **yí gè dàgài de yìnxiàng 一个大概的印象** a general impression **2** adv probably

大会 dàhuì n large meeting, plenary session

大伙儿 dàhuǒr pron we all, you all, everyone; **zhè shì wǒmen dàhuǒr de yìjiàn 这是我们大伙儿的意见** this is the view that we all take

大家 dàjiā pron (often used with **dōu 都** when it's the

subject of a sentence) everybody, everyone; **dàjiā dōu xīhuan tā 大家都喜欢他** everyone likes him

大街 dàjiē *n* main road, boulevard, avenue

大量 dàliàng 1 *adj* large amount of, a great quantity of; **dàliàng de liángshi 大量的粮食** a large quantity of food **2** *adv* in large numbers, by a great quantity; **dàliàng xuējiǎn jīngfèi 大量削减经费** reduce expenses by a large amount

大陆 dàlù *n* mainland, continent

大米 dàmǐ *n* uncooked white rice

大批 dàpī *adj* large quantity/number of; **yí dàpī xuésheng 一大批学生** a large group of students

大人 dàren *n* adult, grown-up

大声 dàshēng *adv* loudly; **dàshēng jiào 大声叫** call out in a loud voice

大使 dàshǐ *n* ambassador

大使馆 dàshǐguǎn *n* embassy

大体上 dàtǐshang *adv* for the most part, generally, more or less

大小 dàxiǎo *n* size

大型 dàxíng *adj* large-scaled, large-sized, large; **dàxíng fādòngjī 大型发动机** large-sized motor

大学 dàxué *n* university, college; **shàng dàxué 上大学** attend university

大衣 dàyī *n* coat, overcoat

大约 dàyuē *adv* approximately, about; **dàyuē yào yí gè xiǎoshí 大约要一个小时** it will take about one hour

呆 dāi 1 *adj* slow-witted, dull; (with fear or amazement) blank, wooden; **tā zhàn zài nàr fādāi 他站在那儿发呆** he stood there staring blankly **2** *vb* stay; **dāi zài jiālǐ 呆在家里** stay

待 dāi *vb* ▶ See also 待 **dài**. stay

大夫 **dàifu** *n* doctor, physician

代 **dài** **1** *n* historical period; **Tángdài** 唐代 the Tang Dynasty; generation; **xīnyídài** 新一代 a new generation **2** *vb* on behalf of; **qǐng dài wǒ wènhòu tā** 请代我问候他 please give him my greetings; acting; **dàizǒnglǐ** 代总理 acting premier

代表 **dàibiǎo** **1** *n* representative **2** *vb* represent

代价 **dàijià** *n* cost, price to pay for

代替 **dàitì** *vb* stand in place of, substitute

带 **dài** **1** *n* belt, ribbon; tyre; region, area; **zài Huáng Hé yídài** 在黄河一带 in the region of the Yellow River **2** *vb* take, bring along, bring; **kěyǐ dài háizi qù ma?** 可以带孩子去吗? can we take children with us?; have with, attached, included; **yí kuài dài rìlì de shǒubiǎo** 一块带日历的手表 a date watch, a calendar watch; (*when talking about children*) look after; bring up; **tā de zǔmǔ bǎ tā dàidà** 他的祖母把他带大 his grandmother raised him

待 **dài** *vb* ▶ See also 待 **dāi**. treat, deal with; wait for, await; **dài dào míngtiān** 待到明天 wait until tomorrow

袋 **dài** *n* bag, sack; **yí dài tǔdòu** 一袋土豆 a sack of potatoes

戴 **dài** *vb* (*on the head, neck, or wrist*) put on, wear

担任 **dānrèn** *vb* assume the responsibility for, hold the position of

担心 **dānxīn** *vb* worry about, be concerned that

单 **dān** **1** *adj* single, of one unit, simple; **dānrénchuáng** 单人床 single bed; (*referring to numbers*) odd; **dānshù** 单数 odd number **2** *adv* singly, separately; **bǎ zhè běn shū dān fàng** 把这本书单放 keep this book in a separate place **3** *n* (*for a bed*) sheet; bill, list; **dānzi** 单子 list

单词 **dāncí** *n* (*as a linguistic unit*) word

单调 **dāndiào** *adj* monotonous, dull, drab

单独 **dāndú** *adj* alone

单位 **dānwèi** *n* unit of measurement; organizational unit; gōngzuò dānwèi 工作单位 work unit

胆量 **dǎnliàng** *n* courage

但 **dàn** *conj* ▶ *See also* 不但 **búdàn** . but, yet, nevertheless

但是 **dànshì** *conj* but, however, yet

但愿 **dànyuàn** *vb* I wish, if only

担子 **dànzi** *n* load, burden, task

诞生 **dànshēng** *vb* be born, emerge, come into being

淡 **dàn** *adj* lacking salt; tā zuò de cài tài dàn 他做的菜太淡 the dishes he cooks are not salty enough; dànshuǐhú 淡水湖 freshwater lake; tasteless, insipid, weak; zhè bēi chá tài dàn 这杯茶太淡 this cup of tea is too weak; (*in colour*) light; dànlǜ 淡绿 pale green; slack, poor; dànjì 淡季 low season, slack season

蛋 **dàn** *n* egg; dànbái 蛋白 egg white, protein; dànhuáng 蛋黄 egg yolk

蛋糕 **dàngāo** *n* cake

当 **dāng** ▶ *See also* 当 **dàng**. **1** *vb* act in the role of, undertake/occupy the position of; dāng lǎoshī 当老师 be a teacher, work as a teacher **2** *prep* (*when referring to a certain time or place*) when, at, whilst; dāng…de shíhòu 当…的时候…, at the time…; dāng wǒ dào de shíhòu, tā yǐjīng zǒu le 当我到的时候, 他已经走了 when I arrived, he had already left

当场 **dāngchǎng** *adv* on the spot, there and then, red-handed

当代 **dāngdài** *n* contemporary, the present age

当地 **dāngdì** *adj* local; dāngdì shíjiān 当地时间 local time

当今 **dāngjīn** *adv* now, at present, nowadays

当年 **dāngnián** *adv* ▶ *See also* 当年 **dàngnián** . in those years

当前 **dāngqián** **1** *adj* present, current **2** *adv* at present

当然 dāngrán *adv* of course, naturally

当时 dāngshí *adv* at that time

当心 dāngxīn *vb* be careful, look out

挡 dǎng *vb* stand in the way of, bar, block; **dǎngzhù dàolù** 挡住道路 bar the way

党 dǎng *n* political party

党员 dǎngyuán *n* party member

当 dàng *vb* ▶ *See also* 当 **dāng** . treat as, regard as; equal to; think that, take it to be that

当年 dàngnián *adv* ▶ *See also* 当年 **dāngnián** . in the same year, that very year

当做 dàngzuò *vb* consider as, take as

刀 dāo *n* knife, sword, razor

刀子 dāozi *n* knife, penknife

岛 dǎo *n* island

倒 dǎo *vb* ▶ *See also* 倒 **dào**. fall, fall down; **tā dǎo zài dìshang le** 他倒在地上了 he fell down to the ground; collapse, be overthrown, close down; go bankrupt; change, exchange; **dǎochē** 倒车 change a train/bus

倒闭 dǎobì *vb* close down, go bankrupt

倒霉 dǎoméi *adj* unlucky, have bad luck

到 dào 1 *vb* arrive, reach, go to! *Often used with* **qù** 去 *or* **lái** 来 *in the pattern* **dào**…**qù** 到…去 *or* **dào**…**lái** 来; **dào Lúndūn qù** 到伦敦去 go to London; **dào Běijīng lái** 到北京来 come to Beijing **2** *vb* (*used after other verbs to indicate successful attainment*) [**mǎi** | **zhǎo** | **bàn**]**dào** [买 | 找 | 办]到 manage to [buy | find | accomplish] something; (*used with the negative* **bù** 不 *to indicate impossible attainment*) [**kàn** | **tīng** | **zuò**]**bú dào** [看 | 听 | 做]不到 be unable to [see | hear | do]something; (*used with the negative* **méi** 没 *to indicate unsuccessful attainment*) **tā méi mǎidào** 他没买到 he was unable to buy it **3** *prep* until, to, towards; **yìtiān-dàowǎn**

一天到晚 from morning to night；huì yìzhí kāi dào bā diǎn zhōng 会一直开到 8 点钟 the meeting lasted until 8 o'clock

到处 dàochù *adv* in all places, everywhere

到达 dàodá *vb* arrive, reach

到底 dàodǐ *adv* after all, really；in the end, at last, finally；to the end, to the finish

倒 dào ▶ *See also* 倒 **dǎo**. **1** *vb* pour, pour out, dump；reverse, go backwards；dàochē 倒车 reverse the car **2** *adv* back, in the opposite direction；upside down；guàdào le 挂倒了 hang upside down；(*for emphasis*) indeed, after all, on the contrary；dàoshì 倒是 (*used in a question to find out the fact of a matter*) (really)...or not?；nǐ dàoshì qù bú qù? 你倒是去不去? are you really going or not?

道 dào 1 *n* road, way, path；way, method **2** *adj* Taoist, Daoist **3** *vb* speak, say, or tell **4** *mw* ▶ **623** (*for orders issued by an authority, questions on an examination*)；(*for things in the shape of a line*)；(*for courses in a meal*)

道德 dàodé *n* morality, ethical code, ethics

道教 Dàojiào *n* Taoism, Daoism

道理 dàolǐ *n* teaching, doctrine, principle；reason, sense；yǒu dàolǐ 有道理 make sense, be reasonable

道路 dàolù *n* way, road, course

道歉 dàoqiàn *vb* apologize

地 de *pt* ▶ *See also* 地 **dì**. (*used after an adjective to form an adverb, equivalent to* -ly *in English*) cōngmáng de jìnlái 匆忙地进来 rush in hurriedly

的 de *pt* ! The particle de 的 *is often used to transform a word, phrase, or clause to modify a noun or noun phrase. It can also be used to transform an adjective into a noun or a verb phrase into a noun phrase: of；* xuéxiào de guīdìng 学校的规定 the rules of the school；(*to*

indicate possession) **wǒ māma de shū 我妈妈的书** my mother's book;（*after an adjective to modify a noun*）**měilì de gūniang 美丽的姑娘** a beautiful girl;（*after a clause to make it modify a noun*）**tā mǎi de shū 他买的书** the books he bought;（*after an adjective to transform it into a noun*）**hóng de shì wǒ de 红的是我的** the red one is mine;（*after a verb phrase to transform it into a noun phrase*）**tā shuō de bù hǎotīng 他说的不好听** what he said was not pleasant;（*in the* **shì … de 是 … 的** *construction for emphasis*）**wǒ shì zuótiān dào de 我是昨天到的** I arrived yesterday

得 de *pt*（*used between two verbs to indicate possibility*）! *Note that the first verb indicates the action, while the second indicates a possible result or attainment;* **bān de dòng 搬得动** able to move it; **zuò de dào 做得到** able to do it！ *In expressions like these, the possibility is negated by the use of* **bu 不** *in place of* **de 得**, *thus the expressions* **bān bú dòng 搬不动**, **zuò bú dào 做不到** *mean* be unable to move *and* be unable to do;（*used between a verb and an adjective or a clause to indicate degree or extent*）**pǎo de kuài 跑得快** run fast; **bìng de hěn lìhai 病得很厉害** be very ill; **lèi de tóutòng 累得头痛** be tired to the point of having a headache;（*used in a negative form to advise someone strongly against doing something*）[**shuō**│**gàn**│**chī**] **bùde** [说│干│吃]**不得** mustn't/can't [say│do│eat]（something）

得 dé *vb* get, have, obtain;（*when used with* **bu 不**）**bùdé 不得** disallow, prohibit

得到 dédào *vb* obtain, receive, gain

得罪 dézuì *vb* offend

德国 Déguó *n* Germany

德文 Déwén *n* German language（usually written）

德语 Déyǔ *n* German language（usually spoken）

得 děi *vb* have to, must; **xuésheng děi niànshū** 学生得念书 students have to study; require; **mǎi zhè běn shū děi duōshǎo qián?** 买这本书得多少钱? how much money will I need to buy this book?

灯 dēng *n* lamp, light; **diǎndēng** 点灯 light a lamp

登 dēng *vb* (*for a bus, train, or other vehicle*) mount, ascend, board; land, alight; **dēnglù** 登陆 land on shore, disembark; publish, print; **dēngbào** 登报 print in a newspaper

登记 dēngjì *vb* register

等 děng 1 *vb* wait, await **2** *n* grade, class **3** *pron* (*used at the end of an enumeration*) etc., and so on; **děngdeng** 等等 and so on, etc.; **děngdeng** 等等 wait a moment

等待 děngdài *vb* wait, wait for

等候 děnghòu *vb* wait, wait for

等于 děngyú *vb* be equal to, be equivalent to; be the same as, amount to, be tantamount to

凳(子) dèng(zi) *n* stool, bench

低 dī 1 *adj* low **2** *vb* lower; **dītóu** 低头 bow one's head

滴 dī *mw* ▶ 623 drop

的确 díquè *adv* indeed, really

敌人 dírén *n* enemy

底下 dǐxia *prep* under, below, beneath; **zhuōzi dǐxia** 桌子底下 under the table

地 dì *n* ▶ *See also* 地 **de**. the ground, floor; earth, soil; place, location

地步 dìbù *n* situation, condition; extent, point

地带 dìdài *n* area, region

地点 dìdiǎn *n* place, location

地方 dìfāng *adj* local

地方 dìfang *n* place

地理 **dìlǐ** n geography

地面 **dìmiàn** n ground, the earth's surface

地球 **dìqiú** n the earth, the globe

地区 **dìqū** n district, area

地铁 **dìtiě** n underground, subway, tube

地图 **dìtú** n map

地位 **dìwèi** n status, social position

地下 **dìxià** n underground

地下室 **dìxiàshì** n basement, cellar

地震 **dìzhèn** n earthquake

地址 **dìzhǐ** n address

地主 **dìzhǔ** n landlord

弟弟 **dìdi** n younger brother

递 **dì** vb hand over, pass

第 **dì** pt (used to indicate ordinal numbers) dì-yī cì 第 1 次 first time; dì-yī míng 第 1 名 number one, champion, winner; dì-èr tiān 第 2 天 the next day; dì jǐ kè? 第几课? which lesson?

颠倒 **diāndǎo** 1 vb reverse, invert, turn upside down 2 adj muddled, confused, upside down

点 **diǎn** 1 n dot, drop, speck; (in decimals) point; sān diǎn liù 三点六 three point six; (used in time expressions, referring to hours on the clock) o'clock; sān diǎn zhōng 3 点钟; (when talking about abstract ideas) point; xiàmian liǎng diǎn 下面两点 the following two points, the two points below 2 mw ▶ 623 (for suggestions, requirements, ideas, opinions) 3 vb touch slightly; mark, punctuate; tick off on a list, check; choose; diǎncài 点菜 select dishes from a menu; (as fire or flame) light; diǎndēng 点灯 light a lamp 4 adv a little, slightly; [hǎo| dà|xiǎo] diǎnr [好|大|小]点儿 a little [better|bigger|smaller]

点名 **diǎnmíng** vb take a roll call, check names on a list,

mention by name

点头 diǎntóu *vb* nod the head

点心 diǎnxin *n* light refreshments, pastry, snacks

电 diàn 1 *n* electricity **2** *adj* electric

电报 diànbào *n* telegram, cable

电冰箱 diànbīngxiāng *n* refrigerator, fridge

电车 diànchē *n* trolley, street car, tram

电灯 diàndēng *n* electric light

电风扇 diànfēngshàn, 电扇 diànshàn *n* electric fan

电话 diànhuà *n* telephone

电脑 diànnǎo *n* computer

电视 diànshì *n* television, TV

电视台 diànshìtái *n* television station

电台 diàntái *n* radio station

电梯 diàntī *n* lift, elevator, escalator

电影 diànyǐng *n* film, movie

电影院 diànyǐngyuàn *n* cinema, movie theatre

电子 diànzǐ 1 *n* electron **2** *adj* electronic

店 diàn *n* store, shop, inn, hotel

吊 diào *vb* pull up by a rope, hang, suspend

钓 diào *vb* fish, angle; diàoyú 钓鱼 fish

调 diào ▶ *See also* tiáo. **1** *n* melody, tune **2** *vb* (*when talking about troops or personnel*) transfer, move, send; change direction, turn, exchange

调查 diàochá 1 *vb* investigate **2** *n* investigation

掉 diào *vb* fall down, drop, come off; (*used after such verbs as* shī 失, qù 去, mài 卖, táo 逃, wàng 忘, miè 灭, rēng 扔, *and* cā 擦 *to indicate loss, end of supply*) shīdiào 失掉 lose; qùdiào 去掉 get rid of; màidiào 卖掉 sell off, sell out, lose, be missing; turn, turn round; diàoguò tóu lai 掉过头来 turn the head round; change, exchange;

diàohuàn 掉换 exchange

跌 diē *vb* fall down;(*of prices*) fall

顶 dǐng 1 *n* top, summit **2** *adj* topmost, extreme; **dǐngtóu 顶头** furthest end, top **3** *adv* very, extremely, most; **dǐnghǎo 顶好** the best, the greatest **4** *vb* carry on the head; push the head against; go against **5** *mw* ▶ **623** (*for hats, caps, or things with a top*)

定 dìng 1 *adv* definitely, certainly **2** *adj* stable, calm **3** *vb* decide, fix, settle

定期 dìngqī 1 *vb* set a date **2** *adv* regularly

订 dìng *vb* make an agreement, cement a relationship; **dìnghūn 订婚** become engaged; **dìng hétong 订合同** make a contract; subscribe to, order, book; **dìng zázhì 订杂志** order a magazine; **dìng fángjiān 订房间** book a room

丢 diū *vb* lose; **tā diūle yí jiàn dōngxi 他丢了一件东西** he lost something; throw, cast, toss; put or lay aside

东 dōng *n* east; **dōng [biān|bù|fāng|miàn] 东 [边|部|方|面]** eastern [side|part|direction|side]

东北 dōngběi *n* northeast; Northeast China, which includes the three provinces of Heilongjiang, Jilin, and Liaoning and the eastern part of the inner Mongolia Autonomous Region

东方 dōngfāng *n* east; the Orient

东南 dōngnán *n* southeast

东西 dōngxi *n* thing, things; **mǎi dōngxi 买东西** go shopping, buy things

冬 dōng *n* winter; **dōngtiān 冬天** winter

懂 dǒng *vb* understand

懂得 dǒngdé *vb* understand, know

懂行 dǒngháng *vb* know a business, be experienced in a profession

懂事 dǒngshì *adj* sensible, wise

动 dòng *vb* move; start action; stir, arouse; use

动静 dòngjing *n* stirring noises, sound of people speaking or moving about; movement, activity

动力 dònglì *n* power; driving force, motive, impetus

动人 dòngrén *adj* moving, touching

动身 dòngshēn *vb* embark on a journey, set off

动手 dòngshǒu *vb* start, make a move to; raise a hand to fight or hit; touch; **qǐng wù dòngshǒu! 请勿动手!** please don't touch!

动物 dòngwù *n* animal

动物园 dòngwùyuán *n* zoo

动员 dòngyuán *vb* mobilize

动作 dòngzuò *n* action, movement

冻 dòng *vb* freeze; **dòngsǐ 冻死** freeze to death

洞 dòng *n* hole, cave

栋 dòng *mw* ▶ **623** (for buildings)

都 dōu! *Can also be pronounced* **dū 都** *with a different meaning*; *adv* all, both; **tāmen dōu hěn hǎo 他们都很好** they are all well; **dōu shì wèile zhuànqián 都是为了赚钱** it's all to make money; (*when used with a negative*)! *Note that* **bù 不** *before* **dōu 都** *means* not all do *or* some don't; *while* **dōu 都** *before* **bù 不** *means* none do; **tāmen dōu bú huì chànggē 他们都不会唱歌** none of them can sing well; **tāmen bù dōu huì chànggē 他们不都会唱歌** they can't all sing well; (*when used with the interrogative* **shénme 什么** what) everything; **nǐ shénme dōu huì 你什么都会** you can do everything; (*when used with the interrogative* **shénme 什么** *and a negative*) nothing, not anything; **tā shénme dōu méi zuò 他什么都没做** he hasn't done anything; (*when used with the interrogative* **shéi 谁** who) everyone; **shéi dōu zhīdào 谁都知道** everyone knows; (*when used with the interrogative* **shéi 谁** *and a negative*) no one; **shéi dōu bù chuān zhè**

zhǒng yīfu 谁都不穿这种衣服 no one wears clothing like this; (*in the pattern* lián…dōu… 连…都…) even！*Note that in practice when the first element of this pattern is omitted, the word* dōu *alone retains the sense of the pattern and means even;* lián zhège wèntí tā dōu bù dǒng 连这个问题他都不懂 he can't even understand this kind of question; tā yīfu dōu méi xǐ 他衣服都没洗 he didn't even wash his clothes; already

斗争 **dòuzhēng** 1 *vb* struggle, fight, strive 2 *n* struggle, combat

豆腐 **dòufu** *n* beancurd, tofu

逗 **dòu** 1 *vb* tease 2 *adj* funny

逗留 **dòuliú** *vb* stay (for a short time), stop over

独立 **dúlì** 1 *vb* be independent, become independent; zhège guójiā dúlì le 这个国家独立了 this country became independent 2 *n* independence 3 *adj* independent; nàge háizi hěn dúlì 那个孩子很独立 that child is very independent

独身 **dúshēn** *adj* single, unmarried

独生女 **dúshēngnǚ** *n* only daughter

独生子 **dúshēngzǐ** *n* only son

独自 **dúzì** *adj* alone, by oneself

读 **dú** *vb* read; read aloud; study (at school, college, or university); dú dàxué 读大学 study at university

读书 **dúshū** *vb* study, read books; attend school

读者 **dúzhě** *n* reader

堵 **dǔ** 1 *vb* obstruct, block up 2 *mw* ▶ **623** (for walls)

肚子 **dùzi** *n* stomach, belly

度 **dù** 1 *n* (*unit or measurement for angles, temperature, etc.*) degree; língxià sān (shèshì) dù 零下 3（摄氏）度 3 degrees below zero centigrade; sānshí'èr huáshìdù 32 华氏度 32 degrees Fahrenheit; occasion, time 2 *vb* spend, pass

度（过）**dù（guò）** *vb* spend, pass

渡 dù vb (*when talking about a body of water*) cross over; **dù** [**hé** | **Cháng Jiāng** | **hǎi**] **渡** [河 | 长江 | 海] cross [a river | the Yangtze River | an ocean]; (*a difficulty, or a period of time*) go through; **dùguò kùnnan shíqī** 渡过困难时期 go through a difficult time

端 duān 1 n (*of a long, narrow object*) end, end point **2** vb hold something level with the hand(s)

端午节 Duānwǔ Jié n Dragon Boat Festival! *It falls on the fifth day of the fifth month of the lunar calendar.*

短 duǎn 1 adj (*in length*) short **2** n weak point, fault

短处 duǎnchù n shortcoming

短期 duǎnqī n short term

段 duàn mw ▶ 623 (*for lengths of road, cable, etc.*) section, segment; (*for periods of time*) period, length; (*for units of writing, articles, speeches, etc.*) piece, passage, paragraph

断 duàn vb break, cut off

断定 duàndìng vb conclude, decide, judge

断断续续 duànduàn-xùxù adv intermittently, on-and-off

锻炼 duànliàn vb do physical training, take exercise, improve one's physical fitness

堆 duī 1 vb heap up, pile up **2** n pile, stack, heap; **yì duī dōngxi** 一堆东西 a pile of things

队 duì n team, group; a queue/line of people

队伍 duìwǔ n troops, ranks

队员 duìyuán n member of a team

队长 duìzhǎng n captain of a team, team leader

对 duì 1 adj correct, accurate, right **2** prep (*introducing a target, aim*) to, towards, with; **duì wǒ shēngqì** 对我生气 angry with me; regarding, about; on; **duì zhè jiàn shì de kànfa** 对这件事的看法 views on this matter; (*in sports*)

against；**Sūgélán duì Yīnggélán** 苏格兰对英格兰 Scotland vs. England **3** vb treat，deal with；face；**chuānghu duìzhe huāyuán** 窗户对着花园 the window faces the garden **4** mw ▶ 623 pair，couple；**duì wǒ lái shuō** 对我来说 in my view，as far as I'm concerned

对比 duìbǐ 1 vb contrast，compare **2** n comparison，contrast；ratio，correlation

对不起 duìbuqǐ vb let someone down，act unworthily toward；**nǐ yǒu shénme duìbuqǐ tā de shì ma?** 你有什么对不起他的事吗？did you let him down in some way?；sorry，I'm sorry，excuse me

对待 duìdài vb treat，handle，deal with

对方 duìfāng n（in negotiations，games，competitions）the other party，opposite side

对付 duìfu vb deal with，cope with；serve for the time being，make do

对话 duìhuà n dialogue

对面 duìmiàn prep opposite

对象 duìxiàng n goal，objective；boyfriend，girlfriend，partner

对于 duìyú prep with regard to

吨 dūn n（a unit of weight）ton

蹲 dūn vb squat

顿 dùn mw ▶ 623（for meals）；（for actions that take place in single sessions）

多 duō 1 adj many，much，more；more than；**wǔshí duō yuán** 五十多元 over fifty yuan（between fifty and sixty）extra，additional；**duōle sān yīngbàng** 多了3英镑 three pounds extra **2** adv（to indicate degree or extent in comparison）much，a great deal；**jīntiān tiānqi hǎo duō le** 今天天气好多了 the weather is a lot better today；（in questions asking for a number，degree，age，etc.）**duō dà**

[niánlíng|suìshù]多大 [年龄|岁数]? how old?；duō dà de [fángjiān|xié]? 多大的 [房间|鞋] [how big a room? | what size shoes?]；(in comparisons, after a verb, expressing a large extent) much, a lot；[hǎo|nán|kěxiào] de duō [好|难|可笑]得多 much [better|harder|funnier]

多(么) duō(me) adv (to exclaim about the high degree to which an action is done) such…！what a…！；nǐ fùmǔ duō(me)ài nǐ a！你父母多(么)爱你啊！your parents love you so much！；(to exclaim or ask about the extent of a quality)duō(me)kě'ài de háizi! 多(么)可爱的孩子！what a lovable child！

多少 duōshao det (as an interrogative) how many? how much?；duōshao [rén|tiān|běn shū|gōnglǐ]多少 [人|天|本书|公里]how many [people|days|books|kilometres]；(to indicate an uncertain amount) how many, how much；wǒ bù xiǎng zhīdào tā yǒu duōshao qián 我不想知道他有多少钱 I don't want to know how much money he has

多数 duōshù n majority, most

多余 duōyú adj extra, excess, surplus

夺 duó vb rob, snatch, seize by force；strive for, win

夺取 duóqǔ vb seize by force

朵 duǒ mw ▶ 623 (for flowers, clouds)

躲 duǒ vb hide oneself away from, avoid, dodge

Ee

俄国 Éguó n Russia

俄文 Éwén n Russian language (usually written)

俄语 Éyǔ n Russian language (usually spoken)

鹅 é n goose

饿 è 1 *adj* hungry；**wǒ è le 我饿了** I'm hungry **2** *vb* starve；**èsǐ 饿死** starve to death

儿童 értóng *n* children

儿子 érzi *n* son

而 ér *conj* (*connecting two adjectives, two verbs, etc.*) and；**cōngmíng ér yǒnggǎn 聪明而勇敢** intelligent and brave；(*connecting an affirmative clause with a negative clause*) but, yet, while；**tā zhǐ xiǎng zìjǐ, ér bù xiǎng biérén 他只想自己, 而不想别人** he thinks only of himself and not of others；(*connecting an adverb of manner with a verb*) **qiāoqiāo ér qù 悄悄而去** depart quietly；(*connecting the cause of an action with the action itself*) because of, on the grounds of；**tā yīnwèi gōngzuò ér fàngqì xiūjià 他因为工作而放弃休假** he gave up his holidays because of his work；**bú shì…ér shì… 不是…而是…** not... but...；**wǒ bú shì Měiguórén ér shì Jiānádàrén 我不是美国人而是加拿大人** I am not an American but a Canadian

而且 érqiě *conj* and also, moreover, in addition；**búdàn… érqiě… 不但…而且…** not only... but also...；**tā búdàn lèi érqiě bù shūfu 他不但累而且不舒服** he's not only tired but also unwell

耳朵 ěrduo *n* ear

二 èr *num* two！ *Note that when used with a measure word*, **èr 二** *usually changes to* **liǎng 两**. ▶ *See also* **两 liǎng**.

二月 èryuè *n* February

Ff

发 fā *vb* ▶ *See also* **发 fà**. send out, issue；**fā hěnduō xìn**

发很多信 send out a lot of letters; start, grow, develop; **fāyá 发芽** put out shoots; get into a state, become; fā [jí|nù |hóng] 发 [急|怒|红] [become agitated | get angry | turn red]; break out in, have a sensation of; fā [má|yǎng] 发 [麻|痒] get [pins and needles | itchy]

发表 fābiǎo *vb* publish, issue; express, state

发财 fācái *vb* get rich, make lots of money

发出 fāchū *vb* send out, issue; fāchū tōngzhī 发出通知 send out notification; give off, give out, give rise to; fāchū guāngliàng 发出光亮 emit light

发达 fādá *adj* prosperous, flourishing, developed

发动 fādòng *vb* launch, start; mobilize

发动机 fādòngjī *n* engine, motor

发抖 fādǒu *vb* shiver, tremble

发挥 fāhuī *vb* give play to, bring into play, give free rein to; fāhuī tā de cáinéng 发挥他的才能 give full play to his talents; (when talking about an idea, a theme, etc.) develop, expand on, elaborate; bǎ zhège tímù zài fāhuī yīxià 把这个题目再发挥一下 develop this topic further

发火 fāhuǒ *vb* catch fire; become angry, lose one's temper

发明 fāmíng 1 *vb* invent **2** *n* invention

发烧 fāshāo *vb* have or run a fever, have a high temperature

发生 fāshēng *vb* occur, happen, take place

发现 fāxiàn 1 *vb* discover, find **2** *n* discovery

发言 fāyán *vb* speak, make a speech/statement

发扬 fāyáng *vb* develop, carry on

发音 fāyīn 1 *vb* pronounce **2** *n* pronunciation

发展 fāzhǎn 1 *vb* develop, expand **2** *n* development

罚 fá *vb* punish, penalize

罚款 fákuǎn *vb* fine, make someone pay a penalty

法 fǎ *n* law, method

法国 **Fǎguó** n France；Fǎguórén 法国人 French people，Frenchman，Frenchwoman

法律 **fǎlǜ** n law

法庭 **fǎtíng** n court of law

法文 **Fǎwén** n French language (usually written)

法语 **Fǎyǔ** n French language (usually spoken)

法院 **fǎyuàn** n court of law

法子 **fǎzi** n way，method

发 **fà** n ▶ See also 发 fā．hair

番茄 **fānqié** n tomato

翻 **fān** vb (when talking about sheets，pages in a book) flip，thumb through；turn，turn over；translate；cross，get over；fānguò nà zuò shān 翻过那座山 cross that mountain；rummage，search；tā zài fān wǒ de shūbāo 他在翻我的书包 he is searching my book bag；multiply；fān yì fān 翻一番 double，increase two-fold

翻译 **fānyì** 1 vb translate，interpret 2 n translator，interpreter；translation

凡(是) **fán(shì)** adv every，all！The term fánshì 凡是 is used at the beginning of a sentence and followed by a noun or noun-clause to mean whatever or whoever. The subject of the sentence，thus defined，is usually followed by dōu 都；fán(shì) tā mǎi de dōu hěn piàoliang 凡(是)她买的都很漂亮 everything she buys is attractive

烦 **fán** 1 adj irritated，annoyed，vexed；tired of 2 vb trouble，bother

烦恼 **fánnǎo** adj worried，vexed

繁荣 **fánróng** 1 adj prosperous 2 vb make prosperous 3 n prosperity

反动 **fǎndòng** adj reactionary

反对 **fǎnduì** vb oppose，object，combat

反复 **fǎnfù** adv again and again，over and over

反抗 fǎnkàng *vb* resist, oppose, react against

反面 fǎnmiàn *n* reverse side, wrong side; negative side, opposite side

反应 fǎnyìng 1 *vb* react **2** *n* reaction

反映 fǎnyìng 1 *vb* reflect, mirror; report, make known, express; **xiàng lǐngdǎo fǎnyìng 向领导反映** make something known to one's superiors **2** *n* reflection

反正 fǎnzhèng *adv* in any case, anyway

返回 fǎnhuí *vb* return, go back

犯 fàn *vb* (*when talking about the law, rules*) offend, violate; (*when talking about a mistake, a crime, etc.*) commit; **fàn cuòwu 犯错误** make a mistake; (*when talking about an old illness*) have another attack of

饭 fàn *n* cooked rice, food, meal

饭店 fàndiàn *n* hotel, restaurant

饭馆 fànguǎn *n* restaurant

饭厅 fàntīng *n* dining hall, dining room

范围 fànwéi *n* scope, sphere, jurisdiction

方 fāng 1 *n* direction; [**dōng** | **nán** | **xī** | **běi**] **fāng** [**东** | **南** | **西** | **北**] **方** the [*east* | *south* | *west* | *north*] side; side, party; **dānfāng 单方** one side, unilateral **2** *adj* square; **fāngkuàizì 方块字** Chinese characters

方案 fāng'àn *n* plan, scheme

方便 fāngbiàn 1 *adj* convenient **2** *vb* go to the lavatory

方法 fāngfǎ *n* way, method

方面 fāngmiàn *n* aspect, respect, side; **yì fāngmiàn… yì fāngmiàn… 一方面… 一方面…** on the one hand... on the other hand...

方式 fāngshì *n* method, style, formula

方向 fāngxiàng *n* direction

方言 fāngyán *n* dialect

方针 fāngzhēn *n* policy, guiding principle

防 fáng *vb* prevent, guard against, defend against

防止 fángzhǐ *vb* prevent

房东 fángdōng *n* landlord

房间 fángjiān *n* room

房子 fángzi *n* house, building, room

房租 fángzū *n* rent

访问 fǎngwèn 1 *vb* visit, call on **2** *n* visit

仿佛 fǎngfú 1 *vb* seem as if **2** *adv* apparently, seemingly

纺织 fǎngzhī *n* spinning, weaving textiles

放 fàng *vb* put down, place; let go, release (*physically*); bié fàng tā 别放他 don't release him (*emotionally or psychologically*) fàngshēng dà kū 放声大哭 burst into tears; (*when talking about something that explodes or fires*) let off, fire, shoot; fàng [pào│qiāng│yānhuǒ] 放 [炮│枪│烟火] [fire a cannon│shoot a gun│let off fireworks]; tend, herd; fàng [niú│yáng] 放 [牛│羊] pasture [cows│sheep]; readjust slightly; dǎnzi fàng dà diǎnr 胆子放大点儿 be a bit braver; (*film, recording, etc.*) show, play

放大 fàngdà *vb* enlarge, magnify

放假 fàngjià *vb* go on holiday/vacation, have a day off

放弃 fàngqì *vb* give up, abandon, forego

放松 fàngsōng *vb* relax, loosen

放心 fàngxīn *vb* feel relieved, set one's mind at rest, be at ease; fàngxīn bú xià 放心不下 can't relax, feel anxious

放学 fàngxué *vb* let out of school, classes are over

飞 fēi *vb* fly

飞机 fēijī *n* aircraft, aeroplane, airplane

飞行 fēixíng *n* flight, flying

非…不可 fēi…bùkě *vb* (*emphatic*) must, have to; fēi qù bùkě 非去不可 must go; will inevitably, will be bound to;

tā fēi chídào bùkě 他非迟到不可 he will definitely be late; insist on

非常 fēicháng *adv* very, extremely, unusually

非洲 Fēizhōu *n* Africa

肥 féi *adj* fat; (*when talking about clothes*) loose, large; (*of soil*) fertile, rich

肥皂 féizào *n* soap

废 fèi *adj* useless, waste, discarded

肺 fèi *n* lungs

费 fèi 1 *vb* expend, consume, waste; fèi shíjiān 费时间 be time-consuming, take a long time **2** *n* fee, fees

费用 fèiyòng *n* expense, expenses, cost

分 fēn 1 *vb* separate, divide; distinguish; bù fēn hǎohuài 不分好坏 not to distinguish the good from the bad; divide, share, receive a share of; fēndào yí fèn jiǎngjīn 分到一份奖金 get a share of the prize money; distribute; bǎ zhèxiē dōngxi fēngěi biérén 把这些东西分给别人 distribute these things to others **2** *adj* (*describing an organization*) branch, sub-; fēngōngsī 分公司 branch company **3** *n* (*of a dollar*) cent; (*of Chinese currency, RMB*) fen; (*of an hour*) minute; (*to represent a point or mark*) point, mark; dé qī fēn 得 7 分 get seven points; fēn zhī… … 分 之…(*to represent a fraction or parts of the whole*) sān fēn zhī èr 三分之二 two thirds

分别 fēnbié 1 *vb* part, leave each other, say good-bye to each other; separate, distinguish, differentiate **2** *adv* differently; separately, respectively

分开 fēnkāi *vb* separate, part

分配 fēnpèi *vb* assign, distribute

分手 fēnshǒu *vb* part company, separate, say good-bye

分数 fēnshù *n* mark, grade

分析 fēnxī 1 *vb* analyze **2** *n* analysis

吩咐 **fēnfù** vb tell, order, instruct

纷纷 **fēnfēn** adv in quick succession, one right after another; in profusion and confusion

坟墓 **fénmù** n grave, tomb

粉笔 **fěnbǐ** n chalk

粉红 **fěnhóng** n pink

份 **fèn** mw ▶ **623** portion, share; (*for copies of newspapers, magazines, or manuscripts*)

奋斗 **fèndòu** vb struggle/strive toward a goal

愤怒 **fènnù** 1 adj angry 2 n anger, indignation

丰富 **fēngfù** 1 adj plentiful, abundant 2 vb enrich

丰收 **fēngshōu** n good harvest, bumper harvest

风 **fēng** n wind, breeze, storm; custom, practice, habit

风格 **fēnggé** n style

风景 **fēngjǐng** n scenery, landscape, view

风力 **fēnglì** n wind power, force of the wind

风水 **fēngshuǐ** n geomancy

风俗 **fēngsú** n social customs

封 **fēng** 1 mw ▶ **623** (*for letters, telegrams*) 2 vb seal, close

封建 **fēngjiàn** adj feudal

疯 **fēng** adj mentally unbalanced, mad, crazy

蜂 **fēng** n bee, wasp

蜂蜜 **fēngmì** n honey

逢 **féng** vb meet, come upon, chance upon; **féngnián-guòjié** 逢年过节 on New Year's Day or other festivals

讽刺 **fěngcì** vb satirize

佛教 **Fójiào** n Buddhism

否定 **fǒudìng** vb deny, negate, decide in the negative

否认 **fǒurèn** vb deny

否则 **fǒuzé** conj if not, or else, otherwise

夫妇 fūfù *n* husband and wife, Mr. and Mrs.

夫妻 fūqī *n* husband and wife

夫人 fūren *n* Mrs., Madam, wife; **Zhōu fūren 周夫人** Mrs. Zhou

扶 fú *vb* support with the hand; **fúzhe lǎorén zhàn qǐlai 扶着老人站起来** help the elderly person stand up; place one's hands on somebody/something for support; **tā fúzhe qiáng zǒu 她扶着墙走** she walked along holding the wall for support

服从 fúcóng *vb* obey, be subordinate to

服务 fúwù 1 *vb* serve, provide service to **2** *n* service

服务员 fúwùyuán *n* attendant, steward, waiter

服装 fúzhuāng *n* costume, outfit, uniform

浮 fú *vb* float, drift

符合 fúhé *vb* conform to, fit, coincide; **fúhé tā de àihào 符合他的爱好** suit his hobby

幅 fú *mw* ▶ **623** (for paintings, works of calligraphy)

福 fú *n* good fortune, blessing, happiness

辅导 fǔdǎo *vb* advise/coach in studies, give tutorials to

腐败 fǔbài *adj* rotten, decayed, corrupt

父母 fùmǔ *n* parents

父亲 fùqīn *n* father

付 fù *vb* pay; **fù [fángzū | shuì | lìxī] 付 [房租 | 税 | 利息]** pay [the rent | taxes | interest]

妇女 fùnǚ *n* woman

负担 fùdān 1 *n* burden, load **2** *vb* bear (a burden), shoulder (a burden)

负责 fùzé 1 *vb* be responsible for, be in charge of **2** *adj* responsible, conscientious; **tā duì gōngzuò bú tài fùzé 他对工作不太负责** he is not very conscientious in his work

附近 fùjìn 1 *adj* nearby, close **2** *adv* closely, nearby, in the vicinity of

服 fù mw ▶ **623** (for doses of Chinese medicine)

复习 fùxí vb review, revise

复印 fùyìn vb photocopy, duplicate

复杂 fùzá adj complicated, complex

副 fù 1 mw ▶ **623** (for things that come in pairs or sets)
set, pair; (for facial expressions) **2** adj deputy, assistant,
vice-; **fùxiàozhǎng 副校长** vice-principal; subsidiary,
secondary; **fùzuòyòng 副作用** side-effect

富 fù adj wealthy, rich

Gg

该 gāi 1 vb should, ought to; **wǒ gāi zǒu le 我该走了** I
must leave now, I have to go; be one's turn to do
something; **gāi wǒ le 该我了** it's my turn **2** det this, that,
the above-mentioned; **gāi xuéxiào 该学校** that school

改 gǎi vb change, transform, alter, correct; **gǎi zuòyè 改作
业** correct students' homework

改变 gǎibiàn 1 vb change, alter, transform **2** n change

改革 gǎigé 1 vb reform **2** n reform

改进 gǎijìn 1 vb improve, make better **2** n improvement

改良 gǎiliáng vb change for the better, improve, reform

改善 gǎishàn 1 vb improve, better **2** n improvement

改造 gǎizào 1 vb transform, reform, remould **2** n
transformation, reform

改正 gǎizhèng vb correct, amend, put right

盖 gài vb build, construct; cover; apply, affix with;
gàizhāng 盖章 apply a chop/seal

盖子 gàizi n cover, lid

概括 gàikuò 1 *vb* summarise, generalise **2** *n* summary

概念 gàiniàn *n* concept, notion, idea

干 gān *adj* ▶ *See also* 干 **gàn.** dry; (*taken into nominal kinship*) **gān'érzi** 干儿子 nominally adopted son

干杯 gānbēi *vb* (*when drinking a toast*) "Bottoms up!"

干脆 gāncuì 1 *adj* straightforward, frank, clear-cut **2** *adv* simply, just

干净 gānjìng *adj* clean

干涉 gānshè 1 *vb* interfere with **2** *n* interference

干燥 gānzào *adj* dry, arid

杆 gān *n* pole, post, stake

肝 gān *n* liver

赶 gǎn *vb* (*an animal, an enemy*) drive, drive away; **bǎ tā gǎnzǒu** 把他赶走 chase him away; catch up; hurry, rush; **gǎn huí jiā** 赶回家 hurry home; catch; **gǎnchē** 赶车 catch the bus

赶紧 gǎnjǐn *adv* speedily, at once, hurriedly

赶快 gǎnkuài *adv* in a hurry, hurriedly, at once

赶上 gǎnshàng *vb* catch up with

敢 gǎn 1 *vb* dare, venture, be certain **2** *adj* bold, daring

感到 gǎndào *vb* feel, sense

感动 gǎndòng 1 *vb* (*referring to the emotions*) move, be moved, touch **2** *adj* moving, touching

感恩节 Gǎn'ēn Jié *n* Thanksgiving, Thanksgiving Day

感激 gǎnjī *vb* feel grateful, be thankful

感觉 gǎnjué 1 *vb* sense, feel, perceive **2** *n* perception, feeling

感冒 gǎnmào 1 *vb* catch cold, have a cold **2** *n* cold, flu

感情 gǎnqíng *n* feelings, emotions, sentiments; affection

感想 gǎnxiǎng *n* impressions, feelings

感谢 gǎnxiè 1 *n* thanks, gratitude **2** *vb* thank, be grateful

感兴趣 gǎn xìngqù *vb* be interested in！*The preposition* **duì** 对 *is used to introduce the object of interest expressed by in in English，and the prepositional phrase comes before the verb：***wǒ duì yǔyán gǎn xìngqù** 我对语言感兴趣 I am interested in languages

干 gàn *vb* ▶ *See also* 干 **gān**. do，work；**nǐ xiǎng gàn shénme?** 你想干什么？ what do you want to do?；**gànmá?** 干吗？ why on earth?；**nǐ gànmá mǎi zhè běn shū?** 你干吗买这本书？ why on earth did you buy this book?；**nǐ gànmá?** 你干吗？ what are you doing?

干部 gànbù *n* cadre，government official

干活(儿) gànhuó (r) *vb* work，work on a job，do some work

刚 gāng *adv*（*referring to something that is happening or about to happen*）just this minute，just now，just about to；**tā gāng yào zǒu** 他刚要走 he is just about to leave；（*referring to something that has just happened*）only a short time ago，just；**tā gāng zǒu** 他刚走 he has just left；（*when talking about suitability*）exactly；**zhè shuāng xié gāng hǎo** 这双鞋刚好 this pair of shoes fits perfectly；（*when talking about quantity*）just，no more than；**gāng shíbā suì** 刚 18 岁 just eighteen years old

刚才 gāngcái *adv* just now，just a few minutes ago

刚刚 gānggāng *adv* just now，just a few minutes ago；just，only，exactly

钢 gāng *n* steel

钢笔 gāngbǐ *n* fountain pen

钢琴 gāngqín *n* piano

港 gǎng *n* port，harbour

港口 gǎngkǒu *n* port，harbour

高 gāo 1 *adj* tall，high；advanced，superior；**gāojí** 高级 high-level **2** *adv* in a high/loud voice，loudly；**gāo hǎn** 高

喊 shout at the top of one's voice

高大 gāodà *adj* tall and big

高等 gāoděng *adj* high level, advanced; **gāoděng jiàoyù 高等教育** higher education

高度 gāodù 1 *n* altitude, height **2** *adv* highly, to a high degree

高速公路 gāosù gōnglù *n* motorway

高兴 gāoxìng *adj* happy, pleased, in high spirits

高原 gāoyuán *n* plateau, highland

高中 gāozhōng *n* (abbreviation of **gāojí zhōngxué 高级中学**) senior middle school, senior high school

搞 gǎo *vb* (*work, a task, etc.*) do, work; **gǎo gōngzuò 搞工作** do work; set up, establish, arrange; be involved in

告 gào *vb* tell, inform, notify; accuse, sue; **gào mǒu rén 告某人** sue someone

告别 gàobié *vb* take leave of, say good-bye to

告诫 gàojiè *vb* warn, admonish

告诉 gàosu *vb* tell, inform, let know

哥哥 gēge *n* elder brother

胳膊 gēbo *n* arm

搁 gē *vb* place, put down; **gēxià 搁下** put down, put aside, put to one side, shelve; **gē zài yìbiān 搁在一边** put aside

割 gē *vb* cut, cut down, lop off

歌 gē *n* song

歌剧 gējù *n* opera

歌曲 gēqǔ *n* song

革命 gémìng 1 *vb* revolt, carry out a revolution **2** *n* revolution

格外 géwài *adv* especially, all the more

隔 gé 1 *vb* divide, separate, partition; be separated by **2** *adv* (*when talking about an interval of time*) later, afterwards, every other; gé yì tiān zài lái 隔一天再来 come back a day later; gé yì tiān dǎ yí cì diànhuà 隔一天打一次电话 phone every other day;(*when talking about a physical distance*) apart, at a distance of; gé yì tiáo mǎlù 隔一条马路 one street apart; géchéng… 隔成 … separate into, partition into; bǎ yì jiān wūzi géchéng liǎng jiān 把一间屋子隔成两间 partition one room into two

隔壁 gébì *n* next door

个 gè *mw* ▶ 623 ! *This is the most common measure word. It can take the place of many nominal measure words, and is handy to use if one does not know the measure word that is specific to a particular noun. It usually has a neutral tone, but has a fourth tone when stressed.*

个别 gèbié *adj* individual; very few, rare

个人 gèrén *n* oneself, one's own; zhè shì wǒ gèrén de yìjiàn 这是我个人的意见 this is my personal view;(*as an abstract concept*) the individual **2** *adj* individual, private; gèrénzhǔyì 个人主义 individualism

个体 gètǐ *adj* individual, self-, private

个子 gèzi *n* height, stature, build

各 gè *det* each, every; gèchù 各处 every place, everywhere

各种 gèzhǒng *pron* every kind, all kinds; gèzhǒng bùtóng… 各种不同… all kinds of... , different kinds of... ; gèzhǒng bùtóng de shuǐguǒ 各种不同的水果 all kinds of fruit

各自 gèzì *det* each, respective

给 gěi ! *Can also be pronounced* jǐ 给 *with a different meaning.* **1** *vb* give; tā gěi wǒ yì běn shū 他给我一本书 he gave me a book; (*used with* jiào 叫, ràng 让, *or* bǎ 把 *before the main verb for emphasis*) tāmen bǎ tā gěi dǎ le 他们把他给打了 they gave him a beating **2** *prep* (*when handing over or transferring something to someone*) to, with, for; [jiāo|sòng|jièshào] **gěi tā** [交|送|介绍] 给他 [hand over|give|introduce] to him; (*when doing something for someone*) for, on behalf of, for the benefit of; **gěi tā** [zuòfàn|mǎi shū|shōushi wūzi] 给他 [做饭|买书|收拾屋子] [cook|buy books|clean his room] for him; (*when introducing the recipient of an action, often translated as* let, allow) **gěi wǒ kànkan** 给我看看 let me have a look; **wǒ gěi nǐ kàn yí jiàn dōngxi** 我给你看一件东西 let me show you something; (*indicating the passive voice*) by; **wǒ de shū gěi xiǎotōu tōuzǒu le** 我的书给小偷偷走了 my book was stolen by a thief; **gěi…kàn** 给…看 show (to someone) **qǐng nǐ bǎ nà shuāng xié gěi wǒ kànkan** 请你把那双鞋给我看看 please show me that pair of shoes

根 gēn 1 *mw* ▶ 623 (*for long, thin objects*) **2** *n* (*of a plant or tree*) root; (*of a structure*) foot, base, basis; cause, origin, source

根本 gēnběn 1 *n* root, foundation, base **2** *adj* basic, fundamental, essential **3** *adv* radically, thoroughly; **tā méiyǒu gēnběn gǎibiàn tā de tàidu** 他没有根本改变他的态度 his attitude hasn't radically changed; (*in the negative*) at all, simply; **wǒ gēnběn bù zhīdào** 我根本不知道 I have no idea

根据 gēnjù 1 *prep* on the basis of, according to, in the light of; **gēnjù tā shuō de huà…** 根据他说的话… according to what he said… **2** *n* basis, grounds; **nǐ yǒu shénme gēnjù shuō zhè zhǒng huà?** 你有什么根据说这种话? on what basis do you say this? **3** *vb* base on

跟 gēn 1 *prep* together with, with; **wǒ gēn nǐ yìqǐ qù** 我跟你一起去 I'll go with you; to, towards; **gēn tā shuōhuà** 跟她说话 speak to her; (*with certain verbs*) from; **gēn tā jièshū** 跟他借书 borrow books from him; **wǒ gēn tā xué Zhōngwén** 我跟他学中文 I am learning Chinese from him **2** *conj* (*when connecting two nouns or noun phrases*) and, with；**wǒ gēn tā shì tóngshì** 我跟他是同事 he and I are colleagues **3** *vb* follow，accompany；**qǐng gēnzhe wǒ shuō** 请跟着我说 please say after me

跟前 gēnqián *n* in front of，near

耕地 gēngdì 1 *vb* plough，till **2** *n* cultivated land，arable land

更 gèng *adv* still more，even more；**gèng** [hǎo|dà|yǒuqù]更 [好|大|有 趣]even [better|bigger|more interesting]

更加 gèngjiā *adv* still more，even more；**gèngjiā kěpà** 更 加可怕 even more frightening

工厂 gōngchǎng *n* factory，plant

工程 gōngchéng *n* (as a field of study or work) engineering；project，engineering project，construction work；**gōngchéngshī** 工程师 engineer

工夫 gōngfu *n* free time，leisure time；**wǒ méiyǒu gōngfu** 我没有工夫 I don't have time；work，effort；**huāle hěn dà de gōngfu** 花了很大的工夫 put in a lot of effort；ability，skill

工会 gōnghuì *n* labour union，trade union

工具 gōngjù *n* tool，instrument

工人 gōngrén *n* worker，workman

工业 gōngyè 1 *n* industry **2** *adj* industrial；**gōngyèhuà** 工 业化 industrialization

工艺品 gōngyìpǐn *n* handicraft item

工资 gōngzī *n* wages，salary

工作 gōngzuò 1 *vb* work **2** *n* work，job，employment

公安 gōng'ān *n* public security；**gōng'ānjú** 公安局 public security bureau

公布 gōngbù *vb* make public，announce

公尺 gōngchǐ *n* metre

公费 gōngfèi *adj* at public/state expense，publicly funded；**gōngfèi lǚxíng** 公费旅行 travel at state expense

公分 gōngfēn *n* centimetre

公共 gōnggòng *adj* public, common, communal

公共汽车 gōnggòng qìchē *n* bus; **gōnggòng qìchēzhàn 公共汽车站** bus stop

公斤 gōngjīn *n* kilogram

公开 gōngkāi 1 *adj* open, public, open to the public **2** *vb* make public

公里 gōnglǐ *n* kilometre

公路 gōnglù *n* highway

公民 gōngmín *n* citizen

公平 gōngpíng *adj* fair, just, reasonable

公社 gōngshè *n* commune

公司 gōngsī *n* corporation, company, firm

公用 gōngyòng *adj* public; **gōngyòng diànhuà 公用电话** public telephone

公元 gōngyuán A. D., the Christian era; or C. E., the Common Era; **gōngyuánqián 公元前** B. C., before Christ, or B. C. E., Before Common Era

公园 gōngyuán *n* park

功夫 gōngfu *n* martial arts, kung-fu, skill

功课 gōngkè *n* schoolwork, homework, assignment

功劳 gōngláo *n* contribution, credit, service

攻击 gōngjī *vb* attack, assault

供 gōng *vb* supply, provide, support; **gōng de qǐ 供得起** be able to support financially

供给 gōngjǐ *vb* supply, provide, furnish; **tā mǔqīn gōngjǐ tā dúshū 他母亲供给他读书** his mother supports his studies

供应 gōngyìng *vb* supply

巩固 gǒnggù 1 *adj* (of a foundation, organization, ambition) strong, firm, solid **2** *vb* consolidate, strengthen

共 gòng *adv* together; **gòngshì 共事** work together; in all,

altogether；**zhège bān gòng yǒu èrshí míng xuésheng**
这个班共有 20 名学生 in all there are twenty students in
this class

共产党 gòngchǎndǎng *n* the Communist Party

共产主义 gòngchǎnzhǔyì *n* communism

共和国 gònghéguó *n* republic

共同 gòngtóng 1 *adj* common **2** *adv* together，jointly

贡献 gòngxiàn 1 *vb* contribute，dedicate，devote **2** *n* contribution

狗 gǒu *n* dog

构成 gòuchéng *vb* constitute，make up

构造 gòuzào *n* construction，structure

够 gòu 1 *adj* enough，sufficient，adequate **2** *adv* rather，quite；**gòulèi 够累** rather tired **3** *vb* (*when referring to a certain standard，etc.*) attain，reach，be up to；**tā [gòu de shàng|gòu bú shàng]hǎo xuésheng** 他 [够得上|够不上]好学生 he [is|is not] good enough to be a good student

估计 gūjì 1 *vb* estimate，appraise，reckon **2** *n* estimate，appraisal

姑娘 gūniang *n* girl，young girl

姑姑 gūgu *n* aunt，father's sister

孤立 gūlì *adj* isolated

古 gǔ *adj* ancient，old，old-fashioned

古代 gǔdài *n* ancient times，antiquity

古典 gǔdiǎn *adj* classical

古迹 gǔjì *n* historic site，place of historic interest

古老 gǔlǎo *adj* ancient，age-old

古文 gǔwén *n* ancient Chinese，classical Chinese

骨头 gǔtou *n* bone；**gǔtou jiàzi 骨头架子** skeleton

鼓 gǔ *n* drum

鼓吹 gǔchuī 1 *vb* advocate **2** *n* advocacy

鼓动 gǔdòng *vb* incite，instigate，agitate

鼓励 gǔlì 1 *vb* encourage，urge **2** *n* encouragement

鼓舞 gǔwǔ 1 *vb* encourage, inspire, hearten **2** *n* inspiration, encouragement

鼓掌 gǔzhǎng 1 *vb* applaud, clap one's hands **2** *n* applause

故事 gùshi *n* story, tale

故乡 gùxiāng *n* home town, native place

故意 gùyì *adv* intentionally, deliberately, purposely

顾 gù *vb* turn round to look at; take care of, look after, manage; pay attention to, attend to, take into consideration

顾客 gùkè *n* customer, client

瓜 guā *n* melon, gourd

刮 guā *vb* scrape; **guā húzi 刮胡子** shave; (*as the wind*) blow

挂 guà *vb* (*when speaking of a painting, poster, etc.*) hang up, suspend; **qiáng shang guàzhe yì zhāng huà 墙上挂着一张画** a picture is hanging on the wall; ring, phone, call; **gěi mǒu rén guà diànhuà 给某人挂电话** phone someone; be concerned about; **guà zài xīnshang 挂在心上** keep in mind; register; hang up a receiver; **guàshang 挂上** (*when speaking of a telephone*) hang up

挂号 guàhào 1 *vb* (*at a hospital, at a doctor's office, etc.*) register, take a number **2** *adj* registered; **guàhàoxìn 挂号信** registered letter

拐 guǎi *vb* (*when speaking of walking, riding, cycling, driving, etc.*) turn; **wǎng zuǒ guǎi 往左拐** turn to the left; limp

怪 guài 1 *adj* strange, odd, peculiar **2** *vb* blame

怪不得 guàibude *conj* no wonder, so that's why

关 guān *vb* close, shut, lock; turn off, shut off; (*as a business, school or factory*) close down; concern, involve; **zhè bù guān nǐ de shì 这不关你的事** it's none of your business, this doesn't concern you; **guāndiào 关掉** close, shut, turn off; **guānshang 关上** close, turn off; **bǎ mén**

guānshang 把门关上 close the door

关怀 guānhuái vb show loving care for, show solicitude to

关键 guānjiàn n (when talking about issues, problems, matters) key, crux

关门 guānmén vb close a door; (when speaking of a shop, store, or business) close, shut

关系 guānxì 1 n relationship, connection, tie; bearing, relevance, consequence; méi (yǒu) guānxì 没 (有) 关系 it doesn't matter, don't worry, never mind; (explaining a cause or reason) yóuyú shēntǐ de guānxì, tā jīntiān méiyǒu lái 由于身体的关系, 他今天没有来 because of his health, he didn't come today **2** vb concern, affect, involve; zhè guānxì dào rénmín de shēnghuó 这关系到人民的生活 this concerns the life of the people

关心 guānxīn 1 vb concern oneself with, pay great attention to **2** n concern, care

关于 guānyú prep about, concerning, with respect to; guānyú jīngjì de wèntí 关于经济的问题 the economic problem

关照 guānzhào vb look after, keep an eye on

观察 guānchá 1 vb observe, examine **2** n observation

观点 guāndiǎn n point of view, standpoint, viewpoint

观看 guānkàn vb watch, view

观念 guānniàn n concept

观众 guānzhòng n audience, spectator, viewer

官 guān n government official, officer; government

管 guǎn 1 vb run, manage, be in charge of; zhè jiàn shì shéi lái guǎn? 这件事谁来管? who will take care of this matter?; mind, attend to, bother about; bié guǎn wǒ 别管我 don't concern yourself about me **2** n pipe, tube

管理 guǎnlǐ 1 vb manage, run **2** n management

管子 guǎnzi n tube, pipe

冠军 guànjūn *n* champion

贯彻 guànchè *vb* implement thoroughly, carry out, put into effect

罐头 guàntou *n* tin, can

光 guāng 1 *n* light, ray; brightness, shine, lustre; glory, honour **2** *adj* smooth, shiny; bare, naked; **guāngzhe tóu** 光着头 be bareheaded; used up; **shuǐguǒ màiguāng le** 水果卖光了 the fruit is completely sold out **3** *adv* solely, merely, alone; **guāng shuō bùnéng jiějué wèntí** 光说不能解决问题 we cannot solve the problem solely by talking

光辉 guānghuī 1 *n* splendour, brilliance, glory **2** *adj* splendid, brilliant, glorious

光明 guāngmíng 1 *adj* bright, promising; open, above-board **2** *n* light

光荣 guāngróng 1 *adj* glorious, honourable **2** *n* glory, honour; credit

光线 guāngxiàn *n* light, ray

广播 guǎngbō 1 *vb* (*on radio or television*) broadcast **2** *n* broadcast; **guǎngbō diàntái** 广播电台 broadcasting station; **guǎngbōyuán** 广播员 announcer, broadcaster

广场 guǎngchǎng *n* public square

广大 guǎngdà *adj* vast, broad, extensive; numerous

广泛 guǎngfàn *adj* wide-ranging, widespread, extensive

广告 guǎnggào *n* advertisement; **guǎnggàopái** 广告牌 hoarding

广阔 guǎngkuò *adj* vast, wide, broad

逛 guàng *vb* stroll, roam; **guàng shāngdiàn** 逛商店 go window shopping

归 guī *vb* go back to, return, give back to; turn over to…, be for…to handle, be up to…; **zhè jiàn shì guī tā chǔlǐ** 这件事归他处理 this matter is for him to handle

规定 guīdìng 1 *vb* regulate, prescribe, stipulate **2** *n* rule, regulation

规律 guīlǜ *n* law（of nature），regular pattern

规模 guīmó *n* scale，scope，magnitude；**dàguīmó 大规模** large-scale

规则 guīzé *n* rule，regulation

鬼 guǐ *n* devil，ghost；（*suffix used in some terms of criticism or abuse*）[lǎn｜jiǔ] **guǐ** [懒｜酒]**鬼**[lazy bones｜drunkard]

贵 guì *adj* expensive，costly；precious，valuable；noble，honoured；**guìbīn 贵宾** honoured guest；（*polite word*）your；**nín guìxìng? 您贵姓?** your surname please?

跪 guì *vb* kneel

滚 gǔn *vb*（*for round things*）roll；（*abusive command*）**gǔn chūqù! 滚出去!** get out of here! shove off!；**gǔnkāi! 滚开!** shove off! scram!

棍子 gùnzi *n* rod，stick

锅 guō *n* pot，pan，cooker

国 guó *n* country，nation，state

国防 guófáng *n* national defence

国籍 guójí *n* nationality

国际 guójì *adj* international

国家 guójiā *n* country，nation，state

国民 guómín *adj* national；**guómíndǎng 国民党** Nationalist Party，Kuomintang（KMT）

国旗 guóqí *n* national flag

国庆 guóqìng *n* National Day；**Guóqìng Jié 国庆节** National Day

国王 guówáng *n* king

国营 guóyíng *adj* state-operated，state-run

国语 guóyǔ *n*（*used primarily in Taiwan*）Mandarin Chinese

果然 guǒrán *adv* indeed，sure enough，as expected

过 guò 1 vb cross, pass, pass over; guò [jiē|hé|qiáo]过 [街|河|桥]cross a [street|river|bridge]; (a series of things, a process) go through; (when talking about time, a holiday, a special day, etc.) spend, celebrate; **guò rìzi 过日子** spend one's days; **guò shēngrì 过生日** celebrate one's birthday; exceed, go beyond; (used after a verb to indicate a result) past, through, over; [tiào|fēi|zǒu]guò [跳|飞|走]过 [jump over|fly over|walk past]; (used after a verb to indicate completion of an action) finished, over; **chīguò fàn yǐhòu 吃过饭以后** after eating; (used after de 得 to indicate potentiality) be better than, surpass, get the better of; [shuō|pǎo|dǎ]de guò [说|跑|打]得 过 can [argue|run|fight] **2** adv exceedingly, excessively, too; guò [dà|duō|gāo]过 [大|多|高] exceedingly [big|many|tall]; over, around, over to the other side **3** prep after, over; **guò yíhuìr zài lái 过一会儿再来** come back in a little while

过程 guòchéng n process, course

过分 guòfèn adj excessive

过来 guòlái vb come over, come here; **qǐng nǐ guòlái ba 请你过来吧** please come over here; (after a verb to indicate a direction towards the speaker) **bǎ shū ná guòlái 把书拿过来** bring the book over (to me); (after a verb to indicate returning to a normal state) **xǐng guòlái 醒过来** wake up, regain consciousness

过年 guònián vb celebrate the New Year, spend the New Year

过去 guòqù 1 n the past **2** adj former, previous

过去 guòqu vb go through, get through; **qǐng ràng wǒ guòqù 请让我过去** please let me get through; (after a verb to indicate a direction away from the speaker) **zǒu guòqù 走过去** walk over (there); (after a verb to indicate changing from a normal state) **tā hūn guòqù le 他昏过去了** he's lost his consciousness; (after a verb to indicate success or attainment) **tā hùn guòqù le 他混过去了** he got through by cheating

过 guo *pt*(*after a verb to indicate or emphasize past experience*) have (ever), have (never); **nǐ qùguo Zhōngguó ma?** 你去过中国吗? have you ever been to China?!*To express this idea in the negative,* **méi**(**yǒu**) 没(有), *rather than* **bù** 不, *is used before the main verb;* **tā méi shàngguo xué** 他没上过学 he has never attended school

Hh

哈哈 hāhā *exc* (*to express laughter*) ha ha!; (*to express satisfaction*) aha!

还 hái *adv* ▶ *See also* 还 **huán**. still, yet; (*when making comparisons*) even more, still more; **tā bǐ wǒ hái gāo** 他比我还高 he is even taller than I am; also, too, in addition; rather, fairly; (*for emphasis*) **zhè hái bù róngyì!** 这还不容易! this couldn't be easier!, this is very easy!; (*indicating something unexpected*) **wǒ hái zhēn wàngle tā de míngzi** 我还真忘了他的名字 I really have forgotten his name; **hái … ne** 还 … 呢 still, yet; (*continuing, in suspense*) **wǒ hái méiyǒu chīfàn ne** 我还没有吃饭呢 I still haven't eaten

还是 háishì 1 *adv* still, all the same, nevertheless, ought to, had better; **nǐ háishì bú qù ba** 你还是不去吧 you'd better not go **2** *conj* or

孩子 háizi *n* child, children, son or daughter

海 hǎi *n* sea, ocean

海岸 hǎi'àn *n* coast, seashore

海边 hǎibiān *n* seashore, beach

海关 hǎiguān *n* customs house, customs

海军 **hǎijūn** *n* navy

海外 **hǎiwài** *adv* overseas, abroad

海峡 **hǎixiá** *n* strait

海洋 **hǎiyáng** *n* seas and oceans, ocean

害 **hài** 1 *n* evil, harm, calamity; disadvantage, damage, injury 2 *vb* harm, impair, cause trouble to; kill, murder; suffer from (an illness or disease), become ill; **hàibìng** 害病 become ill

害处 **hàichu** *n* harm

害怕 **hàipà** *vb* fear, be afraid

含 **hán** *vb* hold in the mouth; contain

寒假 **hánjià** *n* winter holiday, winter vacation

寒冷 **hánlěng** *adj* bitterly cold

韩国 **Hánguó** *n* South Korea

喊 **hǎn** *vb* shout, call, yell

汉语 **Hànyǔ** *n* Chinese language

汉字 **Hànzì** *n* Chinese characters

汉族 **Hànzú** *n* Han nationality

汗 **hàn** *n* sweat, perspiration; **chūhàn** 出汗 sweat, perspire

行 **háng** ▶ *See also* 行 **xíng**. 1 *n* line, row; trade, profession, line of business; **nǐ xǐhuan zhè yì háng ma?** 你喜欢这一行吗? do you like this profession? 2 *mw* ▶ **623** (*for things that form a line*)

航空 **hángkōng** *n* aviation, aeronautics; **hángkōngxìn** 航空信 airmail letter

毫不 **háobù** *adv* not in the least, not at all, not the slightest

毫无 **háowú** *adv* without the slightest

好 **hǎo** ▶ *See also* 好 **hào**. 1 *adj* good, fine, alright; in good health, well; (*in comparisons*) better 2 *adv* well; easy to; **kuàizi hǎo yòng** 筷子好用 chopsticks are easy to use; good to (taste, smell, etc.); **hǎo** [**chī** | **hē**] 好 [吃 | 喝] good [to eat |

to drink]; (*emphatic*) how...! so...! very...!; **hǎo lěng de tiānqì!** 好冷的天气! how cold the weather is!; (*when used after a verb to indicate completion*) done, finished; ready; **wǒ zuòhǎo le** 我做好了 I have finished doing it **3** *conj* so as to, so that; **jīntiān xiàwǔ wǒ yào bǎ zuòyè zuòwán, wǎnshang hǎo qù kàn diànyǐng** 今天我要把作业做完, 晚上好去看电影 this afternoon I want to finish all my homework so that I can go to the cinema this evening

好吃 hǎochī *adj* good to eat, tasty, delicious

好处 hǎochu *n* good point, benefit, advantage; profit, gain

好好儿(地) hǎohāor(de) *adv* properly, carefully, thoroughly; **nǐmen yào hǎohāor de yánjiū yíxià** 你们要好好儿地研究一下 you should research this thoroughly

好久 hǎojiǔ *adv* for a long time, a long time since; **hǎojiǔ bú jiàn** 好久不见 haven't seen you for a long time, 'long time no see'

好看 hǎokàn *adj* good-looking, nice-looking, attractive; (*as a book, movie, etc.*) interesting

好容易 hǎo róngyì, 好不容易 hǎobù róngyì *adv* with difficulty, with great effort

好听 hǎotīng *adj* pleasing to the ear, pleasant to listen to

好玩儿 hǎowánr *adj* interesting, amusing, fun

好像 hǎoxiàng *vb* seem as if, seem as though, be like

好些 hǎoxiē *adj* quite a few, a good many of, a great deal of

号 hào *n* mark, sign, signal; (*of size, house, room, telephone*) number; day, date; **jīntiān shísān hào** 今天 13 号 today is the 13th; horn, bugle, bugle call

号码 hàomǎ *n* number

号召 hàozhào 1 *vb* call, appeal to, attract **2** *n* call, appeal

好 hào *vb* ▶ See also 好 **hǎo**. like, love, be fond of; hàoxué 好学 like studying, be eager to learn; be apt to, be liable to, have a tendency to; **hào shēngqì** 好生气 apt to lose one's temper

喝 hē vb drink; drink liquor, drink an alcoholic beverage; **hēzuì** 喝醉 get drunk

合 hé 1 vb come together, join, combine; (as eyes, etc.) close, shut; **bǎ yǎnjing hé qǐlai** 把眼睛合起来 close your eyes; agree, suit, accord with; be equal to, add up to, be equivalent to; **yì yīngbàng hé shísān kuài Rénmínbì** 1 英镑合 13 块人民币 one pound sterling is equal to thirteen yuan in Renminbi **2** adj suitable **3** adv jointly, together with others; **hébàn** 合办 run jointly

合法 héfǎ adj legal

合理 hélǐ adj reasonable, rational

合适 héshì adj suitable, fitting, appropriate

合算 hésuàn adj worthwhile

合同 hétong n contract, agreement

合作 hézuò 1 vb co-operate, collaborate, work together **2** n co-operation, collaboration

河 hé n river

何必 hébì adv what need...? why bother...?, there is no need to...

何况 hékuàng conj let alone, not to speak of; **zhège wèntí lián lǎoshī dōu bù dǒng, hékuàng wǒmen xuésheng ne** 这个问题连老师都不懂，何况我们学生呢 even the teacher cannot understand this problem, let alone we students

和 hé 1 conj (connects parallel expressions) and, together with **2** prep with; **wǒ hé nǐ yíkuàir qù** 我和你一块儿去 I'll go with you; (denoting relations, comparison, etc.) **tā hé wǒ yíyàng gāo** 他和我一样高 he is as tall as I am

和平 hépíng n peace

和气 **héqi** *adj* polite, kind, gentle

盒 **hé** *n* box, case；yì hé cháyè 一盒茶叶 a box of tea

盒子 **hézi** *n* box, case

黑 **hēi** *adj* black；hēisè 黑色 black in colour；(when talking about weather) dark；tiān hēi le 天黑了 it's getting dark

黑暗 **hēi'àn** **1** *adj* black, dark；hēi'àn de yí miàn 黑暗的一面 the dark side **2** *n* darkness

黑板 **hēibǎn** *n* chalk board, blackboard

嘿 **hēi** *exc* hey!

痕迹 **hénjì** *n* trace, track, mark

很 **hěn** *adv* very, quite, very much

恨 **hèn** **1** *vb* hate **2** *n* hate, hatred, regret

横 **héng** *adj* horizontal, across, sideways

红 **hóng** *adj* red

红茶 **hóngchá** *n* black tea

红绿灯 **hónglǜdēng** *n* traffic lights

红旗 **hóngqí** *n* red flag/banner

洪水 **hóngshuǐ** *n* flood

猴子 **hóuzi** *n* monkey

后 **hòu** **1** *adv* later **2** *adj* rear, back, the latter **3** *prep* after, behind；wǔfàn hòu 午饭后 after lunch **4** *conj* after

后边 **hòubian** *n* back, rear

后代 **hòudài** *n* descendant, later generations

后果 **hòuguǒ** *n* result, consequence

后悔 **hòuhuǐ** *vb* regret, feel regretful

后来 **hòulái** *n* on, afterwards

后门 **hòumén** *n* back door (literally and figuratively)

后面 **hòumian**, 后头 **hòutou** *adv* at the back, in the rear, behind；later

后年 **hòunián** *n* the year after next, two years from now

后天 **hòutiān** *n* the day after tomorrow

厚 hòu *adj* thick；deep，profound；large，substantial，generous

呼 hū *vb* call，call out，shout；exhale，breathe out

呼吸 hūxī 1 *vb* breathe **2** *n* breath，breathing，respiration

忽然 hūrán *adv* suddenly，all of a sudden

忽视 hūshì *vb* ignore，overlook

胡乱 húluàn *adv* blindly，confusedly，recklessly

胡说 húshuō 1 *vb* talk nonsense **2** *n* nonsense；húshuō-bādào 胡说八道 total nonsense，utter rubbish

胡同 hútòng *n* lane，alley

胡子 húzi *n* beard，moustache

壶 hú *n* kettle，pot；yì hú kāfēi 一壶咖啡 a pot of coffee

湖 hú *n* lake

糊涂 hútu，糊里糊涂 húlihútú *adj* confused，muddle-headed

户 hù 1 *n* door **2** *mw* ▶ 623（*for households*）

互相 hùxiāng *adv* mutual，mutually

护士 hùshi *n*（*medical*）nurse

护照 hùzhào *n* passport

花 huā 1 *n* flower，blossom，bloom **2** *adj* multicoloured，variegated **3** *vb*（*of money，time，etc.*）spend，expend；huā [qián|shíjiān]花 [钱|时间] [spend money|take time，be time-consuming]

花费 huāfèi *n* expenditure，expenses

花园 huāyuán *n* flower garden，garden

华侨 huáqiáo *n* overseas Chinese

华人 huárén *n* Chinese person with a non-Chinese nationality

划 huá *vb* ▶ See also 划 huà.（*a boat，etc.*）paddle，row；make a scratch/cut，be scratched/cut

滑 huá *adj* slippery，slick，smooth；cunning，crafty

滑冰 huábīng *vb* skate，ice skate

滑雪 huáxuě *vb* ski

化 huà *vb* transform, change, turn into; melt, dissolve; (*after an adjective or noun to form a verb*) -ise or -ize; xiàndàihuà 现代化 modernization

化学 huàxué *n* chemistry; huàxué chéngfèn 化学成分 chemical composition; huàxué fǎnyìng 化学反应 chemical reaction

划 huà ▶ See also 划 huá. **1** *vb* (*a boundary between regions, classes, etc.*) delineate, draw (a line); appropriate, assign, transfer **2** *n* (*when speaking of a Chinese character*) stroke

画 huà *vb* paint, draw; huà huàr 画画儿 draw/paint a picture

画报 huàbào *n* pictorial, illustrated magazine/newspaper

画(儿) huà(r) *n* drawing, painting, picture

话 huà *n* speech, language, words

话剧 huàjù *n* play, modern drama

怀 huái 1 *n* arms, heart, bosom **2** *vb* cherish, harbour (feelings)

怀念 huáiniàn *vb* miss, cherish the memory of, think of

怀疑 huáiyí *vb* doubt, suspect

怀孕 huáiyùn *vb* be pregnant, get pregnant

坏 huài 1 *adj* bad; broken, ruined; (*as food or other perishables*) spoiled **2** *vb* go bad, become spoiled, get out of order; mǐfàn huài le 米饭坏了 the rice has gone bad **3** *adv* (*when used after an adjective, showing an extreme extent*) [lèi|kě|qì]huài le [累|渴|气]坏了 terribly [tired| thirsty| angry]

坏处 huàichu *n* harm, fault, disadvantage

欢乐 huānlè *adj* happy, merry

欢送 huānsòng *vb* send off; huānsònghuì 欢送会 farewell party, send-off

欢喜 huānxǐ 1 *adj* happy, delighted **2** *vb* like, be fond of, delight in

欢迎 huānyíng *vb* welcome, greet

还 huán *vb* ▶ See also 还 hái. go/come back, return, repay; qǐng nǐ bǎ qián huángěi tā 请你把钱还给他 please return the money to him

环 huán *n* ring, hoop, link

环境 huánjìng *n* environment, surroundings, circumstances

缓慢 huǎnmàn *adj* slow, sluggish

幻想 huànxiǎng *n* fantasy, illusion

唤起 huànqǐ *vb* call, arouse

唤醒 huànxǐng *vb* awaken (someone), wake (someone) up

换 huàn *vb* exchange, trade; huàn yī jù huà shuō 换一句话说 to put it another way, in other words

患 huàn *vb* (*when talking about an illness, etc.*) contract, suffer from

荒 huāng *adj* waste; barren, deserted, uncultivated

慌(张) huāng(zhāng) *adj* flurried, flustered, confused

皇帝 huángdì *n* emperor

黄 huáng *adj* yellow

黄瓜 huánggua *n* cucumber

黄河 Huáng Hé *n* Yellow River

黄昏 huánghūn *n* dusk

黄油 huángyóu *n* butter

谎(话) huǎng(huà) *n* lie, falsehood; shuōhuǎng 说谎 tell a lie

灰 huī 1 *adj* grey **2** *n* ash, dust

灰尘 huīchén *n* dust, dirt

挥 huī *vb* wield, wave

恢复 huīfù 1 *vb* recover, restore, re-establish **2** *n* recovery, restoration

回 **huí** 1 *vb* return，go back；answer，reply，reciprocate；turn round 2 *mw* ▶ 623 (*for times*，*occurrences*)

回答 **huídá** 1 *vb* answer，reply 2 *n* answer，response

回教 **Huíjiào** *n* Islam

回来 **huílái** *vb* come back，return；(*when used after a verb to indicate action coming back toward the speaker*) bǎ yàoshi jiāo huílái 把钥匙交回来 hand back the key

回去 **huíqù** *vb* go back，return；(*when used after a verb to indicate action going back to the place of origin*) bǎ shū huán huíqù 把书还回去 return the book

回头 **huítóu** 1 *vb* turn the head round；repent，change one's ways 2 *adv* later；wǒ huítóu qù kàn tā 我回头去看她 I'll go and see her later

回想 **huíxiǎng** *vb* think back，recollect，recall

回信 **huíxìn** 1 *vb* reply to a letter，write in reply 2 *n* letter of reply

回忆 **huíyì** 1 *vb* recall，recollect 2 *n* reminiscence，recollection

毁 **huǐ** *vb* destroy，ruin

汇 **huì** 1 *vb* remit；converge，gather together，collect 2 *n* compilation，collection

会 **huì** ! Can also be pronounced kuài 会 *with a different meaning*. 1 *vb* know how to，be able to，can；huì yòng jìsuànjī 会用计算机 be able to use a computer；know how to use a computer；be likely to，be going to，be sure to；huì bú huì xiàyǔ? 会不会下雨? is it going to rain?；be accomplished in，be skilful in；tā huì hěn duō zhǒng wàiyǔ 他会很多种外语 he can speak many foreign languages；(*when used after a verb to indicate accomplishment*) acquire，master，command；tā xuéhuìle zhè xiàng jìshù 他学会了这项技术 he has mastered the technique；(*to express future tense*) will，shall；kǒngpà nǐ huì tài lèi le 恐怕你会太累了 I'm afraid you'll be too tired；get together，meet，assemble **2** *n* meeting，conference，party；association，society，union

会场 huìchǎng *n* meeting place，conference centre，assembly hall

会话 huìhuà 1 *vb* engage in a conversation/dialogue **2** *n* conversation，dialogue

会见 huìjiàn 1 *vb* meet with **2** *n* meeting

会客 huìkè *vb* receive a visitor/guest；huìkè shíjiān 会客时间 visiting hours；huìkèshì 会客室 reception room

会谈 huìtán 1 *vb* hold negotiations，talk，discuss **2** *n* negotiation，discussion，talk

会议 huìyì *n* meeting，conference

昏迷 hūnmí 1 *vb* faint，lose consciousness，be in a coma **2** *n* coma

婚礼 hūnlǐ *n* wedding ceremony，wedding

婚姻 hūnyīn *n* marriage

浑身 húnshēn *adv* from head to toe，the whole body

混 hùn *vb* confuse，mix up；pass for，pass off as；tā hùn jìnle huìchǎng 他混进了会场 he conned his way into the conference hall；live aimlessly，muddle along，drift along；tā zài Xiānggǎng hùnle yì nián 他在香港混了一年 he idled away a year in Hong Kong；get along with；wǒ gēn tā hùn de búcuò 我跟他混得不错 I get along with him rather well

混乱 hùnluàn *n* chaos，disorder，confusion

活 huó 1 *vb* live，be alive **2** *adj* alive，lively

活动 huódòng 1 *n* activity，event **2** *vb* move about，get exercise **3** *adj* loose，movable，mobile

活泼 huópo *adj* lively，vivid

活儿 huór *n* work；gànhuór 干活儿 work；product

活跃 huóyuè 1 *vb* invigorate，animate **2** *adj* lively，active，

dynamic

火 huǒ *n* fire；anger，temper；firepower，firearms，ammunition

火柴 huǒchái *n* match

火车 huǒchē *n* train；huǒchēzhàn 火车站 railway station

火鸡 huǒjī *n* turkey

火箭 huǒjiàn *n* rocket

火药 huǒyào *n* gunpowder

伙 huǒ *mw* ▶ 623！ *This measure word usually has a negative connotation*；（*for groups or bands of people*）

伙伴 huǒbàn *n* partner，companion

伙食 huǒshí *n* meals，food，board

或（者）huò（zhě） 1 *conj* or，either...or...；huòzhě zuò huǒchē qù，huòzhě zuò qìchē qù，dōu kěyǐ 或者坐火车去，或者坐汽车去，都可以 we can go either by train or by car **2** *adv* maybe，perhaps，probably

货 huò *n* goods，products，commodities

货币 huòbì *n* money，currency

货物 huòwù *n* goods，products，merchandise

获（得）huò（dé） *vb* obtain，acquire，gain，win，achieve；reap，harvest

祸 huò *n* misfortune，disaster

Jj

几乎 jīhū *adv* almost，nearly

机场 jīchǎng *n* airport

机床 jīchuáng *n* machine tool

机关 jīguān *n* organization，agency

机会 jīhuì *n* opportunity

机器 jīqì *n* machine；**jīqìrén 机器人** robot

机械 jīxiè 1 *n* machinery, mechanism, engine **2** *adj* mechanical

鸡 jī *n* chicken

鸡蛋 jīdàn *n* (*of a chicken*) egg！ *Note that in Chinese the kind of egg has to be specified*；**jīdàn 鸡蛋** *is not used for the egg of any animal other than a chicken.*

积极 jījí *adj* positive, affirmative, optimistic；active, energetic, vigorous

积极性 jījíxìng *n* positive attitude, zeal, enthusiasm

积累 jīlěi *vb* accumulate, build up

基本 jīběn *adj* basic, fundamental, essential

基础 jīchǔ 1 *n* foundation, basis **2** *adj* basic, elementary

激动 jīdòng *adj* moving, exciting；excited, moved

激烈 jīliè *adj* heated, intense, sharp

及 jí *conj* (*used between nouns or noun phrases；the noun after jí 及 is often less important than tho one before it*) and, and including

及格 jígé *vb* (*when speaking of a test or examination*) pass, reach an acceptable standard

及时 jíshí *adj* **1** *adj* timely **2** *adv* on time；right away, promptly, without delay

级 jí *n* grade, rank, quality；(*in school*) year, class, grade

极 jí *adv* extremely, exceedingly, to the highest degree；**…jí le …极了** (*follows an adjective when indicating an extreme degree*) extremely；**hǎochī jí le 好吃极了** extremely delicious

极其 jíqí *adv* extremely, exceptionally

即 jí *vb* (*equivalent to jiùshì 就是*) be, be exactly, be none other than；that is, i. e.

即将 jíjiāng *adv* will, going to, about to

即使 jíshǐ，即便 jíbiàn *conj* even if, even though, even

急 jí *adj* anxious, worried, uneasy; in a hurry; angry, annoyed, impatient; (*as a wind, a storm, or water in a river*) violent, strong, fast; urgent, pressing

急忙 jímáng *adv* in a hurry, hurriedly, hastily

集 jí 1 *vb* collect, gather, assemble **2** *n* collection, anthology; volume, part; market, fair; **gǎnjí 赶集** go to market

集合 jíhé *vb* gather together

集体 jítǐ 1 *n* collective **2** *adj* collective

集中 jízhōng 1 *vb* concentrate, amass, put together; centralize **2** *adj* concentrated, centralized

几 jǐ *det* (*when unstressed*) a few, several! *Note that when used with numerals, the meaning of jǐ 几 changes depending on whether it comes before or after the numeral. The phrase jǐshí bù 几十步 means several tens of steps, i.e., 20, 30, 40, etc. (sometimes translated as) dozens or scores), while the phrase shíjǐ bù 十几步 means more than 10 steps, that is, over 10 but under 20;* (*when stressed*) how many? **xiànzài jǐ diǎn le? 现在几点了?** what time is it now?

己 jǐ *n* oneself, one's own

挤 jǐ 1 *vb* crowd, press, squeeze, push, jostle; (*by squeezing an animal's udder*) milk **2** *adj* crowded

计划 jìhuà 1 *n* plan, project **2** *vb* plan, arrange, map out; **jìhuà shēngyù 计划生育** family planning, birth control

计算 jìsuàn 1 *vb* compute, calculate **2** *n* calculation

计算机 jìsuànjī *n* computer

记 jì *vb* remember, keep in mind; record, note, jot down

记得 jìde *vb* remember

记忆 jìyì 1 *vb* remember, recall **2** *n* memory, memories

记者 jìzhě *n* reporter, journalist

记住 jìzhù *vb* remember, keep in mind, learn by heart

纪录 jìlù 1 *vb* record, take notes, keep minutes **2** *n* (*of*

meetings, *etc*.）minutes，notes，record；（*in athletics*，*etc*.）record

纪律 jìlǜ *n* discipline

纪念 jìniàn 1 *vb* commemorate，observe **2** *n* souvenir，memento，keepsake；**yí ge jìniànpǐn 一个纪念品** a souvenir；commemoration，memorial，anniversary

技术 jìshù *n* technique，skill

技术员 jìshùyuán *n* technician

季(节) jì(jié) *n* season

既 jì *conj* since，now that；jì … yě/yòu … 既 … 也/又 … both... and..., as well as；**zhège rén jì nǔlì，yòu cōngmíng 这个人既努力又聪明** this person is both hardworking and intelligent

既然 jìrán *conj* since，now that，as

继续 jìxù *vb* continue，carry on

寄 jì *vb* send，post，mail

加 jiā *vb*（*as a mathematical function*）add，plus；increase，raise

加工 jiāgōng *vb*（*of raw materials*）process into a finished product

加拿大 Jiānádà *n* Canada

加强 jiāqiáng *vb* strengthen，reinforce

加以 jiāyǐ 1 *vb* add more，apply additionally **2** *conj* in addition，moreover

夹 jiā 1 *vb* pinch，squeeze，compress；（*with chopsticks*，*pincers*，*etc*.）pick up，hold；place between，insert between；mix，mingle **2** *n* tweezers，pincers，pliers，fastener，clip；folder

家 jiā 1 *n* home，family，household；（*when it follows a subject or field*）a specialist，a professional；**kēxuéjiā 科学家** scientist；school of thought **2** *mw* ▶ **623**（*for families*，*enterprises*，*restaurants*，*hotels*，*etc*.）

家具 jiājù *n* furniture

家庭 jiātíng *n* family, home

家乡 jiāxiāng *n* home town, native place

假 jiǎ *adj* ▶ See also 假 jià. false, artificial, fake

价格 jiàgé *n* price, charge

价钱 jiàqian *n* price, charge

价值 jiàzhí *n* value, worth, cost

架 jià 1 *mw* ▶ 623 (for aeroplanes, pianos, cameras, etc.) **2** *n* stand, rack, shelf; structure, scaffold **3** *vb* erect, put up; support, help

假 jià *n* ▶ See also 假 jiǎ. holiday, vacation, leave of absence

假条 jiàtiáo *n* leave permit, permit to take leave, doctor's certificate; application for leave

尖 jiān 1 *adj* sharp, pointed; sharp in sound, shrill; (of the senses) keen, acute; [ěrduo| bízi] jiān [耳朵|鼻子] 尖 have an acute sense of [hearing| smell] **2** *n* sharp tip/point, hook

尖锐 jiānruì *adj* (of objects) sharp, pointed; (of perception, analysis, thought, etc.) penetrating, incisive, sharp; (of sound) shrill, piercing; (of activity, struggle, opposition) intense, acute

间 jiān 1 *mw* ▶ 623 (for rooms) **2** *n* room **3** *prep* between, amongst

坚持 jiānchí 1 *vb* hold firmly to, persist in, insist **2** *adj* persistent, insistent

坚定 jiāndìng *adj* firm, resolute, determined

坚决 jiānjué 1 *adj* resolute, decided, determined **2** *adv* decidedly, determinedly

坚强 jiānqiáng *adj* strong, solid]

肩 jiān *n* shoulder

艰巨 jiānjù *adj* extremely difficult

艰苦 jiānkǔ 1 *adj* hard, difficult, tough **2** *n* hardship, difficulty

拣 jiǎn *vb* choose, pick out, select

捡 jiǎn *vb* pick up, gather

检查 jiǎnchá 1 *vb* inspect, examine **2** *n* inspection, examination

减 jiǎn *vb* subtract, minus, take away; decrease, reduce, cut

减轻 jiǎnqīng *vb* lighten, reduce, mitigate

减少 jiǎnshǎo *vb* diminish, reduce, decrease

剪 jiǎn *vb* (*with scissors*) cut, clip, cut off

简单 jiǎndān *adj* simple, easy, uncomplicated

见 jiàn *vb* see, catch sight of; meet; call on, visit, have an interview with; appear, manifest, be evident; (*used as a suffix to certain verbs to indicate successful perception by the senses*) [kàn | tīng | wén] jiàn [看 | 听 | 闻] 见 [see | hear | smell]

见面 jiànmiàn *vb* meet (face to face), see

件 jiàn *mw* ▶ 623 (for luggage, clothes, furniture, matters, etc.)

建 jiàn *vb* build, construct; establish, found, create

建立 jiànlì 1 *vb* establish, set up, create **2** *n* establishment

建设 jiànshè 1 *vb* build up, construct **2** *n* construction

建议 jiànyì 1 *vb* suggest, recommend, give advice **2** *n* suggestion, recommendation, proposal

建筑 jiànzhù 1 *n* building, structure; architecture **2** *vb* build, construct

健康 jiànkāng 1 *adj* healthy, vigorous, robust **2** *n* health

渐渐 jiànjiàn *adv* gradually, step by step

箭 jiàn *n* arrow

江 jiāng *n* river; the Changjiang (Yangtze) River; Jiāngnán 江南 south of the Yangtze River

将 jiāng 1 *adv* about to, going to; jiāng kāishǐ 将开始 about to begin; (*when indicating future tense*) will, shall, be going to **2** *prep* (*used to introduce a verbal phrase by placing the object before the verb; functions like* **bǎ** 把) jiāng tā de xíngli ná huí jiā 将他的行李拿回家 take his luggage back home

将来 jiānglái 1 *n* future **2** *adv* in the future

将要 jiāngyào *vb* will, be going to, be about to; jiāngyào shàngkè de shíhou… 将要上课的时候 …when the lesson is about to start …

讲 jiǎng *vb* say, tell, remark; talk, discuss, negotiate; explain, interpret; pay attention to, be particular about

讲话 jiǎnghuà *vb* talk, speak, converse

讲座 jiǎngzuò *n* lecture

奖 jiǎng 1 *n* prize, award **2** *vb* praise, commend, reward

奖学金 jiǎngxuéjīn *n* scholarship

降 jiàng *vb* descend, fall, drop; lower, reduce, cut down

降低 jiàngdī *vb* lower, drop, reduce

降落 jiàngluò *vb* (*when talking about an aeroplane*) descend, land

酱油 jiàngyóu *n* soy sauce, soya sauce

交 jiāo *vb* hand in, hand over, give up; meet, join, come into contact with; befriend, associate with; jiāo péngyou 交朋友 make friends

交换 jiāohuàn 1 *vb* exchange, swap, interchange **2** *n* exchange, interchange, swap

交际 jiāojì 1 *n* social interaction, communication **2** *vb* be socially active, interact with people

交流 jiāoliú 1 *vb* exchange, interchange **2** *n* exchange, interchange

交谈 jiāotán *vb* converse, have a chat

交通 jiāotōng *n* communications, transportation; traffic

郊区 jiāoqū *n* suburban district, suburbs

骄傲 jiāo'ào 1 *adj* proud, arrogant, haughty; wǒ wèi nǐ

jiāo'ào 我为你骄傲 I'm proud of you **2** n pride, conceit

教 jiāo ! Can also be pronounced jiào with a different meaning; vb teach, train, instruct; jiāoshū 教书 teach

角 jiāo n (a unit of Chinese money); yì jiǎo qián 一角钱 ten fen, 1/10 of a yuan; corner; (in geometry) angle; (of an animal) horn, antler

饺子 jiǎozi n boiled dumpling filled with meat and vegetable

脚 jiǎo n (part of the body) foot; (of an object, mountain, structure, etc.) base, foot, leg

叫 jiào 1 vb call out, cry out, shout; (as a taxi) summon, order, hire; name, call, address as; tā jiào wǒ lǎoshī 他叫我老师 he calls me 'Teacher'; be named, be called; tā jiào shénme míngzi? 她叫什么名字? what is her name?; tell, order; let, allow, permit; tā bú jiào wǒ kàn tā de shū 她不叫我看她的书 she won't let me read her book **2** n (of a bird or animal) call, cry; [gǒu | niǎo] jiào [狗 | 鸟] 叫 [dog's bark | bird's call] **3** prep (when used to introduce the agent in a passive construction) by; tā jiào lǎoshī pīpíngle yí dùn 他叫老师批评了一顿 he was given a reprimand by the teacher

叫做 jiàozuò, **叫作 jiàozuò** vb (when giving the name or term for something) be called, be known as; zhè jiàozuò làngfèi 这叫做浪费 this is called being wasteful

教材 jiàocái n (textbooks, etc.) teaching materials

教练 jiàoliàn n (in sports, etc.) coach, instructor

教师 jiàoshī n teacher

教室 jiàoshì n classroom

教授 jiàoshòu n professor

教学 jiàoxué n teaching

教训 jiàoxùn 1 vb teach (someone a lesson), lecture (someone for wrongdoing); reproach, reprimand, chide **2** n lesson, teaching, moral; cóng shìgù zhōng xīqǔ jiàoxùn

从事故中吸取教训 learn a lesson from the accident

教育 jiàoyù 1 *vb* teach, educate, inculcate **2** *n* education

教员 jiàoyuán *n* teacher, instructor

较 jiào 1 *vb* compare **2** *adv* comparatively, relatively **3** *prep* compared with, than

阶段 jiēduàn *n* (*of development*) stage, phase

阶级 jiējí *n* (*social*) class

结实 jiēshi *adj* (*when talking about objects*) strong, durable, solid; (*of people*) sturdy, tough, strong

接 jiē *vb* (*when referring to guests or visitors*) meet, receive, welcome, pick up; (*when speaking of a letter, a ball, etc.*) receive, take hold of, catch; (*for the telephone, etc.*) answer, accept, take over; connect, join, unite

接触 jiēchù 1 *vb* touch, come into contact with, meet up with **2** *n* contact

接待 jiēdài 1 *vb* (*when referring to guests or visitors*) receive, host, admit **2** *n* reception

接到 jiēdào *vb* receive

接见 jiējiàn *vb* (*when referring to guests or visitors*) receive, meet

接近 jiējìn *vb* approximate, come close to, approach **2** *adj* close to, near to, on intimate terms with

接受 jiēshòu *vb* receive, take, accept

接着 jiēzhe 1 *vb* follow, carry on, catch **2** *adv* right afterwards, following

街 jiē *n* road, street, thoroughfare; downtown, shopping district

街道 jiēdào *n* road, street

节 jié 1 *n* (*of an object*) segment, section, division; sequence of events, proceedings, programme; festival, holiday **2** *vb* save, economize **3** *mw* ▶ **623** (*for sections of things*) section, length, segment; (*for torch batteries, railway*

carriages, class periods at school)

节目 jiémù *n* (of a performance, or on radio or TV) programme, item on a programme

节日 jiérì *n* festival day, holiday

节省 jiéshěng 1 *vb* save, economize **2** *adj* economical, thrifty, frugal

节约 jiéyuē 1 *vb* economize, save **2** *n* austerity

结构 jiégòu *n* structure, construction, composition

结果 jiéguǒ 1 *n* result, outcome **2** *adv* consequently, finally, as a result

结合 jiéhé 1 *vb* join together, unite, marry; combine, integrate **2** *n* unity, combination

结婚 jiéhūn 1 *vb* marry, get married **2** *n* marriage

结论 jiélùn *n* (of an argument or statement) conclusion; (of a law case) conclusion, verdict

结束 jiéshù *vb* finish, conclude, wind up

姐姐 jiějie *n* elder sister

姐妹 jiěmèi *n* sisters

解 jiě *vb* loosen, untie, unfasten; free, relieve, put an end to; dispel, dissolve, be dissolved; understand, comprehend, realize; solve, explain, interpret

解答 jiědá *vb* answer, explain, solve

解放 jiěfàng 1 *vb* liberate, set free, emancipate **2** *n* liberation, emancipation

解决 jiějué *vb* settle, solve, resolve; dispose of, finish off; **tā bǎ nàxiē shèngfàn quán jiějué le** 他把那些剩饭全解决了 he finished all the food that was left over

解释 jiěshì 1 *vb* explain, clarify, interpret **2** *n* explanation, interpretation

介绍 jièshào *vb* introduce, present, recommend; **wǒ gěi nǐ jièshào jièshào** 我给你介绍介绍 let me introduce you

届 jiè *mw* ▶ 623 (for regular sessions, conferences,

sports tournaments , terms of office , etc .) ; (for students graduating in the same year) year , class , grade

界 jiè n boundary , world , circle ; [zìrán | xuéshù | shāngyè] jiè [自然 | 学术 | 商业] 界 [natural world | academic circles | business circles]

借 jiè vb borrow ; gēn tā jièqián 跟他借钱 borrow money from him ; lend ; wǒ bǎ wǒ de cídiǎn jiègěi tā 我把我的词典借给他 I lent my dictionary to him ; use , make use of , take advantage of

斤 jīn n (*a unit in the Chinese weight system*) 1/2 kilogram

今后 jīnhòu adv from now on , in the future , hereafter

今年 jīnnián n this year , the current year

今天 jīntiān n today ; nowadays , the present

金 jīn 1 n gold **2** adj golden

金属 jīnshǔ n metal , metal product

仅 (仅) jǐn (jǐn) adv only , merely , just ; barely , scarcely

尽 jǐn adv * See also **jìn**. to the greatest extent , to the utmost , furthest ; jǐn [zǎo | dōngbian | shàngmian] 尽 [早 | 东边 | 上面] [as soon as possible | the easternmost | the highest]

尽管 jǐnguǎn 1 adv freely , with no hesitation , without restriction **2** conj in spite of , even though , even if ; jǐnguǎn …dōu/yě/hái… 尽管…都/也/还… although… in spite of… still ; jǐnguǎn tā shēntǐ bù hǎo , kě hái jìxù gōngzuò 尽管她身体不好，可还继续工作 in spite of her ill health , she still continues to work

尽量 jǐnliàng, 尽量 jìnliàng adv to the fullest extent , as much as possible , to one's utmost

紧 jǐn 1 adj tight , taut , tense ; urgent , important , pressing ; near , close **2** adv tightly , closely

紧急 jǐnjí adj urgent , pressing , critical

紧张 jǐnzhāng adj (*of a person*) tense , nervous , intense ;

(*of a situation or supply*) critical, tight, short

尽 jìn ▶ See also 尽 jǐn. **1** *vb* exhaust, use up, come to an end; do one's utmost, try one's best, live up to **2** *adv* exhaustively, exclusively, to the highest degree

进 jìn *vb* enter, go into, come into; advance, move forward, go ahead; (*used after a verb to indicate inward direction*) into, in; zǒujìn shāngdiàn 走进商店 walk into the store

进步 jìnbù **1** *n* progress, advancement, improvement **2** *vb* advance, make progress, improve **3** *adj* progressive

进攻 jìngōng **1** *vb* attack, assault **2** *n* assault, offensive, attack

进化 jìnhuà *vb* evolve, develop

进口 jìnkǒu 1 *vb* (*as goods, products, etc.*) import **2** *n* import

进来 jìnlái *vb* (*when indicating a movement toward the speaker*) enter, come in; zǒu jìnlái 走进来 walk in

进去 jìnqù *vb* (*when indicating a movement away from the speaker*) enter, go in; zǒu jìnqù 走进去 walk in

进入 jìnrù *vb* enter, go into, penetrate; be admitted to

进行 jìnxíng *vb* proceed, go ahead, carry on; undertake, engage in

进修 jìnxiū 1 *vb* receive further training, pursue further studies **2** *n* further training

进一步 jìnyíbù 1 *vb* go a step further **2** *adv* further **3** *adj* better

近 jìn *adj* (*in place or time*) near, nearby, close; intimate, closely related

近来 jìnlái *adv* recently, of late, lately

劲 jìn *n* (*physical*) strength, energy, force; (*mental or spiritual*) vigour, drive, spirit; air, manner, expression; kàn tā nà jǐnzhāng jìnr 看他那紧张劲儿 notice how nervous he is; interest, relish, gusto; xué shùxué zhēn méijìn 学数

学真没劲 I don't have any interest in studying mathematics

禁止 jìnzhǐ *vb* forbid, prohibit, ban

京剧 jīngjù, 京戏 jīngxì *n* Peking opera

经 jīng *vb* (*when talking about a place or an experience*) go through, pass through, via; manage, deal in; stand, endure; **tā jīngbuqǐ zhè zhǒng dǎjī 她经不起这种打击** she can't stand this kind of blow

经常 jīngcháng *adv* frequently, often, regularly

经过 jīngguò 1 *vb* (*when talking about a place or experience*) pass by, pass through, go through **2** *prep* as a result of, after, through; by means of **3** *n* process, course

经济 jīngjì *n* economy, economics; financial condition, income

经理 jīnglǐ *n* manager, director

经历 jīnglì 1 *vb* experience, undergo **2** *n* experience, past career

经验 jīngyàn *n* experience

惊奇 jīngqí *adj* surprised, amazed

惊人 jīngrén *adj* astonishing, amazing, alarming

惊讶 jīngyà *adj* surprised, amazed, astonished

精彩 jīngcǎi *adj* brilliant, splendid, wonderful

精力 jīnglì *n* energy, vitality, vigour

精神 jīngshén 1 *n* mind, consciousness; gist, essence, spirit **2** *adj* spiritual, mental

精神 jīngshen 1 *n* vigour, vitality, drive **2** *adj* vigorous, lively, spirited

井 jǐng *n* well

景色 jǐngsè *n* scenery, landscape, scene

警察 jǐngchá *n* police, police officer, policeman

警告 jǐnggào *vb* warn, caution, admonish

竞赛 jìngsài 1 *vb* compete, race **2** *n* competition, race, contest

竞争 jìngzhēng 1 *vb* compete **2** *n* competition

敬爱 jìng'ài *adj* respectful, honourable, esteemed

敬礼 jìnglǐ *vb* salute, give a salute; give a greeting; (*when closing a letter respectfully*) cǐ zhì jìnglǐ 此致敬礼 with best wishes

静 jìng *adj* quiet, peaceful, still

镜子 jìngzi *n* mirror; zhào jìngzi 照镜子 look at one's reflection in the mirror; lens, glass, spectacles; fàngdàjìng 放大镜 magnifying glass, magnifier

纠正 jiūzhèng 1 *vb* correct (a mistake), put right **2** *n* correction

究竟 jiūjìng *adv* after all, in the end; actually, exactly

九 jiǔ *num* nine

九月 jiǔyuè *n* September

久 jiǔ *adv* for a long time, long since

酒 jiǔ *n* wine, liquor, alcoholic drink

旧 jiù *adj* old, used; former, past; old-fashioned, outdated

救 jiù *vb* save, rescue, help

就 jiù 1 *adv* soon, immediately, right away; (*sooner or earlier than expected*) already, as early as, as soon as; tā zuótiān jiù lái le 他昨天就来了 he arrived yesterday; as soon as, right after; tā chīle fàn jiù zǒu le 他吃了饭就走了 he left as soon as he had eaten; only, just, alone; precisely **2** *conj* (*when used in a complex sentence with the second clause introduced by* yě 也) even if, even though; nǐ jiù bù qǐng wǒ, wǒ yě huì lái 你就不请我，我也会来 even if you don't invite me, I'll still come; (*when introducing a subsequent action*) then; zhǐyào nǐ yuànyì, wǒ jiù gēn nǐ yìqǐ qù 只要你愿意，我就跟你一起去 I'll go with you if you wish; (*when used between two identical words or phrases to indicate that one is making a* *concession*) what's done is done, nothing can be done about it; **tā bù lái jiù bù lái ba**, **fǎnzhèng wǒmen bù néng qiǎngpò tā lái** 他不来就不来吧，反正我们不能强迫他来 if he doesn't come, he doesn't come; anyway, we cannot force him to come; (*when used with* **běnlái 本来**, *to mean all along, from the start*) **tā běnlái jiù bù xiǎng xué Déyǔ** 他本来就不想学德语 he never wanted to study German **3** *prep* according to, with regard to

就是 jiùshì 1 *adv* precisely; (*used with* **le 了** *at the end of a sentence to indicate an affirmative and positive sense*) just; **bié dānxīn nǐ de gōngzuò, huíjiā hǎohǎo xiūxi jiùshì le** 别担心你的工作，回家好好休息就是了 don't worry about your work, just go home and get a good rest **2** *conj* (*when used in the sense of* **either... or...**) or; **búshì... jiùshì...** 不是…就是… either... or...; **tā búshì zài túshūguǎn jiùshì zài shítáng** 他不是在图书馆就是在食堂 he is either in the library or in the dining hall; even if, even; **jiùshì... yě** 就是… 也 even..., even if...; **jiùshì tā qù, wǒ yě bú qù** 就是他去，我也不去 I won't go even if he goes

舅舅 jiùjiu *n* mother's brother, uncle

居住 jūzhù *vb* live, reside, dwell

局长 júzhǎng *n* (*of an office, bureau, department, etc.*) head, director, chairperson

橘子 júzi *n* orange, tangerine; **júzishuǐ/zhī** 橘子水/汁 orange juice

举 jǔ *vb* raise, lift, hold up; (*an example, etc.*) cite, enumerate; **jǔ yí gè lìzi** 举一个例子 cite as an example

举办 jǔbàn *vb* (*when talking about an exhibition, competition, etc*) hold, run

举行 jǔxíng *vb* (*when talking about a meeting, ceremony, discussion, etc.*) hold, conduct

巨大 jùdà *adj* great, enormous, huge

句 jù 1 *n* sentence, line of verse 2 *mw* ▶ 623 (*for lines, sentences, units of speech, poetry, etc.*)

句子 jùzi *n* (*when talking about language*) sentence

拒绝 jùjué 1 *vb* refuse, reject, turn down 2 *n* refusal

具备 jùbèi *vb* (*when speaking of necessary conditions, qualifications, or requirements*) have, possess

具体 jùtǐ *adj* concrete, specific, particular

具有 jùyǒu *vb* have, possess, be equipped with

俱乐部 jùlèbù *n* club

剧 jù *n* drama, play, opera

剧场 jùchǎng *n* theatre

据 jù 1 *vb* occupy, seize 2 *prep* according to; **jùshuō 据说** it is said, they say, I hear

距离 jùlí 1 *n* distance, gap, separation 2 *prep* apart/away from, at a distance from; **wǒ jiā jùlí Běijīng sānshí gōnglǐ 我家距离北京 30 公里** my house is thirty kilometres from Beijing

卷 juǎn 1 *vb* roll up; **juǎn qǐlai 卷起来** roll up; sweep off, carry along 2 *n* roll, scroll

决 jué *adv* (*used before a negative word*) definitely, certainly; **wǒ jué bù tóngyì 我决不同意** under no circumstances will I agree

决定 juédìng 1 *vb* decide, make up one's mind 2 *n* decision, resolution

决心 juéxīn 1 *n* determination, resolution, decision 2 *vb* determine, be determined

觉得 juéde *vb* feel, think

觉悟 juéwù 1 *vb* become aware of, become awakened, realize 2 *n* consciousness, awareness, understanding

绝对 juéduì 1 *adj* absolute 2 *adv* absolutely, definitely

军 jūn *n* (*an armed force as a whole*) the army, the military

军队 jūnduì *n* army, armed force

军事 jūnshì 1 *n* military affairs, military matters **2** *adj* military

----

Kk

咖啡 kāfēi *n* coffee; **kāfēiguǎn** 咖啡馆 café

卡车 kǎchē *n* lorry, truck

开 kāi *vb* open; (*a vehicle or engine*) operate, start, run; **kāichē** 开车 drive a car; (*a business, shop, store*) open, be in business; (*a business, shop, store, factory*) set up, establish, run; (*as a ship, vehicle, or troops on a journey or expedition*) set off, start away; (*land, waterway, etc.*) open up, develop, reclaim; (*flowers, trees, etc.*) blossom, bloom; (*a switch, engine, heat*) turn on; (*as a restriction, ban, etc.*) remove, lift, allow; (*meeting, exhibition, performance, school, class*) hold, begin, start; (*setting out in detail*) write, list, itemize; **kāi yàofāng** 开药方 write a prescription; (*for water*) boil; **shuǐ kāi le** 水开了 the water is boiling; (*after a verb to indicate outward movement, getting out of the way, etc.*) away, off, out; [**chuánkāi** | **zǒukāi** | **duǒkāi**] [传开 | 走开 | 躲开] [spread around | get out of the way | step aside]

开放 kāifàng 1 *vb* open to the public, allow public use; be open; **duìwài kāifàng** 对外开放 be open to the outside **2** *adj* liberal, open

开关 kāiguān *n* switch

开会 kāihuì *vb* hold a meeting

开课 kāikè *vb* (*an academic course or class*) give a course, teach; (*referring to a school or university term*)

begin, start

开明 kāimíng *adj* liberal, enlightened, progressive

开幕 kāimù *vb* raise the curtain, begin the show; open, inaugurate

开辟 kāipì *vb* (*a country, route, road, source of revenue, etc.*) open up, develop, utilize

开始 kāishǐ 1 *vb* begin, start, commence **2** *n* beginning, start, outset

开头 kāitóu *n* beginning, opening

开玩笑 kāi wánxiào *vb* make fun of, crack a joke; **gēn tā kāi wánxiào** 跟他开玩笑 make fun of him

开心 kāixīn *vb* feel happy

开学 kāixué *vb* open/begin/start school

开演 kāiyǎn *vb* begin/start a performance, raise the curtain

开展 kāizhǎn *vb* develop, carry out, launch

看 kān *vb* ▶ *See also* 看 **kàn**. look after, take care of; **kān háizi** 看孩子 look after a child

砍 kǎn *vb* chop, cut, cut down

看 kàn *vb* ▶ *See also* 看 **kān**. look, look at, watch; (*silently*) read; think, consider, regard as; **wǒ kàn tā shòu le** 我看她太瘦了 I think she's too thin; visit, call on; (*in changeable circumstances*) depend on; **yào kàn tā máng bù máng** 要看他忙不忙 that depends on whether he's busy or not; (*after a verb, especially when used in reduplicated form*) just... and see, try... and see; **shìshi kàn** 试试看 try and see (how it is, etc.); **wènwèn kàn** 问问看 ask and see (what the person says, etc.)

看病 kànbìng *vb* (*when talking about a patient seeing a doctor*) see the doctor, have an examination; (*when talking about a doctor seeing a patient*) see, examine, treat

看不起 kànbuqǐ *vb* look down on, scorn, despise; **tā kànbuqǐ wǒ** 他看不起我 he looks down on me

看成 kànchéng vb treat as, regard as, consider as

看待 kàndài vb regard, treat

看到 kàndào vb catch sight of, see, notice

看法 kànfǎ n viewpoint, view, way of thinking

看见 kànjiàn vb (implying perception as well as looking) see; wǒ zuìjìn méi kànjiàn tā 我最近没看见他 I haven't seen him recently! When used to negate the verb, bù 不 comes between the two syllables of this word; wǒ kàn bú jiàn nǐ 我看不见你 I can't see you; (when used in the negative, taking on a passive sense) (dis)appear, become (in)visible; hūrán tā kàn bú jiàn le 忽然他看不见了 he suddenly disappeared

看(起)来 kàn(qǐ)lai, 看样子 kànyàngzi vb it looks as if, it seems that, it appears that; [kànlái | kànyàngzi] yào xiàyǔ [看来 | 看样子]要下雨 it looks like rain

慷慨 kāngkǎi adj generous; vehement

扛 káng vb carry on the shoulder/shoulders

抗议 kàngyì 1 vb protest 2 n protest

考 kǎo vb examine, give/take an examination/test; investigate; kǎoshang 考上 (to attain entry to a school or university) to pass entrance exams; kǎoshang dàxué 考上大学 pass the entrance examination to enter university

考虑 kǎolǜ vb consider, weigh, think over

考试 kǎoshì 1 vb take/give an examination 2 n examination, test

考验 kǎoyàn n test, trial

烤 kǎo vb roast, bake; kǎohuǒ 烤火 warm oneself next to a fire

靠 kào 1 vb lean on, lean against; depend upon, rely on; (a person or a livelihood for a living) depend on; tā kào mài jìsuànjī shēnghuó 他靠卖计算机生活 he relies on selling computers for a living; approach, get near to 2 prep near, towards, along; **kào běibù yǒu hěn duō shān 靠北部有很多山** there are many mountains towards the north

科 kē n area/branch of study; **wénkē 文科** the humanities; **lǐkē 理科** the sciences; administrative unit, section, department

科技 kējì n (abbreviation of **kēxué jìshù 科学技术**) science and technology

科学 kēxué n science

科学家 kēxuéjiā n scientist

科学院 kēxuéyuàn n academy of sciences

科研 kēyán n (abbreviation of **kēxué yánjiū 科学研究**) scientific research

科长 kēzhǎng n section chief

棵 kē mw ▶ 623 (for trees, plants)

颗 kē mw ▶ 623 (for small, round things such as pearls, teeth, and hearts; also for things that appear small such as stars, satellites and planets); (for bullets, bombs, etc.)

咳嗽 késou vb cough

可 kě 1 vb may, can, be permitted; approve **2** adv (for emphasis) indeed, certainly, surely; **kě bié wàng le 可别忘了** mind you, don't forget it **3** conj but, yet, however

可爱 kě'ài adj lovely, beloved, lovable, cute

可靠 kěkào adj reliable, trustworthy, dependable

可怜 kělián 1 adj meagre, inadequate, pitiable; poor, helpless, pitiful **2** vb have pity on, feel sorry for, be merciful to; **wǒ hěn kělián tā 我很可怜他** I feel very sorry for him

可能 kěnéng 1 adj possible, probable; **zhè shì kěnéng de 这是可能的** this is possible **2** vb may, might; **tā kěnéng yào qù 他可能要去** he may want to go **3** n possibility; **méiyǒu kěnéng 没有可能** there is no possibility

可能性 kěnéngxìng n possibility

可怕 kěpà *adj* frightful, terrible, dreadful

可是 kěshì *conj* but, yet, however

可惜 kěxī *n* pity; **shízài tài kěxī le 实在太可惜了** it's really such a shame

可笑 kěxiào *adj* laughable, funny

可以 kěyǐ 1 *vb* may, can, may be permitted to; **nǐ yě kěyǐ cānjiā 你也可以参加** you too can take part in it **2** *adj* fine, OK, not bad; **wǒmen de shēnghuó hái kěyǐ 我们的生活还可以** our life is pretty good

渴 kě *adj* thirsty

克 kè *n* (*unit of weight*) gram

克服 kèfú *vb* (*as a difficulty, hardship, inconvenience*) overcome, surmount, conquer

刻 kè 1 *n* quarter of an hour **2** *vb* carve, engrave, inscribe

刻苦 kèkǔ *adj* hard-working, willing to endure hardships; frugal, austere

客观 kèguān *adj* objective

客气 kèqi *adj* polite, courteous, standing on ceremony; unassuming, modest, humble

客人 kèrén *n* guest, visitor

客厅 kètīng *n* living room

课 kè *n* (*in school or university*) class; [shàng|xià]kè [上|下]课 [start|finish]class; course, subject; lesson; dì-yī kè 第 1 课 Lesson One

课本 kèběn *n* textbook

课程 kèchéng *n* course of study, curriculum; **kèchéng-biǎo 课程表** school timetable, lecture list

课堂 kètáng *n* classroom

课题 kètí *n* question for study, research project

课文 kèwén *n* (*of a lesson or in a book*) text

肯 kěn *vb* be willing to, consent to

肯定 kěndìng 1 *vb* affirm, confirm **2** *adj* affirmative, positive, certain

空 kōng 1 *adj* empty, vacant **2** *adv* in vain **3** *n* air, sky, space

空间 kōngjiān *n* empty space; (*beyond the earth's orbit*) space

空军 kōngjūn *n* airforce

空气 kōngqì *n* air, atmosphere; (*in a figurative sense: social, political, aesthetic, etc.*) atmosphere; jīntiān xuéxiào de kōngqì hěn jǐnzhāng 今天学校的空气很紧张 there is a tense atmosphere at school today

空前 kōngqián 1 *adj* unprecedented **2** *adv* in an unprecedented fashion

空调 kōngtiáo (*abbreviation of* kōngqì tiáojiéqì 空气调节器) air conditioner

空中 kōngzhōng *n* in the sky, in the air; kōngzhōng xiǎojiě 空中小姐 air hostess

孔 kǒng *n* opening, hole, empty space

孔子 Kǒngzǐ *n* Confucius

恐怕 kǒngpà 1 *adv* probably, perhaps **2** *vb* be afraid that, think that; kǒngpà tā bù lái le 恐怕他不来了 I'm afraid he's not coming

空儿 kòngr *n* empty space, vacant space; leisure, spare time; wǒ méiyǒu kòngr 我没有空儿 I don't have time

控制 kòngzhì 1 *vb* control, dominate **2** *n* control, hold

口 kǒu 1 *n* mouth; (*of a river, building, etc.*) opening, entrance; cut, wound, tear **2** *mw* ▶ 623 (*for the number of people in a family or village*); (*for spoken languages, used with the verb "speak" and with the number one,* yì 一)

口袋 kǒudài *n* pocket, bag, sack

口号 kǒuhào *n* slogan

口气 kǒuqì *n* tone, note, implication

口头 **kǒutóu** adj oral

口音 **kǒuyīn** n accent

口语 **kǒuyǔ** n spoken language

扣 **kòu 1** vb button, fasten; deduct, reduce; (for a criminal) detain, arrest **2** n button; kòuzi 扣子 button; kòushang 扣上 button up

哭 **kū** vb cry, weep

苦 **kǔ 1** adj (in taste) bitter; (in life) bitter, difficult, painful **2** adv painstakingly, earnestly, at one's utmost **3** n hardship, suffering, misery **4** vb cause (someone) suffering

苦难 **kǔnàn** n hardship, misery, suffering

裤子 **kùzi** n trousers

夸奖 **kuājiǎng** vb praise, commend

夸张 **kuāzhāng** vb exaggerate, overstate

垮 **kuǎ** vb collapse, fall

跨 **kuà** vb step astride, step across, take a step; (when talking about a horse or other animal for riding) mount; transcend, go beyond, go over; kuà dìqū 跨地区 transregional

块 **kuài 1** n piece, lump, cube; bīngkuài 冰块 ice cubes; (units of money) dollar, yuan; liùbǎi kuài qián 600 块钱 six hundred yuan **2** mw ▶ **623** (for things that come in chunks or solid pieces) (for things that are shaped like sheets) (for slices, sections, divisions, etc.)

快 **kuài 1** adj fast, quick; (of a knife) keen, sharp; zhè bǎ jiǎnzi hěn kuài 这把剪子很快 this pair of scissors is very sharp; (when used with a negative) unhappy, joyful; xīnzhōng búkuài 心中不快 heavy-hearted **2** adv almost, soon, about to; tā kuài yào bìyè le 她快要毕业了 she will graduate soon; quickly; kuài huílái 快回来 come back quickly **3** vb hurry; kuài diǎnr! 快点儿! hurry up! quickly!

快活 **kuàihuo** *adj* happy, cheerful

快乐 **kuàilè 1** *adj* happy, joyful **2** *n* happiness, joy

筷子 **kuàizi** *n* chopsticks

宽 **kuān** *adj* wide, broad; generous, broad-minded, liberal

款 **kuǎn** *n* fund, funds, money

狂 **kuáng** *adj* mad, deranged, crazy

况且 **kuàngqiě** *adv* moreover, besides

矿 **kuàng** *n* ore/mineral deposit; mine, excavation

捆 **kǔn 1** *vb* tie into a bundle, bind up, tie up; **kǔn qǐlai** 捆起来 tie up **2** *n* bundle

困 **kùn 1** *adj* sleepy; in difficulty, stranded, hard-pressed **2** *vb* surround

困难 **kùnnan 1** *n* difficulty, quandary, hardship **2** *adj* difficult, hard to cope with

扩大 **kuòdà 1** *vb* enlarge, expand, spread out **2** *n* expansion

LI

拉 **lā** *vb* pull, drag; haul, transport by vehicle; (*certain musical instruments*) play; **lā** [**xiǎotíqín**] **shǒufēngqín**] 拉 [小提琴] 手风琴] play the [violin] accordion]; extend, extenuate, draw out; implicate, drag in; **lā guānxi** 拉关系 use one's influence/connections; **lā dùzi** 拉肚子 have diarrhoea; **lākāi** 拉开 pull open; space out, widen; **lāshang** 拉上 (*curtains, etc.*) draw, close

垃圾 **lājī** *n* rubbish, garbage, trash

啦 **la** *pt* (a fusion of le 了 and a 啊, which incorporates the function of le 了 while denoting exclamation or interrogation) **tā yǐjīng dāying la!** 他已经答应啦! he has already agreed!

喇叭 lǎbα *n* horn or other brass wind instrument; loudspeaker

蜡烛 làzhú *n* candle

辣 là *adj* hot, spicy, peppery

辣椒 làjiāo *n* hot pepper, chili pepper

来 lái 1 *vb* come, arrive; do; ràng wǒ lái 让我来 let me do it; bring; zài lái yì wǎn fàn 再来一碗饭 bring another bowl of rice; (*when following a verb to indicate direction of action*) qǐng nǐ guòlai 请你过来 please come over here; (*when following de 得 or bù 不 to indicate possibility*) chī [de|bù] lái 吃 [得|不] 来 [it is] it is not] to (someone's) taste! *The word* lái 来 *regularly follows certain verbs as a complement*, *such as* qǐ 起 *in* qǐlai 起来, chū 出 *in* chūlái 出来, guò 过 *in* guòlái 过来, *and so forth. For these expressions*, *see the verbs that precede* lái 来. *In other instances it follows a verb as a directional complement*, *as in* shànglái 上来 come up, *and* xiàlái 下来, come down. **2** *prep* (*with time expressions*) since, for, during; sān nián (yǐ) lái 3 年(以)来 during the past three years **3** *adv* (*following a numeral that acts as an adjective*) about, approximately, over; shí lái gè 十来个 over ten; (*when preceding the main verb*, *to indicate purpose*) to, in order to

来不及 láibují *vb* be unable to do in time, lack sufficient time for

来得及 láidejí *vb* be able to do in time, have enough time for

来回 láihuí 1 *adv* back and forth, to and fro **2** *n* return journey, round trip

来往 láiwǎng 1 *vb* come and go **2** *n* contacts, dealings

来信 láixìn *n* your letter, a letter from...

来自 láizì *vb* come from, originate from

拦 lán *vb* hinder, obstruct, block

蓝 lán *adj* blue

篮球 lánqiú *n* basketball

懒 lǎn *adj* lazy,idle,indolent;sluggish,drowsy

烂 làn *adj* (of fruit,a wound,*etc.*) rotten,over-ripe,festering;(of clothes,cloth) ragged,worn-out;(of meat,stew,*etc.*) well-done,thoroughly cooked

狼 láng *n* wolf

朗读 lǎngdú *vb* read aloud

浪 làng *n* wave

浪费 làngfèi 1 *vb* waste,squander **2** *adj* extravagant,wasteful **3** *n* extravagance,waste

浪漫 làngmàn *adj* romantic

捞 lāo *vb* trawl,dredge,drag for (fish,*etc.*)

劳动 láodòng *vb* work,labour;toil

劳驾 láojià *vb* (polite expression) excuse me...? may I trouble you...? would you mind...?

老 lǎo 1 *adj* old,elderly,aged;long-term,of long standing;**lǎopéngyou 老朋友** an old friend;old-fashioned,outdated;(of vegetation) tough;(of meat) overgrown; (prefix before ordinal numbers to differentiate between children of a family)lǎo（dà|èr…）老 [大｜二…] [eldest｜second eldest...]; (courteous or affectionate prefix to a name,title,or relationship)lǎo（Zhāng|xiānsheng|dàgē）老 [张｜先生｜大哥] [my pal Zhang｜Sir｜dear elder brother] **2** *adv* always,ever,keep on; tā lǎo zhème shuō 他老这么说 he always says this; lǎoshì 老是 always,ever,keep on; (with a negative) hardly ever,rarely,seldom; tā lǎoshì bú niànshū 他老是不念书 he hardly ever studies

老百姓 lǎobǎixìng *n* common people,ordinary people

老板 lǎobǎn *n* boss,employer,shopkeeper

老大妈 lǎodàmā,大妈 dàmā *n* (respectful address for an older woman) Madam,granny,aunty

老大娘 lǎodàniáng n (respectful address for an older woman) Madam, granny, aunty

老大爷 lǎodàye, 大爷 dàye n (respectful address for an older man) Sir, grandpa

老虎 lǎohǔ n tiger

老家 lǎojiā n home town, old home

老师 lǎoshī n teacher

老实 lǎoshi 1 adj honest, frank, trustworthy; well-behaved; simple-minded, naive **2** adv honestly, truthfully

老鼠 lǎoshǔ n mouse, rat

老太太 lǎotàitai n (term of respect for an elderly woman) Madam, old lady

老头儿 lǎotóur n (rude word for an old man) old man

乐 lè ! Can also be pronounced **yuè** with a different meaning; adj happy, joyful

乐观 lèguān 1 adj optimistic, positive **2** n optimism

乐趣 lèqù n pleasure, joy

了 le pt ▶ See also 了 **liǎo**. (indicating a past event) tā shàngge xīngqī qù le 他上个星期去了 he went last week; (indicating a completed action) tā zǒu le 他走了 he has gone; (indicating a change of situation or state) tā bìng le 他病了 he's been taken ill; "huǒchē láile méiyǒu?"—"méi lái"「火车来了没有?"—"没来" 'has the train come?'—'no, it hasn't'! Note that le 了 is usually negated with méi 没, rather than with bù 不; (used with bù 不 to mean no longer, not any more) wǒ bù xiě le 我不写了 I'm not writing (it) any more; (used with búyào 不要 or bié 别 to stop someone from doing something) búyào jiǎng le 不要讲了 stop talking about it, don't talk about it any more

雷 léi n thunder; **léiyǔ 雷雨** thunderstorm

泪 lèi n tear, tears, teardrop

类 lèi 1 *n* category, sort, type **2** *mw* ▶ **623** kind of, sort of

类似 lèisì 1 *vb* resemble, be similar to, be like **2** *adj* similar, like

累 lèi *adj* tired, fatigued, weary

冷 lěng *adj* cold

冷静 lěngjìng *adj* calm, sober, clear-headed

冷饮 lěngyǐn *n* cold drink

厘米 límǐ *n* centimetre

离 lí 1 *vb* leave, part, separate from **2** *prep* from, off, away from; xuéxiào lí zhèr sān yīnglǐ lù 学校离这儿 3 英里路 the school is three miles from here

离婚 líhūn *vb* divorce, be divorced

离开 líkāi *vb* depart, leave, separate

梨 lí *n* pear

礼 lǐ *n* ceremony, ritual; propriety, courtesy, manners; gift, present

礼拜 lǐbài *n* week; (*used for the days of the week*) lǐbài [yī|èr|sān···] 礼拜 [一|二|三···] [Monday | Tuesday | Wednesday···]

礼拜天 lǐbàitiān, 礼拜日 lǐbàirì *n* Sunday

礼貌 lǐmào 1 *n* courtesy, politeness, manners **2** *adj* polite, courteous

礼堂 lǐtáng *n* assembly hall, auditorium

礼物 lǐwù *n* present, gift

里 lǐ 1 *n* (*unit of length*, 1/2 *kilometre*) Chinese mile, li **2** *prep* in, inside, among; wū li 屋里 in the room

里边 lǐbiān, 里面 lǐmiàn 1 *prep* inside, in, within; wūzi lǐbian yǒu sān gè rén 屋子里边有 3 个人 there are three people in the room **2** *n* inside, within; tā zài lǐbian 他在里边 he is inside

里头 lǐtou (*informal, colloquial*) ▶ lǐbian 里边

理发 lǐfà *vb* have a haircut, have one's hair cut/styled

理解 **lǐjiě** **1** *vb* understand, comprehend **2** *n* understanding, comprehension

理科 **lǐkē** *n* (*a branch of learning*) science, natural sciences

理论 **lǐlùn** *n* theory, theoretical idea

理想 **lǐxiǎng** *n* ideal, dream

理由 **lǐyóu** *n* reason, argument

力 **lì** *n* strength, power, force

力量 **lìliang** *n* strength, force, power

力气 **lìqi** *n* physical strength, effort, energy

历史 **lìshǐ** *n* history, record of the past

立 **lì** *vb* stand; establish, set up, erect

立场 **lìchǎng** *n* standpoint, position, point of view

立方 **lìfāng** *n* cube; cubic metre; **sān lìfāng shāzi** 3 立方 沙子 three cubic metres of sand

立即 **lìjí** *adv* immediately, right away

立刻 **lìkè** *adv* immediately, right away

厉害 **lìhài** *adj* (*when talking about the weather, etc.*) severe, extreme; **zhèr de tiānqì rè de lìhài** 这儿的天气 热得厉害 the weather here is extremely hot; (*as a teacher or disciplinarian*) formidable, strict

利息 **lìxī** *n* (*when talking about finance*) interest

利益 **lìyì** *n* interest, benefit

利用 **lìyòng** *vb* utilize, make use of, take advantage of

例 **lì** *n* example, case, instance; **lìrú** 例如 for example, for instance, such as

例外 **lìwài** *n* exception

例子 **lìzi** *n* example, instance

粒 **lì** *mw* ▶ **623** (*for small, round things, such as peas, peanuts, bullets, or grains*)

俩 **liǎ** *num* (*colloquial*) two; some, several

连 **lián** **1** *vb* connect, link, join **2** *adv* in succession, one after the other;even,including;**lián···dōu/yě···** 连···都/也··· even...;**lián tā dōu bù zhīdào** 连他都不知道 even he doesn't know

连接 liánjiē vb join,link

连忙 liánmáng adv promptly,at once

连续 liánxù adv continuously,successively,one after the other;**liánxùjù** 连续剧(on TV or radio) a serial,a series

联合 liánhé vb unite,join together,ally

联合国 Liánhéguó n the United Nations

联欢 liánhuān 1 vb have a get-together/party **2** n social get-together

联系 liánxì 1 vb connect,make connections with,link **2** n connection,link

脸 liǎn n face;self-respect,honour; **diūliǎn** 丢脸 lose face

练 liàn vb train,practise,drill

练习 liànxí 1 vb practise,exercise **2** n practise,drill; **liànxíbù/běn** 练习簿/本 exercise book

恋爱 liàn'ài n love,love affair

良好 liánghǎo adj good,well

凉 liáng ▶ See also 凉 **liàng. 1** adj cool,cold; discouraged,disappointed **2** n cold,flu; **zháoliáng** 着凉 catch cold

凉快 liángkuài adj cool,pleasantly cool

量 liáng vb ▶ See also 量 **liàng.** (for length,weight, distance,etc.) measure

粮食 liángshi n food,provisions,grain

两 liǎng 1 num ! Note that **liǎng** 两 is like **èr** 二 but tends to be used in combination with measure words and nouns to specify two of something; two; **liǎng zhāng zhǐ** 两张纸 two sheets of paper **2** det ! Note that **liǎng** 两 in this sense is usually unstressed;a few,some,a couple of; **shuō liǎng jù** 说两句 speak a few words **3** pron both **4** n (*traditional unit of weight equivalent to* 1.33 *English ounces or* 0.05 *kilo*)；**yì liǎng jiǔ 一两酒** an ounce of liquor

亮 liàng 1 *adj* bright, light, shiny **2** *vb* get light, be light, be switched on

凉 liàng *vb* ▶ *See also* 凉 **liáng.** cool, allow to cool

晾 liàng *vb* dry in the air/sun

辆 liàng *mw* ▶ **623** (*for vehicles*)

量 liàng *n* ▶ *See also* 量 **liáng.** amount, quantity, capacity

聊 liáo *vb* chat idly；**wǒ xiǎng gēn nǐ liáoliao 我想跟你聊聊** I'd like to have a chat with you

聊天儿 liáotiānr *vb* chat to pass the time of day

了 liǎo *vb* ▶ *See also* 了 **le!** *Can also be pronounced* liào *with a different meaning:* finish, end；**wǒ shénme shíhou néng liǎole zhè jiàn shì? 我什么时候能了了这件事?** when will I be able to finish this task?；(*after* dé 得 *or* bù 不 *to indicate the possibility or impossibility of accomplishing or finishing something*)；**zhège bèibāo zhuāng [de|bu]liǎo zhèxiē dōngxi 这个背包装[得|不]了这些东西** this backpack [can|cannot]hold these things

了不起 liǎobuqǐ *adj* extraordinary, astounding, amazing

了解 liǎojiě 1 *vb* understand, comprehend, know；find out, inquire；**liǎojiě yíxià zhèr de shēnghuó 了解一下这儿的生活** find out about the life here **2** *n* understanding, knowledge

列 liè 1 *vb* list, arrange in order, enumerate **2** *mw* ▶ **623** (*for trains*)

列车 lièchē *n* train；**lièchēyuán 列车员** train attendant

邻居 línjū *n* neighbour

临 lín 1 *vb* face, overlook；(*when talking about problems, decisions*) face, confront **2** *adv* on the point of, upon coming to...；**línzǒu 临走** about to depart

临时 línshí 1 *adj* temporary，provisional，last-minute **2** *adv* at the time，at the last moment，when the time comes；**tā línshí juédìng bú qù Běijīng le** 他临时决定不去北京了 he made a last-minute decision not to go to Beijing

淋浴 línyù *n* shower

灵魂 línghún *n* spirit，soul，mind

灵活 línghuó *adj* (*referring to mental capacities，etc.*) quick-witted，resourceful，agile；(*when describing actions， movements，etc.*) nimble，quick；(*when talking about the quality of material objects*) flexible，elastic

铃 líng *n* bell，small bell

零 líng *num* zero，nought

零钱 língqián *n* small change，pocket money

龄 líng *n* age，years；length of time，duration

领 lǐng 1 *vb* lead，command，usher；(*as a prize，award， pension，etc.*) receive，draw，get **2** *n* neck，collar

领带 lǐngdài *n* tie，necktie

领导 lǐngdǎo 1 *vb* lead，be a leader **2** *n* leadership， guidance

领会 lǐnghuì *vb* understand，comprehend

领土 lǐngtǔ *n* territory

领袖 lǐngxiù *n* leader，chief

另 lìng 1 *adj* another，other；**lìng yì fāngmiàn···** 另一方面··· another aspect...，on the other hand... **2** *adv* separately，another；**lìng zhǎo yí gè fāngfǎ** 另找一个方法 look for another method

另外 lìngwài 1 *adj* separate，other，another；**lìngwài yí gè rén** 另外一个人 another person **2** *adv* separately， besides，in addition；**lìngwài xiě yí gè jùzi** 另外写一个句子 write another sentence

留 liú *vb* keep，preserve，save；stay，remain，linger；allow to stay，ask to stay，detain；**wǒ xiǎng liú nǐ zài wǒ jiā zhù jǐ tiān** 我想留你在我家住几天 I would like you to stay at my house for a few days；leave，leave behind；**bǎ shūbāo liú zài jiālǐ** 把书包留在家里 leave the satchel at home

留念 liúniàn 1 vb accept/keep as a souvenir **2** n souvenir，keepsake

留学 liúxué vb study abroad；liúxuéshēng 留学生 student studying abroad

流 liú 1 vb flow **2** n flow，stream，current；［hé｜diàn｜qì］liú ［河｜电｜气］流 ［river｜electric current｜air current］；class，grade

流传 liúchuán vb spread，circulate，pass down

流利 liúlì adj fluent，smooth

流氓 liúmáng n hooligan，gangster，rogue

流行 liúxíng adj popular，fashionable，prevalent

六 liù num six

六月 liùyuè n June

龙 lóng n dragon

聋 lóng adj deaf，hearing impaired

楼 lóu n (of more than one story) building，tower；storey，floor；yī lóu 一楼 ground floor (British English)，first floor (US English)；lóushàng 楼上 upstairs；lóuxià 楼下 downstairs

楼梯 lóutī n stairs，stairway

漏 lòu vb leak，flow/drip out；disclose，divulge；leave out，omit，be missing

露 lòu ▶露 lù

卤鸭 lǔyā n pot-stewed duck

陆地 lùdì n dry land，land

陆续 lùxù adv in succession，one after another

录 lù vb (on tape) record，copy

录像 lùxiàng 1 vb make a video recording，record on videotape **2** n video recording；lùxiàngdài 录像带 video tape；lùxiàngjī 录像机 video cassette recorder，VCR

录音 lùyīn 1 vb make a sound recording，tape-record，tape **2** n sound recording，audio-tape；lùyīndài 录音带 magnetic tape，tape；lùyīnjī 录音机 tape recorder

鹿 lù n deer

路 lù n road，path，route；journey，distance；way，means；(referring to the number of a bus route，etc.) route；yāo líng sì lù (qìchē)104 路(汽车)No. 104 (bus)

路过 lùguò vb pass by/through (a place)

路口 lùkǒu n crossing，intersection

路上 lùshang adv on the way，on the road

路线 lùxiàn n route，line，approach

露 lù vb show，reveal，betray

露天 lùtiān n in the open air，open air，outdoors

旅馆 lǚguǎn n hotel

旅客 lǚkè n traveller，passenger，hotel guest

旅途 lǚtú n journey，trip，route

旅行 lǚxíng vb travel，journey，trip；lǚxíngshè 旅行社 travel service，travel agency

旅游 lǚyóu vb tour，travel

律师 lǜshī n solicitor，barrister，lawyer

绿 lǜ adj green

乱 luàn 1 adj in a mess，in confusion，in turmoil **2** adv in a disorderly manner，recklessly

乱七八糟 luànqībāzāo adj in a mess，in a muddle，in confusion

略 lüè 1 vb omit，leave out **2** adv slightly，a little，briefly

伦敦 Lúndūn n London

轮船 lúnchuán n steamer，steamship，steamboat

论文 lùnwén n thesis，dissertation，treatise

萝卜 luóbo n turnip，radish

落 luò *vb* fall, drop, come down; lower; **bǎ liánzi luò xiàlái 把帘子落下来** lower the blinds; (*referring to the sun or moon*) set, go down; **tàiyáng luòshān le 太阳落山了** the sun has set; lag behind, fall behind, decline; leave behind, result in

落后 luòhòu 1 *adj* backward, behind the times **2** *vb* fall behind, be backward

Mm

妈 mā *n* mother; **māma 妈妈** mother, mum

麻烦 máfan 1 *vb* trouble, bother; **máfan nǐ le 麻烦你了** sorry to have troubled you **2** *adj* troublesome, bothersome, annoying **3** *n* trouble, bother

马 mǎ *n* horse

马虎 mǎhu *adj* careless, casual, in a sloppy manner

马克 mǎkè *n* (*former monetary unit of German currency*) mark

马路 mǎlù *n* street, avenue

马马虎虎 mǎmǎ-hūhū *adj* so-so; careless, casual

马上 mǎshàng *adv* immediately, at once; **wǒ mǎshàng jiù lái 我马上就来** I'll be right there

码头 mǎtou *n* dock, pier, wharf

骂 mà *vb* curse, swear, scold

吗 ma *pt* (*used to turn a declarative sentence into a question*) **shì nǐ ma? 是你吗?** is it you?

嘛 ma *pt* (*used to show that something is obvious*) **zhè shì wǒ de ma! 这是我的嘛!** obviously this is mine!; (*used to mark a pause*) **zhège wèntí ma, wǒ lái jiějué 这个问题嘛, 我来解决** as for this question, let me solve it

埋 mái vb bury, hide in the ground

买 mǎi vb buy, purchase; mǎi dōngxi 买东西 go shopping, buy things! *Note that in expressions denoting buying something for someone, the English word for is rendered as* gěi *or* gěi; nǐ gěi tā mǎi shū ma? 你给她买书吗? do you buy books for her?; mǎi de qǐ 买得起 able to afford

买卖 mǎimai n business, trade; zuò mǎimai 做买卖 do business, engage in a trade

迈 mài vb take a step, stride; màiguò 迈过 step over

麦(子) mài(zi) n wheat

卖 mài vb sell, sell for; nà tái diànshìjī mài duōshao qián? 那台电视机卖多少钱? how much is the TV selling for?; màigěi… 卖给… sell to; nǐ bǎ jìsuànjī màigěi shéi? 你把计算机卖给谁? to whom are you selling the computer?; mài [de|bu]chū(qù) 卖[得|不]出(去) [able to| unable to] sell (well)

馒头 mántou n steamed bun, steamed bread

满 mǎn 1 adj full, filled; whole, entire; mǎn tiān xīngxing 满天星星 the sky is filled with stars; satisfied, content, satisfactory **2** adv quite, rather; mǎn shūfu 满舒服 quite comfortable **3** vb reach, reach the limit of; tā hái bù mǎn shíbā suì 他还不满18岁 he still hasn't reached the age of 18

满意 mǎnyì 1 adj satisfied, pleased **2** vb be pleased, be satisfied

满足 mǎnzú 1 vb be content, be satisfied; fulfill, satisfy, meet **2** adj satisfied, content

慢 màn 1 adj slow **2** adv slowly

忙 máng adj busy, occupied, bustling; nǐ máng shénme? 你忙什么? what are you so busy doing? what are you doing?; diànhuà xiànlù hěn máng 电话线路很忙 the telephone lines are busy; máng bú guòlái 忙不过来

(referring to too much work) unable to manage; **mángzhe …忙着** be busy doing...; **mángzhe xiě zuòwén 忙着写作文** busy writing an essay

猫 māo n cat; **xiǎomāo 小猫** kitten

毛 máo n (a unit of Chinese money) ten fen, 1/10 of a yuan; **wǔ máo qián 5 毛钱** five mao; hair on the body, fur; feather, down; wool

毛笔 máobǐ n writing brush

毛病 máobìng n trouble, defect; **zhè liàng qìchē chángcháng chū máobìng 这辆汽车常常出毛病** this car often breaks down; illness, fault, shortcoming, bad habit

毛巾 máojīn n towel

毛衣 máoyī n jumper, sweater

矛盾 máodùn 1 n contradiction, inconsistency 2 adj contradictory, inconsistent

冒 mào vb risk, brave, take risks; **mào [xuě|yǔ|sǐ] 冒 [雪|雨|死]** [brave the snow | brave the rain | risk death]; falsify, feign; **mào [míng|pái] 冒 [名|牌]** falsify [a name | a brand]; emit, give off, spew forth; **mào [qì|yān|hàn] 冒 [气|烟|开]** [be steaming | emit smoke | sweat]

贸易 màoyì n trade, commerce, economic exchange

帽子 màozi n hat, cap

貌 mào n appearance, looks

没 méi 1 adv (when negating a completed action, an ongoing action, or a past experience) not; **wǒ méi qù 我没去** I didn't go; **tā méi zài kàn diànshì 他没在看电视** he was not watching TV; **wǒ méi qùguo Běijīng 我没去过北京** I have never been to Beijing 2 vb (short for **méiyǒu 没有**) not have, there is not; **méicuò 没错** it's right, you're right; **méifǎzi 没法子** no way, it can't be helped; **méiguānxi 没关系** it doesn't matter, it's alright, don't worry; **méishénme 没什么** it's nothing, it doesn't matter, never mind; **méishìr 没事儿**; it's alright, it's not important, it doesn't matter; be free, have nothing pressing to do; **wǒ méishì, kěyǐ bāng nǐ** 我没事，可以帮你 I'm free, I can help you; **méi xiǎngdào…** 没想到… unexpectedly, I never imagined…, I was surprised that…; **méiyìsi** 没意思 dull, uninteresting, boring; **méi yòng** 没用 useless, of no use; **méi(yǒu) le** 没(有)了 be gone, be used up, have disappeared

没有 méiyǒu adv (when negating a completed action) haven't, hasn't, didn't; **tā hái méiyǒu shuìzháo** 他还没有睡着 he hasn't fallen asleep yet; (when negating a past experience) haven't… before, hasn't… before, hasn't ever…; **nǐ méiyǒu jiànguo tā** 你没有见过他 you haven't met him before; less than; **qián méiyǒu sāntiān jiù huāwán le** 钱没有 3 天就花完了 the money was spent in less than three days; **méiyǒu…yǐqián** 没有…以前 before…; **tā méiyǒu jiéhūn yǐqián hěn jìmò** 他没有结婚以前很寂寞 he was very lonely before he got married

煤 méi n coal

煤气 méiqì n gas, coal gas

每 měi det every, each; **měi cì** 每次 every time; **měi…dōu … 每…都 …** every…, each…; **měi yí gè háizi dōu xǐhuan chī táng** 每一个孩子都喜欢吃糖 every child likes to eat sweets

美 měi 1 adj pretty, beautiful; high-quality, good, happy **2** n beauty, perfection; (short for **Měiguó** 美国) America; [Běi | Nán] **Měizhōu** [北 | 南] 美洲 [North | South] America

美国 Měiguó n the United States of America, USA; **Měiguórén** 美国人 an American, a person from the USA

美好 měihǎo adj good, desirable, bright

美丽 měilì adj beautiful

美术 měishù n art, fine arts

美术馆 měishùguǎn n art gallery

美元 měiyuán, **美金 měijīn** *n* American dollar

妹妹 mèimei *n* younger sister

闷 mēn *adj* ▶ *See also* 闷 **mèn**. stuffy, close

门 mén 1 *n* door, gate, entrance, family, house 2 *mw* ▶ **623** (for academic courses, subjects or disciplines)

门口 ménkǒu *n* doorway, gateway, entrance

闷 mèn *adj* ▶ *See also* 闷 **mēn**. bored, depressed

们 men *pt* (used to make plural forms of personal pronouns or nouns referring to animate entities) [wǒmen | nǐmen | tāmen][我们 | 你们 | 他们][we | you | they]；[xuéshengmen | háizimen | péngyoumen][学生们 | 孩子们 | 朋友们][students | children | friends]

梦 mèng *n* dream；**zuòmèng 做梦** have a dream

迷 mí 1 *vb* be confused, be lost；be fascinated by 2 *n* fan, enthusiast；**wǎngqiú mí 网球迷** tennis fan

迷信 míxìn *n* superstition

谜语 míyǔ *n* riddle, conundrum

米 mǐ *n* husked rice, uncooked rice, grain；metre

米饭 mǐfàn *n* cooked rice

秘密 mìmì 1 *n* secret 2 *adj* secret, confidential 3 *adv* secretly

秘书 mìshū *n* secretary, clerk

密 mì 1 *adj* dense, thick, close；intimate, close, secret 2 *adv* secretly, intimately

密切 mìqiè 1 *adj* (of relationships) close, intimate 2 *adv* carefully, closely, attentively

蜜 mì *n* honey

蜜蜂 mìfēng *n* bee, honeybee

棉花 miánhuā *n* cotton

棉衣 miányī *n* cotton-padded jacket or other items of clothing

免不了 miǎnbuliǎo *adj* unavoidable

免得 miǎnde *conj* so that...not..., so as not to, so as to avoid; **miǎnde shēngbìng 免得生病** so as to avoid getting sick

勉强 miǎnqiǎng 1 *adv* reluctantly, grudgingly; **miǎnqiǎng dāyingle wǒ 他勉强答应了我** he promised me reluctantly; barely enough, narrowly; **tā miǎnqiǎng tōngguòle kǎoshì 他勉强通过了考试** he narrowly passed the examination **2** *adj* inadequate, unconvincing, farfetched; **tā de jiěshì hěn miǎnqiǎng 他的解释很勉强** his explanation is quite unconvincing **3** *vb* force(someone to do something); **bié miǎnqiǎng tā 别勉强他** don't force her; do with difficulty, manage with a great effort; **bìngrén miǎnqiǎng chīle diǎnr fàn 病人勉强吃了点儿饭** the patient has managed to eat some food

面 miàn 1 *n* face; surface, top side, outside; side, dimension, aspect; wheat flour, flour, powder **2** *vb* face **3** *adv* personally, directly **4** *mw* ▶ **623** (*for flat, smooth objects, such as mirrors, flags, etc.*)

面包 miànbāo *n* bread

面对 miànduì *vb* face, confront

面粉 miànfěn *n* flour, wheat flour

面积 miànjī *n* area, surface area

面貌 miànmào *n* (*of people*) facial features, looks, appearance; (*of things*) appearance, look

面前 miànqián *adv* in front of (someone), to one's face; **bié zài lǎoshī miànqián shuō zhè zhǒng huà 别在老师面前说这种话** don't say such things in front of the teacher

面条儿 miàntiáor *n* noodles

描述 miáoshù *vb* describe

描写 miáoxiě *vb* describe, depict, delineate

秒 miǎo *n* second, 1/60 of a minute; **yì miǎozhōng 一秒钟** one second

妙 **miào** adj miraculous, wonderful, excellent; ingenious, clever, skilled

庙 **miào** n temple

灭 **miè** vb (as a light, fire, etc.) extinguish, put out, go out;(by killing) exterminate, obliterate, wipe out

民歌 **míngē** n folk song

民间 **mínjiān** adj of the common people, popular, folk

民主 **mínzhǔ** 1 n democracy 2 adj democratic

民族 **mínzú** n race, tribe, nation; **shǎoshù mínzú** 少数民族 minority nationality, ethnic group

名 **míng** 1 n name; fame, reputation; pretext, surface meaning; **yǐ … wéi míng** 以 … 为名 in the name of..., under the pretext of... 2 adj famous, well-known 3 mw ▶ 623 (for persons with professional or prominent social identities)

名胜 **míngshèng** n famous site, place of interest, scenic spot

名字 **míngzi** n name, given name, first name

明白 **míngbai** 1 adj clear, obvious, plain; frank, explicit, unequivocal; sensible, reasonable 2 vb understand, realize, know

明亮 **míngliàng** adj bright, well-lit, shining; (of understanding) clear

明年 **míngnián** n next year

明确 **míngquè** 1 adj clear, definite 2 vb clarify, specify

明天 **míngtiān** n tomorrow

明显 **míngxiǎn** adj obvious, clear, evident

明星 **míngxīng** n famous person, star

命 **mìng** n life; lot, fate, destiny; order, command

命令 **mìnglìng** 1 n command, order 2 vb command, order

命运 **mìngyùn** n destiny, fate

摸 mō vb touch gently, feel, stroke; grope for, feel for; search for, try to find out, figure out

模范 mófàn n ! *The word mó is sometimes pronounced mú with a different meaning*; model, fine example

模仿 mófǎng 1 vb copy, imitate, model after **2** n copy, imitation, model

模型 móxíng n model, pattern

摩托车 mótuōchē n motorbike, motorcycle, motor bicycle

磨 mó vb rub, wear down, wear away; sharpen, polish, grind; **磨刀 mó dāo** sharpen a knife; waste time, while away time; **磨时间 mó shíjiān** kill time; torment, bother, put through the grind

抹 mǒ vb apply, smear, put on; wipe, erase

陌生 mòshēng adj strange, unfamiliar; **陌生人 mòshēngrén** stranger

墨 mò 1 n ink, ink stick **2** adj black, dark

墨水 mòshuǐ n ink

某 mǒu det certain, some; **某人 mǒu rén** a certain person, someone; **某某 mǒumǒu** ... such-and-such..., so-and-so

模样 múyàng n ! *The word mú is sometimes pronounced mó with a different meaning*; appearance, shape, look

母 mǔ 1 n mother; aunt, elder female relative; [zǔmǔ│gūmǔ│jiùmǔ] [祖母│姑母│舅母][grandmother│aunt (father's sister)│aunt (mother's brother's wife)] **2** adj (of a species) female; [mǔláng│mǔxiàng│mǔmāo] [母狼│母象│母猫][female [wolf│elephant│cat]]

母亲 mǔqīn n mother

亩 mǔ n (unit for measuring land area) 0.0667 hectares, 1/6 of an acre

木 mù 1 n tree, timber; wood **2** adj wooden, made out of wood; (of body or mind) numb, insensitive, dull

木头 mùtou n wood, log, timber

目标 mùbiāo n goal, aim, target

目的 mùdì *n* aim, objective, purpose

目前 mùqián *adv* currently, at present, at this moment

牧民 mùmín *n* herdsman

墓 mù *n* grave, tomb, mausoleum

幕 mù *n* curtain, screen; (*of a dramatic performance*) act

Nn

拿 ná 1 *vb* (*in one's hands*) take, take hold of, carry; (*with* qù 去 *and* lái 来 *to mean* **take** *and* **bring** *respectively*) náqù 拿去 take (it) away; nálái 拿来 bring here; take... as/for; tā méi ná wǒ dāng kèrén 他没拿我当客人 he didn't treat me as a guest **2** *prep* with; ná kuàizi chī 拿筷子吃 eat with chopsticks; ná···láishuō 拿···来说 speaking of..., take... as an example; ná ··· zuò ··· 拿 ··· 做 ··· take...as...; tā bǎ wǒ dāng xiǎoháizi kàn 他把我当小孩子看 he treats me like a child

哪 nǎ 1 *det* which? what?; nǐ yào nǎ kuài biǎo? 你要哪块表? which watch would you like?; (*used with* dōu 都) any, whatever, whichever; nǐ yào nǎ kuài biǎo dōu kěyǐ 你要哪块表都可以 you can have any watch you want **2** *adv* (*used in a rhetorical question*) how is it possible that...?; wǒ nǎ zhīdào tā de míngzi 我哪知道他的名字? how could I know his name?

哪个 nǎge *det* which? which one?; nǎge rén 哪个人? which person?

哪里 nǎli, 哪儿 nǎr 1 *adv* (*in a question*) where?; nǐ de chē zài nǎli? 你的车在哪里? where is your car?; (*with* dōu 都 *in a statement*) anywhere, wherever, everywhere; fàng zài nǎli dōu kěyǐ 放在哪里都可以 you can put it anywhere **2** adv (*used to form a rhetorical question*) how can it be that…?; wǒ nǎli mǎi de qǐ qìchē? 我哪里买得起汽车? how could I possibly afford to buy a car?; you're welcome, don't mention it; " xièxiè nǐ de bāngzhù"—"nǎli,nǎli" "谢谢你的帮助"—"哪里,哪里" 'thanks for your help'—'don't mention it'

哪怕 nǎpà conj even,even if,no matter how; nǎpà…yě… 哪怕…也… even if,even though; nǎpà nǐ bù tóngyì, wǒ yě yào qù 哪怕你不同意,我也要去 I'll still go even if you don't agree

哪些 nǎxiē 1 pron (*plural form*) which? which ones? what?; nǎxiē shì xīn de? 哪些是新的? which ones are new? **2** det which; nǎxiē shū shì nǐ de? 哪些书是你的? which books are yours?

那 nà 1 pron that; nà shì tā de shū 那是他的书 that is his book **2** det (*before a number plus a measure word*) that, those; nà sān zhāng zhuōzi dōu hěn guì 那3张桌子都很贵 those three tables are all very expensive **3** conj then, in that case; nà wǒ yě yào mǎi yí gè 那我也要买一个 in that case I want to buy one too

那边 nàbian adv that side,over there

那个 nàge det that; nàge wèntí 那个问题 that problem

那里 nàli,那儿 nàr adv there,that place,over there

那么 nàme adv in that way,like that,so; nǐ wèishénme nàme zuò? 你为什么那么做? why do you do it like that?; in that case,then; nàme zánmen yíkuàir qù ba 那么咱们一块儿去吧 then let's go together

那些 nàxiē 1 pron (*plural form*) those,that quantity of **2** det those

那样 nàyàng adv like that,so,in that way; nǐ bié nàyàng zuò 你别那样做 don't do it that way

哪 na pt (*when expressing appreciation or confirmation, or when giving advice or encouragement*) kuài lái na! 快来

哪! hurry up!

奶 nǎi *n* milk

奶奶 nǎinai *n* paternal grandmother

耐烦 nàifán *adj* patient

耐心 nàixīn 1 *adj* patient **2** *adv* patiently **3** *n* patience

耐用 nàiyòng *adj* enduring, durable, capable of withstanding heavy use

男 nán *adj* (refers to humans only) man, male

男孩子 nánháizi *n* boy

男朋友 nánpéngyou *n* boyfriend

男人 nánren *n* man, husband

南 nán 1 *n* south **2** *adj* south, southern

南边 nánbian *n* the south, south side

南部 nánbù *n* southern part

南方 nánfāng *n* (as a direction) south; southern part of the country

南极 nánjí *n* South Pole, Antarctic

南面 nánmiàn ▶ 南边 nánbian

难 nán *adj* difficult, hard; (when it precedes a verb) bad, unpleasant; **nán** [chī | tīng] 难 [吃 | 听] [bad tasting | unpleasant to the ear]

难道 nándào *adv* (in rhetorical questions that end with the particle ma 吗) could it be that...? you don't mean to say that...? is it really true that...?; **nándào nǐ lián yí kuài qián yě méiyǒu ma?** 难道你连一块钱也没有吗? do you mean to say you don't even have one *yuan*?! *Note that the speaker doubts or questions the statement that occurs within this pattern.*

难怪 nánguài *conj* no wonder that

难过 nánguò 1 *adj* sad, aggrieved **2** *vb* have a hard time

难看 nánkàn *adj* ugly, unpleasant to look at, disgraceful-looking; unhealthy, pale; embarrassing, shameful

难免 **nánmiǎn 1** *adj* difficult to avoid **2** *adv* inevitably

难受 **nánshòu** *adj* unbearable, hard to stand; uncomfortable, unwell; unhappy, distressed, miserable

脑袋 **nǎodai** *n* (*part of the body*) head

脑筋 **nǎojīn** *n* brain, mind

脑子 **nǎozi** *n* (*part of the body*) brain; (*mental capacity*) brains, mind, intelligence

闹 **nào 1** *vb* make a disturbance, make a noise, cause trouble; suffer bad effects from, be troubled by, undergo; **nào jīhuāng** 闹饥荒 suffer from famine; (*when talking about something disruptive or troublesome*) cause to happen, do, undertake; **nǐ bǎ zhè shì nào fùzá le** 你把这事闹复杂了 you made this matter complicated; (*when speaking of emotions like anger or resentment*) give vent to; **nào qíngxù** 闹情绪 be moody **2** *adj* noisy, loud

闹钟 **nàozhōng** *n* alarm clock

呢 **ne** *pt* (*for questions on a subject under consideration*) "**nǐ hǎoma?**"—"**hǎo, nǐ ne?**" "你好吗?"—"好,你呢?" 'how are you?'—'fine, and you?'; (*to indicate continued action*) **tā zài nàr zuòzhe ne** 他在那儿坐着呢 he is sitting there; (*to indicate emphasis or suspense*) **hái yǒu shí fēnzhōng ne** 还有 10 分钟呢 there are still ten minutes left; (*to introduce a topic*) as for, with regard to; **zhège wèntí ne, wǒmen kěyǐ yǐhòu zài tǎolùn** 这个问题呢, 我们可以以后再讨论 as for this question, we can talk about it later; where?; **wǒ de gāngbǐ ne?** 我的钢笔呢? where is my pen?

内 **nèi 1** *prep* (*when referring to time, place, scope or limits*) within, in, inside; **yì liǎng tiān nèi** 一两天 内 within one or two days **2** *adj* inner, internal

内部 **nèibù** *adj* internal, interior, on the inside ! *This term sometimes refers to something that is for officials only, meaning that it is restricted or exclusive;* **nèibù**

wénjiàn 内部文件 restricted document

内科 **nèikē** n (department of) internal medicine

内容 **nèiróng** n content, contents, the inner part

能 **néng 1** vb can, be able to; **tā néng shuō wǔ zhǒng wàiyǔ** 他能说 5 种外语 he can speak 5 foreign languages **2** n ability, capability, skill; (in science) energy

能干 **nénggàn** adj capable, able, competent

能够 **nénggòu** vb can, be able to, be capable of

能力 **nénglì** n capability, potentiality, ability

能源 **néngyuán** n (in the power industry) energy source, energy

泥 **ní** n mud, clay, mire; puréed/mashed vegetable/fruit

你 **nǐ** pron (singular) you

你们 **nǐmen** pron (plural) you

年 **nián** n year; New Year; person's age; every year, annual, yearly

年代 **niándài** n era, period, age; decade; **qīshí niándài** 70 年代 the seventies

年级 **niánjí** n (in school or university) year, form, grade

年纪 **niánjì**, 年龄 **niánlíng** n (when speaking of a person) age

年轻 **niánqīng**, 年青 **niánqīng** adj young

粘 **nián** ▶ 粘 **zhān**

念 **niàn** vb (a course or subject) study; read, read aloud

念书 **niànshū** vb study, read books

娘 **niáng** n mother, ma, mum

鸟 **niǎo** n bird

您 **nín** pron (polite form of nǐ 你) you

宁可 **nìngkě**, 宁肯 **nìngkěn**, 宁愿 **nìngyuàn** adv would rather, better

牛 **niú** n ox, cow, cattle

牛奶 niúnǎi n cow's milk

牛肉 niúròu n beef

扭 niǔ vb turn, rotate, turn round; twist, wrench, sprain; grapple, wrestle; swing back and forth, sway from side to side

纽约 Niǔyuē n New York

农 nóng n farming, agriculture

农场 nóngchǎng n farm

农村 nóngcūn n village, rural area, countryside

农历 nónglì n traditional Chinese lunar calendar

农民 nóngmín n farmer, farming population, peasant

农业 nóngyè n agriculture, farming

浓 nóng adj (when talking about tea, smoke, colour, atmosphere, fog, etc.) dense, concentrated, thick; **nóng chá 浓茶** strong tea; (when speaking of degree or extent) great, rich, strong

弄 nòng vb do, make, cause; **nòng [huài | cuò | qīngchu] 弄 [坏 | 错 | 清楚]** [ruin | make a mistake | clear up]; handle, manage; obtain, get hold of; **zhè zhǒng yào hěn nán nòngdào 这种药很难弄到** this type of medicine is very difficult to obtain; play with, fiddle with, do for amusement

努力 nǔlì 1 vb work hard, make a strenuous effort, exert oneself 2 adj hardworking, studious, diligent 3 adv studiously, diligently

怒 nù 1 adj angry, furious, indignant 2 n anger, passion, rage

女 nǚ adj female, woman

女儿 nǚ'ér n daughter, girl

女孩子 nǚháizi n girl

女朋友 nǚpéngyou n girlfriend

女人 nǚrén n (less polite than nǚshì 女士) woman

女士 nǚshì n (polite form of address or reference) lady, miss

暖 nuǎn 1 *adj* warm，genial **2** *vb* warm up，make warm

暖和 nuǎnhuo 1 *adj* warm，comfortably warm **2** *vb* warm up，make warm

暖气 nuǎnqì *n* warm air，heating，central heating

Oo

哦 ó *exc* (connoting a sense of doubt；really？or is that really so?) oh!

哦 ò *exc* (showing understanding or realization) oh!

欧元 ōuyuán *n* euro

欧洲 Ōuzhōu *n* Europe

偶然 ǒurán *adv* by chance，accidentally

Pp

爬 pá *vb* crawl，creep；climb

怕 pà *vb* fear，be afraid；be worried/concerned about；(especially when anticipating a negative reaction) think，suppose；**wǒ pà tā bú huì lái 我怕他不会来** I'm afraid he won't come

拍 pāi *vb* beat，clap，tap；take，send，shoot；**pāi [zhào | diànyǐng | diànbào] 拍 [照 | 电影 | 电报]** [take a picture | make a film | send a telegram]

拍(子) pāi(zi) *n* (used in some games) raquet，bat

排 pái 1 *n* row，line **2** *mw* ▶ **623** (for things grouped or set in rows) row **3** *vb* set in a row，line up，arrange in order;(for drama performances, etc.) rehearse

排队 páiduì vb queue (up), line up, form a line

排球 páiqiú n volleyball

牌 pái n sign, signboard; trademark, brand; cards, dominoes; **dǎpái 打牌** play cards

派 pài 1 vb send, dispatch, appoint **2** n school of thought, sect; clique, group, faction

盘 pán 1 n plate, dish, tray;(used in some games) board; **qípán 棋盘** chessboard **2** mw ▶ **623** (for flat things);(for board games)

盘子 pánzi n dish, plate, tray

判断 pànduàn 1 vb decide, judge, assess **2** n judgement, assessment, decision

盼(望) pàn(wàng) vb hope for, yearn for

旁 páng 1 n side; **lùpáng 路旁** roadside;(part of a Chinese character) radical **2** adj side, on the side; other, else

旁边 pángbiān 1 n side, nearby position **2** adv beside, alongside, nearby

胖 pàng adj fat, obese

抛弃 pāoqì vb abandon, forsake, discard

跑 pǎo vb run, run away, escape; do errands, run around busily;(after a verb, indicating quick movement away) **gǎnpǎo le 赶跑了** drive away

跑步 pǎobù 1 vb run, jog **2** n jogging, running

炮 pào n artillery, cannon

陪(同) péi(tóng) vb accompany, be in the accompany of, keep company with

培养 péiyǎng vb train, foster, develop

培育 péiyù vb cultivate, nurture, breed

赔 péi vb lose money, sustain a financial loss; reimburse, compensate, indemnify

配 pèi vb deserve, be worthy of, be qualified; fit; match;

blend, mix, compound; (*when talking about animals*) mate

配合 pèihé *vb* co-ordinate, co-operate

喷 pēn *vb* gush, spurt, spray

盆 pén *n* basin, pot, tub

朋友 péngyou *n* friend

捧 pěng *vb* carry in the hands; flatter, praise excessively

碰 pèng *vb* touch, knock against, collide; encounter, meet, run into; try one's luck

碰见 pèngjiàn *vb* encounter, meet unexpectedly, run into

碰巧 pèngqiǎo *adv* coincidentally, by chance, happen to

批 pī 1 *mw* ▶ **623** (*for people or goods*) group, batch, lot **2** *vb* (*written work, etc.*) correct, mark; criticize

批判 pīpàn 1 *vb* criticize **2** *n* critique, criticism

批评 pīpíng 1 *vb* criticize **2** *n* comment, criticism

批准 pīzhǔn *vb* approve, grant (a request), ratify

披 pī *vb* wear over the shoulders, wrap round

皮 pí *n* skin, hide, leather; bark, peel, outer covering

皮包 píbāo *n* leather handbag, briefcase, portfolio

皮肤 pífū *n* skin

疲倦 píjuàn *adj* tired, fatigued, weary

疲劳 píláo *adj* tired, exhausted

啤酒 píjiǔ *n* beer

脾气 píqi *n* temperament, disposition; **fā píqi 发脾气** get angry, lose one's temper

匹 pǐ *mw* ▶ **623** (*for horses, mules*)

譬如 pìrú *adv* for example, for instance, such as

偏 piān ▶ See also 偏偏 **piānpiān. 1** *adv* (*contrary to expectation*) deliberately, insistently, stubbornly; **nǐ piān yào gēn tā láiwǎng 你偏要跟他来往** you insist on having dealings with him **2** *adj* slanted, inclined, leaning; favouring one side, partial, biased

偏见 piānjiàn *n* prejudice, bias

偏偏 piānpiān *adv* deliberately, stubbornly, insistently; (*contrary to expectation*) yǒu yí jiàn hěn jǐnjí de shìqing yào tā zuò, piānpiān tā bìng le 有一件很紧急的事情要他做, 偏偏他病了 there is a very urgent matter for him to deal with, but he has unexpectedly fallen ill

篇 piān *mw* ▶ 623 (*for papers, articles, written versions of a speech*)

便宜 piányi ! Note that in other uses pián 便 is pronounced biàn. **1** *adj* cheap, inexpensive **2** *n* advantages, gain

片 piàn (*mw* ▶ 623) (*for flat, thin things or things in slices*); (*for expanses or stretches of ocean, desert, mist, fog, etc.*); (*for atmospheres, moods, etc.*)

片面 piànmiàn *adj* partial, incomplete, one-sided

骗 piàn *vb* cheat, swindle, deceive

漂 piāo *vb* (*when talking about something in the water*) float, drift

飘 piāo *vb* float in the air, be borne by the wind

飘扬 piāoyáng *vb* (*when talking about something in the wind*) fly, flutter, wave

票 piào *n* ticket, ballot

漂亮 piàoliang *adj* pretty, good-looking, beautiful

拼命 pīnmìng **1** *vb* give one's all, risk one's life **2** *adv* to the death, with all one's effort

拼音 pīnyīn *n* Chinese phonetic alphabet; combined sounds in syllables

贫苦 pínkǔ *adj* poor, poverty-stricken

贫穷 pínqióng *adj* poor, impoverished

品德 pǐndé *n* moral character, morality

品格 pǐngé *n* (*when talking about a person*) character, morality; (*when talking about literary or artistic works*) quality, style

品质 pǐnzhì *n* character, quality

品种 pǐnzhǒng *n* breed, strain, variety

乒乓球 pīngpāngqiú *n* table tennis, ping-pong

平 píng 1 *adj* flat, level, equal; ordinary, average, common; peaceful, calm, balanced; fair, objective, impartial **2** *vb* even out, level, make even; pacify, bring peace to, calm down; (in a game, match, race, etc.) draw, tie

平安 píng'ān 1 *adj* peaceful **2** *n* peace

平常 píngcháng 1 *adj* ordinary, usual, common **2** *adv* ordinarily, usually

平等 píngděng 1 *adj* equal **2** *n* equality

平凡 píngfán *adj* ordinary, common

平方 píngfāng (in measuring area) square; **yì píng-fāng gōnglǐ 一平方公里** a square kilometre

平静 píngjìng *adj* quiet, peaceful, calm

平均 píngjūn 1 *adj* average, mean **2** *adv* equally

平时 píngshí *adv* ordinarily, usually, normally

平原 píngyuán *n* plain, flatlands

评论 pínglùn 1 *vb* comment on, discuss **2** *n* commentary, comment, review

苹果 píngguǒ *n* apple

凭 píng *vb* go by, take as the basis, base on; rely on, depend on

瓶(子) píng(zi) *n* bottle, jar, vase

坡 pō *n* slope, incline, bank

迫切 pòqiè 1 *adj* urgent, pressing **2** *adv* urgently

破 pò 1 *vb* break, cut, destroy **2** *adj* broken, damaged, in ruins; torn, worn-out

破坏 pòhuài *vb* break, destroy, spoil

扑 pū *vb* rush toward, assault, pounce on; devote all one's energies to; **tā zhěngtiān pū zài xuéxí shang 他整天扑在学习上** he devotes all his time to his studies

铺 pū *vb* spread out, extend, unfold; spread over, cover; pave, lay; pū [chuáng | lù | tiěguǐ] 铺 [床 | 路 | 铁轨] [make the bed | pave a road | lay a railway track]

朴实 pǔshí *adj* simple, plain; down-to-earth, sincere and honest, guileless

朴素 pǔsù *adj* simple, plain

普遍 pǔbiàn *adj* general, common, universal

普通 pǔtōng *adj* general, common

普通话 pǔtōnghuà *n* putonghua, common spoken Chinese

Qq

七 qī *num* seven

七月 qīyuè *n* July

妻子 qīzi *n* wife

期 qī 1 *n* period of time, date, term; due date, deadline, scheduled time; dàoqī 到期 be due; (*of a project, etc.*) stage, phase **2** *mw* ▶ **623** (*for issues of periodicals, magazines, journals, etc.*) issue

期待 qīdài *vb* hope, expect, look forward to

期间 qījiān *n* period of time, course of time

期望 qīwàng 1 *vb* hope, anticipate, expect **2** *n* hope, anticipation, expectation

欺骗 qīpiàn *vb* cheat, deceive

齐 qí 1 *adj* neat, tidy, in good order; complete, ready; similar, alike; together **2** *adv* together, simultaneously, in unison

其次 qícì *adv* (*in order or importance*) next, secondly, secondarily

其实 qíshí *adv* in fact, actually

其他 qítā **1** *pron* the others **2** *adj* other, else

其余 qíyú *n* the rest, the remaining

其中 qízhōng *adv* (*a group or situation*) in which, among whom

奇怪 qíguài *adj* strange, peculiar, surprising

奇迹 qíjì *n* miracle, wonder

骑 qí *vb* (*a horse or cycle*) ride; **qí chē 骑车** ride a bicycle

棋 qí *n* chess, board game

旗子 qízi *n* flag, banner

乞求 qǐqiú *vb* beg, supplicate

企图 qǐtú **1** *vb* try, seek, attempt **2** *n* try, attempt

企业 qǐyè *n* enterprise, business

启发 qǐfā **1** *vb* inspire, stimulate, open the mind **2** *n* inspiration, stimulation

起 qǐ *vb* rise, get up, arise; raise, grow; begin, start; (*after another verb, to indicate upward movement*) up; [ná|tí]qǐ [拿|提]起 [take|lift]up; (*after another verb, to indicate the beginning of an action*) start, begin; **cóngtóu shuō qǐ 从头说起** tell it from the beginning; (*after another verb that is followed by de 得 or bu 不, to mean can or cannot attain a certain standard*) mǎi [de|bù]qǐ 买 [得|不]起 [can|cannot]afford

起床 qǐchuáng *vb* get up, get out of bed

起点 qǐdiǎn *n* starting point

起飞 qǐfēi *vb* take off (as an airplane)

起来 qǐlái *vb* get up, rise, get out of bed; stand up; (*in opposition, rebellion, etc.*) arise, rise up, stand up against; (*after a verb, to indicate upward direction*) raise, lift; (*after a verb, indicate the beginning of an action*) start, begin; (*after a verb, to indicate an accomplishment*) **xiǎngqǐlái…想起来…**think of..., remember...; (*after a* verb, to indicate one's impression in the midst of an activity) tīngqǐlai… 听起来… it sounds…; kàn qǐlai… 看起来… it looks…

气 qì 1 vb become angry, become enraged, fume; make angry, anger, enrage **2** n air, gas, fumes; breath; chuī yì kǒu qì 吹一口气 blow out a puff of air; smell, odour

气氛 qìfēn n atmosphere, ambience

气候 qìhòu n climate, weather; situation, atmosphere

气温 qìwēn n air temperature

气象 qìxiàng n weather, climatic/atmospheric phenomena

汽 qì n steam, vapour

汽车 qìchē n car, automobile, vehicle; bus; qìchēzhàn 汽车站 bus station, bus stop

汽水 qìshuǐ n carbonated drink, soft drink, pop

汽油 qìyóu n petrol, gasoline

器 qì n implement, utensil, instrument, machine; yuèqì 乐器 musical instrument

恰当 qiàdàng adj appropriate, suitable, fitting

恰好 qiàhǎo adv it so happened that, luckily; qiàhǎo tā yě zài nàr 恰好她也在那儿 it just so happened that she was there too

千 qiān num thousand; a large number of

千万 qiānwàn 1 adv (in a warning) please do… at all costs; qiānwàn yào jìzhù! 千万要记住! please do remember! **2** num ten million, millions upon millions

牵 qiān vb lead by the hand, pull

铅笔 qiānbǐ n pencil

签订 qiāndìng vb (as an agreement, etc.) sign, put one's signature on

签名 qiānmíng vb sign name, autograph

签字 qiānzì vb sign, affix signature

谦虚 qiānxū adj modest, self-effacing

前 qián 1 *n* front, the front, ahead **2** *adj* preceding, former; front, first, top **3** *adv* forward, ahead, ago **4** *prep* in front of, ahead of, (*sometimes preceded by* yǐ 以) before

前边 qiánbian,前头 qiántou *adv* in front, ahead

前进 qiánjìn *vb* advance, go forward, move ahead

前面 qiánmian *adv* in front, ahead; (*referring to something mentioned before*) above, the above, preceding

前年 qiánnián *n* the year before last, two years ago

前天 qiántiān *n* the day before yesterday

前途 qiántú *n* the future, future prospects, the road ahead

前夕 qiánxī *n* eve

钱 qián *n* money, coins; (*when talking about cost*) money, cost; píngguǒ duōshao qián? 苹果多少钱? how much are the apples?; táng yì máo qián 糖一毛钱 the sweets cost 10 cents

钱包 qiánbāo *n* purse, wallet

浅 qiǎn *adj* shallow, superficial, not profound; elementary, simple, easy; (*of colour*) light; qiǎnlǜ 浅绿 light green

欠 qiàn *vb* (*debt, gratitude, etc.*) owe, need, be short of, lack

枪 qiāng *n* gun, rifle, pistol

强 qiáng *adj* strong, powerful, better

强大 qiángdà *adj* strong, powerful

强盗 qiángdào *n* robber, bandit

强调 qiángdiào 1 *vb* emphasise, stress **2** *n* emphasis, stress

强度 qiángdù *n* degree of strength, degree of intensity

强烈 qiángliè *adj* strong, intense, fervent

墙 qiáng *n* wall

抢 qiǎng *vb* rob, snatch, loot, vie for; (*in an emergency*) rush, seize the moment; qiǎnggòu shípǐn 抢购食品 rush to buy food

强迫 qiǎngpò *vb* compel, coerce, force

悄悄 qiāoqiāo *adv* silently, quietly, stealthily

敲 qiāo *vb* (*a door, etc.*) knock, tap; (*a drum, gong, etc.*) beat, strike

桥（梁）qiáo（liáng） *n* bridge

瞧 qiáo *vb* see, look at; qiáo [de|bu]qǐ 瞧 [得|不]起 look [up to|down on]

巧 qiǎo 1 *adj* skilful, clever, ingenious; artful, cunning, deceiving; by coincidence, fortuitous, lucky **2** *adv* cleverly; fortuitously, coincidentally

巧妙 qiǎomiào *adj* (*of methods, skills, etc.*) brilliant, ingenious, clever

切 qiē *vb* (*as meat, fruit, vegetables, etc.*) cut, slice

侵略 qīnlüè 1 *vb* invade, encroach **2** *n* invasion, aggression

亲 qīn 1 *n* parent; blood relation, next of kin, relative; marriage, match **2** *adj* close, intimate, dear **3** *adv* in person, oneself **4** *vb* kiss

亲爱 qīn'ài *adj* dear, darling, beloved

亲近 qīnjìn *vb* be close to, be on intimate terms with

亲密 qīnmì *adj* close, intimate

亲戚 qīnqi *n* relative(s), relation(s), kin

亲切 qīnqiè *adj* warm, kind, cordial

亲热 qīnrè *adj* affectionate, intimate, warm-hearted

亲自 qīnzì *adv* in person, personally, oneself

琴 qín *n* (*general name for stringed musical instruments*) xiǎotíqín 小提琴 violin

青 qīng *adj* blue, green

青年 qīngnián *n* youth, young person

青少年 qīngshàonián *n* teenager, youngster

轻 qīng 1 *adj* (*in weight or importance*) light; (*in degree or age*) small; (*when talking about one's work or job*) easy

2 *adv* lightly, softly, gently

轻松 qīngsōng *adj* light, relaxed

倾向 qīngxiàng 1 *n* tendency, trend, inclination **2** *vb* be inclined to, prefer

清 qīng 1 *adj* clear, distinct **2** *vb* (*an account, etc.*) clear up, settle

清楚 qīngchu 1 *adj* clear, distinct **2** *vb* understand, know, have a clear understanding of

清洁 qīngjié *adj* clean

清静 qīngjìng *adj* quiet, peaceful, undisturbed

情节 qíngjié *n* (*when talking about literature*) plot; qíngjié jǐncòu 情节紧凑 a tightly constructed plot; circumstances

情景 qíngjǐng *n* scene, sight; situation, circumstances

情况 qíngkuàng *n* situation, condition, circumstances

情形 qíngxíng *n* situation, condition, circumstances

情绪 qíngxù *n* state of mind, mood, morale

晴 qíng *adj* (*referring to the sky or weather*) clear, fair, fine

晴朗 qínglǎng *adj* fine, sunny

请 qǐng *vb* (*word used in polite requests*) please; qǐng [zuò|jìn|chīfàn]请 [坐|进|吃饭] please [sit down|come in|start eating]; invite, ask, request

请假 qǐngjià *vb* ask for time off, ask for leave of absence

请教 qǐngjiào *vb* ask for advice, consult

请客 qǐngkè *vb* invite someone to dinner, treat, entertain guests

请求 qǐngqiú 1 *vb* ask, request **2** *n* request

请问 qǐngwèn *vb* (*polite way of asking a question*) may I ask…

庆贺 qìnghè *vb* congratulate, celebrate

庆祝 qìngzhù 1 *vb* celebrate **2** *n* celebration

穷 qióng *adj* poor, impoverished

秋(天) qiū(tiān) *n* autumn, fall

求 qiú *vb* seek, request, strive for

球 qiú *n* ball, game played with a ball; sphere, globe, earth

球场 qiúchǎng *n* playing field, court, diamond

球迷 qiúmí *n* (*someone fond of games played with a ball*) fan; zúqiúmí 足球迷 football fan

区 qū *n* area, region, zone; district, precinct, administrative division

区别 qūbié 1 *n* difference **2** *vb* discriminate, distinguish

区分 qūfēn *vb* differentiate, distinguish

趋势 qūshì *n* trend, tendency

趋向 qūxiàng 1 *n* trend, tendency, direction **2** *vb* tend to, incline to

渠 qú *n* drain, ditch, channel

曲子 qǔzi *n* song, tune, melody

取 qǔ *vb* take, fetch, obtain; (*money from a bank, etc.*) withdraw, draw out, take out; (*as a candidate*) accept, admit, select; (*as a course of action*) aim for, choose

取得 qǔdé *vb* obtain, achieve, gain

取消 qǔxiāo *vb* cancel, abolish, call off

去 qù *vb* go, leave, depart; (*after a verb, indicating action directed away from the speaker*) (move) away; náqù 拿去 take away; (*expressing purpose or reason for an action*) to, in order to; ná yìdiǎnr qián qù mǎi dōngxi 拿一点儿钱去买东西 take some money and go shopping; remove, get rid of, discard

去年 qùnián *n* last year

去世 qùshì *vb* die, pass away

趣味 qùwèi *n* interest, delight; taste, liking, preference

圈 quān 1 *n* circle,ring;enclosure **2** *vb* enclose,fence in,encircle

全 quán 1 *adj* whole,entire; complete **2** *adv* completely, entirely,all

全部 quánbù 1 *adj* whole,complete,all **2** *adv* wholly, completely

全面 quánmiàn *adj* overall,all-round,comprehensive

全体 quántǐ 1 *n* as a whole,whole body/group **2** *adj* all, entire,whole

权 quán *n* right;power,authority

权力 quánlì *n* power,authority

泉 quán *n* spring; **wēnquán 温泉** hot spring

拳(头)quán(tóu) *n* fist

鬈 quán *adj* (*when describing hair*) curly,wavy

劝 quàn *vb* persuade,advise,urge

劝告 quàngào *vb* advise,urge,exhort

缺 quē *vb* lack,be short of

缺点 quēdiǎn *n* defect,shortcoming,deficiency

缺乏 quēfá 1 *vb* lack,be short of **2** *n* lack,deficiency

缺少 quēshǎo *vb* lack,be short of

却 què *conj* however,but,yet

确定 quèdìng 1 *vb* settle on,determine,fix **2** *adj* settled, definite,sure

确实 quèshí 1 *adj* certain,true,reliable **2** *adv* certainly, really,indeed

裙子 qúnzi *n* skirt

群 qún 1 *mw* ▶ 623 (*for a group of,many*) group,herd, flock **2** *n* group,crowd,herd

群众 qúnzhòng *n* the masses,the public; **qúnzhòng yùndòng 群众运动** mass movement

Rr

然而 rán'ér *conj* but, however, nevertheless

然后 ránhòu *adv* thereafter, afterwards, subsequently

燃烧 ránshāo *vb* burn

染 rǎn *vb* dye; (*when talking about a disease, etc.*) contract, become infected with; (*when talking about a bad habit, etc.*) acquire

嚷 rǎng *vb* yell, shout

让 ràng 1 *vb* let, allow, permit; **ràng tā qù ba 让她去吧** let her go; make, cause; **zhè jiàn shì ràng tā hěn gāoxìng 这件事让她很高兴** this matter made her very happy; yield, give up, concede; **ràngzuò 让座** give up one's seat **2** *prep* (*when used to introduce the agent in a passive construction*) by; **tā zuò de cài ràng gǒu chī le 他做的菜让狗吃了** the food he made was eaten by the dog

让步 ràngbù *vb* make concessions

饶 ráo *vb* forgive, pardon

扰乱 rǎoluàn *vb* disturb, create confusion, harass

绕 rào *vb* move around, encircle, coil; **rào dìqiú yì zhōu 绕地球一周** go round the world once; bypass, go round; **ràoguò zhàng'ài 绕过障碍** bypass an obstacle

惹 rě *vb* provoke, annoy, tease; (*when talking about trouble, nuisance, attention, etc.*) stir up, incite, attract

热 rè 1 *adj* (*of weather, temperature, etc.*) hot **2** *vb* heat up, warm up **3** *n* heat; temperature, fever; **fārè 发热** have a high temperature; rush, craze; [chūguó | jīngshāng | wǎngqiú] rè [出国 | 经商 | 网球] 热 a craze for [going abroad | business | tennis]

热爱 rè'ài *vb* love, feel warm affection for

热烈 rèliè *adj* enthusiastic, passionate, fervent

热闹 rènao 1 *adj* bustling, lively, boisterous **2** *vb* liven up, have a jolly time **3** *n* excitement, fun

热情 rèqíng 1 *adj* warm-hearted, enthusiastic, zealous **2** *n* passionate feelings, love, ardour

热心 rèxīn *adj* earnest, warm-hearted, enthusiastic

人 rén *n* person, people, humanity; others, other people; tā duì rén bú kèqi 他对人不客气 he is impolite to others; rénrén 人人 everyone, everybody

人才 réncái *n* talent, talented person

人工 réngōng 1 *adj* artificial, man-made **2** *n* manual work; labour; nàr de réngōng hěn guì 那儿的人工很贵 labour there is very expensive

人家 rénjiā *n* household, family

人家 rénjia *pron* others, other people; (*when referring indirectly to a certain person or people*) they, someone; nǐ yàoshi xiǎng qǐng tā chīfàn, nǐ zuìhǎo zǎo diǎn gàosu rénjia 你要是想请他吃饭，你最好早点告诉人家 if you want to invite him to a meal, you had better tell him ahead of time; (*when referring indirectly to the speaker*) someone, one; wǒ cuò le, rénjia xiàng nǐ dàoqiàn hái bù xíng ma? 我错了，人家向你道歉还不行吗? I was wrong and I apologize to you; won't that do?

人口 rénkǒu *n* population; family members, number of family members

人类 rénlèi *n* humankind, humanity; rénlèixué 人类学 anthropology

人们 rénmen *n* people, men

人民 rénmín *n* people, the people

人民币 rénmínbì *n* (*official currency of the People's Republic of China*) Renminbi (RMB)

人权 rénquán *n* human rights

人生 rénshēng *n* life, human life

人物 rénwù *n* personage, figure; (*in a literary work*) character

人员 rényuán *n* staff members, personnel

人造 rénzào *adj* man-made, artificial

忍 rěn *vb* endure, tolerate, be patient

忍耐 rěnnài *vb* be patient, endure, restrain oneself

忍受 rěnshòu *vb* bear, endure

忍心 rěnxīn *vb* be hard-hearted, be callous

认 rèn *vb* (*when speaking of a person, object, etc.*) recognize, know, identify; (*when speaking of a fact, fault, problem, etc.*) admit, acknowledge, recognize; **rèn ⋯ zuò ⋯ 认⋯作⋯** regard. . .as. . . , take. . .for. . .

认得 rènde *vb* be acquainted with, know, recognize

认识 rènshi 1 *vb* (*when speaking of a person*) be acquainted with, know, recognize; (*when speaking of a fact, reason, error, etc.*) realize, understand **2** *n* understanding, knowledge

认为 rènwéi *vb* consider that, think that, take it that

认真 rènzhēn *adj* serious, earnest, conscientious

任 rèn *vb* appoint, assign, be responsible for; let, allow; **rèn (píng) 任（凭）** no matter (who, what, how); **rènpíng tā zěnme hǎnjiào, méiyǒu rén lǐ tā 任凭他怎么喊叫，没有人理他** no matter how much he shouted, no one paid attention to him

任何 rènhé *det* any, whatever; **tā bú rènshi rènhé rén 她不认识任何人** she doesn't know anyone

任命 rènmìng *vb* employ, appoint

任务 rènwu *n* assigned duty, task, responsibility

扔 rēng *vb* throw, throw away, cast aside

仍旧 réngjiù *adv* as before, still, yet

仍（然）réng (rán) *adv* still, yet, as before

日 rì n sun;day,daytime;(*in general*) time;every day,day by day

日报 rìbào n daily paper,daily

日本 Rìběn n Japan

日常 rìcháng adj daily,day to day,everyday

日程 rìchéng n daily schedule,agenda,programme

日出 rìchū n sunrise

日记 rìjì n diary

日历 rìlì n calendar

日落 rìluò n sunset

日期 rìqī n date

日文 Rìwén n Japanese language (usually written)

日益 rìyì adv increasingly,day by day

日用品 rìyòngpǐn n daily necessities,basic commodities

日语 Rìyǔ n Japanese language (usually spoken)

日元 rìyuán n Japanese yen

日子 rìzi n day,date;a period of time,days;way of life, livelihood

容 róng vb allow,let,permit;tolerate;hold,contain

容纳 róngnà vb hold,have the capacity of

容忍 róngrěn vb tolerate,put up with

容许 róngxǔ vb allow,permit

容易 róngyì adj easy；likely,apt；xiàtiān niúnǎi hěn róngyì huài 夏天牛奶很容易坏 in the summer milk goes bad easily

肉 ròu n (*of an animal*) meat,flesh；(*of a person*) muscle, flesh；(*of fruit or vegetable*) pulp,flesh

如 rú 1 vb be like,be as,be similar to；(*when used with a negative*)▶ See also 不如 **bùrú. 2** prep in accordance with,according to **3** conj if,supposing；rú xiàyǔ,wǒmen jiù bú qù le 如下雨,我们就不去了 if it rains,we just won't go **4** rú 如 such as, for example：Běijīng yǒu hěn duō míngshèng，rú Chángchéng，Gùgōng，děngděng 北京有很多名胜，如长城，故宫，等等 Beijing has many famous places，such as the Great Wall，the Forbidden City，etc.

如此 rúcǐ adv so，such，in this way

如果 rúguǒ conj if，supposing that，in case

如何 rúhé adv (in a question or a statement) how，what；nǐ de kǎoshì rúhé? 你的考试如何? how was your examination?；tā bù zhīdào rúhé wánchéng zhè xiàng rènwu 他不知道如何完成这项任务 he doesn't know how to finish this task

如今 rújīn adv these days，nowadays，at the present time

如意 rúyì adj ideal，as one wishes

入 rù vb enter，come in，go in；join，be admitted to，become a member of

软 ruǎn adj soft，gentle，flexible；(when referring to physical weakness) weak，feeble；(when speaking about a person) easily moved/influenced

若干 ruògān det a certain number of，several

若是 ruòshì conj if

弱 ruò adj weak，feeble；inferior，not up to standard

弱点 ruòdiǎn n weakness，weak point

Ss

撒 sā vb let go，let out，cast

洒 sǎ vb sprinkle，spill，spray

赛 sài 1 vb compete，race；rival，overtake，surpass **2** n competition，race，match

三 **sān** _num_ three

三月 **sānyuè** _n_ March

伞 **sǎn** _n_ umbrella, parasol, sunshade

散步 **sànbù** _vb_ take a stroll, go for a walk

嗓子 **sǎngzi** _n_ throat, larynx; voice

扫 **sǎo** _vb_ sweep, clean

嫂子 **sǎozi** _n_ sister-in-law, elder brother's wife

扫帚 **sàozhou** _n_ broom

色 **sè** _n_ colour, look, quality; expression, countenance; sex, physical attraction, sexual passion

森林 **sēnlín** _n_ forest

杀 **shā** _vb_ kill, put to death; weaken, reduce

沙发 **shāfā** _n_ sofa

沙漠 **shāmò** _n_ desert

沙子 **shāzi** _n_ sand, grains of sand; small grains, pellets, grit

傻 **shǎ** _adj_ foolish, stupid, silly

晒 **shài** _vb_ (_when speaking about the sun_) shine upon; (_when speaking about people_) sunbathe, dry in the sun; shài tàiyáng 晒太阳 sunbathe

山 **shān** _n_ mountain, hill

山脉 **shānmài** _n_ mountain range

山区 **shānqū** _n_ mountainous region

闪 **shǎn** _vb_ evade, dodge, duck; (_as a light, lightning, inspiration, etc._) flash; dǎshǎn 打闪 lightning flashes

善于 **shànyú** _vb_ be good at

伤 **shāng 1** _vb_ (_physically, emotionally, etc._) wound, injure, hurt **2** _n_ wound, harm, injury

伤心 **shāngxīn** _adj_ sad, broken-hearted

商场 **shāngchǎng** _n_ market

商店 **shāngdiàn** _n_ shop, store

商量 **shāngliang** _vb_ talk over, consult, discuss

商品 shāngpǐn *n* goods, commodities, merchandise

商业 shāngyè *n* commerce, business, trade

上 shàng 1 *vb* go up, ascend; **shànglóu 上楼** go upstairs; (*when talking about getting on or into a vehicle, mode of transport, stage or platform*) mount, board, get on; **shàng [gōnggòng qìchē|chuán|fēijī]上 [公共汽车|船|飞机]** board [the bus|the boat|the plane]; go, come **2** *adv* (*after a verb to indicate an upward direction or accomplishment*) up; **[guān|dēng|chuān]shang [关|登|穿]上** [close up| climb up| reach| put on]; (*to indicate the beginning and continuity of an action*) **tāmen zhùshangle xīn fángzi 他们住上了新房子** they now live in a new house **3** *adj* up, upper, high; (*in grade or quality*) first, top; first, preceding, previous; **shàng…qù 上…去** go...; **nǐ shàng nǎr qù? 你上哪儿去?** where are you going?; **shàng…[qù|lái]上…[去|来]** [go| come]; **wǒ shàng xuéxiào qù 我上学校去** I am going to the school

上班 shàngbān *vb* go to the office, start work

上边 shàngbian 1 *n* top, above, higher parts; the top of, the surface of; the higher authorities, the higher-ups; aspect, respect, regard; **tā bú yòng zài zhè shàngbian huā hěn duō shíjiān 他不用在这上边花很多时间** he does not need to spend much time on this **2** *adj* above-mentioned, aforesaid, foregoing

上当 shàngdàng *vb* be swindled, be taken in, fall into a trap

上帝 Shàngdì *n* God

上海 Shànghǎi *n* Shanghai (Municipality)

上级 shàngjí *n* upper grade, higher level; higher authority

上课 shàngkè *vb* go to class, attend a lecture; teach a class

上来 shànglái *vb* come up; (*after a verb to indicate a direction up and toward the speaker*) ...up; **ná shànglái**

拿上来 bring up；(*after a verb to indicate accomplishment*) tā dá bú shànglái zhège wèntí 他答不上来这个问题 he is unable to answer this question

上面 **shàngmian** ▶上边 shàngbian

上去 **shàngqù** *vb* go up；(*after a verb to indicate a direction up and away from the speaker*) up；ná shàngqù 拿上去 take up

上头 **shàngtou** ▶上边 shàngbian

上午 **shàngwǔ** *n* morning，a. m.，forenoon

上学 **shàngxué** *vb* attend school，go to school

上衣 **shàngyī** *n* outer garment (worn on the upper half of the body)，jacket

烧 **shāo 1** *vb* burn；heat，cook；bake，stew，roast；have a temperature，have a fever **2** *n* temperature，fever

稍 **shāo**，稍微 **shāowēi** *adv* a little，somewhat，slightly

勺子 **sháozi** *n* spoon，ladle

少 **shǎo**！*Can also be pronounced* **shào** *with a different meaning.* **1** *adj* few，little，scarce；(*in comparisons*) less **2** *adv* seldom，hardly ever，scarcely ever **3** *vb* be short of，lack，be missing；(*used in imperative sentences*) stop，quit，reduce；nǐ shǎo guǎn xiánshì 你少管闲事 stop meddling in other people's affairs

少数 **shǎoshù** *n* minority；shǎoshù mínzú 少数民族 ethnic minority

少年 **shàonián** *n* (*a time of life*) youth；(*a person*) youth，young person

舌头 **shétou** *n* tongue

蛇 **shé** *n* snake，serpent

设备 **shèbèi** *n* equipment

设计 **shèjì 1** *vb* design，plan，draw up plans **2** *n* design，plan，project

社会 **shèhuì** *n* society，community

射 shè *vb* shoot；emit，radiate，send out

谁 shéi *pron* ！ *Also pronounced* shuí；who?；nǐ shì shéi? 你是谁？ who are you?；anybody；yǒu shéi yuànyì qù? 有谁愿意去？ would anyone like to go?；(*used with* dōu 都) everybody；shéi dōu xǐhuan kànshū 谁都喜欢看书 everybody likes to read books；(*used with* dōu 都 *in the negative*) nobody；shéi dōu méi qián 谁都没钱 nobody has any money

伸 shēn *vb* stretch，extend

身 shēn *n* body；life；oneself，personally，itself

身边 shēnbiān 1 *n* one's side，one's person **2** *adv* at/by one's side，at hand，nearby

身体 shēntǐ *n* body，health

深 shēn 1 *adj* (*of water*，*thought*，*etc.*) deep，profound；(*of understanding*，*etc.*) thorough，penetrating；(*of friendships*，*relationships*，*etc.*) close，intimate；(*of forests*，*mysteries*，*etc.*) hidden，inaccessible，obscure；(*of colours*) dark，deep；(*of night*，*season*，*etc.*) late **2** *adv* profoundly，greatly，deeply

深厚 shēnhòu *adj* (*of friendships*，*foundations*，*etc.*) deep，profound，solid

深刻 shēnkè *adj* (*of impressions*，*etc.*) deep，profound

深入 shēnrù 1 *vb* penetrate deeply into，go deeply into **2** *adj* deep，thorough，penetrating

什么 shénme 1 *pron* what? what kind of?；nǐ xué shénme? 你学什么？ what do you study?；wǒ xiǎng jìnchéng mǎi diǎnr shénme 我想进城买点儿什么 I want to go into town to buy something；(*when it comes before* dōu 都) everything；tā shénme dōu chī 她什么都吃 she eats everything；(*when used in the negative before* yě 也 *or* dōu 都) nothing，not anything；tā shénme yě bù zhīdào 他什么也不知道 he doesn't know anything；

(*when enumerating things*) etc.,… and what not;
shénme yīfu a,shípǐn a,wánjù a,nàge shāngdiàn dōu
mài 什么衣服啊,食品啊,玩具啊,那个商店都卖 that
shop sells clothes, food, toys, and what not **2** *exc* (*to
indicate surprise or displeasure*) what? **3** *det* what;
xiànzài shì shénme shíhòu? 现在是什么时候? what
time is it (now)?;… **shénme … shénme** … 什么 … 什么
whatever; nǐ yào shénme jiù mǎi shénme 你要什么就买
什么 buy whatever you want

什么的 shénmede *pron* and so forth,etc.

神 shén 1 *n* spirit,god,deity;spirit,mind;expression,
look **2** *adj* spiritual,supernatural,magical

神经 shénjīng *n* (*of the body*) nerve

甚至(于)shènzhì(yú) *adv* even,so much so that,so far
as to

升 shēng 1 *vb* rise,ascend,move upward;(*in position or
rank*) promote **2** *n* (*unit for measuring liquids*) litre

生 shēng 1 *vb* be born,give birth to,give rise to;grow;
become **2** *adj* living,alive,live,unripe,green,raw;
unprocessed,unrefined;unfamiliar,strange **3** *n* life,
existence;living,livelihood;lifetime

生产 shēngchǎn 1 *vb* produce,make,manufacture;give
birth **2** *n* production

生词 shēngcí *n* new word,new vocabulary

生动 shēngdòng *adj* moving,vivid,lively

生活 shēnghuó 1 *n* life;living,livelihood **2** *vb* live

生命 shēngmìng *n* (*biological existence*) life

生气 shēngqì *adj* angry

生日 shēngrì *n* birthday

生物 shēngwù *n* living beings,organisms;shēngwùxué
生物学 biology

生意 shēngyi *n* business,trade;zuò shēngyi 做生意 do

business

生长 shēngzhǎng vb grow, develop; grow up, be brought up

声 shēng 1 n voice, sound; (as in the linguistic tone of a Chinese word) tone; **sìshēng 四声** the four tones of Chinese **2** mw ▶ **623** (for counting cries, shouts, or other utterances)

声调 shēngdiào n (of words, sentences, speaking) tone, intonation; (of a Chinese character) tone; melody

声音 shēngyīn n sound, voice, noise

绳子 shéngzi n cord, string, rope

省 shěng 1 n province **2** vb (when talking about time or money) economize, save, spare; omit, leave out

圣诞(节) Shèngdàn (Jié) n Christmas (Day)

胜 shèng 1 n victory, success **2** vb conquer, win, defeat; excel, surpass, be better than

胜利 shènglì 1 vb be victorious, be successful, win **2** n victory **3** adv victoriously, successfully

剩下 shèngxia vb remain, be left over, have...left over; leave behind; **shèngxià(lái) 剩下(来)** remain, be left over

失败 shībài 1 vb fail, be defeated **2** n failure, defeat

失去 shīqù vb (when talking about objects, opportunities, friends, etc.) lose

失望 shīwàng 1 adj disappointed **2** vb lose hope, lose confidence

失业 shīyè 1 vb be unemployed, lose one's job **2** n unemployment

师傅 shīfu n master worker, teacher, instructor; a polite term of address to people who have skill or specialized knowledge

诗 shī n poetry, poem, verse; **shīrén 诗人** poet

狮子 shīzi n lion

施工 shīgōng vb be under construction, engage in construction

湿 **shī** *adj* damp, humid, wet

湿润 **shīrùn** *adj* humid, moist

十 **shí** *num* ten, tens, multiples of ten

十二 **shí'èr** *num* twelve

十二月 **shí'èryuè** *n* December

十分 **shífēn** *adv* completely, fully, utterly

十一 **shíyī** *num* eleven

十一月 **shíyīyuè** *n* November

十月 **shíyuè** *n* October

十字路口 **shízì lùkǒu** *n* crossroads

石 **shí**, 石头 **shítou** *n* rock, stone, pebble

石油 **shíyóu** *n* petroleum, oil

时代 **shídài** *n* time, period, age

时候 **shíhou 1** *n* time, length of time; (*when speaking of time on the clock*) time, moment in time, point in time; tā shì shénme shíhou zǒu de? 他是什么时候走的? what time did he leave? **2** *conj* … de shíhou … 的时候 when…, during…, while…; dāng…shíhou 当…时候 when…

时间 **shíjiān** *n* (*as an abstract concept*) time; (*a set period of time*) time, duration; (*point of time*) time; nǐ shénme shíjiān dào de? 你什么时间到的? what time did you arrive?; time zone; Běijīng shíjiān 北京时间 Beijing time; shíjiānbiǎo 时间表 timetable, schedule

时刻 **shíkè 1** *n* time, hour **2** *adv* every moment, constantly, always

时期 **shíqī** *n* time period

实际 **shíjì 1** *n* reality, fact **2** *adj* realistic, practical; shíjìshang 实际上 actually, in fact, in reality

实践 **shíjiàn 1** *vb* put into practice, carry out **2** *n* practice

实事 **shíshì** *n* fact, facts; shíshì-qiúshì 实事求是 seek truth from facts, be realistic

实现 shíxiàn vb (as a hope, dream, plan) realize, come true, actualise

实行 shíxíng vb implement, put into practice, carry out

实验 shíyàn 1 vb experiment **2** n experiment; **shíyànshì 实验室** laboratory

实用 shíyòng adj practical, functional, applied

实在 shízài 1 adj true, real, honest **2** adv actually, really

拾 shí vb pick up, gather, collect

食品 shípǐn n food, provisions

食堂 shítáng n dining hall, cafeteria

食物 shíwù n food

使 shǐ vb use, employ, apply; enable, cause, make

使用 shǐyòng 1 vb utilise, make use of, apply **2** n use, deployment

始终 shǐzhōng adv from beginning to end, all along

世纪 shìjì n century

世界 shìjiè n world

市 shì n municipality, city; market, fair; (pertaining to the Chinese system of weights and measures) yí shìjīn **1 市斤** 1/2 kilo

市场 shìchǎng n market, bazaar

式样 shìyàng n style, type, model

事 shì n affair, matter, event; trouble, accident, work, job; zuòshì **做事** work at a job

事故 shìgù n accident

事件 shìjiàn n incident, event

事情 shìqing n thing, matter, affair

事实 shishí n reality, fact; shìshíshang **事实上** in fact, as a matter of fact, in reality

事务 shìwù n affairs, matters; work, routine, duties

事物 shìwù n thing, object, matter

事先 shìxiān *adv* prior to, in advance, beforehand

事业 shìyè *n* profession, career, cause; enterprise, undertaking

试 shì 1 *vb* try, try out, test **2** *n* test, examination; **shìshi kàn 试试看** try and see

试卷 shìjuàn *n* examination paper, answer booklet, script

试验 shìyàn 1 *vb* test, experiment **2** *n* experiment, test, trial

是 shì 1 *vb* (*the verb* to be) am, is, are; certainly, indeed; **wǒ shì méi qù 我是没去** I certainly did not go **2** *adj* right, correct; (*used to answer the affirmative*) yes, right; **shì, nǐ shuō de duì 是, 你说得对** yes, what you said is correct **3** (*used in certain patterns*) **bú shì…ér shì…不是…而是…** it's not…but…; **yào bú shì…jiù shì…要不是…就是…** if it's not…, it's…; **shì…de 是…的** (*for emphasis*) **tā shì hěn yònggōng de 她是很用功的** she studies hard; (*when giving the details about someone or something, its origin, manufacture, provenance, etc.*) **zhè liàng qìchē shì Rìběn zào de 这辆汽车是日本造的** this car was made in Japan; **shì bú shì… 是不是…** is it?; **shì…háishi… 是…还是…** …or…, whether…or…; **nǐ shì zǒulù lái de, háishì qíchē lái de? 你是走路来的, 还是骑车来的?** did you walk or come by bicycle?; **…shì…, kěshì… …是…, 可是…** (*here* shì 是 *is used in a clause of concession*) yes, it is…, but…, although…, yet…; **zhè bù diànyǐng hǎo shì hǎo, kěshì tài cháng le 这部电影好是好, 可是太长了** although this movie is good, it's too long

适当 shìdàng *adj* suitable, appropriate, proper

适合 shìhé *vb* fit, suit, be appropriate

适应 shìyìng *vb* adapt, suit, fit

适用 shìyòng *adj* suitable, applicable, appropriate

室 shì *n* room

收 shōu *vb* receive, accept; collect, gather, harvest; **shōu huílái 收回来** recover, get back; **shōu qǐlái 收起来** put away, store away

收获 shōuhuò 1 *vb* harvest, gather in the crops, reap **2** *n* (*of hard work, study, etc.*) results, harvest, gains

收入 shōurù 1 *vb* receive, take in **2** *n* income, revenue

收拾 shōushi *vb* put in order, straighten up, tidy; repair, fix, mend

收音机 shōuyīnjī *n* radio

熟 shóu ▶ 熟 shú

手 shǒu 1 *n* hand **2** *adv* by hand

手表 shǒubiǎo *n* watch, wristwatch

手段 shǒuduàn *n* method, means

手工 shǒugōng 1 *n* handicraft, handiwork **2** *adj* manual, handmade **3** *adv* by hand

手绢 shǒujuàn *n* handkerchief

手术 shǒushù *n* surgical operation

手套 shǒutào *n* gloves

手续 shǒuxù *n* procedures, formalities, process

手指 shǒuzhǐ *n* finger; **shǒuzhǐjiǎ 手指甲** fingernail

首 shǒu 1 *n* (*part of the body*) head; (*a person*) leader, chief, head **2** *mw ▶ 623* (*for songs, poems, music*) **3** *adj* first, beginning, most important

首都 shǒudū *n* (*of a country*) capital

首先 shǒuxiān *adv* first, in the first place, above all

受 shòu *vb* receive, accept; suffer, be subjected to; stand, endure, bear; (*used to express the passive voice*) receive, be subject to

售货员 shòuhuòyuán *n* shop assistant

售票员 shòupiàoyuán *n* (*on a bus*) conductor; (*at a*

train station) booking-office clerk; (*at a cinema or theatre*) box-office clerk

瘦 shòu *adj* (*of people*) thin, emaciated; (*of meat*) lean; (*of clothing*) tight

书 shū *n* book; letter

书包 shūbāo *n* satchel, book bag, school bag

书店 shūdiàn *n* bookshop, bookstore

书法 shūfǎ *n* calligraphy

书记 shūjì *n* (*of a political party or a political organization*) secretary

书架 shūjià *n* bookcase, bookshelf

书桌 shūzhuō *n* desk

叔叔 shūshu *n* uncle, father's younger brother; (*a man in one's father's generation*) uncle

舒服 shūfu *adj* comfortable, feeling well

舒适 shūshì *adj* comfortable, cosy

输 shū *vb* transport, transmit, convey; (*when speaking about a game, a gamble*) lose, be defeated

蔬菜 shūcài *n* vegetables

熟 shú ! *Can also be pronounced* shóu. **1** *adj* (*of fruit, etc.*) ripe, mature; (*of food*) cooked, done, processed; (*of people*) familiar, well-acquainted; (*in a subject, a type of work, etc.*) skilled, trained, experienced **2** *adv* (*of sleep*) deeply, soundly; **shúrén 熟人** acquaintance

熟练 shúliàn *adj* expert, adept, proficient

熟悉 shúxī *vb* know well, be familiar with

暑假 shǔjià *n* summer holidays, summer vacation

属于 shǔyú *vb* belong to, pertain to, be part of; Xiānggǎng shǔyú Zhōngguó 香港属于中国 Hong Kong belongs to China

数 shǔ *vb* ▶ *See also* 数 shù. count, enumerate, list; count as, be counted as, be notable for; **shǔdeshàng 数得上**

qualify, count, be counted; **shǔ bù qīng 数不清** unable to count exactly, countless; **shǔ bú guòlái 数不过来** too many to count

鼠 shǔ *n* mouse, rat

束 shù *mw* ▶ **623** bunch

树 shù 1 *n* tree **2** *vb* establish, set up

树林 shùlín *n* woods

数 shù ▶ See also 数 **shǔ. 1** *n* number, figure **2** *det* several, a few

数量 shùliàng *n* number, quantity, amount

数学 shùxué *n* mathematics

数字 shùzì *n* number, figure, digit

刷 shuā *vb* brush, scrub, paint, whitewash, paste up

摔 shuāi *vb* fall, stumble; **tā shuāile yì jiāo 她摔了一跤** she tripped over something and fell; break, smash; **shuāiduàn 摔断** break; throw down, cast

甩 shuǎi *vb* swing, move back and forth; fling, cast away, throw

率 shuài, 率领 shuàilǐng *vb* lead, head, command

双 shuāng 1 *mw* ▶ **623** (for things that come in twos, such as shoes, socks, chopsticks, etc.) pair **2** *adj* double, twin, dual; **shuāngshǒu 双手** both hands; (when talking about numbers) even; **shuāngshù 双数** even numbers

双方 shuāngfāng *n* both sides

谁 shuí ▶ 谁 **shéi**

水 shuǐ *n* water, juice, liquid

水稻 shuǐdào *n* rice grown in a paddy field

水果 shuǐguǒ *n* fruit, fresh fruit

水泥 shuǐní *n* cement

水平 shuǐpíng *n* standard, level

睡 **shuì** vb sleep；**shuìzháo** 睡着 go to sleep，fall asleep，be sleeping

睡觉 **shuìjiào** vb sleep

顺 **shùn 1** prep along，in the direction of **2** vb obey，submit to；follow，accord with，go with **3** adj favourable，successful，smooth，fluent；**shùnzhe** 顺着 along，following

顺便 **shùnbiàn** adv along the way，in passing

顺利 **shùnlì 1** adj smooth，successful，with no obstacles **2** adv smoothly，successfully，well

说 **shuō** vb say，speak，talk；explain；scold，rebuke

说明 **shuōmíng 1** vb make clear，explain **2** n instructions，explanation，directions；**shuōmíngshū** 说明书 directions，instructions，synopsis

司机 **sījī** n driver，chauffeur

丝 **sī** n silk；fine thread，slight amount，trace

私 **sī 1** adj private，secret，confidential；selfish；illegal，underhanded **2** adv privately，confidentially，secretly

私人 **sīrén** adj private，personal

思想 **sīxiǎng** n thought，philosophy，ideas

撕 **sī** vb tear，rip，shred

死 **sǐ 1** vb die，pass away **2** adj dead；stagnant，inflexible **3** adv（when it comes before a verb）to the death；**sǐshǒu** 死守 defend to the death；（when it comes after a verb）die of，to death；[dòng｜yān｜è]sǐ [冻｜淹｜饿]死［freeze／drown／starve]to death；（when it comes after an adjective）extremely；[lè｜qì｜lèi]sǐ le [乐｜气｜累]死了 extremely [happy／angry／tired]

四 **sì** num four

四月 **sìyuè** n April

似乎 **sìhū 1** adv seemingly，apparently **2** vb seem，appear，seem to be；**sìhū tài wǎn le** 似乎太晚了 it seems too late

松 **sŏng 1** n pine tree，fir tree **2** adj loose，lax，slack **3** vb relax, loosen, slacken

送 sòng vb (as a gift) give, present; **sònggěi tā yí jiàn lǐwù** 送给她一件礼物 give her a present; deliver, take, bring; see off, accompany

送行 sòngxíng vb see off, send off, wish someone a safe journey

艘 sōu mw ▶ **623** (for ships)

肃静 sùjìng adj solemn and silent

速度 sùdù n speed, velocity

宿舍 sùshè n dormitory

塑料 sùliào n plastic, plastics

酸 suān 1 adj sour tasting; sad, distressed, sorrowful; (muscles, back, etc.) sore, aching **2** n acid

算 suàn vb figure, count, calculate; include, count in; be counted as, be considered as, be regarded as; **tā suànshì wǒmen de hǎopéngyou** 他算是我们的好朋友 he can be considered our good friend; carry weight, count; **suànshang** 算上 count in, include; **suànle** 算了 forget it, let it be, let's drop the matter

虽然 suīrán conj although, though; **suīrán⋯ kěshì/dànshì⋯** 虽然⋯ 可是/但是⋯ although..., (still, yet)...

随 suí 1 prep along with; **tā suí(zhe) wēndù ér biànhuà** 它随(着)温度而变化 it varies with the temperature **2** vb follow, go along with; (whatever one wishes or finds convenient) **mǎi bù mǎi suí nǐ** 买不买随你 it's up to you whether you buy it or not

随便 suíbiàn 1 adj casual, informal, random; careless, thoughtless, cursory **2** adv following one's convenience, as one pleases, freely, carelessly, in a cursory manner, randomly **3** conj no matter whether, whatever, in whatever way

随时 suíshí adv at any time

岁 suì n year of age, year old; **tā de érzi wǔ suì** 他的儿子 5 岁 his son is five years old

碎 **suì 1** *adj* broken, shattered, fragmentary **2** *vb* break, break in pieces, smash to bits

孙女 **sūnnǚ** *n* granddaughter

孙子 **sūnzi** *n* grandson

损失 **sǔnshī 1** *vb* lose, damage, harm **2** *n* loss, damage

缩 **suō** *vb* (*in size*) shrink, reduce, contract; (*in movement*) shrink back, withdraw

所 **suǒ 1** *mw* ▶ 623 (*for buildings, houses, schools, etc.*) **2** *n* place, site, station; office, bureau, institute **3** *pt* (*used with* wéi 为 *or* bèi 被 *to indicate the passive voice*) bèi dàjiā suǒ chēngzàn 被大家所称赞 be praised by everyone; (*when it precedes a verb*) what, whatever; wǒ suǒ [shuō de | xǐhuan de | zuò de] 我所 [说的 | 喜欢的 | 做的] [what I said | what I like | what I do/did]

所谓 **suǒwèi** *adj* so-called, what is called

所以 **suǒyǐ** *conj* therefore, thus, as a result; tā bìng le, suǒyǐ méi lái 他病了,所以没来 he is ill, so he didn't come; (*when giving a cause or reason*) the reason why...; tā zhīsuǒyǐ shēngbìng shì yīnwèi nà tiān chūqù méi chuān dàyī 他之所以生病是因为那天出去没穿大衣 the reason why he became ill is that he went out that day without a coat

所有 **suǒyǒu 1** *det* all **2** *n* possession

Tt

他 **tā** *pron* he, him; another, other, some other; tārén 他人 other people

他们 **tāmen** *pron* they, them

它 **tā** *pron* (*neuter, for animals and things*) it

它们 tāmen pron (neuter, for animals and things) they, them

她 tā pron she, her

她们 tāmen pron (when referring to females) they

塔 tǎ n pagoda, tower

踏 tà vb step on, tread, set foot on

台 tái 1 n terrace, raised platform, stage; stand, support; broadcasting station **2** mw ▶ **623** (for stage performances, machines, equipment, etc.)

台风 táifēng n typhoon

抬 tái vb lift, raise, carry

太 tài adv too, excessively; extremely; (in the negative) (not) very; **bú tài gāo 不太高** not very tall

太极拳 tàijíquán n taijiquan, traditional Chinese shadow boxing

太空 tàikōng n outer space

太平洋 Tàipíngyáng n the Pacific Ocean

太太 tàitai n married woman, wife; Mrs., Madam

太阳 tàiyáng n sun, sunshine, sunlight

态度 tàidu n attitude, manner, bearing

摊 tān n (for selling things) stand, booth, stall

谈 tán vb talk, discuss, chat

谈话 tánhuà 1 vb talk, chat, carry on a conversation **2** n conversation, discussion

谈论 tánlùn vb talk about, discuss

谈判 tánpàn 1 vb negotiate, talk, discuss **2** n negotiation, talk

弹 tán vb ! Can also be pronounced **dàn 弹** with a different meaning; shoot, send forth; (as fingers, ashes off a cigarette, etc.) flick, flip, snap; (a stringed instrument, piano, etc.) play, pluck

毯子 tǎnzi *n* rug, carpet, blanket

叹气 tànqì *vb* sigh

探 tàn *vb* search out, seek, explore; visit, pay a call on

汤 tāng *n* soup, broth

堂 táng 1 *n* hall **2** *mw* ▶ **623** (*for classes or periods at school or university*) period, class

糖 táng *n* sugar, sweets, candy

躺 tǎng *vb* lie, recline, be lying

烫 tàng 1 *vb* scald, burn; (*clothes*) iron; (*using heat on the hair*) curl, set, perm; heat up, warm **2** *adj* hot to the touch, scalding

趟 tàng *mw* ▶ **623** (*for scheduled services of public transportation*); (*for trips, journeys, visits, etc.*) time, trip

掏 tāo *vb* (*with the hand as from a pocket*) take out, fish out, extract

逃 táo *vb* escape, run away, evade

桃(子) táo(zi) *n* peach

讨论 tǎolùn 1 *vb* discuss, debate, talk over **2** *n* discussion, debate

讨厌 tǎoyàn 1 *adj* disgusting, objectionable; troublesome, annoying **2** *vb* dislike, be disgusted with

套 tào 1 *mw* ▶ **623** (*for sets of books, clothing, tools, furniture, etc.*) set, suit, suite **2** *n* cover, sheath, case

特 tè *adv* specially, particularly, exceptionally

特别 tèbié 1 *adj* special, distinctive, unique *adv* especially, specially

特此 tècǐ *adv* hereby

特点 tèdiǎn *n* special characteristic, special feature

特色 tèsè *n* unique feature

特殊 tèshū *adj* special, particular, exceptional

疼 téng *vb* ache, hurt, be painful; love, be fond of, have affection for

踢 tī *vb* kick; (*when talking about football or other games requiring kicking*) play

提 tí *vb* lift, raise, carry; (*when talking about a subject*) bring up, mention; (*when talking about money in a bank*) draw out, take out, withdraw; (*when talking about a suggestion, an objection, etc.*) put forward, bring up, raise

提倡 tíchàng *vb* advocate, promote

提出 tíchū *vb* put forward, raise, advance

提高 tígāo *vb* raise, elevate, increase, enhance, improve

提供 tígōng *vb* offer, make available to, provide

提前 tíqián 1 *vb* (*when speaking of an appointment or deadline*) bring forward, advance, change to an earlier time/date **2** *adv* in advance, ahead of time, beforehand

提醒 tíxǐng *vb* remind, warn

提议 tíyì 1 *vb* propose, suggest **2** *n* proposal, suggestion, motion

题 tí 1 *n* subject, topic, title **2** *vb* (*on a poem, painting, fan, etc.*) inscribe

题目 tímù *n* (*of a lecture, discussion, essay, etc.*) subject, title, topic

体会 tǐhuì 1 *vb* sense, realize, understand **2** *n* sense, feeling, understanding

体积 tǐjī *n* bulk, physical volume

体系 tǐxì *n* system

体验 tǐyàn *vb* learn through practice/experience

体育 tǐyù *n* sports, physical education, training

体育场 tǐyùchǎng *n* stadium, arena

体育馆 tǐyùguǎn *n* gymnasium, gym

替 tì 1 *vb* substitute for, take the place of, replace **2** *prep*

for, on behalf of

天 tiān *n* sky, heaven; God, Heaven; weather; day; season; nature, world of nature; tiāntiān 天天 every day

天安门 Tiān'ānmén *n* Tian An Men, the Gate of Heavenly Peace

天才 tiāncái *n* talent, gift, genius

天津 Tiānjīn *n* Tianjin (Municipality)

天空 tiānkōng *n* the sky, the heavens

天气 tiānqì *n* weather

天然 tiānrán *adj* natural

天下 tiānxià **1** *n* all under heaven, the whole world, the whole of China **2** *adv* everywhere under heaven, all over the world, all over China

天真 tiānzhēn *adj* innocent, naive, pure

添 tiān *vb* add, supplement with, replenish

田 tián *n* farm, field

田野 tiányě *n* field, open country

甜 tián *adj* (*in flavour, love, dreams, music*) sweet; (*when referring to sleep*) sound

填 tián *vb* (*a hole, a blank space*) fill up, fill in

挑 tiāo *vb* ! *Can also be pronounced* **tiǎo** *with a different meaning*; choose, select; (*with a pole on the shoulders*) carry; tiāo shuǐ 挑水 carry water; (*as heavy responsibilities*) shoulder, carry

条 tiáo **1** *mw* ▶ 623 (*for long, narrow things*); (*for items of news, laws, ideas, views*); (*for limbs of the human body*); (*for human lives*) sì tiáo rénmìng 4 条人命 four lives **2** *n* strip, slip; slip of paper, short note, message; (*in a treaty, constitution, law, contract, or other written document*) item, clause, article

条件 tiáojiàn *n* (*of an agreement*) condition, term, stipulation; requirement, qualification, condition

条约 tiáoyuē *n* treaty，agreement，pact

调 tiáo *vb* ▶ See also 调 **diào**．mix，adjust，mediate

调皮 tiáopí *adj* naughty，mischievous，unruly

调整 tiáozhěng 1 *vb* adjust，reorganize，revise **2** *n* adjustment，revision

挑战 tiǎozhàn ! The character tiǎo 挑 can also be pronounced tiāo with a different meaning． **1** *vb* challenge，challenge to a contest，challenge to battle **2** *n* challenge

跳 tiào *vb* jump，hop，leap；(as a heart，etc.) beat；skip，skip over，miss out

跳舞 tiàowǔ *vb* dance

贴 tiē *vb* paste，stick on；stay next to，nestle close to

铁 tiě *n* iron

铁路 tiělù，铁道 tiědào *n* railway，railroad

厅 tīng *n* hall；office，department

听 tīng *vb* listen to，hear；obey，heed；allow，let

听话 tīnghuà *adj* obedient

听见 tīngjiàn *vb* hear，perceive by hearing

听讲 tīngjiǎng *vb* listen to a talk，attend a lecture

听说 tīngshuō *vb* hear，it is said，hear it said that

听写 tīngxiě 1 *vb* dictate **2** *n* dictation

停 tíng *vb* stop，cease，halt；stay，stop over；(of cars) park；(of ships) anchor，lie at anchor

停止 tíngzhǐ *vb* stop，cease

挺 tǐng *adv* rather，quite，very

通 tōng 1 *vb* go through，pass through；communicate with，get through；**wǒ cháng hé tā tōngxìn** 我常和他通信 I often communicate with him by letter；lead to，go to **2** *adj* open，passable；(of writing，arguments) logical，coherent，grammatical **3** *n* authority，expert；**Zhōngguótōng** 中国通

China expert, old China hand

通常 tōngcháng 1 *adv* usually, normally, generally **2** *adj* usual, normal, general

通过 tōngguò 1 *prep* by means of, by way of, via **2** *vb* pass through; (*by voting*) pass, carry, adopt

通讯 tōngxùn *n* communication; news report, news despatch, newsletter

通知 tōngzhī 1 *vb* notify, inform **2** *n* notice, notification

同 tóng 1 *adj* same, identical, similar **2** *adv* together, in the same way **3** *prep* with

同伴 tóngbàn *n* companion

同情 tóngqíng 1 *vb* sympathize with, be sympathetic toward, share feelings with **2** *n* sympathy, compassion

同时 tóngshí *adv* at the same time, simultaneously, meanwhile; moreover, besides

同事 tóngshì *n* colleague, fellow worker

同屋 tóngwū *n* roommate

同学 tóngxué *n* classmate, schoolmate, fellow student

同样 tóngyàng 1 *adj* same, alike, similar **2** *adv* in the same way, equally

同意 tóngyì *vb* agree

同志 tóngzhì *n* comrade

铜 tóng *n* copper, bronze, brass

童年 tóngnián *n* childhood

统计 tǒngjì 1 *n* statistics **2** *vb* count, add up

统一 tǒngyī 1 *vb* unify, unite **2** *adj* unified

统治 tǒngzhì *vb* control, rule, govern

桶 tǒng *n* bucket, barrel, keg

痛 tòng 1 *vb* hurt, ache, pain **2** *n* pain, sorrow **3** *adv* thoroughly, extremely, deeply; (*when speaking of unpleasant actions*) severely, bitterly

痛苦 tòngkǔ 1 adj bitter, painful **2** n suffering, agony, pain

痛快 tòngkuài 1 adj happy, delighted, refreshed; frank, outspoken, forthright **2** adv frankly, outspokenly; to one's heart's content, with abandon, to one's great satisfaction

偷 tōu 1 vb steal, attack **2** adv stealthily, secretly, illegally

偷偷 tōutōu adv stealthily, secretly, on the sly

头 tóu 1 n head; top, beginning; terminus, end; chief, head **2** mw ▶ 623 (for certain animals); (for garlic bulbs) **3** adj first, leading, the first

头发 tóufa n (on a person's head) hair

头脑 tóunǎo n brains, mind

投 tóu vb throw in/at, put in, drop; (when voting) cast; (when talking about suicide, in a river, sea, etc.) throw oneself into

投入 tóurù vb throw into, put into

投降 tóuxiáng vb surrender, capitulate

投资 tóuzī 1 vb invest **2** n investment

透 tòu 1 vb penetrate, pass through, seep through **2** adj thorough, complete **3** adv fully, thoroughly, completely

突出 tūchū 1 vb stress, highlight, give prominence to **2** adj protruding, projecting; prominent, outstanding **3** adv conspicuously

突击 tūjī 1 vb attack suddenly, assault, take by surprise; attack a job to get it done, go all out to finish a task **2** n attack, sudden attack

突然 tūrán 1 adj sudden, abrupt, unexpected **2** adv suddenly, abruptly

图 tú 1 n picture, map, diagram; plan, scheme **2** vb seek, pursue

图书馆 túshūguǎn n library

涂 tú vb smear, spread on, apply; scribble, scrawl, disfigure by marking; delete, blot out, cross out

土 tǔ 1 *n* earth, soil, dust; land, territory, ground **2** *adj* local, native, locally produced; earthen, made of earth; rustic, crude, unenlightened

土地 tǔdì *n* land, territory

土豆 tǔdòu *n* potato

吐 tǔ *vb* ▶ *See also* 吐 **tù**. spit, spit out; (*as in releasing one's emotions*) speak out, pour out, say

吐 tù *vb* ▶ *See also* 吐 **tǔ**. vomit, disgorge, regurgitate

兔子 tùzi *n* rabbit, hare

团 tuán 1 *n* group of people, organization; lump, round mass **2** *mw* ▶ **623** (*for certain round things*) **3** *vb* unite, round up

团结 tuánjié 1 *vb* unite, band together, rally **2** *n* unity

团体 tuántǐ *n* organization, group, team

团圆 tuányuán *n* (*of a family*) reunion

推 tuī *vb* push, shove; push forward, promote, advance; promote, elect, recommend; (*as a responsibility*) decline, refuse, shirk; put off, postpone

推迟 tuīchí *vb* put off, postpone, defer

推动 tuīdòng *vb* prod, promote, push forward

推广 tuīguǎng *vb* spread, extend; promote, popularise

推荐 tuījiàn 1 *vb* recommend **2** *n* recommendation

腿 tuǐ *n* leg, thigh

退 tuì *vb* retreat, withdraw, step back; return, give back; decline, recede, subside; resign, quit, retire; cancel, break off, quit

退步 tuìbù 1 *vb* regress, slip back, fall behind **2** *n* retrogression

退休 tuìxiū *vb* retire (from work)

托 tuō 1 *vb* (*on the palm of one's hand*) support from underneath, hold up, hold; entrust, rely on; make excuses, give as a pretext **2** *n* tray, stand

托儿所 tuō'érsuǒ *n* nursery, child-care centre

拖 tuō *vb* pull, haul, drag; procrastinate, delay

脱 tuō *vb* (*when talking about clothes, shoes, etc.*) take off, remove, cast off; (*when talking about difficult situations, danger, etc.*) free oneself from, get away from, escape from

脱离 tuōlí *vb* leave, break away from, escape from; separate from, divorce, break off

妥当 tuǒdang 1 *adj* proper, appropriate **2** *adv* properly, appropriately

挖 wā *vb* dig, excavate

袜子 wàzi *n* socks

歪 wāi *adj* crooked, askew, awry; devious, dishonest, immoral

外 wài 1 *n* out, outside; foreign country/countries; duìwài màoyì 对外贸易 foreign trade **2** *adj* outside, other; foreign, external; (*referring to relatives of one's mother, sister, or daughter*) wàizǔfù 外祖父 maternal grandfather **3** *prep* out of, outside, beyond

外边 wàibian *n* outside, out

外地 wàidì *n* (*beyond one's home area or place of residence*) outside area, external region, other parts of the country

外国 wàiguó *n* foreign country; wàiguórén 外国人 foreigner

外汇 wàihuì *n* foreign currency, foreign exchange

外交 wàijiāo *n* foreign affairs, diplomacy; wàijiāobù 外

交部 Ministry of Foreign Affairs

外科 **wàikē** *n* surgical department

外面 **wàimian** ▶ **wàibian** 外边

外头 **wàitou** ▶ **wàibian** 外边

外文 **wàiwén** *n* (*referring primarily to a written language*) foreign language

外语 **wàiyǔ** *n* (*referring primarily to a spoken language*) foreign language

弯 **wān** 1 *vb* bend, flex 2 *n* bend, curve, corner; **guǎiwānr** 拐弯儿 go round a bend, turn a corner 3 *adj* bent, curved, crooked

完 **wán** *vb* finish, complete; (*after a verb to indicate completing an action*) finish..., use up, run out of; **wǒ chīwán le** 我吃完了 I've finished eating

完成 **wánchéng** *vb* complete, finish, accomplish

完全 **wánquán** 1 *adj* complete, whole 2 *adv* completely, fully

完整 **wánzhěng** 1 *adj* complete, perfect, whole 2 *n* wholeness, integrity

玩具 **wánjù** *n* toy, plaything

玩儿 **wánr** *vb* play, play with, have fun; (*for sports and other recreational activities*) play, engage in

玩笑 **wánxiào** *n* joke, jest; (**gēn mǒu rén**) **kāi wánxiào** (跟某人)开玩笑 play a joke (on someone)

晚 **wǎn** 1 *adj* late, late in the day, late in life 2 *adv* late 3 *n* evening, night

晚饭 **wǎnfàn** *n* supper, dinner

晚会 **wǎnhuì** *n* evening party, soirée

晚上 **wǎnshang** *n* evening, night, night time

碗 **wǎn** *n* bowl

万 **wàn** *num* ten thousand; a very great number

万岁 **wànsuì** *vb* long live...!

万一 wànyī 1 *conj* just in case, if by any chance **2** *n* contingency, eventuality

网 wǎng *n* net, web, network

网球 wǎngqiú *n* tennis; tennis ball

往 wǎng ▶ See also 往 **wàng**. **1** *vb* go **2** *adj* past, previous **3** *prep* towards, in the direction of

往往 wǎngwǎng *adv* often, frequently

忘 wàng, 忘记 wàngjì *vb* forget

往 wàng *prep* ▶ See also 往 **wǎng**. to, towards, in the direction of

望 wàng *vb* look up, gaze; hope, expect

危害 wēihài 1 *vb* endanger, harm, damage **2** *n* danger, harm

危机 wēijī *n* crisis

危险 wēixiǎn 1 *adj* dangerous, critical **2** *n* danger

微笑 wēixiào 1 *vb* smile (slightly) **2** *n* (slight) smile

为 wéi ▶ See also 为 **wèi**. **1** *vb* be, equal; do, act; act as, serve as **2** *prep* (*used with* **suǒ 所** *in passive sentences*) by; **wéi rénmín suǒ hèn 为人民所恨** be hated by the people

为难 wéinán 1 *adj* embarrassed, awkward **2** *vb* make things difficult for

违反 wéifǎn *vb* violate, go against

围 wéi *vb* surround, enclose

围巾 wéijīn *n* scarf

围绕 wéirào *vb* surround, circulate, revolve around

唯一 wéiyī *adj* only, sole

维护 wéihù *vb* protect, guard, defend

伟大 wěidà *adj* great, remarkable

尾 wěi *n* tail, end

尾巴 wěiba *n* ! *This word is sometimes pronounced*

yǐba; tail

委员 wěiyuán *n* committee member, designated/appointed official

卫生 wèishēng 1 *adj* clean, good for health, hygienic **2** *n* sanitation, health, hygiene

卫星 wèixīng *n* satellite

为 wèi *prep* ▶ See also 为 **wéi**. (*indicating who will benefit*) for, on account of, for the sake of; **wèi tā mǔqīn mǎi yào** 为她母亲买药 buy medicine for her mother; (*indicating the reason or purpose for an action*) for the sake of, out of concern for, in order to; **wèi shěngqián** 为省钱 in order to save money; **wèi… ér… 为…而…** …for the sake of …; **wèi hépíng ér fèndòu** 为和平而奋斗 struggle for peace

为了 wèile *prep* for the sake of, for the purpose of, in order to

为什么 wèishénme *adv* why, for what reason

未 wèi *adv* not, not yet

未来 wèilái *n* future, time to come

位 wèi *mw* ▶ **623** (*a polite measure word for people*)

位于 wèiyú *vb* be situated in, be located in, lie in

位置 wèizhì *n* position, place, post

位子 wèizi *n* seat, place

味(道)wèi(dao) *n* flavour, taste

胃 wèi *n* stomach

喂 wèi 1 *vb* (*when talking about a person or animal*) feed, give food to **2** *exc* (*as a greeting or to attract attention*) hello!, hey!

温度 wēndù *n* temperature

温暖 wēnnuǎn *adj* warm

文化 wénhuà *n* civilisation, culture; education, schooling, literacy

文件 wénjiàn *n* document, paper

文科 wénkē *n* (*a branch of learning*) liberal arts

文明 wénmíng 1 *n* civilisation, culture, enlightenment **2** *adj* enlightened, civilised

文物 wénwù *n* relic, antique

文学 wénxué *n* literature; **wénxuéjiā 文学家** writer of literary works

文艺 wényì *n* literature and the arts, art and literature

文章 wénzhāng *n* essay, article, literary composition

文字 wénzì *n* written language, characters, script

闻 wén *vb* hear; smell

闻名 wénmíng *adj* well-known, famous, renowned

蚊子 wénzi *n* mosquito

稳 wěn *adj* stable, steady, sure

稳定 wěndìng 1 *adj* firm, stable **2** *vb* stabilize

问 wèn *vb* ask, inquire, question

问好 wènhǎo *vb* send one's regards to, ask after; **xiàng tāmen wènhǎo 向他们问好** send my regards to them

问候 wènhòu *vb* send one's respects to, extend greetings to

问题 wèntí *n* question, problem, issue; trouble, mishap; **tā de qìchē chū wèntí le 他的汽车出问题了** he had trouble with his car; examination question

我 wǒ *pron* I, me, self

我们 wǒmen *pron* we, us

卧铺 wòpù *n* sleeping compartment, berth

卧室 wòshì *n* bedroom

握 wò *vb* grasp, hold fast to

握手 wòshǒu *vb* shake hands, clasp hands

污染 wūrǎn 1 *vb* pollute, contaminate **2** *n* pollution

屋 wū *n* house, room

屋子 wūzi *n* room

无 wú 1 *vb* have not, there is not **2** *n* nothing, void **3** *adj* no **4** *adv* not

无聊 wúliáo *adj* boring; bored; silly, stupid, senseless

无论 wúlùn *conj* no matter what/how; regardless, whether (or not); **wúlùn·rúhé 无论如何** whatever happens, in any case

无数 wúshù *adj* countless, innumerable

无所谓 wúsuǒwèi 1 *adj* indifferent **2** *vb* be indifferent, not matter; cannot be taken as, cannot be designated as

无限 wúxiàn 1 *adj* infinite, boundless, unlimited **2** *adv* infinitely, without bounds

五 wǔ *num* five

五月 wǔyuè *n* May

午饭 wǔfàn *n* lunch, midday meal

武器 wǔqì *n* weapon, armament, arms

武术 wǔshù *n* martial arts

舞 wǔ, 舞蹈 wǔdǎo *n* dance

舞台 wǔtái *n* stage, arena

勿 wù *adv* (*when indicating prohibition*) not, don't

物 wù *n* thing, matter

物价 wùjià *n* price

物理 wùlǐ *n* physics

物质 wùzhì 1 *n* matter, material, substance **2** *adj* (*of resources, etc.*) physical, material

误会 wùhuì 1 *vb* misunderstand **2** *n* misunderstanding

雾 wù *n* fog, mist

西 xī 1 *n* west **2** *adj* west, western

西班牙 **Xībānyá** *n* Spain；**Xībānyárén** 西班牙人 Spaniard；**Xībānyáwén** 西班牙文，**Xībānyáyǔ** 西班牙语（*the language*）Spanish

西北 **xīběi** **1** *n* northwest **2** *adj* northwest，northwestern

西边 **xībian** *n* western side

西餐 **xīcān** *n* Western food

西方 **xīfāng** **1** *n*（*a direction*）the west；（*part of the world*）the West **2** *adj* western

西服 **xīfú** *n* Western-style clothes

西瓜 **xīguā** *n* watermelon

西红柿 **xīhóngshì** *n* tomato

西面 **xīmian** ▶ 西边 **xībian**

西南 **xīnán** **1** *n* southwest **2** *adj* southwestern

西装 **xīzhuāng** ▶ 西服 **xīfú**

吸 **xī** *vb* inhale，breathe；attract，absorb

吸收 **xīshōu** *vb* absorb，take in，assimilate；recruit，enrol，admit

吸烟 **xīyān** *vb* smoke cigarettes，smoke

吸引 **xīyǐn** *vb* attract，draw

希望 **xīwàng** **1** *vb* hope，wish **2** *n* hope，expectation

牺牲 **xīshēng** *vb* sacrifice

习惯 **xíguàn** **1** *n* habit，custom **2** *vb* be accustomed to，get used to

洗 **xǐ** *vb* wash，clean

洗衣机 **xǐyījī** *n* washing machine

洗澡 **xǐzǎo** *vb* have a bath/shower

喜 **xǐ** **1** *adj* happy，pleased，delighted **2** *n* happiness，happy event

喜欢 **xǐhuan** *vb* be pleased with，like，prefer；**tā xǐhuan kànshū** 他喜欢看书 he likes to read

戏 **xì** *n* play，opera，drama

戏剧 xìjù *n* play, drama

系 xì *n* department in a university/college, faculty

系统 xìtǒng *n* system

细 xì 1 *adj* fine, thin, delicate; careful, meticulous, detailed **2** *adv* attentively, carefully, in detail

细菌 xìjūn *n* bacteria, germs

细心 xìxīn 1 *adj* attentive, careful, meticulous **2** *adv* attentively, with concentration

虾 xiā *n* shrimp; **duìxiā 对虾** prawn

瞎 xiā *adj* blind

下 xià 1 *vb* descend, go down from, get off; (*when referring to weather*) fall; xià [yǔ|xuě|báozi] le 下 [雨|雪|雹子] 了 it is [raining | snowing | hailing]; (*as an order*) issue, give, proclaim; (*in making or sending down a decision*) decide, determine; xià [juéxīn|jiélùn|dìngyì] 下 [决心|结论|定义] [make up one's mind | draw a conclusion | give a definition]; (*when speaking of animals or eggs*) give birth to, lay **2** *adv* (*after a verb to indicate downward movement*) down; zuòxià 坐下 sit down; (*after a verb to indicate having space for something*) zhèlǐ fàng bú xià 这里放不下 there's no room to put (it) here; (*after a verb to indicate completion or result*) dìngxià kāihuì de shíjiān 定下开会的时间 fix a time for the meeting **3** *adj* next; xiàge yuè 下个月 next month; lower, inferior **4** *prep* under, below; chuáng xià 床下 under the bed **5** *mw* ▶ 623 (*for brief actions*) time

下班 xiàbān *vb* go off duty, get out of work

下边 xiàbian 1 *n* the bottom, below **2** *adj* next, following **3** *prep* below, under, underneath

下课 xiàkè *vb* class is over, dismiss class

下来 xiàlái *vb* come down; (*after a verb to indicate downward movement*) tiào xiàlái 跳下来 jump down;

(*after a verb to indicate movement away*) bǎ yǎnjìng zhāi xiàlái 把眼镜摘下来 take off your glasses; (*after a verb to indicate completion or result of an action*) wǒ bǎ nǐ de dìzhǐ jì xiàlái le 我把你的地址记下来了 I noted down your address

下面 xiàmian ▶ 下边 xiàbian

下去 xiàqù *vb* go down, descend; (*when referring to the future*) continue, go on; (*used after a verb to express the continuation of an action*) shuō xiàqù 说下去 keep on speaking

下头 xiàtou ▶ 下边 xiàbian

下午 xiàwǔ *n* afternoon, p. m.

吓 xià *vb* frighten, scare; be frightened; intimidate, threaten

夏天 xiàtiān *n* summer, summer season

先 xiān *adv* first, before, in advance; xiān…zài… 先…在… first… and then…; xiān chīfàn zài xiūxi 先吃饭再休息 first eat, then rest; xiān…cái… 先…才… not… until…, must first… before…; nǐ děi xiān gěi wǒ jiěshì yíxià, wǒ cái néng qù bàn 你得先给我解释一下，我才能去办 I can't do it until you explain it to me

先后 xiānhòu **1** *n* order of precedence, priority **2** *adv* successively, one after another

先进 xiānjìn *adj* (*as in techniques, experience, etc.*) advanced

先生 xiānsheng *n* Mr.; husband; (*courteous address to scholars, elders*) sir

纤维 xiānwéi *n* fibre, fibrous tissue

掀 xiān *vb* (*as a cover, etc.*) raise, lift

鲜 xiān *adj* (*as in food or air*) fresh; tasty, delicious; bright, colourful

鲜花 xiānhuā *n* fresh flowers

闲 xián **1** *adj* (*as a person, a room, etc.*) idle,

unoccupied, free; (*when referring to time*) free, leisure **2**
adv leisurely, freely

显得 **xiǎnde** *vb* appear, seem

显然 **xiǎnrán 1** *adj* obvious, clear **2** *adv* obviously, evi-
dently, clearly

显示 **xiǎnshì** *vb* display, show, manifest

显著 **xiǎnzhù** *adj* distinct, prominent, marked

县 **xiàn** *n* district, county

现代 **xiàndài 1** *n* contemporary era, modern age **2** *adj*
modern, contemporary

现代化 **xiàndàihuà 1** *adj* modernized **2** *n* modernization

现实 **xiànshí 1** *n* reality **2** *adj* practical, realistic;
xiànshízhǔyì 现实主义 realism

现象 **xiànxiàng** *n* phenomenon

现在 **xiànzài 1** *n* present, now **2** *adv* now, at present,
currently

限制 **xiànzhì 1** *vb* control, restrict, limit **2** *n* control,
restriction, limit

线 **xiàn** *n* thread, string, wire; line

羡慕 **xiànmù** *vb* admire; envy

献 **xiàn** *vb* offer up, present; donate, dedicate

乡 **xiāng** *n* country, countryside, village; native place, home

乡下 **xiāngxia** *n* country, countryside, village

相 **xiāng** *adv* ! Can also be pronounced xiàng with a
different meaning; mutually, reciprocally, each other

相当 **xiāngdāng 1** *adj* suitable, appropriate **2** *adv* fairly,
quite, rather

相反 **xiāngfǎn 1** *adj* opposite, contrary **2** *adv* on the contrary

相互 **xiānghù 1** *adj* mutual, reciprocal **2** *adv* mutually,
each other

相似 xiāngsì 1 *adj* similar to, like **2** *vb* resemble, be alike

相同 xiāngtóng *adj* alike, the same, similar

相信 xiāngxìn *vb* believe, believe in, trust

香 xiāng 1 *adj* (*of flowers*, *etc.*) fragrant, scented, pleasant smelling; (*of food*) delicious, appetizing **2** *n* fragrance, aroma; perfume, incense, joss stick

香肠 xiāngcháng *n* sausage

香蕉 xiāngjiāo *n* banana

香皂 xiāngzào *n* perfumed soap, toilet soap

箱子 xiāngzi *n* trunk, box, case

详细 xiángxì 1 *adj* careful, meticulous, in detail **2** *adv* carefully, thoroughly, meticulously

享受 xiàngshòu 1 *vb* enjoy **2** *n* enjoyment

响 xiǎng 1 *adj* (as a sound or noise) loud, noisy **2** *vb* make a sound **3** *n* sound, noise

响应 xiǎngyìng 1 *vb* respond, answer **2** *n* response, answer

想 xiǎng *vb* think, consider, ponder; think about, miss, long for; want to, intend to, plan to

想法 xiǎngfǎ *n* viewpoint, opinion, way of thinking

想念 xiǎngniàn *vb* remember, long for, miss

想象 xiǎngxiàng 1 *vb* imagine **2** *n* imagination

向 xiàng 1 *prep* towards, facing **2** *vb* face; incline towards, side with **3** *n* direction, trend

巷 xiàng *n* lane, alley

项 xiàng *mw* ▶ **623** (for work, projects, tasks, requirements, etc.); (for decisions or announcements)

项目 xiàngmù *n* item, project

象 xiàng 1 *n* elephant **2** *vb* be like, look as if

象征 xiàngzhēng 1 *n* symbol, emblem **2** *vb* symbolize, signify, stand for

像 xiàng 1 *vb* be like, resemble, look like **2** *adj* similar, alike

3 *n* portrait, picture, image; **xiàng…yíyàng/yìbān** 像…一样/一般 resemble..., be like...

像片 **xiàngpiàn** *n* photograph, picture

橡皮 **xiàngpí** *n* rubber, eraser

消费 **xiāofèi** *vb* consume; **xiāofèipǐn** 消费品 consumer goods

消化 **xiāohuà** **1** *vb* digest **2** *n* digestion

消灭 **xiāomiè** *vb* wipe out, extinguish, destroy

消失 **xiāoshī** *vb* vanish, disappear

消息 **xiāoxi** *n* news, information

小 **xiǎo** *adj* small, little; young; unimportant, trifling

小吃 **xiǎochī** *n* snack, refreshments

小孩儿 **xiǎoháir** *n* child, children

小伙子 **xiǎohuǒzi** *n* young man, lad

小姐 **xiǎojiě** *n* young lady, Miss, daughter

小麦 **xiǎomài** *n* wheat

小卖部 **xiǎomàibù** *n* small shop, snack bar

小朋友 **xiǎopéngyǒu** *n* child, children

小气 **xiǎoqì** *adj* mean, stingy, petty

小时 **xiǎoshí** *n* hour

小说 **xiǎoshuō** *n* fiction, short story, novel

小偷 **xiǎotōu** *n* petty thief, sneak thief, pilferer

小心 **xiǎoxīn** **1** *adj* careful, cautious **2** *vb* be careful, look out, take care

小学 **xiǎoxué** *n* elementary/primary school

小组 **xiǎozǔ** *n* group

晓得 **xiǎode** *vb* know

校园 **xiàoyuán** *n* school yard, campus

校长 **xiàozhǎng** *n* (*of a school, college, or university*) headmaster, principal, president

笑 **xiào** *vb* smile, laugh; laugh at, make fun of, ridicule

笑话 xiàohua 1 *n* joke, funny story **2** *vb* laugh at, ridicule, make fun of

效果 xiàoguǒ *n* effect, result

效率 xiàolǜ *n* efficiency

些 xiē 1 *det* some, a few; ná xiē shuǐguǒ lái 拿些水果来 bring some fruit **2** *adv* a little, a bit

歇 xiē *vb* rest, have a rest

协会 xiéhuì *n* association, society

斜 xié *adj* slanting, inclined, askew

鞋 xié *n* shoes; xiézi 鞋子 shoes

写 xiě *vb* write, compose

写作 xiězuò *n* writing

血 xiě ▶ 血 xuè

谢谢 xièxie *vb* thank you, thanks

心 xīn *n* heart; mind, feeling; middle, centre

心得 xīndé *n* insight, understanding

心情 xīnqíng *n* feelings, mood, state of mind

心脏 xīnzàng *n* (*the organ in the body*) heart; xīnzàng-bìng 心脏病 heart disease

辛苦 xīnkǔ 1 *adj* laborious, hard, hard-working **2** *adv* with great difficulty and effort, laboriously **3** *vb* work very hard, undergo many hardships, take trouble **4** *n* hardship, laborious work

欣赏 xīnshǎng *vb* enjoy, appreciate

新 xīn 1 *adj* new, fresh, recent; up-to-date, modern **2** *adv* newly, recently, freshly

新郎 xīnláng *n* bridegroom

新年 xīnnián *n* New Year

新娘 xīnniáng *n* bride

新闻 xīnwén *vb* news; xīnwénjiè 新闻界 the press

新鲜 xīnxiān *adj* fresh, new

信 xìn 1 *n* letter, mail, correspondence; message, information **2** *vb* believe, believe in

信封 xìnfēng *n* envelope

信任 xìnrèn 1 *n* trust, confidence **2** *vb* trust, have confidence in

信息 xìnxī *n* information, news, message

信心 xìnxīn *n* confidence, faith

兴奋 xīngfèn *adj* excited

星期 xīngqī *n* week; xīngqī [yī | èr | sān | sì | wǔ | liù] 星期 [一 | 二 | 三 | 四 | 五 | 六] [Monday | Tuesday | Wednesday | Thursday | Friday | Saturday]

星期日 xīngqīrì, 星期天 xīngqītiān *n* Sunday

星星 xīngxing *n* star

行 xíng ! *Can also be pronounced* háng *with a different meaning.* **1** *vb* go, walk, travel; do, carry out, practise **2** *adj* satisfactory, all right, OK; zhèyàng zuò xíng bù xíng? 这样做行不行? is it all right to do (it) this way?; capable, proficient, competent **3** *n* trip, journey; conduct, behaviour, actions

行动 xíngdòng 1 *vb* move, act, take action **2** *n* movement, physical movement, action

行李 xíngli *n* luggage, baggage

行人 xíngrén *n* pedestrian

行驶 xíngshǐ *vb* (*when talking about buses, trains, ships, etc.*) travel, go, run

行为 xíngwéi *n* behaviour, action, conduct

形成 xíngchéng *vb* take shape, take form, form into; develop, evolve, form

形容 xíngróng *vb* describe

形式 xíngshì *n* form

形势 xíngshì *n* situation, circumstances; terrain, lie of the land

形象 xíngxiàng n form, appearance, image

形状 xíngzhuàng n shape, form, appearance

醒 xǐng vb wake up, awaken, be awakened; regain consciousness, sober up

兴趣 xìngqù n interest, interest in; **tā duì lìshǐ yǒu/gǎn xìngqù 她对历史有/感兴趣** she is interested in history

幸福 xìngfú 1 adj happy **2** n happiness, well-being

幸好 xìnghǎo ▶幸亏 xìngkuī

幸亏 xìngkuī adv fortunately, luckily

幸运 xìngyùn 1 adj fortunate, lucky **2** n good luck, good fortune

性 xìng n quality, nature, character; (used at the end of many words to make them nouns) -ity, -ness; **kěnéngxìng 可能性** probability; **chuàngzàoxìng 创造性** creativity; sex, gender; **[nán|nǚ]xìng [男|女]性** the [male|female] sex

性别 xìngbié n sex, gender

性格 xìnggé n personality, character, temperament

性质 xìngzhì n quality, nature

姓 xìng 1 vb be surnamed; **tā xìng Zhào 他姓赵** his surname is Zhao **2** n surname, family name

姓名 xìngmíng n surname and given name, full name

兄弟 xiōngdì n brothers; **xiōngdì-jiěmèi 兄弟姐妹** brothers and sisters, siblings

胸 xiōng n chest, thorax, breast

雄 xióng adj (when referring to animals) male; (in reference to humans) strong, powerful, virile

雄伟 xióngwěi adj magnificent, imposing, grand

熊 xióng n bear

熊猫 xióngmāo n panda

休息 xiūxi vb rest, take a rest

修 xiū vb repair, mend, maintain; build, construct; study, cultivate a knowledge of

修改 xiūgǎi 1 vb correct, revise, amend **2** n revision, modification

修理 xiūlǐ vb repair, mend

袖(子)xiù(zi) n sleeve

虚心 xūxīn 1 adj humble, modest **2** adv humbly, with humility

需要 xūyào 1 vb need, require **2** n need, demand

许 xǔ vb allow, permit, give consent; promise, pledge

许多 xǔduō det a lot of, many, much

叙述 xùshù vb narrate, recount

宣布 xuānbù 1 vb declare, proclaim **2** n declaration, proclamation

宣传 xuānchuán 1 vb propagate, propagandize **2** n propaganda, dissemination

选 xuǎn 1 vb choose, select; elect **2** n selection, election

选举 xuǎnjǔ 1 vb elect, vote **2** n election; **xuǎnjǔquán 选举权** the right to vote

选择 xuǎnzé 1 vb choose, pick out, select **2** n selection, choice

学 xué 1 vb study, learn; imitate **2** n school, institution of learning, level of schooling; [xiǎo|zhōng|dà]xué [小|中|大]学 [primary or elementary school | secondary or high school | college or university]; (added to fields of study, similar to the English ending -ology) study of, field of; [wén|shù|rénlèi]xué [文|数|人类]学 [literature | mathematics | anthropology]; learning, knowledge

学费 xuéfèi n school fees, tuition

学期 xuéqī n term, semester

学生 xuésheng n student, pupil

学术 xuéshù 1 n learning, scholarship, academic research **2** adj academic, learned; **xuéshùjiè 学术界** academic circles

学问 **xuéwen** *n* scholarship, learning

学习 **xuéxí** *vb* study, learn

学校 **xuéxiào** *n* school

学院 **xuéyuàn** *n* academic institution, college, institute

学者 **xuézhě** *n* scholar, learned person

雪 **xuě** *n* snow; xiàxuě le 下雪了 it's snowing

雪花 **xuěhuā** *n* snowflake

血 **xuè** *n* ! Can also be pronounced xiě; blood

血液 **xuèyè** *n* blood

寻找 **xúnzhǎo** *vb* look for, seek, search for

询问 **xúnwèn** *vb* inquire, ask about

训练 **xùnliàn** *vb* instruct, train, drill

迅速 **xùnsù** **1** *adj* fast, rapid **2** *adv* fast, rapidly, at high speed

---

Yy

压 **yā** **1** *vb* press down, apply pressure, crush; (*when speaking of emotions, disorder, rebellion, etc.*) control, suppress **2** *n* pressure

压力 **yālì** *n* pressure

压迫 **yāpò** **1** *vb* oppress, repress, constrict **2** *n* oppression, repression

呀 **yā** *exc* ! Can also be pronounced ya 呀 in a neutral tone with a different meaning; (*indicating surprise*) ah! oh!

鸭(子) **yā(zi)** *n* duck

牙 **yá** *n* tooth, teeth

牙刷 **yáshuā** *n* toothbrush

亚洲 **Yàzhōu** *n* Asia

烟 **yān** *n* smoke；cigarette，tobacco

严格 **yángé** **1** *adj* stern，strict，rigorous **2** *adv* strictly，rigidly

严肃 **yánsù** *adj* solemn，serious，earnest

严重 **yánzhòng** *adj* (*when talking about a situation，a condition，health，etc.*) serious，grave，critical

延长 **yáncháng** **1** *vb* extend，prolong，lengthen **2** *n* prolongation，extension

沿 **yán** *prep* along，alongside

研究 **yánjiū** **1** *vb* study，do research；(*for problems，suggestions，applications*) consider，discuss **2** *n* research，study；yánjiūhuì 研究会 research association；yánjiūshēng 研究生 research student，postgraduate student；yánjiūsuǒ 研究所 research institute；yánjiūyuán 研究员 research fellow；yánjiūyuàn 研究院 research institute，academy

盐 **yán** *n* salt

颜色 **yánsè** *n* colour

眼 **yǎn** *n* eye；hole，opening

眼镜 **yǎnjìng** *n* glasses，spectacles

眼睛 **yǎnjing** *n* eye，eyes

眼泪 **yǎnlèi** *n* tears

眼前 **yǎnqián** *adv* in front of one's eyes，before one's eyes；at the present moment，momentarily

演 **yǎn** *vb* (*when speaking of a play，film，show*) perform，act，show

演出 **yǎnchū** **1** *vb* (*when talking about a play，film，show*) perform，show，put on **2** *n* performance，production

演员 **yǎnyuán** *n* actor，actress，performer

咽 **yàn** *vb* swallow

宴会 **yànhuì** *n* banquet，feast

羊 yáng *n* sheep, goat

羊肉 yángròu *n* mutton, lamb

阳光 yángguāng *n* sunlight, sunshine

仰 yǎng *vb* look up, face upward; look up to, admire, respect

养 yǎng 1 *vb* (*as dependents*) nurture, support, provide for; (*as animals, flowers, etc.*) raise, keep, grow; give birth to **2** *adj* (*as a foster parent, etc.*) foster

样 yàng 1 *mw* ▶ 623 (*for things in general*) kind, sort, type **2** *n* way, manner; form, appearance, shape; pattern, model, sample

样子 yàngzi *n* form, appearance, shape; pattern, sample, model; (*describing how something or someone looks*) tā xiàng shì bìngle de yàngzi 她像是病了的样子 she has the appearance of being ill; manner, air

要求 yāoqiú ! *The word* yāo *can also be pronounced* yào *with a different meaning.* **1** *vb* demand, request, ask for **2** *n* demand, request, need

腰 yāo *n* (*of a person or a garment*) waist; (*of a person*) back, small of the back

邀请 yāoqǐng 1 *vb* (*formal word*) invite **2** *n* invitation

摇 yáo *vb* shake, wag, wave; sway back and forth, rock; (*when talking about a boat*) row; (*when talking about a bell*) ring

咬 yǎo *vb* bite, snap at

药 yào *n* medicine, drug

要 yào 1 *vb* want, wish, desire; need, must; (*when talking about an amount of time*) need, take; dào Lúndūn qù yào yí gè xiǎoshí 到伦敦去要一个小时 it takes an hour to get to London; demand, request; beg; need, must; should; nǐ yào xiǎoxīn 你要小心 you must be careful; (*when talking about what one expects will happen*) will, be going to; tiān kuài yào hēi le 天快要黑了 it's going to get dark soon **2** *conj* (*short for* yàoshi 要是) if; nǐ yào bú qù, tā huì hěn shīwàng 你要不去，她会很失望 if you don't go, she'll be very disappointed **3** *adj* important

要不(然) yàobu(rán) *conj* if not, or else, otherwise

要不是 yàobushì *conj* if it were not for, but for

要紧 yàojǐn *adj* important; (*as an illness*) critical, serious

要是 yàoshi *conj* if, suppose, in case; yàoshi…jiù…(le) 要是…就…(了)；if… then… yàoshi kāichē qù jiù kěyǐ fāngbiàn yìxiē 要是开车去就可以方便一些 if you drive it is slightly more convenient

钥匙 yàoshi *adv* (*to a lock*) key

爷爷 yéye *n* paternal grandfather, grandpa (*a polite and respectful way of addressing an old man, used by children*) grandpa

也 yě *adv* also, too; (*indicating concession*) still; nǐ gěi wǒ qián, wǒ yě bú qù 你给我钱，我也不去 I won't go even if you give me money; yě bù dōu 也不 not either, neither; tā bú huì tánqín, yě bú huì chànggē 他不会弹琴，也不会唱歌 he can neither play the piano nor sing

也许 yěxǔ *adv* maybe, perhaps, possibly

野餐 yěcān *n* picnic

业务 yèwù *n* business affairs, professional work

业余 yèyú **1** *adj* extracurricular, done outside business hours; yèyú huódòng 业余活动 extracurricular activities; amateur **2** *adv* in one's spare time

叶子 yèzi *n* (*of a plant*) leaf, leaves

页 yè *n* (*in a book*) page, leaf

夜 yè *n* night, evening

夜里 yèli *adv* at night, during the night, in the night

夜晚 yèwǎn *n* night, evening

一 yī ! *The tone on* yī — *changes, depending on the tone of the word that follows it. It is pronounced* yì *before words in*

first, second, and third tone, but yí before the fourth tone. When used to count numbers, yī — has the first tone. Because the tone changes for yī — do not indicate any difference in meaning, but only in pronunciation, combinations beginning with yī — are listed in alphabetical order below, regardless of tone. ▶xiii **1** num one **2** det a, an; each, per **3** adj single, alone, only one; the same; together; whole, all, throughout; **yí yè** the whole night **4** adv (indicating a brief action or one taken lightly) briefly; **qǐng nǐ kànyikàn** 请你看一看 please take a look **5** conj once; as soon as; **tā yí kàn jiù xiào le** 他一看就笑了 he laughed as soon as he saw it; **yī…jiù…** as soon as; **yī…yě…** — … 也 … (used with the negative particle **bù** 不 or **méi** 没) (not) slightly, (not) at all; **tā yí gè Hànzì yě bú rènshi** 他一个汉字也不认识 he doesn't know a single Chinese character

一般 yìbān 1 adj alike, the same, just as; general, common, ordinary; so so **2** adv the same as, similarly; **tā hé tā gēge yìbān gāo** 她和她哥哥一般高 she is as tall as her elder brother; generally, in general, ordinarily

一半 yíbàn n half, one-half

一辈子 yíbèizi 1 adv throughout one's life, all one's life **2** n lifetime

一边 yìbiān n one side; **yìbiān…yìbiān…** 一边…一边… (indicating two simultaneous actions) at the same time, simultaneously; **háizimen yìbiān zǒulù, yìbiān chànggē** 孩子们一边走路，一边唱歌 the children are singing while they are walking

一道 yídào adv together, side by side, alongside

一点儿 yìdiǎnr 1 adv a bit, a little; **wǒ yìdiǎnr dōu bù zhīdào** 我一点儿都不知道 I have not the faintest idea **2** pron a little; **zhǐ shèngxia zhème yìdiǎnr, gòu yòng ma?** 只剩下这么一点儿，够用吗？ there's so little left, is it enough for the present purposes? **3** det a little, some;

yìdiǎnr fàn 一点儿饭 a little rice

一定 **yídìng 1** *adj* certain, given, particular; fixed, definite, specified; proper, fair, due **2** *adv* certainly, definitely, surely

一方面 **yì fāngmiàn** *n* one side

一方面…（另）一方面 **yì fāngmiàn…**（**lìng**）**yì fāngmiàn…** *adv* on the one hand... on the other hand...; for one thing... for another...

一共 **yígòng** *adv* altogether, in all, in total

一会儿 **yíhuìr** *adv* in a moment, for a little while, shortly; yíhuìr…yíhuìr… 一会儿… 一会儿… one moment..., the next...

一块儿 **yíkuàir** *adv* together

一路 **yílù** *adv* all the way, on the journey; yílù-píng'ān 一路平安 have a pleasant journey, have a good trip; yílù-shùnfēng 一路顺风 have a pleasant journey, have a good trip

一齐 **yìqí** *adv* together, at the same time, simultaneously

一起 **yìqǐ** *adv* together, in the same place

一切 **yìqiè 1** *det* all, every, whole **2** *pron* all, everything, the whole thing

一生 **yìshēng** *n* all one's life, one's whole life

一时 **yìshí** *adv* for a period of time; for the moment, for a short while, temporarily; by chance, accidentally; it just so happened that; yìshí…yìshí… 一时… 一时… now......one moment and... the next

一同 **yìtóng** *adv* together, at the same time and place

一天到晚 **yìtiāndàowǎn** *adv* all day long, from morning till night, from dawn to dusk

一下（儿）**yíxià(r)** *adv* (*indicating short duration*) once, a bit, for a short while; (*indicating a sudden change*) all at once, all of a sudden, suddenly

一下子 **yíxiàzi** *adv* suddenly, all at once

一些 **yìxiē** *det* some, a few, a little

一样 **yíyàng** 1 *adj* alike, the same, similar 2 *adv* equally, similarly

一月 **yíyuè** *n* January

一直 **yìzhí** *adv* continuously, consistently, all the time; straight, straight on; **yìzhí méi … guo** 一直没 … 过 have never…

一致 **yízhì** 1 *adj* consistent, the same, identical 2 *adv* consistently, unanimously

衣服 **yīfu** *n* clothes, clothing, dress

衣柜 **yīguì** *n* wardrobe

依靠 **yīkào** 1 *vb* depend upon, rely on 2 *n* dependence, support

依然 **yīrán** *adv* still, as before

依照 **yīzhào** *prep* in accordance with, in the light of

医生 **yīshēng** *n* doctor, physician

医务室 **yīwùshì**, 医务所 **yīwùsuǒ** *n* clinic

医学 **yīxué** *n* (*as a field of study*) medicine

医院 **yīyuàn** *n* hospital

仪器 **yíqì** *n* (*usually for scientific use*) apparatus, equipment, instrument

姨 **yí** *n* aunt on one's mother's side, mother's sister

移 **yí** *vb* change position, move, shift; change, alter

移动 **yídòng** *vb* move, shift

遗憾 **yíhàn** 1 *vb* regret 2 *n* regret, pity

疑问 **yíwèn** *n* question, doubt, query

已(经) **yǐ(jīng)** *adv* already

以 **yǐ** 1 *prep* according to; (*indicating implement, instrument, etc.*) with, using 2 *adv* (*indicating purpose*) in order to, so as to 3 *vb* use, take; take, consider; **yǐ … wéi …** 以 … 为 … take … as …, consider … as …

以便 yǐbiàn *conj* in order that, so that, in order to

以后 yǐhòu 1 *prep* after **2** *adv* later, hereafter, afterwards **3** *conj* after

以及 yǐjí *conj* and, as well as, along with

以来 yǐlái *prep* (*sometimes the time-word or cut-off point is preceded by* zì 自 *or* zìcóng 自从, *meaning* from) since, after, until now; (*when it follows a quantity of time*) during the past...in the past..., for the past...; jǐ qiān nián yǐlái 几千年以来 for several thousand years

以内 yǐnèi *prep* within, less than

以前 yǐqián 1 *prep* before, prior to **2** *adv* previously, formerly, ago **3** *conj* before

以上 yǐshàng 1 *prep* over, above **2** *adv* above

以外 yǐwài *prep* outside, beyond; (*when used in the pattern* chú(le)···yǐwài, ···dōu··· 除(了)···以外, ···都···) except, except for; chú(le) tā yǐwài, wǒmen dōu bú huì zuò 除(了)他以外, 我们都不会做 none of us can do it except him; (*when used in the pattern* chú(le)···yǐwài, ···hái··· 除(了)···以外, ···还···) besides, apart from, in addition to; chú(le) Běijīng yǐwài, wǒmen hái qùle Shànghǎi 除(了)北京以外, 我们还去了上海 apart from Beijing, we also went to Shanghai

以为 yǐwéi *vb* think, regard, consider; thought, used to think! Note that in this use, yǐwéi 以为 means that one originally thought something was true, but later found it to be false.

以下 yǐxià 1 *prep* below, under **2** *adv* below

以致 yǐzhì *conj* (*when indicating an unpleasant consequence*) so that, with the result that, consequently

椅子 yǐzi *n* chair

亿 yì *num* hundred million, 100,000,000; shíyì 10 亿 one billion

艺术 yìshù 1 *n* art; skill, technique, craft **2** *adj* artistic, in good taste; **yìshùpǐn 艺术品** work of art, art object; **yìshùjiā 艺术家** artist

议论 yìlùn 1 *vb* discuss, comment, talk **2** *n* opinion, discussion, comment

异常 yìcháng 1 *adj* unusual, abnormal, exceptional **2** *adv* unusually, exceedingly, extremely

意见 yìjiàn *n* idea, opinion, view

意思 yìsi *n* meaning, idea, theme; opinion, wish, desire; interest, fun; **yǒu yìsi 有意思** interesting, enjoyable

意外 yìwài 1 *adj* unexpected, unforeseen, surprising **2** *n* accident, mishap, unexpected development

意味着 yìwèizhe *vb* signify, mean, imply

意义 yìyì *n* significance, meaning

意志 yìzhì *n* will, volition, will power

因此 yīncǐ *adv* therefore, because of this, for this reason

因而 yīn'ér *adv* because of this, thus, as a result

因素 yīnsù *n* element, factor

因为 yīnwèi *conj* because, since, as

阴 yīn *adj* cloudy, overcast, shady

音乐 yīnyuè *n* music; **yīnyuèhuì 音乐会** concert

银 yín *n* (the metal or the colour) silver

银行 yínháng *n* bank

引起 yǐnqǐ *vb* cause, give rise to, bring about

饮料 yǐnliào *n* drink, beverage

印 yìn 1 *vb* print, engrave, replicate **2** *n* imprint, print, mark, stamp, chop, seal

印刷 yìnshuā *vb* print

印象 yìnxiàng *n* impression

应（当）yīng（dāng） *vb* ! The word yīng 应 can also be pronounced yìng with a different meaning; should, ought to

应该 **yīnggāi** *vb* should, ought to

英镑 **yīngbàng** *n* British pound

英国 **Yīngguó** *n* Britain, the United Kingdom

英文 **Yīngwén** *n* English language (usually written)

英雄 **yīngxióng** 1 *n* hero, heroine 2 *adj* heroic

英勇 **yīngyǒng** *adj* heroic, brave, valiant

英语 **Yīngyǔ** *n* English language (usually spoken)

婴儿 **yīng'ér** *n* baby, infant

迎接 **yíngjiē** *vb* welcome, greet, meet

营养 **yíngyǎng** *n* nutrition, nourishment

营业 **yíngyè** *vb* do business

赢 **yíng** *vb* gain, win, beat

影片 **yǐngpiàn** *n* film, movie

影响 **yǐngxiǎng** 1 *vb* influence, affect; shòu…yǐngxiǎng 受…影响 be influenced by… 2 *n* influence

影子 **yǐngzi** *n* shadow, reflection

应用 **yìngyòng** ! *The word* yìng 应 *can also be pronounced* yīng *with a different meaning.* 1 *vb* apply, use, make use of 2 *adj* applied 3 *n* use, application

硬 **yìng** 1 *adj* hard, stiff, tough 2 *adv* by force, stubbornly

拥抱 **yōngbào** *vb* hug, embrace

拥护 **yōnghù** *vb* support, endorse

拥挤 **yōngjǐ** 1 *vb* crowd, push 2 *adj* crowded, packed

永远 **yǒngyuǎn** *adv* always, forever

勇敢 **yǒnggǎn** *adj* brave, daring, courageous

勇气 **yǒngqì** *n* bravery, courage

用 **yòng** 1 *vb* use, employ, apply 2 *prep* with, using 3 *n* use, usefulness; [yǒu|méi] yòng [有|没]用 [useful|useless]; yòngbuzháo 用不着 no need to, have no use

用处 **yòngchu** *n* use, application

用功 **yònggōng** *adj* diligent, studious, hard-working

用力 yònglì 1 *vb* exert one's strength 2 *adv* with all one's strength, with a concentrated effort

优点 yōudiǎn *n* good point, strong point, merit

优良 yōuliáng *adj* fine, good

优美 yōuměi *adj* beautiful, graceful, exquisite

优秀 yōuxiù *adj* outstanding, excellent

悠久 yōujiǔ *adj* long, long-standing

尤其 yóuqí *adv* especially; yóuqí shì 尤其是 especially

由 yóu 1 *prep* from, by, through 2 *vb* follow, obey; let, allow

由于 yóuyú *prep* because of, due to the fact that, as a result of

邮递员 yóudìyuán *n* postman, postwoman

邮局 yóujú *n* post office

邮票 yóupiào *n* postage stamp

犹豫 yóuyù 1 *vb* hesitate 2 *adj* hesitant, undecided 3 *n* hesitation

油 yóu *n* oil, fat, grease

油漆 yóuqī *n* paint

游客 yóukè ▶ 游人 yóurén

游览 yóulǎn *vb* tour, visit, go sightseeing

游人 yóurén *n* tourist, sightseer, excursionist

游戏 yóuxì *n* (for recreation and amusement) game

游泳 yóuyǒng 1 *vb* swim 2 *n* swimming

游泳池 yóuyǒngchí *n* swimming pool

友好 yǒuhǎo *adj* friendly

友谊 yǒuyì *n* friendship

有 yǒu 1 *vb* have, possess; there is, there are, exist; (when making an estimate of age, height, weight, degree, distance, etc.) be about as much as; tā yǒu nǐ nàme gāo 她有你那么高 she is about your height; (used with a noun *to make an adjective*) having..., with...; **yǒuyì** 有意 intentional; have a good deal of, have much; **yǒu xuéwèn** 有学问 learned, knowledgeable; take place, happen, occur; **nàr yǒu hěn dà de biànhuà** 那儿有很大的变化 great changes have taken place there **2** *det* some; **yǒu rén** 有人 some, some people

有的 yǒude 1 *det* some; **yǒude rén** 有的人 some people **2** *pron* some, some people **yǒude…, yǒude…** 有的…, 有的… some..., others...; **yǒude xǐhuan kāfēi, yǒude xǐhuan chá** 有的喜欢咖啡, 有的喜欢茶 some like coffee, others like tea

有(的)时候 yǒu(de) shíhou *adv* sometimes, at times

有的是 yǒudeshì *vb* have plenty of, there's no lack of; **yǒudeshì shíjiān** 有的是时间 there's plenty of time

有点(儿)yǒudiǎn(r) 1 *vb* there is a little/some, have a little/some **2** *adv* somewhat, a little, a bit

有关 yǒuguān 1 *vb* be related to, have something to do with, concern **2** *adj* relevant, concerned

有力 yǒulì *adj* strong, powerful, energetic

有利 yǒulì *adj* beneficial, advantageous

有名 yǒumíng *adj* famous, well-known

有趣 yǒuqù *adj* interesting, amusing, fascinating

有时(候)yǒushí(hou) ▶ 有(的)时候 **yǒu(de) shíhou**

有限 yǒuxiàn *adj* limited

有效 yǒuxiào *adj* effective, efficient, valid

有些 yǒuxiē 1 *pron* some, a few, several **2** *det* some, a few, several

有一点(儿)yǒu yìdiǎn(r) ▶ 有点(儿)**yǒu diǎn(r)**

有意思 yǒu yìsi *adj* interesting, enjoyable, meaningful

有用 yǒuyòng *adj* useful

又 yòu *adv* also, in addition; again; however; **wǒ xiǎng gěi tā xiěxìn, kě yòu bù zhīdào tā de dìzhǐ** 我想给她写信,

可又不知道她的地址 I want to write her a letter but I don't know her address;yòu⋯yòu⋯ 又⋯ 又⋯ both... ...,on the one hand... on the other...

右 yòu 1 *n* right, the right-hand side, the right;(*when speaking of politics*) rightwing **2** *adj* right, right-hand

右边 yòubian *n* right-hand side, right side

幼儿 yòu'ér *n* child, infant; yòu'éryuán 幼儿园 preschool, nursery school, kindergarten

于 yú *prep* in, on, at; from, by; to, than

于是 yúshì *adv* consequently, thus, as a result

鱼 yú *n* fish

娱乐 yúlè *n* entertainment, amusement, recreation

愉快 yúkuài *adj* happy, pleased, joyful

与 yǔ 1 *prep* with, to, for **2** *conj* and

羽毛球 yǔmáoqiú *n* badminton, shuttlecock

雨 yǔ *n* rain

雨伞 yǔsǎn *n* umbrella

雨衣 yǔyī *n* raincoat

语调 yǔdiào *n* intonation, sentence intonation

语法 yǔfǎ *n* grammar

语气 yǔqì *n* tone, tone of voice, manner of speaking

语言 yǔyán *n* language

语音 yǔyīn *n* pronunciation

玉米 yùmǐ *n* maize, corn

浴室 yùshì *n* bathroom, shower room

预报 yùbào 1 *n* forecast **2** *vb* forecast

预备 yùbèi *vb* prepare, get ready

预防 yùfáng *vb* prevent, take precautions against, guard against

预习 yùxí *vb* (*usually referring to an academic lesson*) prepare

遇 yù,遇到 yùdào *vb* meet,encounter

遇见 yùjiàn *vb* meet,meet by chance

欲望 yùwàng *n* desire,wish,lust

元 yuán *n* dollar,yuan

元旦 Yuándàn *n* New Year's Day

元宵 yuánxiāo *n* sweet dumplings made of glutinous rice flour; **Yuánxiāo Jié 元宵节** Lantern Festival (the 15th of the first month in the lunar year)

员 yuán *n* (of a profession, party, or other organisation) member,personnel,staff, [dǎng | hǎi | chuīshì | shòuhuò] yuán [党 | 海 | 炊事 | 售货]员 [party member | sailor | cook | shop assistant]

原来 yuánlái 1 *adj* original, former, previous **2** *adv* it turns out that, as a matter of fact; originally, in the first place

原谅 yuánliàng *vb* forgive,excuse,pardon

原料 yuánliào *n* raw material,source material

原因 yuányīn *n* cause,reason

原则 yuánzé *n* principle; **yuánzéshang 原则上 in** principle

圆 yuán 1 *adj* round, circular **2** *n* circle; (*a unit of Chinese money*) yuan

圆珠笔 yuánzhūbǐ *n* biro,ball-point pen

园 yuán *n* garden,park

远 yuǎn *adj* far away,distant,remote

院 yuàn *n* courtyard, compound; (*public facility*) [yī | diànyǐng | bówù] yuàn [医 | 电影 | 博物]院 [hospital | cinema | museum]

院长 yuànzhǎng *n* (of an academy or organization) director,president,chairman

院子 yuànzi *n* court,yard,compound

愿望 yuànwàng *n* hope,wish

愿(意)yuàn (yì) *vb* wish, would like, want; be willing, be ready

约 **yuē 1** *vb* make an appointment, arrange a meeting, set a time to meet **2** *adv* about, approximately **3** *n* agreement, contract, treaty; appointment, date

约会 **yuēhuì** *n* engagement, appointment, meeting

月 **yuè** *n* moon; month

月亮 **yuèliang** *n* moon, moonlight

月球 **yuèqiú** *n* (*as an astronomical body*) moon

乐器 **yuèqì** *n* musical instrument

阅读 **yuèdú** *vb* read

阅览室 **yuèlǎnshì** *n* reading room

越…越 **yuè…yuè** *adv* the more... the more...; xuéxí yuè nǔlì, chéngjì yuè hǎo 学习越努力, 成绩越好 the harder one studies the better one's marks

越来越… **yuèláiyuè…** *adv* getting more and more..., becoming more and more...; tiānqì yuèláiyuè rè 天气越来越热 the weather is getting hotter

云 **yún** *n* cloud

允许 **yǔnxǔ** *vb* allow, permit, give permission to

运 **yùn 1** *vb* transport, ship **2** *n* luck, fate

运动 **yùndòng 1** *vb* move, exercise, engage in sports **2** *n* movement, motion; sports, athletics, exercise; (*social or political*) movement, campaign

运动会 **yùndònghuì** *n* sports meet, athletic contest, games

运动员 **yùndòngyuán** *n* athlete

运气 **yùnqi** *n* fortune, luck

运输 **yùnshū 1** *vb* transport, move, ship **2** *n* transport, transportation, conveyance

运用 **yùnyòng** *vb* utilize, wield, apply

Zz

杂 zá *adj* miscellaneous, mixed, varied

杂技 zájì *n* acrobatics

杂志 zázhì *n* magazine

砸 zá *vb* break, smash; pound, tamp

灾 zāi *n* disaster, calamity, misfortune

灾害 zāihài *n* disaster, calamity

灾难 zāinàn *n* disaster, calamity, suffering

栽 zāi *vb* plant, grow

再 zài *adv* again, once more, further; even, still; (*when predicting what will happen if an action continues*) still, continue, keep . . .-ing (any) longer; **nǐ zài hē xiàqù huì hēzuì de 你再喝下去会喝醉的** you will get drunk if you continue to drink any longer; (*when preceded by a negative, to indicate that an action will not continue*) (no) longer, (never) again; **wǒ búzài shuō le 我不再说了** I won't ever say it again; (*when one actions follows another*) after, then, only after; **xǐle zǎo zài qù shuìjiào 洗了澡再去睡觉** go to bed after you've had your bath

再见 zàijiàn *vb* good-bye, see you again

再三 zàisān *adv* over and over again, again and again, repeatedly

再说 zàishuō 1 *adv* furthermore, in addition, besides **2** *vb* postpone until some time later, put aside until

在 zài 1 *prep* in, at, on **2** *vb* exist, be alive, be present; depend on, be conditional on **3** *adv* just in the midst of, in the process of doing something; **tā zài mǎi cài 他在买菜** he is shopping for vegetables; **zài . . . shang 在 . . . 上;**

(*referring to a place*) at, above, on top of; (*rhetorically*) in; zài yuánzéshang 在原则上 in principle; zài⋯xià 在 ⋯下; (*referring to physical location*) under, underneath; (*referring to help, leadership, etc.*) with, under; zài tā de bāngzhù xià 在她的帮助下 with her help; zài⋯hòu 在⋯后 after; zài⋯li 在⋯里 inside; zài⋯nèi 在⋯内 within, among, in; zài⋯qián 在⋯前 before; zài⋯shí ⋯时 when; zài⋯wài 在⋯外 out of, outside; zài⋯yídài 在⋯一带 in the region of; zài⋯zhōngjiān 在⋯中间 between

在乎 **zàihu** *vb* (*usually used in a negative sentence*) care about, mind, take seriously

在于 **zàiyú** *vb* lie in, consist in, rest with; be determined by, depend on

咱(们) **zán(men)** *pron* (*used to include only the speaker and those directly spoken to*) we, the two of us, you and I

攒 **zǎn** *vb* save, accumulate, hoard

暂时 **zànshí** 1 *adj* temporary, transient 2 *adv* temporarily, for the time being

赞成 **zànchéng** *vb* agree, agree with, approve

赞美 **zànměi** *vb* praise, sing the praises of, eulogize

赞扬 **zànyáng** *vb* praise, speak highly of, commend

脏 **zāng** *adj* ! This word is pronounced **zàng** when it means **viscera**, **organs**, as in xīnzàng 心脏; dirty, filthy

遭到 **zāodào** *vb* (*usually referring to something unpleasant*) meet with, encounter, suffer

遭受 **zāoshòu** *vb* suffer, be subjected to

糟糕 **zāogāo** 1 *adj* terrible, disastrous, unfortunate 2 *exc* too bad, bad luck

早 **zǎo** 1 *adj* early 2 *adv* early; in advance, beforehand; a long time ago 3 *n* morning; nǐ zǎo! 你早! good morning!；**zǎojiù 早就** a long while ago；**zǎoyǐ 早已** long ago，for a long time

早晨 zǎochén *n* morning，early morning

早饭 zǎofàn *n* breakfast

早上 zǎoshang *n* morning，early morning

造 zào *vb* make，create，manufacture；build，establish

造句 zàojù *vb* make up sentences

则 zé 1 *conj* (*when talking about cause，effect，or condition*) then **2** *n* rule，regulation

责备 zébèi *vb* blame，reproach，reprove

责任 zérèn *n* responsibility，duty

怎么 zěnme *adv* (*in the interrogative*) how，in what way，why；(*in the positive*) however，whatever；**zěnme zuò dōu kěyǐ 怎么做都可以** any way you do it is fine；(*in the negative to indicate inadequacy*) (not) very；**bù zěnme hǎo 不怎么好** not very good；**zěnme le? 怎么了?** what's the matter?；**zěnme huí shì? 怎么回事?** how come? how did this happen? what happened?

怎么样 zěnmeyàng *adv* (*in the interrogative*) how，how about；(*colloquial greeting*) how are you? how's everything? how's it going?；(*in the negative*) (not) very good/well；**nà bù diànyǐng bù zěnmeyàng 那部电影不怎么样** that film is not very good

怎样 zěnyàng *adv* how，in what way

增加 zēngjiā 1 *vb* increase，add **2** *n* increase

增长 zēngzhǎng *vb* increase，grow，become larger

扎 zhā *vb* pierce，prick，stick into

炸 zhá *vb* ▶ See also 炸 **zhà**. deep-fry，fry in deep fat/oil

炸 zhà *vb* ▶ See also 炸 **zhá**. explode，burst；blow up，bomb，blast

摘 zhāi *vb* (*for flowers，fruit，etc.*) pick，pluck；(*for hats，glasses，etc.*) take off，remove

窄 zhǎi *adj* narrow, tight

粘 zhān **1** *vb* stick, paste, glue **2** *adj* sticky

展出 zhǎnchū *vb* show, put on display, exhibit

展开 zhǎnkāi *vb* develop, unfold, open up

展览 zhǎnlǎn **1** *vb* show, put on display **2** *n* exhibition, display; zhǎnlǎnguǎn 展览馆 exhibition centre, exhibition hall; zhǎnlǎnhuì 展览会 exhibition; zhǎnlǎnpǐn 展览品 item on display, exhibit

崭新 zhǎnxīn *adj* brand-new, completely new

占 zhàn *vb* occupy, seize; constitute, make up; hold

战斗 zhàndòu **1** *vb* fight, struggle **2** *n* fight, struggle

战胜 zhànshèng *vb* defeat, win in battle/war, overcome

战士 zhànshì *n* soldier, warrior, fighter

战争 zhànzhēng *n* war, warfare

站 zhàn **1** *vb* stand **2** *n* station, depot, stop

盏 zhǎn *mw* ▶ 623 (for lamps)

张 zhāng **1** *mw* ▶ 623 (for flat things such as paper, paintings, tables, etc.) **2** *vb* open, stretch, extend

章 zhāng *n* chapter, section; rules, regulations; stamp, seal

长 zhǎng ▶ See also 长 cháng. **1** *vb* grow, develop, form; gain, acquire; increase **2** *n* (often used as a suffix) head, chairman, director; [suǒ | shì | xiào] zhǎng [所 | 市 | 校] 长 [director of an institute | mayor | principal]

涨 zhǎng *vb* (of water-level, prices, etc.) rise, go up

掌握 zhǎngwò *vb* grasp, control, master

丈 zhàng *n* (measure of length) 3.3 metres, 10 Chinese feet

丈夫 zhàngfu *n* husband

招待 zhāodài *vb* (of guests, visitors, etc.) entertain, receive, serve

招待会 zhāodàihuì *n* reception, welcoming party

招呼 zhāohu vb call, notify, tell; hail, greet, say hello to; xiàng/gēn mǒu rén dǎ zhāohu 向/跟某人打招呼 say hello to someone

着 zháo vb ▶ 213 See also 着 zhe. touch; (when speaking of an illness) catch, be affected by; zháoliáng 着凉 catch cold; burn; zháohuǒ 着火 catch fire; (after a verb to indicate accomplishment or result) [zháo | diǎn | shuì] zháo [找 | 点 | 睡] 着 [find | succeed in lighting | fall asleep]

着急 zháojí adj worried, anxious

找 zhǎo vb look for, seek; give change, return a balance; tā zhǎo wǒ wǔ kuài qián 他找我 5 块钱 he gave me five dollars change; zhǎodào 找到 find; zhǎozháo 找着 find

召开 zhàokāi vb (when talking about a conference, meeting, etc.) hold, convene

照 zhào 1 vb shine on, put a light on, illuminate; reflect, look at one's reflection; take (a photograph) **2** prep according to; towards

照常 zhàocháng adv as usual, as normally done

照顾 zhàogù vb take care of, look after, attend to; take into account, consider

照看 zhàokàn vb take care of, look after, attend to; keep an eye on

照料 zhàoliào vb care for, look after, attend to

照片 zhàopiàn n photograph, picture

照相 zhàoxiàng vb take a picture or photograph, have a photograph taken

照相机 zhàoxiàngjī n camera

折 zhé vb bend, fold

哲学 zhéxué n philosophy; zhéxuéjiā 哲学家 philosopher, specialist in philosophy

这 zhè 1 pron this **2** det this

这边 zhèbian adv this side, over here

这个 zhège 1 *pron* this, this one **2** *det* this

这么 zhème *adv* by this means, in this way, like this; to this degree, so, such

这儿 zhèr, 这里 zhèli *adv* here

这些 zhèxiē 1 *pron* these **2** *det* these

这样 zhèyàng *adv* in this way, like this, so

着 zhe *pt* ▶ See also 着 **zháo**. (*indicating a continuous state or action, often translated by the present participle* [*-ing*] *in English*) [走│听│唱] zhe [走│听│唱] 着 [walking│listening│singing]

真 zhēn 1 *adj* real, genuine, true **2** *adv* really, truly

真理 zhēnlǐ *n* (*as an abstract concept*) truth

真实 zhēnshí *adj* true, real, factual

真正 zhēnzhèng *adj* genuine, true

针 zhēn *n* needle, pin; stitch; (*as for medical treatment*) injection

针对 zhēnduì *vb* point exactly against, be directed against, be aimed at in view of, in the light of, in accordance with

枕头 zhěntou *n* pillow

阵 zhèn *mw* ▶ 623 (*for events or states of short duration*)

镇 zhèn *n* town

正月 zhēngyuè *n* ! The character zhēng 正 is also pronounced **zhèng** with a different meaning; first month of the lunar year

争 zhēng *vb* fight over, compete; argue about, dispute

争论 zhēnglùn 1 *vb* debate, argue **2** *n* argument, debate

争取 zhēngqǔ *vb* strive for, gain by fighting, win; win over, persuade

征求 zhēngqiú *vb* (*as opinions, advice, etc.*) consult, solicit, seek

睁 zhēng *vb* (*used for the eyes*) open

整 zhěng *adj* whole, entire, complete; (*when talking about the time*) sharp, exact; **bā diǎn zhěng** 8 点整 eight o'clock sharp

整个 zhěnggè *adj* whole, entire

整理 zhěnglǐ *vb* tidy up, put in order, arrange

整齐 zhěngqí *adj* in good order, neat, tidy

正 zhèng ! *Can also be pronounced* zhēng *with a different meaning.* **1** *adj* right, straight, upright; right side up; right side out; chief, main; (*of time*) punctual, exact, precise **2** *adv* precisely, exactly;°(*indicating that an action is in progress*) right in the midst of, just now; **tā zhèng xiězhe nà fēng xìn** 他正写着那封信 he is just writing that letter

正常 zhèngcháng *adj* normal

正当 zhèngdāng *conj* just when, just at the time when

正当 zhèngdàng *adj* proper, appropriate, legitimate

正好 zhènghǎo 1 *adj* (*in time, quantity, etc.*) just right **2** *adv* (*referring to time, quantity, etc.*) just right; happen to, chance to, as it happens

正巧 zhèngqiǎo *adv* it so happens, as it happens, happen to; just in time, just at the right time, in the nick of time

正确 zhèngquè *adj* correct, right

正式 zhèngshì 1 *adj* formal, regular, official **2** *adv* formally

正要 zhèngyào *adv* about to, on the point of

正在 zhèngzài *adv* (*indicating an ongoing action or condition*) in the midst of; **wǒ zhèngzài kàn tā xiě de shū** 我正在看她写的书 I am just now reading the book she wrote

证明 zhèngmíng 1 *vb* certify, prove **2** *n* proof, documentation, certificate

政策 zhèngcè *n* policy

政党 zhèngdǎng *n* political party

政府 zhèngfǔ *n* government

政权 zhèngquán *n* political power, state political power, regime

政治 zhèngzhì *n* politics, political affairs；**zhèngzhìjiā 政治家** politician, statesman

挣 zhèng *vb* earn, make

…之后 zhīhòu *prep* after…, behind…

…之间 zhījiān *prep* between…, among…

…之前 zhīqián *prep* before…, prior to…, in front of…

…之上 zhīshàng *prep* above…, on top of…

…之下 zhīxià *prep* below…, under…

…之中 zhīzhōng *prep* amid…, among…, within…

支 zhī *mw* ▶ 623 (*for stick-like things*)；(*for music, songs, or teams*)

支持 zhīchí 1 *vb* support **2** *n* support

支援 zhīyuán 1 *vb* support, aid, assist **2** *n* support, aid, assistance

只 zhī *mw* ▶ 623 ▶ *See also* 只 zhǐ. (*one of a pair*)；(*for some animals*)；(*for boats*)

知道 zhīdào *vb* know, know how, know that

知识 zhīshi *n* knowledge

织 zhī *vb* weave, spin, knit

枝 zhī 1 *n* (*of a tree or other plant*) branch **2** *mw* ▶ 623 (*for stick-like things*)

执行 zhíxíng *vb* carry out, execute, implement

直 zhí 1 *adj* (*as a line, road, etc.*) straight；(*in expressing opinions, etc.*) straightforward, frank **2** *adv* directly, straight; in a straightforward manner, frankly

直到 zhídào *prep* until, up to

直接 zhíjiē 1 *adj* direct, straightforward, straight **2** *adv*

directly, straightforwardly, frankly

值得 zhídé *vb* be worthwhile, be worth

职工 zhígōng *n* workers, staff

职业 zhíyè *n* profession, occupation

职员 zhíyuán *n* office worker, member of staff

植物 zhíwù *n* plant, vegetation, flora

止 zhǐ 1 *vb* stop **2** *n* end, terminus; **dào xīngqīliù wéizhǐ** 到星期六为止 up to Saturday, until Saturday **3** *adv* only; **bùzhǐ yí cì** 不止一次 not just once

只 zhǐ *adv* ▶ See also 只 zhī. only, merely

只好 zhǐhǎo *adv* have to, can only, the only thing to do is; **yīnwèi tā bú zài, suǒyǐ wǒ zhǐhǎo huíjiā** 因为他不在, 所以我只好回家 since he's not in, I have to go home

只是 zhǐshì 1 *adv* just, only **2** *conj* but, however

只要 zhǐyào *conj* so long as, provided; **zhǐyào yǒu hǎo diànyǐng, wǒ jiù qǐng nǐ qù kàn** 只要有好电影,我就请你去看 as long as there's a good film showing, I'll invite you to see it

只有 zhǐyǒu 1 *adv* only, only if, unless; **zhǐyǒu…cái** 只有…才 only... can...; **zhǐyǒu nǔlì xuéxí, cái néng xuéhuì** 只有努力学习,才能学会 you can master (it) only if you study hard

纸 zhǐ *n* paper

指 zhǐ 1 *vb* point at, point to, point toward **2** *n* finger

指出 zhǐchū *vb* point out, indicate

指导 zhǐdǎo 1 *vb* guide, direct **2** *n* direction, guidance, advice; **zhǐdǎo lǎoshī** 指导老师 supervisor, advisor

指挥 zhǐhuī 1 *vb* (for an army, an orchestra, etc.) direct, command, conduct **2** *n* (of an orchestra) conductor

指示 zhǐshì 1 *n* instructions, directive **2** *vb* point out, indicate; instruct, direct

至 zhì *prep* to, until

至今 zhìjīn *adv* until now, so far, up to now

至少 zhìshǎo *adv* at least

至于 zhìyú *prep* as for, as to；**búzhìyú 不至于** wouldn't go so far as to

质量 zhìliàng *n* quality

治 zhì *vb* rule, govern, manage；(*water, emotions, etc.*) harness, control; heal, cure, treat

治疗 zhìliáo 1 *n* medical treatment **2** *vb* cure, treat

制订 zhìdìng *vb* (*as a scheme, a solution, etc.*) work out, come up with, formulate

制定 zhìdìng *vb* (*as a plan, policy, law, etc.*) draft, draw up, formulate

制度 zhìdù *n* system

制造 zhìzào *vb* manufacture, make, create；(*as a lie, a rumour, etc.*) make up, fabricate, invent

秩序 zhìxù *n* order, sequence

中 zhōng 1 *n* middle, centre；(*short for* **Zhōngguó 中国**) China **2** *prep* in, in the midst of, among **3** *adj* middle, mid-；medium, intermediate；Chinese；**zhōngshì 中式** Chinese style

中餐 zhōngcān *n* Chinese food

中国 Zhōngguó *n* China

中国话 zhōngguóhuà *n* Chinese (spoken) language

中国人 Zhōngguórén *n* Chinese person, Chinese people

中华民国 Zhōnghuá Mínguó *n* the Republic of China

中华人民共和国 Zhōnghuá Rénmín Gònghéguó *n* the People's Republic of China

中间 zhōngjiān 1 *n* middle, centre **2** *prep* amongst, between, in the middle of

中秋节 Zhōngqiū Jié *n* Mid-autumn Festival, Moon Festival (15th of the 8th lunar month)

中文 **Zhōngwén** *n* Chinese language (usually written)

中午 **zhōngwǔ** *n* noon, midday

中心 **zhōngxīn** *n* centre, heart, core

中学 **zhōngxué** *n* middle school, secondary school, high school

中央 **zhōngyāng** *n* centre, middle

中药 **zhōngyào** *n* (*as a drug or remedy*) traditional Chinese medicine

中医 **zhōngyī** *n* (*as a field or department*) traditional Chinese medicine

终于 **zhōngyú** *adv* in the end, at last, finally

钟 **zhōng** *n* bell; clock; (*for telling time*) wǔ diǎn zhōng 5 点钟 five o'clock; wǔ fēn zhōng 5 分钟 five minutes

钟表 **zhōngbiǎo** *n* clock, clocks and watches

钟头 **zhōngtóu** *n* hour

种 **zhǒng** ▶ See also 种 zhòng. **1** *n* seed; breed, species, ethnic group **2** *mw* ▶ 623 kind, type, sort

种子 **zhǒngzi** *n* seed

种 **zhòng** *vb* ▶ See also 种 zhǒng. plant, sow, cultivate

重 **zhòng** ▶ See also 重 chóng. **1** *adj* heavy; important, weighty, serious **2** *n* weight

重大 **zhòngdà** *adj* great, weighty, important

重点 **zhòngdiǎn** *n* point of emphasis, main point

重量 **zhòngliàng** *n* weight

重视 **zhòngshì** *vb* regard as important, take seriously, value

重要 **zhòngyào** *adj* important, significant

周 **zhōu** *n* all around, circumference, circuit; week

周到 **zhōudào** *adj* thoughtful, considerate

周末 **zhōumò** *n* weekend

周围 **zhōuwéi** *n* circumference, surroundings, environment

猪 **zhū** *n* pig, hog

猪肉 **zhūròu** *n* pork

竹子 **zhúzi** *n* bamboo

逐步 **zhúbù** *adv* gradually, step by step

逐渐 **zhújiàn** *adv* gradually, bit by bit

主动 **zhǔdòng 1** *n* initiative **2** *vb* hold/take the initiative

主观 **zhǔguān** *adj* subjective

主人 **zhǔrén** *n* owner; host, hostess

主任 **zhǔrèn** *n* director, chairperson, responsible person

主席 **zhǔxí** *n* chairperson, chair, chairman

主要 **zhǔyào** *adj* main, principal, chief

主义 **zhǔyì** *n* doctrine, -ism

主意 **zhǔyì** *n* idea, plan, decision

主张 **zhǔzhāng 1** *vb* propose, suggest, advocate **2** *n* proposal, suggestion

煮 **zhǔ** *vb* boil, cook

住 **zhù** *vb* live, reside, stay; (*after certain verbs to indicate coming to a halt or grasping hold*) [zhuā | zhàn | jì] zhù [抓|站|记]住 [hold on to | stop | remember]

住院 **zhùyuàn** *vb* be in hospital, be hospitalized

注意 **zhùyì** *vb* pay attention to, take notice of, be careful of

祝 **zhù** *vb* wish, extend wishes

祝贺 **zhùhè** *vb* congratulate

著名 **zhùmíng** *adj* famous, prominent, well-known

著作 **zhùzuò** *n* writings, works

抓 **zhuā** *vb* grasp, seize; catch, arrest; scratch

抓紧 **zhuājǐn** *vb* grasp firmly, pay close attention to, make the best use of

专家 **zhuānjiā** *n* specialist, expert

专门 **zhuānmén** *adj* specialized, special

专心 zhuānxīn 1 *adj* attentive, with undivided attention, with concentration **2** *adv* attentively

专业 zhuānyè *n* specialty, specialized field/profession

砖 zhuān *n* brick

转 zhuǎn *vb* ▶ See also 转 zhuàn. turn, change, shift; (*when speaking of a message, phone call, etc.*) transfer, pass on, forward

转变 zhuǎnbiàn *vb* turn, change, transform

转告 zhuǎngào *vb* (*as a message*) forward, pass on

转 zhuàn *vb* ▶ See also 转 zhuǎn. turn, revolve, rotate; walk around, stroll

赚 zhuàn *vb* (*when talking about money or profit*) make, gain, earn

庄稼 zhuāngjia *n* crop, crops

庄严 zhuāngyán *adj* dignified, solemn, stately

装 zhuāng 1 *vb* install, fit, put in; pack, load; pretend, disguise, play a part **2** *n* clothing, outfit, dress

状况 zhuàngkuàng *n* state of affairs, situation

状态 zhuàngtài *n* condition, appearance, state of affairs

撞 zhuàng *vb* bump/knock against, bump into, collide

追 zhuī *vb* follow, pursue, chase

追求 zhuīqiú *vb* seek, go after, pursue, court, woo

准 zhǔn 1 *adj* accurate **2** *adv* accurately, certainly **3** *vb* permit, allow

准备 zhǔnbèi 1 *vb* prepare, get ready for, prepare to; plan, intend **2** *n* preparation

准确 zhǔnquè *adj* accurate, precise, exact

准时 zhǔnshí *adj* on time, punctual

捉 zhuō *vb* seize, arrest, catch hold of

桌子 zhuōzi *n* table, desk

资料 zīliào *n* information, data

资源 zīyuán *n* resources, natural resources

子女 zǐnǚ *n* sons and daughters, children

仔细 zǐxì 1 *adj* careful of detail, meticulous, attentive **2** *adv* in detail, meticulously, carefully

紫 zǐ *adj* purple

自 zì 1 *pron* oneself, one's own **2** *prep* from, since **3** *conj* since

自从 zìcóng 1 *prep* since, from **2** *conj* since; zìcóng… yǐhòu 自从…以后 from…(that time) on, ever since…; zìcóng…yǐlái 自从…以来 ever since…

自动 zìdòng 1 *adj* automatic, voluntary, self-motivated **2** *adv* automatically, voluntarily, on one's own initiative

自费 zìfèi *adj* at one's own expense, self-funded

自己 zìjǐ *pron* self, oneself

自觉 zìjué 1 *adj* conscious, aware; conscientious **2** *adv* consciously; conscientiously

自来水 zìláishuǐ *n* running water, tap water

自然 zìrán 1 *n* nature, the natural world **2** *adj* natural **3** *adv* of course; naturally

自私 zìsī *adj* selfish

自我 zìwǒ *pron* self, self-, oneself

自行车 zìxíngchē *n* bicycle, bike

自学 zìxué *vb* self-study, study by oneself, teach oneself

自由 zìyóu 1 *n* freedom, liberty **2** *adj* free, unrestrained

自愿 zìyuàn *adj* voluntary, of one's own accord

字 zì *n* word, written character

字典 zìdiǎn *n* dictionary

字母 zìmǔ *n* letters of an alphabet, letter

宗教 zōngjiào *n* religion

综合 zōnghé 1 *vb* synthesize, summarize **2** *adj* comprehensive, overall

总 zǒng 1 *adv* always, in every case, all the time; eventually, sooner or later; inevitably; in any event, anyway, after all **2** *adj* general, total, chief, main, master

总理 zǒnglǐ *n* prime minister, premier

总是 zǒngshì *adv* always, in every case, all the time

总统 zǒngtǒng *vb* (*of a republic*) president

走 zǒu *vb* walk, go; depart, leave; (*for something mechanical*) work, tick, go

走道 zǒudào *n* path, walkway

走后门 zǒu hòumén *vb* get in by the back door; do business or other things by means of backdoor dealings

走廊 zǒuláng *n* corridor, passage, passageway

走路 zǒulù *vb* walk

租 zū *vb* rent, hire, charter; rent out, let out, lease

足球 zúqiú *n* football, soccer

阻止 zǔzhǐ *vb* prevent, stop

组 zǔ *n* group

组织 zǔzhī 1 *vb* organize **2** *n* organisation

祖父 zǔfù *n* grandfather on the father's side

祖国 zǔguó *n* one's native country, motherland, fatherland

祖母 zǔmǔ *n* grandmother on the father's side

祖先 zǔxiān *n* ancestors, forefathers

钻 zuān *vb* drill, bore, enter

钻研 zuānyán *vb* study intensively

嘴 zuǐ *n* mouth

最 zuì *adv* (*indicating the superlative*) most, the most

最初 zuìchū 1 *adj* first, initial **2** *adv* at first, in the beginning, initially

最好 zuìhǎo 1 *adj* best **2** *adv* had better

最后 zuìhòu 1 *adj* final, ultimate, last **2** *adv* at last, finally, eventually

最近 zuìjìn 1 *adj* (*in the recent past*) last, recent; (*in the near future*) next, coming **2** *adv* (*in the recent past*) lately, recently; (*in the near future*) soon, in the near future, coming

罪 zuì *n* crime, guilt; suffering, pain, hardship; **shòuzuì 受罪** have a hard time, endure suffering, be in pain

醉 zuì *adj* drunk, intoxicated, inebriated

尊敬 zūnjìng 1 *vb* respect, honour, esteem **2** *adj* honourable, distinguished

尊重 zūnzhòng *vb* respect, esteem

遵守 zūnshǒu *vb* comply with, observe, abide by

昨天 zuótiān *n* yesterday

左 zuǒ 1 *n* left, letf-hand side, the left; (*when speaking of politics*) left wing **2** *adj* left, left-hand

左边 zuǒbiān *n* left-hand side, left side

左右 zuǒyòu *adv* (*after an expression of quantity*) approximately, about, more or less

作 zuò *vb* do, make; zuò bàogào 作报告 make a report; create, write, compose; zuòqǔ 作曲 compose a piece of music; act as, be, become; regard as, treat as; **tā bǎ wǒ dāngzuò qīnshēng nǚ'ér 她把我当作亲生女儿** she treats me like her own daughter

作家 zuòjiā *n* writer

作品 zuòpǐn *n* literary/artistic work

作为 zuòwéi 1 *vb* serve as, function as, use as; regard as **2** *prep* as, being **3** *n* conduct, action, deed; achievement, accomplishment

作文 zuòwén *n* composition, essay

作业 zuòyè *n* school assignment

作用 zuòyòng *n* purpose, function, role; qǐ hěn dà de zuòyòng 起很大的作用 perform an important function; action, effect

作者 zuòzhě *n* author, writer

坐 zuò *vb* sit; ride on, go by, travel by; zuò [gōnggòng qìchē| huǒchē|fēijī] 坐 [公共汽车|火车|飞机] travel by [bus|train| plane]

座 zuò 1 *mv* ▶**623** (for mountains, buildings, structures, etc.) **2** *n* seat, place to sit

座谈 zuòtán 1 *vb* discuss **2** *n* discussion; zuòtánhuì 座谈会 discussion, symposium, forum

座位 zuòwèi *n* seat, place to sit

做 zuò *vb* do, be engaged in; zuò shìyàn 做试验 do experiments; make, create, manufacture; zuò yīfu 做衣服 make clothes; cook, prepare (food); zuòcài 做菜 cook a meal, prepare a meal; be, act as, take on the role of; tā kuài zuò māma le 她快做妈妈了 she is about to become a mother; (when talking about posts, poslitions, professions, etc.) work as, be, become; tā zuòle sān nián xìzhǔrèn le 他做了3年系主任了 he has been chairperson of the department for 3 years; serve as, be used as; zhège fángjiān kěyǐ zuò wǒ de shūfáng 这个房间可以做我的书房 this room can serve as my study

做法 zuòfǎ *n* way of doing things, method, practice

做客 zuòkè *vb* be a guest

做梦 zuòmèng *vb* dream, have a dream

Basic Chinese measure words

Nominal Measure Words

In Chinese, a numeral cannot quantify a noun by itself. it has to be accompanied by the measure word that is appropriate for the noun that is being used. Each noun has a specific measure word or set of measure words that can be used with it. There is often a link between the measure word and the shape of the object. In expressions of quantification, the numeral comes first, followed by the measure word and the noun. Below is a list of commonly used nominal measure words, along with descriptions of the types of nouns for which they are used, translations (if appropriate), and some examples of their uses. A list of verbal measure words follows this list. Some nominal measure words can also be used as verbal measure words and these are cross-referenced below.

把 **bǎ** (for objects with a handle or with something a person can hold) three [brushes|knives|keys|umbrellas|chairs...]sān bǎ [shuāzi|dāo|yàoshi|yǔsǎn|yǐzi...] 3 把[刷子|刀|钥匙|雨伞|椅子...];(for things that can be grouped in bunches or bundles) bunch, bundle; **a bunch of flowers** yì bǎ* huā 一把 * 花;a bundle of chopsticks yì bǎ kuàizi 一把筷子; handful, a handful of [sand|rice|beans...] yì bǎ [shāzi|dàmǐ|dòuzi...] 一把[沙子|大米|豆子...]

班 **bān** (for scheduled services of public transportation) this train service to London qù Lúndūn de zhè bān huǒchē 去伦敦的这班火车; the next flight to Beijing qù Běijīng de xià yì bān fēijī 去北京的下一班飞机

包 **bāo** package, packet, bundle; **a packet of cigarettes** yì bāo

---

* less formal

xiāngyān 一包香烟；two packages of sweets liǎng bāo táng 两包糖；this bundle of clothes zhè bāo yīfu 这包衣服

本 běn (*for things that are bound, such as books, magazines, etc.*)five books wǔ běn shū 5 本书

笔 bǐ (*for sums of money*) that sum of money nà bǐ qián 那笔钱；(*for deals in business or trade*) this deal zhè bǐ jiāoyì 这笔交易

遍 biàn ▶ *See the list of Verbal Measure Words below.*

部 bù (*for novels, films, etc.*) three[novels | films]sān bù [xiǎoshuō| diànyǐng] 3 部[小说|电影]

册 cè (*for books or volumes of books*)volume, book；this novel has two volumes zhè bù xiǎoshuō yǒu liǎng cè 这部小说有两册；(*for copies of books*) copy；100,000 books shíwàn cè shū 10 万册书

层 céng (*storey, floor*)；a five-storey building yí zuò wǔ céng dàlóu 一座 5 层大楼；(*for a layer, coat, sheet*) a coat of paint yì céng yóuqī 一层油漆；a thin sheet of ice yì céng báobīng 一层薄冰

场 chǎng ▶ *See also the list of Verbal Measure Words below.* (*for the whole process of being ill*) an illness yì chǎng bìng 一场病；(*for a natural disturbance, war, disaster, etc.*) a rain shower, a cloudburst yì chǎng yǔ 一场雨；(*for a show, performance, game, or debate*)[the showing of a film | a performance of Peking opera | a debate] yì chǎng [diànyǐng| jīngjù| biànlùn] 一场[电影|京剧|辩论]；two [football matches | basketball games] liǎng chǎng[zúqiú bǐsài| lánqiú bǐsài] 两场[足球比赛|篮球比赛]

床 chuáng (*for quilts, blankets, sheets*) three[quilts | blankets | sheets] sān chuáng [bèizi| tǎnzi| chuángdān] 3 床[被子|毯子|床单]

次 cì ▶ *See also the list of Verbal Measure Words below.* (*for events such as examinations, accidents, experiments, etc.*)

two [examinations|accidents|experiments...] liǎng cì [kǎoshì| shìgù|shíyàn...] 两次[考试|事故|实验...]

道 dào (*for orders issued by an authority, questions on an examination*) an [order|arithmetic question] yí dào [mìnglìng| suànshùtí] 一道[命令|算术题]; (*for things in the shape of a line*) a [crack|ray of light|wrinkle] yí dào [lièfèng| guāngxiàn| zhòuwén] 一道[裂缝|光线|皱纹]; (*for courses in a meal*) a three-course lunch yǒu sān dào cài de wǔfàn 有 3 道菜 的午饭

滴 dī drop; six drops of blood liù dī xuè 6 滴血

点 diǎn (*for suggestions, requirements, ideas, opinions*) two [suggestions|requirements|ideas] liǎng diǎn [jiànyì| yāoqiú|yìjiàn] 两点[建议|要求|意见]

顶 dǐng (*for hats, caps, or things with a top*) a [hat|tent] yì dǐng [màozi|zhàngpeng] 一顶[帽子|帐篷]

栋 dòng (*for buildings*) ten buildings shí dòng lóufáng 10 栋楼房

堵 dǔ (*for walls*) a wall yì dǔ qiáng 一堵墙

段 duàn (*for lengths of road, cable, etc.*) section, segment; a section of highway yí duàn gōnglù 一段公路; (*for periods of time*) period, length; that period of history nà yí duàn lìshǐ 那一段历史; (*for units of writing, articles, speeches, etc.*) piece, passage, paragraph; a piece of music yí duàn yīnyuè 一段音乐

对 duì pair, couple; a (married) couple yí duì fūqī 一对 夫妻; a pair of vases yí duì huāpíng 一对花瓶

顿 dùn ▶ *See also the list of Verbal Measure Words below.* (*for meals*) three meals every day měi tiān sān dùn fàn 每天 3 顿饭

朵 duǒ (*for flowers, clouds*) a few [flowers|clouds] jǐ duǒ [huā|yún] 几朵[花|云]

份 fèn portion, share; a portion of food yí fèn fàn 一份饭

a gift yí fèn lǐwù 一份礼物；(for copies of newspapers, magazines, or manuscripts) two documents liǎng fèn wénjiàn 两份文件

封 fēng (for letters, telegrams) **eight letters** bā fēng xìn 8 封信

幅 fú (for paintings, works of calligraphy, maps) a landscape painting yì fú shānshuǐhuà 一幅山水画

服 fù (for doses of Chinese medicine) **for doses of Chinese medicine** sì fù zhōngyào 4 服中药

副 fù (for things that come in pairs or sets) set, pair；a set of chess yí fù xiàngqí 一副象棋；a pair of [gloves | glasses...] yí fù [shǒutào | yǎnjìng...] 一副 [手套 | 眼镜...]；(for facial expressions) a [smiling face | serious expression] yí fù [xiàoliǎn | yánsù de biǎoqíng] 一副 [笑脸 | 严肃的表情]

个 gè ! This is the most common measure word. It can take the place of many nominal measure words, and is handy to use if one does not know the measure word that is specific to a particular noun. It usually has a neutral tone, but has a fourth tone when stressed；a [person | problem | month | school...] yí gè [rén | wèntí | yuè | xuéxiào...] 一个 [人 | 问题 | 月 | 学校...]

根 gēn (for long, thin objects) a [rope | needle | pillar | sausage...] yì gēn [shéngzi | zhēn | zhùzi | xiāngcháng...] 一根 [绳子 | 针 | 柱子 | 香肠...]

行 háng (for things that form a line) **two lines of Chinese characters** liǎng háng Hànzì 两行汉字

户 hù (for households) **five Chinese households** wǔ hù Zhōngguórén 5 户中国人

回 huí ▶ See the list of Verbal Measure Words below.

伙 huǒ ! This measure word usually has a negative connotation；(for groups or bands of people) a gang of [people | robbers | hooligans...] yì huǒ [rén | qiángdào | liúmáng...] 一伙 [人 | 强盗 | 流氓...]

家 jiā (for families, enterprises, restaurants, hotels, etc.)
twelve [families|factories|banks|shops...]shí'èr jiā[rénjiā|
gōngchǎng|yínháng|shāngdiàn···]12 家[人家|工厂|银行|商店···]

架 jià (for aeroplanes, pianos, cameras, etc.)
six [aeroplanes|cameras]liù jià[fēijī|zhàoxiàngjī]6 架[飞机|照相
机]

间 jiān (for rooms) a(n) [room|office|kitchen] yì jiān [wūzi|
bàngōngshì|chúfáng]一间[屋子|办公室|厨房]

件 jiàn (for luggage, clothes, furniture, matters, etc.) a
[piece of luggage|shirt|matter] yí jiàn [xíngli|chènshān|shì]一
件[行李|衬衫|事]

节 jié (for sections of things) section, length, segment; a
section of bamboo yì jié zhúzi 一节竹子; (for torch
batteries, railway carriages, class periods at school) four
[carriages|batteries|periods]sì jié [chēxiāng|diànchí|kè]4 节
[车厢|电池|课]

届 jiè (for regular sessions, conferences, sports
tournaments, terms of office, etc.) the tenth[session of
the UN General Assembly|Agriculture Conference|presidency]
dì-shí jiè [Liánhéguó Dàhuì|Nóngyè Huìyì|zǒngtǒng]第 10 届[联
合国大会|农业会议|总统]; (for students graduating in the
same year) year, class, grade; the fourth graduating
class dì-sì jiè bìyèbān 第 4 届毕业班

句 jù (for lines, sentences, units of speech, poetry, etc.)
a [sentence|line of a poem] yí jù [huà|shī]一句[话|诗]

棵 kē (for trees, plants) a [tree|grass|daffodil] yì kē [shù|
cǎo|shuǐxiānhuā]一棵[树|草|水仙花]

颗 kē (for small, round things such as pearls, teeth and
hearts; also for things that appear small such as stars,
satellites and planets) a [pearl|bean|satellite]yì kē [zhūzi|
dòuzi|wèixīng]一颗[珠子|豆子|卫星]; (for bullets, bombs,
etc.) a [bullet|bomb]yì kē [zǐdàn|zhàdàn]一颗[子弹|炸弹]

口 kǒu (for the number of people in a family or village)
eight people bā kǒu rén 8 口人; (for spoken languages,

used with the verb "speak" and with the number **one**，yì
一）to speak Beijing dialect shuō yì kǒu Běijīnghuà 说一
口北京话

块 kuài (*for things that come in chunks or solid pieces*)
three [soaps | sweets | stones] sān kuài [féizào | táng | shítou] 3 块
[肥皂 | 糖 | 石头]；(*for things that are shaped like sheets*)；
five [table cloths | wooden boards | handkerchiefs] wǔ kuài
[zhuōbù | mùbǎn | shǒujuàn] 5 块 [桌布 | 木板 | 手绢]；(*for slices,
sections, divisions, etc.*) **four pieces of** [cake | cloth | land]
sì kuài [dàngāo | bù | dì] 4 块 [蛋糕 | 布 | 地]

类 lèi *kind of, sort of; this type of thing, this kind of thing*
zhè lèi dōngxi 这类东西

粒 lì (*for very small, round things, such as peas, peanuts,
bullets, or grains*) **a grain of** [rice | sand] yí lì [mǐ | shāzi] 一粒
[米 | 沙子]；**three pills/tablets** sān lì yào 3 粒药

辆 liàng (*for vehicles*) **ten** [cars | bikes | lorries] shí liàng
[qìchē | zìxíngchē | kǎchē] 10 辆 [汽车 | 自行车 | 卡车]

列 liè (*for trains*) **a train** yí liè huǒchē 一列火车

门 mén (*for academic courses, subjects or disciplines*) **a**
[course | science | speciality] yì mén [kènchéng | kēxué | zhuānyè]
一门 [课程 | 科学 | 专业]

面 miàn (*for flat, smooth objects, such as mirrors, flags,
etc.*) **a** [red flag | mirror] yí miàn [hóngqí | jìngzi] 一面 [红旗 | 镜
子]

名 míng (*for persons with professional or prominent social
identities*) **seven** [students | doctors | soldiers | workers] qī
míng [xuésheng | yīshēng | shìbīng | gōngrén] 7 名 [学生 | 医生 | 士兵
工人]

排 pái (*for things grouped or set in rows*) **row; a row of**
[seats | trees | houses] yì pái [zuòwèi | shù | fǎngzi] 一排 [座位 | 树
房子]

盘 pán (*for flat things*) **a video tape** yì pán lùxiàngdài 一
盘录像带；(*for board games*) **a game of chess** yì pán qí

一盘棋

批 pī (*for people or goods*) group, batch, lot; a group of people yì pī rén 一批人;two batches of goods liǎng pī huòwù 两批货物

匹 pǐ (*for horses, mules*) three [horses|mules] sān pǐ [mǎ| luózi] 3 匹[马|骡子]

篇 piān (*for papers articles, written versions of a speech*) an [essay|diary|editorial] yì piān[lùnwén|rìjì|shèlùn]一篇[论文|日记|社论]

片 piàn (*for flat, thin things or things in slices*) three slices of bread sān piàn miànbāo 3 片面包;two[tablets| biscuits]liǎng piàn[yàopiàn|bǐnggān]两片[药片|饼干];(*for expanses or stretches of ocean, desert, mist, fog, etc.*) a stretch of sandy beach yí piàn shātān 一片沙滩;(*for atmospheres moods etc.*) a scene of great joy yí piàn huānlè 一片欢乐

期 qī (*for issues of periodicals, magazines, journals, etc.*) the first issue of that magazine nà běn zázhì de dì-yī qī 那本杂志的第 1 期

群 qún (*for a group, crowd, herd, or flock*) group, crowd;a crowd of football fans yì qún zúqiúmí 一群足球迷;a flock of birds yì qún niǎo 一群鸟

声 shēng ▶ See the list of Verbal Measure Words below.

首 shǒu (*for songs, poems, music*) six[songs|poems] liù shǒu[gē|shī] 6 首[歌|诗]

束 shù bunch;a bunch of flowers yí shù huā 一束花

双 shuāng (*for things that come in twos, such as shoes, socks, chopsticks, etc.*) pair;a pair of [shoes|socks| eyes]yì shuāng[xié|wàzi|yǎnjing] 一双[鞋|袜子|眼睛]

艘 sōu (*for ships*)three[ships|oil tankers|warships] sān sōu [chuán|yóulún|jūnjiàn] 3 艘[船|油轮|军舰]

所 suǒ (*for buildings, houses, schools, etc.*) two

[hospitals|schools|houses] liǎng suǒ [yīyuàn|xuéxiào|fángzi] 两所[医院|学校|房子]

台 tái (for stage performances, machines, equipment, etc.) nine [TV sets|washing machines|computers] jiǔ tái [diànshì|xǐyī|jìsuànjī] 9 台[电视机|洗衣机|计算机]; a theatrical performance yì tái xì 一台戏

堂 táng (for classes or periods at school or university) period, class; four periods sì táng kè 4 堂课

趟 tàng ▶ See the list of Verbal Measure Words below. (for scheduled services of public transportation) the next train service to Beijing qù Běijīng de xià yí tàng huǒchē 去北京的下一趟火车

套 tào (for sets of books, clothing, tools, furniture, etc.) set, suit, suite; a set of [stamps|regulations|textbooks] yí tào [yóupiào|guīzé|kèběn] 一套[邮票|规则|课本]

条 tiáo (for long, narrow things) a [towel|boat|pair of trousers|skirt|river|road|street|snake|fish|dog] yì tiáo [máojīn|chuán|kùzi|qúnzi|hé|lù|jiē|shé|yú|gǒu]一条[毛巾|船|裤子|裙子|河|路|街|蛇|鱼|狗]; (for items of news, laws, ideas, views) three [news|laws|ideas] sān tiáo [xiāoxi|fǎlǜ|yìjiàn]3条[消息|法律|意见]; (for limbs of the human body) two [legs|arms] liǎng tiáo [tuǐ|gēbo] 两条[腿|胳膊]; (for human lives) four lives sì tiáo rénmìng 4 条人命

头 tóu (for certain animals) five [cows|pigs|sheep|elephants|lions...] wǔ tóu [niú|zhū|yáng|xiàng|shīzi...]5头[牛|猪|羊|象|狮子...]; (for garlic bulbs) a bulb of garlic yì tóu suàn 一头蒜

团 tuán (for certain round things) a ball of wool yì tuán máoxiàn 一团毛线

位 wèi (a polite measure word for people) a [gentleman|lady|teacher|professor...] yí wèi [xiānsheng|nǚshì|lǎoshī|jiàoshòu...] 一位[先生|女士|老师|教授...]

下 xià ▶ See the list of Verbal Measure Words below.

项 xiàng (for work , projects , tasks , requirements , etc.) a [piece of work | project] yí xiàng [gōngzuò | gōngchéng] 一项 [工作 | 工程] ; (for decisions or announcements) a (n) [decision | announcement] yí xiàng [juédìng | shēngmíng] 一项 [决定 | 声明]

样 yàng (for things in general) kind , sort , type ; three types of tool sān yàng gōngjù 3 样工具

盏 zhǎn (for lamps) a lamp yì zhǎn dēng 一盏灯

张 zhāng (for flat things such as paper , paintings , tables maps , etc.) a [sheet of paper | newspaper | table | bed | picture | ticket | postage | stamp] yì zhāng [zhǐ | bào | zhuōzi | chuáng | huà | piào | yóu] 一张 [纸 | 报 | 桌子 | 床 | 画 | 票 | 邮票]

阵 zhèn (for events or states of short duration) a [downpour of rain | gust of wind | fit of coughing] yí zhèn [dàyǔ | fēng | késòu] 一阵 [大雨 | 风 | 咳嗽]

支 zhī (for stick-like things) a [pen | chopstick | candle | flute] yì zhī [bǐ | kuàizi | làzhú | dízi] 一支 [笔 | 筷子 | 蜡烛 | 笛子] ; (for music , songs , or teams) a piece of music yì zhī qǔzi 一支曲子

只 zhī (one of a pair) a (n) [shoe | eye | ear | hand | foot] yì zhī [xié | yǎnjing | ěrduo | shǒu | jiǎo] 一只 [鞋 | 眼睛 | 耳朵 | 手 | 脚] ; (for some animals) a [chicken | sheep | monkey | bird | cat | crab] yì zhī [jī | yáng | hóuzi | niǎo | māo | pángxiè] 一只 [鸡 | 羊 | 猴子 | 鸟 | 猫 | 螃蟹] ; (for boats) a small boat yì zhī xiǎochuán 一只小船

枝 zhī (for stick-like things) ▶ See 支 zhī above. a long-stemmed rose yì zhī chánggěng méiguihuā 一枝长梗玫瑰花

种 zhǒng kind , type , sort ; two kinds of [people | plants | clothes | dictionaries] liǎng zhǒng [rén | zhíwù | yīfu | zìdiǎn] 两种 [人 | 植物 | 衣服 | 字典]

座 zuò (for mountains , buildings , structures , etc.) a [mountain | bridge | building | palace | cinema] yí zuò [shān | qiáo | lóu | gōngdiàn | diànyǐngyuàn] 一座 [山 | 桥 | 楼 | 宫殿 | 电影院]

Verbal Measure Words

Below is a short list of commonly used verbal measure words. These are generally used to indicate the number of times an action or a state occurs. The numeral and measure word are preceded by the verb and are usually followed by the object if there is one (i. e. if the verb is transitive). Some verbal measure words, such as *shēng* 声 and *xià* 下, imply that the action involved is short and brief. Please note that some verbal measure words can also be used as nominal measure words and therefore also occur in the list of Nominal Measure Words above.

遍 biàn (*to indicate the number of times an action or state occurs*) time! *Note that biàn 遍 is different from cì 次 in that it emphasizes the whole process from the beginning to the end;* I've read that book twice 那本书我看了两遍 nà běn shū wǒ kànle liǎng biàn 那本书,我看了两遍

场 chǎng ▶ *See also the list of Nominal Measure Words above.* (*to indicate the occasion on which a state or an action occurs*) last month she was sick 上个月她病了一场 shàngge yuè tā bìngle yì chǎng 上个月她病了一场; I went back to my room and had a cry 我回到我的房间哭了一场 wǒ huídào wǒ de fángjiān kūle yì chǎng 我回到我的房间哭了一场

次 cì ▶ *See also the list of Nominal Measure Words above.* (*to indicate the number of times an action or state occurs*) time; he came three times 他来了3次 tā láile sān cì 他来了3次

顿 dùn ▶ *See also the list of Nominal Measure Words above.* (*for actions that take place in single sessions*) he received [some criticism | a reprimand | a beating] 他被[批评了|骂了|打了]一顿 tā bèi [pīpíngle|màle|dǎle] yí dùn 他被[批评了|骂了|打了]一顿

回 huí (*for times, occurrences*)! *Note that huí 回 is colloquial and informal;* I'd like to try two more times 我要再试两回 wǒ yào zài shì liǎng huí 我要再试两回

声 shēng (*for counting cries, shouts, or other utterances*)

she called me twice tā hǎnle wǒ liǎng shēng 她喊了我
两声；give me a shout before you go nǐ zǒu yǐqián hǎn
wǒ yì shēng 你走以前喊我一声

趟 tàng ▶ See also the list of Nominal Measure Words
above. (for trips, journeys, visits, etc.) time, trip；**last
month I made three trips to Beijing** shàngge yuè wǒ
qùle sān tàng Běijīng 上个月我去了 3 趟北京；**she came
to my room twice yesterday** zuótiān tā dào wǒ fángjiān
láile liǎng tàng 昨天她到我房间来了两趟

下 xià (for brief actions) time；**I knocked at the˙door
three times** wǒ qiāole sān xià mén 我敲了 3 下门；**he
nodded his head several times** tā diǎn le jǐ xià tóu 他点
了几下头